Surfing Europe

Chris Nelson and Demi Taylor

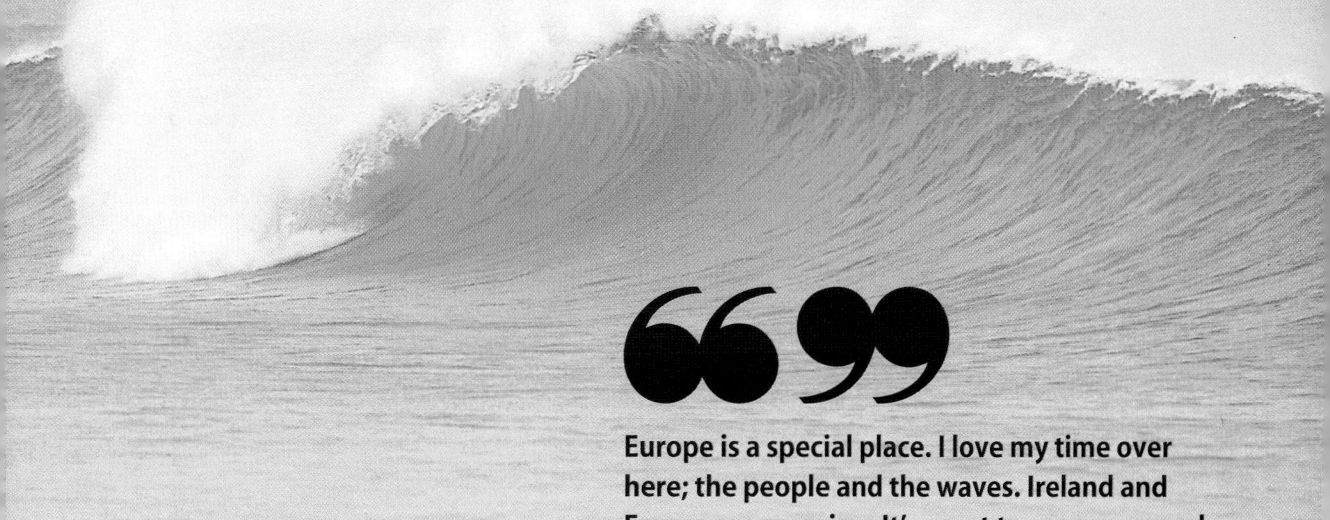

66 99

Europe is a special place. I love my time over here; the people and the waves. Ireland and France are amazing. It's great to see new people and new places.

Mark Richards, 4 x world champion

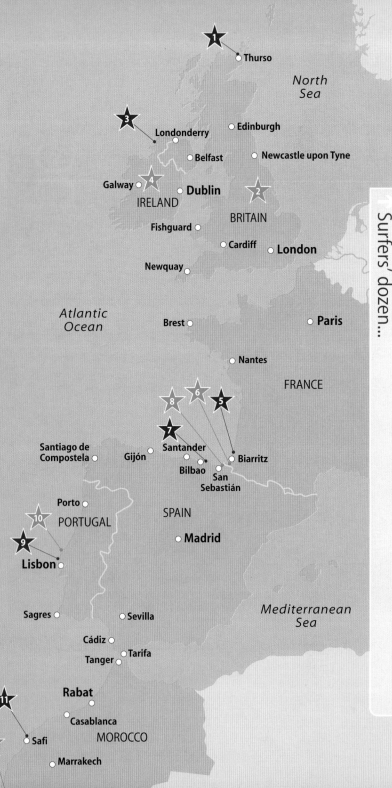

North Sea

Thurso

Edinburgh

Londonderry

Belfast · Newcastle upon Tyne

Galway · **Dublin**

IRELAND

BRITAIN

Fishguard

Cardiff · **London**

Newquay

Atlantic Ocean

Brest · **Paris**

Nantes

FRANCE

Santiago de Compostela · Gijón · Santander · Biarritz

Bilbao

San Sebastián

SPAIN

Madrid

Porto

PORTUGAL

Lisbon

Sagres · Sevilla

Cádiz · Tarifa

Tanger

Rabat

Casablanca

Safi · MOROCCO

Marrakech

Mediterranean Sea

Surfers' dozen...

Britain
Surf Thurso East – a cold water Nias on Britain's 'Norse' shore *p38*.

Don't miss The rest of the country – there's more to Britain than just Cornwall *p100*.

Ireland
Surf The great northwest - step back in time to see how surfing used to be *p116*.

Don't miss A pint of the black stuff with a side order of *craic* *p135*.

France
Surf Hossegor – some of the world's finest beach breaks *p178*.

Don't miss Dinner at the Heteroclito overlooking Guéthary's big-wave spots as the sun goes down *p196*.

Spain
Surf Mundaka – still the daddy, still roaring *p216*.

Don't miss A weekend in San Sebastián – *pintxos*, people, passion *p219*.

Portugal
Surf Coxos – perfect point with grinding barrels *p301*.

Don't miss The Inter Churrasco in Peniche – who needs Michelin stars when you can have chicken and chips like this *p305*.

Morocco
Surf Safi – open for business and doing a roaring trade *p351*.

Don't miss Banana Village souk – this is how oranges are meant to taste *p363*.

200 km
200 miles

Introduction

It was a glorious Scottish spring morning and the air had just about lost its chilly edge. We were standing in long grass, damp with the morning dew, and looking down on the steely blue swell lines wrapping down the point. The waves were as picture perfect as you could imagine. Long, empty, peeling walls that peaked on the edge of the bay and reeled through to the beach, 300 m inside. We were the only surfers looking out at this incredible sight. We were the only surfers on the whole island. We had been on Orkney for a week now – at the most northerly point of our journey. From now on we would be heading south.

Woken by the sun again, we walked out onto the point sipping mint tea. The green ocean was a corduroy of lines marching along the dry orange, rocky point. These wondrous waves hadn't slept for a week now. And then it dawned on us. We had reached the most southerly point on our journey, the desert south of Morocco. It had been eight months since we had left the Orkneys. From now on we would be turning north again, heading back to mainland Europe. Heading home.

We had driven over 30,000 km along the Atlantic coastline of Europe and north Africa. We'd surfed incredible waves, met the most interesting people, eaten a smorgasbord of food, stayed on some dodgy campsites and woken to find a huge rat sitting next to our bed. We'd had rainstorms in Ireland, sandstorms in Morocco, gales in southern Spain, snow in Mundaka and a glorious Indian summer in Biarritz. We'd surfed reefs, beaches, rivermouths and points of every imaginable type. We'd had flat spells and pumping swells. We'd had the time of our lives.

Contents

Essentials

Britain

Ireland

Cover image
Kepa Acero at El Quemao, Lanzarote
by Willy Uribe ▶▶ *p267*
Title page image
Sennen Cove, Cornwall
by Alex Williams ▶▶ *p87*

France

Spain

Portugal

Morocco

About the book

When it comes to surf, there are no guarantees. You can spend two weeks at the world's best break and not get one wave. It can be flat, onshore, too crowded or too big. It is something that we learn to accept as surfers. But imagine the Brazilian football team turning up to play France in the World Cup final only to find the pitch too small to play on. Or too bumpy. Or gone. Entirely. Sorry, try again tomorrow. Maybe they would learn to appreciate the elements more.

As surfers, when everything does come together, when the elements conspire to produce classic conditions for an epic session, that day can stay with us forever. It is the numerous variables of swell, wind and tide that combine to make each surf session so unique. It has helped to make surfers such great travellers and great explorers – if it's onshore here, why not check down the coast? The search for the ultimate wave of the 1970s has gradually given way to a new search – the search for the uncrowded wave, the big wave or the wave near the good beachside bar. Everyone is looking for something slightly different in their surf trips, and everyone is looking in slightly different places.

Europe is a huge continent with waves of every imaginable type breaking on every corner of its shores. There are point breaks in Greece, reef breaks in Italy, beach breaks on the Channel Islands and rivermouth sandbanks in Norway. When setting out to write this book we decided to focus on the regions where surfers would be most likely to get consistently good waves. That's not to say that the areas we have not featured do not have good waves – or good surfers. It is just that the regions in this book allow travellers a better chance of getting some serious water time, more of the time. Wave riders from the Channel Islands, Italy or Northern Ireland probably already have a good idea about the best breaks on their doorsteps. Our aim is to help surfers when they are on the road. More than two decades of searching have gone into this guide, plus an intense year on the road following the Atlantic coastline from the Orkneys in the north to the desert south of Morocco. We have spoken to many of the world's and Europe's top surfers as well as respected local chargers, shop owners and fellow travellers. We asked the world's best shapers to recommend boards for each region and we asked top riders to recommend the best places to grab a post-surf bite. Local chargers contributed tips and advice on their home breaks. All these experiences have been condensed to help make your trip more rewarding. We have also tried to include as many overview photos of the breaks as possible, showing them in a true light. It's easy to include an all-time shot of the one day this decade when the usually weak, dribbling beach was 10 ft and cranking, but that's no use when trying to gauge the true potential of a place. There was obviously discussion about the breaks we chose to include, and the ones we chose to leave out. This was done with the input of many people. The rule of thumb was that if a spot has become widely known – through the internet, magazines, general knowledge – then we would include it. If it is still a genuine secret spot we have left it out. With one or two semi-secret spots, we have not included their location.

Overall this guide has tried to be honest. Honest about the accommodation, honest about the waves and honest about the locations. It is designed to help you to maximize your surfing time – to help you to find the breaks, good places to eat and a selection of surf-friendly accommodation options. These are not the only breaks, the only places to eat or stay or the only bars to drink in. There is still a huge continent out there with waves going unridden. Go explore.

SCOTT WICKING

Secret reef in northeast England

Acknowledgements

There are many people we would like to thank for the invaluable contributions they made to this project. A big thank you is due to The Gill, for his amazing bank of surf knowledge that he keeps filed away along with his best transparencies. Also for shaping the boards which carried us through so many memorable sessions. We also owe a big thank you to the many people who contributed their thoughts, tales and wisdom along the way. These include Willy Uribe, an artist with the camera; Chops Lascelles, an artist with the plane; and Eneko Acero, an artist with the surfboard. Also thanks to Sam Lamiroy; Richie Fitzgerald; Paul McCarthy; Nick Lavery; Nick Gammon; Kepa Acero, our star on the cover; Justin Mujica; Michel Velasco; Tiago Pires; Francisco Garcia; Tony Butt for his insight into the Basque region; Derek McCloud for his Hebridean knowledge; Jools at Gulfstream for his performance under pressure; and Phil Jarratt for telling us we were "F****** crazy" for leaving the comfort of good jobs to embark on this project.

We would like to say a big thank you to the whole Footprint team. Anyone who has ever read a Footprint travel guide will understand immediately why we approached them with this project. Footprint epitomizes the true spirit of travel. This family-run business has integrity – they are honest, have a wealth of knowledge and are always excited about exploring new areas. We would especially like to thank Patrick Dawson, Alan Murphy, Tim Jollands and Debbie Wylde, as well as Rob Lunn, Kevin Feeney and his brother Sean for the amazing maps, and the rest of the Footprint crew.

We would also like to acknowledge the contributions of Mike McNeill and Barry, James Hendy, Pat Kieran, James Stentiford, Minzie, Graham Collins, Ignacio at Pukas, Carlos and Belly at Euroglass, Nick Urrichio at Semente, João da Câmara Valente, Ester Spears, Fernando Muñoz, Franck Corbery, Norbert Pollemans, Franck Lacaze, Frank Goudou, Steve and Nat, Chris and Den at Morrocan Surf Adventures, Toby, Toby and Dave at The Surf Experience, Tom Buckley at Lahinch Surf Shop, Laurent Miramon, Sarah Bentley, Marcus Healen, John Craze, Anthonia Atha, Alex Williams, Alex Dick-Read, Scott Wicking, Andrew 'Harry' Harrison and Ben Pepler at Zero Gravity, Dan Malloy, Dani García, Damian Hobgood, Gabe Davies, George Sohl, Gary Rogers at Saltburn Surfshop, Albert Harris at ODD, Aaron Gray, Chris Gregory, Didier Piter, Fred Robin, Fred Papagaraou, Joe Moran, Nadege Aillotti, Roy Kilfeather, Russell Winter, Sam Carrier, Mark Richards, Rabbit Bartholomew, Peyo Lizarazu, Amine Afal at FAST, Hicham El Ougara at Royal Moroccan Surfing Federation, Marlon Lipke, Andrew Cotton, Hugo Martin, Jay Squire, Jose Gonzales, Mike Brown, Mike Fordham, Nat Young, Paddy and Kit, Jo and Jamie, Pat O'Connell, Roger and Tommo at Secret Spot surf shop, Shaun Thomas, Jes at Gulfstream, Patrick Beven, Joseph Traynor, Claire King, Thierry Organoff, Debbie Taylor, Ian and Sophie Coutanche, Pat Rawson, Peter Daniels, Luke Short, DHD, Al Merrick. Phil Grace, Mark Phipps, Wayne Lynch, Fred Robin, Carwyn Williams, Andrew Cotton, Damien Tate, Sarah Nelson, the Claxtons, Andy Cummins at SAS, Ben at Finn McCools, and Surfrider Europe.

Special thanks go to our parents, Maisie and David, Dick and Bron, who have always been there for us and always will be.

Chris Nelson and Demi Taylor
Porthtowan, Cornwall
June 2004

About the authors

Chris Nelson and Demi Taylor check the Cornish surf from their bedroom window every morning. Chris grew up surfing the frigid reefs of northeast England. He founded and edited two of the UK's most influential boardsports magazines – *Asylum* and *Freeride* – spending almost a decade interviewing surfing's heroes and anti-heroes. He is a freelance writer, but more importantly he's a sucker for a right-hand point break. Demi has travel in her blood – her childhood spanned four continents. She caught her first wave in '92 and has been hooked on surfing ever since. After handling the UK communications for the world's largest surf brand, she left to become a freelance writer/photographer and spend more time surfing those left-hand beach breaks she loves so much.

DEMI TAYLOR

Camera shy? Chris and Demi's wet suits and boards

Bakio in northern Spain
▸▸ *p217*

WILLY URIBE

Essentials

Europe Essentials

European Union (EU)

The EU is an economic, political and judicial collective of countries with certain shared goals and objectives. This 'private members club' of European states initially consisted of six countries: Belgium, Germany, France, Italy, Luxembourg and the Netherlands. In 1973 the group expanded when Denmark, Ireland and the United Kingdom (UK) joined. The number of nations has gradually increased with the entry of Greece in 1981, Spain and Portugal in 1986 and Austria, Finland and Sweden in 1995. A huge enlargement took place in 2004 with ten new countries joining from Eastern Europe and the former communist bloc. The EU has become much more than a trade association. Member countries have agreements and treaties covering security, law, residency and border controls.

The Euro (€)

In 1992 the Treaty of Maastricht agreed the principle of the single European currency but it took another ten years for the euro to come into being in January 2002. It is now the common currency for over 300 million Europeans in 12 countries. You can use the euro in any of the 12 states including Ireland, France, Spain and Portugal. Britain has not yet joined the Eurozone – the Queen's head still adorns its currency. (Note that Northern Ireland is part of Britain and is therefore outside the Eurozone.)

A wave does not occupy a space. It can be waiting, hidden on a point, at the foot of a cliff, on a specific tide, with such-and-such swell direction. It may not be easy to access, but the result can be very rewarding, because in addition to the memory of the good waves you will always be left the pleasure of the search.

Willy Uribe, Spanish photographer

Red tape

Schengen is a small town on the border of Luxembourg where a treaty was signed to remove all border controls from participating states and to introduce a common visa policy. In terms of the regions covered within this guide, France, Spain and Portugal are Schengen States between which you can happily travel with no restrictions. Britain and Ireland are not Schengen States which means that a valid passport is required for travel to and from the UK and Ireland, or an ID card if you are an EU national.

Airlines

It is worth shopping around for flights as prices can vary widely season to season. For the best deals, avoid school holidays and half-term, the summer break and the Christmas period. But if you can find a spare week during the rest of the year, there is a plethora of budget airlines servicing the continent once you are actually in Europe. From outside Europe, budget travel specialists **Trailfinders**, www.trailfinders.com, or student travel specialists **STA**, www.statravel.com, can be an excellent first port of call.

Airline policies towards surfboard carriage are a minefield (see table on page 11). While some take the pragmatic approach that if you have spent your hard-earned cash on a flight to surf-central, you should therefore be allowed to take whatever luggage you want within your quota, others are less accommodating and see surfboards as a quick way to make a fast buck. While **BA** come out on top, **Iberia** will leave you with just enough spending money for one straw donkey between five of you. Airlines are fickle and their policies regarding surfboard carriage are subject to change so make sure you double check terms and conditions before you book your flight.

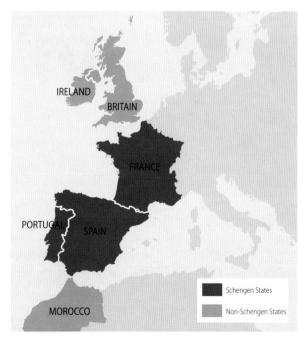

■	Schengen States
■	Non-Schengen States

IRELAND

BRITAIN

FRANCE

PORTUGAL

SPAIN

MOROCCO

Best airlines

DEMI TAYLOR

Airline	Contact	Board carriage policy	Star
Aer Lingus	www.aerlingus.com	▶▶ Within Europe: 1 board per person, charged at €5/kg, not more than 2.77 m. ▶▶ Transatlantic: €50 per board, 1 board plus 1 other piece of luggage only.	✓✓✓
Air France	ww.airfrance.com	▶▶ Boards always attract an additional charge. ▶▶ Within Europe: €1-8/kg. ▶▶ Between US and Europe: €100-130 per board.	✓✓
Air New Zealand	wwww.airnz.com	▶▶ Passengers are permitted to bring 1 board and 1 piece of luggage as part of their 32 kg baggage allowance.	✓✓✓✓✓
Air Portugal	www.tap.pt	▶▶ 20 kg baggage permitted per passenger. ▶▶ If your board falls outside this, charges of €50 per journey up to 2.77 m.	✓✓✓✓✓
Air Southwest	www.airsouthwest.com	▶▶ £10 per flight	✓✓✓✓
BMI	www.flybmi.com	▶▶ 20 kg baggage permitted per passenger. ▶▶ If your board falls outside this you pay £4-10/kg.	✓✓✓✓
British Airways	www.ba.com	▶▶ Boards included in 23 kg baggage allowance for Europe, 32 kg for transatlantic flights.	✓✓✓✓
Continental	www.continental.com	▶▶ US–Europe, US$80 per flight plus 1 additional piece of luggage.	✓✓
easyJet	www.easyjet.com	▶▶ £10 per flight up to 10 kg of sporting equipment.	✓✓✓✓
FlyBe	www.flybe.com	▶▶ £10 per flight. ▶▶ Maximum 2 boards per flight so get there early – not good if travelling in a group.	✓✓✓
Iberia	www.iberia.com	▶▶ Los Banditos! Flights from US to Spain incur charges of US$180-220. ▶▶ Flights between London and Spanish destinations incur charges between £150 and a whopping £215 to Las Palmas.	✗✗✗✗✗
KLM	www.klm.com	▶▶ €40 each way, up to 2.90 m.	✓✓
Lufthansa	www.lufthansa.com	▶▶ Board carriage included in baggage allowance.	✓✓✓✓
Quantas	www.quantas.com	▶▶ 20 kg baggage permitted per passenger. ▶▶ If board falls outside this, excess charged at around A$60/kg up to 32 kg and 2.77 m.	✓✓✓✓✓
Royal Air Maroc	www.royalairmaroc.com	▶▶ 20 kg luggage permitted per passenger. ▶▶ If your board falls outside this, excess to incur fees.	✓✓✓✓✓
Ryanair	www.ryanair.com	▶▶ £15 per flight. ▶▶ Maximum 10 surfboards per flight, so get there early.	✓✓✓✓
United Airlines	ww.united.com	▶▶ Boards charged at 50% excess baggage rate. ▶▶ So from US to UK, board would incur fees of $35-70. Up to 2.77 m and 23 kg.	✓✓✓
Virgin Atlantic	www.virgin-atlantic.com	▶▶ Boards charged at 50% excess baggage rate, approximately £40 on transatlantic flights up to 2.77 m.	✓✓✓

Visas and passports

Visa regulations are subject to change. Everyone entering the EU and Morocco requires a passport that is valid for the duration of their visit.

Britain Citizens of Australia, NZ, Canada, SA and US do not need a visa. The duration of stay can be up to six months, but sufficient funds for the visit must be demonstrated, as well as a booked return ticket. Those wishing to stay longer must contact the Home Office, T020-8686 0688. If you are unsure of entry requirements to the UK, check out www.fco.gov.uk.

Europe For the other European countries, EU citizens and those from the Schengen countries can move freely between states and have no limit to the length of their stay. Citizens of Australia, NZ, US and Canada can enter without a visa for up to 90 days. Other foreign nationals will require a visa for the country they are visiting, which can be obtained from the relevant embassy in their home country. Check that this visa will allow travel to other states if required.

Morocco is outside the EU and Schengen agreements. A valid passport is required but citizens of Britain, US, Canada, Australia and NZ, as well as most EU countries, do not need a visa. If in any doubt check with the Moroccan Embassy. Entry is valid for three months, when an extension must be applied for at the Bureau des Etrangers in larger towns and cities (see page 334).

Health and insurance

Europe is a fairly trouble-free zone when it comes to health but to be on the safe side, check with your healthcare clinic before leaving. Make sure your tetanus is up to date and avoid getting bitten by a rabid animal. For Morocco, check that your polio, tetanus and typhoid are up to date while Hepatitis A and B are also advised.

Within Europe, if you are an EU citizen make sure you have a valid E111 certificate proving your reciprocal rights to free healthcare – in the UK they are available through the Post Office. However, wherever you are travelling from, good travel insurance covering healthcare, flights and personal effects is an essential, especially in Morocco where standards and availability of healthcare are generally poor.

Check that your policy covers you for surfing as well as snowboarding if you are planning to hit the hills. Also check that your insurance extends down to Morocco as well as Europe.

Getting there/getting around

In each chapter, under Essentials, there is specific information detailing travel to and around each destination. As a general rule of thumb, if you're travelling with your surfboard, buses and boards do not mix. Although **Eurolines**, www.eurolines.com, operate a Europe-wide bus service, they will not generally accommodate surfboards. If you have the time, **trains** can be an excellent way to see more of the country you are travelling through and give you a chance to sample a wider cross-section of the culture. But unless you have access to a vehicle at the other end, it may limit you on the surfing front.

DEMI TAYLOR

Top Spanish surfer Eneko's board, San Sebastián

Surfing Europe

"Surfing as we know it today was almost non-existent when I first went to Europe at the end of the summer of 1968. Prior to that date only a handful of die-hard surfers rode waves in Biarritz and at Newquay in Cornwall. Really that was the extent of the surfing world in Europe. Wayne Lynch, Ted Spencer and I were with the photographer Paul Witzig making a surf movie called Evolution. *We drove from Rome direct to Biarritz and discovered some fantastic uncrowded waves in the Basque region. We spent a total of eight weeks in Europe on that trip, driving everywhere along the coasts of Spain, Portugal and Morocco. On that sojourn south from France we stopped at every break we saw, surfing some beautiful waves. Everywhere we pulled up at we were a complete novelty – the way they gawked and laughed at us was like we were from another planet. Upon reflection we really were a different species compared to what they had seen in the past."*

Nat Young, surf pioneer and world champion

To surf in Europe is a truly unique experience. It is not only the quality of the waves, which can be exceptional, or the range of breaks on offer, which can seem endless, but also the whole experience of travelling on a continent so rich in culture and tradition. From the soft purple moorland of northern Scotland through to the fractured volcanic landscape of the Canaries, this continent is as diverse as the people who call it their home.

"I think one of the reasons that Europe is such a great place to surf goes beyond our waves. The history and the culture of the different countries makes one trip that special, I'm sure you won't find that anywhere else in the world. Our waves are really good but I think what attracts a foreign surfer is everything that is around the beaches…"

Tiago Pires, top European surfer

ALEX WILLIAMS

Bundoran peak ▶▶ *p120*

The surfing lifestyle first took off on the beaches of Biarritz, in France, and Newquay, in England, in the 1960s – launched into the Atlantic rollers by American and Australian wave riders. Europe has taken surfing to its heart to such an extent that there are now over 2.2 million surfers on the continent with Eurosima, the European industry's trade association, reporting annual sales figures of around US$1.5 billion. In France, top surfers are swamped on the beach by autograph hunters and in Portugal you can watch the surf contests on terrestrial TV. The surf explosion has had its downsides. Some top breaks are becoming extremely crowded at peak times and there are certain areas where localism has risen its ugly head, but overall Europe provides a unique and rewarding experience that is found nowhere else in the surfing world.

"You can travel for days in Australia and never even leave the state, whereas in Europe, after two days on the road, you could have gone from France, to Spain and on to Portugal. Each has its own unique language and culture. That's what makes Europe so special."

Sam Lamiroy, top European surfer

European directory

The surf industry on the European continent is the largest and most diverse in the world. There are over 20 magazines and hundreds of websites and clubs serving the surfing communities and in each country chapter we have highlighted relevant surf publications. *Surf Europe* is the continent's only pan-European publication and is also on sale in the US, New Zealand, Oz and Reunion, Tahiti etc. They publish English, Spanish,

French, German and Portuguese language editions.

A good first port of call on the web is **Surfersvillage** at www.surfersvillage.com. They have all the latest news and views from the world of waveriding as well as swell and weather information.

Boards and packing

An obvious statement: surfboards are essential for every surf trip. The last thing you want is to arrive at your destination with a broken board or missing a fin or nose from your favourite gun. Everyone has their own tried and tested method for packing – from wrapping your board in your sleeping bag and clothes for the next six months to

O'Neill

Sam Lamiroy making his mark

Surfrider Foundation Europe (SFE)

"Help us keep the oceans clean"

Surfrider Foundation EUROPE

SFE is a non-profit organization dedicated to ocean, wave and seaboard protection. Founded by Tom Curren in 1990, SFE today has 15 European chapters with more than 3,500 members, all with a single purpose – act today for our children's tomorrow.

Members and volunteers are the core of our organization and demonstrate through their action, their ability to defend our common cause: protecting oceans and coastlines. Because marine environment and coastlines constantly suffer from damage caused by human activities, action must overcome indifference.

Since 1997, SFE has published an annual 'black pennants' report, highlighting the most polluted beaches on the French coastline in a name and shame policy. To counter this, SFE is calling for the introduction of appropriate measures to ensure the safety of water users and increased respect towards the ecosystem.

Environmental values are a long-term learning process, for both the young and old. One of the most high-profile campaigns we run is **Initiatives Océanes**. Every spring, the biggest European beach clean-up assembles more than 5,500 people at around 150 clean-up locations. This initiative also takes place in Polynesia, the French Caribbean and Northern Africa.

Surfrider is mainly present in France and Spain and aims to develop all its programs in the rest of Europe. Of course, we cannot do it without you, as we need active members to spread our action.

If you feel concerned about our beautiful oceans, please contact us at:
www.surfrider-europe.org, surfrider-com@wanadoo.fr, T+33 559 235 499.

suffocating it with bubble wrap – but all agree that a well packed board is a one-way ticket to Peace-of-mindsville. "Make sure you have a decent heavy-duty board bag and then add bubble wrap and extra padding to the nose and tail," says Sam Lamiroy. "Also make sure the fins are protected if they're not detachable."

Don't take everything you could ever need on a trip around Europe. "The first time I came to Europe I packed virtually everything I owned," says Pat O'Connell, star of *Endless Summer II*. "Then I realized that I could get everything I needed right here."

Localism and etiquette

Surfing is founded on a set of unwritten rules. During the early years these were loosely interpreted and everyone got on with riding waves and having fun. Today, with increased competition and more surfers in the water, it is important to make sure you travel and surf respectfully. Where there has been localism issues, try to stay friendly and relaxed. Vibing out the locals will gain few friends. If travelling surfers come to your break and are respectful, treat them the same. All surfers have one thing in common: we are all travellers.

"I think the main advice I'd give would be don't take more than your share of waves, even if you are the best surfer in the water. Paddle out and say hi, and never drop in, even on a bad surfer. Just try and stay chilled and enjoy the experience." Gabe Davies

"I would say to not travel in big groups – alone or with one more friend is more then enough, and it's also the best way to meet the local people and a have a real taste of the places you visit! Respect the differences of the different cultures, have a couple of city touring days and just have fun…" Tiago Pires

Europe and the environment

Europe has an incredible and diverse coastline. There are areas of stunning natural beauty – virgin territory and crystal-clear waters. On the flip side, there are regions blighted by heavy industry, waters darkened by pollution, beaches soiled with domestic waste, potato crisp packets floating on the breeze. The beaches and oceans are our playground. As the guys at Quiksilver's environmental programme, *The Initiative*, say, "Don't destroy what you came to enjoy."

DEMI TAYLOR

Give peace a chance

There are organizations out there run by surfers who aim to maintain and improve the quality of our marine environment. The two most prominent in Europe are **SAS** and **SFE** who have provided some information about their organizations – check out the boxes and their websites to find out what you can do to help (see opposite and page 15).

🌊 Surfers Against Sewage (SAS)

In 1990 surfers were getting sick *of* the state of the sea and sick *because* of the state of the sea. A group of surfers met up at the village hall in St Agnes, Cornwall, and SAS was born. At the time the general attitude towards sewage disposal was "pump it out to sea and dump it there untreated". Surfers and other water users were bearing the brunt of this outrageous dumping practice as raw sewage floated back to shore with the winds, waves and tide. The general public however remained unaware of the risk and extent of the problem.

SAS, a bunch of surfers, took on huge industries and Government in order to get the changes everybody deserved. To do this successfully SAS have always strived to present a solution-based argument of viable and sustainable alternatives. SAS highlight the inherent flaws in current practices, attitudes and legislation, challenging industry, legislators and politicians to end their pump-and-dump policies.

The media was used to inform the rate-paying public that their money was being spent on ineffective measures. Water companies were named and shamed for their practices, SAS hit-squads 'crashed' AGMs and demoed at the House of Commons, the Houses of Parliament, the European Parliament and the European Council. These high-profile campaigns attracted the attention of the public, beach users and water users who were appalled at the truth. Public opinion changed about the pump-and-dump polices as SAS highlighted it as harmful to public health, harmful to the environment and harmful to the rate payer's pocket!

Fully treated sewage, UV or microfiltration treatment, was the main aim in 1990, and with the influence of SAS, water companies have improved their performances drastically. There are still areas that don't have the level of treatment that they deserve but on the whole SAS has been very successful.

Some people may now ask the question, is SAS still needed? To answer that you have to ask another question – is pollution still entering the seas and rivers? The answer to that is Yes! So Yes, we do still need SAS.

SAS can only continue the good work that it does if water users support them, so thanks to everybody who has joined, supported and volunteered along the way. But as can be seen above, the war is far from over. SAS still need your help! If you are a member, see if/how you can help in your area; if you are not yet a member, join today.

Remember when you go to the beach, leave nothing but footprints…

T0845-4583001 or www.sas.org.uk

Road trips

Europe is a great continent to explore on the classic road trip, following the seasons south towards the winter sun of the Algarve or Morocco. A good van provides travel and cheap accommodation all rolled into one. In France there are many free-camping areas and campsites can be very cheap in Portugal. If a van is well looked after, it can keep its value when it is sold. We've suggested a couple of itineraries on the back inside cover of the book to tempt you into a van and onto the road; here are a few practical tips.

Finding a van

The UK is the traditional starting point for many Australian and US surfers' road trips. Check out *TNT* magazine in London, www.tntmag.co.uk, or *Auto Trader*, www.autotrader.co.uk, and *MMM magazine*, www.mmmonline.co.uk, in local newsagents.

Paperwork

Make sure all paperwork, insurance and tax is in order and will cover the duration of your journey. Take all relevant papers with you and leave a photocopy with someone at home for emergencies. The correct insurance cover is very important. Without the proper paperwork you may be refused entry to a country, be arrested or have your vehicle impounded. Double check that any insurance policy covers all the countries you will visit, as most have a time limit for Europe and some do not cover Morocco at all. For Spain a bail bond is required in case of an accident, so a good policy will include this. Shop around as policies vary greatly in terms of price and cover. A good source of advice and vehicle insurance is **The Caravan Club**, T01342-336610.

Free-camping

Free-camping is one of the highlights of a European surf trip – pitch up on a suitable patch of land with a sea view – no amenities, no cost, no worries. In Britain, free-camping is not really an option, but continental Europe is more accommodating. In France, there are a number of official free-camping sites (*aire de campings*) that charge a minimal overnight parking fee in season but are usually free off peak. Responsible free-camping elsewhere is generally tolerated. The rule is to treat wherever you pitch up with respect: don't shit in the bushes, don't leave your litter for others to pick up, be mindful of your surrounding environment and other people, and if it says no fires, it does so for a reason. Local surfers and local police are fast losing their patience with disrespectful travellers.

The mix of vastly different cultures in such a small geographical area and the history; not many places in the world you can surf in the shadow of a castle. It's also cool that we still have frontiers, waves are still being discovered.

Roger Sharp, Editor Surf Europe

Crime

Surfers' vans always attract the attention of opportunist thieves who know our vehicles are packed full with boards, wetsuits, walkmans, cameras, passports, wallets, phones and other saleable items. Consider where you are parking, keep any goodies out of view, don't leave your keys on or around your vehicle - the less your van looks like a classic surf-mobile, the less attention it will attract.

Damaged stick

Dings, creases and snaps are all realities of surf travel and without proper planning can cut a surf trip down in its prime. Treat all injuries as soon as possible and avoid the water with open wounds – sea water can seep into the foam through small dings and if not repaired cause serious damage over time. Small dings can be treated instantly with a piece of gaffer tape until a tube of Solar-rez or other fast-drying solution can be found. For serious injuries – dismembered fins, creases, snapped noses etc – seek the immediate attention of a local ding repair practitioner.

DEMI TAYLOR

A great surf experience

Itineraries

1 – 2 weeks

Europe has an amazing range of surfing experiences to suit all surfing tastes and abilities. Whether you are after good waves and good nightlife or a solitary surf experience, this diverse continent will deliver. To simplify things we've divided surfers into two camps: **Soul surfers** are those looking for quiet, quality waves far from the madding crowds while the **Party surfer** wants good surf, a bit of sun but decent nightlife after hours. A couple of suggestions to get you thinking:

	Soul surfer	Party surfer
January	South Morocco ▸▸ *p356* Northern Spain ▸▸ *p210*	Taghazoute ▸▸ *p356* Canaries ▸▸ *p265* Algarve ▸▸ *p317*
February	Southwest Ireland ▸▸ *p136* Taghazoute ▸▸ *p356*	Algarve ▸▸ *p317* Canaries ▸▸ *p265*
March	Northern Spain ▸▸ *p210* Andalucía ▸▸ *p259*	Algarve ▸▸ *p317* Canaries ▸▸ *p265*
April	Hossegor ▸▸ *p178* West Ireland ▸▸ *p126* Northumbria ▸▸ *p60*	Algarve ▸▸ *p317* Spain ▸▸ *p210*
May	Scotland ▸▸ *p34* Hebrides ▸▸ *p52* Central France ▸▸ *p166*	Cornwall ▸▸ *p79* Hossegor ▸▸ *p178*
June	Hebrides ▸▸ *p52* Galicia ▸▸ *p246*	Biarritz ▸▸ *p187* Devon ▸▸ *p72*
July	Galicia ▸▸ *p246* Northwest Ireland ▸▸ *p116*	Hossegor ▸▸ *p178* Lacanau ▸▸ *p176*
August	Hebrides ▸▸ *p52* Northwest Portugal ▸▸ *p286*	Northern Spain ▸▸ *p210* Newquay ▸▸ *p85*
September	Scotland ▸▸ *p34* Northwest France ▸▸ *p159*	Hossegor ▸▸ *p178* Biarritz ▸▸ *p187* Lisbon ▸▸ *p308*
October	Northeast England ▸▸ *p60* Northern Spain ▸▸ *p210*	San Sebastián ▸▸ *p210* Biarritz ▸▸ *p187*
November	Peniche ▸▸ *p297* Morocco ▸▸ *p331*	Canaries ▸▸ *p265* Algarve ▸▸ *p317*
December	South Morocco ▸▸ *p356* Southwest Portugal ▸▸ *p317*	Taghazoute ▸▸ *p356* Algarve ▸▸ *p317* Canaries ▸▸ *p265* Lisbon ▸▸ *p308*

⚲ Tripping up

Weaver fish These small fish are found lurking in the shallows just beneath the sand on sunny, low-tide days. They are virtually impossible to spot and are pretty difficult to avoid. If you do tread on one, they'll greet you with a painful, protein-based injection administered through spines on their backs. Although very painful, their sting is not usually fatal, though certain people may experience allergic reactions to the venom. If you feel dizzy or unwell, let someone (preferably a lifeguard) know.
Treatment: immerse your foot or injured body part into water as hot as can be tolerated, which breaks down the poison and stops the pain. Leave to soak for 10-15 minutes.

Jelly fish Found throughout Europe, jellyfish travel on the wind, tides and currents so they are more prevalent in the shallows following a prolonged period of onshores. Most are relatively harmless, administering a small sting via their tentacles. Don't touch any washed-up jellies as they can still sting. If you experience serious discomfort, feel dizzy, breathless or unwell, seek help as you may be experiencing an allergic reaction.
Treatment: the 'natural' solution is to wee on the affected body part, neutralizing the sting. If the area becomes swollen, antihistamine cream will help reduce the swelling and pain.

Urchins Found on rocky reefs and most prevalent in warmer climes such as Portugal, Canaries and Morocco, urchins have a hard, spiny armour. If you stand on one the spines – brittle like pencil lead – will break off and lodge in your foot.
Treatment: spines can be carefully picked out with a sterile needle but prevention is better than cure – wear boots if in doubt.

Sun Found everywhere, even in Scotland! The sun can cause sunburn, dehydration, heatstroke and even cancer.
Treatment: wear waterproof sunblock. Out of the water, stick on a hat, drink plenty of water and try to avoid the intense midday sun.

Diarrhoea Food poisoning, dirty drinking water, polluted sea water – it can happen anywhere.
Treatment: rest and rehydration are the key. Keep your water levels topped up and keep out of the sunshine. Rehydration salts are also good as they replenish your body's mineral levels. You can buy rehydration salts or make your own by mixing half a teaspoon of salt and four tablespoons of sugar with 1 litre of boiled water. Drugs such as Immodium help bung you up and can be useful if you really have to travel. If you don't need to travel, it's better out than in. If you have diarrhoea for more than three days, pass blood or are in any doubt, seek immediate medical attention.

1 month

A month is a perfect amount of time to really get to know a region, the waves, the culture and the people. If you are lucky enough to have time on your hands, here are some great surfing destinations:

Scotland and the Islands ‣ p34
Best time to go: October.
Beaches, points and reefs all catching those autumn swells.

Tagahzoute and Southern Morocco ‣ p356
Best time to go: February.
The crowds have dropped off, but the points are pumping.

West Ireland ‣ p126
Best time to go: September.
Warm weather, clean swells, cool Guinness.

Peniche and Ericeira ‣ p297
Best time to go: November.
Unrivalled reefs, quality beaches and world-class *churrascarias*.

Hossegor and Landes ‣ p178
Best time to go: September.
The classic 'Old Skool' trip. A van, some mates and living on €10 a day.

It's just so much fun. The whole lifestyle you get when you're a surfer. So much better than football and stuff. I reckon if Zidane started surfing he'd give up football. It's so much fun being out there in the water – it's difficult to explain. I just love it.

Marlon Lipke

Scotland old and new

Minzie deep inside home territory

Atlantic sunset

Northumberian gold

SCOTT WICKING

Cold water Nias
↠ *p38*

Britain

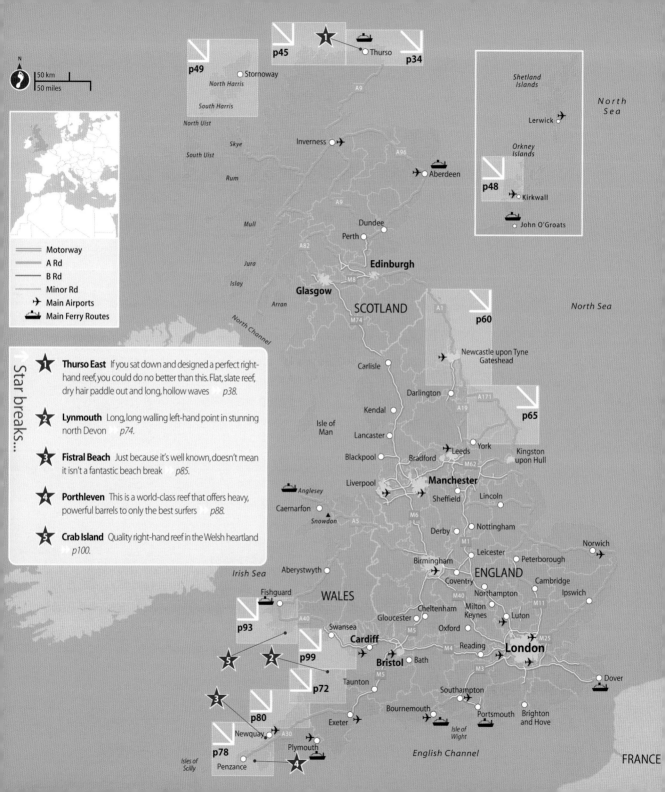

N

50 km
50 miles

Motorway
A Rd
B Rd
Minor Rd
✈ Main Airports
⛴ Main Ferry Routes

North Harris
Stornoway
South Harris
p49
North Uist

p45
★ 1
⛴ Thurso
p34

Shetland Islands

Lerwick ✈
North Sea

Orkney Islands
p48
✈ Kirkwall
John O'Groats ⛴

A9

Skye
South Uist
Inverness ✈
A96
Aberdeen ✈ ⛴

Rum
A9
Mull
Dundee
Jura
Perth
Edinburgh
Islay
Glasgow
M8
SCOTLAND
North Sea
Arran
M74
North Channel
M74
p60
A1
Newcastle upon Tyne
Gateshead ✈

Carlisle
Darlington
A19
A171
p65
Kendal
Isle of Man
Lancaster
York
Blackpool
Leeds ✈
Kingston upon Hull
Bradford
M62
Liverpool ✈
Manchester
Anglesey ⛴
Sheffield
Lincoln
Caernarfon
▲ Snowdon
A5
Derby
M6
Nottingham
Norwich ✈
M1
Birmingham ✈
Leicester
Peterborough
ENGLAND
Aberystwyth
Irish Sea
Coventry
Cambridge
WALES
Northampton
Ipswich
M11
Fishguard ⛴
Gloucester
Cheltenham
Milton Keynes
Luton ✈
p93
A40
Swansea
Cardiff
M5
Oxford
M40
M25
★ 5
★ 2
p99
Bristol ✈
M4
Reading
London ✈
p72
Taunton
Bath
M3
Southampton ✈
M5
Dover ⛴
★ 3
p80
Bournemouth ⛴
Portsmouth ⛴
Brighton and Hove
Exeter ✈
Isle of Wight
Newquay ✈
A30
p78
Plymouth ✈
★ 4
⛴
Isles of Scilly
Penzance
English Channel
FRANCE

North Sea

Star breaks...

★ **1 Thurso East** If you sat down and designed a perfect right-hand reef, you could do no better than this. Flat, slate reef, dry hair paddle out and long, hollow waves ▸ *p38*.

★ **2 Lynmouth** Long, long walling left-hand point in stunning north Devon ▸ *p74*.

★ **3 Fistral Beach** Just because it's well known, doesn't mean it isn't a fantastic beach break ▸ *p85*.

★ **4 Porthleven** This is a world-class reef that offers heavy, powerful barrels to only the best surfers ▸ *p88*.

★ **5 Crab Island** Quality right-hand reef in the Welsh heartland ▸ *p100*.

Introduction

There is no surf in Britain, just ask anyone - apart from a British surfer. They'll tell you that this island is the most flexible surf destination in Europe. You can surf on four coastlines, in swells from any direction, and no British city is more than a two-hour drive from the nearest coastline. Yet Britain is still Europe's most underestimated surfing destination, despite its incredible seafaring history and its 17,820 km of coastline. Britain is home to surf breaks that rival any on the planet - Thurso in Scotland, The Pole in Wales, The Cove in the northeast and Porthleven in the southwest. Waves like these have bred a long line of European champions, and today the likes of Russell Winter, Sam Lamiroy, Nathan Phillips and Alan Stokes compete with Europe's best.

Culturally, London remains one of the world's top tourist destinations, but for a surfer it is merely a gateway to a much more interesting Britain. Whether it's the breathtaking scenery of the Scottish highlands, the cold east coast surf communities that always have a warm welcome to real surf travellers, or the hard drinking, hard charging Welsh heartlands of the Gower, Britain cries out to be truly explored. And even a short trip to the well known beaches of Devon or north Cornwall can leave even the most hardened surf traveller impressed by both the surf on offer and the level of skill and commitment of the locals. Not bad for a country with no surf then.

Best time to visit: Autumn - pumping swells, warm weather and warm water.

Britain Rating

Surf
★★★

Cost of living
★★★★★

Nightlife
★★★

Accommodation
★★

Places to visit
★★★

Essentials

Position

Britain encompasses England, Wales and Scotland and as an island is surrounded entirely by water. On the west coast, the force of the Atlantic Ocean is only softened by the presence of Ireland and the Irish Sea, but continues north through Scotland. On the east coast, the North Sea dominates while the south coast is hemmed in by the English Channel.

Language

English, in a variety of accents and guises, is the official language spoken nationwide. In Wales, road signs are written in both English and Welsh for the benefit of the welsh speakers (they also have a Welsh language TV channel S4C). Although the Welsh language is used, English is widely spoken and understood. In Scotland Gaelic is fairly uncommon except in the Hebrides where it is still used and features on road signs.

Currency

Pound sterling (£), divided into 100 pence (p). There are 1p, 2p, 5p, 10p, 20p, 50p, £1 and £2 coins. Notes are split as £5, £10, £20 and £50. Scotland also produces its own notes which are legal tender nationwide.

Crime/safety

The UK is generally a safe place to travel, however, as with anywhere, do not leave valuables on display in cars and be more vigilant in urban/city environments. Cornwall has recently suffered a spate of summer car thefts resulting from surfers stashing their keys in wheel arches/exhausts – not a great idea.

Health

EU residents need a stamped E-111 from their home country to certify that they are entitled to free (or reduced cost) healthcare. Visitors from outside the EU/reciprocal agreement should invest in travel insurance as the only care they can receive free of charge is emergency treatment in **National Health Service** (NHS) hospitals' Accident and Emergency departments. Chemists are a good first port of call for non-emergencies but can only sell basics over the counter such as painkillers. Antibiotics etc. require a doctor's prescription.

Opening hours

General hours of opening are 0900-1730 Monday to Saturday with limited opening on Sundays for shops and supermarkets.

Sleeping

Accommodation in Britain is expensive when compared to the rest of Europe. **Hotels** are not usually the best option unless you have the finances to go 'haute couture' (£200+ per night) but the occasional

5 best trips

① **London**   History, culture, art and 24/7 nightlife.
② **Edinburgh Festival**   Hosting the world's top comedy festival.
③ **Glastonbury Festival**   The daddy of all music festivals - if you remember it, you weren't there.
④ **Eden Project**   Biotropic gardens of the future.
⑤ **Skara Brae**   Best preserved Neolithic settlement in Europe dating from 3,000 BC ▶ page 55.

DEMI TAYLOR

Skara Brae, Orkney

gem can be found. **Bed & Breakfast (B&Bs)** do exactly what they say on the tin – offering a bedroom in a private house, a slap-up full English breakfast (see below) and a warm welcome. Standards vary from boxy affairs to sprawling rural estates. This is not always reflected in prices which can be anywhere from £35-70 for a double. Prices vary through the season and deals can sometimes be struck if you're staying for more than one night. There are a good number of **hostels** across Britain – independents, YHA (www.yha.org.uk) and SYHA **hostels** (www.syha.org.uk) with beds from around £15 or less per night. **Camping** isn't as cheap as on the continent with some sites charging up to £18 peak season for a van and two people. Groups may also find camping options limited with many sites only accepting families or couples. The cheaper option if you plan to do a lot of camping may be to join either the **Caravan Club**, www.caravanclub.co.uk, or **Camping and Caravanning Club**, www.campingandcaravanning.co.uk, who, alongside plush sites, offer very basic options from £3 a night. Free-camping is not really an option in Britain.

Eating and drinking

As Britain has always been a melting pot of cultures, it follows that Britain's culinary tastes reflect this. It is as much the home of bangers 'n' mash (sausages and mashed potatoes) as it is the home of excellent Chinese, Indian, Thai, Italian and Middle Eastern cooking as well as a growing number of sushi bars. Most of these are available to either eat-in or take away. The **full English breakfast** – eggs, bacon,

→ **Fact file**

Currency Pound sterling (£)
Capital city London
Time zone GMT
Length of coastline 17,820k
Religion Christian
Emergency numbers
General emergency 999 /112
International Operator 1008
Electricity 240v 3 square
pronged adptor

sausage, mushrooms, tomato/baked beans plus toast and a pot of tea or coffee – is a B&B and 'greasy spoon' or café staple and a popular, cheap and filling meal. **Pub grub** can be a cheap eating option with quality varying from filled jacket potatoes to gourmet snacks ranging from £5-10. **Fish and chips** are the standard of any seaside town – battered and fried cod and haddock is served up in paper and smothered in salt and vinegar. Standards vary from excellent to excrement. Dinner (also known as supper by the upper classes and tea by northerners) is the most popular meal of the day except on Sundays when **Sunday lunch** (roast lamb, beef, chicken or pork with vegetables and roast potatoes) rules. Vegetarians are generally well catered for. The major drawback is the eating hours, which are often inflexible – lunch 1200-1400, dinner 1700-2100. The Brits are drinkers and enjoy a pot of tea almost as much as they enjoy a pint of **lager** or **bitter** (flat, brown ale), known as 'heavy' in Scotland. The highlands are also home of the altogether more sophisticated **single malt whisky**.

Festivals/events

Britain has its fair share of events, festivals and fêtes, ranging in size and impact, throughout the year. Some like St David's Day, Guy Fawkes Night and Hogmanay are steeped in history while others, like the Notting Hill Carnival, Glastonbury, Edinburgh Festival and the Urban Games embrace the modern classics of music, theatre, comedy and sport.

Getting there

Road Although an island, Britain is connected to continental Europe via the **Eurotunnel Shuttle Service**, a freight train transporting you and your vehicle between Calais (France) and Folkstone (England) in about 35 minutes, 365 days a year. Singles from about £135 per vehicle – book in advance for better deals, T08705-353535, www.eurotunnel.com.

Rail Hop on the **Eurostar** as a foot passenger from Paris, Brussels or Lille and arrive in London Waterloo in less than 3 hours. Prices vary wildly, anywhere between £65 and £300, so book in advance and look out for special offers, T08705-186186, www.eurostar.com. If you are planning your connecting journey from anywhere else in Europe checkout **Rail Europe**, www.raileurope.com, for details on linking with the **Eurostar**.

Air The main international airports for the UK are London-based Heathrow and Gatwick although there are also limited international services direct to Glasgow in Scotland, Birmingham in the Midlands and Manchester in the North. Off season, flights from the east coast of **America** should cost around $300 and take about 6½ hours – New York is usually cheapest. Flights from the west coast take 9-10 hours and cost around $400 to $600, with LA your best bet for a cheap deal. For cheap flights try **STA Travel**, www.sta-travel.com, or **Air Brokers International**, www.airbrokers.com.

Flights from **Australia** and **New Zealand** are serious business, lasting 20-plus hours and costing from A$1300-1500 off-season. The cheapest routes are usually via Asia, serviced by **Garuda Air**, **Thai Airways** plus pricier **Singapore Airlines**, **Quantas**, **British Airways** and **Air New Zealand** who often offer extras. Try **Trailfinders**, www.trailfinders.com.au, for cheap flights from Australia or **Usit Beyond**, www.usitbeyond.co.nz, for good youth fares from New Zealand.

Travel from **Europe** to a wide range of British destinations (including London Heathrow, Gatwick, Luton and Stansted, Birmingham, Bristol, Cardiff, Edinburgh, Glasgow, Leeds, Liverpool, Manchester, Newcastle, Newquay, Plymouth and Southampton). These destinations are well serviced by the growing number of budget airlines such as www.virginexpress.com, www.ryanair.com, www.flybe.com, www.easyjet.com, www.flybmi.com. Also worth a look are: www.opodo.com, www.expedia.com and

DEMI TAYLOR

Bamburgh Castle, Northumberland ›› *p69*

www.lastminute.com. Fares can range between €10 and €250 but remember most budget airlines do charge for board carriage and they usually need to be booked on when you book your flight.

Sea   The main ports providing links with **France** and **Spain** are based on the south coast of England with Calais to Dover the shortest and cheapest route – singles with **P&O** from £125 for a van and two people. Ferries from northern France and Bilbao also run to Portsmouth, a popular entry point. Plymouth and Poole also offer access from France and Spain. From **Ireland**, ferries run to Scotland – Belfast to Stranraer with **Stena Line** is one of the cheapest routes, about £110 for a van and two people; or to Wales – Rosslare to Pembrokeshire at about £115 with **Irish Ferries** is one of the cheapest. For crossings to England, Dublin–Liverpool takes about 7½ hours with P&O and costs about £120 for a van and two passengers. Ferries from **Northern Europe** run to Hull and Tynemouth in northeast England but take 12-plus hours with a price tag to match. **DFDS Seaways** from Kristiansand in Norway and Gothenburg in Sweden run to Newcastle, T08705-333000, www.dfdsseaways.com. For full listings of routes check out the main carriers **Brittany Ferries**, www.brittany-ferries.com, **P&O Stena Line**, www.posl.com, **Stena Line**, www.stenaline.co.uk, and **Irish Ferries**, www.irishferries.com.

Red tape   Britain is part of the EU (see European Red Tape, page 10).

Getting around

Driving (left-hand side)   A full driving licence or International Driving Permit is required plus adequate insurance. A good network of motorways and primary roads covers the country, all but a couple of which are toll free. However the levels of traffic on these roads, especially rush hour on the M25 and the north's M62, often result in total standstill. In summer and on long weekends the M4 and M5 motorways to the southwest also become clogged making travelling at non-peak times advisable. Distances and speed limits in Britain are indicated in miles not kilometres.

Motorways   These connect the majority of Britain and are signed in blue. Routes from London: M1/A1(M) to Newcastle (northeast England); M4 to Swansea (Wales); M4-M5 to Exeter (southwest England); M40-M6-A74(M) to Glasgow (Scotland). **Speed limit 70 mph (about 110 kph)**. **Primary routes**: A roads take over where motorways leave off and are usually good quality and a mixture of single and dual carriageway. Green on road maps. **Speed limit 70 mph dual carriage, 60 mph single carriage, 30 mph urban areas** (unless otherwise indicated). Speed limits are enforced (resulting in fines) and many of Britain's roads are peppered with speed cameras. **Other roads**   A roads single/dual carriageway. Red on road maps. **B** road single/dual carriageway. Yellow on maps. Secondary roads of varying standards. **Speed limit 70 mph dual carriage, 60 mph single carriage, 30 mph urban areas** (unless otherwise indicated).

Car hire   There are plenty of choices but can be expensive – from

Top tips

● Don't expect much, but bring a couple of boards. Head for one of the surf zones facing a stormy stretch of ocean (ie west- or north-facing), get a job or relax into the local life, and watch the chart. You'll be happily surprised at how often you score proper, powerful waves. Oh, and bring a thick wetsuit unless it's mid-summer, in which case, what you doing here anyway? The real surf here happens in the winter months. *Alex Dick-Read, Editor, The Surfer's Path*

● Don't get stuck in one place, see more and be rewarded. Check the Irish, Welsh and Scottish reefs and enjoy the Cornish beaches and party scene, go camping, save your cash and have more fun. *Joe Moran, Editor, Pit Pilot*

● The main thing I've learned from my travels is not to bring too much stuff. The first time I came here I brought almost everything I owned. Most places have the same stuff as back home, so focus on the basics and you'll be cool. *Pat O'Connell, WCT surfer and Endless Summer 2 star*

● Just be respectful and don't drop litter. As the people at SAS say, leave nothing but footprints. *Sarah Bentley, top British female surfer*

● Make sure you get a good wetsuit because it can get cold in Britain and a bad wetsuit will cut down your time in the water. *Sam Lamiroy, British Champion*

● Get out and explore Britain's coastline. There are some great waves and great communities out there. *Gabe Davies, ex British Champion*

£150 a week for a small car. Fly/drives may offer better deals. All the multinationals operate here but better deals can often be found with local companies if you're prepared to hunt around. You need to be over 21, have held a licence for more than a year and usually have to pay by credit card.

Public transport

Coach companies **National Express** and **Citylink** offer some of the cheapest travel in Britain but board carriage will be in the baggage hold and at the driver's discretion. **Rail** networks cover the majority of Britain but services are often late and tickets pricey unless booked well in advance. Most companies will try to accommodate boards in the guard's van (some, like **South West Trains**, for a fee of £5 each way). For details try **National Rail Enquiries**, T0845-7484950, or www.nationalrail.co.uk. London is well serviced by the underground train service, called the Tube, www.thetube.com. With a good network of airports across Britain, **flying** is a real option and with a bit of pre-planning can sometimes be the cheapest option. Look at the budget airlines as well as national airline **British Airways**, www.britishairways.com.

Surfing Britain

"The UK surf scene is unique because of many factors. The chill, the regular North Atlantic storms, the continental shelf, the fact that there are so many A-grade waves hidden around its coasts and world-class days on offer to those who seek. Also, the unique history of the British coast, UK surfers' close involvement with Australian surf culture, small winding roads, hot pasties and fish and chips. Warm beer helps, too." Alex Dick-Read, Editor, The Surfer's Path

In the early days of European surfing, the British took to water with typical enthusiasm and determination, pioneering the continent's early surf industry and dominating the competition scene. Brands like Bilbo, Tiki, and Gul sprang up in the southwest and surfers like Rodney Sumpter, Nigel Semmens and Ted Deerhurst were the best in Europe. While it was inevitable that the rest of Europe, with their warmer climates, would catch up, the British have managed to build on these strong foundations. Despite the harsh winters, Britain has the second largest surfing community in Europe, with standards to match. A lack of local WQS events has made it harder for British surfers to progress to the upper levels of contest surfing. Many riders, however, are doing just that, with typically British grit and determination, personified by Russell Winter, the first European to make it onto the WCT.

Climate

When it comes to climate and weather, Britain is world class. The British are a people obsessed with weather because they have so much of it – as an island sitting off the coast of continental Europe, it is exposed to maritime, continental and arctic weather systems, which roll across the country at regular intervals. Maritime systems ferry wet weather in off the oceans, continental weather systems filter in from mainland Europe and bring dry weather, while freezing arctic systems can push down cold northerly winds bringing overnight snow and ice.

For the surfer, there are a mixture of benefits and drawbacks to this. Outside the summer season there is a fairly consistent stream of low pressures feeding swell to the Atlantic or North Sea coasts, but accompanying wind and weather can be less than favourable. Cornwall picks up loads of swell, but with dominant trade winds from the southwest, can suffer from onshore winds. The northeast is predominantly offshore, but is less consistent. Scotland has a wave-rich and undulating coastline that means that there is usually somewhere to surf, but in the winter the lack of daylight and cold temperatures make surfing a sport reserved for the seriously committed.

Best seasons to go

In the **summer**, Britain can be a surprisingly warm and pleasant

country. Devon and Cornwall can have long sunny days with water temperatures high enough for shorties or 2-mm spring suits. There can even be years when a consistent stream of lows filter through a steady supply of small, summer waves. Summer also sees the country's one and only WQS event roll into Newquay, and the beaches become jammed with beginners and holidaymakers. Scotland and Wales receive less swell in the summer, but can still have regular waves. The north coast of Scotland has the added bonus of virtually constant daylight in June, allowing maximum use of any summer swells on offer. Unfortunately for the east coast, the low pressures tend to dry up during the summer, and long flat spells can drive the local surf community to near insanity. Luckily for them, autumn is always just around the corner.

THE GILL

Barvas in the Hebrides ▸▸ *p52*

▸▸ *p52*

★ Pros & cons

Pros …

- ✓ Huge coastline facing all points on the compass.
- ✓ Picks up swell from the Atlantic, Arctic and North Sea low pressure systems.
- ✓ It has a massive variety of breaks from sandy beaches to flat slate reefs and secluded rocky points.
- ✓ Spectacular, beautifully rugged Celtic surf spots of Scotland, Wales and Cornwall.
- ✓ High standard of wave riding around surfing hotspots.
- ✓ Great nightlife.
- ✓ Huge surf culture and surf industry.

… and cons

- ✗ Large surfing population so busy breaks.
- ✗ Pollution near cities.
- ✗ Cold and wet outside summer and autumn.
- ✗ Expensive.

Britain Surfing

Ideal chart for Northeast England & Northern Scotland

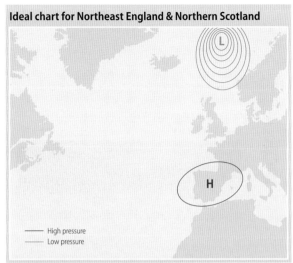

——— High pressure
——— Low pressure

For British surfers, **autumn** is a glorious time of year. The days are still long, the water is still relatively warm, the peak swell season kicks in and the tourists go home. In September and October daytime temperatures can still be in the high teens or low 20s, the water is a mild 15-18°C. The high pressures sitting over Europe force the low pressures to the north, funnelling well travelled groundswells into the Atlantic coastlines. The lows tracking past Iceland send the north shore of Scotland into overdrive, and as soon as the depression passes across the top of the North Sea, the legendary reefs of the northeast reawaken. In the autumn season, for many British surfers, there is nowhere else they would rather be.

The **winter** and **spring** seasons can be a harsh time. Swells pump through the cold months, but water temperatures plummet and air temperatures can regularly dip below freezing. It can be a time of 6-mm suits, hoods, gloves and booties. And although the surf may be classic, few travelling surfers ever venture here to see it and many British surfers seek winter waves in warmer climes.

One thing the British climate has given to local surfers is a great sense

Johnny Jango at Torrisdale ▸▸ *p44*

of appreciation. During good swells, the British will cram in as many sessions as possible, and when travelling, they appreciate any good waves they come across, never taking their next session for granted.

Boards

In Britain, the surf can be just about as varied as it can get, ranging from 2 ft slop to stand-up barrels. So when it comes to boards, flexibility is the name of the game. As the majority of the surf falls into the 3-4 ft category, a good small wave board is a must. Either a fish or a thruster with a bit of extra volume. A good second board would be a flexible performance thruster for when the swells kick in and the waves pick up.

Good charts for surf

A classic chart for the Atlantic coasts of Cornwall, Devon and Wales would be a deep low pressure tracking slowly across the upper North Atlantic. This will pump swell into the westerly breaks for two or three days. As the low tracks above Scotland the north shore should spring to life, and if the depression carries on tracking above the North Sea and sits over the Norwegian seaboard for a couple of days, the Northeast of England will turn on.

Geography and the breaks

Cornwall is a jagged mix of cliff and sandy beaches. Exposed to the pounding of the Atlantic, the slate, granite, and sandstone has eroded in a disjointed way to produce a complex coastline dotted with tiny coves, open bays and hidden reefs. Devon has a less rugged coastline and here, where the forest covered cliffs fall into the sea, sit a couple of excellent points. The beaches are powerful and consistent but the reefs are few and always busy.

The northeast coastline of England is one of the most interesting in Europe for the surfer. Here fingers of flat slate produce some very high quality reef breaks and long, winding points. Its orientation is such that in northerly swells it produces predominantly left-hand breaks. The beaches can be powerful and punchy and the fine sediments ensure the water resembles anything from a weak cup of tea to a pint of Newcastle Brown Ale.

The coastline of Wales offers great diversity. The undulating shore encompasses polluted urban breaks, classic rocky points, huge open sandy beaches, and stunningly beautiful, deserted coves. But for sheer surf potential, it is difficult to beat the north shore of Scotland. The sheltered harbours of Caithness once shipped the local slabstone around the world, paving streets as far away as Argentina and Australia. Today the same slate geography paves the way for quality reefs and points that the region is so famous for. Neighbouring Sutherland has a completely different coastal landscape, one where imposing cliffs give way to deserted bays with golden sand and crystal-clear waters. Seals wait to ambush the leaping salmon in the peaty-brown rivermouths while overhead the puffins shuttle back and forth between the sea and their underground burrows.

5 underground classics

❶ **The Cove** Cold water G-land in the heart of the northeast, a secret spot.

❷ **The Pole** Heavy, fast, long, hollow – and no one will tell you where.

❸ **Gills Bay** Classic and heavy Scottish point break ➤➤ p36.

❹ **The Gare** Reeling, right-hand point in the mouth of the River Tees ➤➤ p66.

❺ **Skaill Bay** Beautiful, walling right-hand point on the Orkney Isles ➤➤ p50.

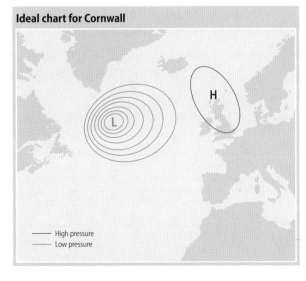

THE GILL

The Cove – a secret spot in the northeast of England

Surfing and environment

The British coastline is a collection of very diverse coastal environments. It is a country where surfers have been at the forefront of the campaign to clean up the seas and protect areas under threat. Some of the most popular breaks sit in polluted waters. Areas of the northeast, like the Gare in Teeside, and parts of south Wales around Aberavon suffer badly from industrial discharge. Other spots, such as St Agnes in Cornwall, suffer due to sewage infrastructure badly in need of updating. In northeast Scotland, Dounreay Nuclear Facility

Ideal chart for Cornwall

—— High pressure
—— Low pressure

casts a blight over the nearby surf spots like Sandside Bay, where radioactive particles have been found. There are however vast areas of the coastline, such as Northumbria, northwest Scotland and southwest Wales, that enjoy pristine line-ups, rich with wildlife.

Localism and surf communities

Overall the British are an honest people, polite to strangers and quick to warm to those with whom they have a common bond. With travelling surfers there is a tendency to give the benefit of the doubt to new arrivals in the line-up, and if no rules are broken and respect is shown, there are rarely any problems.

There are few spots where the mere presence of a stranger in the line-up is enough to spark acts of localism. 'The Badlands' around St Agnes in Cornwall developed a reputation for heavy localism in the 1970s and 1980s, and the label has stuck. These beaches have very tight-knit, very competitive line-ups of high calibre surfers, but aggressive acts of localism are rare these days. Other breaks where tight-knit line-ups dominate include Crab Island on the Gower, Fraserburgh in Scotland and the Cove in the northeast.

Surf directory

Britain supports four main surf magazines *Carve, Wavelength, Pitpilot* and *Surfer's Path*, plus board sports magazine, *Adrenalin*.

DEMI TAYLOR

Porthtowan ►► *p86*

Britain: a brief surf history

1770s → Captain Cook experienced Britain's first brush with surfing while exploring the South Pacific. **1920s** → Surfing becomes the sport of kings with Edward Prince of Wales giving surfing a go in Hawaii. **1930s** → Newquay's Pip Staffien builds and rides one of the first boards in Britain. **1937** → The Countess of Sutherland on a trip to Hawaii wins a trophy in a local surf contest. **1965** → Bilbo, the first British surf company, is established in Newquay by surfers and shapers Bob Head and Bill Bailey. **1969** → The UK's first surf magazine *British Surfer* is founded. **1978** → The British surf team are invited to tea at Buckingham Palace and Prince Charles becomes patron of the BSA. **1978** → British surfer, Viscount Ted Deerhurst, becomes Europe's first professional surfer. **1981** → *Wavelength* magazine launches. **1980s-1990s** → The British surf scene continues to expand and Britain dominates in the European surfing stakes with top surfers including Carwyn Williams, Grishka Roberts, Spencer Hargreaves, Gabe Davies and Russell Winter. **1990** → Surfers Against Sewage (SAS) formed in St Agnes, Cornwall. **1998** → Newquay surfer Russell Winter becomes the first European to take part in the prestigious WCT. **Today** → Britain boasts four surf magazines, a booming surf industry and many of the continent's top riders.

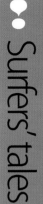

Surfers' tales

A secret spot, somewhere on the British coastline

Names have been changed to protect the innocent…

Secret spots are a phenomenon we think are peculiar to the surfing world. Breaks that we guard and cherish, share with few friends or try to hide. But talk to other people and it soon becomes clear that wherever there is a limited resource, human nature resorts to a primeval instinct, to try to hide a bit away for ourselves. From anglers to wild berry pickers, or climbers to snowboarders, each stores away secret places where they know the pickings are good. Areas away from the competing crowds. The same goes for birdwatchers and hunters. In order to encourage people to talk about their secret spots, the names have been changed to protect the innocent…

"When we first discovered the Cove, if we spotted anyone coming down to one of the nearby breaks, we used to hide under the kelp in the line-up. We managed to keep the crowds away for a few years, but gradually word leaked out. One day a guy from Scarborough paddled out and we knew that was it. The secret was out."

"Now we park our cars and walk round and over the fields so that people won't know where we're surfing. That's the problem you have - if other surfers see a few cars parked together on the coast road, especially if any have surf stickers on, they have a tendency to go and investigate. We've learnt our lessons the hard way."

"I think there are a lot of people who would like to preserve the breaks around here as secret spots, but being a realist, it's getting harder and harder. The numbers of people in the water is pushing people to explore further afield and one thing I've learnt about surfers - they can't keep a good wave to themselves!"

"I think some secret spots have become the stuff of legend. They hardly ever break or are very fickle. But when they do the fishermen's tales keep the legend going, even if the spot isn't that good. Everyone likes to have a secret spot up their sleeves."

"To surf a spot first is really special. Especially today as there aren't that many secret spots left," he said and shuffled towards the edge. The waves look small as we scramble down the cliff face and into the bay. We are somewhere along the massive expanse of the Cornish coastline. The way down to the bay looks impossible, but I'm assured by my companion that there is a trail. We edge our way along the precipice, the crumbling trail just wide enough for my feet, board balanced under my aching arm. I wonder how I'll fare on the way back when my feet and hands are cold and numb. It makes me think about the extent that people go to, to reach places where they can surf away from the crowds, and the risks we take in keeping them secret.

Surfing Caithness

Caithness was once a world leader. It led the field in producing and exporting quality flagstones. Roads as far away as Australia and Argentina are lined by Caithness's finest. In the mid-19th century, ships docked in the solid stone harbours of Ham and Harrow were stacked high with flags and provisions for the long journey to the south Atlantic. But today the harbours are gone, destroyed by the pounding waves of the north Atlantic, just as the waves of modernization destroyed the trade on which they were dependent. The region's biggest source of income is still its countryside – the land from which the slabs were hewn is now a major tourist draw.

"Murkle Point actually means the point on the hill of death – from Morte Hill," the local landowner told us. "It was here that the invading Vikings were driven back into the sea. They still plough up bodies every now and again." Caithness is rich in ancient history. It's a shame then that the region's biggest tourist attraction is the cheap and tacky John O'Groats. But the area is still world famous for one thing – its incredible surf potential. Thurso East is one of the world's premier waves. If it were in southwest France there would be sixty guys on it every day, but luckily for those who make the journey here, the locals are pretty chilled to respectful visitors. "I don't know why there aren't more surfers in Thurso," says former Scottish surf team member, Chris Gregory. "It seemed to be a group of us got into surfing, but then most

Caithness board guide

Kibblewhite Performance Thruster
Shaper: The Gill, ODD Surfboards

» 6'1" x 18" x 2⅛" for Isaac Kibblewhite.
» For average surfer 6'4" x 19" x 2¼".
» Has a screwdiver square tail for extra bite in the face.
» Good for punchy beach breaks and small Thurso and Brims.
» Sunken double concave.
» Ride in clean, medium sized powerful surf.

Semi-gun
Shaper: The Gill, ODD Surfboards

» 6'7" x 18½" x 2⅜" for Isaac Kibblewhite.
» Narrow screwdriver or rounded pintail.
» Double concave bottom for rail to rail down the line speed.
» Designed for 6-8 ft hollow waves, good for Thurso and the Cove.

 Boards by **ODD Boards**
Factory: Freelap Surfboards, Porthcawl, Wales
T00 44 (0)1656-744691
www.oddsurfboards.co.uk
or contact gill@eurotelemail.net

Breaks...

1 Ackergill Reefs
2 Sinclair's Bay
3 Freswick Bay
4 Skirza
5 Gills Bay
6 Queen's
7 Zeppelin Point
8 Skarfskerry Reefs
9 Ham
10 Point of Ness
11 Dunnet Bay
12 Castletown Reefs
13 Murkle Point
14 Backdoor
15 Thurso East ★
16 Shit Pipe
17 Brims Ness Point
18 Brims Ness Bowl and Cove
19 Sandside Bay

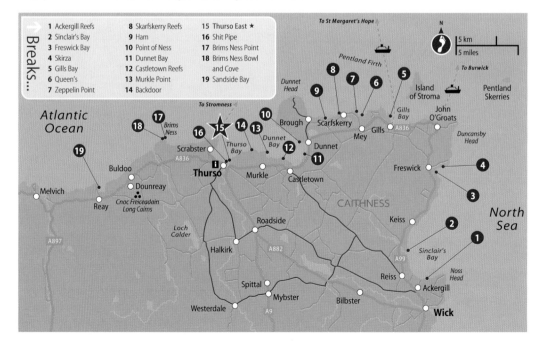

people moved on to somewhere else and others didn't really come through. There's not much of a beach culture in Thurso. You're either walking the dog or scanning for radioactive particles – depending on which beach you're on."

The opening of the Dounreay Nuclear Facility brought much-needed jobs to the area, as well as a deadly legacy. Local surf legend Pat Kieran came north to work at Dounreay, but it was the region's surf that really lured him to Thurso. He moved into a house overlooking Thurso reef in 1977, where he shaped boards in his spare time for local riders. "I lived in a farmhouse cottage overlooking the surf," says Pat. "It was a brilliant spot. I was a single bloke surfing and shaping boards in the barn and the bedroom next door. Surfers from all over the country used to drop in and stay, even when I wasn't home. I never used to lock my door. When I moved out a few years later, I picked up the key to hand it back to the landlord and it left a key shaped hole in the dust." Caithness is one of the few places left on earth where there is still a real spirit of wave sharing left. It's important for travelling surfers to help keep it that way.

Coastline

Heading west from Duncansby Head (the most northeasterly point in mainland Britain), the coastline of Caithness unfolds into series of flat slabstone reefs, which eventually run into the towering cliffs of Dunnet Head, the mainland's most northerly point. The long, open sand of Dunnet Bay sits sheltered in its shadow and the protected dunes are a nature sanctuary and nesting site. From here the coastline opens out into flat slate again. Reef after reef leads into the seclusion of Thurso Bay and the natural harbour at Scrabster. It is from here that ferries depart for Orkney (see page 55) and Shetland. Finally the huge, slab reef at Brims Ness shows that even the Vikings recognized the potential of this spot when they named it Surf Point.

Localism

Caithness remains a place where you can truly escape the crowds. Breaks are usually relatively quiet but while the number of local surfers remains relatively low, Thurso East is now suffering from the 'Mundaka factor'. It has become a world famous break, it is the region's biggest draw and has become the focal point for chart-watching travelling surfers. In a world of internet forecasting, locals who sit through poor surf days patiently can now be swamped by visitors in the line-up just as a good swell arrives. It is not unusual to see Thurso and Brims crowded during bank holiday weekends. While there is no localism here, there is a rising frustration at hassly visitors. Remember the usual rules and etiquette still apply. As Chris Gregory says, "The last person you want to get on the wrong side of is a local farmer or an Orkney fisherman. These guys are hardcore."

Top local surfers While guys like **Pat Kieran** and **Andy Bennetts** helped pioneer surfing in Scotland, and **Neil Harris** oversaw many years' worth of swells rolling into Thurso Bay, the current top surfers

It used to drive me mad. When local people found out I was a surfer, they'd say 'There's no surf in Scotland.' You'd be coming out of the water and it would be perfect 6 ft barrels, and you'd meet someone on the beach and they'd say 'You're not surfing are you? There's no waves round here.'

Chris Gregory, ex-Scottish surf team

any traveller is likely to run into in a Caithness line-up are **Chris Noble** and **Andy Bains**.

Getting around

The roads up here are of very good quality and rarely busy, even in the height of the tourist season. There is a brief rush hour, more like twenty minutes, at knocking-off time at Dounreay, but other than that it is quick and easy to get around by car. The A836 follows the coast and access roads run off it to most of the breaks. Some spots are only accessible via farms or over fields. Remember to be respectful and, if in doubt, ask first.

18 Brims ▸▸ *p40*

Breaks

Caithness

Air —— Sea ——

°F Averages °C

90 — 30

70 — 20

50 — 10

30 — 0

J F M A M J J A S O N D

6mm Boots, hood & gloves | 5/4/3 Boots & gloves | 4/3 | 4/3 Boots

1 Ackergill Reefs

- **Break type** Right reef.
- **Conditions** Medium swells, offshore in westerly/southwesterly winds.
- **Hazards/tips** Good waves in spectacular location.
- **Sleeping** John O'Groats » *p41*.

There are two right-hand reef breaks that sit at the southern end of Sinclair's Bay. These waves are set in a spectacular location overlooked by dark castle ruins. They break in northeasterly or big southeasterly swells with winds from the west. Access is via Ackergill off the A99. Park near the jetty.

2 Sinclair's Bay

- **Break type** Beach break.
- **Conditions** Medium to big swells, offshore in westerly winds.
- **Hazards/tips** Quiet spot, rarely surfed.
- **Sleeping** John O'Groats » *p41*.

This huge, east-facing, crescent-shaped bay works in a big northeasterly as well as easterly swells. It is a good quality break that is rarely surfed. Park at the northern end of the bay at Stain or access via the dunes.

3 Freswick Bay

- **Break type** Beach break.
- **Conditions** Medium to big swells, offshore in westerly winds.
- **Hazards/tips** Quiet spot, pronounced 'Fresik'.
- **Sleeping** John O'Groats » *p41*.

Freswick is a picturesque, small bay with sand and rocks forming lefts and rights in big northeasterly swells. Works through all tides. Great break but not really suitable for beginners.

4 Skirza

- **Break type** Classic left point.
- **Conditions** Big to huge swells, offshore in westerly winds.
- **Hazards/tips** Rocky, fast, heavy waves.
- **Sleeping** John O'Groats » *p41*.

A wonderful, long, peeling, left-hand point, with waves reeling along the rocky headland in the biggest north or northeasterly swells. Skirza can be epic in the right conditions producing leg-numbing rides. Worth checking when the north shore is maxed out. Access from the A99 signposted Skirza. Follow road to harbour and park respectfully. Wave peels towards quay.

5 Gills Bay

- **Break type** Left point.
- **Conditions** Big and huge swells, offshore in southwesterly winds.
- **Hazards/tips** Big, heavy wave for experts.
- **Sleeping** John O'Groats/Dunnet Bay » *p41*.

In a big northwesterly swell, this long point comes to life and can produce huge, heavy barrelling waves that break over a slate reef. Holding waves of over 10 ft, it is one of the north shore's true quality waves. Can be checked from the pier at Gills Bay harbour. This is a wave for experienced surfers only. Northeast charger Del Boy surfed it big and described it as "a Scottish G-Land".

6 Queen's

- **Break type** Left reef.
- **Conditions** Small to medium swells, offshore in southerly winds.
- **Hazards/tips** Overlooked by royal Castle of Mey.
- **Sleeping** John O'Groats/Dunnet Bay » *p41*.

THE GILL

4 Skirza

A low to mid tide slate reef that produces walling lefthanders in clean northwesterly swells. Intermediate and experienced surfers. Access is via left at crossroads after Mey village.

7 Zeppelin Point

- ◐ **Break type** Left point.
- ◑ **Conditions** Medium swells, offshore in southerly winds.
- ❶ **Hazards/tips** Shallow and rocky.
- ◐ **Sleeping** John O'Groats/Dunnet Bay ›› *p41*.

Quality, slate reef point break that produces long, shallow left-hand walls. Works best at mid tide. Walk along the point from the pier. Parking is available at Harrow Pier which, bizarrely, was officially opened by rock legend Jimmy Page, hence the name.

8 Skarfskerry Reefs

- ◐ **Break type** Reef breaks.
- ◑ **Conditions** Small to medium swells, offshore in southerly/southeasterly winds.
- ❶ **Hazards/tips** Rocky reefs, rarely surfed.
- ◐ **Sleeping** Dunnet Bay ›› *p41*.

Check these reefs from the coast road through Skarfskerry. These breaks need a clean northwesterly swell and south or southeasterly wind. Rarely surfed reefs but worth checking.

9 Ham

- ◐ **Break type** Left reef.
- ◑ **Conditions** Big swells, offshore in westerly winds.
- ❶ **Hazards/tips** Shallow reef, breaks in storms.
- ◐ **Sleeping** Dunnet Bay ›› *p41*.

This sheltered left reef can be the only wave working on the north shore in big, stormy surf and westerly winds. Swell wraps around the headland and into the sheltered bay. Best from low to three-quarter tide. Not an epic wave but a decent, if shallow, walling left.

There is also a heavy, shallow left further out on the point – definitely for experienced surfers only. Ham breaks in front of the remains of a massive, two-hundred-year old slate harbour destroyed by violent storms.

10 Point of Ness

- ◐ **Break type** Right point.
- ◑ **Conditions** Medium swell, offshore in southeasterly wind.
- ❶ **Hazards/tips** Fun but rocky reef.
- ◐ **Sleeping** Dunnet Bay ›› *p41*.

This is a quality right point that breaks over a slate reef. It needs a decent, clean northwesterly swell to work and is offshore in

a southeasterly wind. Works best around mid tide and is best left to experienced surfers. Parking available at Dwarwick pier. Access from the rocks.

11 Dunnet Bay

- ◐ **Break type** Beach break.
- ◑ **Conditions** Small swells, offshore in southeasterly winds.
- ❶ **Hazards/tips** Closes out in swells over 4 ft, looks better than it is.
- ◐ **Sleeping** Dunnet Bay ›› *p41*.

Disappointing beach break, which picks up northwesterly swells. Can be good fun in small swells but the lack of good banks

7 Zeppelin Point

THE GILL

9 Ham

DEMI TAYLOR

10 Point of Ness

DEMI TAYLOR

means it tends to close out when the swell picks up. Works on all tides. The middle of the bay by the stream picks up the most swell and has the best banks. Great for beginners.

12 Castletown Reefs

- ◉ **Break type** Reef breaks.
- ☁ **Conditions** Medium to big swells, offshore in south/southwesterly winds.
- ❶ **Hazards/tips** Difficult access on foot, rarely surfed.
- ◉ **Sleeping** Dunnet Bay/Murkle Point ⟿ *p41*.

A series of excellent reefs, starting in the corner of Dunnet Bay with a sheltered A-frame reef. Past the harbour are more exposed, slate reefs that need a big, clean northwesterly swell and southwesterly winds. The reefs are visible from the main A836 Thurso road.

14 Backdoor

13 Murkle Point

- ◉ **Break type** Point break.
- ☁ **Conditions** Medium to big swells, offshore in south/southwesterly winds.
- ❶ **Hazards/tips** Rips, rocks,
- ◉ **Sleeping** Murkle Point ⟿ *p41*.

A pinwheel left point wrapping around the 'Spur' at Murkle Point. This can be an excellent wave but is exposed and susceptible to wind. Needs light winds from a southerly direction. Access is via farm tracks. Definitely a break for experienced surfers only. Exposed, with rocks. Can be awesome though.

14 Backdoor

- ◉ **Break type** Right reef.
- ☁ **Conditions** Small to medium swells, offshore in southerly winds.
- ❶ **Hazards/tips** Shallow, heavy, experienced surfers only.
- ◉ **Sleeping** Murkle Point/Thurso ⟿ *p41*.

This shallow, hollow right-hander comes out of deep water and impacts onto a flat rock ledge, making this a spot for experienced surfers only. An exposed spot, access is via farm tracks, so park respectfully.

12 Castletown Reefs

15 Thurso East

- ◉ **Break type** Right-hand reef.
- ☁ **Conditions** Medium/large swells.
- ◍ **Size** 3-12 ft.
- ◷ **Length** 50-100 m.
- ◉ **Swell** Huge westerly, big northwesterly or any northerly swell.
- ◉ **Wind** Southeasterly.
- ◉ **Tide** All tides, best quarter to three-quarter tide on the push.
- ◉ **Bottom** Kelp covered slate reef.
- ◉ **Entry/exit** Off the rocks, or via the river in big swells.
- ❶ **Hazards/tips** Rocky bottom, can be heavy when big.
- ◉ **Sleeping** Thurso ⟿ *p41*.

Thurso East holds a pretty unique place in European surf lore. For a spot that has been called anything from 'a cold water Nias' to 'the best right reef in the UK', it is amazingly uncrowded. It is also amazingly easy to make it out onto the peak, even on the biggest days. Thurso River feeds into the bay next to the break and the water will carry a surfer out to the peak and deposit them, complete with dry hair, even in a thumping swell. It's once you are on the peak that the fun really begins.

Big swells fresh out of the arctic roll into Thurso Bay and are fanned by southeasterly winds. As a wave approaches the reef it starts to rear up into a peak. "The thing about Thurso is that the take-off is pretty straightforward," says shaper/photographer Paul Gill, credited as the first person to surf the reef back in 1975. "It's what happens next that is interesting." The simple take off leads into either a long, fast perfect wall or a speeding barrel, depending on the swell direction more east in the swell is more walling, more west is more barrelly. "I remember heading up for the British surfing championships," says James Hendy, "and we had it classic for a week before everyone else rolled in. It's such a great wave. Big walls with barrel sections." But the shallow reef is always just one little mistake away.

Catch Thurso perfect, and it's a dream. Driving down the track behind the castle, clouds can be seen rising from the shore, as if

"The thing about Thurso is that the take-off is pretty straightforward …
It's what happens next that is interesting."
The Gill

Britain Caithness Breaks Thurso East

15 Thurso East

great fires are burning to warn of Viking invaders on the horizon. Wind down the window and the rolling thunder of a B52 strike will reverberate inside the confines of the car. But to witness the beauty of a 10-ft swell exploding onto the flat reef at the mouth of Thors River is to see the raw power of an arctic storm condensed into a huge, perfect barrel.

A real Thurso trademark is the peaty brown water, fresh off the Caithness hills. In the winter, this influx of cold water also drops the temperature, testing even the hardiest surfer. "I remember the waves in Thurso were excellent," says top French surfer Didier Piter, "But the water is so cold!"

When it comes to crowds, although the locals are a tight-knit group, they are increasingly having to contend with groups of travellers turning up and hassling on the peak. "It's pretty friendly in the line-up," says local surfer Chris Gregory. "If there's only a few of you then it's not that competitive. Though you do sometimes get people who can't help themselves. They paddle round you, even in an empty line-up!"

So if you are in the Thurso line-up, stay chilled and respectful, and you will find them a friendly lot. If not, your welcome will be as frosty as the water.

(i) **If you like** Thurso East, try *Coxos* in Portugal (see page 301) or *Easkey Right* in Ireland (see page 128).

The Gill discovers Thurso East in 1975. For a different view of him ▸▸ *p93*

16 Shit Pipe

- ◐ **Break type** Right reef.
- ☁ **Conditions** Medium to big swells, offshore in southerly winds.
- ❶ **Hazards/tips** Excellent wave overshadowed by Thurso East.
- ◗ **Sleeping** Thurso » *p41*.

This is an excellent quality, right-hand reef that breaks in front of the pier at Thurso rivermouth. Picks up less swell than Thurso East but can hold a solid swell. Fast, walling waves with occasional barrels peel in southerly winds. Works on all tides except high. The peaty river run-off can make the waves brown and drops the water temperature in the winter. A good wave that is often overlooked due to its proximity to Thurso East. Car park on seafront.

17 Brims Ness Point

- ◐ **Break type** Left point.
- ☁ **Conditions** All swells, offshore in southerly winds.
- ❶ **Hazards/tips** Heavy wave, dangerous rips, experts only.
- ◗ **Sleeping** Thurso » *p41*.

This left point peels along a flat slate reef producing excellent long walls. This exposed spot picks up plenty of swell but the direction of the wind is key. In light southerly winds it will work from low up to three-quarter tide. The point can hold big swells, and is really best left to experienced surfers. Surf is visible from the A836 but as it is a couple of miles away, any sign of white water means that there are waves. Access is via a farm track with respectful parking in the farmer's yard. Remember that you are on private land at the farmer's discretion. Access was nearly withdrawn a couple of years ago after an incident involving a visiting surfer. If there is no access to Brims, we all suffer.

18 Brims Ness Bowl and Cove

- ◐ **Break type** Right reefs.
- ☁ **Conditions** Small swells, offshore in southerly winds.
- ❶ **Hazards/tips** Shallow, powerful and consistent.
- ◗ **Sleeping** Thurso » *p41*.

These two right-hand reef breaks have salvaged many a trip to the north shore, as they hoover up any swell available. The **Bowl** is a fast, hollow, shallow, barrelling right that lunges out of deep water onto a slate shelf. The Bowl can be 4 ft when Thurso is flat. It is best left to experienced surfers as any mistake will be met by the barnacle-encrusted reef (regulars wear helmets!). Works from quarter to three-quarter tide and is offshore in southerly winds.

The **Cove** is to the right of the Bowl and is a short, hollow right-hand wave breaking onto a kelp-covered, slanting shelf. It is also offshore in a southerly wind and is a less heavy wave than the Bowl, but still for experienced surfers only.

Access is the same as the **Point**. This is an exposed spot so wind is important. These breaks can get surprisingly busy in the summer, when they may be the only surfable spot. Watch out for dive-bombing terns in the June nesting season.

19 Sandside Bay

- ◐ **Break type** Reef break.
- ☁ **Conditions** Medium to big swells, offshore in a southwesterly wind.
- ❶ **Hazards/tips** Quality break overshadowed by Dounreay.
- ◗ **Sleeping** Thurso » *p41*.

This is a quality, walling left that breaks over a shallow reef in front of a picturesque slate harbour. Works best when the tide has pushed in a bit, so from mid to high. Although it is offshore in a southwesterly wind, it can handle wind from the west. It needs a big westerly swell or a medium northerly to work. Sandside is a pretty bay overshadowed by Dounreay nuclear power plant. There have been leaks of material from the plant and a sign warns of particles found on the beach. It warns children not to play in the sand and advises owners not to let their dogs dig – so how safe is it to surf there?

THE GILL

18 The Cove

CHRIS GREGORY

THE GILL

18 Brims Ness Bowl

19 Sandside Bay

Listings

DEMITAYLOR

John O'Groats

Grubby, dreary, joyless place on the northeast edge of the mainland with rows of tacky shops claiming to be 'The first and last'. Take your picture by the milemarker sign, get your souvenir piece of rock and get out!

🛏 Sleeping
Camping If you are stuck here you can camp at the basic (and joyless) **John O'Groats Caravan Site**, T01955-611329, Apr-Sep, who charge for showers. The plus point is that you can often see dolphins or orcas swimming off the coast in the Pentland Firth. A better bet is the **Stroma View Caravan & Camping Site**, T01955-611313, about a mile west along the A836. Open Mar-Oct, the site also offers a 4-berth static caravan to rent as well as a great view across to Stroma Island.

Dunnet Bay

Although John O'Groats takes all the glory, Dunnet Head is actually the most northerly point on the British mainland with awesome 300-ft cliffs topped by a lighthouse.

🛏 Sleeping
C Dunnet Head B&B, T01847-851774, is on the B855 to Dunnet Head at Brough. The tea rooms have now closed but they can organise packed lunches or dinners and have a shed to store boards and bikes in.
Camping Dunnet Bay Campsite, T01847-8213129, is beautifully located in the dunes overlooking the eastern edge of the 2-mile crescent. It's a Caravan Club site open Apr-Sep so if you're planning a long stay, it may be worth joining for the discounts.

Murkle

Murkle was the scene of a great battle where the Celts rose up to defend their land, driving the invading Vikings back into the sea. Murkle, derived from Morte Hill or 'hill of death', certainly lives up to its name, with the local farmers still ploughing up Viking skeletons that have lain covered for thousands of years.

🛏 Sleeping
For spectacular seclusion and your own private access to a firing point and a sandy bay, stay at the lovely **C Murkle B&B** in west Murkle, T01847-896405. If you're a Caravan Club member, they also run a certified site with running water for about £3 a night.

Thurso

Thurso takes its name from the Norse, meaning Thor's River. Straight up the A9 from Inverness, it is the most northerly town on the mainland and the only town on this coastline. Although fairly bleak, it is a good base for trips to the north shore as it can service all your basic needs. Thurso has hosted a European Surfing Championships and has been the site of many a legendary surf trip – it is almost as famous for its beer and brawling as it is for its legendary right-hand reef. Thurso acts as a good jumping off spot for trips to Orkney with ferries leaving from Scrabster, a fishing port to the west (see page 55).

✪ Flat spells
Boat charter From Scrabster harbour you can charter boats for sea angling or dolphin spotting. Try **Elana** with John and Malcom, T01847-891112. **Bowling and cinema** The **All Star Factory** on Ormlie Rd has a 2-screen cinema complex, T01847-89080. The factory is also home to the tenpin bowling arena, the **Viking Bowl**, T01847-8905050, open 7 days a week, and houses a bar-cum-nightspot-cum-sports-screening venue with eating options.
Cairns The **Cnoc Freiceadain Long Cairns** overlooking Dounreay nuclear power station are signposted from the A836 heading west. These neolithic ceremonial cairns are worth a visit and provide excellent views along the coast. There are other cairns in the area, notably the partially

reconstructed **Grey Cairns of Camster**, accessed via the A99 south of Wick.

Golf Following the B870 out of town, Thurso's 18 hole golf course is just southwest of the town, green fees £15, T01847-893807.

Sleeping

L-B Royal Hotel on Traill St, T01874-893191, is the best of the bunch and if you want a quiet night get a room at the back. Off season, you may be able to strike a deal for long stays.

B-C Central Hotel, on Traill St, has rooms above the legendary Central Bar ensuring the sounds and smells from the weekend travel up to greet you.

B-C Holborn Hotel, Princes St, T01847-892771, offers a reasonable B&B. With a pool bar showing Sky sports on the big screen downstairs, it can get noisy.

E Sandra's Backpackers, Princes St, T01847-894575, offers good hostel accommodation with no curfews. It has free hot showers and cooking facilities and offers a lock-up for bikes and boards as well as discounts for big groups. They'll also give you a lift to Scrabster to catch the midday ferry to the Orkneys.

E Thurso Hostel, Ormlie Lodge, on Ormlie Rd, T01847-896888, is also open year round.

Camping Campbell Caravan Hire, T01847-893524, is just off the main road into Thurso, overlooking the bay. Open Apr/May-Sep, with up to 6-berth statics to rent, it's a good bet for groups as it can be one of the cheapest options around as well as providing prime views towards the reef. Next door is the council run **Thurso Caravan & Camping Park**, T01847-894631, also open Apr/May-Sep. Thurso town is within stumbling distance but there is also a basic café on site. Opening times vary year to year so call ahead.

Eating/drinking

Safeway supermaket has a good café where you can get an all day breakfast and pot of tea for less than a fiver. Swing by on your way back from the reef. **Le Bistro** opposite the Central is moderately priced and probably your best bet for an evening meal that isn't fish and chips. It also does good cakes and coffee. **Sandra's** and **Robin's** sit opposite each other on Princes St frying up 'with chips' combos. Sandra's also does pizzas and a limited vegetarian menu with 10% off for guests. In Scrabster try the **Fisherman's Mission** (closed Sun) on the seafront for cheap, basic fare. The **Central** is the site of serious drinking sessions while the **Holborn**, complete with pool hall, seems to attract a younger crowd and is your best chance for pulling.

Shopping

Safeway supermarket, junction of A9 and A836, stocks all the basics as well as booze. **Co-Op** supermarket, just off Grove Lane near the river, is the other choice. If you're desperate for a block of wax, try the last shop on the high street, a fishing/outdoors emporium – sometimes you can strike lucky.

Directory

Bank: Royal Bank of Scotland, Olrig St. **Chemists**: two on Traill St. **Doctor's surgery**: Janet St. **Internet**: get on line at Sandra's – a tiny booth in a greasy spoon. **Police**: Olrig St, just down from the campsite. **Post office**: Grove Lane. **Tourist information**: Riverside Rd, fairly helpful, open Apr-Oct, T01847-892371.

Thurso churchyard

Airports → Heathrow T0870-0000123, Gatwick T0870-0002468, Stansted T0870-0000303, www.baa.co.uk. **Buses and coaches** → National Express T08705-808080, www.gobycoach.com; Scottish City Link, T0141-3329644, www.citylink.co.uk. **Car hire** → Avis T0870-6060100; Europcar T0870-6075000; Hertz T0708-448844. **Petrol prices** → £0.85-90/litre. **Ferries** → P&O, T0870-2424999, www.poportsmouth.com; Brittany Ferries,T0870-3665333, www.brittany-ferries.com; Irish Ferries T08705-171717, www.irishferries.com; Sea France, T0870-5711711, www.seafrance.com. **Rail links** → National Rail Enquiries T08457-484950.

DEMI TAYLOR

Surfing Sutherland

Sutherland is as wild and open as any countryside you could imagine. Its rolling hills, open peatland and sheltered coves are home to some of Britain's rarest wildlife. Golden eagles soar overhead, while brown hares dart for cover. In crystal-clear streams otters chase young trout and dragonflies hover over the orchid-strewn blanket bogs. Huge open beaches like Torrisdale can have Mundaka-like rights peeling away from the rivermouth, towards a beach where there are no human footprints. The only locals in the line-up are seals waiting to ambush the salmon returning to spawn.

It's not that the beaches of Sutherland are particularly hard to access - many are visible from the A836. There just isn't the surfing population in the county. Visitors to Scotland's 'North Shore' are usually distracted by the breaks near Thurso, the legendary reef in Caithness (see page ???). Those who stray across the border usually surf the beaches at either Melvich or Strathy, so the breaks to the west generally go unridden. Sutherland's most awesome beach can be found at the end of a 4-mile hike into Sandwood Bay. This huge stretch of sand boasts excellent waves, from quality sandbanks to reefs, but it is a true hardcore mission. The beach is so exposed that it picks up swell even when there appears to be no waves out there. It can also jump overnight into one of the UK's most powerful beach breaks when a good swell hits. It is truly one of European surfing's last great adventures.

Coastline

Following the A836 into Sutherland from Caithness, the change in geography is immediately apparent. The flat sandstone reefs are left behind and an open countryside rolls down to a rock coastline interspersed with stunning sea cliffs and beautiful sandy beaches, usually cut by small rivermouths and backed by pristine grassy dunes. The cliffs provide breathtaking views of the north shore. Strathy Point looks east to the Orkneys and Dunnet Head and across to the storm ravaged Cape Wrath to the west. The beauty of the bays is that, as they all face different directions, in theory there should always be a rideable wave when there is a swell running.

Localism

Find a local if you can.

Top local surfers See above.

Getting around

The A836 follows the coast and access roads run off it to most of the breaks. Once past Melvich there are long stretches where it turns into a single track with passing places. Bear in mind that it takes a lot longer to get between breaks than you think when you look at a map - in particular, the A838 loop around Loch Eriboll is a 40-minute detour.

In Sutherland it's not so much a case of finding a quiet spot, it's more a case of finding someone to go surfing with.

Pat Keiran, Scottish surfing legend

Sutherland board guide

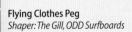

Performance Thruster
Shaper: The Gill, ODD Surfboards

» 6'3" x 18½" x 2¼" for Stephen Phillips.
» Narrow nose for snappy manoeuvres with plenty of curve through the hip.
» Squash tail with strengthening for landing aerials.
» Perfomance board for good waves and for pulling in.
» Following the Aussie trend of narrower noses, this board also has slightly more tail lift and a single concave for stability in hollow waves up to head high.

Flying Clothes Peg
Shaper: The Gill, ODD Surfboards

» 5'7" x 20½" x 2½" for Dan Harris.
» For average surfer 5'8" x 21" x 2½".
» Skip Frye inspired retro fish for any size surf, like Derek Hynd rode at J-Bay.
» Works well either as a twin fin or a two and a half with a small stabilizer to give more drive and feel.
» No rocker makes for extra speed.
» A challenge to tame.

 Boards by **ODD Boards**
Factory: Freelap Surfboards, Porthcawl, Wales T00 44 (0)1656-744691 www.oddsurfboards.co.uk or contact gill@eurotelemail.net

ALEX WILLIAMS

1 Melvich » *p44*

Breaks

1 Melvich

- **Break type**: Rivermouth.
- **Conditions**: Small to medium swells, offshore in southerly winds.
- **Hazards/tips**: Rips when big.
- **Sleeping**: Melvich ▸▸ *p46*.

The brown, peaty river at the eastern end of the bay lays down a sandbar which produces some quality long, walling rights. Other peaks work in the bay in swells up to 6 ft. A great spot that's usually very quiet and works on all tides. Parking available at the western end behind the dunes, or at the eastern end near the Big House. Not suitable for beginners due to rips and isolation. Good water quality.

2 Strathy

- **Break type**: Beach break.
- **Conditions**: All swells, offshore in southerly winds.
- **Hazards/tips**: Beautiful spot, stunning location.
- **Sleeping**: Melvich ▸▸ *p46*.

Walling lefts peel from the rivermouth at the western end of this beautiful bay. The sheltering effect of Strathy Point means that although this spot picks up less swell in northwesterly and westerly swells, it provides shelter from westerly winds. The beach produces lefts and rights, working on all tides. Park by the graveyard and walk down to the beach through the dunes. This is a wonderful, quiet spot. Suitable for beginners, as long as they are supervised by more experienced surfers.

3 Armadale

- **Break type**: Beach break.
- **Conditions**: Medium swells, offshore in a southerly wind.
- **Hazards/tips**: Quiet beach.
- **Sleeping**: Melvich/Bettyhill ▸▸ *p46*.

Quiet, northerly facing beach, which can have good surf in a medium-sized northwesterly or northerly swell. It works on all tides but is rarely surfed. Another quiet beach that is a great spot to escape to. Surfed less than Strathy, but can be checked from the A836 coast road.

4 Farr Bay

- **Break type**: Beach break.
- **Conditions**: Medium swells, offshore in a southeasterly wind.
- **Hazards/tips**: Closes out in big swells.
- **Sleeping**: Bettyhill ▸▸ *p46*.

Farr picks up more swell than Armadale and Strathy due to its northwesterly orientation. It is a small bay that works on all tides, with shifting banks, but tends to close out in bigger swells. Access is via a path from Bettyhill, where parking is available.

5 Torrisdale

- **Break type**: Beach and rivermouth break.
- **Conditions**: All swells, offshore in southerly winds.
- **Hazards/tips**: Isolated spot with rips in big swells.
- **Sleeping**: Bettyhill ▸▸ *p46*.

A big bay that really feels part of the big country. Depending on how the sandbar is working, Torrisdale can produce some epic waves. When the bank is at its best, long, hollow rights peel away from the river at the eastern end of the bay and long hollow lefts peel towards it. This is a very flexible spot as it works in small swells to well over head high and from low to three-quarter tide. There are many lefts and rights along the beach and there is another rivermouth at the western end that generally

Sutherland

Air ——— Sea ———

°F Averages °C

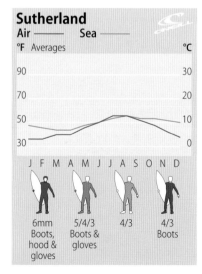

6mm Boots, hood & gloves	5/4/3 Boots & gloves	4/3	4/3 Boots	

DEMI TAYLOR

2 Strathy

picks up less swell, but can also have some great waves. Access via Bettyhill village onto track to rivermouth at the eastern end. For the western end keep on the A836, then turn right to Torrisdale village. Can have big rips but the river can be useful for getting out back in big swells. Experienced surfers only.

6 Kyle of Tongue

- **Break type**: Beach break.
- **Conditions**: Big swells, offshore in southerly winds.
- **Hazards/tips**: Rips.
- **Sleeping**: Tongue ▸▸ p46.

Legend has it that on very big, clean, northerly swells there are long, reeling waves on each side of the bay. Definitely a place to check, but watch out for rips on big tides. Check from the road either side of the inlet.

7 Sango Bay

- **Break type**: Beach break.
- **Conditions**: Medium swells, offshore in southwesterly winds.
- **Hazards/tips**: Quiet beach with average waves.
- **Sleeping**: Durness ▸▸ p47.

Sango is a very pretty beach that sits below the village of Durness. It works on all tides and although it faces northeast, it does pick up plenty of swell. Not a renowned surfing beach but does have some OK waves. You can also visit Smoo Caves.

8 Balnakiel Bay

- **Break type**: Beach break.
- **Conditions**: Medium swells, offshore in southeasterly winds.
- **Hazards/tips**: Very flexible spot.
- **Sleeping**: Durness ▸▸ p47.

An amazing, big U-shaped bay at the mouth of the Kyle of Durness that picks up northwesterly swell but is sheltered from northerly winds. Works through all tides and is best in an easterly wind. Follow road from Durness to Balnakeil. Watch out for rips – not for inexperienced surfers.

9 Sandwood Bay

- **Break type**: Beach break.
- **Conditions**: Small to medium swells, offshore in southeasterly winds.
- **Hazards/tips**: Very isolated spot, rips, no road access.
- **Sleeping**: Kinlochbervie ▸▸ p47.

Definitely not one for the beginner, this beach is very remote and picks up the most swell in northern Scotland. If it's flat here, it's flat everywhere. This is a long, sandy beach set in a stunning location. The surf can be excellent with many peaks and a couple of reefs to chose from. Works on all tides. The only access to this bay is on foot so come prepared. It's a wonderful hike into the bay and a great place to camp for a few days. Check the chart before you make the hike as the last thing you want is to be pounded by a 20-ft swell closing out the beach, which does happen, or get drenched by days of endless rain, which is also a Scottish speciality.

10 Oldshoremore

- **Break type**: Beach break.
- **Conditions**: Medium to big swells, offshore in northeasterly winds.
- **Hazards/tips**: Sheltered break with great views.
- **Sleeping**: Kinlochbervie ▸▸ p47.

A small, southwesterly-facing bay at Oldshoremore that works on all states of tide. Needs a good westerly or northwesterly swell to wrap in around the offshore island. Parking overlooking the break. Stunning location looking across to Lewis.

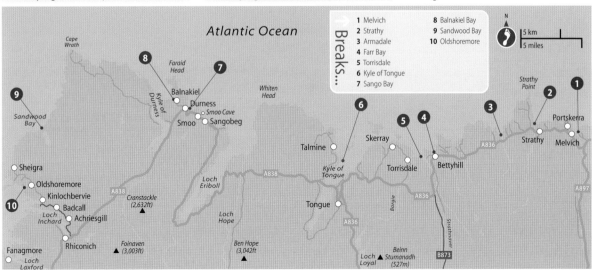

Breaks...

1 Melvich	8 Balnakiel Bay	
2 Strathy	9 Sandwood Bay	
3 Armadale	10 Oldshoremore	
4 Farr Bay		
5 Torrisdale		
6 Kyle of Tongue		
7 Sango Bay		

Atlantic Ocean

5 km
5 miles

Listings

Melvich

Crossing into Sutherland from Caithness via the A836, Melvich is an unassuming entrance.

✖ Flat spells
Golf Get a round in at the 18-hole seaside course at **Reay**, green fees around £20, T01847-811288.

🛏 Sleeping
B **Melvich Hotel**, T01641-531206, on the headland overlooking the bay complete with bar, pool table and eating options. To the west Strathy Point is a stunning location and home to C **Sharvedda**, T01641-541311. As well as a B&B, it's a working croft so no dogs but it does have the bonus of a storage area for boards or bikes and a shed to hang wetsuits. **Camping** Halladale Inn Caravan Park, T01641-531282, is a small site offering basic camping facilities and good showers. It's only a short walk to Melvich Bay and a stroll next door to the **Halladale Inn** where you can grab a pint. Pick up provisions at the **West End Store**, Portskerra.

Bettyhill

Continuing along the A836, the road narrows to stretches of single track with designated passing places. Bettyhill, named after Elizabeth, Duchess of Sutherland, was created following the clearances of the 19th century. The Duchess evicted her tenants or crofters managing smallholdings in the valley of Strathnaver to make way for sheep, a more profitable option.

✖ Flat spells
Leisure centre North Coast Leisure Pool, T01641-521400, has a sauna and jacuzzi to help chill out after a heavy session. **Museum** Strathnaver Museum, open Apr-Oct, clears up any questions about clearances, about £2. **Riding** Torrisdale Pony Trekking, based at the Ferry House, Invernarver, just inland from Bettyhill, T01641-521472, offers trekking.

🛏 Sleeping
C **Bettyhill Hotel**, T01641-521352, offers B&B as well as negotiable rates for longer stays.
C **Dunveaden House B&B**, T01641-521273, also manage the **Craig'dhu Caravan Camping Site**, a pretty average place just off the A836.

🍴 Eating/drinking
The **Far Bay Inn** on the road into Bettyhill does reasonable bar food. **Elizabeth's Café and Crafts** on the main road, overlooking Farr Bay, is open Fri-Sat only during the winter season from 1700-2000 serving cheap, basic grub such as burgers, pizzas and chips to eat in/take away. Formerly the village jail, in the summer the café is open Mon-Sat 1200-2000 also serving good home cooking as well as afternoon teas. The **Bettyhill Hotel** does a range of food from a good all-day breakfast to bar snacks and full 3-course meals.

🛒 Shopping
You can pick up supplies as well as booze, fishing permits and tackle from **The Store**, open every day.

❶ Directory
Tourist information: available seasonally at Elizabeth's Café (see above). **Teleservice Centre**: offers computer/internet access and on Fri 1000-1200 is a stop for the **Royal Bank of Scotland's** mobile service.

Tongue

🛏 Sleeping
C **Rhian Guest House**, from Tongue, head south on the picturesque, single track route towards Ben Hope for this pretty, former gamekeeper's cottage. They have storage for boards/bikes and can also organize packed lunches and evening meals (they're fully licensed and have a good selection of whisky, too).
Camping Just south of the village, **Kincraig Camping & Caravan Site**, T01847-611218, is open Apr-Oct.

5 Torrisdale ▸▸ *p44*

Alternatively, take the causeway across the Kyle of Tongue and head north to **Talmine** and another, smaller, beachfront site, T01847-601255.

Durness

Continuing west, the A838 is a mixture of dual and single track road with passing places. Durness is the most northwesterly village on the mainland, spectacularly located, nestling between coves of blindingly white sand and awesome limestone cliffs.

Flat spells

Cape Wrath Take the ferry across the Kyle of Durness and the minibus onwards (summer only) to the cape which takes its name from the Norse for 'turning place' – the Vikings used the cliffs as a navigation point during their raids on the Highlands. The cliffs, topped by a lighthouse, are still used for navigation. **Golf** Durness GC, T01971-511364, to the west of the town has a 9-hole course. **Smoo Caves** Just east of the town, these awesome limestone, beachfront caves are the area's biggest draw. The caves, 200 ft long, are home to a stunning 80-ft waterfall which bursts through the cave's roof and can be seen from the entrance. Take a walk or the boat trip but be careful after heavy rains.

Sleeping

As a popular spot for green tourism, there are plenty of sleeping options. C **Smoo Falls**, T01971-511228, opposite Smoo caves, is a popular B&B option. Slightly cheaper is C-D **Orcadia**, T01971-511336, a bungalow to the east of Smoo Caves. E-F **Durness Youth Hostel**, T01971-511244, a simple wooden hostel with dorm and lounge a mile east of Smoo with a curfew. F **The Lazy Crofter Bunkhouse**, T01971-511209, may be a better bet. It has kitchen facilities, is close to the village store, has bike/board storage and no curfew.

Camping Try **Sango Sands Oasis**

Campsite, T01971 511761, on the road into Durness which offers statics as well as having a bar and restaurant.

Self catering A good option for groups is **Cranstackie**, T01732-882320, www.norsehaven.com. A short walk from Sango Bay, the cottage sleeps 4 people for £195-360/week.

Eating/drinking

Just north, **Balnakeil** is home to a hippy craft village with a couple of cafés. **Balnakeil Bistro** is only open Easter-Sep, while **Loch Croispol Bookshop & Restaurant** is a bizarre looking affair, serving up good food year round until 2030 (summer), 1730 (winter).

Shopping

Mace supermarket is a one-hit wonder with all the basics plus a cash machine, fuel and a post office.

Directory

Bank: Bank of Scotland mobile branch visits Tue 1115-1300. **Tourist information**: just off the A383, www.visithighlands.com.

Kinlochbervie

On the northwest coast of Sutherland sits the large fishing port and small village of Kinlochbervie. It's not particularly pretty but it's is a handy place to stop off before trekking to Sandwood Bay.

Flat spells

Fishing Buy permits for trout and salmon fishing at Kinlochbervie Hotel or Rhiconich Hotel and catch your own supper. **Sandwood Bay** Park up at Blairmore and make the 4-mile trek to Sandwood Bay. Make sure you've got good footwear as the track follows an old peat road across exposed and often damp moorland. It's a crofting estate with grazing, so no dogs are allowed on the track.

> Sutherland is a true soul surfing experience. The water is crystal clear, there are dolphins and whales, you are lucky to see other surfers, and a big night out would be a couple of pints in a cosy local pub with a peat burning fire.
>
> *Aussie surfer Aaron Gray*

Sleeping

A-B **The Old School Hotel & Restaurant**, T01971-521383, on the B801 between Rhiconich and Kinlochbrevie, serves great lunch and dinner to residents and non-residents at reasonable prices. C **Braeside B&B**, T01971-521325, is fair but unremarkable, as is C **Clashview**, T01971 521733.

Camping Camp to the north at **Oldshoremore**, Apr-Sep, a basic and fairly ugly site with showers, T01971-521281. Heading further north to **Sheigra** along single track you can camp overlooking the beach for a daylight-robbing £5 for no facilities except a tap.

Eating/drinking

Kinlochbervie Hotel has a bar and does reasonable bistro-style meals. **Fisherman's Mission** on the harbourfront is a good place to grab a mug of tea and a bite to eat.

Shopping/directory

London Stores, just south in Badcall, sells all the basics but if you want to pick up some fish get down to the port in the evening. The mobile **bank** visits Mon and Thu.

Orkney & Hebrides

Surfing Orkney & Hebrides

There is a path that leads from the modern, angular visitor centre at Skara Brae on Orkney's Mainland down to the white, sandy beachfront. Subtle plaques mark out relative history as you journey back in time towards the stunning Neolithic village that nestles in the wind-scoured sand dunes 200 yds away. Within a few steps you are past the discovery of the 'New World', the Dark Ages arrive all too quickly and at the halfway mark the pyramids are being built by one of the world's most renowned civilizations. Yet, 100 yds away, sits a village of warm, stone-built residences, a sewage system runs under their paths and stone sideboards decorated with precious ornaments. Within this short journey 5,000 years have melted away and you find yourself transported to an ancient place. Standing stones and ceremonial circles erupt from the pastureland while Viking graffiti, left deep in burial mounds raided for treasure, bear witness to an altogether more violent era in Orkadian history. If there is an overwhelming feeling in the Orkney and Hebrides, it is the relentless pressure of time, weighing heavy on the landscape and the relics of lost civilizations that litter the countryside.

If you look up from the amazing archaeological site at Skara Brae, you will see that the landscape has conspired to produce two wonderful point breaks, unnoticed by the eminent scientists and legions of birdwatchers drawn to these shores. The surf breaks of Orkney and the Hebrides are some of the most unspoilt and pristine in the whole of Britain, offering consistency, quality and, in the summer, near twenty-four hour daylight. The question is, why have you never been?

Coastline

The **Hebrides**, composed of grey Lewisian Gneiss, some of the oldest exposed rock in the world, sit at the far northwestern corner of Britain. Their exposed position means that the rock and boulder reefs and quality beach breaks pick up swell from every low pressure system out in the Atlantic. The islands are home to every conceivable type of wave, from firing rocky point breaks to sheltered white-sand beaches that produce Hossegor-type waves. The rugged coastline and winding roads mean that a week-long trip won't even begin to open up the surf potential of this magical place. However the islands are also renowned for the storms that come lashing through and for the severe, unforgiving winter winds. The east coast of the islands can offer some wonderfully sheltered little gems when the westerlies kick in.

Lying off the northeasterly tip of Britain are the **Orkney Isles**, an extension of the wonderful slabstone geography of the Caithness region and a world-renowned danger to shipping since humans first took to the sea. Add to this the fact that the islands pick up more swell than the mainland and you have a place of amazing surf potential. Mainland Orkney has some wonderful slab and boulder reefs and points that go

Orkney & Hebrides board guide

Performance Thruster
Shaper: The Gill, ODD Surfboards

▸▸ 6'3" x 18½" x 2¼"for Stephen Phillips.
▸▸ Narrow nose for snappy manoeuvres with plenty of curve through the hip.
▸▸ Squash tail with strengthening for landing aerials.
▸▸ Perfomance board for good waves and for pulling in.
▸▸ Following the Aussie trend of narrower noses, this board also has slightly more tail lift and a single concave for stability in hollow waves up to head high.
▸▸ Can be made more gunny for the heavier Hebridean breaks..

Fish
Shaper: The Gill, ODD Surfboards

▸▸ 6'2" x 19½" x 2⅜".
▸▸ For average surfer 6'4" x 19½" x 2⅜".
▸▸ Flat bottomed with a fuller nose to help wave catching and aid stability in manoeuvres.
▸▸ Double concave through the swallow tail for drive, designed for small summer surf.
▸▸ When the surf picks up on the beaches and points, use with bigger fins to create a loose board in good surf.
▸▸ Great fun.

Boards by **ODD Boards**
Factory: Freelap Surfboards, Porthcawl, Wales
T00 44 (0)1656-744691 www.oddsurfboards.co.uk
or contact gill@eurotelemail.net

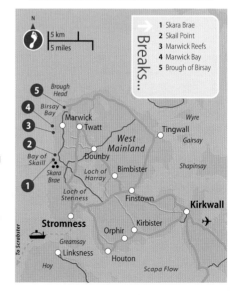

Breaks...

1 Skara Brae
2 Skail Point
3 Marwick Reefs
4 Marwick Bay
5 Brough of Birsay

unridden every day, a big call in the era of boats queuing up to surf reefs deep in the backwaters of the Indonesian archipelago. But if it's beaches you are after, just look at the potential of Sanday.

Localism

The Hebridean Island of Lewis and Harris has a local waveriding population of about twenty surfers and the line-up is now regularly peppered with visiting surfers. This is not the place to breach surf etiquette - it wouldn't be tolerated. Plus the waves here are powerful and the rips can be dangerous, so if you do get into trouble, it will be the locals who bail you out. In the Orkneys, surfers rarely make the journey across the waters.

Top local surfers   The Hebrides has a growing number of committed local surfers, with the local community pioneered by former fisherman **Derek McCloud** (see page 58) and his **Hebridean Surf Camp** which was founded in 1996.

The surf community on Orkney seems to be either very underground or non-existent.

Getting around

The road networks on Orkney and the Hebrides are of pretty good quality but are long, winding and can get clogged with tourists in the summer, especially coaches on Orkney. Always allow way more time to get somewhere than you think.

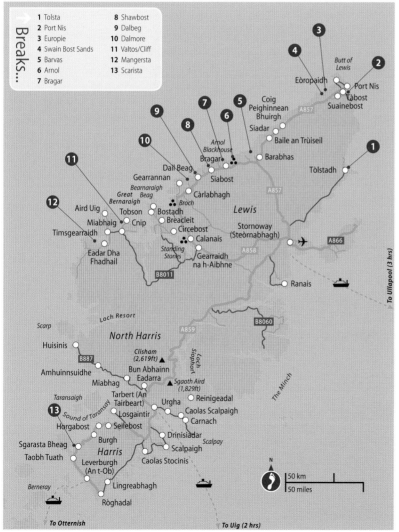

Breaks...

1	Tolsta	8	Shawbost
2	Port Nis	9	Dalbeg
3	Europie	10	Dalmore
4	Swain Bost Sands	11	Valtos/Cliff
5	Barvas	12	Mangersta
6	Arnol	13	Scarista
7	Bragar		

The Hebrides is an instruction in atmosphere. Low, steel grey skies look down on barren landscapes and Byzantine coastal rock formations. Whilst looking for a surf on the sabbath you may be stared at disapprovingly by stern looking men in black suits and their wives in pastel twinsets and chintzy hats going to chapel. You really, truly cannot purchase anything on Sundays – hard to get your head around in this consumer age.

Mike Fordham, Editor, Adrenalin

Breaks

Orkney

1 Skara Brae

- **Break type:** Left point.
- **Conditions:** All swells, offshore in easterly winds.
- **Hazards/tips:** Shallow when small, very quiet spot.
- **Sleeping:** Mainland west coast ▸ p57.

This is a wonderful, pinwheel, left-hand point that breaks over a shallow boulder reef into the calm waters of Skaill Bay. The point sits in front of the amazing Neolithic site at Skara Brae and one look at the postcard selection will show you how consistent this point is. Works in any northwesterly or westerly swell but the wind needs to be from an easterly direction.

DEMI TAYLOR

1 Skara Brae

DEMI TAYLOR

Ring of Brodgar

2 Skaill Point

- **Break type:** Right-hand point.
- **Conditions:** All swells.
- **Size:** 3-10 ft.
- **Length:** 50-200 m.
- **Swell:** West to northwesterly.
- **Wind:** Easterly.
- **Tide:** Mid to low tide.
- **Bottom:** Flat reef.
- **Entry/exit:** Off rocks/from beach.
- **Hazards/tips:** Long walls breaking over rocky reef.
- **Sleeping:** West Mainland ▸ p57.

Skaill Point is a long, walling right-hand point on the northern edge of the bay. In perfect conditions, swell unloads onto flat slabstone reef sending waves reeling through to the beach. The wave can be hollow on the outside, but as it hits the inside section it lines up into a long, long wall perfect for carving turns and cutbacks.

In big swells with little wind, this place is a wonderful, empty, crystal blue, picture book wave the likes of which are very rare in the surfing world these days. At a time when the remotest corners of the globe have surfers scrambling over them, the Orkneys must be one of the few areas where quality surf really does go unridden.

There are good reasons of course. The coastline around Thurso, where the ferry leaves for the Orkneys, is wave rich and uncrowded, meaning there has always been little incentive to splash out on the expensive ferry tickets to the islands. Also conditions in Scotland are notoriously fickle. It really is the land of 'four seasons in one day' and a chart that looks perfect for the Orkneys can quickly change into a week of onshore rain.

However, Skaill Bay is a consistent swell catcher. Get it with light easterly winds and you should hopefully be treated to the sight of two quality point breaks reeling at each side of this wonderful bay, home to a world famous 5,000-year old Neolithic settlement. Skara Brae is probably the only break in the world where surfers are outnumbered by archaeologists.

Orkney & Hebrides

Air ——— Sea ———

°F	Averages	°C
90		30
70		20
50		10
30		0

J F M A M J J A S O N D

6mm Boots, hood & gloves	5/4/3 Boots & gloves	4/3	4/3 Boots

If you like Skaill Point, try Lafitenia in France (see page 193), Anchor Point in Morocco (see page 362) or Ribeira d'Ilhas in Portugal (see page 302).

3 Marwick Reefs

- **Break type:** Reef breaks.
- **Conditions:** Small to medium swells, offshore in easterly winds.
- **Hazards/tips:** Shallow, very quiet bay, experienced surfers only.
- **Sleeping:** West Mainland ⟫ *p57*.

A series of reefs to the south of the bay where waves come out of deep water and break onto a series of flat slab reefs through the tides. Those who have surfed Brims Ness (see page 40) will know exactly what to expect. These reefs throw up powerful, shallow, barrelling waves even in small swells. Experienced surfers only.

4 Marwick Bay

- **Break type:** Right reef.
- **Conditions:** Small to medium swells, offshore in easterly winds.
- **Hazards/tips:** Quiet bay, boulder reef.
- **Sleeping:** West Mainland ⟫ *p57*.

Marwick is a beautiful, quiet bay popular with birdwatchers. It is also home to a nice mid to high tide right-hand reef that breaks over boulders in the middle of the bay. It throws up a quality, walling right that can produce the occasional barrel. Best in small to medium swells. In bigger swells a right will

appear under the cliffs at the northern end of the bay. Rarely surfed spot, so not ideal for inexperienced surfers.

5 Brough of Birsay

- **Break type:** Reefs.
- **Conditions:** Medium to big swells.
- **Hazards/tips:** Rocks, access, shallow, big colony of seals.
- **Sleeping:** West Mainland ⟫ *p57*.

The Brough (pronounced Brock) of Birsay is a small offshore island attached to the

mainland by a low-tide causeway. There are a number of reefs in Birsay Bay that break at different tides and in different swell sizes. Offshore in easterly and southeasterly winds.

4 Marwick Point

3 Marwick Reefs

5 Brough of Birsay

2 Skaill Point setup

2 Skaill Point

Britain Orkney Breaks Marwick Reefs to Brough of Birsay

Hebrides

1 Tolsta

- **Break type:** Beach break.
- **Conditions:** Medium swells, offshore in southwesterly winds.
- **Hazards/tips:** Powerful, hollow waves.
- **Sleeping:** Stornoway ▸ p58.

A mile-long stretch of beach that picks up northerly swell. Tolsta has some quality sandbanks that produce hollow peaks. Faces northeast and works through all the tides. Follow the B895 from Stornoway.

2 Port of Ness (Port Nis)

- **Break type:** Beach break.
- **Conditions:** Small and medium swells, offshore in southwesterly winds.
- **Hazards/tips:** Small bay with some rocks.
- **Sleeping:** Stornoway/West coast ▸ p58.

Port Nis is a sandy bay with rocks that has some excellent low tide rights. There are rocks at mid tide in the middle of the bay and a right breaking at the southern end, which picks up the most swell. There is also a left peeling off the broken pier. Can have bad rips.

3 Europie (Eòropaidh)

- **Break type:** Beach break.
- **Conditions:** All swells, offshore in southeasterly winds.
- **Hazards/tips:** Best beach break, big rips.
- **Sleeping:** Stornoway/West coast ▸ p58.

"Europie is a challenging, A-grade beach break and the most northwesterly break in Britain," says Derek McCloud. "It's very powerful – like big Hossegor. It's board breaking and neck breaking." The best-known break on the Hebrides and a very good beach with hollow, powerful sandbanks. At the southern end there is a sand-covered rocky bank that has some great, hollow waves at low tide. In the middle of the beach are some excellent barrelling rights which break into a channel and work best from low to near high tide. There are also big rights to be had at the northern end of the beach. Europie always looks bigger than it is from the cliffs. Parking available near the cemetery. "It works on all swells. We had Tom Curren and the guys surfing it over twelve foot." Cars need to watch out for sinking sands at the north end of the bay.

4 Swain Bost Sands

- **Break type:** Beach break.
- **Conditions:** Small to medium swells, offshore in southeasterly winds.
- **Hazards/tips:** Rocks and rips.
- **Sleeping:** Stornoway/West coast ▸ p58.

Part of the same stretch of beach as Europie. Low tide rocky sandbanks that lie in a double bay, divided by a rocky reef. **Gunshots** is a massive, heavy left-hand tube for the hardcore. Breaks like Teahupoo when big and is a big paddle.

5 Barvas (Barabhas)

- **Break type:** Reefs and points.
- **Conditions:** All swells, offshore in south/southeasterly/southwesterly winds.
- **Hazards/tips:** A selection of excellent breaks, popular spots.
- **Sleeping:** Stornoway/West coast ▸ p58.

Barvas is a big, right-hand boulder reef that can hold swells up to 10 ft. Works like a reverse Easkey Left (see page 128), breaking through the tides and on all swell sizes. It produces long, walling quality rides and has sections that can combine in the right swell. A south or southeasterly wind is offshore.

Bru is a long left-hand point that has quality walling waves breaking over boulders. Best in a southerly or southwesterly wind. It is one of the island's most recognizable waves due to the large green bus, hence the name **Bus Stops**. Long, walling waves. According to Derek McCloud, "Bru is like a Peruvian point

"As you come down the road to Bru, the coastline opens out in front of you. You don't have to confuse the issue wit break names. The points, the best of them are of Peruvian quality, 500-600 yds long – walling when small, a real challenge when the surf hits 6-8 ft. One year at 'Gunshots' it was 15-ft hell barrels and Derek Hynd laid down the gauntlet to some of the best surfers in the world. Even Tom Curren said he 'Didn't have the right equipment with him.' There are few places in Europe that have waves to match the pure power and energy of the waves here."
Derek McCloud, Hebridean Surf

5 Sarah Bentley at Barvas

break that can peel for 500 yards on its day. When it gets big it is very heavy and challenging with big hold-downs and a hard reef."

Outer Lefts is a left point at the western end of the rocks. It is a rock and boulder reef that is always bigger than the other breaks and can hold a big swell up to 10 ft. Offshore in southerly/southwesterly winds. "Follow the road to Bru and you'll see all the breaks open out in front of you," says Derek.

6 Arnol

- **Break type:** Reef.
- **Conditions:** Big swells, offshore in southwesterly winds.
- **Hazards/tips:** Big wave spot for experienced surfers.
- **Sleeping:** Stornoway/West coast ⇒ p58.

This is a big wave peak that breaks over a boulder and rock reef in the middle of the bay. It is best at low tide when it breaks up to 15 ft plus and there are strong rips. For hellmen only.

7 Bragar

- **Break type:** Rocky left point.
- **Conditions:** Medium swells, offshore in westerly winds.
- **Hazards/tips:** Difficult exit from water in big swells.
- **Sleeping:** Stornoway/West coast ⇒ p58.

A long, left-hand point break that fires along a rocky, bouldery reef. The tide depends on the swell size but in the right conditions rides of up to 300 yds are possible on good quality walling waves. Entry and exit from the water can be difficult over boulders and rocks.

GEORGE SOHL

5 Bus Stops

8 Shawbost (Siabost)

- **Break type:** Rocky left point.
- **Conditions:** Big swell, offshore in westerly winds.
- **Hazards/tips:** Rocky wave, difficult access.
- **Sleeping:** Stornoway/West coast ›› p58.

This point needs a big southwesterly swell to get going due to the rocky nature of the line-up. Best at about 6-8 ft, access can be tricky due to boulders and rocks.

9 Dalbeg

- **Break type:** Beach break.
- **Conditions:** Small to medium swells, offshore in southeasterly wind.
- **Hazards/tips:** Powerful, hollow lefts.
- **Sleeping:** Stornoway/West coast ›› p58.

This beach has a low tide left breaking off a quality sandbank. Dalbeg is a small, sheltered bay with a strong rip at the right end. The wave here is powerful and hollow but closes out on the end section.

THE GILL

10 Sandbar at Dalmore

10 Dalmore

- **Break type:** Beach break.
- **Conditions:** Small to medium swells, offshore in southeasterly winds.
- **Hazards/tips:** Powerful peak.
- **Sleeping:** Stornoway/West coast ›› p58.

The next bay to Dalbeg, this spot has a low tide hollow peak, which produces punchy lefts and rights. As the swell picks up there is a dredging left-hand point. Once you step in the water you have to be committed due to the powerful nature of the waves and the rips.

11 Valtos (Bhaltos) /Cliff

- **Break type:** Beach break.
- **Conditions:** Medium swells, offshore in southeasterly winds.
- **Hazards/tips:** Rips.
- **Sleeping:** Stornoway/West coast ›› p58.

It's a one-hour drive inland and then out along the B8011 to get to the small bay at Valtos. Here there are two peaks to choose from, both producing excellent hollow and powerful waves. The break works on all tides, but better at low to mid. There is parking overlooking the break. "Every year people get into trouble on the western breaks due to the powerful rips," says Derek McCloud, "and there are no lifeguards here. We have to bail them out ourselves."

12 Mangersta

- **Break type:** Beach break.
- **Conditions:** Small swells, offshore in southeasterly winds.
- **Hazards/tips:** Beautiful, white sand bay.
- **Sleeping:** Stornoway/West coast ›› p58.

Crystal clear water and white sand make this pretty beach an excellent destination – it just so happens that it also has an excellent low tide peak producing hollow lefts and rights. Best in small swells when it produces great barrels. Gets nasty when the swell picks up and is exposed to the wind.

13 Scarista

- **Break type:** Beach break.
- **Conditions:** Small to medium to big swells, offshore in southeasterly winds.
- **Hazards/tips:** Beautiful, exposed spot.
- **Sleeping:** Tarbert ›› p58.

This is a big stretch of beach exposed to the wind. There are peaks along the length, with powerful waves from northwesterly and southwesterly swells. A beautiful spot that looks across to Taransay, home of the reality TV show, *Castaway*. A wonderful quiet spot worth checking if the northwest coast is too big and the wind is from the southeast. Quite a long but beautiful drive from Stornoway.

THE GILL

10 Dalmore

Listings

Orkney

Orkney takes its name from the orcas (killer whales) that make their migratory journey through the islands' surrounding waters. There are about 70 islands within the Orkney archipelago, the largest of which is Mainland. Although only a short hop across the water from the tacky John O'Groats, Orkney with its Neotlithic village and standing stones attracts hordes of summer tourists for very good reason.

🛟 Getting there
Ferries **Pentland Ferries**, T01856-831226, www.pentlandferries.co.uk, operate the cheapest service between Gills Bay, just off the A836 west of John O'Groats, and St Margaret's Hope on South Ronaldsay. Foot passengers from £20 return, vans from £50 return. A free bus ferries passengers to the capital, Kirkwall. **Northlink Ferries**, T01856-885500, www.northlinkferries.co.uk, operates year round between Scrabster, near Thurso, and the old fishing port of Stromness on West Mainland. Taking in the Old Man of Hoy, the breathtaking 450-ft sea stacks, the journey takes about 1½ hrs and runs twice daily Mon-Fri with weekend services. Return from £26 foot passenger and £78 van. Northlink also operate ferries year round from Aberdeen on Scotland's east coast to Stromness. Taking 8 hrs, it costs about double the Scrabster service. **John O'Groats Ferries**, T01955-611353, www.jogferry.co.uk, runs a summer passenger service between John O'Groats to

Burwick on South Ronaldsay or Kirkwall with returns from £24. Buses connect with the Burwick ferry and run to Kirkwall.

Air **British Airways**, T0870-8509850, operates direct flights to Kirkwall Mon-Sat from Aberdeen, Edinburgh, Glasgow and Inverness with connections from London Heathrow, Gatwick, Birmingham, Manchester and Belfast. Flights are pricey; ring ahead to make sure there will be room for your board, especially during busy summer months.

❄ Flat spells
There is so much history contained on this tiny island that you won't get bored. Here are just some highlights – see also Kirkwall below. **Churchill Barriers** Constructed between 1940 and 1945 on the order of Winston Churchill, the massive concrete barriers were designed to protect the British Navy based in Scapa Flow from enemy submarine attacks. The barriers, built by Italian prisoners of war stationed on the island, have only limited interest when compared with the exquisitely detailed **Italian Chapel** built by the POWs. The chapel started life as two Nissen huts, while the ornate decorations were crafted from salvaged scrap metal and old pieces of concrete. Follow the A961 south from Kirkwall. **Diving** Scapa Flow, hemmed in by Mainland, South Ronaldsay and Hoy, attracts divers from all over the world to explore in crystal-clear waters the wrecks of the German fleet scuttled during the First World War. **Scapa Scuba**, heading south out of Stromness on Ness Rd, offer lessons, dives and equipment hire to novices and experienced divers, T01856-851218. **Maeshowe** It may look like a hill from the outside but this is one of the most impressive chambered tombs in Western Europe, made even more interesting by the fact it was raided by the Vikings in the 12th century. The plundering Norsemen carved runic graffiti into the walls boasting of their conquests in battle and with women. **Skara Brae** If you only see one thing while you're

Kelp

here, make sure it is this 5,000-year-old village and world heritage site. It's 2,000 years older than the Pyramids, it even predates Stonehenge, but Neolithic man still wanted to utilize the latest technology in his village. Skara Brae has a sewage system and individual dwellings boasted a course of damp-proofing, stone sideboards for displaying treasures, and even cool boxes. Open year round with an excellent visitors' centre, £5. Access via the B9056. **Standing stones** The Stones of Stenness and the bigger Ring of Brodgar are both spectacular ceremonial stone circles dating from the time of Skara Brae. Unlike Stonehenge, you're allowed to walk freely and actually touch the stones. Accessed via the B9055 running northwesterly off the A965, the circles and nearby standing stones run along powerful lay lines.

Stromness

Stromness is a pretty fishing town complete with cobbled streets and a strong seafaring tradition – many of the Atlantic's whaling crews set out from here. On the ferry over from Scrabster, dolphins are often seen playing in the wake, leading the ferries home.

☻ Sleeping
C Mrs Worthington's B&B, 2 South End, T01856-850215, open Apr-Oct, views over Scapa Flow and easy access to the town.
C Bea House B&B, Back Rd, T01856-851043, bea.house@virgin.net, within walking distance of the ferry port and overlooks the town.
F-G Browns Hostel, Victoria St, T01856-850661, independent, popular, open year round and well placed. Beds from about £10.
F-G SYHA Stromness Hostel, on Hellihole Rd, T01856-850589, another cheap option, May-Sep.
Self catering There is plenty of self-catering accommodation which can work out to be the cheapest and easiest option for groups. Traditional stone house on Dundas St overlooking the harbour,

sleeps up to 6 from £200/week. **Contact Mr and Mrs Seater**, T01856-850415. Also on Dundas St, with good town access, is another stone property sleeping up to 4 people for under £200/week, Apr-Oct. **Contact Mrs Boyes**, T01856-850120.
Camping Responsible free-camping is permitted but ask the landowner's permission first.
Point of Ness Caravan and Camping, T01856-873535, is a short walk from town and has great views across the water to neighbouring Hoy (can be a bit windy). Open May-Sep.

☻ Eating/drinking
Julia's café, opposite the ferry terminal, does a good range of reasonably priced food at lunch – soup, sandwiches, salads, jackets etc. The **Ferry Inn,** near the terminal, is a popular spot and does reasonably priced pub grub for lunch and dinner. If you feel like splashing out head to the **Hamnavoe Restaurant** on Graham Place and eat the catch of the day, straight off the boats. This Egon Ronay restaurant is open Apr-Sep, T01856-850606.

☻ Shopping
Argo's Bakery, Victoria St, does fresh bread as well as basic groceries. Swing by **Orkney Mini-labs** on Victoria St to pick up spare camera film.

☻ Transport
Bike hire: Orkney Cycle Hire, Dundas St, hires bikes by the day/week, T01856-850255. **Car hire**: Norman Brass Car Hire, North End Rd, T01856-850850, is based at the Blue Star Filling Station or try Stromness Self Drive Cars, 75 John St, T01856-850973 – both within walking distance of the ferry. See also Getting around, above.

☻ Directory
Bank: Victoria St. **Post office**: corner Boy's La/Victoria St. **Tourist information**: based at the Scrabster ferry port, open year round, T01856-850716, www.visitorkney.com.

Kirkwall

Founded in 1035, Kirkwall is the capital of Orkney, a busy working town that lacks the natural charm of Stromness. However, its redeeming feature is that it does offer basic amenities from chemists to banks to supermarkets.

☻ Flat spells
Golf Orkney Golf Club, just west of Kirkwall on Grainbank, T01856-872457, has an 18-hole course, green fees from £15.
Pickaquoy Centre Pickaquoy Rd, Kirkwall, T01856-879900, is home to the **New Phoenix Cinema** while **The Zone** fitness studio has a sauna, jacuzzi and steam room to help you chill out after a heavy session. The centre also has a café and bar with pool tables and Sky TV.

☻ Sleeping
A-B Albert Hotel, Mounthoolie La, T01856-876000, is centrally located and home to an OK restaurant and a couple of busy bars.
C-D Cumliebank B&B, Cromwell Rd, T01856-873160, is well located, about a 5-minute walk into town. There are several other B&Bs around Cromwell Rd.
F-G Peedie Hostel, on Ayre Rd by the seafront, T01856-875477, is basic and not particularly spacious with beds from £10.
F-G SYHA, Old Skapa Rd, T01856-872243, open Apr-Oct, is basic, about a 15-min walk into town, with a midnight curfew.
Self catering **Mrs Sinclair's** house and flat on Tankerness are about as central as you can get. The house sleeps up to 7 people with prices around £300/week, T01856-872035.
Camping The **Pickaquoy Centre** (see Flat spells above for details) offers basic camping facilities May-Sep with pay showers (get a good haul of 20ps).

☻ Eating/drinking
The **Bothy Bar** at the Albert Hotel is pretty lively, occasionally has live bands and serves a full range of real ales including Dark Island

– an Orcadian-style Guinness – as well as OK bar food. **Busters Diner** on Mounthooliea offers fairly cheap pizzas, pastas and burgers, open lunch/dinner Mon-Sat, dinner only Sun. **Empire Chinese Restaurant** on Junction Rd is pretty good and offers reasonably priced eat-in or takeaway food. The **St Magnus Café** at the community centre is a good and cheap place to grab a sandwich and a cup of tea, as is the **Mustard Seed** on Victoria St who also do home baking.

Transport
Airport: T01856-872421, about 3 miles southeast of town along the A960. **Bike hire**: Bobby's Cycle Centre, Tankerness La, T01856-875777, from £8 a day. **Car hire**: due to a captive audience car hire is pricey, about £150-plus per week. Plenty of options, with firms offering much the same services. **James Peace & Co**, Junction Rd, T01856-872866. **W.R. Tullock** (Fords) with offices on Castle St, T01856-87626, and the airport, T01856-875000. **John Shearer &**

Sons (Vauxhalls), T01856-872950, at the Ayre service station. **Scarth Hire**, Great Western Rd, T01856-872125, also rent vans.

Directory/shopping
Banks: there are a couple of banks off the main Broad St and Albert St. **Chemist**: Boots on Albert St. **Hospital**: Balfour Hospital and Health Centre on New Scapa Rd running south out of town. **Police**: Buttquoy Cres. **Post office**: Junction Rd. **Shopping**: stock up at **Safeway** supermarket on Pickaquoy road. **Tourist information**: Broad St, T0185 872856.

West Mainland

The west coast is home to the major breaks on Orkney and, if you don't mind being away from the pubs and shops, can be a good base for those wanting to escape the tourists. **Sandwick** is a short hop to Skaill Bay with its 2 point breaks and heading north from Skaill is **Marwick Bay** in Birsay, with some excellent reefs and a good point.

Sleeping
Sandwick
D **Netherstove**, a working farm overlooking Skaill Bay, T01856-841625, offers B&B May-Oct and year-round self-catering accommodation from £120/week for 2 people.
D **Hyval Farm**, a family run beef farm in a coastal location near Skaill Bay, T01856-841522, offers B&B Apr-Oct.
Birsay
C **Primrose Cottage**, views over Marwick Bay and comfortable B&B accommodation, T01856-721384.
There are plenty of self-catering facilities here including **Quoylonga Farm**, T01856-721225, open Apr-Oct, which sleeps 4 people from £150/week.

Shopping
Dounby Stores on the A986 has a general store and a petrol station open 7 days a week and stocking good local produce. The petrol here is also cheaper than on the mainland.

DEMI TAYLOR

Sunlit sea across the water from Scrabster

Hebrides

This 130-mile long chain of islands sitting 30 miles off the coast of Scotland is home to Britain's most northwesterly beach, Europie, as well as puffins, golden eagles, dolphins, whales and basking sharks. Tradition has a strong foothold on the islands where Gaelic is still spoken and Sundays really are a day of rest.

⊕ Getting there

Air British Airways, T0870-8509850, operate regular flights Mon-Sat from Glasgow, Edinburgh and Inverness to Stornoway airport.
Ferries CalMac, T01475-650100, www.calmac.co.uk, run regular services year round between Ullapool on Scotland's northwest coast and Stornoway on Lewis. Crossings run 2-3 times daily and take approximately 2 hrs 40 mins – expect to pay from £150 return for a car and 2 passengers.

Lewis (Leodhas)

Stornoway (Steòrnabhagh)

Lewis makes up the top two-thirds of the most northerly island in the chain. The town of Stornoway on the east coast is the focal point for island life and the only major town servicing the islands.

✿ Flat spells

Ancient monuments **Calanais (Callanish) standing stones**, overlooking Loch Roag, are the most spectacular Neolithic monument on the island, forming a Celtic cross. **Clach an Truiseil** near Barabhas is the largest monolith in Europe standing 20-ft tall. **Golf** **Stornoway Golf Club**, Lady Lever Park, just east of Stornoway, T01851-702249, offers an 18-hole course set in the grounds of Lews Castle.

⊜ Sleeping

F-G Stornoway Surf House, Keith St, www.hebrideansurf.co.uk, T01851-705862 (day), T0151-701869 (evening), is run by Derek McCloud and is the best option for visiting surfers. A former fisherman and hardy surfer, Derek's knowledge of this coastline is second to none. £10 will buy you a bed in a dorm and access to a self-catering kitchen. Alternatively you can pay a bit more and have the cooking done for you and be taken to the best breaks every day.
F-G Laxdale Holiday Park, T01851-706966, www.laxdaleholidaypark.com, is about 1½ miles outside Stornoway and has camping facilities as well as caravans and a bungalow for hire Mar-Oct. Their bunkhouse is open year round with beds from £10 per night.

⊘ Eating/drinking

Sunsets Restaurant, near the surf camp, serves tasty and healthy meals using local produce and fresh fish straight off the boats. The **Crown Hotel** on Castle St is a nice place to grab a pint and a bite to eat but there are also plenty of other pubs around the quay. The **Thai Café** on Church St is surprisingly good – and good value. The **Heb** is the nightclub for the islands, so get down there Thu-Sat nights, but remember Sat night finishes early, before midnight, so as not to cross over into Sun.

◐ Shopping

Derek McCloud runs a fully stocked surf shop off Keith St. Head to the **supermarkets** on Cromwell St to pick up your provisions but remember there is no Sun opening.

⊖ Transport

Bike hire: Alex Dan's Cycle Centre on Kenneth St, T01851-704025, hire bikes by the hour, day or week. **Car hire**: Lewis Car Rentals, Bayhead St, T01851-703760, and **Lochs Motors** on Southbeach, T01851-705857, can offer good rates for day and week hire.

ⓘ Directory

Bank: Bank of Scotland, opposite the Tourist info. **Internet**: get online at the **local library** on Cromwell St – connection is expensive from £3.50 per hour – or try **Captions** on Church St. **Post office**: Francis St. **Tourist information**: Cromwell St, www.visithebrides.co.uk, open year round.

West coast

⊜ Sleeping

Port Nis (Ness) Port Nis sits at the northwest tip of the Butt of Lewis, a 45-min drive from Stornoway.
L-A The Cross Inn, T01851-810152, who also have a bar serving food.
C Galson Farm Guest House , 8 miles south of Port Nis off the A857, 18th-century converted farmhouse, T01851-850492.
Barabhas (Barvas) Barabhas sits on the junction with A857 and A858 and gives good scope to explore the coastline.
C Rockvilla B&B, T01851-840286.
Siabost (Shawbost)/Carlabhagh (Carloway) Siabost has camping May-Oct at **Eilean Fraoich Campsite**, T01851-710504. off the A858. If you don't fancy camping try
B-C Airigh B&B in South Siabost, T01851-710478.
Continuing south along the A858 to Carlabhagh, follow the back road towards the coast and the former crofting village of **Garenin**. F-G Garenin Gatliff hostel (non-profit) is open year round with beds in the restored blackhouse from £8. You can't

Airports → Heathrow T0870-0000123, Gatwick T0870-0002468, Stansted T0870-0000303, www.baa.co.uk. **Buses and coaches** → National Express T08705-808080, www.gobycoach.com; Scottish City Link, T0141-3329644, www.citylink.co.uk. **Car hire** → Avis T0870-6060100; Europcar T0870-6075000; Hertz T08708-448844. **Petrol prices** → £0.85-90/litre. **Ferries** → P&O, T0870-2424999, www.poportsmouth.com; Brittany Ferries,T0870-3665333, www.brittany-ferries.com; Irish Ferries T08705-171717, www.irishferries.com; Sea France, T0870-5711711, www.seafrance.com. **Rail links** → National Rail Enquiries T08457-484950.

book ahead and it is heated by coal fire but it is a great place to stay and well located for Dalbeg and Dalmore Bays. Try the **Copper Kettle** at Dalbeg Bay for cheap lunchtime snacks and jacket potatoes.

Isle of Harris (Na Hearadh)

Tarbert (An Tairbeart)

Harris is not a separate island but shares a piece of rock with Lewis to the north and is famous for its Harris tweed. The port of Tarbert, lying in a sheltered bay, is the main settlement on the island and joins north and south Harris.

❂ Flat spells
Golf Get a round in at the 9-hole **Scarista Golf Club**, except on Suns, T01859-502331.

East coast This is worth exploring for the bizzare lunar-style landscape alone.

● Sleeping
B-C MacLeod Motel, near the ferry pier, T01859-502364, offers rooms as well as cottages to rent.
E Rockview Bunkhouse, Main St, T01859-502626, is a cheap, well placed option with kitchen facilities,
F-G Drinishader Hostel, about 5 miles south of Tarbert, has a roaring coal fire, T01859-511255.

❼ Eating/drinking
The Harris Hotel near the ferry terminal does good value bar food as well as a comprehensive dinner menu and serves on Sun. **First Fruits** teahouse, Harbour St Apr-Sep, is a nice place to grab a lunchtime snack, as is **Big D's** on Harbour St which also

does takeaway and dinner. Although not the most lively of places, there are a few pubs on Harbour St including **Tarbert Hotel, Anchor Hotel** and **Corner House**.

❶ Directory/shopping
Banks: on Harbour St. **Pharmacy**: head to the Bannockburn Building on Barmore Rd. **Tourist information**: Harbour St, open Apr-Oct. **Post office**: Campbeltown Rd. **Police**: School Rd. **Shopping**: there's a Co-op on Barmore Rd for all your basic provisions.

An T-ob (Leverburgh)

Continuing south along the A859, Leverburgh has a shop and a few basic facilities including the **F-G Am Bothan Bunkhouse** on Ferry Rd, T01859-520251. An ordinary exterior gives way to a great interior with a drying room and beds from about £12.

The ruined tower of the Earl's Castle

Northeast England

Surfing Northeast England

The northeast was once England's secret realm. A small population of hardcore locals went about their surfing, without shouting about their breaks. Occasional travelling surfers returned with fantastical tales of reeling reefs and points, but these were put down to too much cold water on the head. Even when Newcastle surfer Nigel Veitch took the British title and headed onto the world tour, the east coast still avoided the limelight.

It was not until the surfing boom of the 1990s that the region came into the surf media spotlight. Surfers like Gabe Davies and Sam Lamiroy were making an impression both at UK and European levels and locals like Del and Jesse Davies were featured in surf mags charging big swells at home. Today, spots that at one time saw a small local crew are suffering from overcrowding and breaks that were once secret are common knowledge. This attention has brought surfers from as far afield as Wales to sample some northern soul.

The truth is, the northeast is a complicated area. The region can have classic waves, but it can also be tortuously inconsistent, cold and fickle. In the winter, temperatures in the water can drop below 5°C, with air temperatures often below zero. Breaks can literally work for an

Northeast England board guide

Fish
Shaper: The Gill, ODD Surfboards

▸▸ 6'2" x 19½" x 2⅜".
▸▸ For average surfer 6'4" x 19½" x 2⅜".
▸▸ Flat bottomed with a fuller nose to help wave catching and aid stability in manoeuvres.
▸▸ Double concave through the swallow tail for drive, designed for small summer surf.
▸▸ When the surf picks up, use with bigger fins to create a loose board in good surf.

Semi-gun
Shaper: The Gill, ODD Surfboards

▸▸ 6'7" x 18½" x 2⅜"for Isaac Kibblewhite.
▸▸ Narrow screwdriver or rounded pintail.
▸▸ Double concave bottom for rail to rail down the line speed..
▸▸ Designed for 6-8 ft hollow waves, good for the Cove.

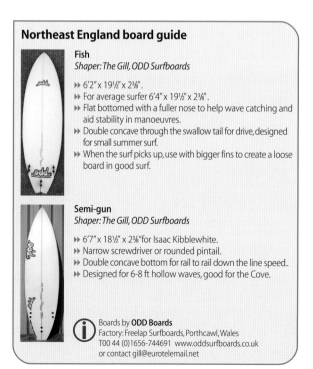

ⓘ Boards by **ODD Boards**
Factory: Freelap Surfboards, Porthcawl, Wales
T00 44 (0)1656-744691 www.oddsurfboards.co.uk
or contact gill@eurotelemail.net

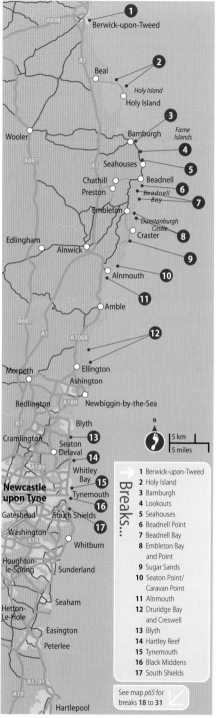

Breaks...

1 Berwick-upon-Tweed
2 Holy Island
3 Bamburgh
4 Lookouts
5 Seahouses
6 Beadnell Point
7 Beadnell Bay
8 Embleton Bay
   and Point
9 Sugar Sands
10 Seaton Point/
   Caravan Point
11 Alnmouth
12 Druridge Bay
   and Creswell
13 Blyth
14 Hartley Reef
15 Tynemouth
16 Black Middens
17 South Shields

See map p65 for breaks 18 to 31

hour or two before becoming unsurfable. As Secret Spot surf shop owner Tommo says: "There's a good variety of waves in the northeast but conditions change so quickly you need to build up a good local knowledge to be on it."

Coastline

The coastline from Scarborough to the Scottish border has England's best surfing terrain. From flat, slate reefs, to long, rocky points to heavy, hollow beach breaks, this area has it all. Northumbria has miles of white sand beaches interspersed with point breaks, whereas Yorkshire has an amazing slate geology that not only attracts fossil hunters from all over the world, but also provides the perfect base for producing quality reef breaks.

A tell-tale trademark of these northern waves is the brown colour of the coastal waters. This is not down to pollution, but more to the silty composition of the soil and coastal sediments. However, north of Newcastle the sea clears, the line-ups clear, and crystal-blue waves peel in front of the silhouettes of once great castles.

Localism

Compared to Cornwall and Devon the northeast is relatively uncrowded. But compared to the mid-1990s, this region has undergone a massive boom in the numbers of surfers in the line-up. This has caused some tension at a few breaks but there have been no incidents of localism. The line-ups here are quite tight-knit, however, and it helps to take a good attitude with you. Problems arise when surfers paddle out at crowded breaks that are well beyond their ability – both dangerous and frustrating.

There was only a handful of us knew about the reef and we did our best to keep it like that. I remember once some surfers came down to check a nearby break and we all ducked down in the line-up and hid under the kelp.

Andrew Harrison, Zero Gravity Surfboards, Whitby

Top local surfers Sam Lamiroy and Gabe Davies are successful WQS surfers, the late Nigel Veitch was a national champion and ex-world champion Martin Potter was born in the northeast. Local chargers include Jesse Davies, Del Boy, Steve Crawford, Robbie Hildreth, Andrew Harrison, Chris Eire, Si Stephenson and Eloise Taylor.

Getting around

The road network in the northeast is very good. Northumbria and Newcastle are serviced by the A1, Saltburn via the A19, while the A64 feeds the Yorkshire coastline. Access to breaks is excellent from the coast road. Check parking as many coastal villages have strictly enforced no parking areas.

Britain Northeast England Surfing

THE GILL

Igor Harris surfing a Northeast point

Breaks

1 Berwick-upon-Tweed

- **Break type**: Beach break.
- **Conditions**: Medium swells, offshore in southwesterly winds.
- **Hazards/tips**: Beware of rips from the river, not for inexperienced surfers.
- **Sleeping**: Beadnell ›› p69.

Peeling along a sandbar near the rivermouth is a left-hander that needs a good clean northeasterly swell but can produce excellent, long walls. Quiet line-up.

2 Holy Island

- **Break type**: Beach break.
- **Conditions**: Medium swells, offshore in southwesterly winds.
- **Hazards/tips**: Quiet spot, access via low tide causeway.
- **Sleeping**: Beadnell ›› p69.

A low tide left-hander breaks towards the northern end of the island. Rarely surfed but can be classic. Needs a good, clean north or northeasterly swell. Park in the car park and walk to the northeast corner of the island. There can also be a left point off the southern tip of the island in big swells. Access to Lindisfarne is only possible at low tide via a causeway that is submerged at high. Make sure you have your tide times or you may find your visit extended longer than you planned.

3 Bamburgh

- **Break type**: Beach break.
- **Conditions**: Small to medium swells, offshore in southwesterly winds.
- **Hazards/tips**: Overlooked by Bamburgh Castle.
- **Sleeping**: Beadnell ›› p69.

Good quality beach break that picks up loads of swell. In a southeasterly the southern end of the beach picks up the most swell; in a northeasterly, the castle end is the place to go. Parking available near castle end of beach behind the dunes. Rocky finger of reef extending towards the Farne Islands has a right-hand point break in southeasterly swells.

4 Lookouts

- **Break type**: Right-hand point break.
- **Conditions**: Big swell, offshore in southwesterly.
- **Hazards/tips**: Can have longshore rips in a big swell pushing north. Clean water.
- **Sleeping**: Beadnell ›› p69.

This good quality, sand-covered rocky point works in a big, clean, southeasterly or easterly swell. Works through the tides but is best from low to mid. In a good swell, long, walling rights peel along the reef. Just to the north, a sandbar peak offers good lefts and rights. Park on the road near the lifeguard tower.

Northeast England

Air ——— Sea ———

°F	Averages			°C
90				30
70				20
50				10
30				0

J F M A M J J A S O N D

6mm Boots, hood & gloves	5/4/3 Boots & gloves	4/3	4/3 Boots & gloves

DEMI TAYLOR

4 Lookouts

5 Seahouses

- **Break type**: Right-hand reef breaks.
- **Conditions**: Medium to big swells, offshore in southwesterly winds.
- **Hazards/tips**: Ledge is shallow and heavy. Experienced surfers only.
- **Sleeping**: Beadnell ►► p69.

A series of reefs, in front of the houses on the coast road that heads north towards Bamburgh, that work best in a big southeasterly swell. There is also a dredging right-hander near the harbour mouth called the Ledge. Parking on seafront and in car park near harbour.

6 Beadnell Point

- **Break type**: Left-hand point break.
- **Conditions**: Big to huge swells, offshore in northerly/northwesterly winds.
- **Hazards/tips**: Park near the sailing club, winter break.
- **Sleeping**: Beadnell ►► p69.

A walling, left-hand point that breaks in front of the old lime kiln at Beadnell Harbour. The point is offshore in northwesterly or northerly winds due to the fact that the waves wrap into the bay, but it needs a big northerly or northeasterly swell to get going. A great place to check when everywhere else is maxed out.

7 Beadnell Bay

- **Break type**: Beach break.
- **Conditions**: Medium to big swells, offshore in westerly winds.
- **Hazards/tips**: Flexible spot, very quiet.
- **Sleeping**: Beadnell ►► p69.

This huge, crescent-shaped bay picks up swells from the south, east and north. It can have some nice waves all the way through the tides. At the southern end is a small bay called **Football Hole** which is worth checking. It is a nice open beach with sand dunes. Parking at northern and southern (Newton) ends.

8 Embleton Bay and Point

- **Break type**: Beach break and rocky point.
- **Conditions**: All swells, offshore in westerly winds.
- **Hazards/tips**: Rips when big, rocky point.
- **Sleeping**: Beadnell ►► p69.

Embleton is a beautiful bay overlooked by the haunting ruins of Dunstanburgh Castle. It is home to some of the best beach-break waves on this coastline, with hollow peaks producing nice barrels in 3-6 ft foot swells. Offshore in southwesterly or westerly winds and works on all tides. At the southern end is a point that comes to life in good southeasterly swells when quality rights peel into the bay at mid to high tide. Beach can be powerful in bigger swells. Park and walk across the golf course.

9 Sugar Sands

- **Break type**: You name it!
- **Conditions**: All swells, offshore in westerly winds.
- **Hazards/tips**: Experienced surfers only, the left is shallow and hollow.
- **Sleeping**: Beadnell ►► p69.

A wonderful, out of the way bay with three points that produce rights, lefts and peaks. At the northern end is **The Box**, a hollow, dredging left reef with low tide barrels. In the middle of the bay, Sugar Sands has left and right reefs peeling towards each other with an easy paddle out in between. They produce good quality waves in northerly swells and light winds. At the southern end of the bay is a long, heavy, exposed left-hander. At low tide it can be big and gnarly with long hollow waves, but needs a clean swell and light winds. Picks up loads of swell. For experienced surfers only.

10 Seaton Point/Caravan Point

- **Break type**: Left-hand point.
- **Conditions**: Big to huge swells, offshore in northerly winds.
- **Hazards/tips**: Shallow, rocky, experienced surfers.
- **Sleeping**: Alnwick/Alnmouth ►► p69.

This very sheltered bay works in massive swells. The beach breaks through the tides but the waves can be a bit weak as the banks aren't great. The point needs a big northerly swell or decent southeasterly swell to get going, but produces nice long lefts, even in northerly winds. Good place to check in big winter storms. Best at low to mid tide. Park by the holiday chalets that overlook the break.

DEMI TAYLOR

9 Sugar Sands

DEMI TAYLOR

11 Almouth ►► p64

DEMI TAYLOR

5 Seahouses

Britain Northeast England Breaks Seahouses to Seaton Point

11 Alnmouth

- **Break type**: Beach break.
- **Conditions**: All swells, offshore in westerly winds
- **Hazards/tips**: Rips by the river.
- **Sleeping**: Alnwick/Alnmouth ⏩ *p69*.

A long, flexible sandy beach that can have excellent waves in northeasterly and southeasterly swells. Alnmouth rivermouth can be classic and produces some good banks depending on the flow of the river, but can have some strong currents – not for inexperienced surfers. This part of the beach is offshore in northwesterly winds. The main beach is a long crescent with some great peaks. Watch rips when bigger. Seafront car park through golf club and in the dunes to the south of the river.

12 Druridge Bay and Creswell

- **Break type**: Beach break.
- **Conditions**: Medium swells, offshore in westerly winds.
- **Hazards/tips**: Suitable for all surfers.
- **Sleeping**: Alnwick/Alnmouth ⏩ *p69*.

Picturesque, dune-backed bay reminiscent of Les Landes in France (see page 173). Facing east, this crescent-shaped bay picks up lots of swell, the northern end best in southeasterly swells and the southern end best in swells from the north. Works on all tides. Has great potential. Worth checking the reef at Creswell on the southern end of the bay. This is where the Northumberland Heritage Coastline ends so from here south the water quality deteriorates. Ellington Colliery marks the start of the industrial Northeast. Coast road to Creswell liable to flooding.

13 Blyth

- **Break type**: Beach break.
- **Conditions**: Medium swells, offshore in southwesterly winds.
- **Hazards/tips**: Rips in big swells.
- **Sleeping**: Alnmouth/Saltburn ⏩ *p69*.

Long, crescent-shaped, sandy bay that can have good lefts and rights. Again, works in northeasterly and southeasterly swells. Quite a consistent spot with the southern part of the beach being the best. Safe for supervised beginners. Access via the A193. Parking at the beach.

14 Hartley Reef

- **Break type**: Reef break.
- **Conditions**: Medium to big swells, offshore in southwesterly winds.
- **Hazards/tips**: Crowds, experienced surfers.
- **Sleeping**: Alnmouth/Saltburn ⏩ *p69*.

Home break to many of the region's top surfers, this flat reef produces excellent quality lefts as well as some good rights. Hartley is a mid to high tide break and can hold decent sized swell. Breaks up to 8 ft producing long, walling waves, with hollow sections. Parking overlooking the break. Popular break that gets crowded when good. Access off the A193 at roundabout with B1325.

15 Tynemouth

- **Break type**: Beach break.
- **Conditions**: All swells, offshore in westerly/southwesterly winds.
- **Hazards/tips**: Road parking near the beach.
- **Sleeping**: Alnmouth/Saltburn ⏩ *p69*.

Longsands is a spot popular with Newcastle surfers and offers decent waves on a northeasterly swell. This beach is where many of the region's surfers learned their trade. Works on all tides. Nearby **Eddies** (King Edwards Bay) is also worth checking at low to mid tide.

16 Black Middens

- **Break type**: Rivermouth reef.
- **Conditions**: Big swells, offshore in westerly winds.
- **Hazards/tips**: Parking near Collingwood's Monument.
- **Sleeping**: Alnmouth/Saltburn ⏩ *p69*.

This left-hand reef break can produce some excellent waves in a big easterly swell. The problem is that it breaks in the mouth of the industrial River Tyne. Although water quality is improving, it is still dire. A wave for experienced and hardened surfers only.

THE GILL

10 Chris 'Guts' Griffiths at Seaton Point ⏩ *p63*

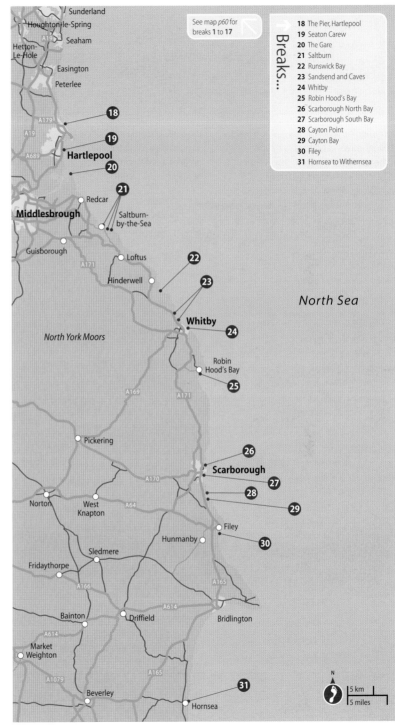

17 South Shields

- 🌀 **Break type**: Beach break.
- 🌊 **Conditions**: Medium swells, offshore in southwesterly winds.
- ❶ **Hazards/tips**: Beachfront parking.
- 🛌 **Sleeping**: Alnmouth/Saltburn ⇒ p69.

A stretch of good quality beach, with nice peaks along its length and fairly clean water. It works on all tides. Good for all surfers.

18 The Pier, Hartlepool

- 🌀 **Break type**: Beach break.
- 🌊 **Conditions**: Small to medium swells, offshore in southwesterly winds.
- ❶ **Hazards/tips**: Good waves but polluted water, bad rips near houses on the seafront, not for beginners.
- 🛌 **Sleeping**: Saltburn ⇒ p70.

Stunning location. Huge, empty sandy beach overlooked by the shells of once mighty northern engineering plants. This huge industrial pier allows sandbars to form either side and produces heavy waves in clean swells on all tides. Can produce epic waves with hollow, powerful lefts and rights. Bleak and industrial backdrop with derelict factories casting their shadows over the dark North Sea. Park on Old Cemetery Road or on the seafront at Hartlepool and walk.

DEMI TAYLOR

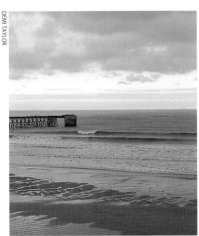

18 Hartlepool Pier

See map p60 for breaks **1** to **17**

Breaks...

18 The Pier, Hartlepool
19 Seaton Carew
20 The Gare
21 Saltburn
22 Runswick Bay
23 Sandsend and Caves
24 Whitby
25 Robin Hood's Bay
26 Scarborough North Bay
27 Scarborough South Bay
28 Cayton Point
29 Cayton Bay
30 Filey
31 Hornsea to Withernsea

Britain Northeast England Breaks South Shields to Hartlepool

North Sea

Sunderland
Houghton-le-Spring
Seaham
Hetton-Le-Hole
Easington
Peterlee
Hartlepool
Redcar
Middlesbrough
Saltburn-by-the-Sea
Guisborough
Loftus
Hinderwell
Whitby
North York Moors
Robin Hood's Bay
Pickering
Scarborough
Norton
West Knapton
Filey
Hunmanby
Sledmere
Fridaythorpe
Bainton
Driffield
Bridlington
Market Weighton
Beverley
Hornsea

5 km
5 miles

19 Seaton Carew

- ◗ **Break type**: Beach break.
- ◔ **Conditions**: Big swells, offshore in southwesterly winds.
- ❶ **Hazards/tips**: Pollution supposed to be getting better.
- ◓ **Sleeping**: Saltburn » p70.

Sheltered beach with harbour at the north end and a groyne with sandbar. Doesn't pick up as much swell as other beaches in the area. Rarely surfed.

20 The Gare

- ◗ **Break type**: Right-hand point break.
- ◔ **Conditions**: Big swells, offshore in southwesterly.
- ◔ **Size**: 3-10 ft.
- ◔ **Length**: 50-150 m.
- ◐ **Swell**: Big easterly or southeasterly swells.
- ◕ **Wind**: From the south or southwest.
- ◒ **Tide**: Works on all tides.
- ◔ **Bottom**: Small, sharp, hard boulders.
- ◔ **Entry/exit**: Off rocks at end of the break.
- ❶ **Hazards/tips**: Bad pollution, heavy wave, long hold downs, cold water.
- ◓ **Sleeping**: Saltburn » p70.

On its day, the Gare is a world-class wave that is the northeast's best right-hander. In big easterly and southeasterly swells, this man-made breakwater inside the mouth of the River Tees is transformed from bleak rocky pier into a brown Jeffrey's Bay with long, walling, hollow waves reeling along the sharp boulders. This is a heavy wave best left

to experienced surfers only. Holds big swells up to 10 ft, and is very powerful – even at 6-8 ft, surfers have had two wave hold-downs. Works through all tides. Water quality has been diabolical with sewage and petrochemical outflows, but this is supposed to be slowly improving. The white water fizzes and has a strong aftershave/chemical smell.

The Gare needs very specific conditions to work – strong southeasterly winds blowing over 24 hours. This means it usually breaks only a handful of times a year, in the depths of winter. However in 2000 the Gare broke for about fourteen days in one month. There were thirty guys out the first day, twenty the second, ten the third . . . there is only so much exposure to the pollution that the human body can take. "Every year we vow not to surf it any more," says northeast surfer Nige Rodwell, "but then you see a chart and know it's gonna break and you find yourself ringing round the crew."

ⓘ *If you like* The Gare, *try* Immessouane *in Morocco (see page 352) or* Coxos *in Portugal (see page 301).*

21 Saltburn

- ◗ **Break type**: Beach break.
- ◔ **Conditions**: All swells, offshore in southwesterly/southerly winds.
- ❶ **Hazards/tips**: Good beach for all surfers.
- ◓ **Sleeping**: Saltburn » p70.

Fairly good quality beach break with the best waves near the pier. Very popular spot due to parking access and surf hire on the beach. Great place for beginners. To the south under the cliffs, the Point is a quality wave that comes to life at low tide in big, clean swells when hollow right-handers reel off the flat reef. In the corner, **Penny Hole** is a low tide peak with short rights and long lefts, which can be excellent.

This beach has been one of the central hubs of northeast surfing due to the beachfront Saltburn Surf Shop first opened in 1987, one of the first surf shops in the Northeast. Pollution was always a problem here but things seem to have improved with a new treatment works.

20 The Gare

The white water fizzes and has a strong aftershave/chemical smell.

20 The Gare backdrop

22 Runswick Bay

⊕ **Break type**: Reefs.

☁ **Conditions**: Medium to big swells, offshore in southwesterly/westerly swells.

❶ **Hazards/tips**: Dangerous rips, Cobbledump is a shallow, rocky reef.

💤 **Sleeping**: Saltburn/Whitby ⇢ p70.

Runswick is a northeasterly facing bay with three quality right-hand reefs found on the southern side. Slabs of flat slate form excellent reefs for fast, walling right-handers that break from low through to mid tide. The inner reef is the most sheltered and it needs more swell to get going; the middle reef is the most popular. Watch out for rips next to the reef, which can be strong. **Cobbledump** is a left-hand reef breaking over rocks, found on the left side of the bay near the village. Runswick is slightly sheltered and so is traditionally surfed when big swells max out the exposed beaches.

23 Sandsend and Caves

⊕ **Break type**: Beach and reef.

☁ **Conditions**: Small to medium swells, offshore in southwesterly winds.

❶ **Hazards/tips**: Heavy beach break, rips, can be crowded.

💤 **Sleeping**: Whitby ⇢ p70.

Caves is a flat, mid tide reef that sits under the headland at the northern end of Sandsend Bay. It is one of the few spots sheltered in a northwesterly wind. Breaks well at 3-4 ft but maxes out easily. Usually looks better than it is. At high tide waves bounce off cliff and exiting the water is difficult. Beware.

Sandsend is a high quality beach that works through the tides. Hollow, powerful lefts and rights spring up on shifting banks. Southwesterly winds are offshore. Works in northeasterly, easterly and southeasterly swells. Groynes were removed a couple of years ago and since then the beach has lost a lot of its fine sand and has become more fickle. Not really for beginners and packs a

punch when big. Parking available by the beach. Used to be a quiet spot but is now getting busy.

24 Whitby

⊕ **Break type**: Beach break.

☁ **Conditions**: Small to medium swells, offshore in southwesterly winds.

❶ **Hazards/tips**: Parking in town or on cliff top.

💤 **Sleeping**: Whitby ⇢ p70.

Popular with grommets in small swells and one of the few spots sheltered in a southeasterly wind due to the harbour wall. Works best on low to mid tide near the harbour. Has a longstanding surf community.

25 Robin Hood's Bay

⊕ **Break type**: Reefs.

☁ **Conditions**: Medium to big swells, offshore in southwesterly winds.

❶ **Hazards/tips**: Rips, rocks, shallow, big tidal range.

💤 **Sleeping**: Whitby ⇢ p70.

There are a number of flat slate reefs in the bay that work on big northeasterly swells.

Best from low to thee-quarter tide as beach disappears. Quiet spot. The point can be good in big swells. Not a good spot for inexperienced surfers. There is a car park in town. Long walk to breaks.

26 Scarborough North Bay

⊕ **Break type**: Beach break.

☁ **Conditions**: All swells, offshore in southwesterly winds.

❶ **Hazards/tips**: Beachfront parking on Marine Drive overlooking the surf.

💤 **Sleeping**: Scarborough ⇢ p71.

North Bay is a northeasterly facing beach with scattered rocky outcrops. It can have some good quality banks, which produce both lefts and rights. It picks up plenty of swell and

23 Sandsend and Caves

21 Saltburn

works in north, northeasterly and easterly swells. The beach is fronted by a sea wall, which means it's only surfable from low to mid tide. These defences have just undergone reinforcement with boulders, but this doesn't appear to have affected the surf. As Billabong rep Shaun Thomas says, "North Bay hasn't been dramatically affected by the new defences in the last twelve months. It still works at low to mid tide with a 2-5 ft swell – any bigger it closes out. I think the defence work is scheduled to finish by the end of the summer 2004 so the long term effects still remain to be seen over the next couple of years."

27 Scarborough South Bay

- **Break type**: Beach break.
- **Conditions**: Big swell, offshore in northerly to westerly winds.
- **Hazards/tips**: Crowds, average waves.
- **Sleeping**: Scarborough ▸ p71.

Poor quality, flat beach fronted by amusements and fish and chip shops. Needs a really big northeasterly to work, so is a

29 Cayton Point

Secret spot

popular spot in huge winter gales. Best peaks are in front of the Spa, from low to three-quarter tide, and there is limited parking here too. Waves are short and pretty weak. Good for beginners. Gets packed when working due to the mellow nature of the wave and the fact that most other spots will be maxed out. Better waves to the south between the Spa and the headland in medium swells.

28 Cayton Point

- **Break type**: Left point.
- **Conditions**: Medium to big swells, offshore in southwesterly winds.
- **Hazards/tips**: Access, crowds, heavy wave, rocks, experienced surfers.
- **Sleeping**: Scarborough ▸ p71.

Excellent and powerful left-hand point that breaks over a bouldery reef. Definitely a wave for experienced surfers, this grinding left breaks up to 10 ft, wrapping around the point at the northern end into the sheltered bay. Too shallow at low, it's best surfed from quarter tide up to high. Needs a good northeasterly swell to get going.

Access is difficult. Check from the A165 where the point is visible through the trees. There is an access path through the woods.

29 Cayton Bay

- **Break type**: Beach breaks.
- **Conditions**: Small to medium swells, offshore in southwesterly winds.
- **Hazards/tips**: Busy spot, suitable for all surfers.
- **Sleeping**: Scarborough ▸ p71.

Bunkers is the most popular and consistent spot with lefts and rights breaking off the sandbanks formed in front of Second World War concrete bunkers. Best from mid to high tide and with a southwesterly wind. There is also the fickle **Pumphouse**, that produces lefts and rights in front of the pumping station, but needs a southeasterly swell. Parking available above the bay.

Popular break with Scarborough surfers and students at the local university and also attracts visitors from as far as Manchester due to the good road links.

30 Filey

- **Break type**: Beach break.
- **Conditions**: Big to huge swells, offshore in southwesterly winds.
- **Hazards/tips**: Rips in big swells, parking on the seafront.
- **Sleeping**: Scarborough ▸ p71.

Filey has a long, flat crescent-shaped beach, the northern end of which is sheltered by Filey Brigg, a rocky headland. The southern end of the bay picks up the most swell, the northern end is popular in big, storm surf. Not renowned for the quality of its waves, but worth checking if everywhere else is maxed out.

31 Hornsea to Withernsea

- **Break type**: Beach break.
- **Conditions**: Medium to big swells, offshore in westerly winds.
- **Hazards/tips**: Dangerous longshore drift in big swells
- **Sleeping**: Scarborough ▸ p71.

These are not really a surfer's first choice but are worth checking in a clean northeasterly or easterly swell if you're in the area. As the groynes show, when the surf picks up there is a longshore drift from the north, so keep a beach marker in view. Better on low to mid tide. Not many surfers here, so not really a good spot for the inexperienced.

Yorkshire secret spot

Listings

Golf on Teeside

DEMI TAYLOR

Beadnell

Beadnell makes for a good base from which to access Northumbria's northern breaks. Sitting just off the B1340 on a sheltered point break, it has great winter surf potential. There is a pretty 18th-century harbour with lime kilns at the head of 3 miles of sandy beach.

✪ Flat spells

Bamburgh Castle Looks impressive as you approach as it dominates the skyline and overlooks an amazing beach; not quite so nice up close though. Open Apr-Oct, www.bamburghcastle.com. **Dunstanburgh Castle** A spectacular ruin overlooking Embleton Bay, open daily. Like a backdrop to a horror film, the jagged keep towers over the crashing sea. **Golf** Dunstanburgh Castle GC at Embleton Bay, 18-hole links, T01665-576562. **Seahouses GC**, heading south out of Seahouses, 18-hole links, T01665-720794.
Holy Island Famous for its monastery founded in AD 634, Holy Island – or Lindisfarne – is well worth a visit but check the tides as it is is separated from the mainland by a tidal causeway and is cut off for about 5 hrs a day.

🛏 Sleeping

B **Low Dover**, Harbour Rd, T01665-720291, is a quiet family-run B&B sitting 30 seconds from the harbour. It also has a self-catering option.
D **Joiners Shop Bunkhouse**, slightly inland at Preston, Chathill, T01665-589245, is good for groups, offering beds from £9 per night.
Camping There are plenty of camping and caravan sites in the area. **Dunstan Hill**, inland from Embleton, T01665-576310, open Mar-Oct. **Beadnell Camping and Caravanning Club**, on the B1340 between Beadnell and Seahouses, T01665-720586. A couple of miles up the coast in Seahouses, the **Seafield Caravan Park**, T01665-720628, offers statics and views across to the Farne Islands, open Apr–Nov. **Newton Hall**, T01665-576239, www.newtonholidays.co.uk,

sits to the southern end of Beadnell Bay in the grounds of Newton Hall.

🍴 Eating/drinking

There are 2 good pubs in the village. The **Towers** offers bar meals and has a slightly more expensive restaurant. The nearby **Craster Arms** is well known for its home cooking and crab sandwiches. The **Village Pantry**, opposite the church, has a selection of provisions as well as coffee and sandwiches.

⭘ Shopping

Nearby Seahouses offers a selection of shops as well as a **Co-Op** supermarket along the main road. It is a surprisingly unattractive village with garish arcades and fish and chip shops. The **Ledge Surf Shop** is actually a corner of an arcade, opposite the Olde Ship Hotel in Seahouses, selling only basic things like wax and T-shirts.

⭘ Directory

Bank: Barclays on Main St. **Internet**: access at the **Village Pantry** in Beadnell. **Post office**: King St. **Tourist information**: in the car park at Seahouses.

Alnwick

Alnwick is a pretty walled town just inland from Alnmouth and is a good base for Northumberland trips. With easy access from the A1, it is close to the breaks and offers a good choice of amenities and has a wonderful castle and gardens.

🛏 Sleeping

C **The Tea Pot**, Bondgate Without, T01665-604473. One of many B&B options.
C **Bondgate House Hotel**, Bondgate Without, T01665-602025.
Camping Bizarrely you can camp at the **Alnwick Rugby Club** in Greensfield Park, T01665-510109. Other options at nearby villages are **Cherry Tree Campsite**, Edlingham, T01665-574635 and **Proctors Steads Caravan and Camping Park**, Craster, T01665-576613.

69

Britain Northeast England Listings Beadnell to Alnwick

🍴 Eating/drinking

The **Grape Vine** offers basic, good value evening food and is on the square on Bondgate Within. On the same square is the pricier **Gate Bistro** where you can get a 3-course, candlelit meal. Opposite, **Chilli's** does good value Tex-Mex while up the road you can grab a cheap takeaway pizza. There's a **Safeway** supermarket on Fenkle St.

⊕ Directory

Banks: a selection with cashpoints in the town square on Bondgate Within. **Chemist**: Boots and **Superdrug** on Bondgate Within. **Internet**: access at **Barter Books** on Bondgate Without, www.barterbooks.co.uk. **Post office**: Wagonway Rd. **Tourist information**: on the Shambles, Market Place, T01665-510665.

Alnmouth

This is a small, quiet coastal village with a couple of pricey B&Bs and hotels and a choice of golf courses.

✇ Flat spells

Golf **Alnmouth GC**, T01665-850231, is an 18-hole course and one of the oldest in England. Handicap certificate needed. **Alnmouth Village GC**, Marine Rd, T01665-830370, is a 9-hole course.

🛏 Sleeping

A-B **Beaches**, on Northumberland St, T01665-830443, offers cosy accommodation and also has the best food in town in their restaurant downstairs
B-C **The Grange**, Northumberland St, T01665-830401, is considered the best and is very popular so book ahead.

🍴 Eating/drinking

The **Tea Cosy Tea Room** offers typical café fair such as jacket potatoes and pretty average sandwiches.

Saltburn

This is a very pleasant Victorian resort town complete with a water-balance cliff tram ferrying people to and from the seafront and the pier.

✇ Flat spells

Golf **Saltburn by Sea GC**, Hob Hill, Guisborough. Also has a snooker room, T01287-622812.

🛏 Sleeping

There are a couple of hotels and plenty of B&B options on the Victorian terraces running down to the cliff top. The most expensive are B **Queen Hotel**, Station St, T01287 625820 and B **Spa Hotel**, on the hill above the beach, T01287-622544.
Camping Try **Hazel Grove Caravan Park**, Milton St, Saltburn, T01287-622014, open Mar-Jan, or the **Serenity Touring Caravan Park**, on the A174 in Hinderwell, T01947-841122, open Mar-Oct.

🍴 Eating/drinking

Gary Rogers of Saltburn Surf Shop recommends **Alessie's** Italian for an evening meal and **Vergo's Café** for good lunchtime food, both on Dundas St. A lot of the local crew drink in the **Victoria**, again on Dundas St. Local surfer Andy Cummins recommends **Windsor's** for a beer and **Signals Café** for a bite to eat.

⊙ Shopping

Saltburn Surf Hire and Shop, on the seafront car park by the pier, T01287-625321, was opened in 1986 and is run by Gary Rogers and Nick Noble. Open year round, they stock hardware and clothing and also hire boards and suits. For a surf update, ring their check line on T09068 -545543 .

⊕ Directory

Shops and **cashpoints** are clustered around the train station, the hub of the town. There are changing and shower facilities in the beachfront car park. **Tourist information**: in the railway station, T01287-622422.

Whitby

One of Yorkshire's seaside gems, this town is now as famous for its Gothic connection with *Dracula* (it hosts an annual Goth Weekend over Halloween) as it is for its picturesque harbour with cobbled streets and excellent seafood.

✇ Flat spells

Golf **Whitby GC**, Sandsend Rd, T01947-600660, an 18-hole clifftop course overlooking the sea. **Whitby Abbey** Climb the hill for great views over the bay. The Abbey was the inspiration for Bram Stoker's *Dracula*.

🛏 Sleeping

B **Shepherd's Purse** on Church St, T01947-820228, has a great location, rooms set around a courtyard to the rear of the shop, and does a good vegetarian breakfast. B **White Horse and Giffin**, also on Church St, T01947-604857, has a number of rooms above the popular restaurant.
There are also a vast number of average B&Bs to choose from on West Cliff.
E-F **Whitby Backpackers**, Hudson St, T01947-601794, has bunks and private rooms and no curfew.
Sandfield House Caravan Site on Sandsend Rd, T01947-602660, overlooks the sea north of Whitby.

 Airports → Heathrow T0870-0000123, Gatwick T0870-0002468, Stansted T0870-0000303, www.baa.co.uk. **Buses and coaches** → National Express T08705-808080, www.gobycoach.com; Scottish City Link, T0141-3329644, www.citylink.co.uk. **Car hire** → Avis T0870-6060100; Europcar T0870-6075000; Hertz T08708-448844. **Petrol prices** → £0.85-90/litre. **Ferries** → P&O, T0870-2424999, www.poportsmouth.com; Brittany Ferries,T0870-3665333, www.brittany-ferries.com; Irish Ferries T08705-171717, www.irishferries.com; Sea France, T0870-5711711, www.seafrance.com. **Rail links** → National Rail Enquiries T08457-484950.

Eating/drinking

The **Magpie Café** has a reputation for serving up the best fish and chips and seafood. Expect big queues during peak times of the year, but it is worth it! **Java** café on Flowergate serves light, cheap snacks and has **internet** access. **Finleys**, also on Flowergate, is worth a check for light meals and live music. **Green's**, Bridge St, T01947-600284, is mid-priced and one of the best spots in Whitby for a sit-down dinner. Another good option is the intimate **White Horse and Griffin**, T01947-604857, with its wide ranging if fairly expensive menu, served by candlelight. **Bar 7** on Pier Rd is recommended as the best night out by Ben Pepler at Zero Gravity. The **Shambles** on Market Place is a popular and busy spot that also has a restaurant attached. Ben also recommends the **Duke of York** at the end of Church St for cheap pub grub. **Elsinore** is a busy pub and popular with visiting Goths. There's a **Safeway** opposite Java on Flowergate.

Shopping

Zero Gravity Surf Shop on Flowergate, T01947-820660, was opened by shaper Andrew Harrison in 1995 and sells the full range of hardware and clothing. 'Harry' is one of the east coast's best known surfers and first started shaping in 1987 for Freespirit Surfboards.

Directory

Banks: there are a number of banks and cashpoints along Baxtergate pedestrian road through town. **Tourist information**: near the train station on New Quay Rd, T01947-602674.

Scarborough

A real Jekyll and Hyde resort. Garish and brash amusements line South Bay, yet explore just a short way from the neon and climb the cliff by way of medieval ginnels. It then becomes clear that Scarborough hides its real light under a bushel.

Flat spells

Scarborough Castle Worth a visit for the spectacular views over North and South bays. **Seafront** Amusement arcades line the seafront of South Bay and include a flight simulator and fairground rides by the harbour.

Sleeping

C **Rockside Hotel**, Blenheim Terr, overlooking North Bay, T01723-374747, is run by well known local surfer, Del. C **Selomar Hotel**, just a few doors up Blenheim Terr, T01723-364964, is also a surfer-friendly establishment with a late bar. E-F **Scarborough YHA**, on Burniston Rd heading north out of town, T017233-61176. **Camping** **Scalby Close Park**, T01723-365908, and **Scalby Manor Caravan Park**, T01723-366212, are both on Burniston Rd and offer camping and van pitches. **Self catering** A good option is **Brompton Holiday Flats**, Castle Rd, T01723-364964.

Eating/drinking

The **Scarborough Tandoori** on Thomas St, T01723-352393, offers great Indian food at very reasonable prices. Roger from Secret Spot recommends **Old Mother Hubbard's**, on Westborough, for the best fish and chips in town, eat in or take away, £4.95 lunchtime special. **Florio's** on Aberdeen Walk off Westborough, T01723-351124, does good Italian food in a central location. **Café Italia** on St Nicholas Cliff near the **Grand** is a great place to grab a coffee and pastry. When it comes to bars, Tommo from Secret Spot recommends **Murray's**, on Westborough, where they have a regular surf night with films, as well as bands, www.murraysmusicbar.com. Also on the list are **Red Square** on Somerset Terr, **Cloisters** wine bar on York Place, and the nearby **Privilege Lap Dancing Club**.

Shopping

Secret Spot Surf Shop on Somerset Terr, T01723-500467, is Scarborough's longest running surf shop and stocks hardware and clothing on their large premises. Roger and Tommo will offer advice to travelling surfers and are happy to give an update on surf conditions. **Surface 2 Air**, Museum Terr, T01723-503762, offer a good range of surf gear. **Cayton Bay Surf Shop**, based on Killerby Cliff, T01723-585585, is something of an institution.

Directory

Banks and ATMs: on Westborough and St Nichols St. **Tourist information**: Pavillion House, Valley Bridge Rd, T01723-373333.

THE GILL

Yorkshire Peak

Devon

Surfing Devon

As well as being one of England's largest counties, Devon has always been one of the UK's biggest tourist destinations. Exit the M5 and the epic, green scenery envelops the traveller like a reassuring blanket. Postcard images of chocolate-box villages with thatched cottages and narrow country lanes attract holidaymakers from all over England and, as fishing and agriculture have become less lucrative, tourism now provides the county's main income.

Despite the image, Devon is not just a sleepy retirement community flooded every August with tourists from the Midlands. There are vibrant, young communities of surfers spread along the north coast in places like Croyde, Braunton, Barnstaple and Bideford. The influx of tourists does have positive effects – unspoilt areas of the coastline are now seen as a resource and are actively preserved, and water quality is improving as beaches have become a valuable commodity.

For such a large county, the north shore of Devon has a surprisingly small coastline. When you think of the number of excellent surfers it produces, the number of visitors it attracts and its influence within the UK surf scene, it is amazing to see only ten breaks listed in this guide. Obviously there are others that we have not included, but this is a graphic illustration of how a limited resource like waves can come under ever increasing pressure.

"The drawback of North Devon is the crowd factor, especially due to its accessibility from London and the Midlands," says James

Devon board guide

Fat Boy Flyer
Shaper: Chops Lascelles of Beachbeat Surfboards

- 7'2" x 20½" x 2⅝".
- Versatile from 6'8" x 19¼" x 2⅛" up to 7'8" x 22 x 3
- An aggressive mid-range retro style thruster that will charge 10 ft and perform in 2-ft surf.
- Built for big guys, beginner shortboarders, a perfect second board or a first board.
- The most popular model I ever made.

Thruster
Shaper: Chops Lascelles of Beachbeat Surfboards

- 6'0" x 18" x 2"for Robin Kent.
- For average surfer 6'6" x 19¼" x 2⅝".
- Based on a fuller plan shape for sloppy summer surf.
- It has a single to double concave with squash tail and tweaks to suit ability of surfer.

Boards by **Beachbeat Surfboards** Factory:Laminations,St Agnes,Cornwall T00 44 (0)1872-553918 www.beachbeatsurfboards.co.uk www.aggiesurf.com or contact Lam2574@aol.com

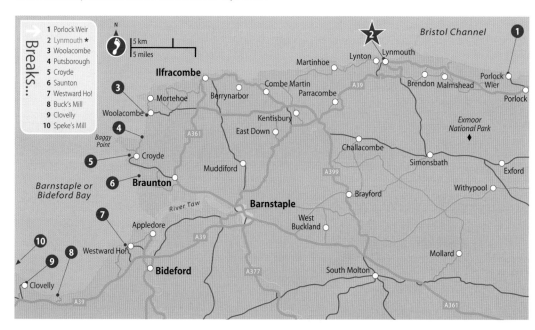

Breaks...
1 Porlock Weir
2 Lynmouth ★
3 Woolacombe
4 Putsborough
5 Croyde
6 Saunton
7 Westward Ho!
8 Buck's Mill
9 Clovelly
10 Speke's Mill

Stentiford, Croyde local and top European pro snowboarder. "On a good day at Croyde you can hardly see the sea for wetsuits and boards. Despite the wide choice of waves, especially for beginners, Croyde seems to be the focus, yet it's not ideal for beginners. On the bright side the vibe is mellow and in general the locals are very welcoming. Although how long that will last is to be seen."

Coastline

The coastline of North Devon can be as spectacular as any in Britain. Forest-shrouded sea cliffs drop off into the Atlantic and small villages like Lynmouth take shelter where stream-eroded valleys meet the sea. Between Ilfracombe and Westward Ho! sit the county's main tourist and surfing beaches. These westerly facing stretches of sand are a heaving mass in the summer months, but in the spring and autumn are home to quality waves. And in the biggest winter storms, sheltered points spring to life, allowing waves to be ridden on even the biggest Atlantic swells.

Localism

Most breaks in Devon will be crowded year round – it's just that they will be less crowded in the depths of winter. In the summer, spots like Croyde will be packed every time there is a surfable wave. The standard of surfing here is very high, and it might be worth checking spots like Putsborough or Woolacombe where there is more room and a more chilled-out vibe. Despite the crowding, it is still unusual to encounter out-and-out localism in Devon, though a surfer breaching the etiquette of the line-up may incur the wrath of the locals.

Top local surfers Devon has produced some of the UK's best surfers. Riders like **Eugene Tollemache** and **Scott Rannochan** perform well in contest jerseys and freesurfing. As **Ester Spears** points out: "There are lots of good underground surfers in Devon, as proved by the fact that Croyde Surf Club and Woolacombe Boardriders are currently the top

> **Devon is still a vast swathe of countryside, it has a laid-back feeling and gentle pace of life. The backdrop of spectacular scenery where Exmoor meets the sea is awe-inspiring and is often taken for granted by the people who live there. There are fabulous beaches and great waves that work in a variety of conditions, the place is small enough so that there is a real community feeling.**
>
> *Ester Spears, Woolacombe local and English Surfing Federation*

two clubs in Britain (British Interclub championships, November 2003). From Croyde there is **Ossian Pleasance, Matt Jenkins, Dan Thornton, Nigel Cross, Matt Saunders, Ralph Freeman, Richard Carter** plus a host of others. From Woolacombe **Neil Clifton** and **Nick Thorn**. From Westward Ho! and all places south **Sophie Hellyer** and her dark horses."

Getting around

The road network in Devon looks great on a map, but in reality it can be a bit of a nightmare. The so-called Atlantic Highway (A39) is a single carriageway road that can be surprisingly narrow in places and frustratingly slow in summer traffic. Allow plenty of time to get to spots and take lots of patience with you. The roads north of Barnstaple, such as the A361, are also very busy during the summer.

THE GILL

5 Nathan Phillips in action at Croyde ▸▸ *p75*

Breaks

Devon

Air —— Sea ——

°F Averages   °C

90   30

70   20

50   10

30   0

J F M A M J J A S O N D

5/4/3   4/3   3/2   4/3
Boots &   Boots
gloves

1 Porlock Weir

- 🌊 **Break type**: Left reef.
- 🌬 **Conditions**: Big to huge swells, offshore in southerly/southwesterly wind.
- ❗ **Hazards/tips**: Crowds.
- 🛏 **Sleeping**: Woolacombe ⟩⟩ p76.

Sitting in the heart of Exmoor National Park, Porlock is actually just over the Devon border in Somerset and has a notoriously steep hill. It is a spot that is surfed on big swells two hours before or after high tide. There is a toll road on the way in, parking above the break.

2 Lynmouth

- 🌊 **Break type**: Long left point break.
- 🌬 **Conditions**: Big swells, offshore in southerly winds.
- ⊕ **Size**: 3-8 ft.
- ⊕ **Length**: 300 m plus.
- ⟩ **Swell**: Northwesterly.
- ⟩ **Wind**: Light southerly/ southeasterly.
- ⊛ **Tide**: Through the tides, best at low.
- ⟩ **Bottom**: Boulders.
- ⟩ **Entry/exit**: Off the rocks.
- ❗ **Hazards/tips**: Crowds, rips, rocks.
- 🛏 **Sleeping**: Woolacombe ⟩⟩ p76.

Lynmouth is one of the UK's finest point breaks. When a big swell hits Devon, long lefts are rideable for up to 300 m. Lynmouth works through all states of the tide, although it is generally better at low, but needs light winds.

As the area's best point break, when it is on it will generally be crowded, especially at weekends or where big swells have been forecast well in advance.

Lynmouth, with long walls and hollow sections, is a break for experienced surfers as there can be bad rips, boulders and crowds to contend with. Car park on the headland to the west of the break.

ⓘ *If you like Lynmouth, try La Fortaleza in Spain (see page 227) or Gills Bay in Scotland (see page 36).*

3 Woolacombe

- 🌊 **Break type**: Beach break.
- 🌬 **Conditions**: All swells, offshore in easterly winds.
- ❗ **Hazards/tips**: Big beach, good place to escape crowds.
- 🛏 **Sleeping**: Woolacombe ⟩⟩ p76.

A two mile stretch of beach with peaks and a high tide right at the northern end. Various peaks work at different states of tide. Can be a good place to escape the crowds at Croyde and ideal for beginners. Parking above the beach.

4 Putsborough

- 🌊 **Break type**: Beach break.
- 🌬 **Conditions**: Medium swells, offshore in easterly winds.
- ❗ **Hazards/tips**: Rips when big.
- 🛏 **Sleeping**: Woolacombe/Croyde ⟩⟩ p76.

The southern end of Woolacombe beach is protected from southerly winds by Baggy Point, so can be the place to check when Croyde and Saunton are blown out. Works at all states of tide. The waves here can be good, so it's worth checking if Croyde is packed as the beach can throw up good banks. Popular with beginners but watch out for rips near the point in larger swells. The road down to the beach is narrow and windy if you are in a van. Parking and toilets above the beach.

2 Lynmouth

5 Croyde

- **Break type**: Beach and reef breaks.
- **Conditions**: All swells, offshore in easterly winds.
- **Hazards/tips**: One of the UK's most crowded beaches.
- **Sleeping**: Croyde ⟫ *p77*.

Croyde is the surf capital of Devon and as such attracts surfers from all around the UK. Add these surfers of mixed abilities to a hungry core of locals and the water can get pretty crowded. Keep your eyes open and don't drop in. The banks here can produce powerful, hollow waves, especially at low tide. If you're not an experienced surfer then it may be better to check out another spot. Croyde was crowded even before the recent surf boom.

The **beach** has some excellent banks and has often hosted the English or British surfing championships. It is offshore in an easterly wind and has the distinction of being privately owned. There are a number of car parks near the beach. Low tide can be a board snapping experience. "Croyde low tide on its day can look like Hossegor – people

4 Putsborough

getting pitted everywhere," says James Stentiford, Croyde local and one of Europe's top pro snowboarders. "Above four foot it's heavy and fast but it needs the right swell direction and good banks to fire."

At the north end of the beach Baggy Point has a right-hand reef, **Baggy End Reef**, which works best on a spring high tide. It gets busy but doesn't really handle crowds well. The reef breaks in bigger swells up to three-quarter tide and is for experienced surfers only.

At the south end of the beach, **Downend Point** is probably the most surfed reef. It doesn't really work below 4 ft and is best from low to mid tide on neap tides. It's also a good spot when it gets too big for the beach. It can be a bit of a cut-back wave but on it's day it can produce a few barrels. It does get crowded but can handle a crowd pretty well. The reefs are shallow and rocky and are popular with locals when they are on.

6 Saunton

- **Break type**: Long beach break.
- **Conditions**: Medium swell, offshore in easterly winds.
- **Hazards/tips**: Very mellow, popular longboard wave.
- **Sleeping**: Croyde/Braunton ⟫ *p77*.

This long stretch of sand runs from the headland south to the mouth of the River Taw and works at all states of tides. It is a very gently sloping beach not renowned for the quality of its sandbanks. A great place for beginners and longboarders as the waves

peel gently and lack punch. Miles of sand dunes and room to spread out. Car park off the main road. It's a pretty safe beach, with lifeguards in the summer.

7 Westward Ho!

- **Break type**: Beach and reefs.
- **Conditions**: Small to medium swells, offshore in easterly winds.
- **Hazards/tips**: Good spot to escape the crowds.
- **Sleeping**: Westward Ho! ⟫ *p77*.

Westward Ho! is the only town in Britain named after a book. It would make for a great review if we could say that the break was a fairy tale, but it's a pretty average spot that can have its good days. The beach works through the tidal range and is much less busy than the breaks north of the Taw. It's a good spot for beginners and inexperienced surfers and those looking to escape the crowds. Easy parking at beach. Laid-back line-ups.

8 Buck's Mill

- **Break type**: Left boulder reef.
- **Conditions**: Big swell, offshore in southerly winds.
- **Hazards/tips**: Not a wave for the inexperienced.
- **Sleeping**: Westward Ho! ⟫ *p77*.

When massive swells hit the West Country, local surfers head for sheltered breaks where quality waves come alive in locations that are usually as flat as a pond. In southwesterly gales

5 Croyde

5 Croyde (Downend)

6 Saunton

Britain Devon Breaks Croyde to Buck's Mill

and huge swells, Buck's Mill has a long left that breaks along a man-made boulder groyne. It's a low tide break and can be crowded due to the quality of wave produced here. Park respectfully in the village.

9 Clovelly

- **Break type**: Left point.
- **Conditions**: Huge swells, offshore in southeasterly winds.
- **Hazards/tips**: Very fickle.
- **Sleeping**: Westward Ho! ⟫ p77.

Clovelly is a fickle left point that is very hard to catch when it's on. Works at low tide on a massive swell, when long, walling lefts peel along a boulder-fringed sandy point. It's a really long walk down to the break from the expensive car park. Very sheltered spot that's offshore in southerly or southeasterly wind. The wave breaks down the point towards the harbour. Access off the boulder beach or harbour if it gets big (once a decade).

10 Speke's Mill

- **Break type**: Left and right reef.
- **Conditions**: Small to medium swells, offshore in easterly winds.
- **Hazards/tips**: Respect locals, difficult to find.
- **Sleeping**: Westward Ho! ⟫ p77.

Once a secret spot, Speke's has always been a popular spot with Devon surfers as it hoovers up swell on small days. It's a shallow, rocky reef, which can get crowded, so not for the inexperienced. Difficult to find the reef (we haven't shown it on the map) so you'll need to do some exploring . Respect the locals if it's on and if it's already busy, head south to Cornwall's Sandy Mouth.

Listings

Clovelly

Woolacombe

Just south of Morte Point sits Woolacombe and the 3-mile stretch of sand leading down to Putsborough.

✺ Flat spells
Cinema Pendle Stairway Cinema, High St, Ilfracombe, T01271-863484, is the nearest place to catch the latest releases. **Golf** There are a couple of 9-hole courses in the area, **Ilfracombe & Woolacombe Golf Range**, Woolacombe Rd, T01271-866222, and **Mortehoe & Woolacombe GC** in Mortehoe, T01271-870255.

◉ Sleeping
L-A Little Beach Hotel, on the Esplanade, T01271-870398, www.surfersworld.co.uk, is the chic boutique end of surf accommodation but they do offer board and wetsuit storage and it's ideal for couples. Open year round they also have a good bar and restaurant.
L-B Headlands Hotel, Beach Rd, T01271-870320, is a small family run hotel offering B&B. Rooms have great views over the bay and, although pricey, they are worth checking out off season as they often do weekend deals.
Camping There are plenty of campsites in the area. **Woolacombe Bay Holiday Parcs**, T01271-870343, have 4 family oriented sites to choose from, with **Golden Coast** open year round. **Woolacombe Sands Holiday Park**, Beach Rd, T01271-870569, a 15-min walk to the beach, have statics, chalets and a bungalow to rent. Open Easter-Oct, they don't take groups. **North Morte Farm**, about a mile north of Woolacombe at Mortehoe, T01271-870381, open Easter-end Sep, statics also available. Further north between Lee Bay and Bull Point is **Damage Barton**, a working farm and campsite, open Mar-Nov, T01271-870502.

◉ Eating/drinking
"The **Red Barn** is just a short walk from the beach and the perfect spot to watch the sun set and have a post-surf beer. It's popular with

locals and the ceiling is covered in some interesting retro boards," recommends Devon local, James Stentiford. They also do good, affordable food with a view. Gulf Stream's Andrew Cotton recommends **West Beach** for good seafood and beach views.

Shopping

Woolacombe is home to **Gulf Stream Surfboards** (shop and factory 12 South St, T01271-870831) who have been shaping since 1993 and make boards for, among others, British Champion Sam Lamiroy, local charger Scott Rannochan and up-and-coming grom Stuart Campbell. There are plenty of surf shops here including **Bay Surf Shop**, Barton Court, **Shore 2 Surf**, West Rd, and a couple of **Hunter** shops, one on West Rd and **Hunter Beach** at the Boat House.

Directory

Banks: a couple of banks and ATMs, including HSBC on Rosalie Terr. **Pharmacy**: Medi-scene, West Rd. **Post office**: as with most things here, head to the main West Rd. **Supermarket**: Woolacombe Food Store on West Rd. **Tourist information**: year round on the Esplanade.

Croyde

Sat on the B3231 Croyde, with its thatched roofs and little streets, has retained its chocolate-box feel despite being a summer tourist Mecca. The village, named after the Norse raider Crydda who landed here, also has a large population of surfers who surf to a high standard.

Sleeping

A-B The Thatch, the central pub and focus of village life, on Hobbs Hill, T01271-890349. They have rooms over the pub or a (slightly) quieter option, over the road.
Other choices geared toward surfers and offering board storage include:
B-C Moorsands House, on Moor Lane between the village and the beach, T01271-890781.
B-C Oamaru, at Down End, T01271-890765.

B-C Sandy Hollow, Sandy Way, T01271-890556, which is available to rent entirely as a self-catering cottage in Jul-Aug.
B-C Crowborough Farm, in Georgeham between Croyde and Putsborough, T01271-891005, is a quieter option which also has board storage facilities as well as an outside tap for rinsing suits.
Camping There are loads of campsites but as it is a popular holiday destination camping is not a particularly cheap option and many places will not take groups. **Bay View Farm**, T01271-890501, has easy access to both the beach and village as well as statics for hire. **Surfers Paradise Campsite**, Sandy La, T01271-890477, open Jul-Aug only but does take groups. **Ruda Campsite** is the older brother of Surfers Paradise and is open to families and couples only.
Self-catering A Croyde Bay Holiday Village at Down End have chalets to rent, T01271-890890.

Eating/drinking

The **Thatch** on Hobbs Hill is the focus for village life and visiting surfers alike as it serves good food at reasonable prices. It's always packed out, especially in the summer, so be prepared to wait for your post-surf pint. **Billy Budd's** just up the road is another popular spot. Ester Spears also recommends **Blue Groove**, a mellow restaurant run by a couple of surfers, for the sea bass.

Directory/shopping

Food store: Brook Stores on St Mary's Rd. **Post office**: St Mary's Rd. **Surf shops**: Little Pink Shop sells all the surfing essentials and does equipment hire including boards, winter suits and women's wetsuits. Or try the **Redwood** surf shop on Hobbs Hill.

Braunton

Off the A361, Braunton is a fair sized market town with most amenities including banks, Somerfield supermarket on Exeter Rd, and a good campsite.

Flat spells

Golf Saunton GC, T01271-812436, has two top-class 18-hole courses for those with handicap certificates. **Skating** SRP Skate Rock Park is an indoor park in Barnstaple with a street course and mini ramp. You need to be a member (£5) to skate it. A day pass is about a fiver. Closed Mon.

Sleeping

Lobb Fields Caravan and Camping Park, Saunton Rd, T01271-812090, mid-Mar-31 Oct.

Westward Ho!

The only town in England to be named after a book and to be punctuated by an exclamation mark!

Flat spells

Clovelly Take in this ridiculously pretty chocolate-box of a village with its ridiculously expensive car park. **Golf** Get a round in at the **Royal North Devon GC** on Golf Links Rd, T01237-473817. **Horse riding** Go for a ride or get a lesson with **Folly Foot** on Burrows Park Rd, T01237-424856. **Skating** Head for **Bideford Skate Park** on Bank End by the River Torridge in Bideford with rails, banks, fun boxes and a spined mini-ramp.

Sleeping

In terms of accommodation, there are plenty of B&B options on Atlantic Way. **Camping Pusehill Farm Camp Site**, in Pusehill, T01237-474295. **Surf Bay Holiday Park**, Golf Links Rd, T01237 471833, open Apr-Oct, rents statics accommodating up to 6 people for less than £500/week. **Self-catering The Old Granary** in Pusehill, T01237-421128, sleeps up to 6 people for £175-425/week. Heading west along the A39 to Clovelly, **Dyke Green Farm Camp Site** in Higher Clovelly, T01237 431279, is open Apr-Oct. Further west at Hartland, **Elmscott Youth Hostel**, T01237 441367, is about half a mile inland, open Mar-Sep, with views over to Lundy Island.

Cornwall

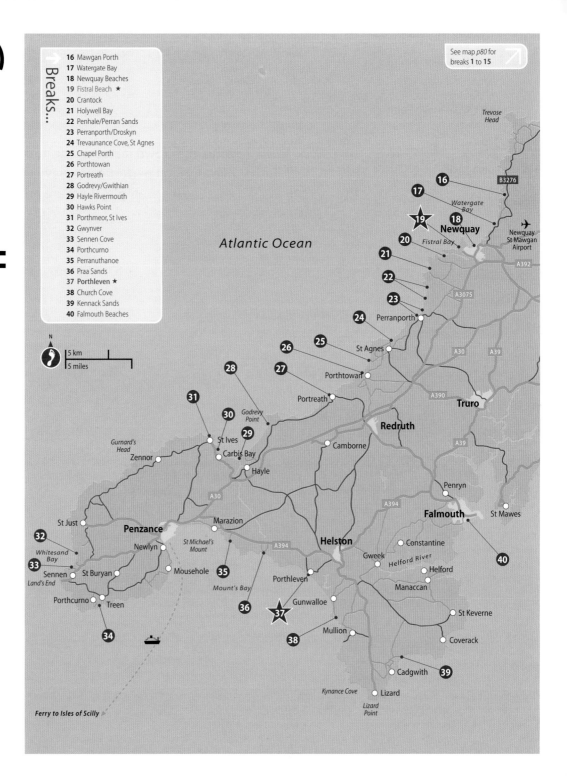

Breaks...

16 Mawgan Porth
17 Watergate Bay
18 Newquay Beaches
19 Fistral Beach ★
20 Crantock
21 Holywell Bay
22 Penhale/Perran Sands
23 Perranporth/Droskyn
24 Trevaunance Cove, St Agnes
25 Chapel Porth
26 Porthtowan
27 Portreath
28 Godrevy/Gwithian
29 Hayle Rivermouth
30 Hawks Point
31 Porthmeor, St Ives
32 Gwynver
33 Sennen Cove
34 Porthcurno
35 Perranuthanoe
36 Praa Sands
37 Porthleven ★
38 Church Cove
39 Kennack Sands
40 Falmouth Beaches

See map *p80* for breaks **1** to **15**

Atlantic Ocean

N
5 km
5 miles

Trevose Head

16
17
19
18
Newquay
20 Fistral Bay
Newquay St Mawgan Airport
21
22
23
24 Perranporth
26
25
St Agnes
27
Porthtowan
28
Portreath
Truro
31
30 Godrevy Point
29
St Ives
Carbis Bay
Redruth
Gurnard's Head
Zennor
Hayle
Camborne
Penryn
Falmouth
St Mawes
St Just
Penzance
Marazion
St Michael's Mount
Constantine
Gweek
Helford River
Helford
32
Newlyn
33
Whitesand Bay
Sennen
St Buryan
Mousehole
Helston
Manaccan
40
Land's End
Porthcurno
Treen
34
Mount's Bay
35
Porthleven
Gunwalloe
St Keverne
36
37
38
Mullion
Coverack
Cadgwith
39
Ferry to Isles of Scilly
Kynance Cove
Lizard
Lizard Point

Surfing Cornwall

Kernow is a rugged land of rolling hills and wooded valleys, a place where the silhouettes of ruined tin mines overlook jagged, rocky coves. Cornwall is a Celtic land in both outlook and landscape. In places you could almost be on the west coast of Ireland, the north coast of Scotland or the northern seaboard of Spain. One thing that Cornwall shares with its Celtic cousins is its excellent surfing potential. And at the heart of the surf scene sits Newquay, a town with a very 'un-Cornish' feel to it.

Newquay would have been very happy to live on as a kind of Torquay of the northern Cornish coast, but what happened in the 1960s changed all that. The seeds were sown long before, due to the town's coastal geography, but the advent of Bilbo surfboards and advances in wetsuits made by Gul meant that surfing had gained a foothold in the town and it has stubbornly refused to let go. Today, with little encouragement from the council, surfing has become big business with the number of surf shops and shapers well into double figures. The annual Newquay Boardmasters attracts over 100,000 spectators and Newquay surfers have reached the highest levels in the sport of competitive surfing, with Russell Winter spending three years on the WCT, Spencer Hargreaves winning the European title and Alan Stokes performing well on the WQS circuit.

But there is more to Cornwall than just Newquay. Some would argue that the spiritual home of Cornish surfing sits to the south, in St Agnes, the heart of the 'Badlands'. This small village grew up around the tin mines, taking to surfing with a fierce passion and a strong will to protect its surf spots, from both outsiders and from pollution. The former spawned the Badlands legend, the latter the national environmental pressure group Surfers Against Sewage. The south coast, with its mix of powerful reefs and beaches, has spawned top British female surfer Robyn Davies – the first woman to grace the cover of *Surf Europe* magazine.

Overall, although Cornish breaks are crowded, the county has a vast coastline and miles of beaches to explore. The region also has a standard of surfing that would rival anywhere in Europe, although in a British, low-key way. "Us Brits are hardcore and surf whatever the weather," says Joe Moran, editor of *Pit Pilot* magazine. "In the past British surfers have been ignored, when we deserve a lot more, but we don't go mad about the hype, we just get it done."

Coastline

The coastline of Cornwall is rugged and crumbling due to relentless onslaught of the North Atlantic. It was along this rocky shore that wreckers lured unsuspecting ships onto the rocks and the myriad tiny coves have, for centuries, been a smugglers' haven. Today it is the tourists who are lured to the Cornish coastline and although the beaches do reach bursting point during the months of July and

On its day Porthleven is as good as any wave in the world, but with such a small take-off zone, the crowd factor can be horrendous. But like any high performance wave in the world, Pipeline for example, there are only a handful of people getting the waves, the really ruthless, focused ones. The rest are floating around just to say they've been in.

James Hendy, top Cornish surfer

Cornwall board guide

The PF Flyer
Shaper: Chops Lascelles of Beachbeat Surfboards

▸▸ 6'2" x 20" x 2³⁄₁₆" the original hotdog shortboard.
▸▸ Models range from 5'4" x 19 x 2½" up to 6'10" x 20½" x 2¾".
▸▸ Double winger spin machine for all sorts of waves and manoeuvres.
▸▸ Aerial attacks a speciality.
▸▸ Single concave under the chest to help paddling in and a spiral V in the tail to help lay it on the rail when required.
▸▸ A great all-round board for Cornish summer waves.

Thruster
Shaper: Chops Lascelles of Beachbeat Surfboards

▸▸ 6'0" x 18" x 2" for Shaun Skilton.
▸▸ For average surfer 6'6" x 19¼" x 2⁵⁄₁₆".
▸▸ Based on a fuller plan shape for sloppy summer surf.
▸▸ It has a single to double concave with squash tail and tweaks to suit ability of surfer.

Boards by **Beachbeat Surfboards**
Factory: Laminations, St Agnes, Cornwall
T00 44 (0)1872-553918
www.beachbeatsurfboards.co.uk
www.aggiesurf.com
or contact Lam2574@aol.com

August, for those who are willing to explore, there are still a few places off the beaten track. Most surfers stay north and only head south in particular conditions, usually in the winter.

Localism

There is no doubt that a lot of Cornish breaks are already very crowded and every summer seems to bring a new influx of people into the water. This can lead to tension in the water. With this in mind, if you are visiting the area, try to be honest about your ability and the types of waves you want to be surfing. Rather than small, tight-knit spots it's probably best to head for the bigger open beaches where there is more room to spread out and less tension in the water. Breaks around the Badlands of St Agnes are crowded, ultra competitive and home to powerful waves. Spots like Perran Sands and Godrevy/Gwithian have good waves, a more mellow vibe and more space. If you're heading to the Newquay area, Watergate holds more of a crowd.

Top local surfers The level of surfing in Cornwall is as high as anywhere in Europe. It has spawned many world-class surfers and also some excellent local riders. **Russell Winter, Lee Bartlett, Spencer Hargreaves, Alan Stokes, Ben Baird, Shaun Skilton, Minzie, Robin and Jake Kent, Ben Skinner, Jake and Sam Boex, James Hendy, Mark Harris** and **John Buchorski** are just the tip of the iceberg. Women surfers include **Robyn Davies, Sarah Bentley, Dominique Munroe, Nicola Bunt** and **Megan Chapman.**

Getting around

The road network in Cornwall is pretty good. The A30 acts as a main artery and access to breaks by car is pretty straightforward. During the peak summer season, especially around the last two weeks in August, the roads can become very congested. Allow more time for journeys into and out of the county and try to avoid travelling at peak periods.

TANGY DREW

25 British longboard champion Dominque Munroe at Chapel Porth ▸▸ p86

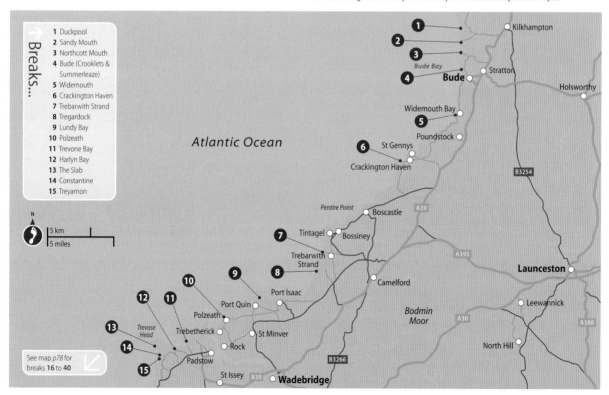

Breaks...

1 Duckpool
2 Sandy Mouth
3 Northcott Mouth
4 Bude (Crooklets & Summerleaze)
5 Widemouth
6 Crackington Haven
7 Trebarwith Strand
8 Tregardock
9 Lundy Bay
10 Polzeath
11 Trevone Bay
12 Harlyn Bay
13 The Slab
14 Constantine
15 Treyarnon

N
5 km
5 miles

Atlantic Ocean

See map p78 for breaks 16 to 40

Kilkhampton
Bude Bay
Bude   Stratton
Holsworthy
Widemouth Bay
Poundstock
St Gennys
Crackington Haven
Pentire Point   Boscastle
A39
Tintagel   Bossiney
Trebarwith Strand
Camelford
Bodmin Moor
Launceston
Leewannick
Port Isaac
Port Quin
Polzeath
Trevose Head   Trebetherick
St Minver
Rock
North Hill
Padstow
St Issey
Wadebridge
B3254
A395
A30
A388
B3266
A39

Breaks

North coast

1 Duckpool

◉ **Break type**: Beach break.
◐ **Conditions**: Small to medium swells, offshore in easterly winds.
❶ **Hazards/tips**: Not really suitable for beginners due to rocks and rips.
◖ **Sleeping**: Bude ▸ *p89*.

A sandy cove flanked by rocky outcrops that works best from low to mid, on an incoming tide. Less busy than the breaks to the south, this spot can have some good waves at low tide, but needs easterly winds to work properly. Picks up plenty of swell. Easy access off the A39 with parking above the break.

2 Sandy Mouth

◉ **Break type**: Beach break.
◐ **Conditions**: Small to medium swells, offshore in easterly winds.
❶ **Hazards/tips**: Watch out for rips and submerged rocks.
◖ **Sleeping**: Bude ▸ *p89*.

With the right banks this cliff-backed beach can produce high quality lefts and rights. Although an extension of the sandy bay leading to Bude, this is a better bet for escaping the crowds. Best from low to mid on a pushing tide – access limited at high tide. National Trust car park plus toilets near the break.

3 Northcott Mouth

◉ **Break type**: Beach break.
◐ **Conditions**: Small to medium swells, offshore in easterly winds.
❶ **Hazards/tips**: Watch out for rips when big.
◖ **Sleeping**: Bude ▸ *p89*.

Good quality beach break that can produce powerful and hollow waves, best from low to mid tide. At high tide the beach can disappear so beginners should bear this in mind. Beach parking.

4 Bude (Crooklets and Summerleaze)

◉ **Break type**: Beach break.
◐ **Conditions**: Small to medium swells, offshore in easterly winds.
❶ **Hazards/tips**: Crowds, rips, rocks.
◖ **Sleeping**: Bude ▸ *p89*.

Summerleaze has a number of waves that work in bigger swells. There is a quality left at low tide and a right at high tide near the swimming pool. There are also shifting sandbanks on the beach. **Crooklets** has a number of waves including sandbank peaks and a good right to the northern end and a left to the south. Watch out for rocky outcrops at high tide. Bude is a popular surfing location with a large local surfing community. Gets busy during the summer and during good swells. Suitable for beginners but watch out for rips near the river.

Britain Cornwall Breaks Duckpool to Bude

Cornwall

Air ——— Sea ———

°F Averages   °C

90		30
70		20
50		10
30		0

J F M A M J J A S O N D

5/4/3
Boots & gloves

4/3
Boots

3/2

4/3

THE GILL

5 Alan Stokes at Widemouth ▸▸ *p82*

"Us Brits are hardcore and surf whatever the weather," says Joe Moran...
But it helps when the surf's up and the sun's shining.

4 Paul Canning at Bude ›› *p81*

5 Widemouth

◉ **Break type**: Beach break.
◔ **Conditions**: Small to medium swells, offshore in easterly/southeasterly winds.
❶ **Hazards/tips**: Crowds, rocks.
◓ **Sleeping**: Bude ›› *p89*.

A long stretch of beach – almost a mile – with some quality banks. It produces lefts, rights and peaks depending on the banks and, as a result, can get crowded. There are also a couple of good reefs worth checking. Easy access off the A39 with a large car park overlooking the break. Beginners should watch out for rocky outcrops.

6 Crackington Haven

◉ **Break type**: Beach break.
◔ **Conditions**: Big swells, offshore in easterly winds.
❶ **Hazards/tips**: Rips, rocks.
◓ **Sleeping**: Bude ›› *p89*.

A sheltered, popular bay at the mouth of a valley, overlooked by 400-ft cliffs of limestone, sandstone and shale. The left-hand point break is surfable in even the biggest surf, with the right winds, hence the name 'Unmaxables'. Tends to work in big winter storms but there is a café in the car park for hot tea and food.

7 Trebarwith Strand

◉ **Break type**: Beach break.
◔ **Conditions**: Small to medium swells, offshore in an easterly/southeasterly wind.
❶ **Hazards/tips**: Beach disappears at high.
◓ **Sleeping**: Tintagel/Polzeath ›› *p90*.

A fairly good beach with lefts and rights, depending on the sandbars. Best surfed at low to mid tide as the beach is covered at high. Suitable for surfers of all abilities. Parking available at the beach. A great place to escape the summer crowds when the tide is out.

8 Tregardock

- **Break type**: Beach break.
- **Conditions**: Small to medium swells, offshore in easterly/southeasterly winds.
- **Hazards/tips**: Good place to escape the crowds.
- **Sleeping**: Tintagel/Polzeath ▸▸ *p90*.

Remote stretch of beach with good peaks from low to mid tide. Access on foot from Treligga. Not suitable for beginners.

9 Lundy Bay

- **Break type**: Beach break.
- **Conditions**: Medium to big swells, offshore in south/southwesterly winds.
- **Hazards/tips**: Worth checking when other spots are blown out.
- **Sleeping**: Polzeath ▸▸ *p90*.

Sheltered north-facing bay that works best at low to mid tide. Needs a big swell to work. No car park near the beach. Follow footpath.

10 Polzeath

- **Break type**: Beach break.
- **Conditions**: Medium to big swells, offshore in southeasterly/easterly wind.
- **Hazards/tips**: Pentire Point provides some shelter in light northwesterlies.
- **Sleeping**: Polzeath ▸▸ *p90*.

Polzeath has a series of lefts and rights that work on all tides. There are peaks in the middle of the bay, with lefts to the south and rights at the northern end by the point. This is a popular and flexible break with parking by the beach. Suitable for surfers of all abilities.

11 Trevone Bay

- **Break type**: Beach break.
- **Conditions**: Big swell, southeasterly winds are offshore.
- **Hazards/tips**: Small bay with good peaks.
- **Sleeping**: Polzeath ▸▸ *p90*.

Small and sheltered bay that faces northwest and needs a decent swell to get going. Has peaks that are best from low to mid tide. Signposted from the B3276.

12 Harlyn Bay

- **Break type**: Beach break.
- **Conditions**: Big swells, offshore in southerly winds.
- **Hazards/tips**: Busy when it breaks, popular spot in winter storm surf.
- **Sleeping**: Polzeath/Newquay ▸▸ *p90*.

A popular beach due to its northerly facing aspect. This means that it works in southwesterly winds with a big swell. Works best from low to three-quarter tide on the push. Parking by the beach. One of the few breaks that works in these conditions so can get crowded.

13 The Slab

- **Break type**: Right-hand reef break.
- **Conditions**: Medium swells, offshore in southeasterly winds.
- **Hazards/tips**: Rips, rocks, crowds.
- **Sleeping**: Polzeath/Newquay ▸▸ *p90*.

Low tide reef that needs a decent swell to fire and has rips when big. Access to the break in Booby's Bay is on foot from Constantine Bay.

14 Constantine

- **Break type**: Reef break and beach.
- **Conditions**: All swells, offshore in easterly winds.
- **Hazards/tips**: Crowds, rips when big.
- **Sleeping**: Polzeath/Newquay ▸▸ *p90*.

To the south of the bay peels a left-hand reef break that can produce long, walling rides. The beach itself picks up any swell going and has some excellent banks. Popular due to the quality of the waves and its consistency. Easterly winds are offshore. Good spot for surfers of all abilities, but beginners should take care when the swell picks up. Parking by the beach.

15 Treyarnon

- **Break type**: Beach break.
- **Conditions**: Small to medium swells, offshore in southeasterly/easterly winds.
- **Hazards/tips**: Parking near the beach.
- **Sleeping**: Polzeath/Newquay ▸▸ *p90*.

A series of peaks along this stretch of sand break from low to high tide. There are also a couple of low tide sand-covered reefs worth checking. A popular spot with quality waves.

16 Mawgan Porth

- **Break type**: Beach break.
- **Conditions**: Small to medium swells, offshore in southeasterly/easterly winds.
- **Hazards/tips**: Popular, rips when big.
- **Sleeping**: Newquay ▸▸ *p90*.

This bay can produce fast, walling lefts and rights and works through all tides. There can also be an excellent left into the rivermouth. Parking off the B3276. It's also worth checking **Beacon Cove** to the south.

17 Watergate Bay

- **Break type**: Beach break.
- **Conditions**: Small to medium swells, offshore in southeasterly/easterly winds.
- **Hazards/tips**: Crowds, popular spot, good spot for beginners.
- **Sleeping**: Newquay ▸▸ *p90*.

Watergate is a huge stretch of sand and a great place to head for when Newquay is heaving. Works on all tides. There are lefts and rights stretching north and south from the car park.

Britain Cornwall Breaks Tregardock to Watergate Bay

DEMI TAYLOR

17 Watergate Bay

Surfers' tales

ESPIX

Melanie Redman Carr

A Year in the Life of Fistral Beach

Fistral beach sits on the western edge of Newquay, an impressive stretch of golden sand backed by a links golf course. To the south sits a row of kitsch hotels and to the north the whole scene is surveyed by the imposing Victorian grandeur of the Headland Hotel. The new National Surfing Centre has arrived. With its decking, wood panelling and alloy struts it has the look and feel of a huge beached cruiser. But its role is that of a glamorous tug, designed to tow the beach into the 21st century.

Fistral is Britain's surfing Mecca and the headquarters of the BSA Surf School. The instructors watch Fistral change through the seasons with the number of surfers in the water constantly fluctuating. Will Giles is a BSA Senior Coach and says that the changes in the beach can be seen in both its physical appearance and the people who come here. "At the start of the year the beach is very quiet and the weather is cold. The sea looks foreboding - it's darker and more aggressive. When the wind really blows, white horses or white caps are whipped up out on the ocean. Because the sun isn't on it, the whole colour changes - the sea takes on a dark steely blue. During the day there may be only about ten to twenty locals, sometimes less than that."

But as the seasons change, so do the numbers of people. "We notice more people on the beach around Easter. At the school we get more kids, although it's still fairly cold around then." But it's not just the young grommets who are braving the elements. "We also get some Stag and Hen parties who are down for the weekend. They come and brave the elements for a couple of hours. We really notice the difference around the beginning of June; it really starts to take off."

During August, the Rip Curl Boardmasters sets up camp on Fistral Beach. It is one of the biggest surf competitions in Europe and attracts over 100,000 people over its duration.

The whole atmosphere of the beach changes. A tent village appears in the car park selling everything from bandanas to boards, from bongos to beads. One of the mobile phone companies erects a massive screen where text messages are broadcast to the whole beach. A stream of innuendos are interspersed with deleted swear words. Legions of adolescents frantically thumb their key pads trying to beat the computerized swear-word filter.

"That's the week when it really gets crazy. It's our peak time. All the car parks are full, even down at south Fistral people are squeezed in."

Once the chaos of the August bank holiday passes, the locals are left to enjoy the beach. "It's a really nice time for the locals. The surf can still be pretty good. And when the sun's on it the water becomes a glassy emerald green."

Autumn is a golden time of warm days and rolling swells. Campervans loiter around the beach and early morning sessions are yet to take on the ice-cold blue of winter. "The summers now are strong through September and even into October some years. We keep giving lessons through to November, but obviously if we get strong bookings we try to cater for them."

When the biting winter winds return, and the boots and gloves are brought out for one more season, groups of surfers huddle around tables in the café in the National Surfing Centre, watching another squall blow in over the dark, mottled ocean. In the days before the new haven, visitors would huddle in their cars, heaters on full, trying to demist their windscreens. "The new surf centre has brought a lot of people here, and also provided jobs. It attracts people from all over the country and helps provide infrastructure for when competitions are on. It helps maintain Fistral's standing as a world-class beach."

The **British Surfing Association** offers lessons and courses for surfers of all levels, T01637-876474.

ESPIX

Rip Curl Boardmasters held in August each year

Although it gets busy in the middle, there are usually some peaks further up the beach. In a good swell there can be excellent, punchy waves here. Watergate is a popular contest site for British and English surfing championships. It also helps take the pressure off Fistral and the Town beaches. Suitable for surfers of all abilities, many surf schools operate from here.

18 Newquay Beaches

- **Break type**: Beach breaks.
- **Conditions**: All swells, offshore in southerly/southeasterly/easterly winds.
- **Hazards/tips**: Crowded beaches, surf schools, flexible beaches.
- **Sleeping**: Newquay » p90.

Newquay is probably Europe's Surf City. It doesn't have the cafés and beach culture of Hossegor (see page 180) or the surf chic of Biarritz (page 195), but it does have a higher density of surf shops and shapers. What it lacks in pastry shops, it makes up for in pasty shops.

Lusty Glaze is a privately owned, cliff-lined cove with some good waves in smaller swells at low to mid tides. Gets narrow near high. Site of an annual night surfing competition.

The **Town Beaches** (Tolcarne, Great Western, Towan) face north and are more sheltered. They work through all tides and need a much bigger swell to get going. There is a left near the harbour wall on Towan and assorted peaks heading east.

The **Cribbar** is a rocky point out past the Headland Hotel and an infamous big-wave spot that comes alive in huge clean swells. It is surfed, but only rarely, and has become the stuff of legends.

19 Fistral Beach

- **Break type**: Beach break.
- **Conditions**: All swells.
- **Size**: 2-8 ft.
- **Length**: 10-100 m.
- **Swell**: Northwesterly/westerly/ southwesterly.
- **Wind**: Easterly/southeasterly.
- **Tide**: All tides.
- **Bottom**: Sand.
- **Entry/exit**: From the beach.
- **Hazards/tips**: Crowds, rocks at Little Fistral.
- **Sleeping**: Newquay » p90.

Fistral is Britain's most famous surfing beach. As the epicentre of the UK scene, it is an often maligned and underestimated break, but it is actually a very high quality spot that can produce hollow and powerful waves. The National Surfing Centre is based there and every year the Rip Curl Boardmasters surf contest attracts the best surfers in the world. The main beach works through all tides and the waves vary with the quality of the sandbanks. Although very busy in the summer, the autumn and winter sees the crowd drop off, but it is rarely quiet here. The beach has produced some excellent surfers including Russell Winter, Lee Bartlett, Alan Stokes, Spencer Hargreaves, Ben Baird – even ex-world champ Martin Potter had a spell here.

Little Fistral is a low tide spot to the north that can produce excellent waves with long walls and barrels. It breaks in front of rocks so is not a good place for beginners.

If you like Fistral, try Santa Cruz in Portugal (see page 300) or Praia Reinante in Spain (see page 248).

20 Crantock

- **Break type**: Beach break and rivermouth.
- **Conditions**: Medium swells, offshore in a southeasterly wind.
- **Hazards/tips**: Worth checking as a less crowded alternative to Fistral.
- **Sleeping**: Newquay » p90.

Just south of Fistral, this beach facing northwest has a rivermouth sandbank that can produce some excellent rights. It needs a decent swell to get going. Works best from low to mid tide. The south end of the beach can produce good lefts.

21 Holywell Bay

- **Break type**: Beach break.
- **Conditions**: Small to medium swells, offshore in southeasterly winds.
- **Hazards/tips**: Less crowded than Newquay area.
- **Sleeping**: Newquay/Perranporth » p90.

Beach break facing northwest that works on all states of tide, producing some good quality lefts and rights. Always worth checking as it can produce excellent waves but is dependent on the banks. Take turning off the A3075 Newquay road.

22 Penhale/Perran Sands

- **Break type**: Beach break.
- **Conditions**: Small to medium swells, offshore in easterly winds.
- **Hazards/tips**: Rips when big, when small OK for beginners .
- **Sleeping**: Perranporth » p91.

A huge, golden beach, stretching from Penhale corner south to Droskyn Head. An endless line-up of lefts, rights and peaks, varying in quality from mellow peelers to reeling, hollow barrels. Works through all tides. A good spot for beginners, intermediates and travelling surfers wanting to escape the crowded and competitive line-ups. Plenty of peaks to go round and a

Britain Cornwall Breaks Newquay to Penhale/Perran Sands

19 Greg Pastusiak at Fistral Beach

much more chilled-out atmosphere. Drive through the holiday camp to the pay and display car park overlooking the beach.

23 Perranporth/Droskyn

- **Break type**: Beach break.
- **Conditions**: Small to medium swells, offshore in easterly winds.
- **Hazards/tips**: Crowds in summer, good for beginners.
- **Sleeping**: Perranporth ▸ *p91*.

Droskyn works best at low through to mid tide. At high the backwash from the cliffs makes the waves bumpy and unpredictable. It can have a good left in front of the cliffs. From here a huge expanse of westerly facing sand stretches out north joining up with Perran Sands and Penhale. The Perranporth beach works on all tides but doesn't handle big swells. Parking on the cliff top at Droskyn or in Perranporth. Chilled line-ups so a good spot for holidaying and travelling surfers to check.

24 Trevaunance Cove, St Agnes

- **Break type**: Beach break.
- **Conditions**: Medium to big swells, offshore in southeasterly winds.
- **Hazards/tips**: Very busy, localism, rips, rocks.
- **Sleeping**: St Agnes ▸ *p91*.

Sheltered sandy and rocky bay that faces northwest. One of the few spots that works in big swells with southwesterly winds. Surfed through to three-quarter tide but best at mid.

A small line-up that easily gets crowded. Can hold a good size swell. A strong rip to the left of the bay and crowds makes this a spot for experienced surfers only. The heart of the large Badlands surfing community, so rarely uncrowded. Parking near the Driftwood Spa pub. The birthplace of SAS and still polluted.

25 Chapel Porth

- **Break type**: Beach break.
- **Conditions**: Small to medium swells, offshore in southeasterly.
- **Hazards/tips**: Crowds, localism.
- **Sleeping**: St Agnes/Porthtowan ▸ *p91*.

Fast, powerful and hollow rights and lefts break in northwesterly or southwesterly swells. Chapel is a small beach that works from low to mid and has a big local crew. The standard of surfing is extremely high here and it is not a place for beginners. Visiting surfers may struggle to get a wave and there have been incidents of localism. Parking by the beach in small National Trust car park.

26 Porthtowan

- **Break type**: Beach break.
- **Conditions**: Small to medium swells, offshore in southeasterly winds.
- **Hazards/tips**: Crowds, dangerous rips, powerful waves.
- **Sleeping**: Porthtowan ▸ *p92*.

Heavy, punchy break that works through all tides, opening out at low tide to reveal Lushingtons to the south. Offshore in a

southeasterly or easterly wind, but at high tide the cliffs provide some shelter from light southerlies. Porthtowan has powerful waves and broken boards are not unusual. Strong rips are a real danger so in anything but small surf it is best left to competent surfers. The excellent banks and beachfront parking have resulted in Porthtowan becoming a very crowded break with a strong local crew, but it is not recommended for the inexperienced.

27 Portreath

- **Break type**: Beach break and reef.
- **Conditions**: Medium to big swells, offshore in southeasterly winds.
- **Hazards/tips**: Sheltered bay.
- **Sleeping**: Porthtowan ▸ *p92*.

Portreath is usually about half the size of Porthtowan, but can be more sheltered from the wind. The right-hand reef that breaks off the rocks in front of the harbour wall is popular with bodyboarders and experienced surfers. The beach break is usually a short, fast right that can easily become a close-out. Works best from low to near high. Car park overlooking break. Can get crowded in the summer.

28 Godrevy/Gwithian

- **Break type**: Beach break.
- **Conditions**: All swells, offshore in southeasterly winds.
- **Hazards/tips**: Relaxed line-up, popular spot.
- **Sleeping**: Hayle ▸ *p92*.

23 Perranporth

22 Penhale / Perran Sands

26 Porthtowan

Huge stretch of sand that extends for 4½ miles from Godrevy south to Hayle, only broken by the occasional cluster of high tide rocks. This exposed beach can be fickle but is a good place for beginners and intermediate surfers on surf trips to head for due to the space and relaxed vibe. Godrevy, the headland at the northern end of the bay, picks up the most swell and can produce some quality waves with easy access from the National Trust car park. Although it does get busy in the summer, there are plenty of peaks to escape the crowds and the atmosphere here is pretty chilled. Good café in the car park. River can be polluted after heavy rains.

29 Hayle Rivermouth

- **Break type**: Rivermouth.
- **Conditions**: Medium to big swells, offshore in southerly/southeasterly winds.
- **Hazards/tips**: Crowds, rips.
- **Sleeping**: Hayle ⟩⟩ *p92*.

Needs a decent swell to get going but can provide good quality waves around the rivermouth. Can get crowded when good. Watch out for rips and pollution after heavy rains. Access from Hayle town.

30 Hawks Point

- **Break type**: Beach break.
- **Conditions**: Big swells, offshore in southwesterly winds.
- **Hazards/tips**: Crowded, difficult access.
- **Sleeping**: St Ives ⟩⟩ *p92*.

28 Godrevy

A good left breaking off the western end of Carbis Bay. Needs a really big swell to get going so it's a great place to check during a big southwesterly swell with southwesterly winds. Works on all tides but if it's on, it will be packed. Access is also difficult.

31 Porthmeor, St Ives

- **Break type**: Beach break.
- **Conditions**: Medium to big swell, offshore in southerly winds.
- **Hazards/tips**: Crowds, parking.
- **Sleeping**: St Ives ⟩⟩ *p92*.

Overlooked by the St Ives Tate Gallery, Porthmeor is a sheltered beach that faces north and needs a decent swell to get going. This beach does get busy in the summer and parking can be a problem.

32 Gwynver

- **Break type**: Beach break with point.
- **Conditions**: Small to medium swells, offshore in easterly winds.
- **Hazards/tips**: Punchy waves, access on foot.
- **Sleeping**: Sennen ⟩⟩ *p92*.

Gwynver is a quality beach break that joins up with Sennen at low tide. It picks up more swell than Sennen and in a good northwesterly swell, right-handers peel off the point at the north end of the beach over a rocky/sandy bottom. Also has a punchy shore break. Works best from low to near high. Watch out for rips. Access is from parking off the A30 and a 20-minute walk down the cliffs.

33 Sennen Cove

- **Break type**: Beach break.
- **Conditions**: Small to medium swells, offshore in easterly winds.
- **Hazards/tips**: Rips in front of car park in bigger swells.
- **Sleeping**: Sennen ⟩⟩ *p92*.

West-facing good quality beach that works well from low through to near high. Due to its location on the toe of Cornwall, it picks up more swell than the other north coast beaches. Suitable for all surfers, but watch out for rips and rocks towards the southern end of the beach in front of the car park. A popular, year-round spot. Surf shop and toilets in car park.

South coast

34 Porthcurno

- **Break type**: Beach break.
- **Conditions**: Medium to big swells, offshore in northerly winds.
- **Hazards/tips**: Beautiful spot, not too crowded.
- **Sleeping**: Sennen ⟩⟩ *p92*.

Cocooned by granite cliffs, at high tide this narrow bay almost disappears. At low the bay opens up with lefts and rights in the emerging bay to the east. Needs a southwesterly swell or a big northwesterly wrapping in to work. With crystal-clear water, this sheltered spot is a great place to see basking sharks on calm, flat summer days. The open air Minack Theatre overlooks the bay.

35 Perranuthanoe

- **Break type**: Beach break.
- **Conditions**: Medium to big swells, offshore in northeasterly.
- **Hazards/tips**: Busy spot.
- **Sleeping**: Sennen ⟩⟩ *p92*.

Underestimated bay with a good right breaking off the rocks at the west. There is an A-frame reef, **Cabbage Patch**, which breaks over boulders to the eastern end of the bay. In between are peaks of variable quality. Works best from low to three-quarter tide as high tide sees the bay virtually disappear. It's usually a couple of feet smaller than Praa Sands. Parking near the beach. Used to be

DEMI TAYLOR

Britain Cornwall Breaks Hayle to Perranuthanoe

very quiet but as Praa has got busier, this spot has taken the overspill. With a more relaxed vibe, it is popular with beginners, intermediate surfers and longboarders.

36 Praa Sands

- **Break type**: Beach break.
- **Conditions**: Medium to big swells, offshore in northeasterly winds.
- **Hazards/tips**: Very crowded, can be heavy, rips.
- **Sleeping**: St Ives ›› *p92*.

A popular, winter break that works in southwesterly or big northwesterly swells to produce powerful, punchy waves. Offshore in northerly or northeasterly winds, it usually draws a big crowd because when Praa is on, the north coast is usually blown out. Gets packed at weekends on good swells. Works on all tides but at high can become a shore dump. Parking overlooking the break.

ⓘ *If you like Porthleven, try Thurso East in Scotland (see page 38) or La Sauzaie in France (see page 167).*

ESTPIX

36 Praa Sands

THE GILL

37 Porthleven

37 Porthleven

- **Break type**: Right-hand reef.
- **Conditions**: All swells.
- **Size**: 3-10 ft.
- **Length**: 50-100 m.
- **Swell**: Southwesterly.
- **Wind**: Northeasterly.
- **Tide**: Three-quarters to just off low.
- **Bottom**: Rock reef.
- **Entry/exit**: Off the rocks.
- **Hazards/tips**: Shallow near low, crowds, crowds and more crowds!
- **Sleeping**: St Ives ›› *p92*.

Porthleven is the most respected reef break in the south of England and, as such, when it is breaking it attracts a large crowd. Although 'Leven' breaks year round, it really comes to life during the big winter swells. The wave breaks onto a reef situated just to the west of the entrance to Porthleven harbour and provides some great vantage points for those watching. It is really a mid-tide break with low tide getting pretty shallow and high suffering from backwash. The reef is famed for its fast, hollow rights which can be board-snappingly ferocious, but it also throws up some lefts.

The biggest factor in surfing 'Leven' is the crowds. Most of Cornwall's best surfers will be in the line-up when it's firing and if you watch you will see that no waves go through unridden. The UK's most competitive line-up is no place for the faint-hearted. Porthleven regular James Hendy says, "The thing about Leven is that when it's good, it's so competitive that there's only a handful of guys actually getting waves. Some people just paddle out to say they were in." The rocks provide a great vantage point to watch all the action.

"Leven can be a real board eater," recalls Minzie. "I remember one session where I'd just snapped my board and I was scooting in on what was left of it and I saw Chops paddling out. He saw me and started laughing. Luckily I had a spare board with me so I grabbed it, put my leash on and jumped back off the rocks. I'm paddling out and guess who I meet coming in on the remains of his board?"

Porthleven and the 500 Quid Dog

I'd seen a little advert for some Jack Russell pups for sale in a farm in Helston. So me and Bub went over there and got this little dog – he was the last one left and only about an inch high. We had our boards in the back and I said, "Well, we might just go over to Porthleven and have a look – it might be OK." So Bub and I went over and all I had in the car was my big 9'6" Dewey Webber – Bub had his board. It was about 4-5 ft and really nice. I was out there surfing this Webber, no leash, and having a great time. The last wave I had was at dead high tide. I lost my board and it went straight into the cave. I got to the mouth and tried to swim in but it was a real pushing tide and my board had gone right up the back so I just got out of the water and left it in there. About three days later they found my board – in about 3,000 little bits. I stopped in at Mike Hendy's on my way back for a cup of tea and he said, "After that, you've got to name the dog Dewey." So that was the day I lost my Dewey Webber board but came home with Dewey the dog.

Chops Lascelles has been surfing in Cornwall since the 1970s. He's a shaper and runs Beachbeat surfboards.

38 Church Cove

- **Break type**: Beach break.
- **Conditions**: Small to medium swells, offshore in northeasterly/easterly winds.
- **Hazards/tips**: Crowds.
- **Sleeping**: St Ives ›› *p92*.

Bay facing southwest on the Lizard Peninsula that can produce some quality waves in southwesterly or big northwesterly swells. Works best from low to three-quarter tide. Winds from the northeast or easterly direction are preferable. Popular break in the winter.

39 Kennack Sands

◉ **Break type**: Beach break.
☁ **Conditions**: Big swells, offshore in northwesterly/northerly winds.
❶ **Hazards/tips**: Crowds.
⊜ **Sleeping**: St Ives ›› *p92*.

Beach facing southeast on the eastern side of the Lizard. There are two beaches separated by a large rocky reef known as the Caerverracks. Only works in massive northwesterly or big southwesterly swells. At low tide the beach opens out with a long stretch to the east and a small section to the west. Can have lefts and rights. Gets busy when working. Parking by the beach.

40 Falmouth Beaches

◉ **Break type**: Beach and reefs.
☁ **Conditions**: Big swells, offshore in north/northwesterly winds.
❶ **Hazards/tips**: Crowds.
⊜ **Sleeping**: St Ives ›› *p92*.

The three beaches closest to Falmouth – Maenporth, Swanpool and Gyllyngvase – can break in big southwesterly swells and the occasional easterly in the channel. Between Swanpool and Gyllyngvase lies Falmouth Reef. Busy when working, large student population.

Listings

17 Sarah Bentley, English Surfing Championships, Watergate Bay, Cornwall ›› *p83*

Bude

The northernmost town in Cornwall, Bude is accessed off the A39 or the optimistically named 'Atlantic Highway' (more byway than highway). Built around a 19th-century canal and a stretch of golden beaches to the north and south, Bude is a pretty town with a relaxed attitude and has been a popular holiday destination since Regency times.

✸ Flat spells
Bowling Ten-pin bowling at **Harlequins**, Stucley Rd, T01288-355366, www.harlequins.com. **Cinema** Rebel **Cinema**, T01288-3614425, miles south of Bude in Poundstock – they may not have the latest films but if it's flat . . . **Golf** Get a round in at **Bude and North Cornwall GC** on Burn View, T01288-352006. Green fees around £30. **Skating** Check out the mini-skatepark on the seafront at Crooklets Beach

⊜ Sleeping
A-B Trevigue, T01840-230418, is a beautiful B&B option serving excellent farmhouse breakfasts and set in the courtyard of a working farm. A short walk from the sea this is ideal for a weekend of loving and surfing.
B-C Widemouth Manor, overlooking Widemouth Bay, T01288-361263, www.widemouthmanor.co.uk, is a popular choice with surfers (but also home to Manorism nightclub).
C Bay View Inn, also over looking Widemouth, T01288-361273, is a quieter B&B option with board storage and a drying room.
C-D Pencarrol, near Crooklets beach on Downs View, T01288-352478.
F-G North Shore Bude Backpackers, T01288-354256, www.northshorebude.com, offer a fair deal with dorm beds from £12 a night. Double rooms also available.
Camping In terms of camping, there are plenty of choices, however many do not take single sex groups so call before you rock up with a van load of 20 mates.
Cornwall Campers, T01208-832927,

DEMI TAYLOR

www.cornwallcampers.co.uk, offer sleeping and transport options in one package – a VW camper van! Van hire from £395/week. **Cornish Coasts**, in Poundstock about 2 miles south of Widemouth on the A39, T01288-361380, open Easter-Oct, are a friendly site, about the cheapest and best option, and offer statics. **Redpost Inn & Holiday Park**, about 4 miles inland from Bude in Launcells, T01288-381305, is a small site, open year round with the option of statics, with the Redpost Inn serving real ale and real food in 16th-century surroundings. **Upper Lynstone Caravan & Camping Park**, just south of Bude on the road to Widemouth, T01288-352017, www.upperlynstone.co.uk, has cabins, is open Easter–Oct to couples and families only. **Budemeadows Touring Park**, T01288-361646, open year round; **Bude Holiday Park**, T01288-355980,summer only; and **Sandymouth Holiday Park**, T01288-352563, Apr-Oct, are very family orientated and don't take same sex groups.

⊘ Eating/drinking

Overlooking Summerleaze, **Life's A Beach** is a popular bistro/bar and chilled place to grab a bite and watch the sun go down. For a more basic approach, **Anne's Corner House** on Queen St is the place to go for a cheap, filling 'with chips' menu, while the **Coffee Pot** on Morwena Terr is a good place to grab a coffee and access the latest charts on the internet. Jay Squire of the **Surf Spot** surf shop recommends **El Barco** on Bencoolen Rd for the 'best steaks in Bude, cooked by a Spanish chef with 30 years' experience'. After dinner, head next door to the **Bencoolen** bar for a drink or to the popular **Carriers Inn** overlooking the River Neet. If it's real ale you're after, head south to the **Bay View Inn** at Widemouth Bay (see also Sleeping above). Also at Widemouth is the **Widemouth Manor** in all its guises as a pub, B&B, restaurant and 'Manorism' club. At Crackington Haven, the **Cabin** on the beach serves a full range of snacks from pizza to cream teas and operates a BYO booze system for eating in.

⊘ Shopping

There are a good number of **surf shops** in Bude including **Surf Spot**, on Belle Vue, www.surfspot.co.uk , who sponsor top rider Joss Ash, and **Zuma Jays**, also on Belle Vue, www.zumajays.co.uk. **Somerfield**, next to the golf club on the Headland, and **Safeway** on Stucley Rd, for all your basic food needs.

✹ Festivals

Aug Bude hosts an annual **Jazz festival** in Aug during which accommodation gets booked up.

⊙ Directory

Banks: most of the main banks are on Lansdown Rd by the river. **Pharmacy**: several on Belle Vue, including a **Boots** chemist. **Post office**: on Morwena Terr. **Tourist information**: centre open year round in the Crescent car park, www.visitbude.info.

Tintagel

Heading south along the A39, Tintagel is signposted from the main road. The castle may or may not be the birthplace of the legendary King Arthur, or the caves below home to the magician Merlin, but the castle ruins clinging to the 'island' are certainly worth exploring. Admission year round £3.20, T01840-770328. There are plenty of tat shops in the one-street town touting myths and magic to the willing.

⊜ Sleeping

Camping The Headland, on Atlantic Rd, T01840-770239, open Easter-Oct, or **Bossiney Farm**, T01840-770481, just north at Bossiney. **YHA Hostel**, at Dunderhole Point, T01840-770334, open 29 Mar-30 Oct, with fantastic views along the coast (also available for hire off season).

Polzeath

In the lea of Pentire Point nestles the seaside resort of Polzeath – popular with middle England's guitar-toting, school-leaving population.

⊜ Sleeping

C-D **Pentire View**, just up from the beach, T01208-862484. **Camping** If you're not in a couple or with a family, camping in Polzeath is going to prove difficult – **The Valley Caravan Park**, T01208-862391, and **Tristram Camping Park** overlooking the bay, T01208-862215, do not accommodate groups. **Trenant Steading**, T01208-869091.

⊘ Eating/drinking

On the beach there are a number of places serving snacks. Just up from the beach sits the **Oyster Catcher**, a lively spot for an evening drink.

⊙ Shopping

Anns Cottage Surf Shop, T01208-863317, stock a full range of gear and also do a surf check on T01208-862162. Shaper **Local Hero** are based just inland in Wadebridge, T01208-814282.

Newquay

Newquay is Europe's self-styled surf capital and deserves the title. There are surf shops on every corner and shapers galore. It even has good surfing beaches – if you can take the crowds. Although not an unpleasant resort, the summer nights can be a throng of stag nights, hen parties and a whole rainbow spectrum of football shirts.

✿ Flat spells

Skate park On Edgecombe Av in the park. **Golf** There are Pitch and Putt greens overlooking Porth and Tolcarne beaches.

⊜ Sleeping

Newquay is awash with hotels, B&Bs and surf lodges. For B&Bs check out Headland Rd for a cheap place to stay within walking access of Fistral Beach. There are also many lodges in town but check the rooms as standards vary from clean and compact to cramped and grubby. **B-D Cribber Green Rooms**, Headland Rd, T01637-875082, overlooks Fistral and has

bunk and room accommodation.
B-D Newquay Surf Lodge, Springfield Rd, T01637-859700, is a self-catering lodge near the centre of town.
C-D Base Surf Lodge, Tower Rd, T01637-874852.
C-D Home Surf Lodge, Tower Rd, T01637-851736, is a lively place that openly welcomes stag nights so might not be the best place if you need an early night. It has a late bar and also does B&B.
C-E Fistral Backpackers, Headland Rd, T01637-873146, is a short walk to the beach. It does dorms and doubles and has a board and drying room and kitchen facilities.
Camping The options are pretty limited for groups due to drunken antics in the past. **Smugglers Haven** at Trevelgue Holiday Park is one of the only places, T01637-852000. Also try **Sunnyside**, T01637-873338, and **Rosecliston**, T01637-830326.

⚲ Eating/drinking
For traditional pub grub try the **Red Lion** on Beacon Rd, a popular hang-out with good value food. The **Fistral Chef Café** over the road is also a good place to grab a meal. Joe Moran from *Pit Pilot* recommends the **Phoenix** on Watergate Beach as a good place to eat day and night – they do a good value daily 'surfers special'. A good lunchtime hang-out is the **Breadline Café** on Beachfield Rd for typical 'caff' food. For a more expensive slap-up meal, the **Lewenick Lodge** on Pentire Headline, has a wide menu from seafood to steaks. **Fistral Blu** on Fistral Beach is also worth trying.
　Newquay is heaving with bars and clubs. The **Chy Bar** and the **Koola Bar** on Beach Rd offer great sounds in a clean modern environment. The **Walkabout** on Cliff Rd is a popular hang-out and **Berties** caters to the younger end of the spectrum. **Sailors**, on

Fore St, tends to be where people gravitate to after a few pints to dance the night away to the latest chart music.

❍ Shopping
There is a massive selection of **surf shops** in Newquay. Here are a few to get started. **Fistral Surf Company**, T01637-850808, is a longstanding surf retailer with a number of shops in town, the biggest on Cliff Rd. **North Shore**, on Fore St, T01637-850 620, offers a good selection of hardware and clothing. **Ocean Magic**, Cliff Rd, T01637-850071, is run by shaper Nigel Semmens. **Revolver**, on Fore St, T01637-873962, is a fairly new shop with a retro twist. **Tunnel Vision**, T01637-879033, is another well established shop and can be found on Alma Place.

❶ Directory
Airport: T01637-860551. **Banks** and ATMs on Bank St. **Chemists**: Kayes Chemist on East St is open 7 days a week in summer. There is a **Boots** and **Superdrug** on Bank St. **Internet**: Tad & Nick's Talk 'N' Surf on Fore St and Cybersurf @ Newquay on Broad St. **Post office**: East St. **Railway station**: on Cliff Rd. **Tourist information**: opposite the bus station on Marcus Hill, T01637-854020.

Perranporth

Perranporth is a pretty unremarkable resort town but it does offer plenty of cheap accommodation and access to a huge beach (complete with beach bar).

⬤ Sleeping
Perranporth has a number of caravan parks including **Perranporth Caravan Holidays** on Crow Hill, T01872-572385, offering static caravans with sea views across Perran Sands. It's just a short scramble down to the

waves. Another budget spot is **D Perranporth Youth Hostel**, T01872-573812. There are also hoardes of cheap B&Bs in town within a short walk of the beach.

St Agnes

This picturesque ex-mining village off the B3277 is the heart of Cornwall's most tight-knit surfing community.

☺ Flat spells
Skate park Nearby **Mount Hawke Skate Park** is an excellent indoor facility and one of the country's best known skate parks.

⬤ Sleeping
A Driftwood Spars, T01872-552428, popular hotel down by picturesque Trevaunance Cove.
C-D Penkerris, T01872-552262, is an ivy-clad house as you enter the village at the top end.
D The Malthouse, T01872-553318, an excellent, surfer-friendly B&B in a central location in Peterville, the lower part of St Agnes. Recommended.
Camping Beacon Cottage Farm, T01872-552347, May-Oct camping and electric hook-ups for vans. **Presingoll Farm**, on the main road into St Agnes near the film studio, T01872-552333, offers Easter-Oct camping and pitches for vans.

⚲ Eating/drinking
The **Tap House** in Peterville is a popular pub and is crammed at weekends, even in winter. The food is excellent and on Wed off-season does half-price pizzas. The **Peterville** is a traditional pub with live soccer. The **Driftwood Spas** has a pool table, live bands and a Sun carvery. The **St Agnes Hotel** also does a good Sun roast and bar meals. For a

Airports → Heathrow T0870-0000123, Gatwick T0870-0002468, Stansted T0870-0000303, www.baa.co.uk. **Buses and coaches** → National Express T08705-808080, www.gobycoach.com; Scottish City Link, T0141-3329644, www.citylink.co.uk. **Car hire** → Avis T0870-6060100; Europcar T0870-6075000; Hertz T08708-448844. **Petrol prices** → £0.85-90/litre. **Ferries** → P&O, T0870-2424999, www.poportsmouth.com; Brittany Ferries,T0870-3665333, www.brittany-ferries.com; Irish Ferries T08705-171717, www.irishferries.com; Sea France, T0870-5711711, www.seafrance.com. **Rail links** → National Rail Enquiries T08457-484950.

splash-out fish supper in the summer, try **Schooners** overlooking Trevaunance Cove.

○ Shopping
St Agnes is the home of Chops Lascelles' **Beachbeat Surfboards**, T01872-553818, who shape boards for some of Cornwall's top surfers including Robin Kent, former Cornish Champion, Sarah Bentley and Longboard Champion Dominique Munroe. Steve Bunt's **Best Ever Surfboards**, T01872-553532, are also based in the heart of the Badlands and shape boards for local chargers including Drustan Ward, Jamie Kent and Nicola Bunt. **Aggie Surf Shop**, T01872-553818, in Peterville has a full selection of hardware and clothing.

Porthtowan

Accommodation is pretty limited in Porthtowan but there is a campsite as you turn into the village at **Rosehill Touring Park** on Rose Hill, T01209-890802. It is in a nice shady valley but does have a slightly authoritarian list of rules. The **Blue** overlooking Porthtowan beach is a great place to enjoy a post-surf beer and has become so popular that it has expanded. It offers a diverse menu of food, which varies between excellent and OK, and has live music on a Sat night.

Hayle

Hayle is an underestimated town that offers loads of potential as a base for a surf trip. It has easy access to St Ives Bay and plenty of accommodation.

● Sleeping
Camping Beachside Holiday Park, T01736-753080, sits in the dunes overlooking the sea and offers chalets and bungalows as well as pitches for vans and tents. St Ives Bay Holiday Park, T0800-317713, also overlooks the sea and has static caravans as well as pitches for tents and vans.

○ Shopping
Market Sq is the base for **Down The Line Surf Co**, T01736-757025, where they stock a good selection of hardware and clothing.

St Ives

The tightly packed streets of St Ives don't make for the ideal base for a surf trip, but it is an excellent place to visit with a number of surf shops as well as great restaurants and bars. Try the **Saltwater Café** on Fish St, T01736-794928, for good seafood at a moderate price. If you're after a bit of culture with a sea view check out **The Tate St Ives** on Porthmeor Beach, T01736-796226.

Sennen

This long, picturesque, crescent-shaped bay is a popular tourist destination and accommodation is pretty limited here. It is, however, one of Cornwall's most consistent beaches, has plenty of room to spread out and a pretty chilled atmosphere. There is a great view of Cape Cornwall, with its chimney stack, some 4 miles to the north.

● Sleeping
C-D **Whitesands Lodge**, T01736-871776, is a pretty good option with dorm accommodation, single and double rooms. It also has a café/restaurant.
C **Myrtle Cottage**, in the village, T01736-871698.
Camping Trevedra Farm Caravan and Camping Site, T01736-871835, offers pitches for tents and vans.

♪ Eating/drinking
The **Beach Restaurant** in the seafront car park does a selection of meals from seafood to burgers, as well as takeaways.

○ Shopping
Chapel Idne Surf Shop, T01736-871192, in the beach car park at Sennen Cove stocks a good selection of hardware and clothing and also has a board hire facility.

ALEX WILLIAMS

33 Sennen Cove ▸▸ *p87*

Surfing Wales

Wales is a country of diverse landscapes, proud people and strong opinions. From the rugged shores of the Pembrokeshire Coast National Park to the stunning peaks of the Brecon Beacons, it is a land of breathtaking scenery and unspoilt beauty. Yet to the south sits the industrial heartland that drove the Welsh economy – the Valleys, with their once great coalmining communities, Port Talbot with its steel plant, Neath and Bridgend, now looking to new technology and new jobs.

To say that the Welsh are a proud people would be like saying the French are known to drink the odd glass of wine. And nowhere is this patriotism better demonstrated than in the national sport of rugby. It's as if all the years of class struggle and the fight for self-determination became distilled into this one sport, a chance to put one over on the

The Gill at Crab Island ▶▶ p100

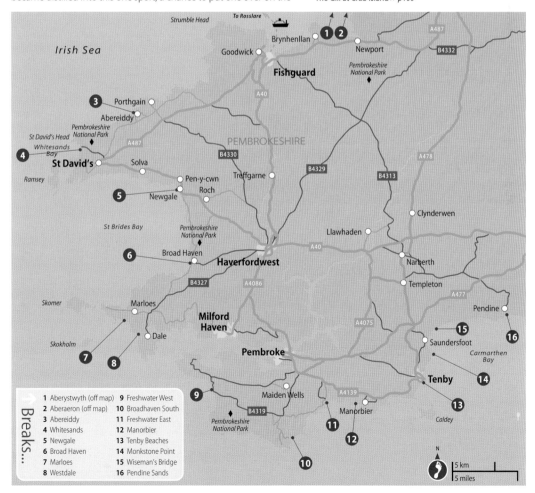

Breaks...

1 Aberystwyth (off map)
2 Aberaeron (off map)
3 Abereiddy
4 Whitesands
5 Newgale
6 Broad Haven
7 Marloes
8 Westdale
9 Freshwater West
10 Broadhaven South
11 Freshwater East
12 Manorbier
13 Tenby Beaches
14 Monkstone Point
15 Wiseman's Bridge
16 Pendine Sands

Irish Sea

Strumble Head
To Rosslare
Brynhenllan
Goodwick
Newport
A487
B4332
Fishguard
Pembrokeshire National Park
A40

3 Porthgain
Abereiddy
St David's Head
Pembrokeshire National Park
Whitesands Bay
4 **St David's**
Ramsey
Solva
A487
B4330
Treffgarne
B4329
B4313
A478
PEMBROKESHIRE

Pen-y-cwn
5 Roch
Newgale
Clynderwen
St Brides Bay
Pembrokeshire National Park
Llawhaden
A40
6 Broad Haven
Haverfordwest
Narberth
B4327
A4086
Templeton
A477
Skomer
Marloes
Pendine
Skokholm
Dale
Milford Haven
A4075
15 Saundersfoot
Carmarthen Bay
16
7
8
Pembroke
Tenby
14
9
Maiden Wells
A4139
Manorbier
Caldey
13
B4319
Pembrokeshire National Park
11
12
10

5 km
5 miles

old enemy, the English. In surfing as well, the Welsh are equally driven. They have produced some of Europe's best surfers, guys like Carwyn Williams, Chris 'Guts' Griffiths, Swinno, Frenchie, Dan Harris and Matt Stephens as well as the new crop like Nathan Phillips, Mark Vaughan and Isaac Kibblewhite.

"The Welsh are a pretty committed lot," says local surf photographer and ODD shaper Paul Gill. "In the winter it can be freezing in those northerly offshore winds, but the line-ups are still busy. There are some quality spots as well. There's a grinding reef that guys have used as practice for Pipeline – very sucky and heavy." And when the surfing is over, the Welsh will give any nationality a run for its money in the partying stakes. As legendary party king Carwyn Williams says, "When it comes to the social scene, Mumbles is madder than anywhere in the world!" And at any international gathering, it won't be long before a rendition of *Land of My Fathers* is heard from the Welsh corner.

I think the most important things you need to be a surfer in Wales is that you have to be very keen to deal with the cold, the wind and the pollution. And you need a good sense of humour! But on the plus side you get to share the ocean with Welsh people.

Carwyn Williams, former World Tour surfer and Welshman

Coastline

The Welsh coastline is broken into distinct communities. Around Llantwit Major and Porthcawl a hardened crew surf in brown water, with pollution from the Bristol Channel and the Port Talbot industrial plant up the coast. Here a mixture of reefs and long beaches lead up to the surfing heartland of Wales, the Gower Peninsula. A series of sandy bays with reefs and points on the Gower provide no end of surfing possibilities. Once out of Mumbles the countryside opens up and the water becomes cleaner. The huge bay at Rhossili has seen surfing for decades and is a spot where many Welsh surfers first learned their trade. To the west the Pembrokeshire coastline is a rugged and spectacular area with no end of coves, bays and reefs, nestled in pristine countryside – a great place to explore and escape from the crowds.

Localism

It would be unusual to experience localism in Wales, but that's not to say that there aren't very tightly knit line-ups. Crab Island is a very competitive spot, and if you turn up at any of the Gower reefs with a minibus full of friends, don't expect a warm welcome. In general, if you are respectful you should have no problems.

Top local surfers Carwyn Williams, Nathan Phillips, Mark Vaughan, Guts, Swinno, Frenchie, Isaac Kibblewhite, Matt Stephens.

Getting around

Most of the breaks on the Welsh coastline are easily accessible and the road network is excellent. The M4 feeds into south Wales over the Bristol Channel and allows easy access to the surfing regions.

Wales board guide

The '66 Dora Model
Shaper: The Gill, ODD Surfboards

▸▸ 8'4" x 22" x 2¾" for Mickey Dora.

▸▸ 9'1" x 23" x 2¾" Classic competition dimensions.

▸▸ Based on a board I shaped for Dora in 1982, which he kept and surfed for nearly twenty years.

▸▸ It has a wide squash tail for smaller surf, wide point in the middle with egg rails.

▸▸ It is a medium weight board with nose concave designed for gliding clean waves.

▸▸ The board has three stringers, two of them curved outer stringers in an old skool style, and is a single fin with a ten inch fin box.

▸▸ Good for peeling summer waves like Llangennith and the points.

▸▸ For a true retro look it has a resin tint and classic paint.

Thruster
Shaper: The Gill, ODD Surfboards

▸▸ 6'2" x 18½" x 2¼" for Reece Maurice.

▸▸ For average surfer 6'4" x 19" x 2¼".

▸▸ Good all-round, everyday board for typical Welsh beaches and reefs.

▸▸ Squash tail with more width and nose.

▸▸ Performs in good surf but with enough area to ride out any slow sections on the beach breaks..

 Boards by **ODD Boards**
Factory: Freelap Surfboards, Porthcawl, Wales
T00 44 (0)1656-744691 www.oddsurfboards.co.uk
or contact gill@eurotelemail.net

Breaks

Wales

Air ——— Sea ———

°F Averages   °C

90   30

70   20

50   10

30   0

J F M A M J J A S O N D

5/4/3   4/3   4/3   4/3
Boots &   Boots
gloves

Southwest coast

1 Aberystwyth

- ◉ **Break type**: Reef break, peak.
- ◕ **Conditions**: Big swells, offshore in easterly/southeasterly winds.
- ❶ **Hazards/tips**: Crowds, backwash at high.
- ◉ **Sleeping**: Aberystwyth ▸▸ p103.

Harbour Trap is a left and right peak with hollow rights at low tide and long lefts at mid tide. This flat reef works from low to three-quarter tide. **Bath Rocks**, a hollow reef for advanced surfers only, is worth trying at high. It needs to be 6 ft on the south coast to work here and it's always busy when it does. Parking on the promenade. Big student surf club so pretty crowded in water.

2 Aberaeron

- ◉ **Break type**: Left point.
- ◕ **Conditions**: Big swells, offshore in southeasterly winds.
- ❶ **Hazards/tips**: Crowds, popular with longboarders.
- ◉ **Sleeping**: Aberaeron ▸▸ p103.

Head south from Aberystwyth on the coast road for 30 minutes. This is a boulder point that breaks about six times a year. Long, walling left-handers break on all tides, good for longboards. Busy when it's on. Only gets to 4-5 ft. Needs to be 6 ft plus on the south coast. Out of village but visible from the road.

---

3 Abereiddy

- ◉ **Break type**: Slab reef.
- ◕ **Conditions**: Big swells, offshore in a southeasterly/southerly wind.
- ❶ **Hazards/tips**: Shallow reef.
- ◉ **Sleeping**: St David's ▸▸ p103.

When Whitesands is too big, check this left-hand reef – it is shallow, wedgy, breaks at mid tide and is really best left to advanced surfers. Found on the south side of bay. Beach car park.

4 Whitesands

- ◉ **Break type**: Beach break.
- ◕ **Conditions**: Medium swells, offshore in southeasterly/easterly winds.
- ❶ **Hazards/tips**: Crowds. Parking near beach.
- ◉ **Sleeping**: St David's ▸▸ p103.

Whitesands is a popular and flexible break that works through the tides. There are peaks from sandbanks along the beach and at low

1 Harry Cromwell at Aberystwyth

3 Bird Point at Abereiddy

2 Aberaeron

tide to the north of the bay is the **Elevator**, a hollow right. There are crowds at the Elevator and surf schools and kayakers on the beach.

5 Newgale

- **Break type**: Beach break.
- **Conditions**: Small to medium swells, offshore in easterly winds.
- **Hazards/tips**: Good for beginners, large uncrowded beach.
- **Sleeping**: St Brides Bay ➤ *p104*.

At the northern edge of St Brides Bay, Newgale is part of the Pembrokeshire Coast National Park so enjoys good water quality, and like Llangennith (see page 97) has plenty of room to spread out (almost 2 miles). When small, it is a good spot for beginners. Faces

11 Freshwater East

west and so picks up plenty of swell. Beach parking, easy access.

6 Broad Haven

- **Break type**: Beach break.
- **Conditions**: Medium swells, offshore in south/southeasterly winds.
- **Hazards/tips**: Not crowded, flexible beaches. Good for beginners.
- **Sleeping**: St Brides Bay ➤ *p104*.

When Newgale gets big, try Broad Haven and Little Haven at the southern end of St Brides Bay. They are good beach breaks and have more protection from the wind. They work on all tides and have plenty of parking.

7 Marloes

- **Break type**: Beach break.
- **Conditions**: Small to medium swells, offshore in northerly winds.
- **Hazards/tips**: Quiet beach, walk from National Trust car park.
- **Sleeping**: Marloes ➤ *p104*.

A peaky beach break that picks up lots of swell and works up to three-quarters tide. Watch out for scattered rocks on the beach. Walk from car park down track. Car crime can be a problem here.

8 Westdale

- **Break type**: Beach break.
- **Conditions**: Small to medium swells, offshore in easterly wind.
- **Hazards/tips**: Quiet bay, intermediate and advanced surfers.
- **Sleeping**: Marloes ➤ *p104*.

Westdale is a bay just north of Milford Haven inlet. It has a left at south and right at north. Best from low to three-quarter tide as it is a bit rocky at high tide. Walk from the village car park. There is a surf school based here.

9 Freshwater West

- **Break type**: Beach break.
- **Conditions**: Small to medium swells, offshore in easterly winds.
- **Hazards/tips**: Rips, rocks, crowds.
- **Sleeping**: Pembroke ➤ *p104*.

Best beach break in Wales with hollow, fast waves like Fistral (see page 85). Picks up the most swell too and is the regular venue for the Welsh Nationals. Works on all states of tide. Although the army used to turn a blind eye to surfers jumping the fence, the firing range beach to the south is out of bounds again. Expect a big fine if you try to sneak in. Beware of rips and rocks in the middle of the bay. The water is clean and Fresh West gets busy when it's on. Beachfront parking.

10 Broadhaven South

- **Break type**: Beach break.
- **Conditions**: Medium swells, offshore in northerly winds.
- **Hazards/tips**: Small take-off zone, crowds.
- **Sleeping**: Pembroke/Manorbier ➤ *p104*.

Swells wrap into this bay and meet in the middle with hollow left wedges. The punchy waves and tiny take-off zone make this a wave for advanced surfers. Watch out for rips in a decent swell. National Trust parking overlooks break. Clean water.

9 Swinno at Freshwater West

11 Freshwater East

- ◉ **Break type**: Beach break.
- ◐ **Conditions**: Big to storm swells, offshore in westerly winds.
- ❶ **Hazards/tips**: Check in westerly storms.
- ◒ **Sleeping**: Pembroke/Manorbier ⇒ *p104*.

Needs a big southwesterly swell to turn this tranquil bay into a hollow, heavy beach break. Gets crowded when it's on and is best around mid tide. Good place to check in a westerly gale. Peaks can throw up excellent lefts and rights with fast barrels. Parking near the beach. Not for beginners when big.

12 Manorbier

- ◉ **Break type**: Beach/reef.
- ◐ **Conditions**: Medium to big swells, offshore in northeasterly wind.
- ❶ **Hazards/tips**: Crowded, easy access, rocks.
- ◒ **Sleeping**: Manorbier/Tenby ⇒ *p104*.

Swells here are always two thirds the size of Freshwater West. There is an average, low tide beach break and a decent high tide right reef. The reef at the western edge of the bay can produce walling right-handers that are always a big draw, but the wave doesn't hold a crowd. Parking is available overlooking the break. Beginners stick to beach.

13 Tenby Beaches

- ◉ **Break type**: Beach breaks.
- ◐ **Conditions**: Big swells, offshore in westerly winds.
- ❶ **Hazards/tips**: Punchy waves, polluted but improving.
- ◒ **Sleeping**: Manorbier/Tenby ⇒ *p104*.

Tenby, with its massive town walls, is the place to head for in huge westerly storms. South beach works on all tides and produces peaks which can be very hollow. Not ideal for beginners. This is a winter break that gets crowded when good. Parking above and at the beach. All amenities in town.

14 Monkstone Point

- ◉ **Break type**: Right-hand point.
- ◐ **Conditions**: Huge swells, offshore in westerly winds.
- ❶ **Hazards/tips**: Winter break.
- ◒ **Sleeping**: Manorbier/Tenby ⇒ *p104*.

This long, walling right-hand point is like a slow Lynmouth (see page 74) so is especially popular with longboarders. Breaking in southwesterly gales from low to mid tide, this sheltered spot is a winter retreat. A long walk out from Saundersfoot harbour car park.

15 Wiseman's Bridge

- ◉ **Break type**: Reef break.
- ◐ **Conditions**: Huge swells, offshore in northwesterly wind.
- ❶ **Hazards/tips**: Alternative spot in winter storms. Parking at break.
- ◒ **Sleeping**: Manorbier/Tenby ⇒ *p104*.

Gentle, walling, long right-hand reef that works from mid to high tide. A good alternative to Tenby in huge winter storms.

16 Pendine Sands

- ◉ **Break type**: Beach break.
- ◐ **Conditions**: Medium to big swells, offshore in northeasterly winds.
- ❶ **Hazards/tips**: Good for beginners.
- ◒ **Sleeping**: Manorbier/Tenby ⇒ *p104*.

This is the nearest break for Carmarthen surfers. Long stretch of sand that produces

gentle waves that are good for beginners. The best surf is near the cliff at the west end of the beach in front of the village at mid to high tide. Sheltered in northwesterly winds. Needs decent swell so only check it when Freshwater is 6 ft plus. This flat beach is used for land speed records, so don't expect good banks. Parking on the beach.

The Gower

17 Broughton Bay

- ◉ **Break type**: Point break.
- ◐ **Conditions**: Big swells, offshore in southerly winds.
- ❶ **Hazards/tips**: Slow wave, dangerous rips.
- ◒ **Sleeping**: Llangennith ⇒ *p104*.

Long, walling, left-hand point break that produces fairly slow waves, popular with longboarders. Worth checking when Llangennith is 6 ft. There is a strong rip, so it's not for beginners. Loads of dogfish in the shallows. Walk through caravan site and be courteous to farmer!

18 Llangennith Beach

- ◉ **Break type**: Long beach break.
- ◐ **Conditions**: Small to medium swells, offshore in easterly winds.
- ❶ **Hazards/tips**: Consistent, popular spot.
- ◒ **Sleeping**: Llangennith ⇒ *p104*.

The beach's 3 miles of relatively flat, featureless sand means that the waves lack punch so this

13 Tenby

17 Broughton Bay

can be a good place for beginners and is relatively safe. It is, however, a consistent spot that gets very busy though quieter peaks can usually be found a short walk down the beach. Works on all tides up to about 6 ft. Pay parking at Hillend Campsite, which has new shop and restaurant facilities. Llangennith is also home to local legend and surf shop owner PJ. When the swell is too big at Llangennith, head south to Rhossili end. This spot is best at mid to high tide and sheltered from strong southerly winds. Parking on top.

19 Mewslade (Fall Bay and Mewslade Reef)

- **Break type**: Beach and reef.
- **Conditions**: Medium swells, offshore in northerly winds.
- **Hazards/tips**: Powerful breaks, not for beginners.
- **Sleeping**: Llangennith/Port Eynon » *p104*.

Fall Bay Wedge is a beach break that works at high tide for spongers, while **Mewslade Reef**, in the middle of the bay, is a sucky, hollow, left reef for experts only. It's a low tide

break best in a northerly wind. Mewslade beach is best from low to mid tide and has powerful, semi close-outs. Park at the farmyard car park. Signed from road.

20 Pete's Reef

- **Break type**: Reef.
- **Conditions**: Small to medium swells, offshore in northerly winds.
- **Hazards/tips**: Very crowded, experts only.
- **Sleeping**: Port Eynon » *p105*.

Low tide hollow peak breaking on shallow limestone reef. Gets very crowded when it's on and holds up to 5 ft. Popular with good local surfers. Breaks like a small Porthleven (see page 88). Long walk. Parking difficult.

21 Boiler Left

- **Break type**: Left reef.
- **Conditions**: Medium swell, offshore in northerly winds.
- **Hazards/tips**: Long walk and parking difficult.
- **Sleeping**: Port Eynon » *p105*.

Low tide, hollow, medium-length left breaking on limestone reef with submerged ship's boiler at the end. Has a big rip and works up to 6-8 ft. Small, sucking take-off zone.

22 Sumpters

- **Break type**: Right-hand reef.
- **Conditions**: Medium to big swells, offshore in northeasterly wind.
- **Hazards/tips**: Popular wave with deep channel for paddle out.
- **Sleeping**: Port Eynon » *p105*.

Quality right and another peak nearby. Easier access. Best from low to mid tide producing long, walling rights with the occasional barrel. Not too shallow. Popular wave that holds swells up to 8 ft. Paddle out in deep channel after walking along sewer pipe.

23 Port Eynon Point

- **Break type**: Right-hand reef point.
- **Conditions**: Medium to big swells, offshore in northerly winds.
- **Hazards/tips**: Access is a walk south from Port Eynon beach car park.
- **Sleeping**: Port Eynon » *p105*.

Powerful, sucky, low tide point break which peels in front of rock ledges. Popular spot that breaks consistently. Quality wave that is best left to the experts.

24 Horton Beach

- **Break type**: Beach break.
- **Conditions**: Medium to big swells, offshore in northerly wind.
- **Hazards/tips**: Parking at the beach.
- **Sleeping**: Port Eynon » *p105*.

Sheltered beach that needs a good swell to work, but produces dumpy, hollow waves that can close out at high. Works on all tides but is better at low to mid. An alternative to crowded Langland. Good spot for intermediates and a safe beach for beginners. Also popular with kitesurfers and windsurfers.

THE GILL

18 Llangennith Beach

THE GILL

20 Frenchie at Pete's Reef

THE GILL

21 Boiler Left

THE GILL

22 Sumpters

25 Oxwich Bay/Point

- **Break type**: Beach break.
- **Conditions**: Storm swell, offshore in southwesterly winds.
- **Hazards/tips**: Safe beach, scenic, Oxwich Bay Hotel for refreshments at a price.
- **Sleeping**: Oxwich ›› *p105*.

A hollow beach break that's best at high tide. Gets busy when breaking as it can be the only spot in storms. Breaks up to 6 ft, but is usually about 3 ft.

26 Three Cliff Bay

- **Break type**: Beach break.
- **Conditions**: Medium swell, offshore in northwesterly winds.
- **Hazards/tips**: Dangerous rips.
- **Sleeping**: Oxwich ›› *p105*.

This is a mid to high tide beach break with some good sandbanks, producing lefts and rights. It's the most scenic bay on the Gower and features on many postcards. Park near Penmaen post office, on South Gower Road, and make the long walk to the beach. Usually uncrowded so an alternative to Langland.

27 Hunts Bay

- **Break type**: Reef break.
- **Conditions**: Medium swell, offshore in northerly wind.
- **Hazards/tips**: Difficult access.
- **Sleeping**: Oxwich/Mumbles ›› *p105*.

A right-hand reef where there is difficult access in and out of the water due to rocks. Produces walling rights, with sections. Access from Southgate, a long walk along cliffs. Quiet break.

28 Caswell Bay

- **Break type**: Beach break.
- **Conditions**: Small to medium swells, offshore in northerly winds.
- **Hazards/tips**: Popular spot near Mumbles.
- **Sleeping**: Mumbles ›› *p105*.

THE GILL

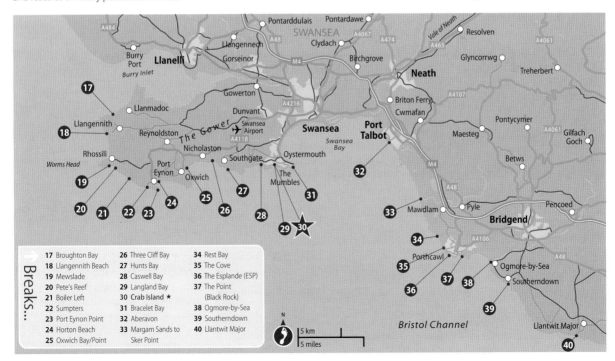

26 Three Cliff Bay

Britain Wales Breaks Oxwich Bay to Baswell Bay

Breaks...

17 Broughton Bay	26 Three Cliff Bay	34 Rest Bay
18 Llangennith Beach	27 Hunts Bay	35 The Cove
19 Mewslade	28 Caswell Bay	36 The Esplande (ESP)
20 Pete's Reef	29 Langland Bay	37 The Point
21 Boiler Left	30 Crab Island ★	(Black Rock)
22 Sumpters	31 Bracelet Bay	38 Ogmore-by-Sea
23 Port Eynon Point	32 Aberavon	39 Southerndown
24 Horton Beach	33 Margam Sands to	40 Llantwit Major
25 Oxwich Bay/Point	Sker Point	

5 km
5 miles

Smallish bay popular with tourists and beginners with a beachfront car park. Works from mid to high tide. Produces short peaky waves that can get crowded.

29 Langland Bay (Langland Point/Langland)

- **Break type**: Reefs/beach/point.
- **Conditions**: All swells, offshore in northerly winds.
- **Hazards/tips**: Many spots for surfers of all abilities, gets crowded.
- **Sleeping**: Mumbles ›› p105.

The **Outside Point** is a reef, but not dangerous. It works at low tide only, best from 2-8 ft, and is not too challenging. A popular spot with longboarders and doesn't get too crowded.

The **Inside Point** and **Shit Pipe** (Huttons) is a mid tide reef break with long, walling right-handers. Again a popular longboard wave, nicknamed the 'Malibu of the Gower'. It has a friendly line-up, is sheltered from strong westerly winds but can be rocky and shallow.

26 Three Cliff Bay

29 Langland

Langland Shorebreak is a virtual close-out, popular with shortboarders on a big swell. It's really a one manoeuvre wave that works at high tide only. Crowded with locals in solid swells and generally ridden in stormy conditions.

Langland Reef (Kevs) breaks at mid tide, a crowded peak with a mixture of boards and abilities. It's a very busy, short left and long right that is shallow on the peak.

Middle of the Bay (MOTB) is a left that breaks into strong rip, opposite **The Reef**. This sandbank breaks from low to half tide, producing lefts that can be hollow. Gets very crowded and can be ridden in all winds as it is quite sheltered.

Rotherslade Left is further out than MOTB, producing walling lefts with sections, over a low tide sandbank. Works best in medium swells when it can be crowded.

The **Sandbar** is a low tide, very shallow reef. It has a dangerous, dropping take-off and is best left to advanced surfers only. "This is where Carwyn used to practice for Pipeline," explains Mumbles local The Gill. The peak splits into a left and right, the left is the most hollow. It's a heavy wave where you don't want to get caught inside as it unloads onto the shallow reef. Breaks up to 10 ft.

Gas Chambers is a cocktail of sand, rock and air, for boogie boarders and the brave. At mid tide, **Inside Crab** produces left-hand barrels up to 5 ft.

The **Shallow Peak** is a shallow, rocky reef that works up to 5 ft. It produces lefts and rights, sucky all the way.

30 Crab Island

30 Crab Island

- **Break type**: Right-hand reef.
- **Conditions**: All swells.
- **Size**: 2-10 ft.
- **Length**: 50-100 m.
- **Swell**: Southwesterly.
- **Wind**: Northerly.
- **Tide**: When Crab Island appears out of the water at low tide.
- **Bottom**: Rocks.
- **Entry/exit**: Off the rocks.
- **Hazards/tips**: Rocks on take-off.
- **Sleeping**: Mumbles ›› p105.

Nestled in Langland Bay sits one of the country's best waves, the legendary Crab Island. This wave is home to a long established and respected surf community including the likes of Guts Griffiths, Frenchie, Matt Stephens, Swinno, Tim Page and The Gill. This is a long, powerful wave which peels along a reef formed by a small island just offshore – hence the name. The peak is an elevator drop with the danger of nearby rocks always in the back of the mind. It then walls up into a fast section, with barrels opening up in the right conditions. There is a strong rip pushing away from the peak in good swells, which can become quite tiring. If you are going to go and surf Crab, it's best to be respectful and try not to snag too many waves.

If you like Crab Island, try Thurso East in Scotland (see page 38) or Easkey Right in Ireland (see page 128).

31 Bracelet Bay

- **Break type**: Right-hand reef.
- **Conditions**: Medium to big swells, offshore in northwesterly winds.
- **Hazards/tips**: Strong rips.
- **Sleeping**: Mumbles.

Nestled under the coastguard station is this low to mid tide right-hand reef. It produces walling rights with sections, breaking up to 8 ft. Has strong rips. Last of the Gower breaks.

The entertainer

When Crab is breaking, local surfers drop everything and appear in the line-up, as if drawn by a silent call to prayer. Jobs are put on hold, weddings held up, births missed. The roll call is a who's who of the great, the good and the eccentric of Welsh surfing. Paul Henry is a local institution. A Crab regular, shortboards and modern leashes are not his thing. One cold winter's day in 2003 and not only was Crab Island 6-8 ft and pumping, but Paul Henry was paddling off the rocks and into the line-up on a battered old longboard, as heavy as the Ark Royal, with a leash that attaches to the fin and has all the elasticity of an anchor chain. But that wasn't what made people turn and stare. To the guys in the line-up, they were confused by the sight of what appeared to be Al Jolson paddling out towards them. For Paul Henry is an entertainer by trade and had arrived fresh from a gig at an old peoples' home. In his haste to make it into the water he was still sporting his full Black and White Minstrel Show make-up and wig.

A set swung in and started to rear up. Henry was in position and got the huge barge under way, paddling into the 8-ft peak. He popped to his feet, angled the board but as he was taking the drop, he caught an edge and was propelled forward off his board and the huge lip detonated on top of him. As the churning white water eventually subsided, a head appeared, now minus the wig, long grey hair framing the jet-black face. Bobbing nearby was a single fin, the board was nowhere to be seen. As the next wave was about to unload on the lonely figure in the impact zone, a voice was heard to shout, "It could have been worse, people could have recognized me."

Southeast Coast

32 Aberavon

- **Break type**: Breakwater.
- **Conditions**: All swells, offshore in easterly winds.
- **Hazards/tips**: Dirty water, heavy when big, access off the jetty when big.
- **Sleeping**: Porthcawl » p105.

Short right and long left, spoiled by new sea defence in the corner. It's difficult to get back in at high tide when it's big. This sandbar is a real industrial surf spot, breaking next to steelworks and deepwater docks. Very unscenic and crowded.

33 Margam Sands to Sker Point

- **Break type**: Beach breaks.
- **Conditions**: Small to medium swells, offshore in easterly winds.
- **Hazards/tips**: Pollution.
- **Sleeping**: Porthcawl » p105.

Best at mid to high tide, this long stretch of beach break peaks are hollower at the Sker end. Park at Kenfig Pools, a long walk through the dunes. A quiet spot with better waves towards the Sker end.

34 Rest Bay

- **Break type**: Beach break.
- **Conditions**: Small to medium swells, offshore in easterly winds.
- **Hazards/tips**: Pollution, parking in beach car park, strong parallel rips.
- **Sleeping**: Porthcawl » p105.

This popular beach produces great peaks, with some excellent waves, which many consider to be some of the best in the area. Works best from low to three-quarter tide on the push. Can have lefts and rights up and down this long beach. The southern peaks are the most popular.

35 The Cove

- **Break type**: Beach break.
- **Conditions**: Small to medium swell, offshore in easterly winds.
- **Hazards/tips**: Heavy wave with rips.
- **Sleeping**: Porthcawl » p105.

This spot is accessible at low tide from Rest Bay. It has heavy peaks, with lefts and rights breaking on a sand bottom. Strong rips.

36 The Esplande (ESP)

- **Break type**: Reef.
- **Conditions**: Medium swell, offshore in northeasterly winds.
- **Hazards/tips**: Crowds, shallow reef.
- **Sleeping**: Porthcawl » p105.

This is a shallow, hollow and fast left reef where the locals dominate. Park on seafront overlooking break. Only works at high tide.

THE GILL

32 Aberavon

THE GILL

36 The ESP

37 The Point (Black Rock)

- **Break type**: Reef point.
- **Conditions**: Medium to big swell, offshore in northerly winds.
- **Hazards/tips**: Drive through caravan park to front.
- **Sleeping**: Porthcawl ⏵ p105.

This is a high tide right-hand reef point that breaks over knobbly rocks. After a shallow take-off the wave is fast and sucky before becoming a long wall. This is a crowded spot best left to Porthcawl locals and experts.

38 Ogmore-by-Sea

- **Break type**: Rivermouth break.
- **Conditions**: Medium swells, offshore in easterly winds.
- **Hazards/tips**: Can be excellent, watch out for rips.
- **Sleeping**: Porthcawl ⏵ p105.

A fickle spot that can be a classic, right-hand rivermouth if the banks are right. Best at high tide, the spot can be quite busy, but watch out for rips out from river. Park overlooking break. Locals will be on it when it's good.

39 Southerndown

- **Break type**: Beach break.
- **Conditions**: Small to medium swell, offshore in easterly winds.
- **Hazards/tips**: Consistent spot.
- **Sleeping**: Porthcawl ⏵ p105.

A popular break with Bridgend/Cardiff surfers. The beach peaks can produce good, walling waves, suitable for all surfers. A consistent spot that picks up a lot of swell, so gets quite busy. Similar to Llangennith (see page 97).

40 Llantwit Major

- **Break type**: Selection of reefs.
- **Conditions**: All swells, offshore in a northerly wind.
- **Hazards/tips**: Good quality spot, crowds, pollution.
- **Sleeping**: Porthcawl ⏵ p105.

A large triangular boulder reef on the Glamorgan Heritage Coast producing a number of waves at different states of tide. The peak works at low tide in small to medium swells. Perfect right peels off the left edge of the reef at low to mid tide and can be classic on its day. At mid to high tide there are hollow peaks on the boulders near the car park. This is a crowded spot that breaks in swells between 3 ft and 8 ft. Best on incoming tides, but beware of rips. Signposted to beach. Home of Nathan Phillips, Mark Vaughan and the Bright brothers.

THE GILL

39 Southerndown

THE GILL

39 Southerndown

THE GILL

39 Lloyd Cole at Southerndown

Listings

Aberystwyth

Set on the west coast on the A487, Welsh nationalism and the Welsh language is alive and kicking in this Victorian resort town appropriated by students during term time.

⚙ Flat spells
Cinema Catch a movie at the **Commodore** on Bath St. **Golf** Get a round in at the 18 hole **Bryn-y-Mor** in Aberystwyth, T01970-615104, or **Borth &Ynyslas**, 5 miles north in Borth, T01970-871202. **Riding** Try **4Trek** in Bontgoch, T01970-832291, and if horses aren't your thing you can always saddle up a quad bike.

😴 Sleeping
C **Yr Hafod** on South Marine Terr just back from the seafront, T01970-617579. **C-D Mrs Williams** on Bridge St, T01970-612550. E **Borth Youth Hostel**, 5 miles north in the village of Borth overlooking the bay, T01970-871498, open Apr-Oct. F **Aberwystwyth University** rents out single rooms out of term time in self-catering student flats, **T01970-621960. Camping** There are plenty of sites scattered around the area. You can camp next to the river at **Aberystwyth Holiday Village**, Penparcau Rd, T01970-624211, open Mar-Oct, who also rent statics. **Oceanview Caravan Park**, T01970-828425, overlooks North Bay and is open Mar-Oct, also with statics. Heading about 5 miles north, **Borth** also has a couple of camping options: **Swn-y-Mor Holiday Park**, off the B4345, T01970-871233, open Apr-Oct, and **Brynrodyn Caravan and Leisure Park** in Upper Borth, T01970-871472, open Jan-Oct. Both have statics available.

🍴 Eating/drinking
As a student town there are plenty of cheap places to grab a bite to eat. The **Treehouse** on Baker St combines an organic shop with a lovely lunchtime café where you can get a tasty bowl of soup and a roll for about £3.50 or something more filling for about £6. It can get packed out but is worth waiting for. **Gannets Bistro** on St James Sq is more expensive but a relaxed place serving good home cooking using local fish and meat – the steak is very good. In terms of cafés, the **Dolphin** on Great Darkgate is a winner for bacon and eggs combos while the **Blue Creek Café** on Princess St serves up good veggie and more 'exotic' café food. There is no shortage of pubs here and many enjoy extended summer licensing hours including **Rummers** with its beer garden next to the river on Bridge St.

🛍 Shopping
The **Stormriders surf shop** on Alexandra Rd is near the train station and well stocked. There are plenty of supermarkets here, including a **Somerfield** and **Kwik Save** on Park Av.

ℹ Directory
Banks: ATMs on Terrace Rd, Great Darkgate and North Parade. **Internet**: pricey connection at **Biognosis** on Pier St or head to the library just off Corporation St. **Post office**: on the main Great Darkgate St. **Tourist information**: open year round on Terrace Rd running up towards North Beach.

Aberaeron

Heading south on the A487 this pretty fishing port is home to the **Aeron Coast Caravan Park** on Norton Rd, T01797-4 202247. It's a bit more pricey than other sites in the area, offers statics and is open Mar–Oct.

St David's

What seems like a tiny village on the A487 is actually a city (it has a cathedral) and provides easy access to Whitesands Bay as well as having good ammenities.

⚙ Flat spells
Golf Get 9 holes in at **St David's City GC** at Whitesands Bay, T01437-721751.

😴 Sleeping
Ma Simes Surf Hut have a cottage to let by the beach from about £275/week, T01437-720433. Near the beach is the **St David's Youth Hostel**, T01473-720345,

open Easter-Oct. **Camping** There are plenty of campsites in the area including, to the south, **Caerfai Farm**, T01437-720548, with an organic shop, open May-Sep, and the large **Caerfai Bay Caravan and Tent Park**, Caerfai Rd, T01437-720274, open Mar-Nov, with statics to rent. Handier for Whitesands however is **Lleithyr Farm Caravan & Tent Park**, T01437-720245, open Easter-Oct.

Directory
Shaper: Simon Noble Surfboards (SNS) are based at Trehenlliw Farm, St David's, T07866-737935.

St Brides Bay

With **Newgale** to the north and **Broad Haven** to the south, this pretty bay is a popular draw for tourists in the summer and sits at the heart of the **Pemrokeshire Coast National Park**, stretching from Cardigan to Amroth.

Sleeping
D **Penycwm Youth Hostel**, T01437-721940, in Penycwm, has excellent facilities and is always very popular, so it is advisable to book ahead. E **Broad Haven Youth Hostel**, T01437-781688, provides an affordable place to stay in the village. You can camp at **Newgale Camp Site**, T01437-710253.

Marloes

Sleeping
C **Clockhouse B&B**, T01646-636527, has a wetsuit drying area.
C **Foxdale Guesthouse**, opposite the church on Glebe Lane, T01646-636243, also offers a camping area.
D-E **Marloes Sands YHA Hostel**, T01646-636667, is a cheaper option and has easy access to the beach.

Pembroke

The market town of Pembroke has plenty of facilities and amenities mainly centred around Main St, making it a good base, with

easy access to the breaks on the south coast as well as Fresh West.

Flat spells
Castle Pembroke castle was originally built in 1093 in wood before being modernized in stone in 1204. **Golf** Head to Military Rd overlooking the Pembroke Dock to the 18 hole **South Pembrokeshire GC**, T01646-621453.

Sleeping
D **Beech House B&B**, on Main St, T01646-683746 and D **Merton Place House**, on East Back, T01646-684796. Both recommend. **Camping** Year round camping south of Pembroke at St **Petrox Caravaning and Camping**, near St Petrox village.

Eating/drinking
You'll find unexceptional food at moderate prices here. Check out **Henry's** on Westgate Hill and **Brown's** on Main St for basic food for around a fiver. For good fish and chips try **Rowlies** on Main St.

Shopping
For surf shops, **Waves 'N' Wheels** on Commons Rd, **The Edge** on Main St. South, in Maiden Wells, is **Outer Reef**. There's a **Somerfield** supermarket on Main St.

Directory
Banks: Banks and ATMs on the western end of Main St. **Post office**: Main St. **Tourist information**: Pembroke Visitors' Centre, Commons Rd, T01646-622388.

Manorbier/Tenby

Manorbier is a pretty village with a well known surf break. The Norman castle is in a pretty good state of repair and overlooks the sea.

Flat spells
Golf Head east to Tenby: **Trefloyne GC** in Trefloyne Park off the A4139, T01834-842165, or **Tenby GC**, off the A478, T01834-842787, the oldest course in Wales, handicap certificate required.

Sleeping
Manorbier Youth Hostel, T01834-871803, open Mar-Oct, also offer camping facilities.

Shopping
Tenby has a couple of **surf shops**, heading east on the A4139 – **The Edge** on Tudor Sq and **Underground** on Church St.

Llangennith

Llangennith is at the western edge of the beautiful Gower Peninsula – the first place in Britain designated an area of outstanding natural beauty. Llangennith sits just inland from Rhossili Bay, a huge flat beach that opens out in front of a vast area of sand dunes. Popular with holidaymakers and beachgoers, this area has been at the forefront of the British surf scene since the very early days and is now home to the Welsh Surfing Federation Surf School.

Flat spells
Arthur's Stone Head to Reynoldston where this 25-tonne stone marks a Neolithic burial mound and gives awesome views right across the Gower. **Riding** Pilton **Moor Trekking**, Pitton Cross, Rhossili, T01792-390554, offer treks for all abilities.

Sleeping
C **Western House**, just down the road from the King's Head pub, T01792-386620, run by a surfing family or C-D **Bremmel Cottage**, T01792-386308, also surf friendly.
Camping There are plenty of campsites in the area, the most popular of which is **Hillend Camping Site** overlooking the beach and housing the newly opened Eddy's Restaurant, T01792-386204. Another option in Llangennith is **Kennexstone Camping and Touring Park**, T01792-391296, open Apr-30 Sep. Heading towards Broughton Bay is **Broughton Farm Caravan Park**, T01792-386213, open Apr-Oct with statics to hire. They also run the **Cross**, a year-round self-catering cottage sleeping up to 8 people from £350/week, within walking distance of the

King's Head. South at Rhossili is the reasonably priced **Pitton Cross Caravan & Camping**, T01792-390593, open Apr-Oct .

🍴 Eating/drinking
The **King's Head** is the place to grab a pint and some pub grub and sit outside to soak up some rare Welsh sunshine. The recently opened **Eddy's** at Hillend Camping Site is also a good place to grab a cheap bite to eat.

⭕ Shopping
PJ's Surf Shop Opposite the King's Head, PJ's has been up and running since 1978 and sells and hires out surf equipment. PJ (Pete Jones) is a dedicated surfer and in his time has been the Welsh, British and European Champion.

ⓘ Directory
Welsh Surfing Federation: the WSF surf school based at Hillend Campsite has been giving lessons since 1981, T01792-386426, www.wsfsurfschool.co.uk.

Port Eynon

🛌 Sleeping
On the A4118 from Swansea, Port Eynon has a couple of camping options. **Bank Farm Leisure Park**, T01792-390228, overlooks the Bay and is within walking distance of Horton. **Carreglwyd Camping & Caravan**, T01792-390795, is open Apr-Oct. As an alternative, **Port Eynon Youth Hostel**, T01792-390706, is right on the beachfront and open Apr-Oct.

Oxwich

🛌 Sleeping
Oxwich Bay is a nature reserve as well as a popular surf beach and has a couple of camping options, the small **Bay Holme Caravan Site**, T01792-401051, with statics to hire, and **Oxwich Bay Camping Park**, T01792-390777, open Apr-Sep. Further east, overlooking the next beach, is **Three Cliffs Bay Caravan and Camping Park**, T01792-371218, open Mar-Oct, who also run a self-catering cottage.

Mumbles

Mumbles is the general term given to the village of Oystermouth. The name actually came about as a bastardization of 'mamelles' or breasts – the word French sailors used to describe the 2 offshore islands nearby.

✪ Flat spells
Golf Get a round in at **Langland Bay GC** just off the B4593, T01792-361721. **Skate park** Head to Swansea's Cwmdu Industrial Estate on Camarthen Rd and the **Swansea Skate Park**, T01792-578478.

🛌 Sleeping
A Langland Cove Guest House, Rotherslade Rd, T01792-366003, gill@eurotelemail.net. Overlooking Langland Bay and within walking distance of the beach, the B&B is run by legendary shaper and surf photographer The Gill who keeps the breakfasts and stories flowing. In Mumbles try **B Coast House**, Mumbles Rd, T01792-368702.

🍴 Eating/drinking
There are some good eating options in Mumbles, as recommeded by The Gill. **CJ's** on Mumbles Rd is a lively bar/restaurant where you can eat for about £5–10. The **Village Inn** further along the road mixes good pub grub with bad karaoke. For something a bit different, try the **Mediterranean Restaurant** who do 2 sittings a night at 1900 and 2100. **Castellamare** pizzeria overlooking Bracelet Bay is a great place to spend an evening. The **Antelope** on Mumbles Rd is a lively pub with a beer garden and is just one of the places Welsh poet Dylan Thomas is said to have frequented. **Bar Mex** on Newton Rd has something for everyone. As the Gill puts it, 'there's scantily clad barmaids for the men and firemen for the ladies'. The **Rock and Fountain** at the top end of Newton Rd is a locals' pub with live music. **Bentley's Night Club** is popular with local surfers and comes complete with sticky carpet and cut-glass mirror ball.

Surf shop **Big Drop** is on Tivoli Walk. **JP Surfboards** is on Woodville Rd, Mumbles, T01792-521149. John Purton has been shaping boards since he was 13 and now shapes for some of the UK's top surfers including Carwyn Williams and Gabe Davies. There's a **Somerfield** supermarket on Mumbles Rd.

ⓘ Directory
Banks: Barclays on Newton Rd. **Post office**: Mumbles Rd. **Tourist information**: Dunn La, summer opening only.

Porthcawl

Accessed via junction 37 on the M4, Porthcawl is an unspectacular seaside resort town with a couple of camping options and plenty of amusement arcades.

✪ Flat spells
Golf There are a couple of courses here, the expensive 18-hole **Royal Porthcawl GC** at Rest Bay, T01656-782251, and the more reasonable **Grove GC**, off the A4229 at South Cornelly, T01656-788771.

🛌 Sleeping
Camping **Trecco Bay Holiday Park**, just east of the town, T0870-2204645, is open Mar-Nov. **Happy Valley Caravan Park**, off the main A4106, T01656-782144, is open Apr-Sep and has a bar and café on site.

⭕ Shopping
There are a couple of **surf shops** in the town, **Black Rock** and **Porthcawl Marine** on New Rd. Just inland at Bridgend's South Cornelly Industrial Estate is **Freelap Custom Surfboards**, T01656-744691, who put out boards under the **ODD** logo. Freelap is run by glasser Albert Harris who has been involved in the surf industry since the 1970s. ODD's Paul Gill has been shaping since 1977 and has made boards for modern chargers such as Wales's Isaac Kibblewhite and old school hero Mickey 'Da Cat' Dora.

Northwest Ireland: the grass is always greener ...
▶▶ *p118*

Ireland

THE GILL

p116

p119

p126

p130

p136

Star breaks...

⭐1 **Bundoran** Ireland's most famous wave, the Peak, is still under threat, despite the positive influence surfing has on the local economy ▶ *p120*.

⭐2 **Pampa Point** Awesome ▶ *p121*.

⭐3 **Easkey Right** Beautiful right-hand reef, with long walls and a mirror-image left looking on ▶ *p128*.

⭐4 **Crab Island** Ireland's answer to Pipeline, like playfighting with Mike Tyson – don't overstep the mark ▶ *p130*.

⭐5 **Inch Reef** Fickle wave that break for miles – literally! ▶ *p141*.

Motorway
A Rd
B Rd
Minor Rd
✈ Main Airports
⛴ Main Ferry Routes

N
20 km
20 miles

Atlantic Ocean

North Channel

Celtic Sea

Green hills roll down to a cluster of brightly painted fishing cottages nestled around a harbour. The drizzle has passed and a rainbow provides a stunning backdrop to the Kerry Mountains. This is the Ireland of the posters: a timeless scene that hasn't changed in decades. Only it has. Ireland is booming. Business, tourism, population. The economy has skyrocketed, as have standards of living. Surfing was not about to buck the trend. With such glorious reefs and reeling points, it was only a matter of time before wave-hunting nomads came across this potential and word got out. The influx of foreign surfers opened many local eyes to the amazing emerald jewels right here under their noses. They couldn't be held back by a lack of boards or surf shops. The industrious Irish had caught the wave.

Ireland has always been legendary for the *craic*. Sit by the fire in O'Connor's in Doolin nursing a pint of the black stuff and soon you will find yourself part of the band. If the surf is flat, you can take your hangover on a short trip up onto the Burren with its incredible, bleak limestone pavement and wonderful flora and fauna. It is one of only a handful of these fragile ecosystems left, and Europe's finest. To the south, Dingle is a lot more 'easy on the eye', with rolling hills, tranquil bays and, in the summer, the hedgerows erupt with fuchsias and wild flowers.

The clover is the national emblem of Ireland. Its three leaves stand for the holiest of trinities – great surf, great people and great *craic*.

Best time to visit: Spring - cool Atlantic swells and warm peat fires. **Autumn** - glassy waves and firey sunsets.

Ireland Rating
Surf
★★★★
Cost of living
★★★★
Nightlife
★★★★★
Accommodation
★★★
Places to visit
★★★

Essentials

Position

The island of Eire lies in the Atlantic Ocean, taking the full brunt of the ocean's force on its western flank. Separating it from Britain, the Irish Sea and St George's Channel cover Ireland's eastern side. The northeastern part of the island is taken up by Northern Ireland, a much fought-over entity that remains removed from the surrounding republic. Northern Ireland is under British control and as such has not adopted the euro.

Language

English, in a soft, rounded, lilting tone is spoken throughout Ireland – in varying degrees of strength. Irish or Gaelic still survives in the everyday lives of the *Gaeltacht* communities – a collective term for the communities, predominantly west coast based, where Irish is spoken as a first language. But even in the *Gaeltacht*, English is used. The most common Irish phrase you will see written or hear spoken is *Cead mile failte* – a thousand welcomes.

Crime/safety

Ireland is a fairly hassle-free place to be, with the usual problems focused around city centres. If you do need to report anything, head for the Garda – the Irish police force. While Ireland's drink driving laws used to be fairly relaxed, in recent years they have stepped up their action in even the smallest villages. Terrorism is unfortunately a reality in most places in today's world. Ireland's past has been tainted with domestic terrorism issues – Chops Lascelles remembers attending the 1985 European Surfing Championships in Bundoran under armed escort. Following the Good Friday agreement tensions have eased. However, it is advisable to avoid passing through Northern Ireland into the Republic during the marching season around mid-July when occasional violence erupts.

Health

EU residents need a stamped E-111 from their home country to certify that they are entitled to free (or reduced cost) healthcare.

Opening hours

Unlike continental Europe, lunch is not the focal point of the day, it merely slots in around everything else. As a result, business hours are generally Monday to Friday 0900-1700 with shops opening on Saturdays and big supermarkets in big towns suppressing Catholic guilt to open on Sundays.

Sleeping

Like Britain, accommodation in Ireland can seem pricey when compared to continental Europe. At the top end of the scale, hotel rates are usually highest in the summer months of July and August. More reasonable rates

5 best trips

1. **The Pub** Any pub. Buy a pint of Guinness and strike up a conversation with one of the locals ▸▸ *p135*.
2. **The Burren** Stunning landscape ▸▸ *p114*.
3. **Cliffs of Moher** The mother of all vertical drops. Test your vertigo ▸▸ *p135*.
4. **A night out in Limerick, or Sligo, or any other town** Enjoy the *craic* with the locals ▸▸ *p144*.
5. **Giants Causeway** One of the wonders of the natural world ▸▸ *p115*.

Brandon Bay view ▸▸ *p139*

can often be negotiated off peak – during the cold, wet months of November-February. **Bed & Breakfasts (B&Bs)** – usually offering a warm welcome, a bed for the night in a private home and a full Irish breakfast in the morning – can be a good option for a short stay. Rooms range in quality, style – from chintzy to cheap – and price (€30-80 for a room). Around popular holiday resort areas such as Bundoran, **self-catering** is a good and readily available option. It can also often be the cheapest solution for groups, especially off peak when prices following the summer season can practically halve. There is plenty of **hostel** accommodation throughout Ireland, much of which is run independently. Check out www.holidayhound.com and www.hostels-ireland.com for details. **An Oige**, affiliated to Hostelling International, also have a good network of sites across the country. In terms of **camping**, it is extremely difficult to find a site open off season. Even during the summer, there is not the number of sites you find on the continent. However, it is often worth asking about camping opportunities in the pubs – sometimes you can find a farmer who'll let you pitch for a couple of euros a night.

Eating and drinking

The climate and economy have shaped both the people and the cuisine of Ireland – times have been hard and the weather harder. So it's no surprise that the diet is more about filling, affordable food than fine, flashy fare.

Served with every meal in a multitude of guises, in Ireland the **potato** is king – despite the famine of the 1800s. **Colcannon** (mashed potato and cabbage) is a common occurrence, served as an accompaniment or with grilled cheese on top as a meal on its own. Another staple is the

→ **Fact file**

Currency Euro (€)
Capital city Dublin
Time zone GMT
Length of coastline 3,172km
Religion Catholic
Emergency numbers
  General emergency 999
Electricity 220v flat 3 pin

bread, particularly **soda bread**, a dense white loaf with a consistency similar to scones – nothing beats a slice of it with a mug of tea after a surf! Warming, hearty **stews** of lamb, beef or pork and veg are an everyday staple. Surrounded by the sea, Ireland is also a place to sample excellent seafood. **Crabs' toes** (or crab's claws to you and me), **oysters**, and the **Dublin Bay prawn** (or lobster) as well as some good, old fashioned **fish 'n' chips** – battered, smothered in salt and vinegar and wrapped up in paper. Similar to a full English, the **Irish cooked breakfast** is the real selling point of a B&B and a hearty way to start the day. Cafés will very often serve an all-day Irish breakfast – so get ready for the cholesterol-raising bacon, fried egg, sausages, black pudding, tomatoes and toast all washed down with an industrial-strength mug of tea. And while we're on washing things down, it is important to note that drinking here is a near-professional pursuit. You can get lager and wine here but you are better off sampling some of Ireland's famous 'black stuff' – held in such high regard that pregnant women used to be advised to take a half of **stout** at regular intervals. Stout is black with a thick, creamy head, the body is rich and thick, with a hint of iron about it – practically a whole meal in itself. It takes time to pour a perfect pint of **Guinness** or **Murphy's** but it is definitely worth the wait. To round off an evening where the beer and conversation flows in equal proportions, enjoy a nip of **Irish whiskey** neat or in an Irish coffee – a coffee revved up with a shot of whiskey and a blob of cream on top.

Festivals/events

Festivals, festivals everywhere, and always a drop to drink! On 17 March, just about everything that does or doesn't move is painted green, topped with a leprechaun and finished with a clover. **St Patrick's Day** is the only national holiday in Ireland and is more than a saint's day festival, it's a celebration of all things Irish, a time of street parties, music, dancing and plenty of Guinness. Best place to catch it is Dublin. Although St Patrick is the patron saint of Ireland, he actually came from Scotland. He was kidnapped by an Irish raiding party and sold as a slave in Ireland. St Patrick is famous for banishing snakes from Ireland and coming up with 'the analogy' – well, he used the three leaves of the clover to explain the holy trinity.

Ireland Essentials

DEMI TAYLOR

Bally Ferriter on the Dingle Peninsula

Getting there

Air There are no direct flights between Ireland and Australia/New Zealand. Usually, the cheapest and easiest way is to fly via the UK and look at the opportunities with one of the budget airlines. There are plenty of services from the US. Irish national airline **Aer Lingus**, www.aerlingus.com, run regular flights from Boston, Chicago, LA, New York and Washington to Dublin and Cork with returns to Dublin starting at about US$650. They also offers excellent services across Europe to Dublin, Cork and Shannon. **Ryanair**, www.ryanair.com, also run regular, reasonable services between Dublin or Shannon and Paris or Brussels. Services from Faro and Málaga to Dublin are less frequent. They also run between Frankfurt and Kerry or Shannon. **Easyjet**, www.easyjet.com, also run a regular shuttle from Paris, Amsterdam or Málaga to Dublin. To keep prices down, avoid travelling on a Monday morning or a Friday evening – popular with business commuters – and try to book well in advance.

From UK: Aer Lingus, T+353(0)818-365000, run flights between Ireland and the UK at prices which can often rival budget airlines. The cheapest route is usually Gatwick–Dublin. **Ryanair** offer an awesome range of services from a plethora of UK destinations. Dublin is serviced by almost every conceivable UK airport, while flights to Knock, Kerry, Shannon and Cork run from London only. A twice-daily flight also runs between London Stanstead and Derry in Northern Ireland and provides good access to the north shore. Ryanair flights to Ireland cost £0.99-99.00 depending on offers and how far in advance you book. Other airlines to consider include **Easyjet**, who run flights to Belfast in Northern Ireland (handy for the north) and **Flybe**, www.flybe.com, who run daily flights between Exeter and Dublin from £40.

Sea There is a wide range of services between the UK and Ireland, fares varying according to how far in advance you book and the season in which you travel. **Irish Ferries**, T08705-171717, www.irishferries.com, run between Pembroke and Rosslare in southeast Ireland (3 hours 45 minutes, flexible returns for a car and two adults £220-350). They run two services on the Holyhead–Dublin route, the swift ferry (1 hour 50 minutes, flexible returns £280-400) and the slower *Ulysees* (£240-360). **Stena Line**, T08705-707070, www.stenaline.com, run Holyhead–Dublin, Fishguard–Rosslare, and Stranraer–Belfast services. **P&O Irish Sea**, T0870-2424777, www.poirishsea.com, run Cairnryan–Larne, Fleetwood–Larne and Liverpool–Dublin services.

From France, **Brittany Ferries**, www.brittany-ferries.com, run a weekly service between Roscoff in the northwest and Cork. It takes 14 hours and has a price tag to match. **Irish Ferries**, T0818-300400, www.irishferries.com, run Roscoff–Rosslare and Cherbourg–Rosslare services.

Red Tape: Ireland is a Schengen state (see European Red Tape).

Top tips

- Travelling surfers compare Ireland to Indo - except for the cold water. Bring a quiver of boards and a rain jacket because you never know what the surf or the weather is going to do. *Roy Kilfeather, Sligo surfer*

- In Ireland we depend on the goodwill of landowners and local residents to access many of the spots we surf on a regular basis. Please respect our access and show respect to landowners and local residents. Do not damage fences or leave gates open. If you are unfamiliar with a break check with local surfers regarding access. If you see other surfers jeopardizing access bring the matter to their attention. Please take your litter home. *Irish Surfing Association*

- Talk to the local people, the local surfers, and get involved a bit. It's definitely the way to get the most out of Ireland. In a village, if you're staying for a couple of days you only need to get talking to a few people before everyone knows you. Plus you might be talking to the old fisherman at the bar and he'll be telling you about these 'rollers' in a cove up the coast, you never know what you might find out. *Martin 'Minzie' Mynne – top UK surfer and southwest Ireland pioneer*

- If you show respect, you will gain respect. Irish surfers on a whole are a friendly, laid-back bunch and this is pretty rare in world surfing terms. Hopefully we can hold on to this tradition long into the future. Be patient - good things come to those who wait. *Richie Fitzgerald, Surfworld, Bundoran*

- At all breaks please remember that there are people other than yourself using the narrow roads, including local farmers. Do not cause obstructions with cars - local farmers have been known to use tractors to tow cars and lock them inside fields if they are in the way of local traffic. *Tom Buckley, Lahinch Surf Shop*

Getting around

Driving (left-hand side) A full driving licence or International Driving Permit is required plus adequate insurance and ownership papers. Since Ireland received a massive EU cash injection, they've been building new roads and resurfacing old roads like there's no tomorrow! Having said that, the roads are extremely windy and smaller roads badly potholed. Journeys anywhere will always take longer than you think.

Motorway: there are snatches of motorway, mainly focused around the Dublin area, but more roads are being upgraded all the time. Speed limit 112 kph.
Other roads: N roads act as motorways and connect the majority of

the country. Their standard is improving but some stretches will test even the most robust suspension. **Speed limit 96 kph/48 kph in urban areas.**

Car hire   Car hire can be expensive, from €160 a week for a small car. Fly/drives may offer better deals as will booking ahead if you are coming over from the US. You need to be over 21, and very often companies won't rent to anyone under 23. You also need to have held a licence for more than a year. **Budget** have bases here, including Dublin airport, T01-8400800, www.budgetcarrental.ie, as do **Thrifty**, T01-8400800, www.thrifty.ie.

Public transport

The national **rail** company, Iranrod Eireann, T01-836 3333, www.irishrail.ie, has a fairly limited rail network. Main routes fan out from Dublin to Sligo and Ballina in the north, Galway in the west and Tralee, Cork, Waterford and Rosslare Harbour in the south. They don't charge for board carriage, provided you put the board on the train yourself. If you are going to be doing a lot of train travel, it may be worth looking at the Irish Rover train pass (5 days' travel out of 15 consecutive days costs around €90). If you want a few days in the city without your board, you can always send it on ahead of you for a small fee. Price is worked out by weight, contact the freight department on T0185-767676 for details.

Bus Eireann, T01-8366111, www.buseireann.ie,the national **bus** company, do have a fairly extensive network across Ireland for both long-haul and short-haul trips. However they charge for surfboard carriage a whopping €9 and they can't guarantee that your board will get on – 'luggage' gets priority – making this mode of transport really only viable for long journeys. If you are going to be doing a lot of bus travel, it may be worth investing in an Irish Rover bus pass (3 days' travel out of 8 consecutive days costs around €55). Alternatively you can get a combined bus and train pass.

Galarus oratory

Pros ...
- Picks up loads of swell.
- Undulating coastline with loads of potential for surf in all conditions.
- Excellent quality reefs.
- Unsurfed breaks waiting to be discovered.
- Great pubs.
- Friendly locals.
- Beautiful Celtic countryside.
- Lots to do on flat days.

... and cons
- Famous breaks are crowded.
- Inconsistent.
- Cold and wet in winter and spring.
- Journeys between breaks time -consuming.
- Relatively expensive.

Pros & cons

Surfing Ireland

"I think surfing changed forever in Ireland in the early 1990s. The combination of a booming Irish economy, more time and money being spent on leisure pursuits, the general TV and movie exposure of surfing worldwide and in Ireland, from Baywatch *to* Litmus *it was all over our screens, and printed media. It brought it to the attention of Irish and foreign enthusiasts, plus surfing became a real possibility for the Irish general public, and so developed the culture of the weekend city surfer. They flocked to places like Bundoran, Easkey, Strandhill, Tramore, Lahinch and Portrush for a two day fix of surfing. These coastal towns themselves have changed – benefiting from the economic growth. Surf shops, surf schools and clubs sprang up all over the country catering to the new surf appetite." Richie Fitzgerald, top Irish surfer*

Ever since the first shaky steps were taken on a surfboard in Irish waters by Kevin Cavey back in the mid-1960s, surfing and Ireland were always destined to have a special relationship. What was surprising about the surf boom was that it took so long to happen. Although the rest of Europe had a good head start on the Irish, many local wave riders are catching up quickly. One area in which they really charge is big-wave surfing. Taking the full brunt of the Atlantic low pressure systems, the swells that hit the Irish coastline only serve to wake the sleeping points and reefs. Bundoran's Richie Fitzgerald, along with his tow-in partner Gabe Davies, watch the charts and wait patiently to take them on. In the south Paul McCarthy uses the giant walls of Madeira as a winter training ground for the big points back home. If you are heading to Ireland to take on the grinding reefs, or to hone your

5 underground classics

① **Doolin Point** So overlooked but soooo good ▸▸ *p131*.

② **Inishcrone** Irish J-Bay ▸▸ *p129*.

③ **Pollacheeny** Fickle, fast, hollow ▸▸ *p129*.

④ **Ballydavid Point** Cranking right-hander in massive swells ▸▸ *p140*.

⑤ **Doughmore** A beautiful beach that maxes out easily, but when there's no swell around, this baby could save your trip ▸▸ *p132*.

Chris Nelson at Doolin ▸▸ *p131*

skills on one of the many excellent beaches, remember to bring with you an open mind and a friendly smile and you'll take away some amazing memories. The waves, the awe-inspiring landscape, the open people, the hospitality, a drop of the black stuff and the sense of a good *craic* are all part of what makes it such a great destination.

Climate

Green. That's one word that describes Ireland. Go there in the summer and you'll be amazed by how warm and mild it is. The sun can shine for weeks and daytime temperatures can demand shorts and T-shirts. In the golden sun the heather takes on a wonderful purple hue and hidden flowers are suddenly revealed. But within ten minutes the whole scene can be turned on its head. When the wind and rain kick in, Ireland can be transformed into shades of grey– bleak and barren under a blanket of cloud. In the summer the days are long, but surf trips can still be either blessed with glass or cursed with gales. One thing you can guarantee is that on an evening, beside the peat-burning fire, there is always enough music, stories and drink to go round.

Best seasons to go

Summer in Ireland means taking the luck of the draw. Some years will be blessed with constant swells, others will be inconsistent. To optimize the chance of a wave, head for the more exposed coastlines. One drawback to this time of year is that Ireland has become a very popular tourist destination and holidaymakers from all over the world will be sharing the narrow roads and pushing the price of B&Bs. The

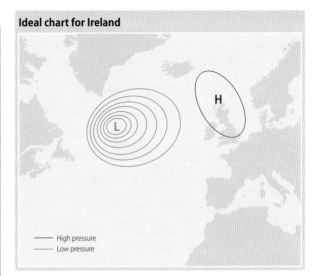

Ideal chart for Ireland

— High pressure
— Low pressure

plus side is that you'll have a fair chance of catching some sunshine.

Autumn is a glorious time. While the breaks remain quite busy at peak times, it is still possible to score good uncrowded, clean waves. Prices for accommodation drop as the swells increase, coaxing the reefs and points out of hibernation.

In winter it can be bleak but there will be a huge amount of swell hitting the coast. This is the time to head for the sheltered coastline and breaks. Although the days will be short, the line-ups will be quiet and some of the sleeping beauties will awaken. They will also be cold, so pack your 5/4/3, boots and gloves. The warming currents of the Gulf Stream help to keep the winter temperatures reasonably mild and also make spring a good time to check out the Emerald Isle. Although this is generally a very wet time of year, the line-ups are fairly quiet and there will be plenty of swell around allowing maximum surfing possibilities. Head for a flexible coastline at this time of year.

Good charts for surf

You don't have to be a trained meteorologist to predict when swells will hit Ireland. Any good low, below about 988 mb, will push swell into the Irish coastline. Watch for a blocking high over Europe and pray for the gentle offshores to kick in.

Geography and the breaks

Ireland has some spectacular landscapes and amazing countryside. The bleak limestone pavements of the **Burren** are a rare and fragile environmental ecosystem found in few places in Europe. Swathes of flat carboniferous rock hide unique plants within the cracks in the open rock slabs. The stunning mountains of the southwest, the biggest of which is Carrauntuohil in Kerry, provide a wonderful backdrop to the breaks of this region. Much of the west coast of Ireland is jagged and undulating. There are inlets, huge sandy bays and towering cliffs. Just to south of Doolin, the Cliffs of Moher tower above the Atlantic. These huge vertical faces are a popular tourist destination, but definitely not for those who suffer from vertigo. And yet in the northwest, the Mullet Peninsula has a huge sandy stretch of beach where visitors can really escape the crowds. The limestone that gives this land its distinctive make-up also shapes the reefs and points, providing wonderful hollow playgrounds for the adventurous, but also jagged punishment for the careless.

Surfing and environment

Western Ireland has a wonderfully diverse coastline. Its main industry is tourism and it has been lucky enough to avoid the blight of heavy industry that has scarred so many European coastlines. Water quality is improving although, as several towns lack proper water treatment facilities, raw or partially treated sewage is still being discharged into the sea.

There have been other issues that have affected surfers, such as a proposed marina development in Bundoran. "As most surfers know, The Peak has been under the threat of a marina development for the last eight years," explains Richie Fitzgerald. "The Irish Surfing Association, local surfers and concerned residents, using a number of tactics, have managed to fight off any development so far. As the years go on and the visable popularity and financial benefit of surfing to this area become more obvious, the marina project looks less and less likely. But when dealing with big money and politics you let your guard down to your peril, so the ISA and locals have been keeping the pressure on the local council to drop the idea entirely."

Localism and surf communities

There is little in the way of localism in Ireland. The boom in surfing has caused some growing pains, as numbers in the line-ups increase year on year. Originally there was a big influx of travelling surfers keen to surf the pristine waters and quiet breaks of the Irish coast. But in recent years there has been an exponential growth in Irish surfers – the coast can be reached in a couple of hours from many of the cities, and weekends are becoming crowded at the major breaks. "The *craic* is still mighty in the water," says Graham Collins. "It's still very mellow. It's so laid-back it's almost horizontal. It's getting more competitive at the more glamorized spots – like anywhere in the world really. I've

also noticed that it's getting busier when it gets bigger, as people's abilities get better. It's definitely pushed the level of surfing up. Wherever surfing has touched in the world it keeps on growing. What else would you be doing anyway?"

Surf directory

Ireland is home to a comparatively new and small surf community. As a result, it currently has no specialized surf publications – although with a rapidly expanding surf scene, this is sure to change.

Surfing in Northern Ireland

The northern shore of Northern Ireland is home to good quality surf. Its consistency and ease at picking up northerly swells accounts for its popularity as a surf location. The coastline is home to some excellent beach breaks, most spots working in a southerly wind and a northerly swell, interspersed with several quality reefs, if you can find them. The break at **Portrush** is the region's biggest pull. To the west lies the 10-km stretch of **Magillian/Benone Strand** and, to the east, Ballycastle Bay - just follow the B15 and A2 along the coast to explore the possibilities.

Stop off at the helpful **Troggs Surf Shop** on Portrush's Main St, T028-70825476, to stock up on hardware and to find out about local surf spots. If you're in the market for a new board or need to get a ding fixed contact Richard at **Westbay Surfboards**, www.westbaysurfboards.co.uk , or via Troggs.

Sleep at **MacCools Hostel** on Causeway St, Portrush, T028-70824845, who have internet access and beds in dorm rooms from £10 and twin rooms from £14. To the west, **Downhill Hostel**, T028-70849077, is in an excellent location overlooking Benone Strand. It has a kitchen, lockers, a garden, beds from £8 and private rooms from £25.

Don't miss the geological phenomenon, **The Giant's Causeway**. At the far end of East Strand Beach, perfect hexagonal columns comprise this 60 million year old rock formation leading from the cliffside to the sea.

Ireland: a brief surf history

1960s → Kevin Cavey becomes the first Irishman to surf on the Emerald Isle. **1966** → Ireland are invited to attend the World Surfing Championships – Kevin Cavey is their representative. Roger Steadman and Kevin Cavey establish C&S Surf Board Company, the first Irish surf company. **1967** → Surf Club of Ireland is established in Mount Herbert, Bray, and hosts the first National Championships in Tramore. **1968** → First Irish Intercounty Championships, won by County Down , are held at Rossnowlagh. **1969** → Ireland attends the first European Surfing Championships in Jersey. **1970** → Irish Surfing Association established as the sport's governing body to look after the 400 surfers in the country. **1972** → Ireland host the European Surfing Championships at Lahinch, without any surf! **1979** → The Smirnoff International is held in Easkey, Co Sligo, in perfect surf. **1985** → Ireland hosts the Guinness Eurosurf at Bundoran and Rossnowlagh. **1987** → Grant Robinson wins the European Masters title in France. **1996** → *Litmus* – the ultimate film for soul surfers – brings breaks like Pampa Point to world prominence. **2001** → Quiksilver hold the World Masters Championships in Bundoran, attended by a host of former world champions including Tom Curren, Rabbit, Kanga, Simon Andersen, Jeff Hakman and local heroes, Henry Moore and Grant Robinson. **Today** → Surfing in Ireland is going through a boom and is establishing itself as a big-wave spot. The ISA estimates that there are 5,000 surfers in Ireland, 35 surf shops, 27 surf schools, 10 affiliated surf clubs and 5 surfboard shapers nationwide.

Northwest Ireland

Surfing Northwest Ireland

Donegal is a land of surfing extremes. To navigate the tangle of roads leading to the craggy inlets and hidden reefs of its northern seaboard is to return to the days before the surf boom – a time of pristine waters and empty peaks. The weathered coastline, sandy beaches and quiet line-ups are the playground of a small but dedicated surfing population. This is wave riding like it used to be. In contrast, Bundoran to the south is a bustling holiday resort. Gone are the rows of painted cottages and quiet, snug pubs with three locals and a dog. The town expanded on the back of tourism and has continued to expand with the influx of surfers. The town is peppered with surfing iconography, its line-ups are littered with wave riders on any given day, and it boasts one of only two surfing reserves in the world (although the future of this Irish reserve currently hangs in the balance while plans for a new marina development are discussed).

The region is the cradle of Irish surfing. The surf club at Rossnowlagh is one of Ireland's most established. The Britton family has been part of surfing here since the beginning of the scene and has seen this love affair continue down the line and into the next generation through Easkey Britton, who is fast becoming one of Ireland's top female surfers.

It is also on the northwest shore that Irish surfing is taking steps into the next realm. Local surfer Richie Fitzgerald has been tackling the big-wave spots around the region. With friend Gabe Davies, the pair

Northwest Ireland board guide

Semi-gun
Shaper: Chops Lascelles of Beachbeat Surfboards

▸ 6'8" x 18½" x 2⁵⁄₁₆"

▸ This is a mid range semi-gun excellent for when the swell gets over 6 ft at spots like Pampa Point and the Peak.

▸ It is a flexible performance pin tail as shaped for Mike Morgan, Willie Britton or Richie Fitz.

Semi-gun
Shaper: Chops Lascelles of Beachbeat Surfboards

▸ 6'3" x 18½" x 2¼"

▸ Good all-round performance squash tail thruster that's perfect for small days at the Peak or good days at Tullan.

ⓘ Boards by **Beachbeat Surfboards**
Factory: Laminations, St Agnes, Cornwall
T00 44 (0)1872-553918
www.beachbeatsurfboards.co.uk
www.aggiesurf.com
or contact Lam2574@aol.com

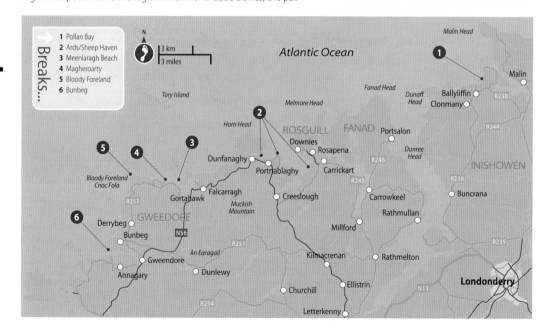

Breaks...
1 Pollan Bay
2 Ards/Sheep Haven
3 Meenlaragh Beach
4 Magheroarty
5 Bloody Foreland
6 Bunbeg

have been paddle and tow-in surfing huge Atlantic swells as they hit the region's reefs. "We have been on the road of discovery along the coast, where we have accessed some fantastic unsurfed big-wave spots and outer reefs," says Richie. "I know we are only scratching the surface of Ireland's big-wave potential, and I feel privileged to be in this pioneering position."

"It's great just being here in Ireland. The whole place has such an amazing atmosphere. It's great to see the likes of Simon Anderson, Tom Curren, Jeff Hakman surfing with Grant Robinson and Henry Moore. The surf hasn't been brilliant, but we've managed to hit a few balls on the golf course, and have a few pints of Guinness."
Rabbit Bartholomew, ASP director and former world champ, at the 2001 Quiksilver Masters in Bundoran

Coastline

Northwest Ireland has two distinct surfing communities. Around Bundoran and Rossnowlagh are probably the country's biggest surfing groups, with a history that goes back to the roots of Irish surfing. To the north, heading out of Donegal Bay, the coastline can be summed up in one word – potential. Just the beaches alone would keep an explorer busy for weeks. Hidden among the islands there must be points and reefs that have yet to be ridden. It's crying out to be explored. Head out onto the N56 with a good map and a compass and don't tell a soul what you find.

Localism

"My advice to any surfer coming to visit our shores, would be the same to any travelling surfer. If you show respect, you will gain respect. Irish surfers on a whole are a friendly laid-back bunch and this is pretty rare in world surfing terms, and hopefully we can hold on to this tradition long into the future. Be patient and good things come to those who wait."
Richie Fitzgerald

Top local surfers Richie Fitzgerald, Grant Robinson, Danny Clarke, the Britton family and Mikey Morgan and female surfers Easkey Britton, Nicole Morgan and Shauna Ward.

Getting around

The N56 will take you north away from Bundoran on a true surf adventure. Be patient, be friendly and remember that it always takes much longer to reach your destination than you think.

It was the Europeans in Bundoran in 1985. On our last day there, I got up really early – about three in the morning – and took the entire English surfing team to this Bundoran secret spot that I'd first surfed in the 1970s. We had a great day there but was I popular with the local boys! I was pilloried there for years for giving out the local secret spot! But to this day I don't think any of those kids has been back there or told anyone where it is – because they wouldn't have a clue. It's just another one of those Irish spots that either you know how to get to or you'll never find your way. It's like a maze up there.

Chops Lascelles, Beachbeat Surfboards

THE GILL

Northwest Irish coast

Breaks

1 Pollan Bay

- **Break type**: Beach break.
- **Conditions**: Small to medium swells, offshore in easterly/southeasterly winds.
- **Hazards/tips**: Open exposed beach.
- **Sleeping**: Malin Head/Ballyliffin ▶ p123.

Heading north on the R240, take the R238 at Carndonagh to **Pollan Bay**, or continue through Malin to **White Strand Bay**. Both are exposed beaches that pick up westerly and northwesterly swell. The banks here can be very good with powerful, hollow waves on all tides. If the swell has more north, or is big, head to **Tullagh Bay** to the west of Pollan.

2 Ards/Sheep Haven

- **Break type**: Beach and point.
- **Conditions**: All swells, offshore in southeast/southwesterly winds.
- **Hazards/tips**: Inlet that comes alive in northwesterly swells.
- **Sleeping**: Rosguill/Dunfanaghy ▶ p123.

A series of breaks that work in swells from the northwest or west. In a straight northwesterly swell, **Rosapenna** is a quality beach break with fast and hollow waves. It is a massive crescent-shaped bay and works in any wind with east in it. **Ards** has a sandy point that's worth seeking out and, to the north, **Portnablaghy** has a sheltered beach that needs southwesterly winds. **Dunfanaghy** is a very flexible spot that picks up north and northeasterly swell, but is offshore in any westerly wind. Rivermouth banks at the northern end of the beach.

Northwest Ireland

Air ——— Sea

°F	Averages		°C
90			30
70			20
50			10
30			0
	J F M A M J J A S O N D		

| 5/4/3 Boots & gloves | 5/4/3 Boots & gloves | 3/2 | 4/3 |

THE GILL

Secret spot in County Mayo

I love the whole Irish experience. The surfing is amazing but it's like a bonus on top of everything. It's a whole different thing to surfing in Hawaii or California. It's freezing, but that's one of the things I like about it. In Ireland I like having the days when you don't surf.

Dan Malloy, pro surfer

3 Meenlaragh Beach

- **Break type**: Beach break.
- **Conditions**: All swells, offshore in easterly/southeasterly winds.
- **Hazards/tips**: Works well in westerly and southwesterly swells.
- **Sleeping**: Falcarragh ▶ p123.

Found at the western end of a 10-km stretch of beach, Meenlaragh is a quality beach that works well in westerly and southwesterly swells. It curves round from facing due west to face due north, so is a flexible spot.

4 Magheroarty

- **Break type**: Reef break.
- **Conditions**: All swells, offshore in southeasterly winds.
- **Hazards/tips**: Needs a northwesterly or westerly swell
- **Sleeping**: Falcarragh ▶ p123.

A left-hand reef that sits in front of the harbour and works in a northwestly or westerly swell. Best surfed mid to high tide when walling waves can break up to 6 ft. Easy paddle out. A quality spot. Between here and Bloody Foreland are a couple of left reefs worth checking.

5 Bloody Foreland

🌀 **Break type**: Boulder reef.

🌊 **Conditions**: All swells, offshore in southeasterly wind.

❶ **Hazards/tips**: Boulders, rips, powerful waves.

🛏 **Sleeping**: Falcarragh/Bunbeg ▸▸ p123.

This exposed headland gets its name from the fact that the rocks turn blood red at sunset. There is a bouldery right-hand point that breaks in northwesterly swells. Can be a quality wave in the right conditions and picks up heaps of swell. Needs to be over 3 ft to surf as it is a bouldery reef, but it can hold a big swell of up to 10 ft.

6 Bunbeg

🌀 **Break type**: Beach break.

🌊 **Conditions**: All swells, offshore in southeasterly swells.

❶ **Hazards/tips**: Northwest facing beach with offshore islands.

🛏 **Sleeping**: Bunbeg ▸▸ p124.

Inishfree Bay is to the southwest of Bunbeg and picks up plenty of swell from a northwesterly direction. Although the bay is littered with offshore islands, the swell still filters through. Works on all tides and has some excellent banks. Very quiet spot.

7 Gweebarra Bay

🌀 **Break type**: Beach break.

🌊 **Conditions**: All swells, offshore in easterly and southeasterly swells.

❶ **Hazards/tips**: Rips in rivermouth.

🛏 **Sleeping**: Dungloe/Ardara ▸▸ p124.

It's a bit of a walk into the bay but it is worth it. A beautiful location with a river at the southern end of the bay. There is a sandbar which forms here and can have excellent lefts and rights on an incoming tide. Watch out for rips as the tide drops. To the north and south there are plenty of banks to explore. Check out the bay in front of the golf course by Inishkeel.

8 Tramore /Loughros More

🌀 **Break type**: Beach break.

🌊 **Conditions**: Medium to big swells, offshore in easterly/northeasterly winds.

❶ **Hazards/tips**: Rips by rivermouth.

🛏 **Sleeping**: Ardara ▸▸ p124.

Tramore beach is the northern beach, which has some excellent rights at the top end of the beach in good swells. It is offshore in northeasterly as well as easterly winds. **Loughros** is the next beach to the south, a huge bay with a rivermouth to the south. The sandbanks change with the tides, but there are usually waves near the rivermouth. Part of the Spanish Armada ran aground here.

9 Loughros Beg

🌀 **Break type**: Beach break.

🌊 **Conditions**: Medium to big swells, offshore in southeasterly winds.

❶ **Hazards/tips**: Quiet bay, rips by rivermouth.

🛏 **Sleeping**: Ardara ▸▸ p124.

This is a wonderful beach with many sandbanks spread along its length. The rivermouth usually has a decent sandbar, but is best on a pushing tide. A good place to check in southwesterly winds as the south of the beach is overlooked by the Slieve League Peninsula which gives it plenty of shelter.

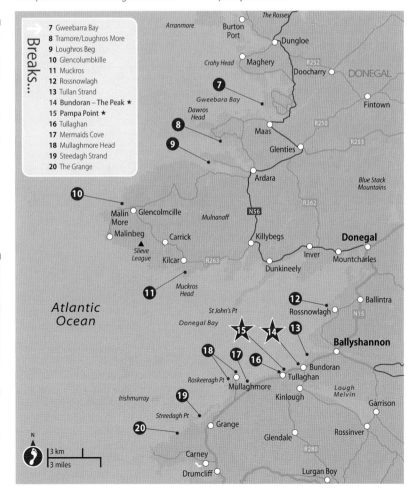

Breaks...
7 Gweebarra Bay
8 Tramore/Loughros More
9 Loughros Beg
10 Glencolumbkille
11 Muckros
12 Rossnowlagh
13 Tullan Strand
14 Bundoran – The Peak ★
15 Pampa Point ★
16 Tullaghan
17 Mermaids Cove
18 Mullaghmore Head
19 Steedagh Strand
20 The Grange

Ireland Northwest Breaks Bloody Foreland to Loughros Beg

10 Glencolmcille

- **Break type**: Beach break.
- **Conditions**: Small to medium swells, offshore in easterly winds.
- **Hazards/tips**: Picks up heaps of swell, very exposed.
- **Sleeping**: Glencolmcille ⟩⟩ p124.

Follow the road out towards the end of the headland and stop off at the bay. This small beach picks up heaps off swell and although the waves might not be epic, there can be some great little peaks.

11 Muckros

- **Break type**: Beach break.
- **Conditions**: Big swells, offshore in northeasterly winds.
- **Hazards/tips**: Works in northerly wind.
- **Sleeping**: Glencolmcille ⟩⟩ p124.

A good beach break that is popular when a northerly wind is blowing out the breaks around Bundoran. Needs a decent northwesterly or a medium westerly or southwesterly swell. Works on all tides.

12 Rossnowlagh

- **Break type**: Beach break.
- **Conditions**: Medium to big swells, offshore in easterly winds.
- **Hazards/tips**: Big surfing tradition.
- **Sleeping**: Rossnowlagh ⟩⟩ p125.

This long beach has a big surfing tradition. It was one of the first places to be surfed in the 1960s and has been home to the Intercounties Surfing Contest since 1968. It needs a decent northwesterly or a medium westerly swell to get into the beach where there are some decent banks. An ideal spot for beginners and intermediates to polish their skills.

THE GILL

15 Pampa Point

13 Tullan Strand

- **Break type**: Beach break.
- **Conditions**: All swells, offshore in easterly winds.
- **Hazards/tips**: Long beach with rips by the cliffs at the south.
- **Sleeping**: Bundoran ⟩⟩ p125.

Parking on the cliffs overlooking the bay. There are usually better waves near to the cliffs, where a consistent left breaks. Tends to take the overspill from Bundoran, so gets crowded, but there are more peaks along the beach to spread out onto. Works on all tides and picks up plenty of swell, so it may be worth checking for waves here when other spots are flat. Inexperienced surfers should watch out for the rip in front of the cliffs.

14 Bundoran – The Peak

- **Break type**: Reef break.
- **Conditions**: All swells.
- **Size**: 3-8 ft.
- **Length**: 50-100 m.
- **Swell**: West/northwesterly.
- **Wind**: Southeasterly.
- **Tide**: Low.
- **Bottom**: Flat reef.
- **Entry/exit**: In the channel/over the reef.
- **Hazards/tips**: Shallow reef, gets very crowded, experienced surfers.
- **Sleeping**: Bundoran ⟩⟩ p125.

One of Ireland's most famous waves, the Peak has hosted the Quiksilver Masters and is a very popular destination for travelling surfers. The reef works best at low tide, when long, hollow lefts reel off. There are also quality rights, the length depending on the swell direction. Walk out along the reef, access from the car park on the seafront. The wave has been under threat from a proposed marina development which has been on and off for years now and has yet to be resolved. The fact that the wave is one of only two surfing reserves in the world seems to have little bearing on the case. "We've been trying to save the Peak by demonstrating that

THE GILL

> ⓘ *If you like Bundoran, try The Bubble in Fuerteventura (see page 271) or Pointe de Chassiron in France (see page 169).*

15 Duncan Cook at Pampa Point

"Be patient and good things come to those who wait."
Richie Fitzgerald

(i) *If you like Pampa Point, try Gills Bay in Scotland (see page 36) or Les Alcyons in France (see page 192).*

surfing brings a lot into this town, that we're not just a bunch of hippies," says Richie Fitzgerald. "There are businesses and holiday accommodation that are supported by visiting surfers. By highlighting the excellent quality of the wave, it has made it more crowded, but we'd rather have a Peak that's more crowded than no wave at all."

15 Pampa Point

- ◉ **Break type**: Left-hand reef break.
- ◉ **Conditions**: Medium to big swells.
- ◉ **Size**: 4-12 ft.
- ◉ **Length**: 25-75 m.
- ◉ **Swell**: Northwesterly.
- ◉ **Wind**: Southerly.
- ◉ **Tide**: Mid to high.
- ◉ **Bottom**: Ledge reef.
- ◉ **Entry/exit**: Off the rocks and round the back.
- ◉ **Hazards/tips**: Heavy wave, experts only.
- ◉ **Sleeping**: Bundoran ⟩⟩ *p125*.

Pampa is an awesome wave. In a big swell it offers Pipeline-like tubes as the wave jacks up onto the shallow ledge, opening up into a wicked barrelling left. Starts working at about 4 ft but will dredge away at 10-12 ft. The take-off is steep and sucky and it is a race to the channel. It really is a wave for the most experienced surfers only. There are rips pushing east. Best from mid to high tide.

16 Tullaghan

- ◉ **Break type**: Right point.
- ◉ **Conditions**: Medium to big swells, offshore in southerly winds.
- ◉ **Hazards/tips**: Breaks over boulders.
- ◉ **Sleeping**: Bundoran ⟩⟩ *p125*.

Quality right-hand point that works in even the biggest swells when it takes on Sunset Beach-like proportions. Featured in the film *Litmus* that helped bring Ireland to the attention of surfers outside Europe. The waves break over boulders, which is fine in bigger swells but can be a problem in smaller swells.

17 Mermaids Cove

- ◔ **Break type**: Beach break.
- ◔ **Conditions**: Medium to big swells, offshore in southerly winds.
- ❶ **Hazards/tips**: Quiet beach.
- ◔ **Sleeping**: Bundoran ›› *p125*.

This beach break is found in front of the caravan park at the eastern end of Mullaghmore beach. A good place to check in a bigger swell. As the swell picks up, move closer to Mullaghmore Head where the beach is more sheltered from swell and wind. Works on all tides.

18 Mullaghmore Head

- ◔ **Break type**: Reef break.
- ◔ **Conditions**: Big swells, offshore in southeasterly winds.
- ❶ **Hazards/tips**: Big-wave spot.
- ◔ **Sleeping**: Bundoran ›› *p125*.

Needs a big swell to get going due to the rocks in the line-up. Starts getting ridable in the 8-10 ft range. Definitely for advanced surfers only. Has been a tow-in spot. West Mullaghmore has a right reef further round the headland which gets going when the swell is over 4-5 ft.

19 Steedagh Strand

- ◔ **Break type**: Beach break.
- ◔ **Conditions**: All swells, offshore in southeasterly winds.
- ❶ **Hazards/tips**: Exposed beach, picks up loads of swell.
- ◔ **Sleeping**: Bundoran ›› *p125*.

This is great stretch of beach and a fantastic place to escape the crowds. The beach is very consistent. It picks up loads of swell – in bigger swells, check out the peaks near Steedagh Point, which are more sheltered. Offshore in southeasterly and southerly winds. Park and walk along the beach. There are bits of reef and a rivermouth to check.

20 The Grange

- ◔ **Break type**: Reef breaks.
- ◔ **Conditions**: All swells, offshore in southeasterly winds.
- ❶ **Hazards/tips**: A series of reefs.
- ◔ **Sleeping**: Bundoran ›› *p125*.

This area has some excellent Easkey-like lefts that break over rocky reefs with boulders. They are best from mid to high tide. Take a right after Grange and explore the headland.

Big wave

Secret reef Northwest Ireland

Listings

Malin Head

Over the border from neighbouring Northern Ireland, the Inishowen Peninsula is the first port of call in County Donegal. Banba's Crown on Malin Head, which juts out into the Inishtrahull Sound, is the Republic of Ireland's most northerly point and was a strategic lookout point during the Second World War. Pick up provisions, have a beer or a bite to eat at the **Seaview Tavern**. Otherwise you'll need to head into the main town of Carndonagh to the south which has facilities including tourist info and a bank.

● Sleeping

F **Malin Head Hostel**, T074-9370309, is a relaxed spot, open year round with dorm rooms and doubles. It can organize bike hire for €9 a day, sells fresh vegetables grown in the garden and offers reflexology and aromatherapy treatments. F **Sandrock Holiday Hostel**, at Port Ronan Pier, T074-9370289, is right on the water and another good year-round choice.

Balllyliffin

Heading west from Carndonagh, the town of Ballyliffin on the R238 offers good access to the 3-mile stretch of Pollan Bay, the site of a bloody battle for the lordship of Inishowen in the 16th century. Grab a €5 all-day breakfast at the **Village Diner**.

☸ Flat spells

Golf Ballyliffin GC, T074-9376119, green fees €60, cheaper in winter.

● Sleeping

Camping **Tullagh Bay Campsite**, just behind Tullagh Bay, T074-9378997, open May-Sep.

Rosguill

This pretty peninsula is a popular summer spot with tourists and locals.

☸ Flat spells

Golf Rosapenna GC, T074-9155301, if you can stomach the €50 green fees.

● Sleeping

Camping Camp Apr-Sep at the popular **Casey's Carvan and Camping Park** in Downings, T074-915 5376. The site overlooks the beach but is just 200 m from shops, bar etc. The drawback is that you do have to pay for showers. In Jul-Aug only, there's also the tiny **Rosguill Park** campsite on Melmore Rd.

Dunfanaghy

On the N56, this pretty, unassuming town is on the western edge of Sheep Haven and has a fantastic year-round hostel. For a cashpoint or provisions head to **Ramsey's** in town.

☸ Flat spells

Golf Get a round in at the par 68, 18 hole Dunfanaghy links course T074-9136335. Green fees around €28. **Mountain walks** Head to Muckish Mountain and climb the 670-m monster for some great views of the area (when it's not covered in cloud!).

● Sleeping

E-F **Corcreggan Mill Hostel**, on the road to Falcarragh, T074-9136409, combines 200 year old, kiln-house accommodation with rooms in a converted railway car to create an awesome sleeping experience in dorms and doubles. For campers, there's a converted stable complete with kitchen and dining area plus shower block. There is a handy Chinese in the grounds – what more do you want?

Falcarragh

This town has a significant Irish-speaking community and some beautiful sand dunes to the northwest.

☸ Flat spells

Bloody Foreland Drive out to Cnoc Fola

and watch the sunset turn the rocks here blood red. Legend has it that Balor of the evil eye, the Celtic God of Darkness, was slain on these hills, with his blood colouring the landscape, giving Bloody Foreland its name. **Golf** Get 9 holes in at the par-70 **Cloughaneely GC** at Ballyconnel, Falcarragh, T074-9165416, €14.

⬤ Sleeping

E **Shamrock Lodge**, Main St, T074-9135859, dorm accommodation 15 Jan-15 Dec.

✆ Eating/drinking

The hostel is above a popular pub of the same name, which is big at the weekends for traditional music. They also have a pool table and screen the Gaelic matches. For cheap grub, head to **Damien's Café** further along Main St. Try the home made soup from €2.75 or the burger with an egg on top, with chips, for €5.75.

Bunbeg

Thevillages of Bunbeg and Derrybeg have expanded to meet one another on the R257.

❂ Flat spells

Golf Get 9 holes in at the par-71 **Gweedore** links course in Magheragallon, Derrybeg, T074-9531140, green fees from €15, or splash out on the 9-hole **Cruit Island GC** to the southwest, T074-9543296, green fees from €22. **Tory Island** 11 km north of the mainland, Tory Island is the place to rub shoulders with royalty. They have their own king – currently Patsy-Dan – who more than likely will greet you off the ferry. **Donegal Coastal Cruises**, T074-9531320, www.toryislandferry.com, run between Bunbeg and Tory Island throughout the year, returns around €20.

⬤ Sleeping

F **Backpackers Ireland Seaside Hostel** in Derrybeg, T074-9532244, is open Mar-Oct. Groups might try **Bunbeg Holiday Homes**, T074-9531402, which are pretty soulless-looking affairs but have

accommodation sleeping 4-8 people at reasonable off-season rates.

✆ Eating/drinking

Head south to Annagary for a drink in **Leo's Tavern**, owned by the parents of Irish singers Clannad and Enya whose memorabilia cover the walls.

Dungloe

Heading south on the N56, Dungloe is the capital of The Rosses. With good facilities and amenities, it makes a good base to explore northwest Donegal.

❂ Flat spells

Arranmore This island is all about the scenery and the atmosphere. The Arranmore ferry from Burtonport takes 25 mins, T079-520532. **Mary** If you're in town for the last week of Jul you can catch, or be caught up in, the Mary from Dungloe Festival – an annual mini-Rose of Tralee affair when a new 'Mary' is crowned amidst music and mayhem.

⬤ Sleeping

F **Greene's Holiday Hostel**, on Carnmore Rd, T074-9521943, is centrally based, open year round, hires out bikes (cheaper for guests) but does have a curfew. Round the back of the hostel is **Greens's Caravan and Camping Park**, T074-9521943, open Apr-10 Oct, free hot showers. Alternatively head south to out of the way Crohy Head and the **Crohy Head An Oige Hostel**, overlooking Boylagh Bay, T074-9521950, basic facilities, open Jun-Sep. To the north along the R259 try **Cois Na Mara Hostel** in Burtonport, open Mar-Oct, with internet access for a fee.

✆ Eating/drinking

Grab a bite to eat in the average **Doherty's** café on Main St.

❶ Directory

Bank: Bank of Ireland, Main St. **Pharmacy**: Main St. **Post office**: Quay Rd. **Supermarket**: a couple including

SuperValu on Carnmore Rd. **Tourist information**: Main St, summer only.

Adara

If you're in the market for some Donegal tweed, you've hit upon the right place! And as a tweed-tourist magnet, there are a couple of good accommodation options as well as banks, a pharmacy and post office around Main St.

❂ Flat spells

Golf Narin and Port Noo GC, off the R261, T074-9545107, has an 18-hole, par-69 links course, green fees around €30.

⬤ Sleeping

C **Green Gate B&B**, T074-9541546, is a lovely, relaxed place just out of town, a good spot to escape to with your significant other. For a cheaper option, try the small F **Drumbaron Hostel**, on the main square, T074-9541200.
Camping Head up to **Tramore Beach Caravan & Camping Park**, T074-9551491, just behind Tramore beach with easy access to the break.

✆ Eating/drinking

Head to **Nancy's** on Front St for good seafood or **Charlies Café** on Main St for basic grub at basic prices.

Glencolmcille

There are a couple of good hostels near this breathtaking settlement.

⬤ Sleeping

F **Dooey Hostel**, T074-9730130, is a friendly, inviting, cliff-top place for all- comers – from campers to couples and groups.
F **Malinbeg Hostel**, to the south in Malinbeg, T074-9730006, swanky, with dorms and doubles.
Further south still at Kilcar,
F **Derrylahan Hostel**, T074-9938097, very handy for Muckros Head, with dorms, private rooms and camping facilities.

Rossnowlagh

Rossnowlagh is home to one of Ireland's oldest surf communities and one of Ireland's largest surf clubs. With a great swathe of sand known as the Heavenly Cove, this is a popular spot with holidaymakers but quiet off season.

● Sleeping

Accommodation here is fairly pricey, so you are probably better off biting the bullet and staying in Bundoran.
Camping Manor House Camping Park, just north of the town on the seafront, T071-9851477, summer opening.

● Eating/drinking

Smugglers Creek Inn, an old beamed bar/restaurant/B&B overlooking the beach on Cliff Rd, T071-9852366, is a great place to eat some good seafood even if you can't afford to stay here. Drink at the **Surfers Bar**, Easter-Oct, attached to the **Sand Hotel**, overlooking the beach.

Bundoran

Bundoran is not your typical Irish village. It doesn't have the multi-coloured terraced houses, it doesn't have the cobbled street, old world charm. But what this 1970s-style resort town does have is far more appealing. Bundoran is home to some of Ireland's most famous waves and a serious surfing community with an infrastructure to match.

✿ Flat spells

Bowling Get a strike at **Mac's Glow Bowl** on Main St, T071-9842111, open 1100-0000.
Cinema Head to Ballyshannon's **Abbey Centre**, T072-9852928, to catch a film.
Crazy Golf and Pitch 'n' Putt Tyrconnell **Holiday Homes**, T071-9842277, from €4.
Golf Bundoran GC, T071-9841302, is an 18-hole, par-70 links course, green fees from €30. **Waterworld** Atlantic Way, T071-9841172.

● Sleeping

E **Homefield Hostel**, Bayview Av, T071-9841288, is part of an equestrian centre but offers dorm accommodation year round, breakfast included.
Self-catering Tyrconnell Holiday Homes, a low-rise holiday village with a good range of houses and apartments, about 10 mins walk from the break. Off-season rates are reasonable – a 4-bed house for around €400/week – but summer prices are more than double. Contact Matt Britton for details, www.donegal-holidays.com, T071-9842277. Heading north out of town on the Tullan Strand Rd, **Surfers Cove Holiday Village**, T071-9842286, www.surferscove.com, offers a similar deal.
Camping Easter-Oct at the fair-sized **Dartry View Caravan Park**, East End, T071-9841794.

● Eating/drinking

The **Ould Bridge** bar on Main St does a good range of reasonably priced food – the veggie burgers are great and around €7. Food comes with a view – if you peer through the church-style windows you can check the break. **Suzies** on Main St does a fair fish 'n' chips and there's even a **KFC** on the road to Tullan Strand. Richie Fitzgerald advises dropping by the **Astoria Wharf** on Atlantic Way or, "For the best pint of Guinness in Ireland (and yes they have won the award five times), no night would be complete without a visit to **Brennans Bar**, Main St, Bundoran – it's a Guinness drinker's Nirvana!"

○ Shopping

Fitzgerald's Surf World on Main St, T071-9841223, surfworld@eircom.net, www.surfworldireland.com, is run by the knowledgeable Richie Fitzgerald who stocks hardware as well as accessories. Richie is a committed surfer who, along with Gabe Davies and the assistance of a jet-ski, has been pioneering big-wave spots along the coastline. Shaper Jim Barnes's **Legend Surfboards** is based in Bundoran, T087-9711718. There are **Mace** and **Spar** supermarkets in East End.

⊙ Directory

Bank: Allied Irish Bank on Main St has an ATM. **Bike hire**: Hire and Sell Centre, East End. **Pharmacy**: a couple on Main St. **Police**: Garda Station on Church Rd, T071-9841203. **Post office**: Quay St. **Tourist information**: Bundoran Bridge.

Airports → Dublin T01-8141111, www.dublinairport.com; Shannon T061-712000, www.shannonairport.com; Cork T021-4313131, www.corkairport.com; Kerry T066-9764644, www.kerryairport.ie; Aer Lingus T0818 365000, www.aerlingus.com. **Coaches** → Bus Eireann T01-8366111, www.buseireann.ie. **Car hire** → Avis T0870-6060100; Europcar T0870-6075000; Hertz T08708-448844. **Petrol prices** → €0.95/litre. **Ferries** → P&O T0870-2424999, www.poportsmouth.com; Brittany Ferries T0870-3665333, www.brittany-ferries.com; Irish Ferries T08705-171717, www.irishferries.com; Sea France T0870-5711711, www.seafrance.com. **Rail links** → Iranrod Eireann www.irishrail.ie, T01-8363333.

West Coast Ireland

66 99

One of the great things about this area is the huge variation of waves. From Crab Island, to Lahinch, to Spanish Point, to further south. Most swell directions will hit something around here. Most of the time there will be somewhere working.

Tom Buckley, Lahinch Surf Shop

Surfing the West Coast

Although stories of Irish surf had been around since the 1960s, it was only when surf magazines featured the likes of Spanish Point, Lahinch and Easkey Right that the words took on a physical form. Ireland had it all. Perfect reefs, uncrowded line-ups and the *craic* was always good. Hell, even the legendary Mickey Dora had set up camp there. For a time it seemed like the whole world was Ireland bound.

The west coast of Ireland is still one of Europe's top surfing destinations. The coastline has classic reefs that receive regular swells from a constant stream of Atlantic lows. The prevailing winds are offshore at many of the breaks, and while numbers in the line-up have risen in Ireland, they have risen everywhere else too. The lush green landscape and friendly villages only

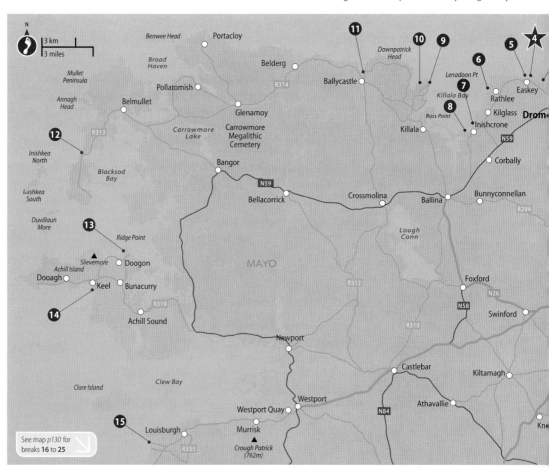

add to the experience. If you visit here with a relaxed outlook and chat to the locals, both in and out of the water, your stay will be one of the most rewarding surf trips you could imagine.

Coastline

From Easkey heading west, this coastline has a geology and geography perfectly suited for surfing. The rock forms some wonderful flat limestone reefs and point breaks interspersed with sheltered sandy beaches that have generally built up around rivermouths or inlets. The undulating coastline allows for almost any swell to be surfed as there is usually somewhere offshore. But the amazing thing is that for such a well known stretch of coastline, there are still hidden beauties. "The beauty of Ireland is that with a little effort and a map you can still find world-class waves," says Nick Gammon.

Localism

Surfing in Ireland has boomed. The number of local surfers is rising exponentially each year, and the number of visitors from all over Europe is at an all-time high. The country's surfing population had a lot of catching up to do, in terms of surfing infrastructure and in terms of coping with all the extra bodies in the water. When your local break goes from four guys in the line-up to forty, it is bound to cause frustration in some quarters. However, the bottom line in Ireland is that if you turn up to surf with a chilled outlook, there will be no problems. Don't try to take more than your share of waves, even if you are the best surfer in the line-up. Enjoy the surfing and the company and you won't go far wrong.

Top local surfers Irish Champion and Enniscrone local **Cain Killcullen** is leading the charge. Other stand-outs include **Alan Coyne** and **Ollie O'Flaherty**.

Getting around

The roads in western Ireland are not built for speed. Always factor this into the equation when working out how long it will take to reach anywhere.

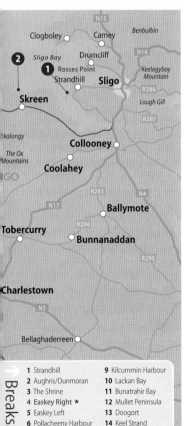

Breaks...

1 Strandhill	9 Kilcummin Harbour
2 Aughris/Dunmoran	10 Lackan Bay
3 The Shrine	11 Bunatrahir Bay
4 Easkey Right ★	12 Mullet Peninsula
5 Easkey Left	13 Doogort
6 Pollacheeny Harbour	14 Keel Strand
7 Inishcrone Point	15 Emlagh Point
8 Inishcrone Beach	

West coast board guide

PF Flyer
Shaper: Chops Lascelles of Beachbeat Surfboards

▸ 6'0" x 20" x 2³⁄₁₆"

▸ Good for Strandhill and Easkey Left and Right.

▸ An excellent beach break board. Loose yet drivey, with double wings and a swallow tail for performance.

Semi-gun
Shaper: Chops Lascelles of Beachbeat Surfboards

▸ 6'6" x 18½" x 2⅜"

▸ Break out this board when Easkey and the reefs are pumping.

▸ Gets you into waves early and with a pintail for steep and hollow waves.

Boards by **Beachbeat Surfboards**
Factory: Laminations, St Agnes, Cornwall
T00 44 (0)1872-553918
www.beachbeatsurfboards.co.uk
www.aggiesurf.com
or contact Lam2574@aol.com

I think we were drawn to Ireland because we felt a connection from the Northeast (of England). Many Northeast surfers made the trip over to surf the reefs around Easkey. You could drive across to the overnight ferry at Larne and be in the line-up the next morning. We heard all the stories about the epic surf that was just a short hop away.

Sam Lamiroy, pro surfer

Most trips will take longer than you think, and firing down the country lanes will not do your suspension any favours. Also be warned that the *garda* are clamping down on drink driving and will often set up checkpoints heading out of towns or even in the smallest villages.

Breaks

1 Strandhill

- **Break type**: Beach breaks.
- **Conditions**: All swells, offshore in easterly winds.
- **Hazards/tips**: Popular beach.
- **Sleeping**: Strandhill ▸▸ p133.

Strandhill has a variety of waves including rights breaking at the north off the bouldery point. This point needs a northeasterly wind. The main beach has banks all along it, the most popular is by the car park. These work best in easterly or northeasterly winds and through all tides. Rivermouth can also have excellent waves breaking on the sandbar.

2 Aughris/Dunmoran

- **Break type**: Beach break.
- **Conditions**: Medium to big swells, offshore in southerly winds.
- **Hazards/tips**: Quiet spot.
- **Sleeping**: Strandhill/Easkey ▸▸ p133.

Good place to escape the crowds. This beach break is pretty mellow and less intense than the reefs to the west. A good spot for beginners and intermediate surfers. Works on all tides with the west of the beach being sheltered in bigger swells and westerly winds.

3 The Shrine

- **Break type**: Left reef break.
- **Conditions**: Medium swells, offshore in south/southwesterly winds.
- **Hazards/tips**: Shallow and heavy.
- **Sleeping**: Easkey ▸▸ p133.

Follow the road to the shrine of St Farnan where you will find a ledgy, hollow left-hand reef. It needs a decent swell to get going but produces quality waves around mid tide.

4 Easkey Right

- **Break type**: Right reef break.
- **Conditions**: All swells.
- **Size**: 3-10 ft.
- **Length**: 50-100 m.
- **Swell**: Northwesterly.
- **Winds** : Southerly.
- **Tides**: Low tide.
- **Bottom**: Flat reef with boulders.
- **Entry/exit**: Paddle round or off the point.
- **Hazards/tips**: Rock reef, crowds.
- **Sleeping**: Easkey ▸▸ p133.

Easkey and Bundoran were the top destinations for travelling surfers after the Irish explosion in the surfing media. The reason it was so popular, and why people keep coming back, is that it's very easy to find, consistent, not a particularly heavy wave and great quality. Swells hit the flat reef and throw up long, walling right-handers that can get hollow. There's an easy paddle out and it can handle swells up to 8-10 ft. Works best at low tide. It is rarely quiet. With a good chart, it will be busy during holidays, bank holiday weekends and the summer.

If you like Easkey Right, try Thurso East in Scotland (see page 38) or Crab Island in Wales (see page 100).

5 Easkey Left

- **Break type**: Left reef break.
- **Conditions**: All swells, offshore in southerly winds.
- **Hazards/tips**: Crowds.
- **Sleeping**: Easkey ▸▸ p133.

Facing Easkey Right is another quality reef breaking left. It starts to work in smaller swells and has some excellent waves. There is an easy paddle out from the harbour wall that overlooks it. It also has the advantage that it works through all the tides. Again, very busy and very popular.

West Ireland

Air ——— **Sea**

°F	Averages												°C
90													30
70													20
50													10
30													0
	J	F	M	A	M	J	J	A	S	O	N	D	

5/4/3 Boots & gloves	5/4/3 Boots	3/2	4/3

THE GILL

Secret Spot Irish Summer Glass

6 Pollacheeny Harbour

- **Break type**: Right reef break.
- **Conditions**: Medium to big swells, offshore in southeasterly winds.
- **Hazards/tips**: Quality wave, heavy when big.
- **Sleeping**: Easkey/Inishcrone ➤ p133.

Follow the bumpy track down to the bouldery natural lagoon. There are two waves that break here, the outside and inner point. They are both quality hollow waves breaking over a bouldery reef. Works best in a southeasterly wind and at low tide.

7 Inishcrone Point

- **Break type**: Point break.
- **Conditions**: Medium to big swells, offshore in southeasterly winds.
- **Hazards/tips**: Fast, quality reef.
- **Sleeping**: Inishcrone ➤ p133.

Just outside the harbour at Inishcrone sits a quality right-hand point break. In a good swell and southeasterly winds, fast hollow waves reel down the point over the shallow reef. A very nice wave that has been largely overlooked, but those in the know enjoy a speedy wave that challenges the surfer. Best at low tide. Park near the harbour.

8 Inishcrone Beach

- **Break type**: Beach break.
- **Conditions**: Medium swells, offshore in southerly winds. Works on all tides.
- **Hazards/tips**: Good all-round beach.
- **Sleeping**: Inishcrone ➤ p133.

A good sized beach with plenty of peaks. Not too powerful or heavy so a good spot for beginners and intermediates.

9 Kilcummin Harbour

- **Break type**: Left-hand point.
- **Conditions**: All swells, offshore in southerly winds.
- **Hazards/tips**: Crowds, reef.
- **Sleeping**: Ballycastle ➤ p134.

Looking north from the harbour wall you will see a quality left peeling down the point towards you. This wave has excellent walls and barrel sections but it does get busy in a westerly wind as it can be one of the few waves working.

10 Lackan Bay

- **Break type**: Beach break.
- **Conditions**: Medium swells, offshore in southerly winds.
- **Hazards/tips**: Big beach.
- **Sleeping**: Ballycastle ➤ p134.

Lackan tends to stay uncrowded and is a good place to check if there is a westerly wind as it is sheltered by the headland. It is a long beach with banks that change with the tides. A great location and suitable for surfers of all abilities. Check the headland to the west for a left-hand reef break.

11 Bunatrahir Bay

- **Break type**: Reef break.
- **Conditions**: Medium swells, offshore in southerly wind.
- **Hazards/tips**: Quiet break.
- **Sleeping**: Ballycastle ➤ p134.

Another point break located by a harbour, Bunatrahir has a nice little left-hand reef to the north of the breakwater. The wave needs a medium swell from a northerly direction to really fire. Park responsibly near the harbour.

12 Mullet Peninsula

- **Break type**: Beaches and reefs.
- **Conditions**: All swells, offshore in easterly winds.
- **Hazards/tips**: A huge variety of breaks.
- **Sleeping**: Belmullet ➤ p134.

The Mullet Peninsula has amazing potential. The beaches on the western side are exposed to the full force of the Atlantic so would make ideal spots to check out in the summer. It is a long sandy beach, with plenty of peaks to choose from, and virtually no surfers. The southern tip is more sheltered and worth checking when the swell really kicks in.

Ireland West Coast Breaks Pollacheeny Harbour to Mullet Peninsula

THE GILL

7 Inishcrone Point

THE GILL

6 Pollacheeny Harbour

13 Doogort

- ◉ **Break type**: Beach break.
- ◉ **Conditions**: Medium to big swells, offshore in southeasterly winds.
- ◉ **Hazards/tips**: Access over the fields from the village.
- ◉ **Sleeping**: Achill Island ▸▸ p134.

It's a long drive round from Belmullet to this flexible spot. There are a couple of beaches here that work in big swells and winds from easterly through to southwesterly. Ridge Point picks up the most swell whereas the western beach is more sheltered. Works on all tides.

14 Keel Strand

- ◉ **Break type**: Beach break.
- ◉ **Conditions**: Medium to big swells, offshore in northeasterly winds.
- ◉ **Hazards/tips**: Likes a southwesterly swell.
- ◉ **Sleeping**: Achill Island ▸▸ p134.

Keel is a small village at the northern end of this open stretch of beach. It is exposed to the wind but flexible as it works in an easterly, northeasterly or northerly winds. This is a long beach facing southwestely so a southwesterly swell hits the sandbanks perfectly. Also worth checking in massive northwesterlies.

15 Emlagh Point

- ◉ **Break type**: Beach break.
- ◉ **Conditions**: All swells, offshore in southeasterly winds.
- ◉ **Hazards/tips**: Long open beach.
- ◉ **Sleeping**: Louisburgh ▸▸ p134.

This is an amazing beach about as far away from the crowds as you can get. Between Emlagh Point and Tonakeera Point lie nearly 10 km of beaches broken by the occasional reef and rocky point. There are plenty of high quality sandbanks to check out in an easterly or southeasterly wind.

16 Crab Island

- ◉ **Break type**: Right reef break.
- ◉ **Conditions**: All swells.
- ◉ **Size**: 3-12 ft plus.
- ◉ **Length**: 50-75 m.
- ◉ **Swell**: Northwesterly.
- ◉ **Wind**: Easterly/southeasterly.
- ◉ **Tide**: All tides, better around low to mid.
- ◉ **Bottom**: Jagged reef.
- ◉ **Entry/exit**: Paddle out in the channel from the harbour.
- ◉ **Hazards/tips**: Long paddle offshore, heavy wave, shallow reef.
- ◉ **Sleeping**: Doolin ▸▸ p134.

Standing on the harbour at Doolin, the small offshore island looks quite close and the waves a lot smaller than they really are. It's a long paddle (20 mins) round to the back of the island where this serious right-hander breaks on a shallow reef. The swell jacks up out of deep water and unloads onto a ledge producing long and very hollow waves. Best at

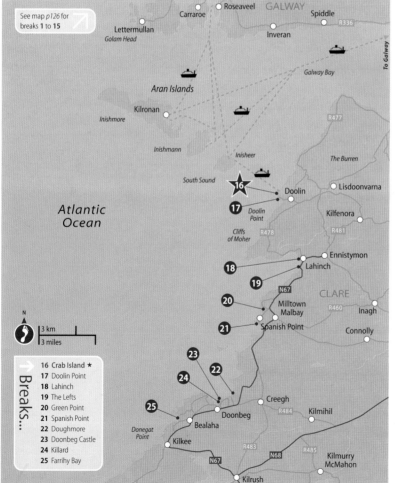

Breaks...

16 Crab Island ★
17 Doolin Point
18 Lahinch
19 The Lefts
20 Green Point
21 Spanish Point
22 Doughmore
23 Doonbeg Castle
24 Killard
25 Farrihy Bay

9 Kilcummin Harbour ▸▸ p129

4-6 ft but will break over 10 ft, when it is for the serious hellmen only. Definitely for experienced surfers only. The wave is often likened to Pipeline and can cause serious damage. "Do not overestimate your ability," warns Tom Buckley of nearby Lahinch Surf Shop. "It is a serious wave and has broken many boards and leashes, dislocated a few shoulders and put out a few backs. If you lose your board then the swim home can be very, very difficult due to the currents in the channel between the island and the mainland."

(i) **If you like** Crab Island, try Coxos in Portugal (see page 301) or El Basurero on Isla Graciosa (see page 269).

21 Matt Jones at Spanish ▸▸ p132

17 Doolin Point

Secret reef

17 Doolin Point

- ◉ **Break type**: Right reef point.
- ◉ **Conditions**: All swells, offshore in easterly winds.
- ◉ **Hazards/tips**: Long walling wave, entry and exit can be tricky in big swells.
- ◉ **Sleeping**: Doolin ▸▸ p134.

This is a long walling right that breaks over a jagged limestone reef, a very underestimated spot. While surfers turn up and eye Crab Island, most miss the pearl of a right that breaks nearby. It has long, walling waves that are ridable up to 8 ft. The wave is best surfed at low to mid tide, before the waves start to push onto the ledges making exit difficult. The reef at these breaks is sharp and dangerous. Best left to experienced surfers.

18 Lahinch

- ◉ **Break type**: Beach break.
- ◉ **Conditions**: Medium to big swells, offshore in easterly winds.
- ◉ **Hazards/tips**: Excellent beach for beginners to advanced surfers.
- ◉ **Sleeping**: Lahinch ▸▸ p135.

A very popular beach that is the centre of the local surf community. It works through the tides and can have good to excellent banks. Good place for beginners and advanced surfers. Busy peaks by town, spread out north and south.

16 Swinno at Crab Island

Ireland West Coast Breaks Doolin Point to Lahinch

19 Cornish Left

19 The Lefts

- **Break type**: Left reefs.
- **Conditions**: Medium to big swells, offshore in easterly winds.
- **Hazards/tips**: Good quality waves, experienced surfers.
- **Sleeping**: Lahinch ▸▸ p135.

Heading south from Lahinch, there are a number of left reefs that pick up more swell as you go. The first is **The Left**, which sits at the end of the beach and is the most popular. In good swells it produces long walls up to 300 m and is best from low to mid tide. Just to the south is **Cornish Left**, a faster, hollower wave that works through the tides. **Cregg** has a left and right that works through the tides, and a low tide right. Next is **Aussie Left**, a quality wave that needs a big swell to fire.

20 Green Point

- **Break type**: Right.
- **Conditions**: Big swells, offshore in easterly winds.
- **Hazards/tips**: Advanced surfers only.
- **Sleeping**: Lahinch/Kilkee ▸▸ p135.

A huge right-hand peak that comes alive in massive swells. One to watch and admire, unless you have your tow-in set up with you.

21 Spanish Point

- **Break type**: Reef break.
- **Conditions**: All swells, offshore in easterly winds.
- **Hazards/tips**: Series of excellent reefs.
- **Sleeping**: Lahinch/Kilkee ▸▸ p135.

There are three right-hand reefs here. The **outer point** picks up a massive amount of swell and can be huge. It can look perfect but upon closer inspection its size can be awesome. The **middle point** is a high quality right-hand reef. It picks up a medium swell and has some great walls and hollow sections. There is an easy paddle out. Best at mid tide. The **inside point** needs a large swell to get going. It is a fast, walling wave that tends to be the most sheltered from the wind.

The houses around Spanish Point are frequently swamped by surfers parking there for the breaks. Make sure you park respectfully and don't rock up with the stereo pumping. This will quickly lose what little goodwill is left. Farmers have been known to move cars that have parked irresponsibly with their tractors.

22 Doughmore

- **Break type**: Beach break.
- **Conditions**: Small to medium swells, offshore in southeasterly winds.
- **Hazards/tips**: Difficult access.
- **Sleeping**: Kilkee ▸▸ p135.

A wonderful, dune-backed beach that picks up heaps of swell. There are some excellent

21 Roystone's Right at Spanish Point

fast and hollow banks but when the swell hits head-high it tends to close out. Works on all tides. Access is a bit tricky here as you have to cross farmland to reach the sea. Always check with the farmer first and make sure you don't block any of the access roads.

23 Doonbeg Castle

- **Break type**: Reef.
- **Conditions**: Big swells, offshore in southwesterly.
- **Hazards/tips**: Great spot when other breaks closing out.
- **Sleeping**: Kilkee ⟫ p135.

This is a pretty good left-hand reef that produces walling lefts in massive swells. The corner by the castle is sheltered and allows surfing here when other breaks are closing out. Take the turn by the church, just south of the village. Works on all tides except low.

24 Killard

- **Break type**: Beach break.
- **Conditions**: Big swells, offshore in southwesterly.
- **Hazards/tips**: Sheltered spot.
- **Sleeping**: Kilkee ⟫ p135.

Another sheltered spot to check in big swells, this time offshore in southwesterly or westerly winds. Easy parking. Works through all tides and can produce walling lefts and rights, depending on the sandbanks.

25 Farrihy Bay

- **Break type**: Beach break.
- **Conditions**: Small to medium swells, offshore in easterly winds.
- **Hazards/tips**: Consistent spot.
- **Sleeping**: Kilkee ⟫ p135.

Just north of Kilkee, this bay picks up heaps of swell and can have some great beach-break waves in small swells. Tends to close out in bigger swells. Take the turning for Corbally and follow it to the bay.

Listings

THE GILL

22 Doughmore

Strandhill

This is a popular beach resort for surfers and families from the Sligo area. It has a great stretch of beach and a large surfing community, including **Perfect Day** surf shop, T071-9128488.

✴ Flat spells

Ancient monument **Carrowmore Megalithic Cemetery**, just to the southwest of Sligo, is a collection of over 60 tombs, half of which are open to the public. **Golf** Check out **Strandhill GC**, T071-9168188, a par-69 links course.

Sleeping

E **Strandhill Lodge and Hostel**, Shore Rd, T071-9168313, is on the seafront and popular with surfers, with doubles and bunk rooms.
Camping **Strandhill Caravan and Camping Park**, on the airport road, T071-9168111, open Easter to mid-Sep.

Easkey

This is a pretty, traditional Irish village centred around the main street. It has been heavily influenced by the influx of surfers – Mickey Dora once lived here. The surf breaks have proved so popular that changing facilities have been installed by the reefs.

Sleeping

Easkey Surfing and Information Centre on the main street, T096-49020, will have an up-to-date list of surfer-friendly rooms and apartments.
Camping **Atlantic 'N' Riverside Caravan and Camping Park**, in the village, open Apr-end Sep, is a 5-min walk from the breaks. Register at the Post office, T096-49001.

Inishcrone (Enniscrone)

Popular holiday resort with the Irish that really only opens from Easter, but if you do turn up off season ask in the pubs as very often they'll be able to help you find B&B accommodation. **Walsh's Pub** on Main St has live music and does good food. It also has internet access. During Easter weekend you may find the pubs closed, but one of them may have a crafty lock-in.

Flat spells
Golf Enniscrone GC, T096-36297, is a par-72 championship links course. There is also a pitch and putt course in the village for those who prefer to fool around than play a round.
Spa To unwind, check out **Killcullen Bath House**, T096-36238, where you can get steam baths, massage and seaweed baths.

Sleeping
D **Gowan House B&B**, on Pier Rd, T096-36238, is worth checking out.
Camping **Atlantic Caravan Park**, on the seafront, T096-36132, has excellent access to the beach. It has static caravans as well as room for vans.

Ballycastle

This small and pretty village, with its sloping central street, is a popular tourist destination with people drawn to the Céide Fields site.

Flat spells
Céide Fields An extensive 5,000-year-old settlement first uncovered in the 1930s. There is an impressive visitors' centre at this very important archaeological site, T096-43325.

Sleeping
D **Céide House**, Main St, T096-43105, is a lively pub with good value rooms open year round.
D **Suantrai**, Killala Rd, T096-43040, has great rooms in a central location but is only open during the peak summer months.

Mullet Peninsula

An awesome stretch of pristine coastline with huge sand beaches and many undiscovered reefs. A ship from the Spanish Armada was scuttled in Blacksod Bay. Ardelly Point was also home to a whaling station in the early 20th century. The main settlement is **Belmullet**, a small town with a few places to eat and drink. The **Square Meal Restaurant**, on Carter Sq, offers hearty post-surf food.

Sleeping
D **Chez Nous**, Church Rd, T097-82167, has 3 double rooms with showers.
F **Kilcommon Lodge Hostel**, just off the peninsula in Pollatomish, 20 mins to the east of Belmullet via the R314 towards Ballycastle, T097-84621, offers the cheapest accommodation, with excellent dorm and double rooms.

Directory
Bank: Ulster Bank, on Main St, has an ATM.
Tourist information: on Barrack St, T097-81500, can offer advice on accommodation.

Achill Island

This windswept peninsula juts into the Atlantic, forming a beautiful and typically Celtic landscape – when the sun is out it is stunningly pretty, when the sky is grey and the wind blows, it is harsh and bleak. Even during the summer the beaches are amazingly quiet with few tourists venturing this far.

Sleeping
C-D **Wave Crest Hotel**, in Dooagh, T098-43115, is very reasonable off season and has a lively bar.

F **Valley House Hostel**, T098-45392, is another good choice and can be found on the road out to Dugort from Bunacurry. Good access to the beach.
F **Wild Haven Hostel**, in Achill Sound, T098-45392, is an excellent hostel offering good food and a welcoming fire.
Camping **Seal Caves Caravan and Camping Park**, T098-43262, open May-Sep, is well placed by the beaches at Dugort.

Eating/drinking
For a good evening meal check out **Calvey's Restaurant** in Keel. It has good seafood and locally produced steaks. There is a **Spar** supermarket in Keel if you need to stock up on supplies.

Directory
There is a Bank of Ireland ATM and **Tourist information** at Achill Sound.

Louisburgh

This is a small town with a population of about 500, named after the American battle of Louisburgh (1758).

Sleeping
Camping Old Head Forest Caravan and Camping Park, by the beach at Clew Bay, T087-648688, open Jun-Sep, has mobile homes to let from €320/week.

Doolin

This tiny village that stretches out along the valley, has become a centre of Irish music. The pubs have regular live bands that play to audiences including locals, surfers and US tourists. Boats run from the quay to the Aran Islands. There are no banks or ATMs in Doolin.

Airports → Dublin T01-8141111, www.dublinairport.com; Shannon T061-712000, www.shannonairport.com; Cork T021-4313131, www.corkairport.com; Kerry T066-9764644, www.kerryairport.ie; Aer Lingus T0818 365000, www.aerlingus.com. **Coaches** → Bus Eireann T01-8366111, www.buseireann.ie. **Car hire** → Avis T0870-6060100; Europcar T0870-6075000; Hertz T08708-448844. **Petrol prices** → €0.95/litre.
Ferries → P&O T0870-2424999, www.poportsmouth.com; Brittany FerriesT0870-3665333, www.brittany-ferries.com; Irish Ferries T08705-171717, www.irishferries.com; Sea France T0870-5711711, www.seafrance.com. **Rail links** → Iranrod Eireann www.irishrail.ie, T01-8363333.

❂ Flat spells

Aran Islands Catch the ferry that runs from the harbour out to the Aran Islands for a great day out when the swell hasn't materialized. **Caves** Peer into the sea caves to the north of the harbour. One is called Hell and is a drop into a maize of sea caves, called the Green Holes of Doolin, that only the most experienced cavers should enter. **Cliffs of Moher** Spectacular and a test of anyone's head for heights.

☺ Sleeping

C-D Atlantic View House, Pier Rd, T065-7074189, is a large, comfortable B&B with great views of the sea.
C Rainbow's End, T065-7074900, is a comfortable, clean B&B.
E Doolin Hostel, T065-7074006, is popular with walkers and just a short stagger from the pubs. It has dorms and double rooms.
F Aille River Hostel, by the river at the top end of the village, T065-7074260, is a converted farmhouse and very popular.
Camping Nagles Doolin Camping and Caravan Park, T065-7074458, open May-end Sep, is a great place for campervans. It is within walking distance of the breaks, has fully equipped kitchens, a phone and a shop.

◑ Eating/drinking

McDermott's is where the locals go for good beer, pub grub and live music. **Doolin Café** serves excellent dishes including seafood specials, good if a bit pricey, while **Doolin Deli** is definitely worth checking if you need to stock up on provisions or snacks.

Lahinch

Lahinch is a popular tourist centre with a long sandy beach backed by sea defences. It is also one of Ireland's main surfing centres with a surf club of over 50 members. The beach is pretty safe for beginners, but Tom Buckley from the Lahinch Surf Shop urges that beginners take care. "Two hours before full tide the beach is covered and if there is a

big swell it can be very difficult getting out of the water. For beginners the area between O'Looney's pub and the first lifeguard tower is the safest area." You can find the surf shop on the Old Promenade, T065-7081543. They also do a surf report on T0818-365180, www.lahinchsurfshop.com.

❂ Flat spells

Golf There is a highly impractical (if world class) golf course with prices to match. The Castle course has green fees of €110 and reservations need to be made 3 months in advance! There is a great seafront pitch 'n' putt course on the way into town from Doolin. **Sea World and Leisure Centre** Claims to have "enough activities for a full day out". Pool, jacuzzi and sauna – perfect for a post-surf chill out – plus some fish in tanks.

☺ Sleeping

E St Mildred's B&B, Church St, near the sea, T065-7081489, great rooms, beach views and very reasonable prices.
F Lahinch Hostel, Chuch St, T065-7081040, clean and comfortable.
Camping Lahinch Camping and Caravan Park, on the southern edge of town a short walk from the sea, T065-7081424, open May-Sep.

◑ Eating/drinking

Mrs O'Brien's for pub grub and very pricey internet access – luckily the live music and match screenings are free! **O'Looney's** looks out over the sea and offers good pub grub and a nightclub after sundown. For a chilled-out pub with music head to **Flanagans** or, if you want to give it large, get down to **Coast** – a modern club open at weekends.

❶ Directory

Banks: no banks, but there is an **ATM** at the northern end of Main St. Also on Main St are the **Post office**, a petrol station and a pharmacy. **Surf school**: John McCarthy runs Lahinch Surf School, T096-09667, and also rents equipment. **Tourist information**: on

Main St, T065-7082082, can book accommodation.

Kilkee

Packed in the summer, Kilkee is best avoided, but out of season it is a much more attractive proposition. O'Curry St boasts a **Bank of Ireland** and ATM.

☺ Sleeping

C-D Bayview B&B is in a good location and open year round, T065-9056058.
F Kilkee Hostel, O'Curry St, T065-9056209, has comfortable dorm rooms and is close to the seafront.
Camping Green Acres Caravan and Camping Park at Doonaha, T065-9057011, open Apr-Sep, sits on the coast and offers beach access and static caravans.

Virgin in a greenhouse

DEMI TAYLOR

Southwest Ireland

Surfing in southwest Ireland is a young sport in an old land. The vast open countryside is breathtaking, with weathered mountain peaks looking down on the green, lush wind-sculpted landscape. The craggy coastline can change from plunging cliffs to wide open beaches at the turn of a headland. The surfers in this region may lack a long surfing tradition, but they make up for it in sheer enthusiasm. Many drive for hours to reach the breaks that are catching the swell, a test of endurance not helped by the narrow and twisting roads of the region.

While the surf may not have the consistency of the north, it has many other things going for it. The line-ups are friendly and open to travelling surfers who arrive with a smile and a nod, and who take their place at the edge of the line-up. There are waves of amazing quality that come to life when the swell does kick in, including legendary Inch Reef that breaks for a mile and Ballydavid Point with its huge grinding walls. If the surf is flat, the countryside is a joy to explore. In Dingle, sit outside Dick Mack's pub with a pint of the black stuff and hear stories of when Dolly Parton dropped by, incognito (if that's possible). Or the day Julia Roberts was in town. Stars seem to love the region because, whether you're a Hollywood A-list celebrity or a surfer sitting out a flat spell, everyone is treated the same way. There are many spots around Europe that are more consistent than

Southwest Ireland board guide

Fatboy Flyer
Shaper: Chops Lascelles of Beachbeat Surfboards

▸▸ 6'10" x 19¾" x 2½"

▸▸ Great all-round board that catches waves yet is flexible and manoeuvrable.

▸▸ At this size good for advanced surfers, but available from 6'8" to 7'7" depending on ability.

Performance shortboard
Shaper: Chops Lascelles of Beachbeat Surfboards

▸▸ 6'3" x 18½" x 2¼"

▸▸ Good, high performance shortboard that is great for Inch Reef and hollow breaks like Coumeenole.

ⓘ Boards by **Beachbeat Surfboards**
Factory: Laminations, St Agnes, Cornwall
T00 44 (0)1872-553918
www.beachbeatsurfboards.co.uk
www.aggiesurf.com
or contact Lam2574@aol.com

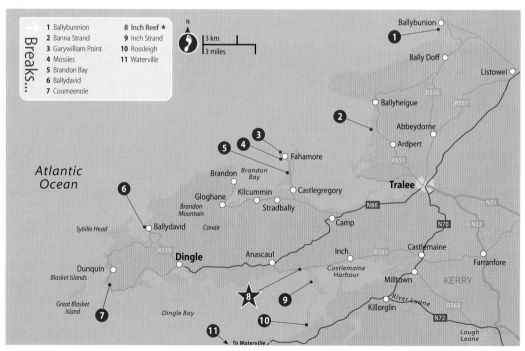

Breaks...

1 Ballybunnion	8 Inch Reef ★
2 Banna Strand	9 Inch Strand
3 Garywilliam Point	10 Rossleigh
4 Mossies	11 Waterville
5 Brandon Bay	
6 Ballydavid	
7 Coumeenole	

southwest Ireland, but when it comes to the people, the places and the potential, there are few places better.

"Local surfers on the peninsula are very few. In the winter it's pretty quiet, but in the summer the number of surfers from France, England, Cornwall, Wales or guys from Cork has grown a lot. On bank holidays, nearly every car has got boards on the roof."
Ben, Finn McCool's surf shop, Dingle

Coastline

The southwest corner of Ireland has a wonderful green and rolling landscape, windswept countryside topped by towering hills and jagged coastline scoured by the raging Atlantic. Summers here are warm and mild and the blue waters around Dingle have the clarity of a Caribbean bay. The many hidden bays and open beaches provide rich surfing when the northwesterly swells roll in. Brandon Bay to the north is the most consistent area. Hidden in the fjord-like Dingle Bay, Inch and other less obvious reefs are like sleeping giants, waiting for a westerly swell to hit. And to the south, the amazing Ballinskelligs Bay has a whole raft of boulder reefs waiting for the southwesterly swell lines to roll in. In this region, if you're willing to get out and explore, you will truly be rewarded.

Localism

The most famous wave in the area is Inch Reef, which can be busy and hassly when it's breaking on a weekend or bank holidays. "Inch works so infrequently that you really have to be on the peninsula to be on it," says Ben from Finn McCool's. "All the Cork surfers will come up and be here by lunchtime, 'cause it takes so long to get here, so the line-up starts to fill up by lunchtime." But generally, around the southwest there is a pretty mellow vibe in the water. Travelling surfers who are friendly and chilled will find they get a lot more out of the experience than ones who go charging and hassling and aiming to catch more waves than anyone else in the line-up.

Top local surfers Paul McCarthy and Tom McCormack are two of the few year-round surfers on the Dingle Peninsula. As Paul says, "There is still a very small surfing population here. Just a couple of guys really on the peninsula and about ten guys in Tralee. A couple of the guys in Tralee are pretty handy, but we have nothing the likes of Cain Killcullen, but young guys will come through." In Cork the stand-out surfers include Graham Collins and Jason Conroy, in Kerry Alan O'Reardon, Alan Hanson, Jason Malone are leading the way. Further east, in the Tramore region, John McCarthy and Dave Blunt are among the region's best.

Getting around

The roads in Ireland are not built for speed but to get you there eventually. Some go by the longest, most convoluted way you could imagine. Even the relatively easy task of reaching the next bay around

What's the surf like on the Dingle Peninsula? Inconsistent. When it's good it's very good, but when it's bad, it's horrid. It can be good for like two hours of the day at a certain stage. I've seen tourists driving around for a whole week saying they've had no waves, and I've been surfing every day. They turn up to spots at the wrong tides, with the wrong wind directions or swell directions. Even whether it's a spring or neap tide can have an effect. That's why most people who are in Ireland just for a week head north. But then again, I have just surfed perfect Coumeenole for the past three weeks.

Paul McCarthy, Dingle local surfer

the headland can become a lengthy trek inland before turning back to the coast. But once you accept that most trips will take longer than you think, you can sit back and enjoy the scenery.

Dingle Harbour

DEMI TAYLOR

DEBBIE TAYLOR

Minzie Mynne in action

was it. The only surfers I'd seen. Gone, into the sunset. I just wanted to find out where they were going surfing and have someone else to go surfing with.

"The next day I went down the coast 40 miles with my boss for a spot of fishing and chucked my board in the back of the van, on the off chance. We got down to this spot and it was like 3 ft, perfect, clean surf on this mile-long beach at Castlefreak and nobody in the water. I got changed and into the water and about ten minutes later I looked up to see the car that I'd chased the day before, pull up and the guys pile out. We met in the water, exchanged numbers and I started surfing with them in western Cork and Kerry. Every weekend we'd just go off and explore. There were about eight to twelve surfers in the Cork area, about half a dozen of the old guys – Dave Nagle, Fred Jump, Robin Hodger. The guys in the car were Graham Collins (one of the major reps for the Irish surf industry now), Jason who runs Tubes Surf Shop and Johnny Buggler, a friend of theirs, an artist. I've kept in touch with those guys ever since. We had a party a couple of years ago – a sort of tenth anniversary of when we met. And they're still really good friends to this day."

Martin 'Minzie' Mynne

Friends: scary ...

"What makes Ireland special? The people – they're really welcoming people. I went to Cork, Crosshaven, in 1992 for a two-week boat building job and ended up staying for three years. I went without surfboards and the first week I was there, on the south coast I went up the cliffs and saw these perfect 8-ft waves, nobody in. So I flew home that weekend and came back out with three surfboards. I surfed there for eleven months without seeing another surfer. There were surfers there 40 or 50 miles down the coast just on beaches but there were these points and reefs around that I just came upon by chance. The three main waves I surfed I walked to – I didn't have any transport. I'd just see the swell out on the island from where I was working and I'd go and surf. Alone.

"One day I was going into Cork City. I got off the bus and was walking up the road as I saw this car come round the corner with surfboards on the roof. So I'm waving at them madly, just trying to wave them down. These were the first surfers I'd seen in months and they went past me, all just looking at me like 'Whose this lunatic?' – I had long hair at the time. They stopped at the traffic lights so I start giving chase, running down the road after them. As I get to the car, they're looking back at me through the window and they drive off. I don't think the lights had even changed. And that

... or what?

"We had to wait for my mate's mum to get home from Mass so we could use the car to go surfing. As we set off there was this guy walking along the road with big long dreadlocks and dungarees on. We were parked up at some traffic lights and looked behind to see this guy running down the road after us, waving, and we were all like, who is he? So we drove off.

"Back then we didn't know about tides, wind, swell. We went to the beach every day just hoping there would be some waves. There was nobody surfing then – you would have fitted the whole surfing population of the southwest in one car. So we pulled up at our local beach the next day and there was Martin – the guy we'd seen chasing us down the road the day before. It was like 3 ft and he shredded it big time. And that's how we met. He pretty much taught us how to surf – about winds, tides, swell charts. He used to plague us with video footage of him surfing Nias and Bali and say, 'When you've finished school you should go there – you should go there just once in your life to see the perfection.' We were probably all destined to do something else, but he really did teach us to love surfing."

Graham Collins, Irish surfer

Breaks

1 Ballybunnion

- **Break type**: Beach and reef.
- **Conditions**: All swells, offshore in easterly winds.
- **Hazards/tips**: Three popular breaks.
- **Sleeping**: Ballybunion ›› *p143*.

There is a good stretch of beach with easy access and some fairly good banks. It has lefts and rights at all states of tide. Towards the southern end of the beach is a left that breaks over rocks and boulders. This spot produces good walls and the odd barrel section. It likes a low tide otherwise it gets too fat. At the northern end of the beach is a right that starts breaking in front of the cliff and peels through to the inside with nice walls to attack. The right works on all tides except low.

2 Banna Strand

- **Break type**: Beach break.
- **Conditions**: All swells, offshore in easterly winds.
- **Hazards/tips**: Beautiful beach.
- **Sleeping**: Ballyheigue ›› *p143*.

This massive, open beach is exposed to a medium westerly and northwesterly swell. The beach offers some great peaks with the northern end being the most sheltered and the southern end picking up the most swell. There are a couple of rivermouths worth checking out for sandbanks. Follow the R551 from Tralee or Ballybunnion.

3 Garywilliam Point

- **Break type**: Reef break.
- **Conditions**: Small to medium swells, offshore in southeasterly winds.
- **Hazards/tips**: Exposed reef for experienced surfers.
- **Sleeping**: Dingle Peninsula ›› *p143*.

Out on the end of the point breaks this exposed right-hand reef. It picks up plenty of swell but is easily affected by winds and is best checked when there is little wind or it is coming from the southeast. The wave hits and throws out sending fast, hollow barrels racing along the shallow reef. Best at low tide.

4 Mossies

- **Break type**: Reef break.
- **Conditions**: Medium swells, offshore in southeasterly winds.
- **Hazards/tips**: Offshore reef with mellow waves.
- **Sleeping**: Dingle Peninsula ›› *p143*.

A mellow reef break that has both lefts and rights peeling along a reef just inside Brandon Bay. It's a bit of a paddle out to the wave, which is best at low to mid tide. Follow the road out towards Fahamore.

5 Brandon Bay

- **Break type**: Beach break.
- **Conditions**: All swells, offshore in southeasterly/southerly swells.
- **Hazards/tips**: Huge bay exposed to northwesterly swell.
- **Sleeping**: Dingle Peninsula ›› *p143*.

This is the most likely spot to have waves on the Dingle Peninsula as it faces due northwest. Take a drive up from Dingle and park on the pass at Conair to check the bay. Just south of Mossies is **Dumps**, a section of hollow peaks that works at all tides. It picks up plenty of swell producing short, barrelling lefts and rights. Further round the bay at Stradbally is **Peaks**, a section of good banks that work from mid to high tide. At

THE GILL

3 Garywilliam Point

Southwest Ireland

Air — Sea

°F Averages
°C

90	30
70	20
50	10
30	0

J F M A M J J A S O N D

5/4/3 Boots & gloves | 5/4/3 Boots | 3/2 | 4/3

Kilcummin is a popular area that is offshore in southerly winds, but the waves here aren't as powerful nor the banks as good.

6 Ballydavid

- **Break type**: Right point break.
- **Conditions**: Big swells, offshore in southerly winds.
- **Hazards/tips**: Heavy wave.
- **Sleeping**: Dingle Peninsula ▶ *p143*.

This right point is a real quality wave that only comes to life in the biggest swells. Definitely a spot for experienced surfers as it has a difficult take-off, heavy, hollow waves and long hold-downs. Works on all tides. Check it from the harbour in the small village of Ballydavid. If it's on, break out your gun. On the other side of the bay is **Black Strand**, a left that breaks at high tide. This part of the beach picks up more swell.

7 Coumeenole

- **Break type**: Beach break.
- **Conditions**: All swells, offshore in northeasterly winds.
- **Hazards/tips**: Hollow powerful break, not for beginners.
- **Sleeping**: Dingle Peninsula ▶ *p143*.

This is a very popular spot with local surfers, a beach break that really packs a punch. There are some great banks here including a hollow, heavy right that works from low up to three-quarter tide. A board breaker. There's a steep road down the cliffs to the beach, demanding careful parking – check your handbrake!

"Ireland is cold, wet, inconsistent – but perfect."
Graham Collins, Cork surfer

7 Coumeenole

5 Brandon Bay ▶ *p139*

8 Inch Reef

- **Break type**: Right reef.
- **Condition**: Medium to big swells.
- **Size**: 3-8 ft.
- **Length**: Up to 800 m (according to legend).
- **Swell**: Westerly or big northwesterly.
- **Wind**: Northeasterly.
- **Tide**: Not high.
- **Bottom**: Flat, rock reef.
- **Entry/exit**: Over the rocks from the cliff.
- **Hazards/tips**: Rips, tricky entry and exit.
- **Sleeping**: Dingle Peninsula ▸▸ p143.

A great name for a reef that can break for nearly half a mile in perfect conditions. Inch needs a big northwesterly swell or a solid westerly swell to get into Dingle Bay. Check it from the R561 that runs above the break. It will be packed if it breaks on a weekend as all surfers from the greater area converge here. "You can still get it pretty quiet during the week, early morning or in the winter," says local surfer Paul McCarthy. There can be punishing rips pushing away from the peak. Spectacular location with views all down the peninsula.

If you like Inch Reef, try Immessouane in Morocco (see page 352) or Ribeira d'Ilhas in Portugal (see page 302).

8 Inch Reef

6 Ballydavid Bay

Ireland: hate it or love it

Southwest Ireland: March 1991
It became clear after five minutes in the brown, woodchipped toilet that I didn't want the house. Rain lashed against the windows, whilst outside a group of daggy and forlorn sheep stuck their arses into the squall. Snapping and cracking, polythene bags snagged on the barbed-wire fence in the wind. Later, I steered the Land Rover up a muddy track near the pier, where unmistakably, despite the 90 mph onshore, there was a cranking right-hander.

"Maybe we should check out the house again in better weather," I said.

Southwest Ireland: January 2003
"I guess this'll be the last time you surf this," Paul McCarthy said bluntly, as we sat in the line-up during a lull at Ballydavid. I stared at him in disbelief and then at the village looking like a postcard under Mount Brandon. On the right Sybille Head and the Blaskets in their grandeur against the blue water in the low sun. This wave, the one I found, the line-ups I worked out... my wave.

And I miss it. And I miss the 5 a.m. call with K2 buoy reading 18 ft and rising, the wind in the right direction and a four-hour drive to a smoking boulder point.

But, living here now in southwest France, I do not miss the daggy sheep.

Nick Gammon is a respected surfer and painter (see example below) who spent more than ten years living on, exploring and surfing the Dingle Peninsula.

Ocean © Nick Gammon

8 Inch Reef

10 Glenbeigh

Men only

11 Waterville

9 Inch Strand

○ **Break type**: Beach break.
◐ **Conditions**: Big swells, offshore in easterly winds.
❶ **Hazards/tips**: Mellow beach.
● **Sleeping**: Dingle Peninsula ›› p143.

A stunning location looking down Dingle Bay with spectacular scenery on both sides. The beach is quite mellow and has a feel of Llangennith or Saunton as the waves lack real punch. A good spot for beginners or longboarders. Parking available at the beach.

10 Rossleigh

○ **Break type**: Beach break and boulder point.
◐ **Conditions**: Medium to big swells, offshore in southeasterly winds.
❶ **Hazards/tips**: Mellow beach.
● **Sleeping**: Glenbeigh ›› p144.

On the south side of the bay there is another stretch of beach and a boulder point accessed at Glenbeigh Wood. Picks up more swell than Inch, and is offshore in winds from the southeast.

11 Waterville

○ **Break type**: Beach break.
◐ **Conditions**: Big swells, offshore in northeasterly winds.
❶ **Hazards/tips**: Sheltered bay.
● **Sleeping**: Waterville ›› p144.

This bay only works in medium or big southwesterly or big westerly swells. To the west of Waterville is a stretch of average beach break. To the left of the village are a number of boulder reefs that work at various stages of tide. At low there is a left that breaks out from the house towards the edge of the cliff. At low to mid there is a right that breaks towards the house into a channel. At half to high there is a walling left and inside that is another left that breaks at the same time towards the beach.

Listings

Ballybunnion

In order to avoid a mammoth drive around the Shannon Estuary – a circuit of about 140 km – hop on the Killimer–Tarbert ferry (see Transport for details). The handily placed year-round **Ferry House Hostel** in Tarbert's square has dorms and twins, T068-36555. Heading along the R551 to the resort town of Ballybunion, the **Parklands Holiday Park** on Listowel Rd, T068-272275, open May-Sep, has mobile homes to rent.

⊖ Transport
Shannon Ferry, T065-9053124, www.shannonferries.com. The Killimer–Tarbert crossing takes about 20 mins, regular services throughout the day (last ferry from Killimer 2100, from Tarbert 2130), single for a car load €14, return €22.

Ballyheigue

Heading south along the R551, Ballyheigue has a couple of camping options and all the basic amenities you need including a supermarket, post office, pubs and takeaways.

⊜ Sleeping
Camping   Sir Roger's Caravan & Camping Park, just back from Banna Beach, T066-7134730, is a full-on holiday park, open May-Oct, with mobile homes also available. **Casey's Caravan & Camping Park**, Main St, T066-7133195, open 29 Apr-15 Sep, have pitches for tourers and tents as well as mobile homes.

Tralee

To the south lies Tralee, capital of Kerry and home of the world-famous Rose of Tralee, the beauty pageant/festival that takes over the town in August.

✿ Flat spells
Aqua Dome   Go mad in the waterpark or chill out in the sauna or steam room, T066-7128899. **Cinema**   Hit the **Kerry**

Omniplex Cinema just next to the tourist information office to catch the latest movie. **Dogs**   Head to the **Kingdom Greyhound Stadium** in Oakview, at the north of the town, for an evening at the dogs. Races are held Tue and Fri, from 2000, T066-7180008. **Golf   Tralee GC** is an 18-hole links course whose green fees are a snip at €150. If you 'forgot' to hit the cashpoint and only have some spare change, you could always try **Aqua Golf**, an 18-hole miniature course at the Aqua Dome.

Dingle Peninsula

In a country that has taken Europe to its heart, Dingle in all its beauty sits at the most westerly point of this new superstate. The harbour here is the adopted home of Fungie the dolphin and a whole micro-industry has sprung up around him. The town of Dingle is itself small and cosmopolitan, lying within the *Gaeltacht* or Irish-speaking community. The town is based around Main St and Goat St where traditional painted shopfronts and bars blend with businesses.

✿ Flat spells
Blasket Islands   The Blaskets, a group of islands off the coastline, were inhabited until 1953 and are now home to colonies of puffins, gannets and guillemots. Along the way you may spot dolphins, porpoises and whales. In the autumn, Atlantic seals make their annual trip to Great Blasket. Ask at the tourist office for details.
Cinema   Catch a movie at the **Phoenix** on Dykegate. **Diving   Dingle Marina Diving Centre**, T066-9152422, offers everything from try dives for first-timers to open water dives for the more experienced.
Fishing   Sea angling is available out of Dingle harbour for about €35 for a half day. Shore angling is also popular with some excellent spots near Coumeenole and Ballydavid.
Fungie the dolphin   There are boat trips out of the harbour to see Fungie the dolphin, but you can also see him from the nearby beach. The dolphin first appeared as

THE GILL

Reef watch Southwest Ireland

a young adult in 1984 and has become the region's major attraction. If Fungie stimulates your interests in all things aquatic, you can visit **Oceanworld** on Dingle Harbour, which has a shark tank and an ocean tunnel tank.

Golf Dingle is home to an 18-hole, par-72 links course near the Three Sisters, out towards Ballyferriter, T066-9156255. For the less serious golfer, there's a pitch and putt course just outside Dingle on the road to Ventry (R559). **Massage Dingle Natural Therapy Centre**, Coast Guard Cottage, Cooleen, T066-9152474, offers acupuncture, reiki, shiatsu, chiropractic and individual yoga sessions to revive your body after a gruelling session. **Mountain Mt Brandon** is Ireland's second largest peak, situated on the north coast of the Dingle Peninsula. At 950 ft, it is a serious trek, but the views it reveals are worth the walk.

Sleeping

There are plenty of sleeping options on the Dingle Peninsula but the best place to base yourself is Dingle itself which has a plethora of B&Bs.

B **An Capall Dubh**, Green St, T066-9151105, is an excellent option, especially for couples. The 6 B&B rooms are bright and clean with en suite bathrooms. They also have 2 reasonably priced self-catering apartments for 6-8 people with board storage facilities. C **O'Collian**, Dykegate, T066-9151937, is a centrally located and well run B&B with en suite facilities.

There is plenty of hostel accommodation on the peninsula.

E-G **Ballintaggart House Hostel**, on Racecourse Rd to the east of the town, T066-9151454, is an excellent option. Originally a hunting lodge in the 1700s, it has been well converted into a hostel with spacious dorms, €13 a bed, and double

rooms from €40. It also has camping pitches. A free shuttle service runs between the town and hostel.

F-G **Grapevine Hostel**, centrally located on Dykegate, T066-9151434, is pretty pokey, with dorms available from €13.

Ballydavid

On the north shore at Ballydavid, **Tigh An Phoist Hostel**, on Bothar Bui, T066-9155109, is open Apr-Oct and offers good access to Ballydavid Point as well as bike hire. Beds from €12. Also near Ballydavid, at Gallarus, is **Teach An Aragail Campsite**, T066-9155143. This friendly spot is open May-Sep and is Europe's most westerly site.

Eating/drinking

Adams, on Main St, is a pub/restaurant and as traditional as they come. This mid-priced, dark, cosy bar serves, among other more basic fare, excellent locally caught crab salad. **Café Po'oka**, on Goat St, dish up reasonably priced, locally grown organic produce wherever possible – it's a great place to grab a coffee or an all-day breakfast and listen to some top tunes. The walls double as a gallery for original paintings. **An Café Lit Er Tha**, Dykegate St, is a café-bookshop that serves great, affordable soups and snacks. For an evening meal, try mid-priced **Global Village** on Main St, open Mar-Nov, which fuses foods from across the world to create a varied menu. **Dick Mack's** is one of Ireland's most famous pubs with a Hollywood Boulevard-style pavement outside with all their famous visitors recorded in stone. They include the likes of Dolly Parton, Julia Roberts and the Hothouse Flowers. Its interior has remained unchanged from the days when it doubled as a bar and hardware store.

Bars and clubs

"Once a month we run a hip-hop, funk and soul night that attracts a lot of local surfers," says Ben of Finn McCool's. "Those nights rock, we call it '**The Big Pay-back**'. Drop by for details. Or try the **Conair Bar** on Spa St who have a cool funk band on a Sat night."

Shopping

Stock up at **Garvey's Supervalu** on Holy Ground. **Finn McCool's – The Surf Company**, on Green St, T066-9150833, www.finmccools.ie, sells hardware and accessories and also rents out equipment.

Directory

Banks: a couple on Main St. **Bike hire**: try Foxy John's on Main St from €9 a day. **Internet**: Dingle Internet Café, Main St, open 7 days a week, €5/hr. **Pharmacy**: Holy Ground. **Post office**: Main St.. **Tourist information**: Strand St, next to the pier.

Glenbeigh

Heading south on the N70, Glenbeigh sits on the Iveragh Peninsula, home of the stunning road circuit known as the Ring of Kerry. Camp in the village within site of Rossbeigh beach at **Glenross Caravan and Camping Park**, T066-9768451, www.killarneycamping.com. Open May-Sep, they also have mobile homes available from €220 for 6 people.

Waterville

This is a popular seaside resort on the western edge of the Ring of Kerry.

Sleeping

There are loads of pricey B&Bs on Main St. Alternatively, try
E **Peter's Place Hostel**, Main St,

Airports → Dublin T01-8141111, www.dublinairport.com; Shannon T061-712000, www.shannonairport.com; Cork T021-4313131, www.corkairport.com; Kerry T066-9764644, www.kerryairport.ie; Aer Lingus T0818 365000, www.aerlingus.com. **Coaches** → Bus Eireann T01-8366111, www.buseireann.ie. **Car hire** → Avis T0870-6060100; Europcar T0870-6075000; Hertz T08708-448844. **Petrol prices** → €0.95/litre. **Ferries** → P&O T0870-2424999, www.poportsmouth.com; Brittany FerriesT0870-3665333, www.brittany-ferries.com; Irish Ferries T08705-171717, www.irishferries.com; Sea France T0870-5711711, www.seafrance.com. **Rail links** → Iranrod Eireann www.irishrail.ie, T01-8363333.

T066-9474608, overlooking the sea with dorms, doubles and camping opportunities. **Camping** South along the N70 at Caherdaniel are Wave Crest, an excellent year-round campsite overlooking Kenmare Bay, T066-9475188, www.wavecrestcamping.com, and **Glenbeg Caravan and Camping Park**, right on the beach at Kenmare, T066-9475182, open Apr-Oct 7 – a great location even if they do charge for showers.

🍴 Eating/drinking

Grab basic fare (pizzas, sandwiches etc) at basic prices at the **Beach Cove Café** on the beachfront at Waterville. If you want to splash out on some quality seafood, look no further than **Sheilin**, T066-9474231, a restaurant that turns a local catch into a fine affair – try the chunky fish soup.

Rosslare

If you are on your way in or out, a night here is just fine, otherwise there are more interesting places to be based on the south coast. Grab provisions at the **Supervalu** or head out to **MacFadden's** pub/restaurant, a bit of a trek along the N25 – food, beer, *craic*, job done.

😴 Sleeping

E **An Oige Rosslare Harbour Hostel**, Goulding St, T053-33399, is fine for a night and clean with dorm rooms for around €15. For a more sumptuous affair try the old fashioned, pretty C **St Martins B&B** on St Martins Rd, T053-33133.

Camping **Burrow Holiday Park**, 15 minutes north of the ferry port along the N740, T053-32190, www.burrowpark.com, open 15 Mar to 3 Nov, also offers mobile homes to rent.

DEMI TAYLOR

Killimer-Tarbert ferry

France

Six times world champion Kelly Slater at Bourdaines
▶▶ *p179*

THIERRY ORGANOFF

ENGLAND

English Channel

Calais
St Omer
Boulogne-sur-Mer
Arras
Dieppe
Amiens
Cherbourg-Octeville
Le Havre
Beauvais
Caen
Rouen
Roscoff
Dinard
St Malo
NORMANDY
Evreux
Versailles
Paris
Brest
Lisieux
Dreux
Quimper
Rennes
Fougères
Alencon
Chartres
BRITTANY
Laval
Le Mans
Etampes
Montgaris
St-Nazaire
Angers
Tours
Orléans
Blois
LOIRE VALLEY
BURGUNDY
Dijon
Nantes
River Loire
Cholet
Bourges
La Roche
Poitiers
Châtearoux
Nevers
Macon
Niort
LIMOUSIN
La Rochelle
Vichy
Rochfort
Saintes
Limoges
QUERCY
Clermont-Ferrand
Lyons
Royan
St Etienne
Vienne
Atlantic Ocean
Lacanau
Brive-la-Gaillarde
Bordeaux
River Dordogne
THE DORDOGNE
Cahors
LANGUEDOC
PROVENCE
ITALY
Monte-de-Marsan
Orange
Avignon
Hossegor
Montauban
Nimes
Arles
Aix-en-Provence
Nice
Biarritz
Auch
Toulouse
Montpellier
Cannes
Pau
Tarbes
Béziers
Narbonne
Marseille
Lourdes
Foix
ROUSSILLON
Toulon
SPAIN
Perpignan

p158
p165
p172
p179
p187

Star breaks...

1 La Sauzaie Quality A-frame reef that is the heart of the Vendée surf community ▸▸ p167.

2 Lacanau Heaving summer-holiday destination and traditional centre of surfing in the Gironde, its sandbanks have been the stage for surf competitions since the early days of French surfing ▸▸ p176.

3 La Gravière A thumping sandbank with heavy, hollow barrels on the golden beaches of Hossegor ▸▸ p180.

4 Les Cavaliers Another outstanding sandbank that offers year-round barrels. One of the original 'old skool' surf spots from the 1970s ▸▸ p189.

5 Lafitenia Classic right-hand point in the heart of the Côte Basque ▸▸ p193.

Motorway
A Rd
B Rd
Minor Rd
✈ Main Airports
⛴ Main Ferry Routes

N

50 km
50 miles

With endless kilometres of golden sand, perfect hollow peaks, and eternal sunshine, it's not hard to see why France has always had a such a special place at the heart of European surfing. The surf industry's leading brands were not slow to set up their European headquarters around Hossegor and Biarritz, and soon southwest France became *the* summer destination. In contrast, the northwest corner has managed to avoid the glare of the surf media spotlight, but its awesome coastline is home to many quality breaks and word is gradually filtering out about the potential of the area.

Visiting professional surfers enjoy the beach culture and chic lifestyle on offer on the Gallic coastline. Many are household names in a country that has truly taken surfing to its heart. La Republique has developed a fine tradition for producing home-grown talent. Micky Picon, Patrick Beven and Fred Robin are all high flyers on the WQS, Tim Boal is an up-and-coming talent, while Eric Rebière is only the second European male to qualify onto the WCT. Emmanuelle Joly is one of France's top female surfers, along with Marie Pierre Abgrall who became Europe's first woman to join the competitive WCT.

There are few countries to rival the French when it comes to pride in their culture. When it comes to dining, the French will never concede that any other national cuisine could rival their fish and meat dishes, garnished with fine sauces and accompanied by myriad fine wines. If it flies, crawls or walks, it will go well with garlic and lemon…

Best time to visit: **Autumn** – beautiful surf, beautiful weather and beautiful people.

France rating

Surf
★★★★

Cost of living
★★★★★

Nightlife
★★★

Accommodation
★★

Places to visit
★★★★

Essentials

Position

The largest country in western Europe, France is shaped like a massive hexagon and borders, moving anti-clockwise from its northwest flank, the Channel, the Atlantic, Spain, Andorra, the Mediterranean, Italy, Switzerland, Germany, Luxembourg and Belgium.

Language

French, as spoken by about 122 million people worldwide, is the official language of France. Although English is understood in cities and many coastal resorts, it is really important to try out your linguistic skills, even if it is just for the amusement of the French. They will either correct your appalling pronunciation, look bored and pretend they don't understand or, worse still, reply in fluent English to your best efforts. In Brittany, the Celtic language of Breton is just about surviving while the Basque influence in the southwest is flourishing.

Crime/safety

France is a relatively crime-free country. The biggest problem is with car break-ins – especially tourist cars, which are generally thought to be packed with holiday goodies, passports etc. Leaving anything visible in your car or hidden in the boot will make it an easy target. If you do need to report anything, head for the Police Nationale or Gendarmerie Nationale (same but different). Out and about, the police do have amazing powers of search and are happy to use them.

Health

EU residents need a stamped E-111 from their home country to certify that they are entitled to free (or reduced cost) healthcare. If you do need treatment, or to call out an ambulance, be aware you'll be charged (although you can claim this back later). For minor ailments head to the local *pharmacie* –there will always be a local 24-hour chemist open on rotation.

Opening hours

As lunch is generally the most important meal of the day, banks and businesses tend to open Monday to Saturday 0800-1200 and 1400-1700. For most businesses Sundays are a day of rest (which can often stretch over into Monday as well).

Sleeping

From *première classe* to designated free-camping sites, France has a good range of *l'herbergement* or accommodation options. With accommodation already pricier than its continental cousins, a *tax de séjour* is also usually levied on top of the room rates/camping prices so be prepared for this when settling the bill. **Hotels** are graded 1-4 star with an 'L' thrown in for good measure at quality establishments. At

5 best visits

① **Arcachon Dune** Surf Europe's largest sand dune ▶▶ *p184*.
② **Paris** Tour d'Eiffel, Place de la Concorde, l'Arc de Triomphe, The Louvre, Notre Dame, Disneyland… Paris has it all.
③ **The Pyrénées** The world's best snowboarding around La Mongie ▶▶ *p196*.
④ **Cesta Punta** Basque extreme squash with huge, curved, wicker claws! ▶▶ *p188*.
⑤ **Guéthary** Sit on Mickey Dora's bench and watch the old guys charge the hallowed big waves at Parlementia ▶▶ *p115*.

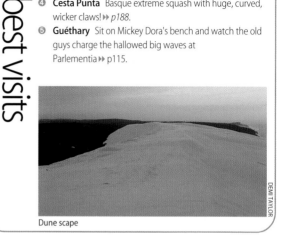

DEMI TAYLOR

Dune scape

the lower end of the scale, Formule 1, www.hotelformule1.com, are worth checking out. They offer a chain of clean, basic, budget, usually out of town, hotels with rooms sleeping up to three people for around €30. There are plenty of *auberges de jeunesse* dotted around but for many you will need an HI card.

Camping is king in France with thousands of sites in fantastic locations all over the country. Camping is not always a particularly cheap option (especially if you head to one of the popular super-sites on the coast) and many sites do shut over the winter period. In many popular areas, however, especially in Les Landes/Côte Basque, you can find *aire de campings*, regulated free-camping style sites, where a minimal fee of around €1 is charged (but seldom checked) for overnight parking. There are also usually facilities including water and electric hook-up available at a minimal charge.

Eating and drinking

Food is to the French what technology is to the Japanese – not just a necessity but an art form. Even a McDonald's in France is more civilized and has a *pâtisserie* section. *Pain au chocolat*, buttery *croissants* or even a bit of last night's *baguette* washed down with *un grand café au lait* or *chocolate chaud* – this is, quite simply, breakfast heaven whether sitting outside a café or on the beach following a stop by a *boulangerie* (bread shop). Lunch can be a simple affair involving a *pain* (a fatter bread stick than a *baguette*) and a wedge of your favourite *fromage* (cheese) – be it a creamy Camembert, a salty Roquefort or a sublime Brie de Meaux. If you want something more

Fact file

→ **Currency** Euro (€)
Capital city Paris
Time zone +1hr GMT
Length of
coastline 3,430km
Religion Catholic & Muslim
Emergency numbers
General emergency 115
Police 17
Ambulance 15
International Operator 1008
Electricity 220v continental

serious, try an *'Américan'* – a *baguette* stuffed with hamburger patties, salad and french fries – or a *croque-monsieur* – a cheese and ham toastie, French-style – at a café.

For something more civilized, head to a café or restaurant for lunch (1200-1430) or dinner (1900-2230) and grab a *menu* or *formule* – a two or three course meal, often reasonably priced. But no French trip is complete without sampling some of the excellent seafood on offer, whether it's *huîtres* (oysters) in Arcachon or the staple *moules et frites* (mussels and chips) available countrywide for around €10. As a snack or an after-dinner sweetener, you can do no better than a *crêpe* – a thin pancake topped off with a range of fillings from sugar or Nutella to Calvados and apples, or even something savoury. Here no meal would be complete without a glass of something to wash it down with. Home to some of the world's most celebrated vineyards, France has something for everyone: sparkling Champagne from the northeast, fruity Beaujolais from the

southeast, full-bodied reds from Bordeaux, light Sancerre from the Loire Valley and Cognac from just north of the Gironde to finish off a good evening. *Le bière blonde* (lager) also flows freely in France.

Festivals/events

France enjoys a good party as well as the next country and has its fair share of *fêtes* (festivals) and *foires* (fairs). **Bastille Day** on the 14 July is a national holiday commemorating the start of the French Revolution in the 1700s and sees some good parties. France has also truly embraced surf culture, with events such as the annual Biarritz Surf Festival or Lacanau Pro enjoying prominence in the community. June sees a little town in the heart of the Loire Valley explode into noise and action with the **24 hour Le Mans** race which has been held since 1923.

Getting there

Air France's two main international airports are Paris Orly and Paris Charles de Gaulle, with other airports dotted around the country connecting mainly with European destinations. Paris receives direct flights from east and west coast USA as well as from Australia and New Zealand with carriers including **Air France**, www.airfrance.com, and **British Airways**, www.british-airways.com. Flights can vary widely in price according to season and availability. From Ireland, **Ryanair**, www.ryanair.com, run regular flights to Paris from Shannon and Dublin.

DEMI TAYLOR

Reef girls with 2001 World Champion CJ Hobgood at Biarritz

From UK: the handiest route into southwest France is the daily Stansted-Biarritz flight with **Ryanair** whose fares run from 1p to about £120 return. They also run regular flights from Stansted to Dinard in the northwest and La Rochelle in the middle of the west coast, randomly charging for board carriage. Budget airline **Fly Be**, www.flybe.com, run daily flights between Southampton and La Rochelle and between Bristol and Bordeaux.

Rail   From the UK, if you don't fancy Dover-Calais by sea, you can always hop on the **Eurotunnel** train, T08705-353535, www.eurotunnel.com, with your car or van at Folkestone which will deposit you just south of Calais 35 minutes later. This can, however, be double the price of a ferry crossing, unless you look out for special offers. Alternatively, as a foot passenger, you can hop on the **Eurostar**, T08705-86186, www.eurostar.com, at London Waterloo to Calais, Lille or Paris. Returns can cost anything from £100 upwards depending on time of travel and can often be a more expensive option than flying. They charge £20 for surf-board carriage and can only guarantee a 24-hour service so unless you want to arrive in Paris without your board, they advise you book it in the day before. For onward connections, or journeys across Europe, check out routes with **Rail Europe**, www.raileurope.com.

Road   Surrounded by countries to the east and south, there are plenty of overland routes into France from the Continent. From Northern Spain, the coastal N1 becomes the N10 as it trickles over the border at Irun/Hendaye, as does the E5 toll road. From Belgium, Luxembourg/Germany and Switzerland, the main E17, E50 and E60 run to Paris respectively. From Italy the E80 crosses into France by Monte Carlo, following the coast round past Marseille to Perpignan, from where it's just a short 450-km hop past the Pyrénées to Biarritz!

Sea   From the UK there are various routes to France. The cheapest (around £200 return for a van and two people) and shortest (about 1¼ hours) crossing is Dover-Calais, operated year round by **Sea France**, www.seafrance.com, and **P&O Stena Line**, T08705-202020, www.posl.com. **Hoverspeed**, T0870-2408070, www.hoverspeed.co.uk, also operate a seacat service March-December taking just 50 minutes. Another popular route is the Portsmouth-Cherbourg crossing (about 4¾ hours) run by both **P&O Portsmouth**, www.poportsmouth.com, and **Brittany Ferries**, T08703-665333, www.brittany-ferries.com. Returns cost slightly more than the Dover-Calais route. The showcase route into France is the Portsmouth-St Malo crossing with Brittany Ferries. The journey takes 8-11 hours (St Malo suffers massive tides) and may cost slightly more (around the £300 mark) but on the plus side you can make the crossing overnight, thus maximizing 'away' time, the boat has a cinema and St Malo makes a beautiful entry point. Companies do operate other routes into France – check websites for details.

From Ireland, **P&O Ireland**, T08702-424777, www.poirishsea.com,

run a service three times a week between Rosslare and Cherbourg which takes 20 hours. A return for a van and two people – including a cabin and meals – costs around €600 off peak, but special offers are available. **Irish Ferries**, T00353-5333158, run Rosslare-Cherbourg between March and January and Rosslare-Roscoff between April and September for a similar price. **Brittany Ferries**, T00353-214 277801, also operate a weekly service between Cork and Roscoff.

Red Tape: France is a Schengen state (see European Red Tape).

Getting around
Driving (right-hand side)   A full driving licence or International Driving Permit is required plus adequate insurance and ownership papers. The roads in France are of a generally good standard making travel in this large country fairly straightforward, if not a little monotonous. The French themselves make road travel a more

Top tips

- Enjoy every minute, speak to the locals, be respectful towards them, wake up early for the offshore morning sessions and if the surf's flat, party and meet the mademoiselles. And don't forget to taste frogs' legs! With parsley and garlic, there's nothing as good, trust me. *Franck Lacaze, Editor in chief, Trip Surf magazine*

- France has some crazy waves - some of the best beach breaks in the world - plus there is the added advantage of having semi-clad French women on the beach. So learn as much French as possible as the culture is unique. *Carlo, Euroglass*

- Don't expect to get all the waves. Sometimes there is a problem with some of the guys who come from non-European countries like Australia or America. Yes, the average level of surfing may be higher there than the average level in France but there are some very good surfers in France. As a visitor in France, don't think you will get all the waves because you will face some big problems. *Peyo Lizarazu, Basque surfer*

- In France people often say "not possible", like when you're asking for no onions on your pizza they say, "It's not possible". Of course it's possible. But you can't let it bother you, you just need to shrug it off. *Dan Malloy, US pro surfer*

- If you're in southwest France for the first week of August don't miss the Bayonne festival. Bull runnings, fireworks, street parties. *Antonia Atha, UK surfer*

- In the summer in Biarritz, it can get pretty crowded. But you can always find uncrowded waves, just head north into Les Landes and explore. *Patrick Beven, top French surfer*

high-octane experience as they hate getting stuck behind slow moving or foreign vehicles – especially vans. So they'll speed up close behind you, lights flashing, and wait to overtake.

Motorway (*autoroute*): France has an extensive and efficient motorway system, spreading out like spiders' legs from Paris, much of which is made up of *péages* (toll roads). Check out www.autoroutes.fr for pricing details. Autoroutes are peppered with excellent motorway services, complete with cafés serving real food and pretty, wooded picnic areas. **Speed limit 130 kph.**

Routes nationales: N or **RN** roads are of a good standard, often with stretches of dual carriageway, but can get extremely busy with motorists avoiding the *péages*. **Speed limit 110 kph dual carriageway, 90 kph single carriage, 50 kph urban areas.**

Other roads: local roads are of a generally good standard and can be a great way to explore the countryside and get off the beaten track. **Speed limit 90 kph/50 kph urban areas.**

Car hire There are plenty of car-rental companies operating in France including **easyCar** in Paris, www.easycar.com, as well as all the big multinationals such as **Hertz**, www.hertz.com, and **Europcar**, www.europcar.com, who have offices in all the main towns, ports and airports. Rental starts at about €450 for two weeks but usually you do need to be over 25. Hire cars are especially attractive propositions to thieves so be extra vigilant and try to remove obvious signs, stickers and logos.

Public transport

The SNCF train network of France offers a quick and easy way to travel with a surf board. The fastest services are on the TGV and the slowest on autotrains, which generally stop in every one-horse town. Remember to get your ticket date stamped at one of the orange machines before you hop on board to avoid a fine. Check out www.sncf.com for route details.

THE GILL
La Gironde shoot

Key phrases

Key words/phrases

Yes	oui
No	non
Please	s'il vous plaît
Thank you	merci
Sorry	pardon
Hello	bonjour
Goodbye	au revoir
Good	bon
Bad	mauvais
I don't understand	je ne comprends pas
I'd like…	je voudrais…
Do you have…	avez vous…
How much is it?	c'est combien?
Where is…	où est…
Mens	hommes
Ladies	femmes
Left	gauche
Right	droite
Straight on	tout droite
Night	nuit
Room	chambre
Pitch	emplacement
Shower	douche
Toilet	toilettes
The bill	l'addition
White coffee	café au lait
Beer	bière
Red wine	vin rouge
white wine	vin blanc
Mineral water (sparkling)	l'eau minérale (gazeuse)
Orange Juice	jus d'orange
Sandwich	sandwich
Ham	jambon
Cheese	fromage
Grilled cheese/ham	croque-monsieur
Help!	au secours!
Beach	la plage
Point	pointe/cap
River	rivière
Wind	vent
Wave	vague
Board	planche
Wax	cire
Tide	marée
High	haut
Low	bas
Mid	milieu
North	nord
South	sud
East	est
West	ouest

Numbers

0	zero
1	un
2	deux
3	trois
4	quatre
5	cinq
6	six
7	sept
8	huit
9	neuf
10	dix
11	onze
12	douze
13	treize
14	quatorze
15	quinze
16	seize
17	dix-sept
18	dix-huit
19	dix-neuf
20	vingt
21	vingt et un
22	vingt-deux
30	trente
40	quarante
50	cinquante
60	soixante
70	soixante-dix
80	quatre-vingt
90	quatre-vingt-dix
100	cent
200	deux cent
1000	mille

Days of the week

Monday	lundi
Tuesday	mardi
Wednesday	mercredi
Thursday	jeudi
Friday	vendredi
Saturday	samedi
Sunday	dimanche

Surfing France

"Well, we've got some of the best beach breaks in the world around Hossegor and some decent reef breaks around St-Jean-de-Luz. The climate is not too bad either. Brittany and the Mediterranean offer some incredible waves. But, above all, what makes France so special as a surf destination is probably its lifestyle with great food, great wine, a good nightlife, and nice-looking women for the singles. There's nothing better than an October in southwest France."
Franck Lacaze, *Editor in chief*, Trip Surf

The original seeds of European wave-riding were sown in the wave-rich, sun drenched southwest of the country, and now France has booming surf communities along its entire coastline, from the resorts of the Med to the chilly waters of the Channel. Physically, the Atlantic coastline has it all. The miles of endless beach that stretches out like a spine connecting Biarritz to Arcachon is a natural wonder and the backbone of French surfing. An Indian summer of beach breaks, barrels, baguettes, bronzed, beautiful bodies and *bière* is a European surfing rite of passage not to be bypassed. Then the complex rocky coastline to the north opens up into a classic Celtic landscape, with an almost limitless potential of surfing possibilities, mirroring its Cornish cousin across the water. And after the surfing is done, there are few things in life to rival sitting at a table outside one of the chic cafés of Biarritz or Hossegor, sipping milky coffee, eating a *pain au chocolat*, and watching the world go by as you relive the filthy barrels you scored that morning.

Climate
There are many factors that combine to draw surfers to the French coast, but the climate is definitely one of the main reasons. The temperate maritime conditions that prevail here provide for hot summers and mild, damp winters, but even in December, when the sun comes out in Hossegor, so can the shorts and T-shirts.

Best seasons to go
"I remember one summer in Hossegor and the surf stayed flat for two months," says top pro surfer Sam Lamiroy. "Everyone was going down to the beach every morning praying for surf. One day the surf was shin high and we were trying to persuade ourselves it was surfable." The **summer** surf season in France is a bit of a lottery. Some years there can be consistent swell, offshore winds, and hot sunny days broken only by the occasional thunderstorm rolling in off the Pyrénées. Other years can be blighted by persistent onshore winds or long flat spells. July and August can be notoriously fickle. Add to this the hordes of holidaying surfers that descend on the west coast and, unless there is a promising chart, this time of year can be very frustrating. However,

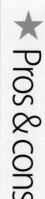

Pros ...
- The best beaches in the world.
- Rugged and varied breaks in the northwest.
- Consistent swell outside the summer months.
- Plenty of *aire de camping* locations.
- Great seafood, chocolate and wine.
- See the world tour come to town in September.
- Still quiet breaks in Gironde and Les Landes.
- Good climate.
- Wonderful cafés.

... and cons
- The straight, southwest coast is easily blown out by westerly winds.
- Busy breaks in the summer around the southwest.
- Quite expensive.
- Wet in the winter.
- Competitive line-ups.

these two months are when resorts like Hossegor come to life. The bars and clubs will be heaving, the cafés packed and the beautiful French women will still want nothing to do with you.

For surf quality, **autumn** and **spring** are the times to visit. Spring is a quieter option as the seas have yet to warm up, but in the autumn the weather can stay hot and sunny into November, and the swells can be clean and glassy.

Winter is the time when the quiet little secret spots of Brittany and Vendée come to life, the jagged coastline providing some real gems that break when the surf pumps. In the southwest, travelling surfers are few and far between. The resorts are quiet, and the wind and rain can lash the coastline for days on end. But there are still occasions when the short days offer up heavy winter swells, powerful and punishing in the cold green waters. "The other good thing about the southwest is that you can always head for the Pyrénées and have a day snowboarding in resorts like La Mongie," says James Stentiford, pro snowboarder. "January and February are the best times. But it's not like in the Alps, if it dumps, you have to be on it, because the powder doesn't last."

Boards
A classic board for a French trip would be a flexible beach break board. It should be fuller and wider for the summer – a good wave catcher, but can be more performance orientated for the autumn and spring when the swells kick in. A squash tail or swallow tail will give the board more drive in smaller waves. This would work well on the beaches of Les Landes and Brittany/Vendée as well as the reefs when they are up to head high. When the serious swells hit and the points and reefs of the north or the big banks around Hossegor fire, a longer board with a pin or rounded pin tail will come into its own.

Good charts for surf

A classic France chart has two components. A deep low tracking across the north Atlantic and a nice high pressure sitting over France. The low will pump swell towards the whole French coast as it travels west to east and the high will bring good weather and light offshores. A low pressure with a more southerly track across the Atlantic, heading towards Portugal, will push a southwesterly swell up into the south-facing breaks around Britanny/Vendée. However, southwest France can suffer if the swell is too big as the exposed beaches can max out.

Geography and the breaks

When seen from the air, the coastline of Les Landes and Gironde is a stunning natural phenomenon. A line of huge sand dune stretches from the River Gironde south to Hossegor, forming a coastal spine separating the emerald-green ocean on one side from the deep green pine forests on the other. The elements of wind and sea conspire to create this barrier, the defining symbol of an area that truly is the backbone of French surfing. The banks and channels here are constantly changing and the local surfers seek out the areas that are consistently the best, or the rogue 'superbanks' that spring up from time to time, offering the select few perfect waves that will be added to the folklore of the region's surf history.

To the north, the rugged and jagged coastline of south Brittany, Loire Atlantique, Vendée and Charantes has always been dominated by the power and force of the ocean. The Bai des Trépassés, or Bay of Death, where the bodies of dead sailors would regularly be washed up, symbolizes the spirit of a coastline once ransacked by pirates, but

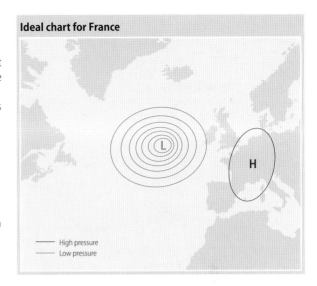

Ideal chart for France

—— High pressure
—— Low pressure

now plundered by modern day wave-riding buccaneers, searching out hidden gems among the many headlands and bays.

Surfing and environment

The coastline around northwestern France has always been some of the most treacherous in Europe. In 1999 an oil tanker sank off the coast off the Gulf of Morbihan, spilling thousands of tonnes of oil onto the shore. Luckily it was not quite on the scale of the Prestige oil

THE GILL

Micky Picon at VVF ▶▶ *p182*

5 underground classics

❶ **Biscarrosse Plage** Wonderful stretch of Les Landes beach break that the crowds have bypassed ▸▸ *p177*.

❷ **Casernes** Beaches to the north of Hossegor with quality banks and quiet peaks ▸▸ *p178*.

❸ **Côte Sauvage** Beautiful sandy bays with more than a passing resemblance to the north coast of Cornwall ▸▸ *p162*.

❹ **Bud Bud** Consistent and high quality stretch of the Longville beach north of La Tranche ▸▸ *p168*.

❺ **Le Gurp** Flexible beach in northern Gironde, great waves away from the crowds ▸▸ *p175*.

THIERRY ORGANOFF

Bud Bud ▸▸ *p168*

France Surfing

❝❞

I love it here because I spend my days at the beach. I pack a bag and an umbrella, food for the day, put on some sun block and just surf all day. Hike down the beach and look for sandbars. It's fun to check it out, be on it, eat lunch, then be on it again when the tide drops.

Dan Malloy, US pro surfer

Localism and surf communities

Southwest France has some of the busiest surf breaks in Europe during the summer and early autumn. Anglet, Biarritz, Cavaliers, Hossegor and Lancanau are notoriously crowded. Line-ups can be jammed with locals and travellers scrambling over waves, a situation made worse by any flat spell. With the locals so outnumbered by visitors in the summer, it is unlikely that any of these breaks will have any localism issues . However, at other breaks, locals have seen the situation developing and may be less than enthusiastic about the presence of non-locals. Fred Papagaraou has been surfing in Biarritz for twenty years and says that Grande Plage is a very competitive beach. "It is very busy here in the summer and can be very intense. There are many local surfers who all want to get their waves." Another local, pro rider Patrick Beven, says, "Many people come here and the local surfers get frustrated, which doesn't make for a relaxed atmosphere. Visitors should be relaxed and also check out the less crowded beaches." Luckily though, there are few places where localism exists, and if travelling surfers show respect, they will generally be treated with respect.

Surf directory

France supports two excellent surf magazines, *Surf Session* and *Trip Surf*.

disaster in Spain in 2002, from which France is still recovering, but it shows the potential for environmental disasters in European waters and unfortunately, there is always the possibility that this kind of event may reoccur.

France, like most countries, has problems with water quality around the mouths of major rivers, like the Loire and the Gironde, and around heavily urbanized areas. It is best to avoid surfing these breaks after heavy rains – talk to the locals who will offer advice. Luckily the beaches of Les Landes are clean and free of most pollution. There are occasional factories dotted along the coastline, but luckily the importance of the tourist industry and the preservation of the beaches has held most industrial development in check. The environmental organization, the Surfrider Foundation, has its European headquarters based firmly in southwest France where it campaigns hard for improved water quality, www.surfrider-europe.com.

France: a brief surf history

1956 ➔ While filming in Biarritz with actress wife Deborah Kerr, scriptwriter Peter Viertel surfs the waves of Biarritz, lending his board to interested locals – George Hennebutte, Joel de Rosney, Rott and Barland. **1958** ➔ Barland Surfboards (Barland & Rott) set up shop as France's first surfboard shapers. **1959** ➔ Deborah Kerr becomes patron of Waikiki, France's first surf club. **1964** ➔ The French Surfriding Foundation establishes itself in Biarritz. **1966** ➔ Guéthary hits the world stage after featuring in *US Surfer* magazine. **1968** ➔ *Evolution*, staring Nat Young and Wayne Lynch, highlights the surf potential of Europe, featuring among other spots the beach break at La Barre, Anglet. **1971** ➔ France hosts the European Surfing Championships. **1979** ➔ The Lacanau Pro is established as an annual event and becomes an international affair with everyone from Rabbit, to Carroll, to Curren to Slater winning the event. **1984** ➔ Quiksilver set up offices in southwest France and other international brands quickly follow suit. **1985** ➔ France wins the European Surfing Championships and goes on to win more than ten times. **1986** ➔ France's first magazine *Surf Session* sets up shop in Biarritz. **1987** ➔ Biarritz hosts its first pro contest, the Surf Masters. **1989** ➔ François Payot founds the EPSA in Capbreton, France, in order to support and promote European surfing. France today remains the nerve centre for European surfing. **1990** ➔ Tom Curren founds environmental pressure group Surfrider Foundation Europe in France in order to protect Europe's seas and coastline. Today SFE has more than 15 chapters operating across Europe. **1994** ➔ Eric Chauche sets up *Trip Surf* magazine in Biarritz, edited today by Franck Lacaze. **Today** ➔ Southwest France, playing host to both a number of prestigious WCT events and the European headquarters for many of surfing's International organizations, remains at the heart of the European surf scene. In recent years, France has seen several of its riders take to the world stage. In 2003, French surfer Marie Pierre Abgrall became Europe's first female surfer to join the competitive WCT while in 2004 Eric Rebière became the first Frenchman to join the elite 44 on the world tour.

Surfers' tales

THE GILL

Capbreton ▶ *p182*

France Surfing

Rites of Passage

By top professional surfer Sam Lamiroy

Hossegor and Lacanau are almost like my surfing parents. I spent about eight years going there every single summer. It was funny how my relationship with the places changed, and how the places themselves changed. Even just over the short time I've been going there, and we're not talking twenty odd years, the whole atmosphere is different and the role surfing plays has changed as well. It used to be a fringe sport, even as recently as ten years ago, and then in the last five years it's become the lifeblood of that area. It used to survive purely on the French going there on holiday, the odd German tourist - because they have great beaches and they love the nudism. It's quite bizarre to find yourself suddenly as part of the majority. Surfing used to be something different. Now everybody surfs.

Because surfing has suddenly become quite respectable, the kind of gypsy or 'feral' van existence is kind of frowned upon now. I don't mean to say "back in the good old days" because quite frankly sleeping in the dirt and having a budget of twenty francs for the day isn't exactly my idea of heaven. It was an experience, it was a rite of passage. I guess it was so popular because it was so cheap. You could buy a second hand van, chip in with three or four of your mates, split the petrol, split the ferry and fire down there and live like paupers, but get to go surfing every day.

We used to go down to the Rock Food bar in Hossegor and we used to be green with envy at all the top pros who were in there during the contest time. They could afford the beers in

the Rock Food, which was something quite special, because if you've got twenty francs for the day you have a choice of either malnourishing yourself and getting a beer, or eating something semi-decent. We used to buy six franc flagons of wine, get blind drunk, then go to the Rock Food and make the most of the atmosphere they so generously provided. The pros were our idols. When we were standing next to them in the bar, with our Kronenbourg bottle full of cheap wine, and them with their beers that they'd bought at the bar, and you're literally rubbing shoulders with them.

I remember being in Lacanau with a few of my mates. We used to live on 'baguette frite'. Some of my mates lived on beefburgers from a tin and things like that. It's funny to look back on how my relationship with the place has changed. It seems to have provided everything from camping, to free-camping at Casernes to living in swanky pads by the beach. It caters for everyone from kids on their first trip with fifty pounds to see them through the whole summer, to London stockbrokers who've discovered the thrills of surfing. But I think you see the free-campers less and less. It got too big. From like 15 vans it got to more like 150, all parked up in the forest. It sounds a bit like The Beach, it was paradise for a few years, but then it was ruined. I think the authorities are reluctant to let it reach that size again. But France is still the place to really experience surfing, whatever your budget, accommodation or mode of transport. It has something for everyone. I think your first trip to France will always be a rite of passage, whatever your age.

Northwest France

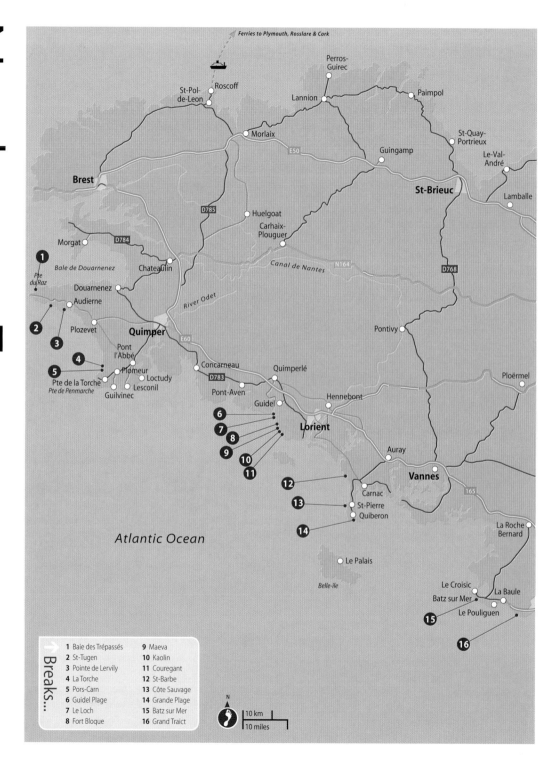

Ferries to Plymouth, Rosslare & Cork

Perros-Guirec

St-Pol-de-Leon
Roscoff

Lannion

Paimpol

Morlaix

E50

Guingamp

St-Quay-Portrieux

Le-Val-André

Brest

St-Brieuc

Lamballe

D785

Huelgoat

Carhaix-Plouguer

Morgat

D784

Chateaulin

Canal de Nantes

N164

D768

1

Bale de Douarnenez

Pte du Raz

Douarnenez
Audierne

Plozevet

2

3

River Odet

Quimper

Pontivy

E60

Pont l'Abbé

4

Concarneau

Quimperlé

Ploërmel

5

Plomeur

Pte de la Torche

Loctudy

D783

Pte de Penmarche

Lesconil

Pont-Aven

Hennebont

Guilvinec

Guidel

6

7

8

Lorient

9

10

Auray

11

Vannes

12

Carnac

165

13

St-Pierre

14

Quiberon

La Roche Bernard

Atlantic Ocean

Le Palais

Belle-île

Le Croisic

La Baule

Batz sur Mer

15

Le Pouliguen

16

→ Breaks...

1 Baie des Trépassés	**9** Maeva
2 St-Tugen	**10** Kaolin
3 Pointe de Lervily	**11** Couregant
4 La Torche	**12** St-Barbe
5 Pors-Carn	**13** Côte Sauvage
6 Guidel Plage	**14** Grande Plage
7 Le Loch	**15** Batz sur Mer
8 Fort Bloque	**16** Grand Traict

N

10 km
10 miles

Surfing Northwest France

There is a common bond between southwest Britain and Brittany. The two share many elements: storm-lashed jagged coastlines, beautiful secluded coves, a hardy people and landscape, sculpted by the elements. Not only is the southwest region of Brittany known as Cornouaille (Cornwall) but they are also linked by the legend of King Arthur. Each have their own unique languages (Cornish and Breton) that were once widely spoken but are now kept alive by a determined few. The roots of Brittany lie not in mainland France but in Celtic Britain and Ireland. The region's inhabitants migrated from these parts and maintained close social and economic links.

While Ireland and Cornwall have become renowned surf destinations, northwest France has managed to maintain a low profile. Occasionally the region will come up in conversation over a few quiet pints in the corner of the bar. "Oh yes, I was there a few years ago and the potential of this area is amazing." "Yes we should go and check it out . . . maybe next year." But soon the conversation moves onto safer ground. And that's just the way the local surfers like it. Hordes of travellers bypass their breaks on the way south to the crowded line-ups around Hossegor and Biarritz. There are few opportunities left in Europe to really go and explore. Why pass it by?

Coastline

The northwest of France takes the full brunt of the Atlantic storms that roll in off the bay of Biscay – the jagged coastline is a testament to this. Sandy coves, powerful beaches and crumbling cliffs culminate in the Pointe du Raz, a French version of Land's End. In fact the region in which it lies, Finistère, literally translates as the end of the world. Heading south, the undulating and rocky coastline has been littered with wrecks for centuries. Fishing villages nestle in rivermouths away from the storms and treacherous currents. On the Quiberon peninsula, the west-facing Côte Sauvage has banned all swimming due to the number of drownings. Further south, the major surfing area of La Baule demonstrates how powerful the ocean can be. The rocky island, once free floating and independent, has been snared by a long sandy peninsula, and quickly colonized by beach homes and holiday cottages.

Localism

There are breaks in this region that do draw a crowd but little out-and-out localism. Visiting surfers who surf respectfully should have no problems.

Top local surfers There are some very good surfers from northwest France. These include Greg Salaun, Thom Joncourt, Dan Billon, Aurelien Jacob and Florian Talouarn.

Powerful breaks, sandy beaches hidden below crumbling cliffs. A lot like the area around St Agnes. But they also have some really nice reefs, like the Gower. It's the kind of place where the outside world knows only a fraction of the surf spots.

Paul Gill, surf photographer

Northwest France board guide

M4
Shaper: Al Merrick, Channel Islands Surfboards

- 6'0" x 18¼" x 2"
- Al's new shortboard design for 2004.
- Explosive performance shortboard first ridden by Dane Renolds in the 2003 X-Games.
- A favourite with surfers on tour for riding the small to medium waves that are often found in Brittany.
- Flat entry rocker to increase tail kick, full rail and single concave.

Mutant
Shaper: Phil Grace, Quiksilver Surfboards

- 7'0" x 21½" x 2½".
- A combination of traits, from shortboards through to mini mals, join forces in a mutation more suited for larger or mature surfers, femlins or advanced beginners.
- Flatter rocker and slightly wider nose allows easier paddling and better all round performance.

 Boards by **Euroglass**
(Quiksilver Surfboards and Channel Islands European distributor)
81 Av des Artisans, 40150, Soorts-Hossegor, T00 33 (0)5584 34185
www.quiksilver.com/surfboards, www.cisurfboards.com
or contact euroglass90@aol.com

Getting around

When it comes to the roads west of Quimper, think Celtic and you'll know what to expect. It takes longer to reach places than you would think, especially in the summer when tourists hit the area. The N165 provides a good fast link between the cities, but there is excellent coastal access via minor roads.

Breaks

1 Baie des Trépassés

- **Break type**: Beach break.
- **Conditions**: All swells, offshore in easterly/southeasterly winds.
- **Hazards/tips**: Beautiful location.
- **Sleeping**: Audierne ⟩⟩ p163.

This northwesterly facing Brittany beach has a dramatic 'end of the world' feeling, picks up loads of swell and is sheltered from south or southwesterly winds by the Pointe du Raz. Has some good quality peaks overlooked by magnificent cliffs – popular with walkers and holidaymakers in the summer. Breaks up to 8 ft producing some great right-handers.

2 St-Tugen

- **Break type**: Beach break.
- **Conditions**: All swells, offshore in northeasterly winds.
- **Hazards/tips**: Quality waves.
- **Sleeping**: Audierne ⟩⟩ p163.

Heading east along the D784, this good quality beach break can have excellent hollow and powerful waves, especially when a southwest swell kicks in. Works through the tides, though better at low.

3 Pointe de Lervily

- **Break type**: Reef/point break.
- **Conditions**: All swells, offshore in north/northeasterly winds.
- **Hazards/tips**: For experienced surfers.
- **Sleeping**: Audierne ⟩⟩ p163.

A walling right-hand point/reef that works in southwesterly swells. Found to the south of the break water.

4 La Torche

- **Break type**: Beach break.
- **Conditions**: All swells, offshore easterly/southeasterly winds.
- **Hazards/tips**: Most famous break in region.
- **Sleeping**: Pointe de la Torche/Pont l'Abbé ⟩⟩ p164.

This is a rocky point flanked by beach breaks and the home of Breton surfing. It has good exposure to northwesterly swells which makes it one of the area's most consistent breaks. As well as good beach-break waves, there is also a good quality wave by the point. Right breaks towards the rip, left away. Easy paddle out in rip. The waves here work

Northwest France

Air ——— Sea ———

°F Averages °C

	90													30
	70													20
	50													10
	30													0

J F M A M J J A S O N D

5/4/3 Boots & gloves | 4/3 Boots | 3/2 | 4/3

DEMI TAYLOR

4 La Torche

on all tides. Gets crowded when it's on. Try Tronoën just to the north if it's too crowded.

5 Pors-Carn

- **Break type**: Beach break.
- **Conditions**: All swells, offshore in a southeasterly wind.
- **Hazards/tips**: Popular spot.
- **Sleeping**: Pointe de la Torche/Pont l'Abbé ›› p164.

Less swell gets in at Plage Pors-Carn to the south of the point, but a powerful right-hander breaks here at low tide. The wave is punchy and can be hollow. It is worth checking in a big southwesterly storm as the headland offers some protection. If the wind is northerly, head east along the D53 and south on the D102 to Lesconil where there is a reef near the harbour.

6 Guidel Plage

- **Break type**: Beach break.
- **Conditions**: All swells, offshore in northeasterly winds.
- **Hazards/tips**: Inconsistent spot.
- **Sleeping**: Lorient ›› p164.

To the west of Lorient, this spot varies between distinctly average to excellent depending on the sandbanks. If a good southwest swell hits when the Laïta rivermouth sandbanks have built up, it can be classic. Works best at low tide.

7 Le Loch

- **Break type**: Beach break.
- **Conditions**: All swells, offshore in easterly/northeasterly winds.
- **Hazards/tips**: Popular spot.
- **Sleeping**: Lorient ›› p164.

South on the D152, this is generally considered to be the best beach break in the area. It can have some good banks, especially at low tide. Can get very busy, particularly in the summer. Needs a southwesterly swell or a big northwesterly swell to work.

8 Fort Bloque

- **Break type**: Beach break.
- **Conditions**: All swells, offshore in easterly winds. Works on all tides.
- **Hazards/tips**: Average break.
- **Sleeping**: Lorient ›› p164.

A pretty sluggish break, good for beginners. Needs a good southwesterly swell.

9 Maeva

- **Break type**: Reef break.
- **Conditions**: All swells, offshore in easterly winds.
- **Hazards/tips**: Average break.
- **Sleeping**: Lorient ›› p164.

A reef break peak with walling lefts and rights that work up to 6 ft. Works best at high tide when it can be busy with local surfers.

10 Kaolin

- **Break type**: Reef break.
- **Conditions**: All swells, offshore in easterly/northeasterly.
- **Hazards/tips**: Heavy, hollow break.
- **Sleeping**: Lorient ›› p164.

This is a short, powerful, hollow reef break. Swell comes out of deep water lunging onto this flat slab reef producing heavy right-hand barrels. Needs a big westerly or a southwesterly swell to work. Best from low to three-quarter tide and offshore in an easterly. A serious wave respected by the locals.

11 Couregant

- **Break type**: Reef break.
- **Conditions**: All swells, offshore in easterly winds.
- **Hazards/tips**: A long paddle, experienced surfers only.
- **Sleeping**: Lorient ›› p164.

Continuing along the D152, this heavy peak breaks over a rocky reef, a long way off the point at Couregant. It is worth the paddle though as it is a quality long wave. Works best at low tide in a big westerly or southwesterly swell.

12 St-Barbe

- **Break type**: Beach break.
- **Conditions**: All swells, offshore in easterly winds.
- **Hazards/tips**: Popular beach, crowds.
- **Sleeping**: Quiberon ›› p164.

This is a long beach on the western side of a sandy peninsula connecting the mainland with the rocky Côte Sauvage. It is pretty

7 Le Loch

1 Baie des Trépassés

Fisherman in Brittany

consistent as it is well exposed to westerly and southwesterly swells. It has lefts and rights that can be long and walling, and very popular with longboarders. Heading south along the peninsula, there are several other beach breaks worth checking out – **Tata, Les Crevettes, Les Palisades** and **L'Isthme**.

13 Côte Sauvage

- 🌊 **Break type**: Beach breaks with rocks.
- 🌀 **Conditions**: All swells, offshore in easterly winds.
- ⚠ **Hazards/tips**: Dangerous currents.
- 🛏 **Sleeping**: Quiberon ⟩⟩ *p164*.

The exposed western side of the 'Wild Coast' is a treacherous part of the coast where swimming is banned due to the dangerous waters. It is home to a series of quality breaks that sit in front of cliffs and join up at low tide. There is parking at Port Blanc and access along a path to Port Blanc, Port Maria, Port Rhu and Port Bara. **Port Blanc** has peaks breaking over sand and rock, works well in westerly swells in northeasterly winds and is popular with locals. **Port Maria** produces some good lefts and rights, but to the south **Port Rhu** is the most powerful break, with quality peaks breaking over sand and rock. **Port Bara** has a good left, sand-covered reef.

13 Port Bara

14 Grande Plage

- 🌊 **Break type**: Beach break.
- 🌀 **Conditions**: Big swells, offshore in northwesterly winds.
- ⚠ **Hazards/tips**: Very popular tourist beach in the summer.
- 🛏 **Sleeping**: Quiberon ⟩⟩ *p164*.

This spot on the southern tip of the Quiberon peninsula needs a very big swell to work. Best at low to mid tide, the waves become a close-out shore break at high tide. Good in westerly through to northwesterly winds.

15 Batz sur Mer

- 🌊 **Break type**: Reef.
- 🌀 **Conditions**: Big swells, offshore in northeasterly winds
- ⚠ **Hazards/tips**: Rocky.
- 🛏 **Sleeping**: La Baule ⟩⟩ *p164*.

West of St-Nazaire, **La Govelle** is a right and left walling sand-covered flat rock reef. Best at mid tide when there can be some good waves in decent swells. Works up to 8 ft. Gets crowded when good. In a large swell you can head to the versatile and popular crescent-shaped beach at **La Baule**.

16 Grand Traict

- 🌊 **Break type**: Rocky reef.
- 🌀 **Conditions**: Big swells, offshore in northeasterly winds.
- ⚠ **Hazards/tips**: Rocks.
- 🛏 **Sleeping**: La Baule ⟩⟩ *p164*.

This spot near St-Marc needs a big swell to produce long, walling right-hand waves. Best mid to low tide. A break that comes to life during the winter season as it is quite protected from the wind.

13 Côte Sauvage

DEMI TAYLOR

Listings

Calais

Dover-Calais by sea is the shortest route into France. Calais is fine for a night's stopover on your way in or out.

🛏 Sleeping

Camping **Camping Municipal**, west of the ferry terminal on Av Raymond Poincare, T0321-978979, open year round.
Auberge de jeunesse, just back from the campsite on Av Marechal Lattre Tassigny, T0321-345940, beds from €15.

Cherbourg

Cherbourg is a busy but unglamorous port of entry into France from Portsmouth or Poole.

🛏 Sleeping

D-E Moderna, R de la Marine, T0233-430530, is handy for the ferry port.
Auberge de jeunesse, R de l'Abbaye, T0233-781515, is a big hostel offering B&B with no curfew, convenient for those with late arrivals or early departures. €15 in dorm. Stock up on palettes of '33' at the **Carrefour Supermarket** on the Quai de l'Entrepôt.

St-Malo

Another probable and preferable port of entry is St-Malo, a pretty town with an impressive *citadelle*. It's worth arriving early to spend an evening or afternoon walking around the 17th-century ramparts.

🛏 Sleeping

D-E Le Croiseur, within the walls on Pl de la Poissonnerie, T0299-408040. All are en suite.

Camping **La Cité d'Aleth**, T0299-816091, overlooks the bay and is housed in a Second World War fort, complete with bullet-riddled emplacements. Open year round, it is advisable to book ahead in the summer.

🍴 Eating/drinking

There are plenty of good eating options within the walls – most have a similar set menu involving *moules et frites* along the way. Be warned they do fill up pretty quickly around lunch and dinner.

🛍 Shopping/directory

Check out **Le Continent Hypermarket** on the outskirts of town if you want to stock up on food and drink. **Tourist information**: Esplanade St Vincent.

Audierne

In the heart of Finistère, this pretty fishing town is set back from the sea on the Goyen estuary.

🛏 Sleeping

D L'Horizon, R J.J. Rouseau, T0298-700991.
Camping **Le Loquéran**, near the bridge on Bois de Loquéran, T0298-749506, is reasonably priced, open May-Sep. **La Corniche Camping**, heading south on the D784 to Plozevet, T0298-913293, is open Apr-Sep and offers cabins. Heading west towards Pointe du Raz, campervans free-camp in the car park behind the dunes at **Baie de Trépassés**.

Pointe de la Torche

This spot is popular with surfers and windsurfers and has plenty of surf shops and a good campsite.

🛏 Sleeping

Camping **Pointe de la Torche**, southwest of Pont l'Abbé on the Plomeur-Pointe de la Torche road, T0298-586282, about 2 km from the sea, open Apr-Sep, also has cabins.

🛍 Shopping

Juanito Surfboards, on the Meju-Roz Route de Tronöen, sponsor local ripper, Thomas Joncourt. **Twenty Nine** surf shop is next door to the *crêperie* at Pointe de la Torche. There is also the **Atlantic** surf shop on Route Pointe de la Torche.

Pont l'Abbé

This is the main town of the region and a good base for reaching the breaks combined with some nightlife.

☼ Flat spells

Phare d'Eckmühl Standing on the Pointe de Penmarche, this lighthouse offers awesome views out across the bay.
Quimper Head inland along the D785 to the oldest city and heart of Brittany. Sitting on the banks of the Oder, it's all about the ambience.

⬤ Sleeping

D **Hôtel de Bretagne**, Pl de Republique, T0298-871722, is probably the best option in town with good rooms on the main square.
Camping Out of town there are several seasonal camping options. Heading southeast on the D2 to the relaxed town of Loctudy, there is **Les Hortensias**, T0298-874664, just 300 m from the beach, open Apr-Sep, cabins available. Following the coast road on towards Lesconil, **Les Sables Blancs**, T0298-878479, open Apr-Sep, is set 800 m back from the seafront and also offers caravans. Also to the south, **La Greve Blanche**, T0298-589313, on the coast road between Guilvinec and Penmarche, is a summer-only campsite with caravans.

Lorient

The port town of Lorient is a huge natural harbour that was flattened during the Second World War and rebuilt in a very bland manner. It has a massive naval base housing nuclear submarines. If you still want to stay . . .

⬤ Sleeping

Camping There are several campsites just

to the west by the surfing beaches including the year-round **Plage du Forte Bloque**, T0297-059546, next to the beach of the same name. It is reasonably priced and has statics for rent. Heading north on the coast road, **Pen er Malo**, at Guidel Plage, T0297-059986, is slightly cheaper, open year round, with statics to rent. Also try the **Parc de Loch Malo**.

○ Shopping

Actionline surf shop at Guidel Plage stocks hardware as well as all the basics.

Quiberon

The Presqu'île de Quiberon peninsula, with the port Quiberon at its southern tip, is a massive tourist draw in the summer as it offers excellent beaches on 2 sides.

☼ Flat spells

Belle-Île This spectacularly beautiful and rugged island is just 20-km long and very popular in the summer. Regular ferries run between Port Maria in Quiberon and Le Palais on the Belle-Île (returns about €20 with **SMNN**, T0820-056000). Hire a bike at the port for around €10 and explore. There are a couple of campsites on the island as well as a hostel near the port, T0297-318133.
Carnac Tucked away behind the Quiberon peninsula lies Carnac and its Neolithic monuments. Predating the Pyramids and Stonehenge, rows upon rows of *menhirs* (standing stones) stretch northwards and eastwards from Carnac in lines and grids or 'alignments'. It is a spectacular site and believed to be Europe's oldest settlement.

⬤ Sleeping

The tourist office is able to offer advice on available rooms.
E **Hôtel Restaurant au Bon Accueil**, Quai de Houat in Port Maria, T0297-502862, is

reasonably priced, closed Jan.
Camping Plenty of options on the Presqu'île de Quiberon. At St-Barbe, just inland, try **Kersily**, T0297-523965, open Easter-Oct, statics available. South on the peninsula at Sables Blancs is the massive **Camping Muncipal**, T0297-523715. At Kerhostin is **L'Ocean**, T0297-309129, open Apr-5 Nov, cabins to rent. Continuing south along the D768 to St-Pierre Quiberon is the pricier **Park er Lann**, T0297-502493.

❷ Eating/drinking

Try the nearby **Joaquina Café**, a great latino café/bar with a relaxed vibe, complete with pool table.

○ Shopping/directory

Authentic surf shop, on Av General de Gaulle, stocks hardware and accessories.
Tourist information: R de Verdun.

La Baule

Just north of the Loire, this popular holiday resort was once an island until, in 1779, a huge storm lashed through and deposited a sandy peninsula. The crescent-shaped bay is a bustling tourist beach in the summer and a popular surfing spot.

⬤ Sleeping

The tourist office on Pl de la Victoire will advise on accommodation options.
D **Marini**, on Av Clemenceau, T0240-602329, close to the railway station, has clean, comfortable rooms.
Camping There are plenty of campsites around La Baule and Batz sur Mer. Between Le Pouliguen and Batz, on the coast, there is the summer-only **Camping Govelle**, R de la Côte Sauvage, T0240-239163. **Camping Ajoncs d'Or**, on Chermin du Rocher, T0240-603329, open Apr-Sep, is close to the sea.

Airports → Paris Orly, T01 49 751515, www.adp.fr; Paris Roissy Charles de Gaulle, T01 48 622280; Nantes-Atlantique, T02 40 84 80 00, www.nantes.aeroport.fr; Bordeaux, T05 56 345050, www.bordeaux.aeroport.fr; Biarritz-Anglet-Bayonne, T05 59 438383.
Buses and coaches → SNCF, www.sncf.com. **Car hire** → Avis, T0870-6070100; Europcar, T0870-6075000; Hertz, T08708-448844. **Ferries** → P&O, T0870-2424999, www.poportsmouth.com; Brittany Ferries, T0870-3665333, www.brittany-ferries.com; Sea France, T0870-5711711, www.seafrance.com. **Rail links** → SNCF, www.sncf.com; TGV, www.tgv.fr. **Petrol prices** → €1/litre.

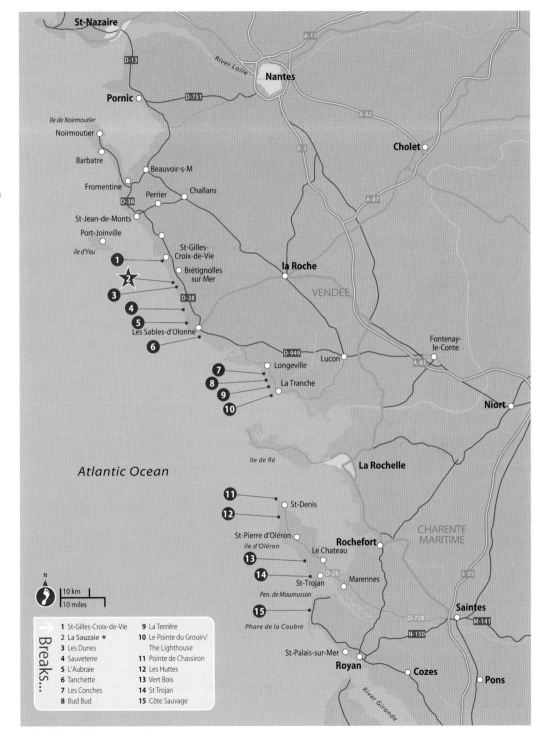

Central France

St-Nazaire

River Loire

A-11

Nantes

Pornic

D-13

D-751

E-62

île de Noirmoutier

Noirmoutier

Cholet

Barbatre

E-3

A-87

Beauvoir-s-M

Fromentine

Perrier

Challans

D-38

St-Jean-de-Monts

Port-Joinville

île d'Yeu

St-Gilles-Croix-de-Vie

1

2 ★

Brétignolles sur Mer

la Roche

3

D-38

VENDÉE

4

5

Les Sables-d'Olonne

6

Fontenay-le-Conte

D-949

Lucon

A-83

7

Longeville

8

La Tranche

9

10

Niort

Atlantic Ocean

île de Ré

La Rochelle

11

St-Denis

12

CHARENTE MARITIME

St-Pierre d'Oléron

Rochefort

île d'Oléron

Le Chateau

13

E-05

14

D-26

Marennes

St-Trojan

Pen. de Maumusson

15

Saintes

D-728

M-141

Phare de la Coubre

N-150

St-Palais-sur-Mer

Royan

Cozes

Pons

River Gironde

N

10 km
10 miles

Breaks...

1 St-Gilles-Croix-de-Vie
2 La Sauzaie ★
3 Les Dunes
4 Sauveterre
5 L'Aubraie
6 Tanchette
7 Les Conches
8 Bud Bud

9 La Terrière
10 Le Pointe du Grouin/ The Lighthouse
11 Pointe de Chassiron
12 Les Huttes
13 Vert Bois
14 St Trojan
15 Côte Sauvage

Surfing Central France

Learning to read the sea, to predict the weather and how conditions can change almost instantly . . . these people have spent years with saltwater-crusted skin, that year-round tan of a waterman. Their sport has become their passion and their lifestyle. But that's where the similarity with surfers ends. They are here for the Vendée Globe Challenge, a non-stop, single-handed round the world yacht race that attracts the sport's best sailors. It's not by chance that this prestigious race starts from Sables d'Olonne in the Vendée region of France. It has always had a strong link with the sea. As boats leave the harbour they pass the lighthouse, and head south. Surfers in the line-up at L'Aubrai, Les Conches and La Terrière watch the sails disappear on this epic challenge.

Being a surfer in Vendée and Charente is like going back a few years to an age when wave riding was popular, but not overwhelming. Before every car in the car park at the beach had a board on the roof. In the autumn, when the *grandes vacances* is over, the line-ups are more chilled and a traveller can enjoy exploring this excellent region. With such undulating terrain, there is always the potential for the next curve in the coastline to yield a hidden gem.

Coastline

This spectacular coastline is a patchwork of coastal features, a geographer's delight. Dense, pine-fringed beaches demonstrate the classic features of succession – the naked beach, the dunes colonized by marram grasses, the pine tree forests that are quick to follow. Tidal rivermouths have rich mud flats and cities like La Rochelle, Rochefort and Royan have sprung up in their calm waters. Sitting offshore are a series of islands with their own raison d'être. While Île de Ré has a unique microclimate and receives the most sunshine in western France, Île d'Oléron is second only to Corsica in size.

This physical complexity makes the region a diverse surfing destination. There is a healthy mix of reefs, beach breaks and even some rivermouth sandbars. To the south, the River Gironde marks the start of one of the world's longest beaches – heaven or monotony, depending on your point of view. But one thing's certain, you won't reach coastline as diverse as Vendée and Charente until you cross the border into Spain.

Localism

Outside the main summer tourist season, breaks will be pretty chilled. While you won't be welcomed with open arms and a champagne reception, it would be unusual to experience any problems in the water. It pays to try a bit of French and pass the time of day in the line-up.

Top local surfers Local surfer Gregory Pastusiak is a former French Champion. Other regional standouts include Anthony Guibert and Sylvain Grégoire.

Getting around

The road links in Vendée and Charente are very good, with the coastal areas all served by main D roads. Getting around outside the busy summer season should be no problem. Watch out for bridge tolls between islands – in the summer they can be as high as €16.

Secret break

Central France board guide

C1 Fish
Shaper: Al Merrick, Channel Islands Surfboards

» 5'11" x 19+" x 2½".
» A fish by definition, with two fins and a deep swallow tail.
» Designed not just as an exercise in nostalgia, but to be user friendly.
» Al has put his experience and input from the world's best surfers to make an incredibly fast and fun board.
» Fins have cant while the bottom is light single to double concave to allow manoeuvrability uncommon to the fish design.
» Ride this one small, shorter than your shortboard.

Mongrel
Shaper: Al Merrick, Channel Islands Surfboards

» 6'1" x 18+" x 2½".
» The Mongrel is a crossbred fusing 1980s full volume, low entry rocker and outline, with a modern bottom consisting of single concave to a pronounced 'vee' concave.
» While ridden by pro-level surfers in all kinds of surf, the Mongrel excels in small to medium surf due to the wide nose, wide tail and full rails.
» Should be ordered one to three inches shorter and a little wider than your all-round shortboard.

 Boards by **Euroglass**
(Quiksilver Surfboards and Channel Islands European distributor)
81 Av des Artisans, 40150, Soorts-Hossegor, T00 33 (0)5584 34185
www.quiksilver.com/surfboards, www.cisurfboards.com
or contact euroglass90@aol.com

DEMI TAYLOR

France Central

Breaks

1 St Gilles-Croix-de-Vie

- **Break type**: Beach break.
- **Conditions**: All swells, offshore in northeasterly winds.
- **Hazards/tips**: Popular with longboarders and beginners.
- **Sleeping**: St-Gilles-Croix-de-Vie » *p170*.

Crumbly, mellow beach break with lefts and rights that is protected from big swells. A real longboarders' wave, making it an ideal location for the Vendée Longboard Pro Am. An urban spot with a breakwater at the northern end. At hightide there is backwash from the concrete defences, so best at low to mid.

2 La Sauzaie

- **Break type**: Reef break.
- **Conditions**: All swells.
- **Size**: 3-8 ft.
- **Length**: 50-100 m.
- **Swell**: Northwesterly or westerly.
- **Wind**: Northeasterly.
- **Tide**: Quarter to high tide.
- **Bottom**: Rocky reef and sand.
- **Entry/exit**: In the channel.
- **Hazards/tips**: Busy break.
- **Sleeping**: St-Gilles-Croix-de-Vie/Les Sables-d'Olonne » *p170*.

Head south from St-Gilles on the D38 and turn right at La Sauzaie. This A-frame reef is one of the region's premier spots and hosts the annual WQS Pays de La Loire Surf Pro contest. When swell hits the reef, it produces powerful and hollow lefts and rights and can have nice barrel sections. As you would expect at such a good break, it does get busy year round, with a committed group of local surfers. Best surfed from mid to high tide. There are other reefs in the area worth checking out.

If you like La Sauzaie, *try* Bundoran Peak *in Ireland (see page 120) or* The Bubble *in Fuerteventura (see page 271).*

Central France

Air —— Sea ——

°F Averages °C

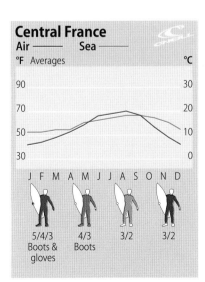

J F M	A M J	J A S	O N D
5/4/3 Boots & gloves	4/3 Boots	3/2	3/2

2 La Sauzaie

France Central Breaks St-Gilles-Croix-de-Vie to La Sauzaie

3 Les Dunes

- **Break type**: Beach break.
- **Conditions**: All swells, offshore in easterly/northeasterly winds.
- **Hazards/tips**: Popular longboarders' wave.
- **Sleeping**: St-Gilles-Croix-de-Vie/Les Sables-d'Olonne » *p170*.

This beach break has lefts and rights and is a touristy spot with lifeguards in the summer. A fairly weak wave, popular with longboarders, its swamped when small, better at 4-5 ft.

4 Sauveterre

- **Break type**: Reef/beach break.
- **Conditions**: All swells, offshore in easterly/northeasterly winds.
- **Hazards/tips**: Lovely location, busy in the summer.
- **Sleeping**: Les Sables-d'Olonne » *p171*.

Follow the small coast road north from Sables-d'Olonne into the pine forests and in a good swell you will see the surfers' cars parked by the footpath through the pine forest to the sea. There are a couple of options to chose from, **Pic du Large** and **Pic du Phoque**. Both are right-hand, sand-covered reefs with nice long walls that work well in big northwesterly swells.

5 L'Aubraie

- **Break type**: Beach break.
- **Conditions**: All swells, offshore in easterly/northeasterly winds.
- **Hazards/tips**: Beach break with rocks.
- **Sleeping**: Les Sables-d'Olonne » *p171*.

These spots sit about 2 km north of Chaume in a beautiful forest location. At low tide there are good rights on the beach. There are a couple of sand-covered rocky breaks – **Pic de L'Abraie** is the best and has a fast hollow left, considered one of the best waves in the region, which works best at mid tide. Watch out for the rocks.

6 Tanchette

- **Break type**: Beach break.
- **Conditions**: All swells, offshore in northeasterly winds.
- **Hazards/tips**: Good potential.
- **Sleeping**: Les Sables-d'Olonne » *p171*.

Average beach break at Sables-d'Olonne with good, long right-hander breaking off the rocks. The right can handle a big swell but be careful with the rips and currents.

7 Les Conches

- **Break type**: Beach break.
- **Conditions**: All swells, offshore in easterly/northeasterly winds.
- **Hazards/tips**: Very pretty location.
- **Sleeping**: La Tranche » *p171*.

Beach break in the middle of Longeville, a stretch of beach that resembles Les Landes. It has peaks, lefts and rights and varies with the swells, from mellow and cruisey to punchy and powerful. Less busy than the spots to the south. Works on all tides. This access point serves as a good indicator as to whether the rest of the Longville beaches are working.

8 Bud Bud

- **Break type**: Beach break.
- **Conditions**: All swells, offshore in easterly/northeastery winds.
- **Hazards/tips**: Can get busy, can be powerful when big.
- **Sleeping**: La Tranche » *p171*.

Vendée and Charente have some really nice breaks. Around Lacanau and Hossegor it's mainly beachbreaks, but up there you have spots like La Sauzaie – a really quality reef. They don't get as much swell as the breaks to the south, but when they do it gets really good. And it's not that far north from Lacanau either, but there's a different atmosphere. Surfing's not quite as big up there – it's more relaxed. It's more quintessentially French.

Sam Lamiroy, British Champion

Head south from Les Conches to this popular beach break that can have excellent waves and produces some of the best barrels in the area. It has both lefts and rights and is often compared to the Landes region by visiting surfers. Works on all tides. Worth checking when there is a good swell running.

DEMI TAYLOR

4 Sauveterre

9 La Terrière

- **Break type**: Beach break.
- **Conditions**: All swells, offshore in easterly/northeasterly.
- **Hazards/tips**: Popular tourist beach in the summer.
- **Sleeping**: La Tranche ‣‣ *p171*.

There is easy beach access to this part of the beach. It can have some good peaks with plenty of room to spread out if there is a crowd. Works on all tides and has a pretty chilled vibe.

10 Le Pointe du Grouin/The Lighthouse

- **Break type**: Point break.
- **Conditions**: Big swells, offshore in northeasterly winds.
- **Hazards/tips**: Check here in the biggest swells.
- **Sleeping**: La Tranche ‣‣ *p171*.

This is the place to check when the swell is too big for Bud Bud and the other beach breaks. There is a good, long right-hand point break out by the lighthouse on the coast road. Sand and rock at high tide. There is also a weak right-hander by the jetty called Embarcadère.

11 Pointe de Chassiron

- **Break type**: Reef breaks.
- **Conditions**: Medium to big swells, offshore in southerly/southeasterly winds.
- **Hazards/tips**: Low tide, shallow reef, strong rips.
- **Sleeping**: Île d'Oléron ‣‣ *p171*.

The northern tip of the Île d'Oléron comes to life in decent swells when the reef produces some good quality lefts and rights breaking over a flat reef at low tide. Head for the lighthouse and check out the peak. Boots are needed for the long walk out over the reef. There are strong currents round here as the tide pushes in. In a massive swell check out the left points at St-Denis and Les Boulassiers.

12 Les Huttes

- **Break type**: Beach break.
- **Conditions**: Medium to big swells, offshore in easterly winds.
- **Hazards/tips**: Rips.
- **Sleeping**: Île d'Oléron ‣‣ *p171*.

In a big southwesterly or good northwesterly swell, this stretch of beach really comes into its own with powerful and hollow waves breaking through the tides. Park and walk

over the dunes. The best beach break on the island when it's on, but watch out for powerful rips.

13 Vert Bois

- **Break type**: Beach break.
- **Conditions**: Medium swells, offshore in northeasterly winds.
- **Hazards/tips**: Very popular break.
- **Sleeping**: Île d'Oléron ‣‣ *p171*.

This stretch of beach is the most popular spot on the island and main surf check point. It can have some excellent waves on all tides, but needs a decent clean swell. The beach stretches south so check it out if the main peaks are crowded.

14 St-Trojan

- **Break type**: Beach break.
- **Conditions**: Medium swells, offshore in easterly winds.
- **Hazards/tips**: Quiet spot.
- **Sleeping**: Île d'Oléron ‣‣ *p171*.

7 Les Conches

11 Pointe de Chassiron

8 Bud Bud

Take the D126 and walk down the Grande Plage, which is dune-backed and has massive potential. Can be busy by the main access points in the summer but is such a big stretch of beach that there are always empty peaks to be had. A beautiful and quiet spot that has a real Les Landes feel to it. Watch out for rips and currents, especially near the southern Maumusson end.

15 Côte Sauvage

- **Break type**: Beach break.
- **Conditions**: All swells, offshore in an easterly wind.
- **Hazards/tips**: Rips, can be polluted.
- **Sleeping**: Royan ▶▶ p171.

Access points through the forest lead to the dune-backed beaches. The southern end near the lighthouse, Phare de la Coubre, is the busiest, but try to the north where it is much quieter. The banks can be excellent with hollow, powerful waves in clean swells. Watch out for powerful rip currents.

15 Côte Sauvage

Longville

Listings

Le Foie Gras Passion

St-Gilles-Croix-de-Vie

A pretty town on the D38, this is the venue for the Vendée Longboard Pro Am and makes a good base for exploring the quality reefs to the south

Flat spells
Golf Get a round in at **Fontenelles GC**, 6 km east of the town, T0251-541394. **Île d'Yeu** Drive north along the D38 to Fromentine and get the ferry across to Port-Joinville on Île d'Yeu which – with forest, beaches and rocky outcrops – is like a sampler of France. **Vedettes Inter-Îles Vendeenes**, T0251-390000, do a day return for around €25. Hire a bike from Port-Joinville for around €10.

Sleeping
Camping Bahamas Beach, on R des Sables, T0251-546916, open Apr-end Sep, is 2 km from the town centre and 600 m from the beach. Just to the south, at Givrand, is **Domaine des Beaulieu**, T0251-555946, about 1 km from the sea, open year round with cabins to rent.

Eating
Casa Pizza, by the church on R Achard, serves pizzas and good grills. "Drop by the Pointe Break and talk to Gregory and he'll give you the low-down on the best places to eat," says pro surfer Sam Lamiroy.

Shopping
Pointe Break Surf Shop, in town centre on Quai des Greniers, is run by Gregory Pastusiak.

Directory
Tourist information: on Blvd de L'Egalité – has good accommodation list and can advise on where to stay.

Bretignolles sur Mer

Just south of St-Gilles and close to the quality break of La Sauzaie, check out **Atlantic Lezard** surf shop on R de Plage.

Les Sables-d'Olonne

This popular holiday destination is the starting point for the Vendée Globe Challenge..

Sleeping
E **Hôtel les Voyageurs**, R de la Baudere at Pl de la Gare, T0251-951149, spacious rooms with baths. E **Hôtel de Depart**, also near the station on Av De Gaulle, T0251-320371, is comfortable and good value. **Camping Dune des Sables**, just by the sea at La Paracou, T0251-323121, open Apr-Sep, cabins. **Camping Roses**, R des Roses 500 m from Rembai beach, T0251-951042, open Apr-Oct.

Shopping
The **Bahia Surf Shop**, R de Ramparts, stocks hardware and accessories.

Directory
Tourist information: on Promenade Joffre in a glass-fronted building near the seafront.

La Tranche

This is a picturesque town, sheltered in the natural harbour behind Pointe du Grouin du Cou. It is quiet off season, but just to the north sits Longeville, a long stretch of pine-fringed beach with a number of campsites.

Sleeping
Camping Clos des Pins, 250 m inland from Les Conches, T0251-903169, open Apr-Oct. Also try **Brunelles** at Le Bouil, T0251- 335075, open Easter-Sep, and **Dunes**, 6 km south of Longeville off the D105, T0251- 333293.

Shopping
If you need a **surf shop**, try **Le Palmier**, on R Pertuis Breich in Tranche sur Mer.

La Rochelle

La Rochelle is a city on the up. It has an attractive old port area with lively cafés and bars and the university population ensures that there is always some decent nightlife to be had. It's only a short, if expensive, hop over the bridge to the beautiful, beach-fringed Île de Ré.

Sleeping
D **Hôtel de Bordeaux**, in a great location on R St Nicolas above a café, T0546-413122, is good value with clean and comfortable rooms with shower and toilet. D **Hôtel Terminus**, R de la Fabrique, T0546-56969, is another value option. **Camping** Municipal **Camping Port-Neuf**, on Bvd Aristide Rondeau, Port-Neuf, T0546-438120, is open all year.

Eating/drinking
La Provençale Pizzeria, R Jean du Perot, serves Italian and French cuisine including good seafood, steaks and duck. There are plenty of seafood restaurants around the old port serving reasonably priced set menus.

Shopping
There are a couple of **surf shops** here including a **Quiksilver Boardriders** on R des Templiers and **Neway** on R Bonette.

Directory
Internet: access at the wonderfully named Cyber Squat on R St Nicolas. **Post office**: Pl de Hôtel de Ville. **Tourist information**: Pl de la Petite Sirène can reserve rooms.

Île d'Oléron

This 30-km long island is joined to the mainland by a 3-km bridge. Fringed by 20 km of beautiful beaches, it gets very busy in the summer. Le Château on the southeast of the island is a popular base with easy access to the breaks on the western coast.

Sleeping
D-E **Le Castel**, R Alsace-Lorraine, T0546-752469, has comfortable and clean rooms. **Camping** There are plenty of campsites on the island. **Phare Ouest** in St-Denis, T0251-975550, open Apr-Sep, is about 1 km south of the lighthouse at the northern tip of the island. Nearby **Soleil Levant**, just off the D734, T0546-478303, is open year round. In the middle of the island, at picturesque St-Pierre, **Trois Masses**, T0546-472396, open Easter-Sep, offers good access to all the breaks.

Shopping
Check out **Island Surf Shop** on R Bouline, in St-Pierre. Head to the town **market** on Sun morning to stock up on local produce.

Directory
Post office: on Blvd Victor Hugo. **Tourist information**: on Pl de la République.

Royan

Royan sits at the mouth of the River Gironde and makes a good base to explore the beaches of the Côte Sauvage. It is also a good place to bisect the river: take the ferry across to the start of Gironde.

Flat spells
Cognac The N150 to Saintes leads onto the M141 and the booze heaven that is Cognac – it's all about the distilleries! Henessey, T0545-357268, is the biggest and the best. Ask at the tourist office on R 14 Juillet for more details. **Golf** The 18-hole **Golf de Royan**, to the west of the city in St-Palais-sur-Mer, on Maine Gaudin, T0546-231624.

Sleeping
C-E **Hermitage**, on the seafront overlooking Plage Grande Conche, T0546-385733, has excellent deals available off season and is handy for an overnight stop. **Camping** Plenty available in and around Royan. **Clairfontaine**, a well-equipped site 300 m from the beach in Pontaillac, T0546- 390811, open May-Sep. **Camping Chenes**, 2 km to the north at Medis, T0546-067138, open Mar-Oct. **Camping La Triloteie**, on Av Alienor d'Aquataine just out of town on the road to Bordeaux, T0546-052691, is open year round.

Shopping
Quiksilver Boardrider, R Gambetta. There are several shops on Blvd de la Republique, including **American Box**. There is also **Europlanche** on Esp du Bac.

Girondes & Les Landes

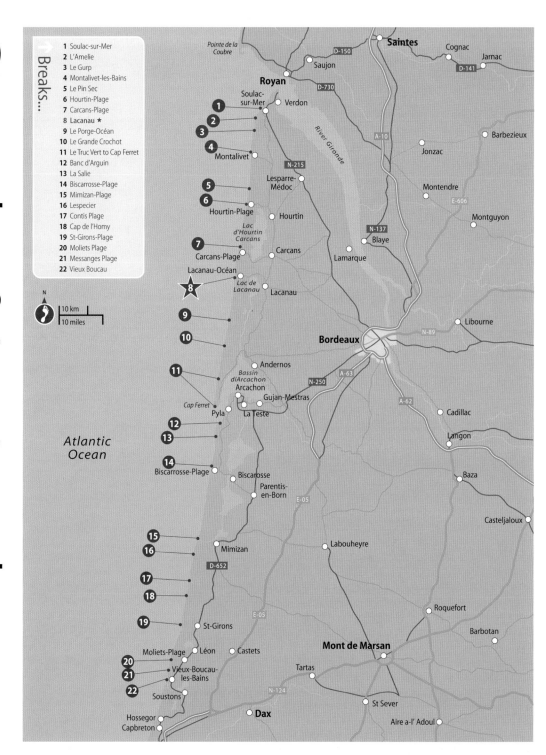

Breaks...

1 Soulac-sur-Mer
2 L'Amelie
3 Le Gurp
4 Montalivet-les-Bains
5 Le Pin Sec
6 Hourtin-Plage
7 Carcans-Plage
8 Lacanau ★
9 Le Porge-Océan
10 Le Grande Crochot
11 Le Truc Vert to Cap Ferret
12 Banc d'Arguin
13 La Salie
14 Biscarrosse-Plage
15 Mimizan-Plage
16 Lespecier
17 Contis Plage
18 Cap de l'Homy
19 St-Girons-Plage
20 Moliets Plage
21 Messanges Plage
22 Vieux Boucau

N

10 km
10 miles

Atlantic
Ocean

Surfing Girondes & Les Landes

Gravière. Estagnots. Capbreton. Le Penon. Lacanau. Names that go right to the heart of surfing. For a lifestyle that only arrived on these shores relatively recently, this region has a history that goes back almost to day one. Small surfwear companies from Down Under landed on this strip of the Gallic coastline with little money and even less French vocabulary. They soon saw their businesses grow to become multinational organizations at the very core of the Hossegor community. At one time there were so many ex-pat Australians living here that the town became known as Aussiegor. For decades, the first trip to these hallowed beaches has been a rite of passage that every grommet had to experience. Sleeping in the back of a van, drinking cheap wine, seeing the beautiful French women on the beach and feeling too pasty and white to even make eye contact. This region has taken surfing to its heart like no other in Europe. Pros are recognized on the street and asked for autographs while walking past surf shops that are more like surf boutiques.

Yet, venture north into Les Landes and although the landscape remains the same, the beaches become steadily quieter, and the lifestyle and atmosphere more relaxed. The top of the Dune de Pyla, a 120-m high mountain of sand and the biggest in Europe, offers an awesome perspective. To the north and to the south stretches one long, continuous beach – as far as the eye can see. Occasional lighthouses stick their heads above the dense green pine forests, whose aroma fills the air. This long spine of sand dunes has become the backbone of European surfing. In a lifestyle where history plays such an important role, this region has a track record that few places in the world can match. And when it comes to quality beach breaks, it is second to none.

Coastline

There is 225 km of straight beach from Pointe de Grave to Anglet, broken only by the Bassin d'Arcachon. The west-facing strip has a huge ridge of sand dunes behind which stretches a dense pine forest. An extreme example of this can be found to the south of Arcachon, where the amazing Dune de Playa dominates the landscape. This huge sand dune towers above the forest and is slowly encroaching landward, swallowing massive pine trees as it advances.

The immense amount of sand moving around this coastline means one thing – sandbanks and lots of them. Currents and storms can create and destroy perfect sandbars with amazing regularity. However, as one bank is swept away, another will come to life.

The only drawback to this open coastline is that when a big swell hits, there are few sheltered spots. Capbreton will always be crowded

There was a sandbar near Hossegor, I got it one morning, it was bit overhead and no one else was out. For like three hours I surfed alone and this big storm started on the horizon, with lightning and thunder – it was amazing. It was sunny where I was, and I watched the storm in the distance but the waves were just clean and perfect. It was one of my best sessions ever.

Dan Malloy, US pro surfer

Girondes & Les Landes board guide

Kong model
Shaper: Mark Phipps, Quiksilver Surfboards

» 6'0" x 19" x 2+".
» This board has been designed by the king of power surfing, Kong!
» The idea behind the board is that there are a lot of solidly built surfers looking for a board with a full plan shape, flat deck and low rocker.
» With boxy rails and deep triple concaves, the Kong model is not a conventional looking board, yet is incredibly fast and responsive.
» Highly suited to surfers chasing greater paddling power.
» "It's the board that most surfers need, the right equipment to get more waves and have fun out there." Gary Elkerton

Mark 11
Shaper: Mark Phipps, Quiksilver Surfboards

» 6'6" x 18¼" x 2¼".
» A board created purely with performance in mind.
» Thin and narrow with a deep single concave and accentuated rocker, this board is very popular with the Quiksilver Surfboard team.
» These boards are for surfers looking to blow up in the water.
» Perfect for when Hossegor and Capbreton get a little bigger and more powerful, and you don't quite need a gun.

 Boards by **Euroglass**
(Quiksilver Surfboards and Channel Islands European distributor)
81 Av des Artisans, 40150, Soorts-Hossegor, T00 33 (0)5584 34185
www.quiksilver.com/surfboards, www.cisurfboards.com
or contact euroglass90@aol.com

in big swells and the breaks around Soulac-sur-Mer are also popular. If all else fails, head south into the Basque region where the bays will have plenty to offer.

Localism

This region is home to some of the busiest breaks in Europe. There will also be many top riders in the water, especially when the world tour is in town in September/October. The breaks will be very competitive around Hossegor but as you head north the spots get quieter and more chilled. Many spots in Les Landes and Gironde can be empty, even in early Autumn. The moral is, get out and explore – if you're prepared to walk, you can have your pick of empty peaks.

Top local surfers Many of France's top surfers can be found around Hossegor. The likes of **Micky Picon, Fred Robin, Eric Rebière** as well as a host of ex-pats including **Robbie Page, Carwyn Williams, Gabe Davies** and **Sam Carrier**. When the WCT events are on you will find the whole top 44 and many WQS surfers swelling the ranks in the water.

Getting around

For a fast north to south journey the N10 inland is the best bet. There is a whole series of D roads that follow the coastline and allow easy access to every resort along this huge beach. There is always ample parking by the beach, and a short walk should yield a decent bank to surf.

CHRIS NELSON

France Girondes & Les Landes Surfing

18 Cap de l'Homy

Breaks

Gironde

1 Soulac-sur-Mer

- **Break type**: Beach break.
- **Conditions**: Medium to big swells, offshore in easterly winds.
- **Hazards/tips**: Good spot in big swells.
- **Sleeping**: Soulac-sur-Mer ›› p183.

Sitting 9 km south of Pointe de Grave, Soulac marks the start of an epic stretch of sand running south to Biarritz, only broken by the Bassin d'Arcachon. Soulac's area of fine beaches is affected by offshore sandbars deposited by the River Gironde. These cut out a lot of swell and make this a good area to check in big swells. Works on all tides but best from low to three-quarters.

2 L'Amelie

- **Break type**: Beach break.
- **Conditions**: Medium swells, offshore in easterly winds.
- **Hazards/tips**: Rips when big.
- **Sleeping**: Soulac-sur-Mer ›› p183.

Follow the D101 south to this quiet beach. L'Amelie has some good peaks and works best in medium swells. As with most spots along this stretch of coastline, it works through all tides. However when a big swell hits it can have strong rips and be difficult to paddle out. In small swells these beaches are suitable for supervised beginners.

3 Le Gurp

- **Break type**: Beach break.
- **Conditions**: Medium swells, offshore in easterly winds.
- **Hazards/tips**: Quiet beach.
- **Sleeping**: Soulac-sur-Mer ›› p183.

The beaches here have some great banks in clean swells. Can take a bigger swell but banks tend to move around quickly and change with tides.

Central France

Air ——— Sea

°F Averages

°C

90 — 30
70 — 20
50 — 10
30 — 0

J F M A M J J A S O N D

| 5/4/3 Boots & gloves | 4/3 Boots | 3/2 | 3/2 |

4 Montalivet-les-Bains

- **Break type**: Beach break.
- **Conditions**: Small to medium swells, offshore in easterly winds.
- **Hazards/tips**: Good beach break.
- **Sleeping**: Montalivet-les-Bains ›› p183.

An extension of this huge stretch of beach, again can have some good banks. Popular in the summer but very quiet off season.

5 Le Pin Sec

- **Break type**: Beach break.
- **Conditions**: Small to medium swells, offshore in easterly winds.
- **Hazards/tips**: Good beach break.
- **Sleeping**: Montalivet-les-Bains/Hourtin Plage ›› p183.

Another quiet spot with various quality peaks. Doesn't handle a big swell. Plenty of scope for exploration around here.

6 Hourtin-Plage

- **Break type**: Beach break.
- **Conditions**: Small to medium swells, offshore in easterly winds.
- **Hazards/tips**: Good beach break.
- **Sleeping**: Hourtin Plage ›› p184.

A popular summertime beach with many tourists and day trippers from Bordeaux. Plenty of room up and down the beach – pack a lunch and head off.

DEMI TAYLOR

7 Carcans-Plage ›› p176

7 Carcans-Plage

- **Break type**: Beach break.
- **Conditions**: Small to medium swells, offshore in easterly winds.
- **Hazards/tips**: Good beach break.
- **Sleeping**: Carcans-Plage ▸▸ *p184*.

Small village with amenities and parking near to the beachfront. Not so busy or commercial as Lacanau but still a popular spot in the summer. The peaks near the village fill up first but a short walk should provide quieter peaks.

8 Lacanau

- **Break type**: Beach break.
- **Conditions**: Small to medium swells.
- **Size**: 2-8 ft.
- **Length**: 20-75 m plus.
- **Swell**: Northwesterly to westerly.
- **Wind**: Easterly.
- **Tide**: All tides.
- **Bottom**: Sandbanks.
- **Entry/exit**: From the beach.
- **Hazards/tips**: Heavy when good, very busy.
- **Sleeping**: Lacanau-Océan ▸▸ *p184*.

The popular resort town of Lacanau-Océan has been on the surfing map since the early, hazy days of French wave riding, and for good reason. Sandbanks build up,

assisted by the occasional groyne, to produce miles of consistent, powerful, sometimes hollow beachbreak. The Lacanau Pro has been an annual feature since 1979 and has been won by just about every big name on the circuit from Rabbit, through to Carroll, Curren, Occy and Pottz. Lacanau is slowly expanding and spilling into the generous pine forests that fill the gap between ocean and lake. In the summer months, the beach and town throngs with the bronzed and the beautiful, the pros and the poseurs, but in the autumn months, the crowds die back and the swells kick in to reveal the true beauty of the area.

> **ⓘ** *If you like* Lacanau, *try* Praa Sands *in England (see page 88) or* Praia de Fontella *in Spain (see page 248).*

9 Le Porge-Océan

- **Break type**: Beach break.
- **Conditions**: Small to medium swells, offshore in easterly winds.
- **Hazards/tips**: Good beach break.
- **Sleeping**: Lacanau-Océan ▸▸ *p184*.

Another good section of beach backed by pine trees which is quiet except during the peak summer season. Works on all tides.

10 Le Grande Crochot

- **Break type**: Beach break.
- **Conditions**: Small to medium swells, offshore in easterly winds.
- **Hazards/tips**: Good beach break.
- **Sleeping**: Lacanau-Océan/Cap Ferret ▸▸ *p184*.

The D106 leads the Bordeaux surfers straight to this popular beach. Another stretch of golden sand that can have excellent banks through the tides. There will be surfers here year round, but very popular in the summer.

11 Le Truc Vert to Cap Ferret

- **Break type**: Beach break.
- **Conditions**: All swells, offshore in easterly winds.
- **Hazards/tips**: Good beach break.
- **Sleeping**: Cap Ferret ▸▸ *p184*.

The huge stretch of beach from Le Truc Vert to Cap Ferret, with roads down through the pines to a series of spots, is a great place to lose the crowds. Cap Ferret is worth checking in a big swell on an incoming tide as the cape cuts out the swell. There are nasty rips on an outgoing tide as water empties from the Basin d'Arcachon, a massive lagoon.

12 Banc d'Arguin

- **Break type**: Beach break.
- **Conditions**: Small to medium swells, offshore in easterly winds.
- **Hazards/tips**: Huge offshore sandbank.
- **Sleeping**: Dune de Pyla ▸▸ *p184*.

Overlooked by the towering sand dune, Dune de Pyla, the biggest in Europe, the Banc d'Arguin is a huge sandbank sitting in the mouth of the Bassin d'Arcachon. Boats leave from Dune de Pyla for the sandbank. Worth exploring for a unique surf session. Watch out for rips in big tides and big swells.

DEMI TAYLOR

8 Lacanau

13 La Salie

- ◉ **Break type**: Beach break.
- ◉ **Conditions**: Medium swells, offshore in easterly winds.
- ❶ **Hazards/tips**: Quiet spot.
- ◉ **Sleeping**: Dune de Pyla ▸▸ *p184*.

Heading south on the D218, there is a turning that leads through the pines to the beach. Protected by the Pointe d'Arcachon and the sandbanks in the river, this area doesn't pick up as much swell as Biscarrosse to the south and the banks shift around due to the currents. Nice quiet location.

Les Landes

14 Biscarrosse-Plage

- ◉ **Break type**: Beach break.
- ◉ **Conditions**: Small to medium swells, offshore in easterly winds.
- ❶ **Hazards/tips**: Excellent beach break.
- ◉ **Sleeping**: Biscarosse ▸▸ *p185*.

The first stop in Les Landes, this is an excellent quality beach break with plenty of banks. From the top of the dunes you can see banks all the way north and south, with the ones by the main beach access getting busy. There are also nice hollow peaks by the northern access point. Busy at weekends but with a chilled vibe in the water.

15 Mimizan-Plage

- ◉ **Break type**: Beach break.
- ◉ **Conditions**: Small to medium swells, offshore in easterly winds.
- ❶ **Hazards/tips**: Rips when big.
- ◉ **Sleeping**: Mimizan ▸▸ *p185*.

Between Biscarrosse and Mimizan is a restricted military zone. There is a rivermouth here and beachfront parking by the surf club. The most popular banks are in front of the surf club, but there is a good vibe in the water. There are two groynes with banks. There is a very smelly factory by the river on the road in, so water quality at the rivermouth may not be the best.

16 Lespecier

- ◉ **Break type**: Beach break.
- ◉ **Conditions**: Small to medium swells, offshore in easterly winds.
- ❶ **Hazards/tips**: Beautiful, quiet location.
- ◉ **Sleeping**: Mimizan ▸▸ *p185*.

This is a secluded spot reached by quite roads through the Forêt de Mimizan, either from Mimizan to the north or Bias inland. Good quality beach break with numerous banks to the north and south.

17 Contis Plage

- ◉ **Break type**: Beach break.
- ◉ **Conditions**: Small to medium swells, offshore in easterly winds.
- ❶ **Hazards/tips**: Beautiful, quiet location.
- ◉ **Sleeping**: Mimizan ▸▸ *p185*.

This tiny resort has a rivermouth and stone groyne to check out for banks. There are also some excellent waves in front of the old bunker. You can check out the surf from the car park on top of the dunes just to the north of the village. A summer resort, quiet outside the holidays. Great lighthouse marooned in the middle of the woods. The car park is a popular autumn free-camp spot.

18 Cap de l'Homy

- ◉ **Break type**: Beach break.
- ◉ **Conditions**: Small to medium swells, offshore in easterly winds.
- ❶ **Hazards/tips**: Beautiful, quiet location.
- ◉ **Sleeping**: Mimizan/Moliets Plage ▸▸ *p185*.

There is a campsite overlooking the sea with some great banks stretching to the north and south. The bank in front of the access fills up first but a short walk should yield empty waves. Chilled-out location.

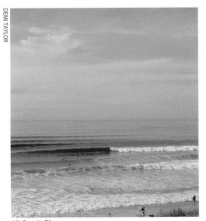

17 Contis Plage

14 Biscarrosse-Plage

France Girondes & Les Landes Breaks La Salie to Cap de l'Homy

19 St-Girons-Plage

- **Break type**: Beach break.
- **Conditions**: Small to medium swells, offshore in easterly winds.
- **Hazards/tips**: Beautiful, quiet location.
- **Sleeping**: Moliets Plage ▸▸ p185.

Accessed via the D42, this is another small resort village, quiet out of season with a slightly run-down feel about it, with some great waves in the right conditions.

20 Moliets Plage

- **Break type**: Beach break.
- **Conditions**: Small to medium swells, offshore in easterly winds.
- **Hazards/tips**: Pleasant resort with good waves.
- **Sleeping**: Moliets Plage ▸▸ p185.

The D117 hits the coast at one of the most pleasant resorts on this stretch of Les Landes' endless sandy coastline. The banks here shift around but there are generally some great peaks to be had.

21 Messanges Plage

- **Break type**: Beach break.
- **Conditions**: Small to medium swells, offshore in easterly winds.
- **Hazards/tips**: Excellent spot, quiet off season.
- **Sleeping**: Moliets Plage/Vieux Boucau ▸▸ p185.

Excellent series of banks, plenty of peaks to choose from in a good swell. Low tide sees some hollow, grinding barrels jacking up onto the sandbars. In a bigger swell it can be a hell of a paddle without a decent channel. Works through all tides, and although busy in the summer, off season it is quiet.

22 Vieux Boucau

- **Break type**: Beach break.
- **Conditions**: Small to medium swells, offshore in easterly winds.
- **Hazards/tips**: Popular spot with strong surf community.
- **Sleeping**: Vieux Boucau ▸▸ p178.

There are great banks here and a much more mellow scene than at Hossegor. The breaks by the surf club and main access are the busiest but there are plenty of waves up and down the beach. The surf club in the dunes (founded in 1973) has a new clubhouse shaped like a breaking wave, in tune with the natural surroundings.

23 Plage des Casernes

- **Break type**: Beach break.
- **Conditions**: Small to medium swells, offshore in easterly winds.
- **Hazards/tips**: Beautiful, quiet location.
- **Sleeping**: Seignosse/Hossegor/ Capbreton ▸▸ p186.

The place to go to find quiet banks during the high season. This long stretch of beach has miles of banks and endless possibilities. From the car park, follow the tracks through the pines.

Hossegor

24 Le Penon

- **Break type**: Beach break.
- **Conditions**: Small to medium swells, offshore in easterly winds.
- **Hazards/tips**: Quality beach break.
- **Sleeping**: Seignosse/Hossegor/ Capbreton ▸▸ p186.

First of the renowned Seignosse/Hossegor breaks. Park in front of the apartments and check the surf from the dunes. Banks cluster around the pier and also further to the north where it is a bit quieter. Works on all tides.

26 Estagnots

18 Cap de l'Homy ▸▸ p177

25 Bourdaines

- **Break type**: Beach break.
- **Conditions**: Small to medium swells, offshore in easterly winds.
- **Hazards/tips**: Less busy than the breaks to the south.
- **Sleeping**: Seignosse/Hossegor/ Capbreton ▸▸ *p186*.

This stretch of beach starts to the south of the jetty and heads south to Estagnots. A good option in the summer, when it is less busy than the breaks to the south. Can have some excellent banks, some of which will be working at all states of tide.

26 Estagnots

- **Break type**: Beach break.
- **Conditions**: All swells, offshore in easterly winds.
- **Hazards/tips**: Heavy shore break at high tide.
- **Sleeping**: Seignosse/Hossegor/ Capbreton ▸▸ *p186*.

Traditional home of the Rip Curl Pro, this bank has a reputation for producing quality left-hand waves. At low there can be long walling waves, which break closer in at high when it can have a punishing shore break, especially in bigger swells.

27 Les Culs Nuls

- **Break type**: Break type.
- **Conditions**: All swells, offshore in easterly winds.
- **Hazards/tips**: Nudist beach.
- **Sleeping**: Seignosse/Hossegor/ Capbreton ▸▸ *p186*.

Sandwiched between Estagnots and La Gravière, this spot always attracts a crowd. The fact that this is also the official nudist beach for Hossegor may help to swell the crowd. It is home to some quality sandbanks which work through the tides. It can also hold a large swell. Punishingly heavy shore break at high tide.

19 Moliets Plage

21 Messanges Plage

24 Le Penon

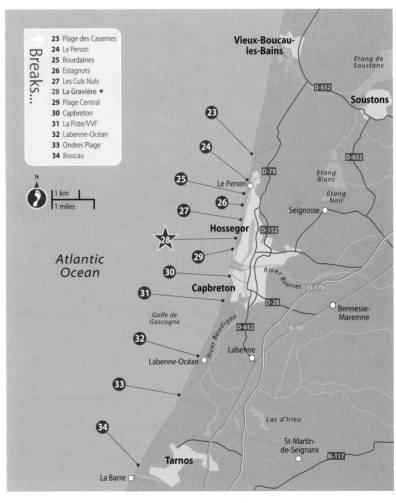

Breaks...
23 Plage des Casernes
24 Le Penon
25 Bourdaines
26 Estagnots
27 Les Culs Nuls
28 La Gravière ★
29 Plage Central
30 Capbreton
31 La Piste/VVF
32 Labenne-Océan
33 Ondres Plage
34 Boucau

1 km
1 miles

Atlantic Ocean

Vieux-Boucau-les-Bains
Etang de Soustons
Soustons
23
24
25 Le Penon
27 26
Seignosse
Etang Blanc
Etang Noir
28
Hossegor
29
30
Capbreton
31
Golfe de Gascogne
River Bourret
Bennesse-Maremne
Labenne
32
Labenne-Océan
33
River Boudigau
Lac d'Irieu
34
Tarnos
La Barre
St-Martin-de-Seignanx

France Girondes & Les Landes Breaks Bourdaines to Les Culs Nuls

28 La Gravière

- **Break type**: Beach break.
- **Conditions**: All swells.
- **Size**: 2-12 ft.
- **Length**: 25-75 m.
- **Swell**: Northwesterly/westerly.
- **Wind**: Easterly winds.
- **Tide**: All tides.
- **Bottom**: Sandbar.
- **Entry/exit**: Off the beach in the channel (if there is one).
- **Hazards/tips**: Heavy, hollow, crowded.
- **Sleeping**: Seignosse/Hossegor/ Capbreton ▸▸ *p186*.

Known as one of the world's best beach breaks, the famous bank here can throw up very heavy, very hollow lefts and rights. The swell comes out of deep water and really packs a punch, breaking even in big swells. Definitely a break for experienced surfers when it's on. Will be crowded with some of the world's best surfers. Regular haunt of the top 44 when the contests are on and, off season, the likes of Robbie Page, Tom Curren, Micky Picon, Martin Potter, Carwyn Williams and Sam Carrier. Has a heavy shore break at high tide.

ⓘ *If you like* La Gravière, *try low tide* Croyde *in England (see page 75) or* Supertubos *in Portugal (see page 299).*

Occy at Hossegor

Occy at Bunkers

Pottz

28 Gravière at sunset

Fred Robin

"I love Capbreton. I have a place there near VVF, my favourite spot to surf. This region has such a great lifestyle, great food, good bars and the waves are crazy. In the summer there are so many people, but then it gets much better in the autumn. To get waves here you just have to be patient – there are plenty of waves to go around."

Fred Robin, pro surfer

France Girondes & Les Landes Breaks La Gravière

29 Plage Central

◉ **Break type**: Beach break.
◉ **Conditions**: All swells, offshore in easterly winds.
❶ **Hazards/tips**: Crowds when small, heavy when big.
◉ **Sleeping**: Seignosse/Hossegor/ Capbreton ⟫ p186.

In big swells, **L'Epi Nord**, an outside sandbank, can come to life with some huge rideable waves for the area's big-wave chargers. In smaller swells the banks near the rivermouth breakwater are popular, throwing up some decent lefts.

30 Capbreton

◉ **Break type**: Beach break.
◉ **Conditions**: Medium to big swells, offshore in easterly winds.
❶ **Hazards/tips**: Sheltered in big swells.
◉ **Sleeping**: Seignosse/Hossegor/ Capbreton ⟫ p186.

A series of groynes breaks up the beach just south of the river. The area nearest the river is known as **Kiddies Corner** as it is very sheltered and surfable in the biggest swells. The other beaches get very busy when the surf is big. Sandbanks build up by the groynes and can produce good rights peeling off the south side of them.

31 La Piste/VVF

◉ **Break type**: Beach break.
◉ **Conditions**: Small to medium swells, offshore in easterly winds.
❶ **Hazards/tips**: Hollow banks in front of the WW2 bunkers.
◉ **Sleeping**: Seignosse/Hossegor/ Capbreton ⟫ p186.

An excellent stretch of beach, heading south from the old bunkers, with many banks that work through the tides. Popular place to surf with some very hollow rights in clean swells and light offshores. Gets busy in the summer.

32 Labenne-Océan

◉ **Break type**: Beach break.
◉ **Conditions**: Small to medium swells, offshore in easterly/southeasterly winds.
❶ **Hazards/tips**: Much less crowded than Hossegor.
◉ **Sleeping**: Seignosse/Hossegor/ Capbreton ⟫ p186.

A great place to escape the crazy summer days in Hossegor. Take the D126 off the N10 and a whole range of quiet peaks are available. Works best in a small to medium swell on a low to three-quarter tide. The sandbanks around the main access points fill up first. Pack a picnic and take a hike – you'll be surprised at how quiet it can be.

33 Ondres Plage

◉ **Break type**: Beach break.
◉ **Conditions**: Small to medium swells, offshore in easterly/southeasterly winds.
❶ **Hazards/tips**: Good option for quiet waves.
◉ **Sleeping**: Seignosse/Hossegor/ Capbreton ⟫ p186.

Amazing to find such quiet waves in the heart of the surfing southwest. If the main peaks are busy, a short walk north or south will yield something quieter. Banks change with tides, but lower tides seem to be better.

34 Boucau

◉ **Break type**: Left-hand jetty.
◉ **Conditions**: All swells, offshore in easterly/southeasterly winds.
❶ **Hazards/tips**: Not for beginners.
◉ **Sleeping**: Seignosse/Hossegor/ Capbreton ⟫ p186.

Not to be confused with Vieux Boucau, this spot is a left-hand, walling wave that breaks along the sandbar built up along the northern side of the concrete jetty at the mouth of the River L'Adour. The jetty also offers some protection from southerly winds. The waves here can be pretty awesome in the right conditions, though the locals like to keep quiet about the spot. Parking available in front of the break.

30 Capbreton – it's a dog's life

30 Capbreton

31 VVF

Listings

22 Vieux Boucau surf club ▶▶ *p178*

Gironde

Getting there

The drive around the Gironde – south to Bordeaux and then north along the N215 to Soulac-sur-Mer – is a serious commitment of over 200 km. But the endless line of sandbanks stretching as far as the eye can see soon makes up for it. The alternative entry route into the Gironde is a lot less painless, especially off season. A year-round ferry service connects Royan (T0546-383515) on the north bank of the mouth of the Gironde with Verdon (T0556-733773) on the south bank in just 20 mins. The service runs regularly in the summer , every couple of hours in winter, €3 passengers, from €35 for a van. In the height of the summer, queuing may send you over the edge. Otherwise drive two-thirds of the way down the river and hop on the Blaye-Lamarque ferry (20 mins, about €3 passengers, from €19.50 vans, T0557- 420449) which can shave almost 100 km off your journey.

Soulac-sur-Mer

Sitting on the northern tip of Médoc, this resort town all but closes in winter months. As with the majority of towns and villages on this stretch, the beach is the focal point, with most amenities on the handily named R de la Plage. This includes a couple of surf shops, **Cangoo** and **Aloha Beach**, as well as the post office, tourist information office, daily food market and a plethora of cafés, bars and restaurants.

🛏 Sleeping

There are a couple of sleeping options on R de la Plage including the unexceptional **D-E Hôtel La Dame de Coeur**, T0556-098080, open year round. **Camping** There are a couple of seasonal camping options. **Palace**, Blvd Marsan de Montbrun at northern end of town, T0556-098022, open May-15 Sep. Heading south on the D101 to L'Amélie sur Mer, the smaller **Les Sables d'Argent**, T0556-098287, nestles in pine forest on the beachfront, open Apr-Sep, with the option of cabins and statics. The slightly cheaper and larger **Amélie Plage**, T0556-098727, is a less level site on the seafront, open Mar-Jan.

Montalivet

This truly seasonal resort all but shuts down outside Apr-Sep. In summer they hold a massive daily market selling goods from across the region but the area is better known for the nearby **Euronat**, Europe's largest naturist park.

🌀 Flat spells

Skating Walk north along the beach to the skate park behind the beachfront car park.

🛏 Sleeping

C-E L'Océan, beachfront, T0556-093005, you pay more for a seaview. They also have apartments for 4 at €300-510/week, again you pay more for a room with a view, and one of the only restaurants open out of season. **Camping Le Chesnays**, about 6 km inland, T0556-417274, open Apr-Oct. **Camping Municipal**, south of the town on Av de l'Europe, T0556-093345, open May-Sep.

🍴 Eating

There are plenty of seasonal cafés and restaurants on the main drag including the excellent **La Guinguette** pizzeria where you can eat in or take away. **Globetrotter**, Av de l'Océan, are open year round (sometimes only weekends) and do a mean chicken fajita.

○ Shopping

Spyder Surf Shop, on Av de l'Océan, is open year round while **Surf & Co**, who also hire out bikes and skateboards, are open summer only. The **market** is on Av de l'Océan.

❶ Directory

Tourist information: on the main Av de l'Océan.

Hourtin-Plage

Heading south on the coast road you pass plenty of right turns to the beach with endless possibilities. At the top of Forêt d'Hourtin sits the summer resort of Hourtin-Plage with its own surf shop, **Surf & Co**, on R Jean Lafitte.

● Sleeping

Camping In a pine forest just back from the beach is the massive **Côte d'Argent**, T0556-091025, open mid-May to mid-Sep, fairly pricey with statics available. At Hourtin, 9 km inland, cheaper camping options include **Les Ourmes**, on Av du Lac by the massive Lac d'Hourtin (which attracts more than its fair share of mozzies), T0556-091276, open Apr-Sep, statics available.

Carcans-Plage

Backed by the largest freshwater lake in France, Carcans-Plage is another seasonal seaside resort which offers a little relief for those trying to escape the Lacanau hordes. Grab a pizza to restore you post-surf at **Le Galipo** on Av de Plage. Try **Camping Municipal**, just back from the beachfront, T0556-034144, open Mar-Sep; or, inland at Carcans, **Le Lierre**, on Route de Philibert, T0556-034009, is open year round.

Lacanau-Océan

Follow the D6 from Bordeaux or the coast road south from Carcans-Plage to the summer resort of Lacanau-Océan. Slowly expanding between awesome dunes and pine forest, this is a popular, busy summer resort for families and surfers and has played host to the annual Lacanau Pro since 1979.

✿ Flat spells

Bordeaux Head inland along the D6 to the home of vin rouge and learn how to truly appreciate the plonk you've been necking at the **Maison du Vin** on 1 Cours de 30 Julliet – about €20 for a 2-hr course. If this has whetted your appetite, they can also recommend a selection of nearby châteaux where you can

sample more wine.
Casino Bright lights, slot machines, roulette . . .
Golf Get a round in at **Golf d'Ardilouse International Golf** on the main road in from Lacanau town, T0556-039298. **Lac de Lacanau** Bike round the lake, avoiding the mozzies! **Massage** Revive yourself after a heavy session with a professional rub down at **Lineavital** at Domaine Aplus, T0556-039244.

● Sleeping

E-F Villa le Zenith, just a short walk from the beach on Av Adjudant Guittard, T0684-608808, open Apr-Sep, acts as the local hostel, with beds from €16 and kitchen facilities. **Self-catering** The pretty 2-bed villa **Raphael Marguérite**, on R Gabriel Dupuy, a short walk to the beach and town, T0556-034678, offers a good rate – from €250/week – off season. There are a couple of private cottages available year round at **Ardilouse Golf Course**, T0044(0)1444-455081, www.ourcottagesinfrance.com, a couple of miles from the beach, one sleeping up to 7, the other sleeping 4 people. Off season the rates are very reasonable, from around €320/week; in high summer the prices almost quadruple. **Camping Airotel de l'Océan**, R du Repos, T0556-032445, open May-Sep, statics available. **Grands Pins**, T0556-032077, open Apr-Dec, is an excellent site set in the pine forests with private access across the dunes to Plage Nord – about a 15-min walk into town along the beach. It also has a good, reasonably priced on-site restaurant serving anything from pizzas to coquilles St-Jacques. **Free-campers** regularly pitch in the dunes between the campsite and the town with little bother.

◑ Shopping

There are several **surf shops** here including Lacanau's first surf shop, **Surf City**, on the main Blvd de Plage, which opened in 1978 and sells everything from boards to boardies. There is also **Pacific Island** on Allées Pierre Ortau.

◐ Directory

Bike hire: Locacycles, Av de l'Europe, have

both 'touring' bikes and VTT (*vélo tout terrain*) or mountain bikes. **Tourist information**: on Pl de l'Europe, also offering summer internet access.

Cap Ferret

This thin finger of land found at the mouth of the Bassin d'Arcachon marks a pause in the stretch of sand dunes and beach breaks. To the north, on the Route de Forestière, is camping **Truc Vert**, T0556-608955, open May-Sep, back from the beach in the pine trees. In the main town is **Camaro** surf shop, Blvd de la Plage, who can service your basic needs.

Dune de Pyla

From Cap Ferret, the road goes round the triangular Bassin d'Arcachon before heading south towards the natural wonder, Dune de Pyla, which – at over 100 m – is Europe's highest sand dune.

✿ Flat spells

Bikes Head into Arcachon and hire bikes at **Locabeach 33**, on the main Blvd de Plage, and explore the cycle routes around the basin. **Boats** Hop on a boat from Dune de Pyla to Banc d'Arguin, T0557-722828 for details. **Casino** Check out Arcachon's casino on Blvd de Plage. **Dune** Grab your board, take the fins out, climb the dune, and take the drop! **Oysters** Head to the port of Gujan Mestras, home of Banc d'Arguin oysters, for a sampling session. A dozen freshly shucked oysters will set you back around €2.50. **Skating** Head for the mini-ramp at La Teste on the N250.

● Sleeping

Camping There are a couple of seasonal campsites here, all on the D218 Route Biscarosse. **La Fôret**, T0556-227328, nestled between the forest and the imposing sand dune, open Apr-Nov, has statics and swanky wooden chalets. Continuing along the road, **Panorama**, T0556-221044, is on the edge of the dune, open May-Sep, also has statics. **Petit Nice**, a terraced site with easy beach access, T0556-227403, is open Apr-Sep.

Les Landes

Biscarrosse-Plage

Heading south on the D218-D83, Biscarrosse is the first town in Les Landes an area of flat, sandy pine forest. With good amenities and a good atmosphere, it makes an excellent base. Off season, the town closes. There are few locals and most of the travelling surfers focus on the fabled beach breaks of Hossegor to the south.

✪ Flat spells

Aventure Parc Get in training for your next session at this wooded, army assault course style, fun park on the Route de la Plage, T0558-825340, entry from €18. **Casino** Gamble, gamble, gamble on the Blvd des Sables. **Golf** Get a round in at the par-68 **Golf de Biscarosse** on the Route des Lacs, T0558-098493 – cheaper during the week. **Karting** Drive inland to Chemin d'en Hill, Biscarrosse-Bourg, for a go at some serious driving, T0558-788850. **Kitesurfing** Well, if the wind really won't stop blowing you can get some lessons in on the lake at Port Navarosse with **Kikeo Windstation**, T0672-998306, open Mar-Oct. **Skating** Head for the skate park – complete with midi-ramp, rails and fun box – in Biscarrosse-Bourg at the roundabout on Av Daudet.

⊕ Sleeping

Camping Aire de camping: year round, vans can park up at the Le Vivier Aire de Camping, R de Tit, Biscarrosse-Plage. It is free to camp except in peak (Jul-Aug) season, when it is pay and display. From 1 May, vans can park overnight inland at the **Porte de Navarrosse Aire de Camping**, which has a multi-service point and electric hook-up (30 Jun -31 Aug). In terms of 'proper' sites, **Camping Maguide**, Chemin de Maguide, T0558-098190, is open year round and has statics. Another good, but seasonal, option is **Campeole Plage Sud**, R Becasses, T0558-782124, open May-Sep, chalets available.

① Eating/drinking

In season there is a plethora of seafood restaurants and cafés lining Av des Plages. For everything else – pizza, pasta, takeaway – there's **La Florentin**, open year round. You know it's wrong but there is a **McDonald's** in Biscarrosse-Bourg on Av Laouadie. Also check out the nearby **Globe Trotters Café**.

○ Shopping

Surf shops There are a couple in town including **Blue Hawaii** off the main square open Apr-Sep and **Tamaris Surf Shop** on rue des Tamaris. **Supermarket** The **E.Leclerc** supermarket on the north edge of Biscarrosse Ville, is a good place to stock up on rations and fill up with petrol.

① Directory

Banks: several ATMs including a **Credit Agricole** in the semi-pedestrianized centre. **Bike hire**: Au Velo Pour Tous, Av de la Plage. **Internet**: the surf club may check the charts for you, if not, head into the Bourg to **Cyber Café L'Estela**, Av de la République, where access is slow and fairly pricey. **Police**: Gendarmerie, Av de la Plage, T0558-782291. **Tourist information**: Pl de la Fontaine.

Mimizan

Mimizan is another seaside town of 2 halves, Bourg and Plage. There are several good camping options here including the swanky **Club Marina**, just back from the front at Plage Sud, T0558-091266, open mid May-mid Sep, cabins available. **Camping de la Plage**, Blvd de l'Atlantique, T0558- 090032, open 15 Apr-Sep, is slighly cheaper and also offers cabins. As a fall back, **Camping La Lande**, T0558-824662, is open year round but well back from the beach on the D44.

○ Shopping

Karukera surf shop, on the beachfront Av Côte d'Argent, sells hardware as well as clothes. In Mimizan-Bourg there is a **Netto** discount shop and a **Leclerc** on Av de Bordeaux as well as an **Intermarché** on the R de Baleste (heading south) with a 24-hr service station.

① Directory

Pharmacy: on Av Maurice Martin.

Moliets Plage

Heading south along the D652 you pass a handy Aire Natural (free-camping spot) on the way into this inviting seaside resort, laid out in 'garden city' style. On Av de l'Océan, **Camping Saint Martin**, T0558-485230, which has a pool, and **Les Cigales**, T0558-485118, are both open Apr-Sep. Off season however the town follows form and shuts down, including **Guaratiba surf shop** opposite the campsites. **Café de l'Océan**, on the beachfront, is one of the only decent cafés that stays open off season – except for Tue.

Vieux Boucau

The pretty resort town of Vieux Boucau is a popular yet relaxed spot with an excellent beachfront campsite. The town centre has plenty of amenities, even off season, including **Locacycles** renting bikes on Grand' Rue and the **Wishbone surf shop** on Av des Pêcheurs – open half days and weekends from Nov depending on the weather. There is also a nice **skate park** in the town near the sports centre, opposite the *pelote* stadium, complete with rails, midi-ramps, quarter ramps, spined ramps and a fun box.

⊕ Sleeping

Camping Camping Les Sableres, Blvd de Marensin, open Apr-15 Oct, is just a short walk from the beach with statics from €185/week for 4.

Hossegor

Seignosse-Hossegor-Capbreton

This affluent, sprawling, modern collection of low-rise resort towns – with 2 golf courses, 1 lake, hundreds of bars and cafés and a similar number of surf shops – has become the focal point for surfing in the southwest, for surfers and international businesses alike. While Hossegor forms the centre and focal point, Seignosse and Capbreton take up the flanks to the north and south respectively.

❄ Flat spells

Bowling Get a strike at **Bowling du Port**, Av Maurice Martin, Capbreton, which also has a pool table. **Casino** Make a killing at **Le Sporting Casino**, Av Maurice Martin, Capbreton. **Golf** There are a couple of courses to choose from, the par-72 **Golf de Seignosse**, T0558-416830, or the par-71 **Golf Club d'Hossegor**, T0558-435699. **Go-karting** Burn round the 855-m outdoor track on Blvd des Cigales, Capbreton, T0558-418009. **Skating** Seignosse Car Park has nice concrete banks. **Hall 04**, Zone Artisanale, Soorts-Hossegor, is home to an excellent pay-to-play wooden skate park with bowls, banks, rails, fun boxes etc. **Capbreton skatepark**, with a midi-ramp, fun box, rails and banks, overlooks the Port de Plaisance.

● Sleeping

There are hundreds of apartments available to rent but they are best booked through the tourist office or an agent such as **Seignosse Immobilier**, T0558-433226. **Camping Aire de Campings**: there's an Aire de Stationnement Pour Surfeurs, just off the CD79 Le Penon-Seignosse route. Continuing south just past Seignosse Golf Club is an Aire du Stationnement, as well as one in Hossegor just off the Route des Lacs. The most popular

one is by VVF which becomes a bit of a surf commune over the long summer. Most cost around €4 in the summer months but are free off season. In terms of established campsites, there is a good selection including several year-round sites. **Seignosse**: just inland from Plage Cascernes at Le Penon, and within a short stroll of the nudist area, is the all-singing **Les Oyats**, T0558-434280, open 15 May-15 Sep, with cabins. **Camping Hourn Naou**, Av Tucs between the golf club and Estagnots, T0558-433030, open Apr-Sep, is closer to the action. In the Village Vacances, Estagnots, is **Camping Les Estagnots VVF La Forêt**, T0558-416850, open 12 Jun-2 Sep, with swimming pool and cabins to rent. **Hossegor**: Camping du Lac, on the Route des Lacs, T0558-435314, is open Apr-Sep while the more basic **La Forêt** is behind the golf course on Av de Bordeaux, T0558-437592, open May-Sep. **Capbreton**: crossing the river into Capbreton, summer-opening **Labarthe**, R des Campeurs, T0558-720234, has chalets. **Municipal Bel Air**, Av du Bourret, T0558-894479, is open year round and well placed.

❷ Eating/drinking

There are all the usual seaside eateries and watering holes here as well as a few firm favourites. **Le Rock Food**, on Pl des Landais (the main square), is like a self-styled Hard Rock Café for the surfing fraternity – surf memorabilia line the walls and you can watch the sun go down on your last session with a beer for comfort. Opposite, **Dick's Sand Bar** is another more relaxed watering hole, with sea views. **Seaside Restaurant**, not actually on the seaside but on Av de la Dune, is run by an Aussie and is a great place to head for a weekend meal, where you can get anything from veggie enchilada

to nasi goreng to seafood. After the eating's done, drinking goes on until about 0200. British surfer and professional snowboarder, James Stentiford, recommends going Japanese, dropping by **Phil's Sushi Bar** (home to a ping-pong table) opposite Estagnots for eat in or take away (€8-10) or **Nori Sushi** opposite the Billabong Factory and Factory Shop in Soorts. "Or, if you want a French experience at little expense, head to Chez Manu's just over the bridge in Capbreton. It's always busy and they serve up things like salads, chips, grilled sardines, moules …you can get dinner for about €10," says James.

○ Shopping

Hossegor has more **surf shops** than you can shake a stick at including **Billabong Surf Central** on Av Paul Lahary; **Hos'oyat** on Plage Sud; **Neway Lasaosa, Rusty Pro Boutique** and **Rip Curl** on Av Touring Club; **Surf Bazaar** on Pl Louis Pasteur; and **O'Neill** on R de la Paix. For provisions, **E. Leclerc** on the main Blvd des Cigales, Capbreton, has all the basics as well as an on-site café serving reasonable snacks. Alternatively, the **Intermarche** is based up on the Route de Seignosse in Soorts-Hossegor.

❶ Directory

Bike hire: Locavelo, Av Paul Lahary, Hossegor, and Av M. Leclerc, Capbreton, hire out touring bikes and serious off-roaders. **Internet**: get on line at France Telecom just back from the lake on Av Point d'Orgue. **Post office**: Pl Castille au Penon , Seignosse; Av de Paris, Hossegor; Blvd Dr Junqua, Capbreton. **Tourist information**: Av du Lac, Seignosse; Pl des Halles, Hossegor; Av G Pompidou, Capbreton.

Surfing Southwest France

To sit on the benches above the Hetero Clito restaurant and look down on the famous right-hand peaks, swinging onto the reef at Guéthary, is to experience what surfing on the Côte Basque is all about. Out in the water sits a pack of surfers, including many who cut their teeth on the north shore of Hawaii back in the day. The boards they are riding are big; classic designs for a classic big wave. As a wide set rolls in, the pack paddles into position. A surfer drops down the huge face and sets the rail into a long bottom turn out towards the shoulder. This is not a wave for slashing. It's all about the size of the wave and the style with which it is ridden.

The French Basque region has a real old school feeling to it. The grand old resort of Biarritz, where Napoleon liked to relax between wars, has a feeling of quiet contentment with its chic bars, ornate hotels and

DEMI TAYLOR

Rusty boards

Southwest France

Breaks...

1	La Barre	7	Plage de la Côte des Basques	12	Cenitz
2	Les Cavaliers ★	8	Ilbarritz	13	Lafitenia ★
3	Anglet Beaches	9	Bidart	14	Peyo's left
4	Sables d'Or & Le Club	10	Guéthary	15	Erromardie
5	VVF	11	Les Alcyons/ Avalanches	16	Sainte Barbe
6	Grande Plage			17	Socoa
				18	Hendaye

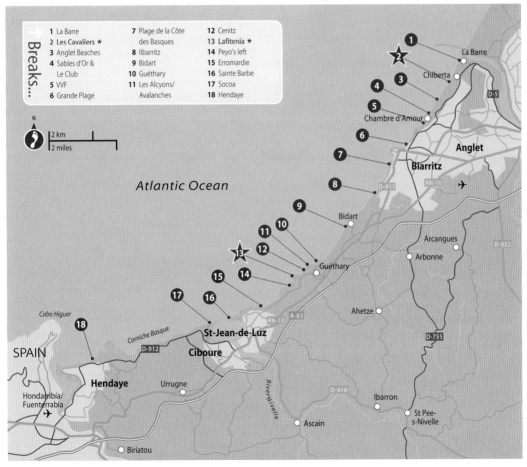

stylish boutiques. Basque flags adorn windows and billboards. The surrounding picture postcard villages are decorated in a universal white and terracotta colour scheme, but the Côte Basque does not have that edge of militancy that their Spanish cousins have south of the border. However Basque traditions do still run deep here, and sports halls and outside courts around the region resound to nightly games of pelota and **cesta punta**. The Basque region even gave France its national headdress, the beret.

It was in Guéthary that the original surf rebel, Mickey Dora, spent his last few years. Surfing the right, sitting outside the Bar Basque, drinking in the relaxed atmosphere of the place. His memorial bench looks out over the break, inviting people to sit and watch and absorb a bit of what surfing on the Côte Basque is all about.

Coastline

The Côte Basque is a wave-rich and varied coastline with excellent beaches and fine reefs. The rivermouth at La Barre was the site of one of the original great European waves, until a stone groyne was built through its heart. To the south stretches nearly 5 km of golden beaches reaching all the way to VVF in Anglet. Below Biarritz, the rocky coastline comes alive when a good swell hits. The beaches of Bidart can be a great place to lose the crowds. The reefs of Guéthary stretch far out to sea and can work in 20-ft swells. The two rock fingers with deep water channel allows access on the biggest days. To the south of St-Jean-de-Luz there are offshore reefs that only wake during monster swells. It was here that a group of French surfers shocked the wave-riding world and the judges of the Billabong XXL Tow In surfing contest.

Localism

There are areas on the Côte Basque where breaks are dominated by local surfers. These tend to be spots like Lafitenia, which used to be a localized spot but is now just plain crowded, or less well known breaks that the locals would like to keep that way. If you surf respectfully, you should have no problems. "Compared to what I've seen in Hawaii, the French are pretty friendly and cool," says Peyo Lizarazu. "Especially if guys are really respectful and say 'Hi' when they paddle out. Obviously don't expect to take all the waves, even if you are a better surfer."

Top local surfers   This region has many excellent surfers. These include **Patrick Beven, Tim Boal, Manu Portet, Louise Caron, Roman Laulhé** from Anglet. Top female surfer **Emmanuelle Joly Thomas** is also from Anglet. There are also many ex-pats such as ex-world champ **Martin Potter** and Masters champ **Gary Elkerton**.

Getting around

Very painless, even in the summer. The main coastal N10 is excellent and stays just inland from the sea down to St-Jean-de-Luz, before carrying on to the Spanish border. The only real bottlenecks are probably getting through Biarritz at rush hour and around St-Jean-de-Luz on a Sunday evening when everyone is heading home.

I started surfing in Biarritz twenty years ago and back then we were a small group on the edge, we were considered hippies. But now, everyone wants to surf. The image of surfing has completely changed. It is big in the media, and guys like Kelly Slater are very famous here now. Parents can see he's a clean guy. Surfers are no longer considered dangerous.

Fred Papagaraou, Biarritz surfer

Southwest France board guide

Evolution
Shaper: Wayne Lynch, Quiksilver Surfboards

▸▸ 7'2" x 19" x 2½".

▸▸ This board has performance and comfort in mind for the larger, beginner or older surfer, yet can be ridden in a great variety of waves.

▸▸ The best Evolution is slightly wider and thicker than regular shortboards.

▸ Performs best in waves from 2-7 ft.

▸▸ Would be great for waves such as Lafitenia.

High performance
Shaper: DHD, Quiksilver Surfboards

▸▸ 6'4" x 18¾" x 2+"

▸▸ The Executive is designed for surfers who can't find time for three surfs a day.

▸▸ It has lots of rocker, which helps control and manoeuvrability.

▸▸ The extra thickness and width helps out-paddle those groms.

 Boards by **Euroglass**
(Quiksilver Surfboards and Channel Islands European distributor)
81 Av des Artisans, 40150, Soorts-Hossegor, T00 33 (0)5584 34185
www.quiksilver.com/surfboards, www.cisurfboards.com
or contact euroglass90@aol.com

Breaks

1 La Barre

- 🌀 **Break type**: Left sandbar.
- 🌊 **Conditions**: Big swells, offshore in easterly winds.
- ❗ **Hazards/tips**: Pollution.
- 🛏 **Sleeping**: La Barre/Anglet ▸▸ *p194*.

La Barre was once a classic wave breaking by the mouth of the river Adour. It starred in several 1970s surf films, being ridden by the likes of Nat Young and Wayne Lynch, and was one of the first European waves to feature in *Surfer* magazine. Today two block breakwaters have somewhat ruined the wave. There is still a good left-hander that breaks in big swells from low to three-quarter tides. The water quality isn't the best and the break is, unsurprisingly, quiet.

2 Les Cavaliers

- 🌀 **Break type**: Beach break.
- 🌊 **Conditions**: All swells.
- 🔵 **Size**: 3-10 ft.
- 🔵 **Length**: 50 m plus.
- 🌀 **Swell**: Northwesterly.
- 🌀 **Wind**: Offshore in easterly winds.
- 🌊 **Tide**: All tides, better low to three-quarters.
- 😎 **Bottom**: Sandbar.
- 🌀 **Entry/exit**: From the beach.
- ❗ **Hazards/tips**: Rips, heavy wave, crowds.
- 🛏 **Sleeping**: La Barre/Anglet ▸▸ *p194*.

Pull into the car park at Cavaliers and walk through to the seafront and on a good day you will be greeted by a perfect A-frame peak fanned by gentle offshores. This area has

2 Les Cavaliers

2 Les Cavaliers

Southwest France

Air ——— Sea ———
°F Averages °C

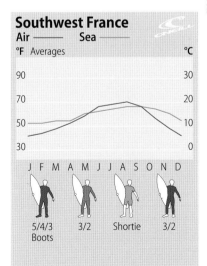

2 Kelly Slater at Les Cavaliers

90 — 30
70 — 20
50 — 10
30 — 0

J F M A M J J A S O N D

5/4/3 | 3/2 | Shortie | 3/2
Boots

always held a quality sandbank, which subtly changes through the year with swells and currents. On its day, Cavaliers can be one of the best waves in the country forming hollow, fast lefts and rights. The bank works through all tides, but is best from low to three-quarter tide. This break has been a regular site for WCT and WQS surf contests due to the quality of the wave and its consistency. It can work in small swells providing fun walls, right up to thundering swells when huge, hollow, cavernous waves can pound the beach.

ⓘ **If you like** Cavaliers, try **Supertubos** in Portugal (see page 299) or **Fistral** in England (see page 85).

3 Anglet Beaches

- **Break type**: Beach breaks.
- **Conditions**: Small to medium swells, offshore in easterly winds.
- **Hazards/tips**: Rips, crowds.
- **Sleeping**: Anglet ›› p194.

A series of beaches that run between Sables d'Or and Cavaliers, broken by huge rock groynes. Sandbanks build up alongside the breakwaters forming good lefts and rights at all tides. In big swells the paddle out is a mission and in the summer the breaks become very busy. Plage des Dunes and Plage de l'Océan are the best bets for less busy summer waves.

4 Sables d'Or and Le Club

- **Break type**: Beach breaks.
- **Conditions**: Small to medium swells, offshore in easterly winds.
- **Hazards/tips**: Crowds.
- **Sleeping**: Anglet ›› p194.

Two beaches separated by block groynes in front of the bars and surf shops of Sables d'Or. These breaks are busy year round due to the parking and easy access. **Le Club** is popular with young local surfers as it is in front of the surf clubhouse. Le Club disappears at high tide when the sea reaches the concrete sea defences. Try heading north to Marinella, Corsaires or Madrague or south to VVF.

5 VVF

- **Break type**: Beach break.
- **Conditions**: Medium to big swells, offshore in easterly winds.
- **Hazards/tips**: Crowds.
- **Sleeping**: Anglet ›› p194.

VVF is the most southerly of the Anglet beaches and sits in the lee of the cliffs. Works well at high tide in big swells, 6-10 ft, when all the other beaches are maxed out. There is a large car park right in front of the break which means it's always crowded, especially in the summer.

6 Grande Plage

- **Break type**: Beach break.
- **Conditions**: Medium swells, offshore in southeasterly winds.
- **Hazards/tips**: Crowds.
- **Sleeping**: Biarritz ›› p195.

A beautiful beach in central Biarritz, overlooked by the casino and Hôtel du Palais, this is home to the annual Reef Trophy contest and a large and committed crew of surfers. In a medium, clean swell, the beach can produce excellent hollow waves. Works on all tides with the southern, casino end, being the busiest.

4 Sables d'Or and Le Club

3 Marinella Plage, Anglet

7 Plage de la Côte des Basques

DEMI TAYLOR

7 Plage de la Côte des Basques

◉ **Break type**: Beach break.
◉ **Conditions**: Small to medium swells, offshore in easterly winds.
❶ **Hazards/tips**: Popular with longboarders.
◉ **Sleeping**: Biarritz ▸▸ p195.

The waves on this large beach are less powerful and heavy than on the rest of the beaches in the area. Hence this has traditionally been a popular beach with longboarders and beginners. As a result the vibe in the water is friendly, even though it does get crowded in the summer. Best from low to mid tide – at high the beach disappears. Parking on the Boulevard du Prince de Galles.

8 Ilbarritz

◉ **Break type**: Beach break.
◉ **Conditions**: Small to medium swells, offshore in easterly winds.
❶ **Hazards/tips**: Rocky.
◉ **Sleeping**: Biarritz ▸▸ p195.

A series of beaches heading south from Plage Marbella that have various sandbars and rocky reefs. Great place to explore and get away from the heaving crowds in the summer. There are no hidden classic waves here but there are a few OK rides if you check them through the tides. They are visable from the cliff top at Avenue Notre Dame.

9 Bidart

◉ **Break type**: Beach break.
◉ **Conditions**: Small to medium swells, offshore in southeasterly winds.
❶ **Hazards/tips**: Quieter beach, closes out easily.
◉ **Sleeping**: Bidart ▸▸ p196.

The beaches around Bidart traditionally pick up less swell, but this is a good thing as they tend to close out easily. Can be excellent on their day, or frustratingly fickle. Definitely worth checking in a small or medium clean swell. Home of the annual Roxy Jam.

10 Guéthary ▸▸ p192

🔴 **Chez Gammon at Guéthary**

We'd surfed Guéthary a few times, but the day after the '74 European Championships finished, the swell picked up and it seemed like the entire contest had decamped to the left at Les Alcyons. It was one of those smoky afternoons in Guéthary, hot and heavy, where the sea's like oil and you can't tell where it ends and the sky starts. Nobody was surfing the right at Parliamentia, but it seemed like there were 300 on the left. So I jumped into the rip and paddled out at Parliamentia. I caught a few waves in the 10-ft range – I was sixteen and I felt pretty smug. Then a monster set showed up, making the horizon black. I paddled like a clown for about two minutes . . . for really a long time, just hoping to scrape over. But then it arrived, majestic and feathering, and I spun around, only because it was the most beautiful wave I had ever seen. That elation evaporated fast, giving way to cringing fear, because then I had to catch the wave. I was on a 7' 2", diamond tail, single fin Creamed Honey and as I took off I went into free-fall for the first 5 ft. When I reconnected I immediately developed big speed wobbles. It was like a car crash with everything in slow motion. I could think of about five things at once. I shuffled forwards to cure the wobbles until I realized I was so far forward that Dave Friar's monk logo was between my feet, so I shuffled back again. The wave fanned out around me like a football stand, with a horrible boil on the left. I tried to concentrate on not turning too soon. But above all I forced myself not to jump off and start running. When I got back onto dry land I couldn't speak for an hour.

It was only a drop, but it's a wave I never got over. I've returned to it in dreams and bleak nights in London where I could half convince myself that the thrum of traffic was the sea. And perhaps it's the reason I live here, in Guéthary, so close to the break it's like being in a boat. We live in a crumbling hotel full of ghosts from 'the roaring twenties' and on some quiet winter nights I imagine I can hear the scuff of the dancers' soft-soled shoes above the roar of the wave. Sometimes the following morning I'll paddle out early and alone. I'll stroke out from the cold shadows of the cliff into the pink sunlight and the blue water, where the waves feather with rainbows.

Nick Gammon is a respected painter and surfer, a Welshman who lives in Guéthary, via Ireland. Check out www.nickgammon.com.

10 Guéthary

- **Break type**: Reef break.
- **Conditions**: Medium and big swells.
- **Hazards/tips**: For experienced surfers only.
- **Sleeping**: Guéthary ▸▸ *p196*.

Legendary big-wave spot and showpiece attraction that dominates the view from the heart of this traditional Basque village that overlooks it. The reef is 400 m offshore and swell comes out of deep water to form huge, shifting peaks. This is not a wave for shortboarders. The experienced locals jostle around, paddling their big boards into the elevator drops. The wave then fattens out into either a short left or, more often, a right-hander. The right can sometimes connect through to the inside section where the wave walls up again. It is a pretty straightforward paddle out in the channel, but be warned, the wave looks easier and smaller than it is.

11 Les Alcyons/Avalanches

- **Break type**: Left reef breaks.
- **Conditions**: Medium to big swells, offshore in southeasterly winds.
- **Hazards/tips**: Big wave, heavy, crowded.
- **Sleeping**: Guéthary ▸▸ *p196*.

On the left-hand side of the harbour breaks a heavy, hollow reef break. It has a jacking take-off followed by a barrelling left that reels along the shallow reef toward the channel. Can break up to 12 ft when it is an awesome sight. Outside sits a true big-wave spot, Avalanches, a left reef that works in the biggest swells. It's a long paddle and a heavy wave for true big-wave chargers only.

12 Cenitz

- **Break type**: Reef breaks.
- **Conditions**: Small to medium swells, offshore in easterly/southeasterly winds.
- **Hazards/tips**: Popular local spot.
- **Sleeping**: Guéthary ▸▸ *p196*.

Cenitz is a popular break with Basque locals. It has a left point at the south of the bay that works best at mid tide. It is a walling wave that peels into a deep channel opposite a right-hander that breaks from low to mid tide. To the north of this is another right that breaks way out the back. It is a long paddle from the rocky beach and there are rips to negotiate. This is a break where locals come to get away from the excesses of Lafitenia and Anglet. If you surf respectfully and share the waves you will be OK; if you come to hassle and drop in you will not be tolerated.

10 Guéthary

Oil from the *Prestige* disaster at Guéthary beach

13 Lafitenia

13 Lafitenia

- **Break type**: Right-hand point.
- **Conditions**: All swells.
- **Size**: 3-10 ft.
- **Length**: 50-200 m plus.
- **Swell**: Northwesterly.
- **Wind**: South/southeasterly.
- **Tide**: Low to three-quarter tide.
- **Bottom**: Reef and sand.
- **Entry/exit**: Paddle off the beach.
- **Hazards/tips**: Heavy when big, crowded in the summer.
- **Sleeping**: Guéthary/Lafitenia » p196.

This renowned right-hand point sits in a secluded, sheltered bay in the heart of the French Basque lands. The excellent break peels along a sand-covered reef and is always crowded with local surfers. In big swells it has a shifting, heavy take-off out over the rocky reef on the point. The wave then walls into a fast middle section, perfect for big carves. The inside section can get fast and hollow. It is a classic point set-up with a dry hair paddle out from the beach. This is one of the area's most popular breaks and gets crowded when it's firing, especially in the summer. It is one of Patrick Beven's favourite waves: "I like Lafitenia because it's such a special place and you can work your line and do big manoeuvres." Lafetenia was the venue for the Quiksilver Masters, bringing together the legends of surfing. Ex-world champion Barton Lynch loved the wave: "It was a shame to have to wait between heats. It's the kind of wave you just wanna go out and surf with your mates. It's a real surfers' wave. Great walls, just great fun."

ⓘ *If you like Lafitenia, try Devil's Rock in Morocco (see page 363) or Skaill Bay in Orkney (see page 50).*

DEMI TAYLOR

14 Peyo's Left

- **Break type**: Big wave left.
- **Conditions**: Big to huge swells.
- **Hazards/tips**: Experts only.
- **Sleeping**: Guéthary/Lafitenia.

The point facing Lafitenia has an enormous left-hander that wakes in the biggest swells. There is a huge peak leading into a massive wall. During the Masters, Kelly Slater, Tom Carroll and Peyo Lizarazu surfed the left, both paddle surfing and tow-in.

15 Erromardie

- **Break type**: Beach break.
- **Conditions**: Small to medium swells, offshore in southeasterly winds.
- **Hazards/tips**: Quiet beach.
- **Sleeping**: St-Jean-de-Luz » p197.

Just to the north of St-Jean-de-Luz sits this beach break, overlooked by campsites. It is a fairly average break which can have decent rights at the north end of the beach.

16 Sainte Barbe

- **Break type**: Right breakwater.
- **Conditions**: Big swells, offshore in southeasterly winds.
- **Hazards/tips**: Peaks at end of breakwater.
- **Sleeping**: St-Jean-de-Luz » p197.

When big swells pound the coast, a right-hander peels from outside the jetty at Sainte Barbe and wraps its way through into the

14 Peyo's Left

18 Hendaye

> I think this region is wonderful. I think it is rich in culture. It's incredible to see the mountains and the ocean so close. Most people when they come, all they see is the coastline, but they should go inland. There are many beautiful places to visit.
>
> *Peyo Lizarazu, Basque surfer*

sheltered bay. In these conditions, it can get very crowded.

17 Socoa

- **Break type**: Sand-covered reef breaks.
- **Conditions**: Big swells, offshore in southerly winds.
- **Hazards/tips**: Crowds.
- **Sleeping**: St-Jean-de-Luz » p197.

Big northerly or northwesterly swells thread their way through the harbour entrance and find a few banks to break on inside the bay. If everywhere is maxed out, check it out.

18 Hendaye

- **Break type**: Beach break.
- **Conditions**: Medium to big swells, offshore in southerly winds.
- **Hazards/tips**: Long, flat safe beach.
- **Sleeping**: St-Jean-de-Luz » p197.

"I learnt to surf at Hendaye," says top Basque surfer Peyo Lizarazu. "It is basically the flattest beach on all the coast, with the weakest waves." This is a good beach for beginners and a good place to check out in big swells. There can be decent waves here with peaks.

DEMI TAYLOR

Grand Plage at Biarritz ►► *p190*

La Barre

The once-famous sandbank at La Barre was ruined long ago by a huge breakwater. Sitting on the south bank of the Adour, La Barre offers an Aire de Camping (a couple of euros a night in summer, free off season) that is basically just part of the **Ice Hockey Rink** car park. Convenient place to stay with good access to Cavaliers. There is a **McDonald's** handy for breakfast.

Anglet

The beaches to the north of Biarritz belong to the town of Anglet and boast some excellent beach breaks and great places to stay. Much of the action is centred around Chambre d'Amour where there are surf shops, bars and restaurants overlooking the sea.

✪ Flat spells

Bowling Cyberbowling on Allée du Cadran, accessed off the RN10. **Golf** Get a round in at the 18-hole, par-70 **Golf de Chiberta**, Blvd des Plages, T0559-525110. **Mini golf** Get a mini round in at Pl de Docteurs Gentilhe in Chambre d'Amour. **Ice skating** Patin Oire, Plage de la Barre, T0559-571730. Have a go at ice skating, or watch the experts at the professional ice hockey games. **Spa** Revitalize yourself after a long session with a trip to **Hôtel de Chiberta et du Golf** fitness centre – jacuzzi spa, hydrotherapy, sauna and massaging shower, €10.

🛏 Sleeping

C Villa Clara, Blvd des Plage, T0559-520152. A chilled hotel with tiled floors and views over the dunes to the sea. Used to surfers. Open year round, they also have apartments to rent, with basic kitchen facilities.
C-D Hôtel Residence Mer & Golf, Blvd de la Mer, just back from Plage de VVF, T0559-527000. Apartments for 2-6 people, all with balconies overlooking either the sea or the golf course. Very reasonable outside the summer holidays.

D-E Arguia, Av des Cretes, T0559-638382, open 15 Apr to 15 Oct, is reasonably priced and a 10-min walk to the beach. Rooms are light and airy if a little basic, but excellent value. They also do group rooms and breakfast.
Camping Camping Fontaine Laborde, Allée Fontaine Laborde, T0559-034816, is open Easter to end-Sept. **Camping de Parme**, out by the airport on R de l'Aviation, T0559-230300, is the only year-round site in the Biarritz/Anglet area. That said, it is relatively expensive with basic facilities and has little going for it.

🍴 Eating/drinking

There is a good selection of bars/cafés/restaurants focused around Sables d'Or and the beachfront. **Mama Nature** is a lively beach café that serves large portions of great food at reasonable prices, a popular spot with local surfers, as is nearby **Balthazar**, a bar that also serves *tapas* and light food. **Croq des Sables** does a showcase post-surf takeaway feast. The Americana is awesome – a baguette filled with burgers, fries and salad. Excellent value lunch.
Also worth trying out on the strip are **El Mexicano, Pizzeria Pinocchio** and **Pollo Asado**.

🔵 Shopping

Stock up on provisions at the massive **Leclerc** hypermarket, at the Anglet Centre Commercial on Blvd du Bab heading towards Bayonne, or head for **Carrefour** signposted off the RN10. **Surf shops** centred around Chambre d'Amour include the **Rusty Boutique, Billabong** shop and **Waimea Surf Shop**. All stock hardware, accessories and clothing. **JP Stark**, Allée Louis de Foix, T0559-639478, www.starksurf.com, are surfboard shapers who do new custom boards and board repairs.

🔵 Directory

Banks: there is an ATM at Av de l'Adour at Le Barre and a **Crédit Agricole** ATM at

Chambre d'Amour. **Car hire**: all the major companies – **Avis, Hertz** and **Europcar** – have offices at BAB airport but it is advisable to book in advance. **Internet**: access available at the **Cyber Bowling** in Anglet just off the N10. **Post office**: in Anglet centre on R du 8 Mai, about 10 mins' drive from the beaches. **Tourist information**: Av de Chambre d'Amour.

Biarritz

This grandiose resort has been reinvented as a surf chic city. The impressive Hôtel du Palais overlooks the Grande Plage, the home of the annual Reef Biarritz Pro competition. On any given day, people meander along the esplanade, with its boulevard cafés and casino.

✿ Flat spells
Aquarium Musée de la Mer, on the seafront on Esplanade du Rocher de la Vierge, is open year round and comes complete with sharks, seals etc.
Chocolate Biarritz is a real chocoholic's heaven, with a **Chocolate Museum** above Côte de Basques. **Party** Check out the **Casetas**, a 5-day festival that takes place in the summer and again in the winter. All the local bars set up under one huge marquee and a massive party takes place into the early hours. **San Sebastián** Head over the border to the town that never sleeps, about an hour away on the E5 motorway (see page 219). **Skating** Head to R 8 Mai by the Lycée College for some mini-ramp, fun box action at this small skate park

◗ Sleeping
In Jul-Aug, prices sky rocket but there are still a couple of bargains to be found.
C-D Hôtel Argi Eder, R Peyroloubilh, T0559-242253, is a peach building near the top of Côte de Basque. They also offer rooms for up to 4 people.
E Hôtel Palym, R du Port Vieux, T0559-242583, is a warren of a hotel above a pizzeria. There are an amazing number of rooms of varying size and layout, all eclectically decorated. Some rooms are en suite. Parking available by the harbour, free off season.

Camping Biarritz Camping, off Av de Milady on the R d'Harcet, T0559-230012, open May-Sep. **Aire de Camping Cars**, just off the Av de Milady opposite the turning for Plage de Marbella, is free for motorhomes off season and even has limited electric hook-up points and water and toilet emptying facitlities.

☕ Eating/drinking
La Pizzeria, opposite the Casino on Av Edouard V11, is the showcase place to eat in Biarritz. That's why there is always a queue, but it's worth the wait. Fantastic pizzas, amazing tarts and very reasonable – about €30 for 2 plus a *pichet* or jug of wine. The **Milk Bar** on the seafront behind the Casino offers snacks and drinks at outside tables overlooking the sea. Good coffee.
Taco'Mex, R Lavernis, is a great little Tex-Mex restaurant with a small menu of excellent food including help yourself fajitas. Down in the fishing port are 2 great seafood restaurants. **Chez Albert** is an excellent eatery with prices to match. **Juan Carlos** has great food at good value.
"For a special treat head up to the **Hôtel Grande Palace** and order a hot chocolate in the beautiful café area," recommends local surfer Nadege Aillotti.

♪ Bars and clubs
If you fancy a late night there a couple of places to choose from – the **Play Boy** nightclub near the Casino and the **Blue** Cargo in Ilbarritz which offers food, music and dancing.

○ Shopping
There's a handy **Leclerc** supermarket on Av de la Milady at the southern end of town. There are plenty of **surf shops** including **Rip Curl** on Av Reine Victoria. The **Volcom** skate shop is on Av Edouard VII. **Wilbur** stocks smaller brands and can be found on R Gambetta. **Unity Skate Shop**, R de la Bergerie, is confined to skate brands. **Rainbow Girl**, Av de la Chambre d'Amour, is a surf shop for women stocking purely female lines. The **Gotcha** shop is on R Mazagran, near the **Roxy** store.

● Directory
Aéroport International de Biarritz-Anglet-Bayonne: T0559-438383. **Internet**: available in the **Games Store**, corner of Av Edouard VII

DEMI TAYLOR
The breast bar in town

DEMI TAYLOR
Rest In Pieces

Airports → Paris Orly, T01 49 751515, www.adp.fr; Paris Roissy Charles de Gaulle, T01 48 622280; Nantes-Atlantique, T02 40 84 80 00, www.nantes.aeroport.fr; Bordeaux, T05 56 345050, www.bordeaux.aeroport.fr; Biarritz-Anglet-Bayonne, T05 59 438383.
Buses and coaches → SNCF, www.sncf.com. **Car hire** → Avis, T0870-6070100; Europcar, T0870-6075000; Hertz, T08708-448844. **Ferries** → P&O, T0870-2424999, www.poportsmouth.com; Brittany Ferries, T0870-3665333, www.brittany-ferries.com; Sea France, T0870-5711711, www.seafrance.com. **Rail links** → SNCF, www.sncf.com; TGV, www.tgv.fr. **Petrol prices** → €1/litre.

🔵 Snowboarding in the Pyrénées

Running the entire length of the France/Spain border, the Pyrénées offer some excellent snowboarding opportunities. While not matching the consistency and quality of the Alps, if you keep an eye on the weather you can still have some excellent powder days. "When you get powder in the Pyrénées, it doesn't stick around as long as it would in the Alps – it's not as cold so if it does dump, you have to be on it immediately. Resorts like La Mongie are probably your best bet – it was the original staging post for the triple 'S' Quikcup event," explains pro border James Stentiford. Day passes at the resorts cost around €20 as does snowboard hire.

Follow the A64-E80 from Bayonne east towards Tarbes then the N21 south through the holy city of Lourdes and D920 on to the resort and spa town of **Cauterets**. About 200 km from the coast, it has some of the region's most consistent snowfall throughout the season (usually Dec-Apr). Before heading off, check the conditions with the tourist office T0562-925027. Camping is available at **Le Mamelon Vert** on Av Mamelon Vert, T0562- 925156, Jan-Sep, or try D **Le Pas de l'Ours** on R Raillère, T0562-925807, who offer both dorms and room.

To the east on the D918, which runs along the Parc National des Pyrénées, is the resort **La Mongie** – one of the biggest snowfields in the Pyrénées and therefore an excellent spot for freeriding. If the D918 is closed, access the resort from the north via the D935 through Bagnères. Contact the tourist office for accommodation details, T0562-955071.

and Av de la Reine Victoria. **Post office**: R de la Poste. **Tourist information**: Square d'Ixelles, behind the Hôtel de Ville and police station.

Bidart

This is a pretty Basque village with a wonderful beach, with quick and easy access to Biarritz and Anglet. Many of the houses are painted in traditional Basque style, white with red timbers and shutters, representing the Basque national colours. At one time ox blood was used to stain the timbers.

🛏 Sleeping

There are some great hotels in Bidart, either on the beach side of the main road or inland.
D **Motel Mil**, R d'École, T0559-547171, offers clean and comfortable rooms at reasonable prices. They also have chalet/apartments.
Camping There are plenty of camping options around Bidart. **Camping Berrua**, just outside the village on R d'Arbonne , T0559-549666, open Apr-2 Oct. **Camping Pavillion Royal**, Av Prince de Galles, T0559-230054, is a well kept site next to the sea.

🍴 Eating/drinking

For a cheap bite to eat, check out **La Pizzeria** on R Erreteguia. For wonderful seafood, served in an awesome location, splash out at **La Tantina** on Plage du Centre, T0559-265356. A fantastic seafood restaurant – epecially for the gambas or

grilled monster prawns – that is very popular so it's worth booking ahead.

Guéthary

One of the villages at the heart of the Côte Basque, Guéthary's streets are lined with beautiful houses, the steep seafront overlooking one of the world's most famous breaks. The square just behind is an amazing place to sit and chill and drink coffee. In the evening head down to **le trinquet**, the venue for pelota. If you've brought your skateboard, there is also a shallow **concrete bowl** nearby on Cemin de Tranchet.

🛏 Sleeping

D **Hôtel Madrid** is right on the square, with an old skool feel to the beamed rooms, at reasonable rates.

🍴 Eating/drinking

Bar Basque, on the square, is a wonderful place for a drink or a bite to eat. Sit outside on the terrace and watch the world go by. Don't miss **Hetero Clito** with its eclectic decoration, great food, awesome view and random opening hours. Try to nab one of the outside tables for sunset. Unfortunately the legendary **Surf Hut** is no more, replaced by **Kafe Loco Restaurant**, next to the railway station.

🔵 Directory

Surf schools: Ecole de Surf Christophe Reinhardt, T0556-249396, offers accommodation and/or lessons. **Ecole de**

Biarritz airport

Anglet: camping at Sable D'Or

Surf de Guéthary, T0608-688854. **Tourist information**: excellent centre next to the railway station. If the surf's flat, get the map showing the route around Guéthary and its beaches.

Lafitenia

Home of the amazing right-hand point break, but little in the way of accommodation. However, **Camping Playa**, T0559-265585, open Apr-Oct/Nov (depending on demand), must have one of the most amazing views in the surfing world as this terraced site overlooks the break. Feel your tent shake when the surf's big.

St-Jean-de-Luz

This is a wonderful, picturesque Basque fishing town. Basque privateers (pirates) sailed under the French flag, attacking British merchant ships, and many of the fine houses were paid for this way. Check out the fishing port – one of the busiest in France – and grab a coffee in one of the cafés on the main square. Ciboure, on the south side of the River Nivelle, was an area settled by whalers, fishermen and privateers thought to be too inferior for St-Jean. Ravel, of *Bolero* fame, was born here.

⊜ Sleeping

D **Hôtel Bolivar**, R Sopite, T0559-260200, is close to the beach and has some great rooms, clean and comfortable.
E **Hôtel Verdun**, on Av Verdun just across from the train station, T0559-260255, is just about the only budget option in town, with good clean rooms and friendly staff.
Camping There are many campsites around St-Jean. **International d'Erromardie**, to the north by the sea, T0559-263426, open Mar-Oct, has terracing

and takeaway food. **Juantcho**, R de la Corniche on the D912, T0559-471197, open Apr-Sep, is nearer to town .

❷ Eating/drinking

The traditional Basque cuisine at **Restaurant Chez Pablo**, R Mlle Etchoto, is definitely worth trying. The seafood and pork are excellent. Check out the great seafood restaurants in Ciboure, including **Arrantzaleak** on Av Jean Poulou, T0559-471075. **Buvette de la Halle**, Blvd Victor Hugo, is very good value serving regional dishes like Gateaux Basques and great seafood dishes.

◐ Shopping/directory

On R Gambetta there is a **supermarket** for provisions and a surf shop, **Le Spoton**. **Post office**: Blvd Victor Hugo. **Tourist information**: Pl Maréchal Foch, T0559-260316.

DEMI TAYLOR

Patrick Beven on camera

Spain doing a good impression of Tahiti. El Basurera and Yellow Mountain (Graciosa) in the background. ≫ *p269*

WILLY URIBE

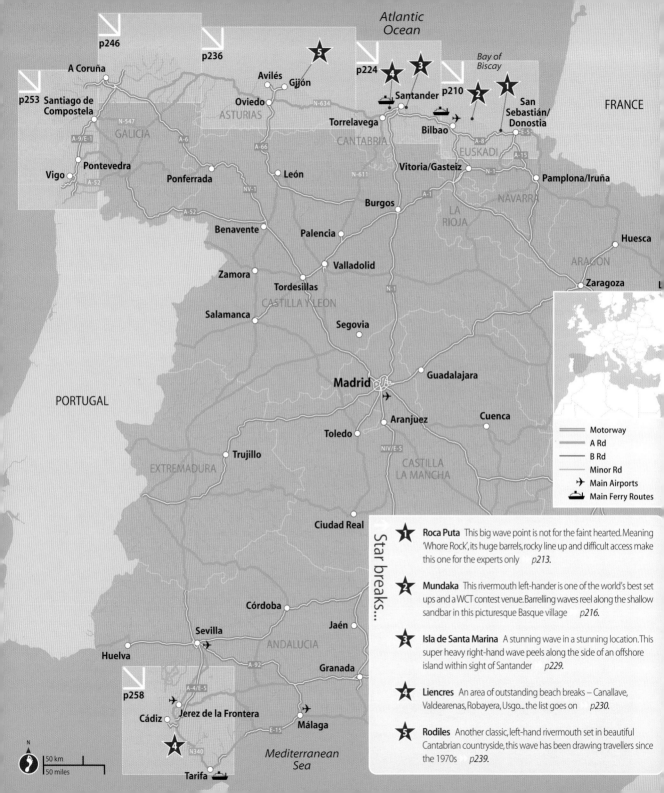

Atlantic Ocean

p246

p236

p224

Bay of Biscay

p210

p253

A Coruña

Santiago de Compostela

Avilés

Gijón

Oviedo

Santander

San Sebastián/ Donostia

FRANCE

ASTURIAS

Torrelavega

Bilbao

Vigo

Pontevedra

GALICIA

Ponferrada

CANTABRIA

León

Vitoria/Gasteiz

Pamplona/Iruña

EUSKADI

NAVARRA

Huesca

Burgos

LA RIOJA

Benavente

Palencia

Zamora

Valladolid

Zaragoza

Tordesillas

CASTILLA Y LEÓN

Salamanca

Segovia

Madrid

Guadalajara

PORTUGAL

Cuenca

Toledo

Aranjuez

Trujillo

CASTILLA LA MANCHA

EXTREMADURA

Ciudad Real

Córdoba

Jaén

Sevilla

ANDALUCIA

p258

Huelva

Granada

Cádiz

Jerez de la Frontera

Málaga

Mediterranean Sea

Tarifa

Star breaks...

★1 **Roca Puta** This big wave point is not for the faint hearted. Meaning 'Whore Rock', its huge barrels, rocky line up and difficult access make this one for the experts only   *p213*.

★2 **Mundaka** This rivermouth left-hander is one of the world's best set ups and a WCT contest venue. Barrelling waves reel along the shallow sandbar in this picturesque Basque village   *p216*.

★3 **Isla de Santa Marina** A stunning wave in a stunning location. This super heavy right-hand wave peels along the side of an offshore island within sight of Santander   *p229*.

★4 **Liencres** An area of outstanding beach breaks – Canallave, Valdearenas, Robayera, Usgo... the list goes on   *p230*.

★5 **Rodiles** Another classic, left-hand rivermouth set in beautiful Cantabrian countryside, this wave has been drawing travellers since the 1970s   *p239*.

N

50 km

50 miles

Motorway

A Rd

B Rd

Minor Rd

✈ Main Airports

⛴ Main Ferry Routes

Spain is Europe's best kept surfing secret. Although Mundaka attracts surfers in their droves from all over the world, the breaks along the rest of the Biscay coastline offer an unrivalled variety of surfing options. Many pristine spots with crystal clear waves are waiting for a passing travelling surfer. Galicia at Europe's western tip, attracts more swell than anywhere on our continent and is a surfer's paradise, with countless beaches, coves and points that never sleep. Spanish riders now top the European surfing tree with professionals like Eneko Acero, Jonathan González, Pablo Solar, Pablo Gutiérrez and Kepa Acero brought up on a diet of some of the best breaks in the surfing world.

Out of the water, Spain is truly Europe's party capital. In cities like San Sebastián the term 'early night' is not in people's vocabulary, and during the summer, when the fiestas roll from village to village, the streets of Pamplona resound to the pounding of hooves as the famous running of the bulls draws huge crowds. When it comes to food Spain has the opposition licked with seafood as good as anywhere in the world and Tapas bars where snacking has become an art form.

Best Time to Visit: Autumn – great waves, warm weather and plenty of festivals.

Spain rating
Surf
★★★★
Cost of living
★★
Nightlife
★★★★
Accommodation
★★★
Places to visit
★★★★

Essentials

Position

Spain stretches out westward from continental Europe and south towards Africa, with access to both the Atlantic and Mediterranean. It is the second largest country in Western Europe after France.

Language

For the majority, the main language is Spanish (Castellano or Español) spoken at breakneck speed. A grasp of basic Spanish isn't just a nicety, it's a necessity. Even in the tourist hubs of Bilbao and San Sebastián, English is not widely understood – so pick up a few handy phrases before you go.

In Euskadi (Basque country) the regional language 'Euskara' is making a comeback and appears on all road signs. In Galicia you may come across a smattering of 'Galego' and in Asturias 'Babel' raises its head on road signs, (with a helping hand from some locals who change the j to x).

Crime/safety

This is a relatively safe destination with car break-ins causing the most problems for visitors. Just be aware and don't leave anything valuable on display.

If you need to report anything lost/stolen see the **Policía Nacional** who deal with most urban crimes. The **Guarda Civil** handle roads, borders and law and order away from towns while the **Polícia Local/Municipal** deal with traffic issues and some crime in large towns and cities. The Basques have their own force, **Ertzaintza**, who deal with local issues.

Health

EU residents, fill in an E-111 before you go to certify that you are entitled to free (or reduced cost) healthcare. Visitors from outside the EU should invest in travel insurance. In towns at least one pharmacy will be 'on-call' and open round the clock. Manned by highly trained staff, they can be a good first port of call as many prescription drugs (like antibiotics) can be bought over the counter after a consultation with the pharmacist.

Opening hours

Lunchtime governs the country. General opening hours are 1000-1400 and 1700-2000 Monday to Saturday with banks opening at 0830 and large supermarkets staying open throughout the day.

Sleeping

There are plenty of accommodation – *alojamientos* – options here but the thing to remember is that you can never judge a place from the outside – always request to see the room first. **Hotels** are the priciest, listed as H or HR and often charge a 7% tax on top of the asking price. The quality of lower end *Hostals* (listed Hs or HsR) is often similar to *Pensiones* (P) which are usually cheaper, family run places or rooms

5 best trips

① **Pamplona** Historic town with the world famous 'Running of the Bulls' festival ›› *p220*.

② **San Sebastián** Party town with great bars, clubs and people ›› *p219*.

③ **Bilbao** More than just the Guggenheim ›› *p223*.

④ **A Coruña** Beautiful maritime city with great nightlife and top soccer team ›› *p256*.

⑤ **Picos de Europa** Beautiful mountains with tiny villages and a real celtic feel ›› *p243*.

Gijón Harbour ›› *p244*

above bars. Offering good rates for double and twin rooms, *pensiones* are the accommodation of choice. Off the beaten track *casa rurales / agroturismos* – cottages rented out or run as hotels – can prove a popular and affordable option but may not be near many amenities. *Albergues* (youth hostels) are few and far between and when compared with *pensiones* are not usually the best, or most affordable choice. There are plenty of *campings* (campsites) across Spain although many are summer opening only. Responsible free-camping away from tourist spots (and 1km away from official campsites) is widely tolerated although in many areas isn't safe and the local police may move you on.

Eating

Breakfast is not the most exciting of meals with many favouring coffee and a pastry. The sugar rush option is *chocolate con churros*. The hot chocolate is thick enough to stand your spoon in, and churros are fried dough sticks covered in sugar. In Spain lunch, from 1330-1530, is the most important meal of the day. The best and cheapest way to eat is to grab a three-course *menú del día* from a local café, workers bar or *venta*. Either wine or water as well as bread is usually included in the €5-9 cover price. Quality varies but if the café's full it's usually a good sign. Dinner is eaten late – usually 2200 onwards (later at weekends) which can send you over the edge if you've been surfing and need to refuel. To combat this, head to a café and grab a *plato combinado* – usually chicken and chips or steak and chips or – embrace the *tapas* culture. *Tapas* (or *pintxos* in Euskadi) are normally eaten from about 1930 onwards and are little nibbles ranging from *tortilla* (potato omelette) to glamorous regional delights with seafood, ham or sausage. They should only cost about €2-3 each. You either help

Fact file

Currency Euro (€)
Capital city Madrid
Time zone +1hr GMT
Length of coastline 5,000km
Religion Catholic
Emergency numbers
General emergency 112
Police 092
Local Police 091
International Operator 1008

yourself from the selection on offer and keep a note of what you've had for when you come to pay, or ask the bartender to serve you. The Spanish favour a 'food crawl' – soaking up the ambience, having a bite to eat and a small drink at each stop.

Spanish surf photographer Willy Uribe spends his time travellng the coast of Northern Spain and recommends sampling some of the local food including *bacalao a la pil-pil* (salt cod in garlic) in Euskadi. In Cantabria try the *quesada* (like a cheesecake), in Asturias the **faves** (large butter beans that go into the *fabada* or bean and pork stew) and in Galicia the *pulpo a feira* (octopus).

Festivals/events

Spain must be the festival capital of Europe. In the summer there always seems to be a celebration on somewhere, whether on a small local scale, or a huge national fiesta. It's worth checking as sometimes accommodation will be scarce around festival weekends.

Getting there

Air Madrid is the main international airport although for most it is often easier, quicker and cheaper to connect via another European destination, with the UK offering a good variety of low cost options direct to the north and south coasts. For many European destinations, Bilbao is the main entry point into the north.
From UK: Budget airline **easyJet**, www.easyjet.com, offers the cheapest flights to Bilbao, which can be anywhere between €30 (£20) and €180 (£120) depending on time of year and availability. They do charge for carriage of boards (somewhat randomly) so cram as many as you can into one bag. **British Airways** and **Iberia** also fly into Bilbao and can sometimes be a cheap option depending on season. For northern Spain, flying into Biarritz with **Ryanair**, www.ryanair.com, is a great budget alternative. The airport is about half and hour from the Spanish border and flights are available off season from around €1 plus taxes up to about €180 (£120). They again have a random policy of charging for board carriage. For the south coast, easyJet offers budget flights between London and Málaga (more expensive in peak periods) while Ryanair flies between Stanstead and Jerez (near Cádiz).

Ajo steam train ›› *p234*

Road The main route into northern Spain is through southwest France via the E5/E70 motorway heading towards San Sebastián. You can avoid the tolls and take the slower but more scenic N-10, which becomes the N-634.

Rail Using Paris as the European connection, the best and cheapest way to get to Spain by train is to catch the TGV to Hendaye and use the Spanish **RENFE** or **FEVE** systems to get to your destination.

Sea P&O run a year round ferry service between Portsmouth and Bilbao which, with pool, sauna, casino and two day journey time, is closer to a cruise than a channel crossing. Because of this, they can charge a heavy premium – a van and two people can make the crossing for upwards of about €450 (£300). A return ticket with a large motorhome can be anything up to about €1350 (£900), depending on when you book. Check www.poportsmouth.com as they run occasional off peak special offers. **Brittany Ferries** offers a twice-weekly service between Plymouth and Santander, which takes around 24 hours. It only runs from mid March through mid November, but with singles for a van and two people from about €375 (£250) can be cheaper than the P&O offering. Try www.brittanyferries.com.

Red Tape Spain is a Schengen state (see European Red Tape page 10).

Getting around

Driving (right-hand side) A full driving licence (photo type or International Driving Permit) is required plus liability insurance – you need a 'green card' certificate to prove this. You also need to carry two warning triangles. Since its transition to democracy and entry into the European Union, Spain has been a country that has been modernising quickly. New and improved road links are opening regularly, and the motorway network is expanding rapidly right across the country. The coastal routes are generally very good and now that the motorways have taken the strain of the goods vehicles, they are a pleasant and scenic alternative. However the tolls in Euskadi are nothing short of rude.

Motorway – *autovía/autopista* – stretches across the majority of Northern Spain and is signed in blue. Running southwards, the motorway connects both Cádiz and Huelva to the north via Madrid. Toll roads are indicated by a red circle and are reasonable (except in Euskadi). **Speed limit 120 kph.**

Rutas Nacionales – N roads – are main roads that take over where the motorway finishes and are of a good or fair standard. **Speed limit 100 kph/50 kph urban areas.**

Secondary/provincial roads – B, C or province initials (AS Asturias) –

Top tips

- The police are inflexible. The papers of the vehicle and your insurance must be in order, if not your vehicle will be immobilised, and you will receive a hefty fine. Do not try and bribe the police. *Willy Uribe, Spanish surf photographer*

- Be careful when you surf city breaks, don't leave anything of any value out on show in your van. Some guy watched us and waited until we were in the water and the took everything - our passports, wallets, stereo, mobile phone. The police weren't exactly helpful. *Jo and Jamie, travelling surfers, Aberdeen, Scotland*

- Pick up a new board in Sopelana – they've got some good brands which are pretty cheap – I picked up a new short board for around €300. *Martin Beelert – travelling surfer, North Germany*

- Talk to the locals, although we may not shave and have long hair, the majority of us are good people. We can help you or may even tell you how to find some good waves. In the towns there are bars where the surfers meet, which have a great atmosphere so try and find them. *Willy Uribe*

vary but provide access to many hard to reach spots. **Speed limit 100 kph/50 kph urban areas.** Urban speed limits are vigorously enforced and heavy fines are not uncommon.

Car hire: This is not a big issue here although it seems pretty pricey when compared to other living costs – from about €400 for two weeks. All the big boys operate in Spain including **Hertz**, www.hertz.com, **Europcar**, www.europcar.com and **Avis**, www.avis.com with convenient offices at airports and ferry ports. You'll need your license plus credit card and if you've booked ahead prepare yourself for other charges they'll try to slip in such as extra insurance.

Public transport

If you need to go public, although the bus routes are quicker with greater access you'll have little joy getting on with a board under your arm. The other choice is the rail network, where you may get charged for board carriage. **RENFE**, www.renfe.es, are useful on major routes offering, among others, services between Madrid and the coast as well as across the North – San Sebastián to A Coruña will take roughly 12 hours and cost about €37.50. In the North, **FEVE**, www.feve.es, takes the scenic route offering greater coverage of the coast. **EUSKOTREN**, www.euskotren.es, services the Basque region while Bilbao relies on its efficient metro service, www.metrobilbao.net.

Islas Canarias (Canary Islands)

The volcanic Islas Canarias archipelago erupted from the Atlantic and lies more than 1,000 km from the Iberian peninsula and just 100 km from the coast of Africa. While the islands are very much part of Spain, Africa still manages to influence their make up, the Sirocco winds depositing tonnes of Saharan sand on the islands. Lanzarote and Fuerteventura are the least mountainous of the seven main islands and so receive very little rainfall. This leaves them dependent on desalinated seawater for drinking.

Getting there

Air Lanzarote and Fuerteventura have international airports at Arrecife and Puerto del Rosario respectively. There are no direct flights from the US or Australasia, connections will need to be made via Madrid or the UK. There are regular flights between the Islands and Madrid with **Spanair**, www.spanair.com, **Iberia**, www.iberia.es (who, be warned, can charge heavily and randomly for board carriage) and **Air Europa**, www.air-europa.com. **Air Europa** also run regular services to Lanzarote from Barcelona in Cataluña, Bilbao in Euskadi and weekly flights from Santiago de Compostela in Galicia.

　　From UK: British Airways and **Iberia** run regular services between London and the Canaries but better deals can often be found with package holiday companies like **Thomsons**, www.thomsonflights.com, or **First Choice**, www.firstchoice.co.uk, T0870 850 3999.

Sea Transmediterranea, www.transmediterranea.es, run a weekly ferry service between Cadiz, on the southwest coast of mainland Spain, and the Canary Islands. Setting sail on a Tuesday, the journey to Las Palmas (then onwards to Fuerteventura or Lanzarote) takes around 36 hours and has a hefty price tag to reflect this. A single journey including meals and obligatory cabin costs around €320 per person, with a van costing from €400 upwards. **Fred Olson**, www.fredolson.es, T902 100107 and the slightly cheaper **Naviera Armas**, www.naviera-armas.com, T902 456 500, run regular, reasonably priced inter-island ferry connections between the big seven. Journeys between Playa Blanca, Lanzarote, and Corralejo, Fuerteventura, take about 20 minutes and cost around €12 for a single journey.

Key phrases

Key words/phrases

Yes	sí
No	no
Please	por favor
Thank you	gracias
Sorry	perdon
Hello	Hola
Goodbye	Adiós
Good	buenoBad　mal
I don't understand	no entiendo
I'd like…	quería…
Do you have…?	¿tiene…?
How much is it?	¿cuánto es?
Where is…	¿dónde está?
Mens	caballeros
Ladies	señoras
Left	a la izquierda
Right	a la derecha
Straight on	todo recto
Night	noche
Room	habitación
Pitch	espacio
Shower	ducha
Toilet	servicio
The bill	la cuenta
White coffee	café con leche
Beer	cerveza
Red wine	vino tinto
White wine	vino blanco
Mineral water (still/sparkling)	agua mineral (sin/con gas)
Orange Juice	zumo de naranja
Sandwich	bocadillo
Ham	jamón
Cheese	queso
Help!	socorro
Beach	playa
Point	punta/cabo
River	río
Estuary	ría
Wind	viento
Wave	ola
Board	tabla
Wax	cera
Tide	marea
High	alta
Low	baja
Mid	media
North	norte
South	sur
East	este
West	oeste

Numbers

0	cero
1	uno
2	dos
3	tres
4	quatro
5	cinco
6	seis
7	siete
8	ocho
9	nueve
10	diez
11	once
12	doce
13	trece
14	catorce
15	quince
16	dieciséis
17	dieciseite
18	dieciocho
19	diecinueve
20	veinte
21	veintiuno
22	veintidós
30	treinta
40	cuarenta
50	cincuenta
60	sesenta
70	setenta
80	ochenta
90	noventa
100	cien
200	doscientos
1000	mil

Days of the week

Monday	lunes
Tuesday	martes
Wednesday	miércoles
Thursday	jueves
Friday	viernes
Saturday	sábado
Sunday	domingo

Surfing Spain

"There's more to Spain than Mundaka." Eneko Acero, European
Surfing Champion

After years of domination, first by British surfers in the early 90s,
then by French surfers in the late 90s, the European surfing tree is
now topped by the Spanish. And when you look at the waves
they call home, it's easy to see why. The 2003 European Team
Champions have the continent's most consistent and varied
coastline, with pristine beaches, classic rivermouths and reeling
point breaks. The regular, sizeable swells that bombard these
shores have also produced a committed and hard charging big
wave community. Add to this the Spanish propensity for fiestas,
late nights and general partying and you can see why travelling
surfers have been drawn here since the 60s.

Pros & cons

Pros ...
- Long and rugged coastline which picks up loads of swell
  from the Atlantic low pressure systems.
- It has a massive variety of breaks from classic rivermouths
  and sandy beaches, to reeling points and hollow reefs.
- Spectacular, beautiful deserted surf spots.
- Bustling, urban breaks.
- High standard of wave riding around surfing hotspots.
- Great nightlife.
- Excellent food.

... and cons
- Some localism at busiest breaks.
- Oil residue from the *Prestige* disaster.
- When Portugal is basking in the sun, the Basques can be
  shivering in the rain.
- Some breaks polluted by industrial waste.

Climate

When it comes to climate and weather, northern Spain exhibits a
classic temperate maritime climate. This is characterised by relatively
mild winters, warm summers and a high level of rainfall throughout
the year. You'll hear this said time and time again but they don't call
this region 'Green Spain' for nothing – it can have an annual rainfall
higher than northern Scotland. Moist winds roll in off the Bay of Biscay,
hitting the mountains that fringe the ocean. This causes the air mass
to rise to a higher altitude where it cools. The colder air holds less
moisture and releases the excess as rainfall. Good news if you're a
farmer, bad news if you're a sun worshipper.

For the surfer, the benefits of this are that the rainfall has helped to
carve a varied and jagged coastline punctuated by many rivermouth
breaks. The mountains are being slowly eroded and some of the
debris carried by the water ends up deposited as rivermouth
sandbanks at breaks like Mundaka or Rodiles. It also keeps away those
surfers who need a guaranteed helping of sun with their waves. But if
it's pure wave quality you are after, the odd cloudy or drizzly day is a
price well worth paying.

Andalucía on the other hand, is the exact opposite. Hot summers
of small surf and mild winters make this a popular stop on the surfers
trail to Morocco.

Best seasons to go

When it comes to northern Spain, if swell was the only criteria for a
trip, the question would not when is the best season to go, but where
is the best spot. In the summer this area is one of Europe's most
consistent swell catchers and if there is going to be surf anywhere in
Europe, stretches of northern Spain will be getting it. As a general rule,
the breaks on the areas of coastline that face northwest pick up the
most swell. Spots around Sopelana in the Basque region, Liencres and
Suances in Cantabria, and Asturias west of Gijón are some of the most

consistent summer breaks while the coastline north of Ferrol in Galicia
picks up every ocean ripple. Combined with ocean temperatures of
between 18 and 20°C and air temperatures in the 20s, you can see
why this region is a real surfing hotspot. The stunning scenery,
beautiful beaches and towering mountains provide a stark contrast to
the over-developed costas of the Mediterranean and prove a big draw
to holidaying Spaniards. Consequently, breaks around resort towns
become very busy. Noja, Reinante, Zarautz and Laredo are typical. "In
summer the beaches are overrun by tourists and surf contests, the
prices rise and the highways become clogged," explains Spanish surf
photographer Willy Uribe. "It's a good time for fiestas, but if you've
come to surf you'll have to share half-meter waves with a hundred
other surfers." But this is not to say that there isn't the odd uncrowded
beach to enjoy. If you don't mind the odd rainy day, this is great time
to be here. Long, warm days filled with surfing and nights filled with
fiestas and tapas. You may need a holiday to recover.

Most travelling surfers head for Spain for the autumn swell season.
In September and October daytime temperatures can still be in the
high teens or low 20s, the water is a mild 17-18°C. Swells start to kick
in from the lows tracking across the North Atlantic and while
well-known breaks like Mundaka, Rodiles and Pantín prove to be the
biggest draws, there are countless other reeling spots going unridden.
This is the time of year that the ASP world tour chooses to role into
Mundaka, Tapia and Pantín for their professional surfing contests.

The winter and spring seasons are left to the local surfers and just a
handful of hardy travellers. But whilst the coastline can be battered by
storms for days on end, the geography of the coastline means that
there are always spots working in even the most severe weather. In
between the storms, cool, crystal clear swells can break under crisp,
sunny, winter skies while the snow-topped Picos de Europa look on
impassively. If you want empty line-ups, this is the time to go.

In Andalucía, Autumn is again the most popular time with the swells picking up and warm weather still dominant.

Boards

A good two board selection for Spain would have a beach break board as its mainstay. Something flexible for small days through to overhead. A good rounded squash tail or swallow-tailed thruster, about 18½" wide will give plenty of range. For the big days, or for when the points fire, a good semi-gun will definitely be a help, something like a nice 6'8" to 7'0" pin tail. For board advice check out the Pukas website at www.pukassurf.com.

Good charts for surf

The classic northern Spain chart has always meant one thing – the classic Mundaka chart. A deep low pressure, tracking slowly across the North Atlantic, far enough away to allow the swell to clean up and for the wind to be offshore at the legendary rivermouth break.

However, there is more to northern Spain than just Mundaka. Most of coastline is open to the predominant northwesterly and northerly swells generated by a low pressure passing through the North Atlantic. The deeper the low, and the further away, the bigger and cleaner the swell.

Geography and the breaks

In general, northern Spain is a rugged mountainous region with a thin strip of land acting as a buffer between the towering peaks and the raging Bay of Biscay. In these green and fertile areas, wide rivermouths and large beaches can be found, often with excellent breaks peeling along the white sandy bay in front of pristine sand dunes. In some areas

the mountains fall directly into the sea. Here the surfer's only options are low tide coves that shelter under towering cliffs or rivermouths where thousands of years of erosion have opened up some breathtaking surfing possibilities. Many of Europe's best point breaks peel along this coastline – some hidden deep in the eucalyptus forest, some within plain view of the coastal highway. Many are rocky, sleeping giants needing a big swell to bring them to life. In Andalucía the wide open coastline has huge stretches of sandy beach interspersed with rocky points, while overhead vultures and storks soar on warm thermals.

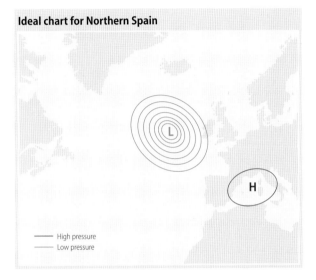

Ideal chart for Northern Spain

L

H

—— High pressure
—— Low pressure

WILLY URIBE

Playa de Deba (Santiago) ▸▸ *p214*

5 underground classics

❶ **Laga** Close to Mundaka, this is an excellent beach break ⇢ *p214*.

❷ **Oriñon** Another Cantabrian rivermouth in a picturesque setting that fires in big autumn swells ⇢ *p226*.

❸ **Ajo** Consistent Cantabrian beach break that picks up loads of swell ⇢ *p228*.

❹ **Galizano** Low tide rivermouth with an excellent, hollow right-hander ⇢ *p228*.

❺ **Esteiro** Quiet Galician beauty with perfect A-frame sandbank ⇢ *p249*.

Esteiro ⇢ *p249*

Surfing and environment

There are parts of the coastline where the industrial landscape rivals any region in Europe. Smoke stacks belch noxious fumes that are wafted by offshore winds into the line-up and burning chimneys illuminate the night sky. Franco's hatred of the northern territories that had dared to hold out against his rule, meant that little thought went into the environmental impact of the steel works, petrochemical plants and power stations that sprung up as the struggling Spanish economy tried desperately to modernise. Playa de la Arena, Playa de la Concha and the breaks north of Gijón are typical of this kind of development which led, not just to a visual blight on the landscape, but to a legacy of air and water pollution.

Luckily this is not the norm and a visitor is more likely to see areas that look like they have completely missed the industrial revolution. Mules can be seen pulling ploughs on smallholdings, while crops dry nearby in the Autumn sun. The oceans around are some of the cleanest in Europe. Northern Spain missed the 70s holiday boom and is desperate to protect its natural habitat. Unfortunately the events of 19 November 2002 have left a lasting impression on the coastline. It was on this date that the oil tanker *The Prestige* broke in two and sank, a hundred miles off the Galician coastline, causing one of Europe's worst environmental disasters. It has become, not only the biggest environmental issue in Spain, but also one of the biggest issues in Spanish politics. The clean up operation is still ongoing and environmental organizations predict the oil may have an impact for the next decade. Local surfers have been hit hard with oil washing up as far south as Portugal and as far north as the Channel Islands. Beaches along the Spanish north coast and French west coast were closed as the oil was scraped and scrubbed from the shore. On the anniversary of the disaster tens of thousands of protesters congregated in Madrid and oil could still be found on the beaches of Spain and France. Environmental organizations claim that another *Prestige* disaster could still occur as old, single-hulled tankers move through the same waters that the *Prestige* went down in.

Localism and surf communities

The Spanish are passionate about life and passionate about their surfing. With an ever-increasing number of surfers, some breaks are suffering greater tensions in the water. Only a few suffer out-and-out localism, but this number is on the increase. Usually surfers riding respectfully will have no problems. Tensions grow at breaks that are very busy, only break at one state of tide, have a small take-off point, rarely break, are dangerous or all of the above. A good example of this is the rivermouth at Rodiles. A low tide break popular with travelling surfers since the 70s, Rodiles has a small take off zone and large local surfing population. Some people surf there and have the session of their lives. Others come away with tales of intimidation and drop-ins.

At some spots a breach of etiquette may be treated harshly due to the dangerous nature of the break. Spots like Roca Puta and Menakoz are for experienced surfers and fools are not suffered lightly. There are, however, urban breaks where surfers who are less experienced become frustrated by being pushed down the pecking order by a more experienced outsider. Picking up a few words of Spanish can help defuse potential conflicts. The thing to remember is that all surfers have two things in common. We like people who visit our home breaks to surf respectfully, and we like to be treated respectfully when we visit other areas – because all surfers travel.

Surf directory

Spain supports five surf magazines *360*, *Surfer Rule*, *Surfari*, *Radical Surf* and free surf newspaper, *Surf Time*.

Spain: a brief surf history

1963 → Having got his hands on a Barland surfboard from the French Basque region, Jesús Fiochi becomes the first Spanish surfer at Sardinero, Santander. **1964** → The surf scene begins to spread through Cantabria. **1965** → Basque surfer Raul Dourdil and friends begin surfing at Bakio. **1969** → José Merido begins making Spanish surfboards under the MB mark. **1969** → Surfing spreads to Galicia with the discovery of breaks like Ferrol and Doniños. **1970s** → Surfing goes national travelling south to Cádiz and across the water to the Canaries. **1973** → Following on from Santa Marina and Geronimo surfboards, the first Pukas boards are shaped. **1987** → The first Spanish surf magazine, *Tres60*, is launched. **1988** → Spain holds its first International surf contest the Pukas Pro. **1989** → The first international surf contest, organized by the EPSA is held at Mundaka, helping to project the wave onto the world stage. **1990** → *Surfer Rule* magazine launches. **2001** → Spain's successes in competitive surfing culminate in Euskadi's Eneko Acero being crowned European surfing champion. **Today** → Spain hosts one of the WCT's most prestigious events, the Mundaka Pro, as well as several WQS events including rounds held at Tapia and Pantín.

THE GILL

Lavery styling at Mundaka » *p216*

Mundaka heaven and hell

British surfer Nick Lavery was brought up in Mundaka and soon developed a talent for surfing. By charging on the biggest days, Nick became one of Mundaka's most respected surfers. He has experienced the highs and lows of this awesome wave.

The Mundaka Surf Classic was an annual event that brought many of the world's finest surfers to the tiny Basque village. But in 1989, the surf went off the Richter scale, with 10 ft sets reeling along the sandbar. Unfortunately for Nick, he wasn't even in the country. "I had only just started my first year at Cambridge University, and hadn't been in the water for weeks," says Nick. "But Craig Sage (Mundaka surf shop owner and my sponsor) and my Dad paid my airfare to Spain so I could get back for the competition."

"One moment I was daydreaming in a boring lecture room, the next my Dad was swinging the car round the bendy mountain roads of Sondica. I was rolling around in the back trying to get into my wetsuit, desperately hoping to make it to my heat which was already underway." "A group of Aussies were watching as Nick jumped out of the car and straight into the water," says surf photographer Paul Gill. "They were all laughing going 'Who's this guy?' 'He's gonna drown'."
"I jumped off the jetty into the water," says Nick. "The rest of the guys were already in the line-up – I didn't even know what the surf was like! That Friday evening saw the swell peak in what was one of the most 'Classic' of the Mundaka Surf Classics."

"This huge set rolled into view and everybody started scratching for the horizon," says Paul. "Suddenly Nick turned and started paddling for this wave. The whole place went quiet. He dropped down the face and disappeared into this massive barrel. We all started looking for him in the white water. The commentator was going 'Where's the Pommie gone?' Then he pops out of the barrel on the inside and rides over the back of the wave. The whole place erupted!"

"Without thinking, I dropped into my first wave," says Nick "and it must have been 8-10 ft plus, and I just stood in this massive barrel. I've always been nervous in competition, so maybe not having the chance to be involved in the build-up and hype allowed me to surf at my peak. I won the heat on the strength of that first wave alone."

"The next morning I had the chance to surf in an expression session with legends Gary Elkerton and Tom Curren. It was the heat immediately after this that I pulled off the barrel with my hands behind my back." This classic moment was captured and went on to become the image on the following year's contest posters. "I went on to a storming run, beating Maurice Cole and Wayne Lynch along the way, ending up 3rd in the semi-finals. I was chuffed. Good memories."

However, Mundaka is not all good memories for Nick. "I dislocated both my shoulders there, Christmas 1991, and I've had loads of problems with them since. It was a small day, about 6 ft, really perfect. Most of the guys, Alfonso Fernández, Craig, Bruce etc were out or had been out. I'd had quite a good day with a couple of long barrels, but it was a bit nerve-wracking with all the crowds. Often guys who haven't surfed there before will drop in on you while you're in the barrel. Anyway, I was in the barrel and I saw this guy frantically paddling up the wave, and kicking with his feet (another no-no as it brings a curtain down). I wasn't sure if he was taking off on me, or had been caught in the lip. Anyway, this curtain closed down and I broke through it too low. I put my hands over my head, expecting the guy to land on me. The lip landed on my arms, shoving them behind my head, the force dislocating both my shoulders. Very painful!"

"After that it was a bit of blur. A couple of guys helped me out of the impact zone. I could just about grip the side of the board with my left arm, which had popped back into the socket, but my right arm was just floating around like a spare part. My father and the village sports coach got me into the rowing club, where they proceeded to cut through my wetsuit with a pair of scissors! I had a bumpy hour's drive to Baracaldo hospital in Bilbao. Ten hours later I was still waiting for them to put me under anaesthetic. I think that at that time I was the last regular on the peak who didn't have an injury. Mundaka can be a punishing wave. Locals have their injuries to prove it. Backs, shoulders and especially knee injuries are the norm. So treat it with respect."

Euskadi

Surfing Euskadi

Euskadi – the Basque Country (El País Vasco) – is home to a proud and patriotic people. Suppressed under Franco, Basque culture is now booming. The beret is on show in every harbour-side bar and city café as the headwear of choice for young and old and is used at surf contests to crown new champions. The Basque language, once illegal, has also been reborn through a new generation of young, brought up speaking Europe's oldest language as their first. Euskara words usually bear no relation to their Spanish equivalents (which on road signs have often been sprayed over) so a few choice terms will not only impress but will also come in very handy when you're looking for the *hondartza*.

There is a strong independence movement here, with the terrorist group ETA an extremist offshoot. However, surfers are probably unique in that, if asked for the first thing they associate with the Basque region, it would not be the bombings that have hit the world headlines. Wave riders will forever associate this region with the reeling left-hander that peels in the mouth of the Ría de Mundaka. But even here, in the small, picturesque fishing village, occasional colourful murals – either pro or anti ETA – illustrate the political debate in a universal language. However, this is probably the only sign you will see of the politics of Euskadi and this region is renowned as one of the friendliest areas in Spain.

One drawback to the Basque region for the budget traveller is that Euskadi is also one of Spain's most expensive regions, even in the off season. Whereas cities like San Sebastián have plenty of good quality,

Euskadi board guide

Short board
Shaper: Rawson for Pukas

▸▸ 6'2" x 18" x 2".
▸▸ For beach breaks such as Sopelana, Zarautz, Gros.
▸▸ Hyper Skate model. Bump squash tail.
▸▸ Perfected in many of my trips to California.
▸▸ For flatter conditions and features a slight bonzer bottom and forgiving entry forward, for skatey moves in crap waves.

Semi-gun
Shaper: Peter Daniels for Pukas

▸▸ 6'3" x 18" x 2⅛" for Aritz Aranburu.
▸▸ Perfect for Mundaka.
▸▸ Smooth rocker and narrower tail to get into wave early and pigdogging barrels.
▸▸ Version for a 75 kg surfer, normal level will be 6'6" x 18" x 2⁵⁄₁₆".
▸▸ Version for big guys: 7'2" x 19" x 2".

ⓘ Boards by **Pukas**
Factory: Olatu, Oyarzun, Euskadi, Spain
T00 34 (0)943-493255
www.pukasurf.com

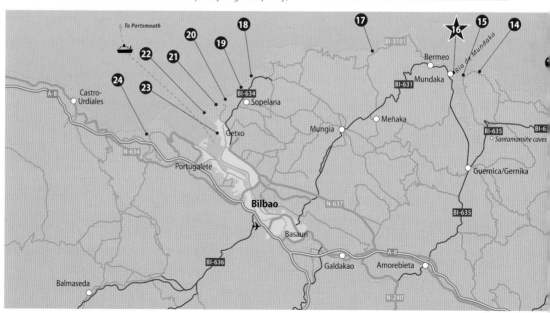

cheap *pensiones* costing between €22 and €30 for a double room in low season, smaller towns and villages could have prices nearer €40 to €45 – even more in Mundaka.

Localism

The standard of surfing in the Basque region is as high as anywhere in Europe. Euskadi is also the busiest region in Spain. "As a travelling surfer, the locals will either welcome you with a friendly sense of curiosity, or they will ignore you," says Tony Butt. "Extreme localism is not prevalent here, unlike, say, the Canary Islands. Obviously though, if you come with an aggressive attitude, you will be met with aggression." As top Basque surfer Eneko Acero says, "In the past few years there has been a change at Mundaka. It's not like thirty or forty people in the water – it's like a hundred people. I think some of the local guys get a bit tired of it because it's so crowded. You can't get so many waves, a lot of people are dropping in. It's getting more localised now than it was years ago."

Tony explains: "The locals are understandably concerned that some of the other breaks will 'end up like Mundaka', particularly some world-class big-wave spots in the area." So, as Eneko explains, follow the golden rule and you'll have no problems: "Surf respectfully and you'll be respected."

Top local surfers Eneko and Kepa Acero, Iker Fuentes, Alfonso Fernández, Ibon Amatriain and female surfer Estitxu Estremo.

Getting around

The minor road networks are of good quality and provide good access to the Basque coastline. The motorways are a fast way to cross the region, if a bit pricey. The bus and rail networks are also a convenient way to get around and provide access to all the major cities.

Euskadi chart by The Gill

"The Basque region will pick up swell from any decent low pressure system tracking through the north Atlantic. The further away the low pressure, the cleaner the swell, and the longer the fetch, the bigger the surf. Ideally this should be coupled with local high pressure for light southerly winds giving offshore conditions. For classic Mundaka, an oval-shaped low of 985 or lower sitting off the coast of Ireland will have everyone frantically checking the web and clearing their diaries."

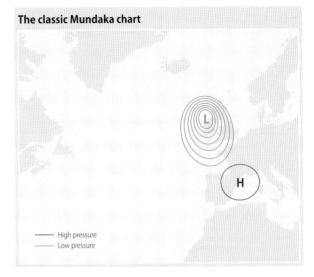

The classic Mundaka chart

—— High pressure
—— Low pressure

Spain Euskadi Surfing

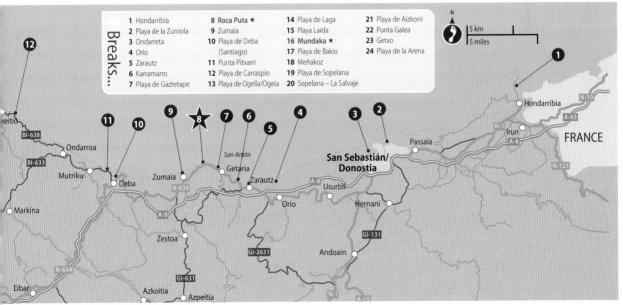

Breaks...

1 Hondarribia
2 Playa de la Zurriola
3 Ondarreta
4 Orio
5 Zarautz
6 Karramarro
7 Playa de Gaztetape
8 Roca Puta ★
9 Zumaia
10 Playa de Deba (Santiago)
11 Punta Pitxarri
12 Playa de Carraspio
13 Playa de Ogella/Ogeia
14 Playa de Laga
15 Playa Laida
16 Mundaka ★
17 Playa de Bakio
18 Meñakoz
19 Playa de Sopelana
20 Sopelana – La Salvaje
21 Playa de Aizkorri
22 Punta Galea
23 Getxo
24 Playa de la Arena

5 km
5 miles

Breaks

1 Hondarribia

- **Break type**: Beach break.
- **Conditions**: Big swell, offshore in south/southwesterly.
- **Hazards/tips**: Moderately polluted.
- **Sleeping**: San Sebastián ›› *p219*.

Sheltered town beach that needs big north or northwesterly swell to work. On the push it can produce good waves. A place to look at in massive storms when everywhere else is maxed out.

2 Playa de la Zurriola

- **Break type**: Beach break.
- **Conditions**: Small to medium swells, offshore in southerly winds.
- **Hazards/tips**: Crowds, urban break.
- **Sleeping**: San Sebastián ›› *p219*.

A large, crescent shaped, sandy beach in San Sebastián working through the tide. Zurriola produces good quality peaks along the beach and a right-hander that breaks at the eastern end near the sea wall. Can have excellent waves in small and medium swells but tends to close out in bigger swells. The east end plays hosts to a WQS contest. Has a strong local crew so there can be some localism on crowded days and water quality is sometimes poor. A pleasant urban beach with showers and drinking water.

3 Ondarreta

- **Break type**: Beach break.
- **Conditions**: Big swells, offshore in south/southwesterly winds.
- **Hazards/tips**: In San Sebastián parking is a problem.
- **Sleeping**: San Sebastián ›› *p219*.

This is the second town beach at San Sebastián and is sheltered by a headland and the small island – Isla de Santa Clara. There are two stretches of sand. To the east, **La Concha** is not renowned for its waves. **Ondarreta** works on the push and also has a high tide point break.

4 Orio

- **Break type**: Beach break.
- **Conditions**: Big swells, offshore in southwesterly/southeasterly winds.
- **Hazards/tips**: Antilla is visible from the motorway viaduct, has a massive car park, a beachfront campsite, cafés and showers.
- **Sleeping**: Orio ›› *p220*.

Playa de la Antilla is a pleasant sandy beach break that works through the tides and is situated slightly out of the town of Orio at the rivermouth. Although quite a small beach, in large swells it can have a peak towards the west and a right towards the east. The breakwater at Orio cuts out a lot of swell but gives shelter in large westerly storms. Not too crowded or polluted.

5 Zarautz

- **Break type**: Beach break.
- **Conditions**: Small to medium swells, offshore in southerly winds.
- **Hazards/tips**: Crowds, parking, has skatepark.
- **Sleeping**: Zarautz ›› *p221*.

Zarautz is a pretty town with a beach that is busy throughout the year. It has a variety of peaks working on all tides along its long shore, with a popular peak near the skatepark. A WQS contest is often held here in September. A local hotspot, Zarautz has a high standard of surfing and can be crowded. Parking is difficult at peak times but off season you should be able to find a spot on the road running parallel to the beach. The seafront is lined with modern art and has showers.

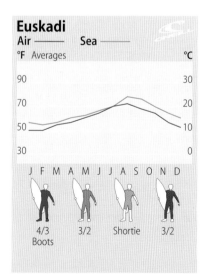

Euskadi

Air ——— Sea ———

°F Averages   °C

4/3 Boots	3/2	Shortie	3/2

2 Playa de la Zurriola

6 Karramarro

- **Break type**: Left-hand reef break.
- **Conditions**: Big swells, offshore in southerly winds.
- **Hazards/tips**: May be some localism on busy days, experienced surfers only.
- **Sleeping**: Zarautz » p221.

This low tide, rocky reef works in big northwesterly swells. Waves of up to 10 ft draw surfers from Zarautz and beyond. For experienced surfers only. Check the N-634 just north of Zarautz.

7 Playa de Gaztetape

- **Break type**: Beach break.
- **Conditions**: Small to medium swells, offshore in southerly winds.
- **Hazards/tips**: Not too crowded or polluted, parking available overlooking the break.
- **Sleeping**: Zarautz/Zumaia » p221.

Just west of the San Antón headland at Getaria, this is a small, quiet crescent-shaped bay that all but disappears at high tide when the waves break onto the rocky sea defences. At low through to mid tide, in small to medium northwesterly swells, it produces peaks along the picturesque, sandy beach. It is offshore in southerly winds, but the surrounding hills provide good protection from westerlies and easterlies.

8 Roca Puta

- **Break type**: Right-hand point break.
- **Conditions**: Medium to big swells, offshore in southerly winds
- **Size**: 4-12 ft.
- **Length**: 200 m plus.
- **Swell**: Northerly.
- **Wind**: Southerly.
- **Tide**: Low-mid.
- **Bottom**: Boulders.
- **Entry/exit**: Off the rocks on the inside.
- **Hazards/tips**: Rocks, crowds, heavy wave for experienced surfers only.
- **Sleeping**: Zumaia » p221.

One of the region's most famous big-wave spots, Roca Puta can see huge right-hand waves reeling off the rocky point near Punta Izustarri. This break really comes to life in big swells and has a hard-core crew of big-wave chargers. Meaning 'Whore Rock', the wave breaks along rocky coastal defences and needs to be over head-high to start working, otherwise large boulders pepper the line-up. Once a big swell kicks in, the point is transformed. This low tide spot should really only be tackled by experienced surfers. Clean water but rocky line-up. A great spectacle when it's working, the lay-by on the coast road provides a good vantage point.

If you like Roca Puta, try Isla de Santa Marina in Spain (see page 229) or Safi in Morocco (see page 351).

It was very special to me when I became the European champion – I am a Basque surfer so it meant a lot to me to win on home soil.

Eneko Acero, 2001 European Champion

9 Zumaia

- **Break type**: Beach break.
- **Conditions**: Small to medium swells, offshore in southerly winds.
- **Hazards/tips**: Parking can be a problem at peak times.
- **Sleeping**: Zumaia » p221.

Playa de Itzurun is a beautiful bay with a sandy beach and fingers of reef that reach out into the Bay of Biscay. It is a consistent break that picks up lots of swell and works on all tides except high where it can be prone to backwash from the cliffs. To the west, a red sandstone cliff of vertical slabs stretches out to the headland and to the east lies a blue slate cliff with sandy beach between. The fingers of reef act like groynes and allow the build-up of sand. Contest venue on the Euskadi circuit.

Spain Euskadi Breaks Karramarro to Zumaia

4 Orio

5 Zarautz

8 Roca Puta

10 Playa de Deba (Santiago)

- **Break type**: Right-hand reef and sandy beach.
- **Conditions**: Big swells, offshore in southerly winds.
- **Hazards/tips**: Heavy wave for experienced surfers.
- **Sleeping**: Deba/Mutriku » *p221*.

The low tide reef is a fairly consistent big-wave spot, that breaks best at 6-9 ft (but up to 15 ft) in big northwesterly swells. Considered by local surfers as a dangerous spot suitable for experienced big-wave surfers only. The reef sits at the east end of a sandy beach that works through all tides producing lefts and rights. At the western end of the beach is a sheltering rocky groyne. There are toilets and plenty of parking at the beach.

11 Punta Pitxarri

11 Punta Pitxarri

- **Break type**: Left-hand point.
- **Conditions**: Medium swells, offshore in southerly winds.
- **Hazards/tips**: This rocky reef is shallow when small. Park just off the GI-638 and scramble down the disused track.
- **Sleeping**: Deba/Mutriku » *p221*.

Quality left-hand rocky point break that works best at low tide/on the push in southerly offshore winds. Pitxarri needs a bigger swell from a more northerly direction to form long, peeling walls that spin off the point along the rocky reef.

12 Playa de Carraspio

- **Break type**: Beach break.
- **Conditions**: Medium swell, offshore in southerly winds.
- **Hazards/tips**: Popular weekend and evening break, just off the coast road east of Lekeitio.
- **Sleeping**: Lekeitio » *p221*.

A very pretty beach break with an island at the western end and a rocky point at the east. A left breaks near the island, along a rivermouth sandbar. There can also be peaks on the beach in a medium swell. Can break on all tides depending on swell size and sandbars. The river flow affects sandbar deposition.

13 Playa de Ogella/Ogeia

- **Break type**: Sand-covered reef.
- **Conditions**: Medium and large swells, offshore in southerly winds.
- **Hazards/tips**: Very difficult to find, off small back roads, not signposted (or signposts have been removed).
- **Sleeping**: Lekeitio » *p221*.

Situated west of Lekeitio in beautiful countryside, this low tide peak produces fast, hollow rights and fast walling lefts. Quality break. Fairly localized.

14 Playa de Laga

- **Break type**: Beach break.
- **Conditions**: Small to medium swells, offshore in southerly winds.
- **Hazards/tips**: Crowds when good and weekends/lunchtime.
- **Sleeping**: Mundaka » *p221*.

Sitting so close to Mundaka, Laga tends to get overlooked by travelling surfers but is a high quality beach break that works on all tides. This fact has not escaped the local surfers, so when it is on expect there to be a strong local crew. Sitting under a spectacular cliff, the beach provides some excellent banks with hollow lefts, rights and peaks. It works best at low to mid tide. Car parking area, toilets and bar.

10 Playa de Deba (Santiago)

12 Playa de Carraspio

15 Playa Laida

- **Break type**: Beach break.
- **Conditions**: Small to medium swells, offshore in southerly winds.
- **Hazards/tips**: Can produce nice waves, but it's not what people come to Mundaka for.
- **Sleeping**: Mundaka ▸▸ p221.

Laida is an extension of the beach at the ría de Mundaka. It is a break that can produce some pretty good waves through the tides and, at any other location, would probably be surfed a lot more. Access from Mundaka village means paddling across the river or driving inland to Gernika and then following the river road back out to the coast – a bit of a trek. In the summer you can hop on a foot passenger ferry.

9 Zumaia ▸▸ p213

14 Playa de Laga

Surfers' tales

18 Tony Butt at Meñakoz ▸▸ p217

Olatu Handien Txapelketarik Ez, Eskerrik Asko
(Big-Wave Contests, No Thanks) by Tony Butt

The Basque Country, or Euskal Herría to give it its proper name, differs in almost every way from its neighbours; culturally, topographically, oceanographically and linguistically. The harsh, steep morphology is a stark contrast from the flat pine forests of Les Landes or the rolling hills of coastal Cantabria. The frontier between Euskal Herría and its neighbours is a natural one, strikingly evident as one enters Iparralde from the north. Here, after miles of flatness, large mountains suddenly spring up out of nowhere, and the main surf spots briskly change from beaches to reefs.

The reefs tend to have slightly different features according to their particular location. In Iparralde (on the French side of the border) to the north, they tend to be quite flat and spread out, making rides long and take-offs relatively easy. Things become difficult here when the swell starts to get really big, as the playing field quickly grows and the peaks start to shift. Moving into the Guipúzkoa region, the coastal geology tends to favour faja-type boulder reefs, which sometimes give rise to huge waves breaking just a few metres from the shore. Then, in Bizkaia, the folded rock strata so typical of Spain's north coast, starts to become evident, with the uneven and dangerous reef formations often resembling rows of giant shark's teeth sticking out of the ocean floor.

The locals are neither Spanish nor French: they are Euskaldunes – Basques. They are brutally proud of their heritage and culture, and some resort to desperate measures in their paranoia about losing it. There is a degree of xenophobia here and, although less prevalent among the surfing community, any surfer living here who was not born in the Basque country, or even one who has a non-Basque name, will always remain an outsider.

Almost every year, some corporation proposes a big-wave contest, or somebody suggests using a jet-ski to tow in to the waves. The locals are fiercely against these types of activities; they see no advantage to them, only increased aggressiveness, contamination and stress in the water.

Tony Butt lives in the Basque Country and holds a PhD in Physical Oceanography and big-wave riding. His excellent book *Surf Science* explains all about waves from a layman's point of view. It is available from most surf shops or through Tony's website: www.swell-forecast.com.

WILLY URIBE

16 Mundaka

- **Conditions**: Medium to big swells.
- **Size**: 2-4 ft.
- **Length**: 200 m plus.
- **Swell**: Northerly/northwesterly.
- **Wind**: Southerly.
- **Tide**: Low to three quarters.
- **Bottom**: Shallow rivermouth sandbar.
- **Entry/exit**: Entry via harbour, exit on rocks south of harbour.
- **Hazards/tips**: Crowded, powerful, rips, experienced surfers only.
- **Sleeping**: Mundaka ►► *p221.*

When the waters of the Ría de Mundaka finally flow into the Bay of Biscay, the loss of momentum causes the suspended sediment they have been carrying down from the mountains to be deposited here at the rivermouth. Currents help produce a long sandbank perfectly angled to produce fast, hollow left-hand waves when struck by a northerly or northwesterly swell. These factors conspire to produce a wave that is famous the world over. It is not the longest wave in the world.

The wave at Mundaka breaks anywhere from half a metre to 2-12 ft. The nature of the sandbar allows the wave to break, even in massive swells, when other spots might simply close out. Surfers access the line-up by paddling out from the harbour, until the river currents drop them at the peak. This channel is kept open in all but the biggest swells. However, you must keep an eye open for outside sets. Although Mundaka is, in effect, a beach, it breaks like a shallow reef. If you have not surfed here before, it's best to watch a couple of bigger sets come through. The locals dominate the peak and will take the best waves, but even a half-decent wave at Mundaka is special. Some waves do sneak through unridden. Make sure you double-check the wave is free before you drop in. It is not uncommon to see inexperienced surfers drop in on a surfer who is deep in the barrel.

ⓘ *If you like* Mundaka, *try* Rodiles *in Spain (see page 239) or* Gills Bay *in Scotland (see page 36).*

18 Meñakoz

Mundaka top tips *by Nick Lavery*

The best time to go to Mundaka is late autumn, as it's still warmish and you can get long spells of offshore winds. Its a very unpredictable wave, which is part of what makes it so fun, but the crowds have always been a problem – even in the early 80s it wasn't uncommon to get over a hundred guys out on the weekend.

As far as boards are concerned, things change a lot, and it depends on your build. Generally you want enough length to get you into the take-off, but because it is so steep, hollow and down the line, you don't want anything over a 7'6" - 7'8". I personally like a 7'6" with boxy rails and a bit of rocker for anything up to 10-12 ft. If your board is too long, you increase the chances of snapping it, and it won't trim so well in the barrel.

I used to love surfing it an hour before low tide, as the wave was more hollow at that stage, but beware of the super strong rip from the river. Check your leash, because if it snaps, you can't always get across the river to the safety of the rocks, and I have seen quite a few people end up a good mile out to sea with a growing swell and getting dark. The estuary is **very** treacherous, so be careful.

In as far as water etiquette goes, try not to hassle the locals on the peak. Try to pick off waves a bit further down the line. Understand why they get annoyed as there are always 'giris' travelling throughout the whole year! Also don't turn up with two car loads of guys ... usual stuff. There are plenty of great places to stay in Mundaka, and if you are there in the summer try to go to some of the fiestas and remember that the Basques drink at a steady pace for a long night, and do not appreciate loud, drunk foreigners. Try to speak a bit of Basque and they may open up some more.

Nick Lavery grew up surfing the hallowed waves of Mundaka and beat many of the world's best, including the likes of Wayne Lynch and Maurice Cole, in the Mundaka Surf Classic competitions.

17 Playa de Bakio

- **Break type**: Beach break.
- **Conditions**: Small to medium swells, offshore in southerly winds.
- **Hazards/tips**: Crowds.
- **Sleeping**: Mundaka ▸▸ *p221*.

This is a quality beach break that works through all tides. As a town beach it is usually crowded and can suffer some localism. In big swells there can be a large, hollow, right-hander at the western end of the beach. The town end of the beach is open and sandy with peaks running along its length. From the stream east the beach has rocky outcrops, but the sand builds up into some quality banks. This is an alternative contest site for the Mundaka Pro competition. Good beach for surfers of all abilities. Park in bays on main road from east. Has showers.

18 Meñakoz

- **Break type**: Right-hand reef.
- **Conditions**: Big swells, offshore in southeasterly winds.
- **Hazards/tips**: Dangerous wave; for experts only.
- **Sleeping**: Sopelana ▸▸ *p221*.

Along with Mundaka, Meñakoz is the region's most famous spot. It is a big wave with a big reputation. This is definitely an 'experts only' wave as the powerful right-handers break up to 18 ft in height. Works from mid to high tide. It also has a highly localized line-up with rocks, tricky access, long hold downs and very powerful waves.

17 Playa de Bakio

Spain Euskadi Breaks Playa de Bakio to Meñakoz

DEMI TAYLOR

20 Sopelana - La Salvaje

THE GILL

16 Mundaka line-up ▸▸ *p216*

WILLY URIBE

16 Wayne Lynch 1989 Mundaka pro ▸▸ *p216*

WILLY URIBE

23 Gexto

19 Playa de Sopelana

- **Break type**: Beach breaks.
- **Conditions**: Small to medium swells, offshore in southeasterly winds.
- **Hazards/tips**: Car crime has been a problem here with vans broken into.
- **Sleeping**: Sopelana ▸▸ *p222*.

Playa de Atxibiribil and **Playa de Arrietara** are two beaches in Sopelana that break through the tides. They offer a variety of peaks and reefs that break either left or right along and near rocky fingers. This area has a large and very committed surf population and boasts some of Europe's top surfers. Surf shops nearby on road to beach, Loiola Ander Deuna.

20 Sopelana – La Salvaje

- **Break type**: Beach break.
- **Conditions**: All swells, offshore in southwesterly winds.
- **Hazards/tips**: A very popular spot, which may have some localism and car crime.
- **Sleeping**: Sopelana ▸▸ *p222*.

Heading west from Playa de Sopelana lies Salvaje, a good quality beach break boasting some excellent waves at all states of tide. **La Triangular** is a rocky finger that produces, as the name suggests, both lefts and rights. These can be fast, long and have barrel sections. This break attracts the area's best surfers so standards are high.

21 Playa de Aizkorri

- **Break type**: Beach break and point.
- **Conditions**: All swells, offshore in southeasterly.
- **Hazards/tips**: Due to its proximity to Getxo the water quality is not good.
- **Sleeping**: Getxo ▸▸ *p222*.

The next bay west boasts nice quality peaks and an excellent left-hand point at the west of the bay that pumps in large swells. Tends to be less crowded than Sopelana. Access from car park at eastern end of the beach.

22 Punta Galea

- **Break type**: Rocky right-hand point break.
- **Conditions**: Big swell, offshore in southeasterly winds.
- **Hazards/tips**: Dangerous spot where access is a problem.
- **Sleeping**: Getxo ▸▸ *p222*.

A huge right-hand point breaks here in big swells. Close to the cliffs and rocks, this is a spot that even experienced surfers would think twice before tackling. Works on mid to high tide and is offshore in south and easterly winds.

23 Getxo

- **Break type**: Beach and point breaks.
- **Conditions**: Medium swells, offshore in southeasterly winds.
- **Hazards/tips**: Busy and very polluted.
- **Sleeping**: Getxo ▸▸ *p222*.

The two beaches inside Punta Galea are **Arrigunaga** and **Ereaga**. Both are rocky and sand-covered rock. Through the tides Arrigunaga can have good quality right-hand waves whereas Ereaga boasts both lefts and rights. Both are popular breaks due to their proximity to Getxo and Bilbao.

24 Playa de la Arena

- **Break type**: Beach break.
- **Conditions**: Small to medium swells, offshore in southeasterly.
- **Hazards/tips**: Polluted, smelly, busy.
- **Sleeping**: Bilbao ▸▸ *p223*.

This beach is just to the west of Bilbao and can have some good quality waves with various peaks along the beach at different states of tide. However, the drive-in will give you a clue as to why this may be a beach to avoid. Huge petrochemical plants belching noxious fumes are not the prettiest backdrops, and in an offshore wind from the south the smell is pretty hideous. Parking and camping available near the beach. Suitable for all surfers.

Listings

San Sebastián/Donostia

Crossing the French border and following the N-1 in from the Pays Basque, San Sebastián is a great first port of call on the Guipúzcoan Coast and excellent introduction to Euskadi. A young, vibrant city of tightly packed bars and cafes, San Sebastián is cocooned by three beaches. Ondarreta and Playa de la Concha stretch out to the west and Playa de la Zurriola to the east.

✖ Flat spells

Aquarium Complete with sharks and a glass walk way through the tank, it's just west of Monte Urgallon on Plaza Carlos Blasco de Imaz. At €8 it's pretty pricey and closed on Mon. **Drinking** From Jan-Apr an afternoon spent at a *sidrería* or **sagardotegiak** is not a wasted one. The Basque cider, which is flat and tart, is brewed in massive barrels and as part of the traditional *sidrería* menu (from about €20) you can help yourself to as much as you need to wash down your slab of meat, cheese and walnuts. Note: pour your cider from a good height for a professional finish. **Football** At the Estadio de Anotea watch **Real Sociedad**, San Sebastián's home grown team, go head to head with some of Spain's finest. Tickets available from the stadium at €25–40. **Funfair** Catch the funicular railway up to the top of Monte Igueldo for €1.50 return – great views, cheesy funfair. **Golf** There are a couple of courses. Green fees are around €40. The 18-hole **Real San Sebastián GC** is 14 km eastbound on the Hondaribbia/San Sebastián motorway, T943 61 68 45/46 or the more centrally located Golf Basozabal is on the Camino Goyaz-Txiki, T943 46 76 42.

🛏 Sleeping

If you want to sample the bars and cafés of San Sebastián, for ambience and access the best place to base yourself is in the Parte Vieja or 'Old Town'. Crammed full of cheap *pensiones* and good tapas bars, it's only a short walk over the bridge to Zurriola.
D **Pension Edorta**, www.pensionedorta.com,

on Puerto with lovely old beamed rooms from €40 in the low season
F **Pensión Fermin,** on Fermin Calbeton, with a fridge in the rooms and a shared bathroom down the hall.
F **Pensión Loinaz**, on San Lorenzo, www.infobide.com/pensionloinaz, with shared bathrooms and laundry room.
F **Pensión Amaiur**, on 31 de Agusto, the only street to survive the great fire of 1813, reservas@pensionamaiur.com.
F **Pensión San Lorenzo**, on San Lorenzo, the rooms come with all the mod cons, TV, fridge, kettle, making it a popular option.
B&B **Isabella**, www.roomsisabella.com, near Ondarreta has apartments which can house up to either 2 or 6 people respectively.
Camping There's only one campsite here and, stuck way out west behind the Monte Igueldo, is not very convenient. **Camping Igueldo**, on the Paseo Padre Orkolaga is open year round to tents only, T943 21 45 02, www.campingigeldo.com.

🍴 Eating

Eating tapas, or pintxos, as they are known in Euskadi, is *the* thing to do in San Sebastián so don't fight it. The Parte Vieja is humming with great bars all serving their own variety of pintxos, which you can sample all day starting just after breakfast. The best time to hit the tapas trail is from about 1930 onwards when the bars are beginning to pack out. Locals go from bar to bar having a bite and *txikiteo* (small drink) at each stop. Almost anywhere you go is going to be good but a couple of popular spots include **Beti Jai, Bar Egosari** and **Bodega Donostiarra**, on Fermin Calbeton, where a couple of pintxos and *zuritos* (small beers) for 2 will set you back about €5. Another great spot, with a full complement of hanging hooves, is **Bar/Restaurant Portaletas**, where the wine flows freely and the pintxos are as good as any. For cheap eats there are also plenty of places to choose from in the Parte Vieja including an average Italian, **Capriccosa Trattoria and Pizzeria** and a bright, clean Tex Mex, **Cantina Mariachi**, on Fermin Calbeton. For a more traditional approach try the restaurant below **Txalupa**

DEMI TAYLOR

bar on Calbeton which does a good *menú del día* for about €10. In the Egia district, just east of the train station on Ametzagana, is **Garraxi**, a vegetarian restaurant, offering a fair weekday menu for €8.

⚙ Festivals
19–20 Jan, Feast day of San Sebastián 'Tamborrada'. **Mid Aug** *Gran Semana* or Big Week. **Sep** International Film Festival.

◐ Shopping
There are plenty of **surf shops** in San Sebastián including a couple of **Pukas** stores – one in the Parte Vieja on Nagusia and another on the sea front at Zurriola. A few doors down **Maru Jo** stocks hardware as well as clothing. Back from Zurriola is **Stock Island** on San Francisco and on the west side near Playa de la Concha is **Hawaii** on San Bartolomé. If you need a new board, **Pukas** have their factory, Olatu, east of here in Oyarzun. It opened in 1988 and has world-class shapers, T0034 943 493255, www.pukassurf.com.

⊖ Parking
There is no access by cars through the old town but there are a couple of underground car parks near the Almeda del Boulevard. Parking can be a nightmare in San Sebastián, as can driving. You can try and scour the town for a parking spot – doubtful unless you want to go native and try double parking on the pedestrian crossing. The Paseo Nuevo on the headland just west of the river is a bit of a walk into town but you can usually find a spot and it's free off-season. It's also a good place to park vans. Alternatively bite the bullet and park in one of the central underground car parks (cars only) which limit the chances of getting broken into. They're about €1.50 an hr or €14 for 24 hrs, a good option if you're staying overnight.

❶ Directory
Emergency number: T112. **Hospitals**: Hospital Nuestra Señora de Aranzazu on Av Doctor Begiristain near the Plaza de Toros, T943 00 70 00. **Police**: the main police station Policía Municipal San Sebastian is on Larramendi, T943 45 00 00. Dialling 091 will get you the help of the local police. **Tourist information**: www.sansebastianturismo.com, on Reina Regente in Parte Vieje and open year round. **Internet**: in the Parte Vieja there are a couple of options including **Zarr@net** on San Lorenzo from €3 an hr and 2 **Donosti-NETs** on Embletran with connections from €3.30 per hr and a luggage storage facility. **Post office**: Plaza Guipúzkoa.

Pamplona/Iruña

South from San Sebastián the N-1 joins the A15 to take you down to Pamplona. Since the sixties Pamplona's Fiesta de San Fermín has proved to be an irresistible attraction for surfers. The 7 July sees the usually dignified streets of the capital of Navarra overrun by a heady mixture of adrenaline, alcohol and thundering hooves, as the now world famous 'running of the bulls' takes place. At 0800, for 7 days, 6 bulls are released from pens at Santo Domingo to run a course through the city to the Plaza de Toro. But they are not alone. Dressed in white and accessorized with red neckties, are the runners who have chosen to accompany the bulls on their journey. The bulls charge headlong through a tight warren of streets, while the accompanying masses try to stay ahead of the game, or at least out of horns' reach. With each bull weighing more than a family car, serious injury can and does regularly happen. So if you've come to run, make sure you've got decent shoes on – the cobbled streets quickly become a skid pan. It's also worth picking up some tips from seasoned locals the night before. Also check

out the excellent www.sanfermin.com for details on every aspect of this event.

⊜ Sleeping
Fiesta time sees prices for everything sky-rocket and rooms get booked up months in advance, although there may be the odd room going spare if you're willing to pay – ask at the tourist office. The weekend is the busiest time when attendance nearly doubles. Parking in town is a problem. A popular, free and relatively hassle-free option is sleeping out in one of the parks. **Camping Ezkaba** is 5 km from town and open all year, T948 33 03 15. A left luggage store is set up for the duration of the festival on the Plaza San Francisco, next to the tourist office.

❷ Eating
Tapas is probably the way forward with a good variety of eateries and bars centred around the Plaza del Castillo.

Orio

Heading west from San Sebastián, just off the N-634, is this beach with showers, toilets, bars and cafés as well as a large campsite, **Playa de Orio**, open from 1 Mar-1 Nov, T943 83 48 01.

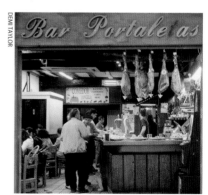
On the tapas trail

Airports → Madrid T913-936000; Bilbao T944-869661; Málaga T952-048804. **Buses and coaches** → Eurolines, T020-7730 8235, www.gobycoach.com. **Car hire** → Avis, T0870-6060100; Hertz, T08708-448844; National, www.nationalcar.com. **Ferries** → Brittany Ferries, T08705-360360; P&O, T0870-242 4999, www.poportsmouth.com. **Rail links** → RENFE, www.renfe.es. **Petrol prices** → €0.80-95/litre.

DEMI TAYLOR

Zarautz

On the N-634, Zarautz marks the start of the truly coastal route. The seafront is littered with candy-striped change tents and sculptures, which bleed back into the town. With its combination of long sandy beach and pretty old town, it is a popular and pricey seaside resort – heaving in the summer – and regular staging post for WQS and European events.

✺ Flat spells

Drinking Head to Getaria and sample the local txakoli – a tart, dry, sparkling white wine. **Golf** Get 9 holes in at the Royal Golf Club, Zarautz, T943 83 01 45. **Skating** On the beach front there's a good concrete midi-ramp with banks, ledges and rails.

⬤ Sleeping

The old town is set back from the beachfront and has plenty of places to eat, drink and sleep. D **Txiki Polit**, at the edge of Musika Plaza, is a nice option. www.euskalnet.net/txikipolit, T943 83 53 57.

Camping Open year round the large **Gran Camping Zarautz** gets packed out in the summer T943 83 12 38. Just inland there's also the summer-only **Talai-Mendi** on the N-634, T943 83 00 42.

❶ Eating

For cheap eats head to the old quarter which has a good range of options including **Bar/Restaurant Klery** on Azahara where a chicken and chips *plato combinado* will set you back €6 or you can fill up on tapas.

10 Playa de Deba (Santiago) ▶▶ *p214*

⊖ Parking

Off season you can park on the streets near the sea front but when it gets busy try the car park at the west end of the beach.

❶ Directory

The **tourist office** is on Nafarroa, the main road through town, as is the first **Pukas** shop, opened in 1977. Next door to Txiki Polit, at the Vodafone shop, you can get **Internet** access from €2 an hr and the **post office** is on Herrikobarra.

Zumaia

Built around the harbour, Zumaia is a little off the beaten track.
E **Bar/Pension Goiko**, on Erribera Kalea, T943 86 13 91, is the focal point of the town and open year round. **Apartments Tomas**, on Eusebio Gurrutxaga Plaza, T943 86 19 16, is a cheaper option at €50-75 for groups of 4-6. **Cafeteria Kaia** on the riverfront does a mean *chocolate con churros* for breakfast. For surf essentials drop into **Gaztesurf** on Baltasar Etxabe where grommets clog up the shop front watching videos through the windows.

Deba

Nestled in a valley with a mountainous backdrop, Deba – pretty but functional – is a typical Basque working village. **Camping Itxaspe** on the N-634, T943 19 93 77, www.campingitxaspe.com, is open Apr-Sep with the option of 2-6 person bungalows.

Mutriku

The most westerly village on the coast of Gupuzkoa, this place is a camper's paradise with 4 sites to choose from: **Aritzeta**, T943 60 33 56; and **Santa Elena**, T943 60 39 82, are both open all year and based on the Deba–Gernika route; **Galdona**, is on the same road, T943 60 35 09, open Jul-Sep; and there's also **Saturraran**, T943 60 38 47, open Jun-Sep.

Lekeitio

A traditional Basque village complete with a bustling fishing port. Lined with bars and cafés, this is a hotspot for holidaying locals. Accommodation is fairly pricey. D **Pinupe**, on Pascal Abaroa, T946 84 29 84. The cheapest option for groups are the self-catering apartments attached to **Hotel Zubieta** on Portal de Atea from €73 for 4 people. **Leagi** has year round camping on the Lekeitio–Mendexa route, T946 84 23 52, www.campingleagi.com. **Endai** on the same road is open summer only, T946 84 24 69.

Mundaka

Surfing has had a big impact on this Basque fishing village with a year round influx of surfers and annual surfing contest. But that's not to say that the legendary left is all Mundaka has to offer. Lying on the west bank of the Ría de Mundaka, and at the neck of the Urdaibai Biosphere Reserve, the geography of the surrounding countryside lends itself as a sanctuary to local flora and fauna as well as a steady stream of migrating birds. The winding, cobbled streets of the village lead you on to the pretty fishing harbour and surrounding bars – a great place to watch the world go by. Offshore the Isla de Izaro has a reeling right-hander that breaks only in the biggest swells.

✺ Flat spells

If you're trapped in Mundaka without surf, you may get that 'Groundhog Day' feeling, so head the 12 km south along the estuary to **Gernika**, both the birthplace of Basque nationalism and the site of the most notorious act of the Spanish Civil war. 26 April 1937 was just another busy market day when Jerónimo Alonso, from the village of Elantxobe, was sitting on the hill overlooking the Ría de Mundaka. "I looked across to see planes banking into the Ría and following the river south to Gernika. The sky seemed to be filled with them. I had never seen planes like these before." As the Nationalists and the Republicans battled for control of Bilbao, Franco ordered the German Condor squadron to bomb Gernika, the seat of power in Euskadi. He hoped that the strike would demoralize the Basque population and drain support away from the Republican movement. The planes swung in low over a packed town. It was market day and the square was swarming with men, women and children. During the 3 hr assault, incendiary devices rained fire on the streets and shrapnel ripped through the fleeing population. Over 1,650 people died. The raid so affected Picasso that he immortalized it in a painting named after the town, a tile replica of which is on display on Allende Salazar. Other attractions in Gernika include **The Parque de Los Pueblos de Europa** – this free park is dedicated to peace and filled with sculptures of Henry Moore and E Chilida. **The caves at Santamamiñe** can be found by following the BI-638 to Lekeitio, then taking the road to Santamamiñe and Oma. Although closed, the caves house the 12,000 year old art of prehistoric man as well as some awesome rock formations nearby. The forest at Oma has been converted by visionary painter Agustín Ibarrola, into the 'Bosque Pintado de Oma' – a living work of art. Both are free and worth the short trip out.

A trip to **Bilbao** from here is a little over an hour by train or bus, departing about every half hour – pick up time tables from the tourist office. The train station is at the back edge of town (www.euskotren.es). The bus stop is on Goiko Kalea, the main road through Mundaka.

Sleeping

Hotel accommodation in Mundaka is a little bit pricey. There are a couple of hotels, the favourite with WCT surfers being **B-C Hotel Mundaka**, on Florentino Larrinaga, T946 87 67 00, www.hotelmundaka.com.
F Albergue Islakale on Banutegúi, T946 87 60 71, www.islakale.com, has hostel-style accommodation as well as a gym and bar/restaurant. Price per person.
Camping The year-round campsite

Portundo, on the BI-635 road into Mundaka, T964 87 77 01, www.campingportundo.com, has pitches and cabins and comes complete with an Aussie-style communal seating area. It's fairly pricey and the only choice for miles around – but the showers make up for it.

Eating

Hotel El Puerto has a nice little café which, as the name suggests, is on the harbour front. They do great *bocadillos de jamón* – serrano ham in a lightly warmed baguette. Just on the main square, **Batzoika** does a good value, three-course *menú del día* for about €6 and is always busy. There is a nice bread shop on Florentino Larrinaga (follow your nose) and a couple of basic food stores on Goiko, the main village road, with larger ones in Bermeo.

Shopping

The world famous **Mundaka Surf Shop** on Txorrokopuntako is owned by ex-pat Aussie Craig Sage and has been serving surfers since 1983. If you've come ill equipped, there's always a good selection of second-hand and new semi-guns perfect for tackling the legendary left. Their own brand is MSC, shaped by Bruce Smith.

Parking

Across the Ría, Playa Laga, with a few bars and seasonal toilets, has always been a popular stopping point for vans – despite the signs prohibiting overnight camping.

Directory

The little **tourist office** is on Kepa Deuna Kalea near the harbour front, handily placed in a block with the **post office** and **police**. Hotel Mundaka has pricey **internet** access at about €4 an hr.

Sopelana

Marking the end of the rural Basque country, this busy, grey, urban town services a thriving surf community, who try to keep the number of visiting surfers in check by

removing and altering the hondartza (beach) signs.

Flat spells

Bilbao is within easy reach, as Sopelana is a stop on the city's metro system.

Sleeping

Sopelana is not exactly overrun with places to stay. **Camping Sopelana** – with cabins available for 1-6 people – is probably the best option. It's open year round and is signed posted off the main road. T946 76 21 20. **C 'Hotel' Goizalde**, on the beach road, Av Atxabiribil, T946 76 39 37, www.hotelgoizalde.com, is pricey and not especially nice.

Bars and cafés

El Sitio is a good café to sit and watch the surf at Atxabiribil and on the road to Arrietara is **La Triangu**, a busy bar popular with local surfers, complete with boards on the walls, sport on the screens and table football.

Shopping

Follow the signs to Arrietara for **Motion Surf Shop**, which sells everything from boards and hardware to clothing and videos. On Loila Ander Deuna, the main road through town, there's a whole row of surf shops including **Waves & Wind**, **Eukaliptus** and **Uhaina**.

Parking

There's plenty of parking in front of hondartza Atxabiribil and parking overlooking La Salvaje, which, despite a series of break-ins, is a popular spot for free-camping.

Getxo

Separated by the Ría Nervion, and joined by the awesome hanging bridge, Puente Vizcaya (€1 per car), Getxo and Portugalette are two very different towns. While Getxo, all relaxed elegance, is home to an international jazz, blues and folk festivals, Portugalette has always been more hardworking, giving over her bank of the river to industry and functionality.

✪ Flat spells

Sport They're big on *pelota* here and hold national contests throughout the year so if you want to try your hand at it, or just fancy a game of tennis or a dip in the pool, head to the **Fadura Sports Centre** on Av Los Chopos, T944 30 80 70.

● Sleeping

There's no campsite in Getxo and the *pensiones* are usually cheaper at the weekends – during the week they are packed with business travellers from Bilbao. D **Areeta**, on Mayor near the bridge in the popular Las Arenas district, T944 63 81 36, is one of the cheapest options.
E **Pensión Basagoita**, to the north, in the Algorta district, on the avenue of the same name, near the church San Nicolás, T608 57 74 46. Fairly average.

○ Shopping

There are a couple of surf shops in Getxo including **Dream** on Algorta Etorbidea and **Getexa Cuadro** on Ollarretxe, both in the Algorta district.

▢ Parking

There is plenty of parking in Getxo on the beachfronts of Arrigunaga and Ereaga.

❶ Directory

The **tourist office** is on the seafront at Ereaga and open year round.

Bilbao

Set back from the sea front and spread across the two banks, or 'bi albo', of the Nervion, the capital of Bizkaia has shown the world it is more than just a working port. From agriculture, to heavy industry, to sophisticated metropolis, Bilbao's ability to adapt and change with the times has secured both its fortune and on going success. One of its greatest successes to date, the opening of the Guggenheim Museum Bilbao, has transformed it into both a tourist hotspot and thriving cultural capital.

✪ Flat spells

Set on the banks of the river, the **Guggenheim** museum, created by architect Frank Gehry, has to be seen to be believed – the curved lines of the building created in granite, glass and titanium create wave-like contours. T944 35 90 80, Tue-Sun, €8.
Football Head to the Campo de San Mames for an **Athletic Bilbao** game. Tickets available from the stadium at €25-50

● Sleeping

A lot of the accommodation gets pretty booked up so if you want to be sure of somewhere to lay your head, call ahead. The Casco Viejo, over the river from the train station, has the best selection of cheap sleeping options as well as a dense population of bars and cafés.
F **Pensión Laredo** on Lotería, T944 15 09 32, is probably the cheapest with rooms with shared bathrooms from about €23.
On Bidebarrieta, there are a couple of hostels: E-F **Gurea**, T944 16 32 99; and E-F **Arana** T944 15 64 11.

❼ Eating

Hit the pintxos path – you know the drill. In the old town start out at the Plaza Nueva then head along Arenal to the art deco **Café Boulevard** and on to C Santa María, which has its fair share of bars. Cutting across it, C Jardines is home to **Berton**, which is packed

with hooves on the ceiling and people at the weekend. The **Siete Calles** (7 streets) is the oldest part of town with fantastic ambience and pintxos to match.

◉ Festivals

Mid Aug, big Week of Celebrations.

◉ Transport

An easy way to get round the city, apart from on foot, is using the metro – a day pass will set you back about €3. **Parking** Bilbao has double and even triple parking down to a fine art, although there are a few underground car parks, including one near the train station on Bailén and another handy one in the pedestrianized Casco Viejo, or Old Town, near the Plaza Nueva.

❶ Directory

Emergency numbers: T112. **Hospital**: Hospital de Basurto on Av Montevideo, T944 00 60 00. **Internet**: on Sendeja, just up from the tourist office in the Casco Viejo is **Laser Internet** which charges by the min and offers fax and photocopy services. **Police**: Policía Municipal on Luis Brinas – emergency number T092. **Post office**: there are 2 – 1 in the centre on Alameda Urquijo and 1 in the Casco Viejo on Epalza. **Tourist information**: the main tourist office is just off the river in the Casco Viejo on Arenal and open year round, www.bilbao.net.

DEMI TAYLOR

Signs of Basque nationalism are everywhere

Cantabria

Surfing Cantabria

From the moment you leave behind the sulphurous air and petrochemical plants around La Arena in Euskadi, the border crossing is a breath of fresh air. With some of the most beautiful landscapes and coastline in the country, Cantabria's crystal clear ocean teams with life and offers endless surfing possibilities. Here variety is the name of the game. "You can always find a place to surf in any swell from one to twenty feet, in any wind direction and at any tide," says one of Spain's top professional surfers, Dani García. "There are beach breaks, rocky breaks and reef breaks, some waves are short and hollow others are really long – last week I surfed waves 600 metres long at Fortaleza, maybe the longest wave in Europe. The surf in Cantabria is incredible."

Cantabria has a less turbulent past than the neighbouring states of Asturias and Euskadi. The region benefited from the prosperity brought in through the principal port of Santander, as the huge sea-front villas in the city prove. Santander is still a first port of call for many entering via the regular ferry link from the UK. While not as lively as San Sebastián, it is home to some great *tapas* bars and seafood restaurants.

The region's principal draw, aside from the stunning coastline, are the towering Picos de Europa, a mountain range that squeezes western Cantabria towards the sea. The beautiful limestone peaks are popular with walkers, birdwatchers and nature buffs alike, and, towering over the coastline, provide a breathtaking backdrop to many breaks. The

Cantabria board guide

Hi performance
Shaper: Peter Daniels for Pukas

» 6' 0" x 18" x 2⅛" for Hodei Collazo.
» High bumpwing squash for beach breaks like Los Locos.
» Fast turning, curvy bottom for looseness, boosting big airs and pulling into barrels.
» No rail catching, no problemas. S-concaves.
» Version for a 75 kg surfer, normal level 6' 3" x 18⅜" x 2⁵⁄₁₆".
» Version for big guys: 6'8" x 19" x 2".

Big gun
Shaper: Rawson for Pukas

» 8'6" x 19¼" x 2¾' rounded pin.
» Big wave gun for Santa Marina formulated from boards for the north shore spots like Sunset beach and Waimea bay.
» Has paddle power necessary for this type of wave, but a flowing rocker that will enable the rider to always "ride in the pocket"...something my Rawson guns are known for around the world.
» Also good for Meñakoz, Roca Puta....

ⓘ Boards by **Pukas**
Factory: Olatu, Oyarzun, Euskadi, Spain
T00 34 (0)943-493255
www.pukasurf.com

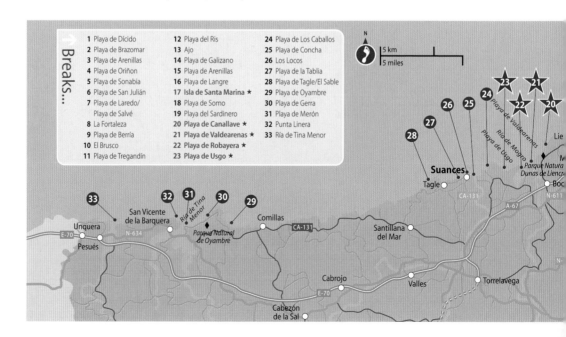

Breaks...

1 Playa de Dícido
2 Playa de Brazomar
3 Playa de Arenillas
4 Playa de Oriñon
5 Playa de Sonabia
6 Playa de San Julián
7 Playa de Laredo/ Playa de Salvé
8 La Fortaleza
9 Playa de Berría
10 El Brusco
11 Playa de Tregandín
12 Playa del Ris
13 Ajo
14 Playa de Galizano
15 Playa de Arenillas
16 Playa de Langre
17 Isla de Santa Marina ★
18 Playa de Somo
19 Playa del Sardinero
20 Playa de Canallave ★
21 Playa de Valdearenas ★
22 Playa de Robayera ★
23 Playa de Usgo ★
24 Playa de Los Caballos
25 Playa de Concha
26 Los Locos
27 Playa de la Tablia
28 Playa de Tagle/El Sable
29 Playa de Oyambre
30 Playa de Gerra
31 Playa de Merón
32 Punta Linera
33 Ría de Tina Menor

5 km
5 miles

Picos are one of the reasons the county is such a popular holiday destination for the Spanish.

Coastline

Cantabrian breaks east of Laredo sit in pristine countryside, but protected by the headland between Noja and Santander, pick up less swell than those to the west. Breaks around Galizano and Suances are some of Europe's best and their northwesterly orientation means they pick up heaps of swell. Further west, the surf spots around Oyambre sit in beautiful national parkland and have a relaxed atmosphere. The jagged coastline, with its coves and inlets, means there will always be waves to surf somewhere – if you don't mind a bit of a drive.

Localism

Many of the breaks around Cantabria sit in countryside and during the week, can be surprisingly quiet and laid-back. As local pro, Michel Velasco says: "Normally, most of the people here are friendly in the water, so with a good attitude you won't have any problems and you will really enjoy it." However, there are a couple of surfing hotspots that draw big crowds. Breaks like Los Locos and Los Caballos get busy during peak times and there can be some tension in the line-up. Car crime has also been a problem at Los Caballos. Noja is a popular resort town that can get very busy during the summer. To the east of Noja, El Brusco is always busy when it's working and has developed a reputation as a localized spot.

More common in the countryside areas is the strategic removal of signs to the beach, so a bit of exploring is sometimes needed to actually find the break.

Cantabria is one of the best places to surf in the north of Spain. You have a real variety of waves for all the surfing levels (from beginners to experts). You can surf all the year due to the swell's consistency and you can always escape the crowds.

Michel Velasco, Spanish Pro Surfer

Top local surfers Cantabria has some of the best surfers in Spain. It has produced riders such as **Pablo Gutiérrez**, **Dani García**, **Pablo Solar**, **David Echagüe**, **Michel Velasco** and female surfer **Mirka Martín Solar** as well as many good local riders.

Getting around

The road system through Cantabria is very good. The coastal roads, like the N-634 in the east, the CA-141 from Noja, the CA-231 from Santander, and the CA-131 from Suances all provide good access to the coastal break. The A-8 motorway dissects the county and provides a fast, toll-free route that stays close to the coastline. Much of the road system is of a good standard with an ongoing motorway improvement programme.

Spain Cantabria Surfing

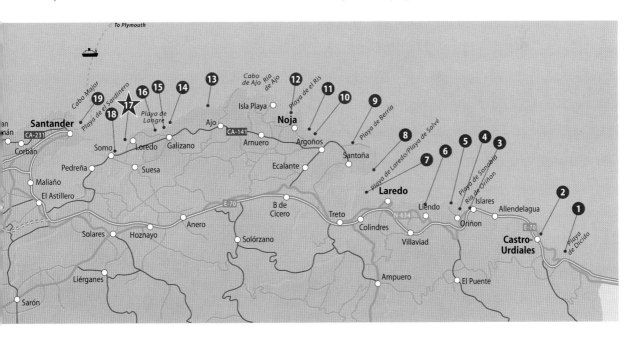

Breaks

1 Playa de Dícido

- **Break type**: Beach break.
- **Conditions**: Medium to big swells, offshore in south/southwesterly wind.
- **Hazards/tips**: Suitable for all surfers.
- **Sleeping**: Castro Urdiales ▸▸ p233.

This small, sheltered, crescent-shaped sandy bay is visible from the N-634. Works in big northwesterly swells with hollow peaks that are best at low tide. It's usually uncrowded and offshore in a southerly wind. Small village with a climbing wall outside the local sports centre.

2 Playa de Brazomar

- **Break type**: Beach break.
- **Conditions**: Big swell, offshore in southeasterly winds.
- **Hazards/tips**: Parking available near the beach.
- **Sleeping**: Castro Urdiales ▸▸ p233.

This is one of the town beaches at the popular summer vacation spot of Castro Urdiales. The bay is quite sheltered from swell and so only usually comes to life out of the tourist season. When it works there are peaks on this sandy beach, best at low tide.

3 Playa de Arenillas

- **Break type**: Beach break.
- **Conditions**: Medium swells, offshore in southerly winds.
- **Hazards/tips**: Rips can be present in big swells on a dropping tide.
- **Sleeping**: Islares/Oriñón ▸▸ p233.

At the Ría de Oriñón the mountains drop off dramatically into the sea framing this picturesque rivermouth. Right-hand waves peel towards the river from the western bank and work best in medium swells at low to mid tide. Can have some very good waves but maxes out in big northwesterly swells. Waves break in front of rocks. Parking is available by the Lantarón Hosteria, which is a popular eatery.

4 Playa de Oriñón

- **Break type**: Beach break.
- **Conditions**: Medium swell, offshore in southerly wind.
- **Hazards/tips**: Rips near the river.
- **Sleeping**: Oriñón ▸▸ p233.

On the opposite bank to Arenillas is a wide beach where good quality waves can be found. Left-hand waves peel into the rivermouth, from low on the push, but not at high tide. There are also peaks to the west. Waves here are of better quality but need a bigger swell to get going. This is a popular holiday spot that is very quiet out of season. Can be seen from the motorway and the N-634.

5 Playa de Sonabia

- **Break type**: Beach break.
- **Conditions**: Medium swells, offshore in southerly winds.
- **Hazards/tips**: Quiet, picturesque spot.
- **Sleeping**: Oriñón ▸▸ p233

A quiet, cliff-lined beach that works best at low tide producing peaky waves. Follow the road round from Oriñón.

4 Playa de Oriñón

Cantabria

Air ——— Sea ———

°F Averages		°C
90		30
70		20
50		10
30		0

J F M A M J J A S O N D

4/3 Boots	3/2	Shortie	3/2

6 Playa de San Julián

- ◉ **Break type**: Beach break.
- ◉ **Conditions**: Medium to big swells, offshore in southwesterly winds.
- ❶ **Hazards/tips**: Beautiful and quiet location, perfect to escape the crowds.
- ◉ **Sleeping**: Liendo/Laredo ›› p233.

This small, crescent-shaped sandy beach nestles under impressive cliffs. In a big northwesterly swell it can have either a peak or hollow, wedgy right-handers. Offshore in a southwesterly or westerly wind, but the oppressive hills provide a lot of shelter. Better on low tide. This bay can be hard to find as local surfers have removed the signs. Turn right leaving Liendo and then right again. You will pass the shrine to San Julián on the way to the cliff-top parking that is littered with condoms.

7 Playa de Laredo/Playa de Salvé

- ◉ **Break type**: Beach break.
- ◉ **Conditions**: Big swells, offshore in westerly winds.
- ❶ **Hazards/tips**: Suitable for all surfers. A good place to head for in stormy, westerly conditions.
- ◉ **Sleeping**: Laredo ›› p233.

The resort town of Laredo has a huge stretch of sandy shore that faces northeasterly. In big conditions the swell wraps into the beach, which is unusual in that it is offshore in south, southwesterly and westerly winds. Wave quality varies with conditions, but this is a popular beach with local surfers. Works through all the tides. This is a fairly dirty beach with lots of litter and condoms. In the winter drizzle it's a bleak, urban break but it comes to life in the summer as a popular holiday spot – though it is usually flat then. Banks vary and huge sections of the beach can close out. The middle of the beach is worth checking. A road runs along the length of the massive crescent-shaped beach, one block back from the seafront, providing easy access and good parking off season.

8 La Fortaleza

- ◉ **Break type**: Point break.
- ◉ **Conditions**: Big, clean swells, offshore in southerly winds.
- ❶ **Hazards/tips**: Known as Spain's Chicama.
- ◉ **Sleeping**: Laredo/Santoña ›› p233.

This is one of Spain's premier surf spots, but it very rarely breaks. When conditions are perfect, long, long, left-hand point break waves come to life – but only in the biggest swells. The walling lefts attract a large local crew when it's on and there may be some localism. Works best from low to mid tide with light or southerly winds.

9 Playa de Berría

- ◉ **Break type**: Beach break.
- ◉ **Conditions**: Small to medium swells, offshore in southerly/southwesterly winds.
- ❶ **Hazards/tips**: Eastern end of the bay picks up the most swell, cliffs offer protection from easterly wind.
- ◉ **Sleeping**: Santoña ›› p233.

Berría is a long, sandy beach that works through all states of tides. Can have some excellent, hollow waves and consequently is popular with local surfers. This break hoovers up any swell in the Laredo/Santoña area. A pretty beach that is overlooked by an imposing prison, a campsite compound (that looks worse than the prison) and a cemetery.

10 El Brusco

- ◉ **Break type**: Beach break.
- ◉ **Conditions**: Small to medium swells, offshore in southerly winds.
- ❶ **Hazards/tips**: Localism, heavy waves, crowds. Access along the beach road until you can drive no more.
- ◉ **Sleeping**: Santoña/Noja ›› p233.

Situated at the far eastern end of Tregandín beach (where the rocks stop), this beach break produces waves of excellent quality –

fast hollow barrels and reeling walls. Works best at high tide and in a southerly wind, when board-snapping lefts will be visible from the car park. Unfortunately it also has a reputation as a highly localized spot, so bear this in mind. Picks up less swell than Ris.

11 Playa de Trengandín

- ◉ **Break type**: Beach break.
- ◉ **Conditions**: Big swell, offshore in southerly winds.
- ❶ **Hazards/tips**: Rocks!
- ◉ **Sleeping**: Santoña/Noja ›› p233.

Needs a big northwesterly swell to produce

6 Playa de San Julián

7 Playa de Laredo

9 Playa de Berría

DEMI TAYLOR

12 Playa del Ris

DEMI TAYLOR

13 Ajo

DEMI TAYLOR

15 Playa de Arenillas

DEMI TAYLOR

14 Playa de Galizano

left-hand walls along a low tide sandbar, offshore in southerly or southeasterly winds. This beach has scattered jagged rocks that look like tank traps on a Normandy landing beach. Excellent skatepark with concrete bowl, midi, rails and even concrete cars to skate. Also basketball courts and a climbing wall.

12 Playa del Ris

- **Break type**: Beach break.
- **Conditions**: Small to big swells, offshore in south/southeasterly winds.
- **Hazards/tips**: Crowds, localism.
- **Sleeping**: Noja ▶ *p233*.

North of Noja is the popular and consistent crescent-shaped beach break of Ris. It picks up a lot of swell and can produce some excellent hollow waves. Works through the tides, but best at high. Gets crowded when good. Very sheltered from the wind and probably picks up the most swell in the Noja area. Campsites found at the western end.

13 Ajo

- **Break type**: Beach break.
- **Conditions**: Small to medium swells, offshore in southerly winds.
- **Hazards/tips**: Left breaks off the western end of the beach when big.
- **Sleeping**: Ajo ▶ *p234*.

Playa de Cuberris and **Playa de Antuerta** both consistently produce good waves in small and medium northwesterly swells. Both work best at low to mid tide. This is a good sized beach which picks up lots of swell. Suitable for all surfers. Beach parking.

14 Playa de Galizano

- **Break type**: Beach break.
- **Conditions**: Small to medium swells, offshore in southeasterly winds.
- **Hazards/tips**: Locals have removed sign to beach. Also known as La Canal.
- **Sleeping**: Loredo ▶ *p233*.

Galizano is a low tide, rivermouth beach break with powerful, hollow rights at the east and lefts at the western side. Can produce excellent waves in a medium swell and works up to 6 ft, where stand-up barrels are common. Doesn't usually get crowded. This small bay disappears at high tide.

15 Playa de Arenillas

- **Break type**: Beach break.
- **Conditions**: Small to medium swells, offshore in south/southwesterly winds.
- **Hazards/tips**: Take the CA-441, hang a left at the 1 km marker.
- **Sleeping**: Loredo ›› *p233*

This small, sandy bay is surrounded by cliffs and can produce some excellent, long walling or barrelling waves. At the west end a left peels off a sandbar formed on a rocky outcrop and on the eastern end right-handers can be found. Works best from low to mid tide and is offshore in a southerly or southwesterly wind. Can hold up to a 6 ft swell. Popular fishing spot. Find it via track through farm.

16 Playa de Langre

- **Break type**: Beach break.
- **Conditions**: Small to medium swells, offshore in south/southwesterly winds.
- **Hazards/tips**: Picturesque and quiet stretch of coastline.
- **Sleeping**: Loredo ›› *p233*

A cliff-lined bay immediately west of Arenillas, which again works best from low to mid tide. The cliffs here offer some protection from the wind. Good peaks. Larger yet more sheltered bay with a good left that can be found at the western end.

(i) If you like *Isla de Santa Marina,* try *Meñakoz* in Spain *(see page 217)* or *Tullaghan* in Ireland *(see page 121).*

17 Isla de Santa Marina

- **Break type**: Sand/reef breaks.
- **Conditions**: Big swells, offshore in southeasterly winds.
- **Size**: 6-12 ft plus.
- **Length**: 50-200 m plus.
- **Swell**: North/northwesterly.
- **Wind**: Southeasterly.
- **Tide**: Mid-high.
- **Bottom**: Sand and rock.
- **Entry/exit**: Paddle out from beach.
- **Hazards/tips**: Just about all the difficulties you could imagine, expert surfers only.
- **Sleeping**: Loredo ›› *p233*.

Isla de Santa Marina is an offshore island, wildlife sanctuary that also doubles as the region's premier big-wave spot. A powerful right-hander peels down the western side and a left-hander down the eastern side in big swells. The right is dominated by local big-wave surfers and access is via a long paddle from Playa de Loredo. The surf is always way bigger than it looks and without someone in the line-up to give it some scale you may find the 3 ft surf you were expecting is nearer 9. Surfers at this break have long hold-downs, broken boards and rocks to contend with, but the payback is some awesome, huge barrelling waves. Access from Loredo, out past the campsite and then turn left onto the headland.

Santa Marina
By Michel Velasco

With good conditions, Santa Marina is a high quality wave. At the beginning you have a long and powerful wall for good manoeuvres and the inside has an excellent section for big barrels. It is not really dangerous, but when the tide is low, if you fall at the beginning you will go straight into the rocks. At mid and high tide there's no problem with that – just be prepared for a big hold-down.

I feel really good surfing at Santa Marina – the bigger the better. It's a huge rush of adrenalin and I always enjoy it out there. I remember that day I snapped my board. It wasn't really big compared to how it can be – but it was really good fun and perfect for doing big carves.

DEMI TAYLOR

17 Isla de Santa Marina

DEMI TAYLOR

17 Michel Velasco at Santa Marina

Spain Cantabria Breaks **Playa de Arenillas to Isla de Santa Marina**

18 Playa de Somo

- ◉ **Break type**: Beach break.
- ◉ **Conditions**: Small to medium swells, offshore in southerly winds.
- ❶ **Hazards/tips**: Crowds from Santander.
- ◉ **Sleeping**: Loredo/Santander ›› p233.

A high quality beach break that can deliver excellent waves. Works through all tides. The consistency of the waves and the fact that the beach looks over to Santander means that it always draws a crowd. This big sandy beach is suitable for surfers of all abilities. A pretty, dune-backed shoreline that joins up with Loredo to create a massive beach. Maxes out in surf over 6 ft.

19 Playa del Sardinero

- ◉ **Break type**: Beach break.
- ◉ **Conditions**: Big swells, offshore in westerly winds.
- ❶ **Hazards/tips**: Crowded beach suitable for all surfers.
- ◉ **Sleeping**: Santander ›› p234.

Sardinero is one of the town beaches in Santander and works in big north or northwesterly swells. It usually has some surfers here, even when small and onshore, and can be very crowded on good weekends. Needs a westerly or northwesterly/southwesterly wind. Surfing is banned in the summer but there is usually no swell here in any case.

22 Playa de Robayera

DEMI TAYLOR

20-23 Liencres

The breaks around the small town of Liencres, about 15 km to the west of Santander, sit in the stunning Parque Natural Dunas de Liencres. It harbours the longest stretch of beach in Cantabria and is home to some world-class beach breaks. **Playa de Canallave** and **Valdearenas** are both consistent high quality spots set in beautiful pine forest and the rivermouth at **Robayera** is a hidden gem. In the summer they are bustling tourist beaches and the line-ups are crowded, but out of season the waves are much quieter and the atmosphere much more chilled.

ⓘ *If you like Liencres, try Les Landes in France (see page 177) or Costa da Caparica in Portugal (see page 312).*

20 Playa de Canallave

- ◉ **Break type**: Beach break.
- ◉ **Conditions**: Small to medium swells, offshore in south/southeasterly winds.
- ❶ **Hazards/tips**: Crowds in summer, localism.
- ◉ **Sleeping**: Liencres ›› p235.

After the hustle and bustle of the Santander town beach, Canallave is a stark contrast. Access to this spot is through a beautiful national park of evergreen trees and sand dunes, **Parque Natural Dunas de Liencres**.

This excellent beach break is one of the area's most consistent and high quality spots. It works through the tides, except for high. **La Lastra** produces fast, hollow right-handers.

This is quite a large beach with plenty of banks to spread out to. Like a lot of breaks in this area, **Canallave** has many local surfers and there may be localism issues when very crowded.

However the good news is that there is loads of parking and the facilities are also pretty good.

21 Playa de Valdearenas

- ◉ **Break type**: Beach break.
- ◉ **Conditions**: Small to medium swells, offshore in south/southeasterly winds.
- ❶ **Hazards/tips**: Crowded spot in the summer, some localism, quieter out of season.
- ◉ **Sleeping**: Liencres ›› p235.

A high quality, sandy beach that spreads out to the west of Canallave. It picks up loads of swell and produces hollow, fast and powerful waves in northwesterly swells. Works through all tides. Again, a big beach where the peaks nearest to the car park fill up first. Doesn't handle a big swell.

22 Playa de Robayera

- ◉ **Break type**: Rivermouth break.
- ◉ **Conditions**: Medium swells, offshore in south/southeasterly winds.
- ❶ **Hazards/tips**: Can be crowded spot, rips in big swells and dropping tides, not suitable for inexperienced surfers.
- ◉ **Sleeping**: Liencres ›› p235.

This sandy, rivermouth break has excellent, fast and hollow left-hand waves. These peel from the rocky stack at the western, rivermouth end of the beach, with peaks further to the east. This is quite a consistent spot where a quality sandbank is formed in the Ría de Mogrois. Best at low to mid tides on the push.

23 Playa de Usgo

- ◉ **Break type**: Beach break.
- ◉ **Conditions**: Small to medium swells, offshore in south/southwesterly winds .
- ❶ **Hazards/tips**: Usually uncrowded.
- ◉ **Sleeping**: Liencres ›› p235.

Usgo is a crescent-shaped beach that works best on a small to medium swell but tends to close out over 5 ft. At low to mid tide, wedgy rights break off the banks with some powerful, hollow waves on offer.

24 Playa de Los Caballos

- **Break type**: Reef and beach break.
- **Conditions**: Small to medium swells, offshore in south/southeasterly winds.
- **Hazards/tips**: Crowds, localism, car crime.
- **Sleeping**: Liencres ›› p235.

This crescent-shaped bay is an excellent spot with high quality waves to be had at low to mid tide. A left peels off a sand-covered rocky finger of reef and beach-break peaks can be found in the bay. Above 5 ft there tends to be too much water moving around to work properly. Can be crowded and may have some localism. Car crime has been a problem so park carefully. Take the road to Playa de Cuchia and bear right.

25 Playa de Concha

- **Break type**: Beach break and rivermouth.
- **Conditions**: Big swells, offshore in southerly swells.
- **Hazards/tips**: Very poor water quality due to the polluted river.
- **Sleeping**: Suances ›› p235.

From Los Caballos to Concha is a frustrating 30-minute round trip just to reach the other side of the narrow river. The road heads inland, crosses the bridge, before heading back out to the coast – you will notice the factories. Although Concha needs a big swell to get going, when it does work, quality lefts and rights peel at low tide and the beach works through the tides and can have good rights. A good place to check is from the road out to Los Locos.

26 Los Locos

- **Break type**: Beach break.
- **Conditions**: All swells, offshore in southerly winds.
- **Hazards/tips**: Consistent beach, gets busy, localism.
- **Sleeping**: Suances ›› p235.

Check this spot from the top of the cliffs and in a northwesterly groundswell you will see an excellent beach break producing fast hollow barrels and long walls. Always popular in small and medium swells in the summer, at weekends and during lunch, though it is still possible to score it pretty uncrowded early in the day and out of summer season. Works through the tidal range and areas of the bay are offshore in south, southeasterly, easterly and northeasterly winds, making this a very flexible beach. Has a reputation for localism when busy. Follow the signs from Suances. Parking available on top of the cliffs.

27 Playa de la Tablia

- **Break type**: Beach break.
- **Conditions**: Small to medium swells, offshore in south/southeasterly winds.
- **Hazards/tips**: Crowds in summer, car crime.
- **Sleeping**: Suances ›› p235.

Next bay along from Los Locos, La Tablia has peaks in the middle of the bay and lefts at the western end. Works from low tide on the push, but not at high, when the beach disappears. Again, another high quality break that can get busy, especially at weekends. As

25 Playa de Concha

26 Los Locos

24 Playa de Los Caballos

with all the previous breaks, it is advisable to be careful about where you park your car and what you leave visible inside. Follow coast road west and look for La Tablia building, park on cliff top.

28 Playa de Tagle/El Sable

- **Break type**: Beach break.
- **Conditions**: Medium swells, offshore in south/southeasterly winds.
- **Hazards/tips**: Picturesque, quiet beach.
- **Sleeping**: Suances » *p235*.

Follow the signs down to this smallish bay overlooked from the headland by a wind-ravaged ruin. Tagle is a sandy beach with good lefts and rights in medium swells. Waves can be fast and powerful with barrels at low tide, but the beach disappears at high. This picturesque location can be a quiet spot off season. The car park has a little touch of Malibu with some great and subtle 'Da Cat Vive' graffiti as well as a café and shower.

29 Playa de Oyambre

- **Break type**: Beach break.
- **Conditions**: Medium to big swells, offshore in southerly/southwesterly winds.
- **Hazards/tips**: Sheltered in big westerly storms.
- **Sleeping**: Oyambre » *p235*.

This long, flat sandy beach is set in the beautiful countryside of the Parque Natural de Oyambre. It is quite sheltered from northwesterly swells and works on all tides, but is best from low to mid. Needs a big north or northwesterly swell and winds from the south, southwest or west, to produce lefts and rights.

Average waves along most of the beach, but the banks can throw up high quality peaks. The western end is very sheltered and is the place to hit in big westerly storms.

30 Playa de Gerra

- **Break type**: Beach break.
- **Conditions**: Small to medium swells, offshore in south/southeasterly swells.
- **Hazards/tips**: Excellent banks, big beach, in national park.
- **Sleeping**: Oyambre » *p235*.

Gerra is a real gem of a beach break. Overlooked by green pasture, this break has some excellent banks and throws up consistent hollow waves. Off season it is a good place to escape the crowds, although a surf school has now opened here. This pretty location has peaks along its 1-km length and works through all states of tide. You can park in front of the surf school where there are some really nice peaks or there is beachfront parking just to the west. This beach is also part of the Parque Natural de Oyambre.

31 Playa de Merón

- **Break type**: Beach break
- **Conditions**: Medium swells, offshore in south/southwesterly winds
- **Hazards/tips**: Town beach in San Vicente.
- **Sleeping**: Oyambre/San Vicente de la Barquera » *p235*.

The beach from Gerra joins up with this sandy, rivermouth break, a popular place for local and travelling surfers. Banks can produce excellent, fast and hollow waves at

all states of tides. It has a rocky jetty with a lighthouse. These sucky waves are slightly sheltered from a westerly wind.

32 Punta Linera

- **Break type**: Point break.
- **Conditions**: Medium swell, offshore in southerly winds.
- **Hazards/tips**: Beautiful, rugged, typically Celtic spot.
- **Sleeping**: San Vicente de la Barquera » *p235*.

Fairly consistent, flat rock point that produces fast and sometimes hollow lefts. Worth checking as the waves can be excellent and the crowds quite small. Is offshore in south and southeasterly winds. Works from low on the push with long rides possible. Drive out of town following signs to the *punta*. Park overlooking the break in a small car park.

33 Ría de Tina Menor

- **Break type**: Point break.
- **Conditions**: Small clean swells, offshore in southerly winds.
- **Hazards/tips**: Very quiet, crystal clean water, difficult access.
- **Sleeping**: San Vicente de la Barquera » *p235*.

This low tide, rivermouth right-hander breaks over a sandbar and occupies the most spectacular setting – the *ría* winds through a plunging gorge to the sea where hanging cliffs overlook this very sheltered break. This spot needs a small, clean swell and is offshore in a south or southwesterly wind. Access – now there's the trick!

30 Playa de Gerra

31 Playa de Merón

32 Punta Linera

Listings

DEMI TAYLOR

Castro Urdiales

Travelling west out of Euskadi along the N-634 or E-70/A-8 the first coastal town you hit is Castro Urdiales, complete with gothic church, working harbour, castle cum lighthouse and a beach – Brazomar.

Sleeping

There are quite a few *pensión* options around the port. **F Losio** on Los Huertos to the west of the harbour is one of the cheapest, T942 860 299. **Camping Castro**, Jun-Sep, is about 1 km from the beach.

Eating

As a harbour town, the fish here is excellent. Good cheap eats can be found on Bilbao, La Mar and Ardigales with **Bajamar** on La Mar offering an excellent *menú del día* for €7.

Shopping/ directory

Banzai Surf is back from the harbour on Ardigales. **Emergencies:** T092. Police: Arturo Duo Vital, T942 869 278. **Tourist information**: open year round on Av de la Constitución near the harbour, www.turismo.cantabria.org.

Islares and Oriñón

Sleeping

Just off the N-634, Playa de Arenillas is serviced by campsite **Playa Arenillas** from 1 Apr-30 Sep and also offers bungalows, T942 863 152, www.cantabria.com/arenillas.asp. **E Hostería Lantarón**, right on the beach, has reasonable accommodation as well as being a popular lunchtime spot, T942 871 212. Across the river, campsite **Oriñón** overlooks the beach. Not the prettiest of campsites, Apr-Sep, T942 878 630.

Laredo

This lively summer resort town is home to Salvé – a 5-km stretch of golden sands and decent waves. In winter, the town pretty much shuts down and condoms, dog shit and litter replace towels and tourists on the beach.

Flat spells

Caves Ramales de La Victoria is southbound on the N-629 and home to a series of caves. Covalanas has the most impressive cave paintings while Cullalvera lets nature do the talking with some serious stalagmites and stalactites.

Sleeping

There are plenty of summer opening campsites including the small **Carlos V**, Ctra. Residencial Playa, May-Sep, T942 605 593, and **Playa del Regatón**, on the Laredo-Regatón road, Mar-Sep, T942 606 995, www.campingplayaregaton.es.org. **Laredo**, on Irun-A Coruna road, mid-Apr-mid-Sep, offers bungalows, T942 605 035, www.campinglaredo.com. **F Cantabria**, T942 605 073, and **E Salomón**, T942 605 081, both on Menéndez Pelayo, are the most reasonable of the many places to stay.

Shopping

Surf shops include **Atlantic** and **New Wind**, on Marquís Comilla, the main town road, and **Chacahua**, where you can pick up all your surf essentials, on Menéndez Pelay.

Directory

Tourist information: open year round on Alameda de Miramar.

Santoña

The camping compound **Playa de Berría** may be hemmed in by a prison to its rear and a cemetery to the east, but it does have an awesome view and fantastic access to the beach. Open Easter and Jun-15 Sep, the site is basic but functional, T942 662 248.

Noja

This is another popular seaside resort which all but closes during the off season.

Flat spells

Skating In front of Playa de Tregandin is a great concrete skatepark with bowl, midi ramp and concrete cars to abuse.

⊖ Sleeping

The camping is centred around Playa Ris, to the west of the town, including: **Playa de Ris**, Apr-Sep, T942 630 415; **Suaces**, 15 Apr-30 Sep, T942 630 324; and the massive **Playa Joyel**, 15 Apr-30 Sep, offering bungalows and mobile homes. **Los Molinos**, 1 Jul -30 Aug, offers bungalows and is based further west on La Ría, T942 630 426, www.campinglosmolinos.com. E **Ris**, Playa de Ris, May-Sep, T942 630 131, and E-F **Dorada**, Av de Ris, Jul-30 Sep, T942 630 043, are 2 of the cheapest *pensiones*.

❼ Eating

The main square has a couple of good breakfast choices – **El Horno** bakery or **Plaza Cafetería** for an eat-in option. **Lupa** supermarket on the main town road.

Ajo

Travelling west along the CA-141, the small village of Ajo is serviced by a couple of **campsites**: summer opening **Cabo de Ajo**, T942 670 624, and year-round **Arenas**, just 100 m from the beach, T942 670 663. In terms of food, local pro surfer Michel Velasco recommends sampling the paella at **Restaurante Labu**.

Loredo

⊖ Sleeping

Across a small stretch of water from Santander, hidden among the trees, Loredo has plenty of camping options as well as basic amenities to satisfy the steady influx of visitors and holidaymakers: **El Arbolado**, open year round, T942 504 414, on the Loredo-Ribamontan al Mar road, about 500 m from the beachfront. **Rocamar**, larger, good access to Isla de Santa Marina and a half pipe opposite, open year round, T942 504 455.

Somo

Just down the road from Loredo, Somo also services the area and is home to the summer opening **tourist office** on Av de Trasmiera.

⊖ Sleeping

There are a couple of campsites: **Somo Parque**, just inland towards Suesa, open year round, offers bungalows sleeping 5-6, T942 510 309; while **Latas**, 15 Jun-15 Sep, T942 510 249, is just 200 m from the beach. E **Hong Kong**, on Las Quebrantas, is one of the cheapest *pensiones*, T942 510 013.

❼ Eating

Michel Velasco recommends hitting **Mar Salada** for some great post-surf fare and ambience: "The owners are surfers and a lot of surfers go there, so you will feel at home."

◎ Shopping

Xpeedin' surf shop on Edificio las Brisas, which has been around since the 1970s.

Santander

Sticking out into the Cantabrian Sea, Santander is a peninsula surrounded by water on 3 sides. If you've just stepped off the ferry, this is a gentle introduction to Spain – there are plenty of cheap places to stay and plenty of good places to eat and drink. If however you've been travelling along the west coast and are expecting a Cantabrian version of San Sebastián, think again.

✪ Flat spells

Caves Travelling south out of Santander on the N-632, **Puente Viesgo** is both a spa town and home to a series of caves in the heart of Castillo Mount featuring the paintings of Palaeolithic man. Open to the public through guided tours. 45 min, €2. **Golf** Real Golf Club de Pedrena, offering both 9 and 18 hole courses, is about 20 km out of the city on the CA-141, T942 500 001. **Skiing/snowboarding** " Head to the ski resort **Alto Campo**, it's only an hour and a half from the coast," advises Michel Velasco. Drive south to Reinosa – they're building a motorway straight down from Santander – then take the CA-183 eastbound to the resort. Check there's snow before you go, T942 77 92 22, or www.altocampoo.com.

⊖ Sleeping

Santander can be extremely pricey, especially in the summer and especially around the upmarket Sardinero area. For cheap accommodation, it's best to head for the area around the bus station and ferry port. E **La Corza**, on Hernán Cortés, is a good but more expensive option, with great access for underground parking, eating, drinking and the ferry. Some rooms come with enclosed balconies overlooking the plaza, T942 212 950. F-G **Gran Antila**, on Isabel II, large, basic and cheap, T942 213 100. F-G **Los Caracoles**, on Marina – just off Hernán Cortés, T942 212 697. Not glamorous but another cheap option well located for eating and drinking. **Camping** If you've just driven your van off the ferry and want to camp over, **Cabo Mayor** to the north of Sardinero is well located, offers bungalows, but is only open Apr-15 Oct, T942 391 542. Further out of town on the CA-231 San Román–Corbán road is **Virgen del Mar** which is smaller and open year round, T942 342 425. Bungalows are available as are mobile homes sleeping up to 8 people.

❼ Eating/drinking

Santander is still an important fishing port so for some of the freshest, cheapest but not necessarily chicest dishes around, get down to the Barrio Pesquero (fishing port). There's plenty of *tapas* to sample – head for the Plaza Canadio and check out the roads leading off it, including Daoiz y Verlade, home to the heaving **Casa Ajero**. Hernán Cortés also has a great selection of *tapas* bars and bodegas which also sell nibbles and plates – good examples are **Bodega Bringas** and **Bodega Mazón**. An easy and surprisingly busy place to grab a drink and a bite to eat is at the **La Casa del Indiano** in the Mercado del Este (which also houses the tourist office). Close by, **Café del Mercado** on the corner of Medio and San José is also a popular spot to grab snack. Whatever you do, don't make the mistake of going into the local Chinese while you're here. For the best *chocolate y churros* in Spain don't miss **Chocolatería Aliva** on Daoiz y Verlade – an old school parlour, open 0700-1200 and 1700-2130, where fur coats rub shoulders with overalls.

⊖ Parking

Off season it's easy to find roadside parking along the beach – high season is a different matter. One of the underground car parks may prove a better bet for cars.

⊙ Shopping

Santander has a thriving surf community and as such has plenty of specialist stores. Near the bus station and off Cádiz are **Surf 33** and a **Quiksilver Boardriders** with all the usual necessaries. Heading east, back from the harbour is **Andalucía** on Reina Victoria. Further along the road, Primera Playa plays host to **Black Ball**. If you're in the market for a new board, **Full & Cas Surfboards** are based just south of Santander in the Camargo and shape boards for some of Spain's top surfers including Pablo Solar.

❶ Directory

Internet: Heladería Lugano on Hernán Cortés takes the relaxed approach as a café cum cyber bar. In the shopping district try **La Copia Copistería** on Lealtad or **Insistel** on Méndez Nuñez. **Post office**: back from the ferry port off the main Av Calvo Sotelo. **Tourist information**: extremely efficient and open year round with info on the whole region, it's based in the Mercado del Este.

Liencres

Heading west along the CA-341 Liencres is only 15 km from Santander but, harbouring Cantabria's longest stretch of sand dunes and a nature reserve – Parque Natural Dunas de Liencre – it is worlds apart.

⊖ Sleeping

The campsite **Playa de Arnia** is small and only open 15 May-15 Sep but is right on the beach at Arnia, T942 579 450. To the west of the national park, Playa Mogro offers a camping alternative, **La Picota**, 15Apr-30 Sep, T942 576 432, handy for Robatera, Usgo and Caballos.

Suances

Crossing the Río Saja is a mammoth task – about half an hour's drive to cross a 50-m gap, which is a hideous traffic nightmare in the summer. Once there, Suances sprawls out from the marina to the headland with plenty of places to eat, drink and sleep throughout the year. Due to the proximity to Santander, it can be fairly pricey.

✹ Flat spells

Despite the name, **Santillana del Mar** is actually 4 km from the sea. It is a beautiful medieval town complete with cobbled streets, gothic towers and a 12th-century church. Don't be tempted to go on a midsummer weekend – you won't be able to move for day trippers. A couple of kilometres down the road are the **Altamira caves** which house 14,000 year old paintings of bison, boar, deer. The caves are closed to the public to preserve the paintings but in its place is the newly opened Neocueva – a replica cave and museum. It's not the real thing so is only so interesting. Closed Mon, admission €2.40. T942 818 815. **Camping Santillana del Mar** is open year round and pretty central with bungalows and mobile homes available, T942 818 250.

⊖ Sleeping

D/E **Posada Marina**, is the showcase. It may be more than 1 km from the beach on Plaxa de la Cuba, but more than makes up for with its views over La Concha, T942 811 474. E **Posada del Mar**, on Cuba de Arriba, is reasonable with off-season rates from €24, T942 811 233. E **Pensión Consuelo**, on La Guerra, open Jul-Sep and with just 5 rooms worth booking ahead, T942 810 458. In season the cheapest place to stay. **Camping** Suances is on the road into town and open Easter and Christmas week as well as 15 Jun-15 Sep, T942 810 280.

❷ Eating

If you're after a simple bite head to **Pier Pizzeria & Pasta** on the Paseo de la Marina – it does what it says on the tin. On the

headland the café at hotel **El Caserío** overlooks both Los Locos and La Concha and offers decent *tapas* and breakfast.

Oyambre

The Parque Natural de Oyambre encompasses pasture, cliffs, estuaries, dunes and beach, making this a clean and beautiful stretch of coastline.

✹ Flat spells

Golf There's a golf course next to the beach at Oyambre. South on the N-621 is **Potes**: "Potes near Los Picos de Europa has plenty of activities for flat days – kayak, rafting, paragliding," recommends Dani García. Check out one of the tour agencies for details – **Europicos**, T942 730 724, www.europicos.com, or **Picostur**, T942 738091, www.picostur.com. "The nearby **Picos de Europa** are also an incredible place to walk and climb with some peaks up to 2500 m high."

⊖ Sleeping

A popular summer draw, there are 3 campsites here. **La Playa**, on the beach, is the largest and open year round. You can park up, pitch a tent or rent one of the statics or rooms, T942 722 616. **Rodero** is just inland, 300 m from the beach, open year round with cabins and mobile homes available, T942 722 040. **Playa de Oyambre**, open Apr-Sep with bungalows, T942 711 461, www.oyambre.com.

San Vincente de la Barquera

San Vincente has banks, supermarkets and a castle and is popular with day trippers and locals alike. There are plenty of places to stay over if the mood grabs you including a summer opening campsite, **El Rosal**, T942 710 165, www.campingelrosal.jazztel.es. Eat on the harbour front – **Dulcinea** is a popular local spot for *tapas* and a glass of wine and **Urquiza** does a great range in food from a substantial *menú del día* for about €8 to a lobster menu for 2 at about €60.

Asturias

Surfing Asturias

The 2500-m summits of the Picos de Europa look down upon the stunning coastline as you cross into eastern Asturias. The mountains that surround this region allowed the Asturians to hold out against the all-conquering Moors, the only area not to fall under the north Africans' rule. This set a trend for the centuries that followed and the region developed a strong will and proud people. In 1934 the army was sent in to put down a strike by the local miners and during the Civil War the region fought against Franco and his Nationalist troops.

The Asturian countryside still has vast swathes of ancient woodland and some pristine coastline. Wolves and bears still roam the Parque Nacional de los Picos de Europa and the region has managed to preserve much of its natural heritage. And although the area around Gijón and Avilés is home to some heavy industry, this is the exception.

When it comes to socializing the *sidrería* is the heart of the local community. Raised voices, cigarette smoke and card games are the order of the day, and glasses are kept full with a constant stream of still cider poured from above the bartender's head. As a result, the cuisine in the region also differs, with bean and sausage stews, excellent meats as well as the staple seafoods on offer.

Coastline

The Asturian coastline has a distinctly Celtic feel to it with small

Asturias board guide

Semi-Hi performance
Shaper: Luke Short for Pukas

▸▸ From 5'10" to 6'6".
▸▸ Great board for Salinas.
▸▸ Freeglide model has to be ordered 1-2" smaller than your regular short board.
▸▸ Slightly less rocker combined with a touch more nose and tail area for glide and speed over those flat dead sections.
▸▸ A smaller wave board, yet still maintains plenty of hold and drive in bigger waves with its smooth continuous plan shape.
▸▸ Beachy air board. This year the tail concave has been increased for extra lift and liveliness.

Mini gun
Shaper: Peter Daniels for Pukas

▸▸ 6' 0" x 18⅛" x 2⅛" for Pablo Gutiérrez.
▸▸ Ideal for Rodiles.
▸▸ Round tail, even rocker, low boxy rail, s-concave for powerful backside gouging and forehand cutbacks.
▸▸ Version for a 75 kg surfer, normal level 6' 6" x 18" x 2".
▸▸ Version for big guys: 6'10" x 19" x 2⅜".

ⓘ Boards by **Pukas**
Factory: Olatu, Oyarzun, Euskadi, Spain
T00 34 (0)943-493255 www.pukasurf.com

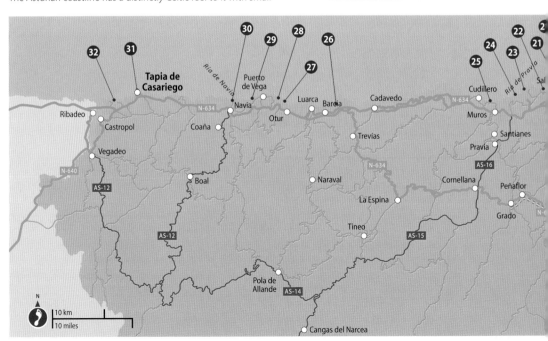

villages, clean sandy beaches and rugged, rocky points. Between the towns there may be nothing but smallholdings, rolling green fields and sheltered bays. If you want to escape the crowds, this is one of the few places in Europe where you can truly have a beach to yourself.

The drive into Rodiles takes you through some beautiful scenery and coastal villages like Luarca and Cudillero, with its picturesque harbour front, make great places to overnight. To the west, Tapia, with its small rivermouth break, is home to one of Spain's oldest surfing communities and is a regular European contest site. As for the rest of the coastline, it is a surf explorer's dream, with break after break just waiting to be discovered.

Localism

Unfortunately, the region's best and most famous break has developed a reputation for not just its high quality waves, but the levels of localism in the water. Rodiles is an excellent break but due to circumstance and the attitudes of some locals, confrontations, thefts and a general bad vibe in the line-up has followed the break's increased profile. However, even in the 1970s it had a reputation. "We pitched our tent by the beach front and decided to sleep with our boards in the tent, attached to our ankles by our leashes," says shaper and photographer Paul Gill. "When we woke in the morning our leashes had been cut and our boards were gone."

Aside from Rodiles, Asturias is very laid-back and has few places where localism is a problem although Salinas and some spots around Avilés can get crowded and may have tension in the water.

We were winding down these tiny country roads looking for the *playa,* but all the signs had been removed. You could still see where the posts had been left behind. Eventually we stumbled onto the rivermouth break and it was low tide, six foot and pumping with no one out. I think in northern Spain you can tell how good a break is by how many signs have been removed to it.

Aaron Gray, Aussie surfer.

Top local surfers Fernando Pérez, Iván Villalba, Fernando Ferrao, Lucas García and David Sastre.

Getting around

The A-8 motorway follows the coast through eastern Asturias until Avilés. The N-634 and then the N-632 provide good access to the coastal breaks. The N-634 between Avilés and Cudillero can be a real bottleneck during rush hour with big queues of traffic. The rest of the coastline through to Ribadeo is pretty plain sailing on the N-634.

Spain Asturias Surfing

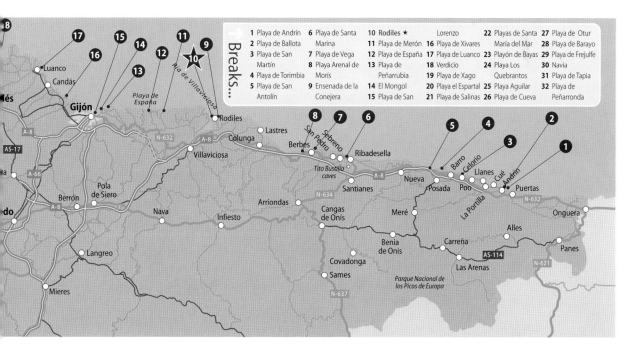

Breaks...

1 Playa de Andrín	6 Playa de Santa Marina	10 **Rodiles ★**	Lorenzo	22 Playas de Santa María del Mar	27 Playa de Otur
2 Playa de Ballota	7 Playa de Vega	11 Playa de Merón	16 Playa de Xivares	23 Playón de Bayas	28 Playa de Barayo
3 Playa de San Martín	8 Playa Arenal de Morís	12 Playa de España	17 Playa de Luanco	24 Playa Los Quebrantos	29 Playa de Frejulfe
4 Playa de Torimbia	9 Ensenada de la Conejera	13 Playa de Peñarrubia	18 Verdicio	25 Playa Aguilar	30 Navia
5 Playa de San Antolín		14 El Mongol	19 Playa de Xago	26 Playa de Cueva	31 Playa de Tapia
		15 Playa de San	20 Playa el Espartal		32 Playa de Peñarronda
			21 Playa de Salinas		

Breaks

Asturias

Air —— Sea ——
°F Averages °C

[chart showing air and sea temperature averages over months J F M A M J J A S O N D, °F axis 30 50 70 90, °C axis 0 10 20 30]

J F M A M J J A S O N D

4/3 Boots | 3/2 | Shortie | 3/2

1 Playa de Andrín

- **Break type**: Beach break.
- **Conditions**: Medium swell, offshore in south/southeasterly winds.
- **Hazards/tips**: Quiet, sheltered bay with wedgy waves.
- **Sleeping**: Andrín/Llanes ›› p243.

Andrín is a small, cliff-lined, crescent-shaped bay. This quiet, sandy cove is a beautiful location to escape the crowds. The offshore island of Isla de Ballota blocks out a lot of the swell which wraps around the rocky outcrop and enters the bay at two angles, converging on a wedgy peak in the middle of the bay. Worth checking in small to medium swells. The banks produce both lefts and rights through all tides. Follow the signs from the N-634.

2 Playa de Ballota

- **Break type**: Beach break
- **Conditions**: Medium swell, offshore in south/southeasterly winds.
- **Hazards/tips**: Quiet spot.
- **Sleeping**: Andrín/Llanes ›› p243.

This picturesque bay is the next cove round from Andrín and a twin brother. It faces more easterly so needs more swell to get going but it is sheltered from all winds but dead onshore. Both bays are very picturesque and, overlooked by a popular tourist viewing point, are a great introduction to Asturias.

3 Playa de San Martín

- **Break type**: Beach break.
- **Conditions**: Small swells, ofshore in south/southeasterly winds.
- **Hazards/tips**: Worth checking Poo out for the novelty value and postcards.
- **Sleeping**: Llanes ›› p243.

Although the nearby Playa de Poo sounds tempting, you are more likely to find waves at low tide in this pretty, sandy cove. Works best in smallish swells.

4 Playa de Torimbia

- **Break type**: Beach break.
- **Conditions**: Small to medium swells, offshore in south/southeasterly winds.
- **Hazards/tips**: Quiet spot.
- **Sleeping**: Llanes ›› p243.

Sandy bay that works well in small and medium swells, is an attractive location for a day's surfing and is usually uncrowded. Has a powerful peak in the middle of the bay and a right at the eastern end. Very pretty location with parking overlooking the bay.

5 Playa de San Antolín

- **Break type**: Beach break.
- **Conditions**: Medium swells, offshore in south/southeasterly winds.
- **Hazards/tips**: Visible from road, rips when big, rivermouth.
- **Sleeping**: Llanes ›› p243.

A large beach with numerous peaks that works through the tides. Can have fast and hollow lefts and rights. There is a sandbar formed by the *ría* that enters the sea on the beach near the car park. Access from the AS-263 under the railway line.

DEMI TAYLOR

1 Playa de Andrín

DEMI TAYLOR

2 Playa de Ballota

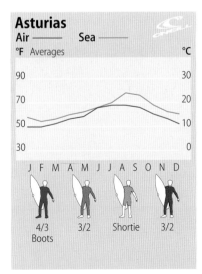

6 Playa de Santa Marina

- ◉ **Break type**: Beach break.
- ◐ **Conditions**: Medium swell, offshore in southerly winds.
- ❶ **Hazards/tips**: Rivermouth can be polluted.
- ◯ **Sleeping**: Ribadesella ▸▸ p243.

Sandy beach close to Ribadesella with good waves at all tides apart from high. Picks up a reasonable amount of swell.

7 Playa de Vega

- ◉ **Break type**: Beach break.
- ◐ **Conditions**: Small to medium swells, offshore in southerly winds.
- ❶ **Hazards/tips**: Water quality can be poor.
- ◯ **Sleeping**: Ribadesella ▸▸ p243.

This long beach picks up lots of swell and will produce good quality peaks through all tides. Doesn't get overly crowded.

8 Playa Arenal de Morís

- ◉ **Break type**: Beach break.
- ◐ **Conditions**: Small to medium swells, offshore in south/southeasterly winds.
- ❶ **Hazards/tips**: Quiet spot.
- ◯ **Sleeping**: Ribadesella ▸▸ p243.

Long beach that is worth checking on all swells. Consistent beach which can have good banks at low tide. Has parking.

9 Ensenada de la Conejera

- ◉ **Break type**: Point break.
- ◐ **Conditions**: Big swells, offshore in south/southwesterly winds.
- ❶ **Hazards/tips**: Access is difficult. Found to the east of Punta Rodiles.
- ◯ **Sleeping**: Rodiles ▸▸ p244.

Sand and rock point along which high quality, left-hand waves peel. Breaks up to 8 ft in big northwesterly swells. Best at low to mid tide but needs a big swell to get going. Semi-secret spot that is difficult to find.

10 Rodiles

- ◉ **Break type**: Rivermouth.
- ◐ **Conditions**: All swells.
- ◉ **Size**: 2-10 ft.
- ◉ **Length**: 200 m plus.
- ◉ **Swell**: North/northwesterly.
- ◉ **Wind**: Southerly/southwesterly.
- ◉ **Tide**: low to mid.
- ◉ **Bottom**: Sandbar.
- ◉ **Entry/exit**: Beach.
- ❶ **Hazards/tips**: Crowds, rips, localism, car crime.
- ◯ **Sleeping**: Rodiles ▸▸ p244.

A perfect, left-hand rivermouth break that is the region's most famous spot. In medium and big northwesterly swells, long, hollow lefts reel away from the rivermouth and short, barrelling right-handers sometimes break towards the river. Works best at low to mid tide. The rivermouth break is busy when it's on and there have been incidents of localism and vehicles are frequently broken into. A world-class wave when it is on and the region's biggest draw. The beach also has some excellent waves with sandbars producing lefts and rights through the tides. Get there early morning to beat the crowds. Parking in the eucalyptus trees overlooking the dune-backed beach, or in the car park near the river. There is a picnic area, showers and toilets. An outstanding break in beautiful countryside. Rips in big swells.

ⓘ *If you like Rodiles, try Mundaka (see page 216) and Barbate in Spain (see page 261).*

10 Rodiles

11 Playa de Merón

- **Break type**: Beach break.
- **Conditions**: Small to medium swells, offshore in southerly winds.
- **Hazards/tips**: Picks up more swell than Rodiles.
- **Sleeping**: Rodiles/Playa de España» *p244*.

High quality right-handers break on this sandy beach at low tide. A good quality break worth checking if Rodiles is packed. Good water quality and more chilled.

12 Playa de España

- **Break type**: Beach break.
- **Conditions**: Medium swells, offshore in southerly/southeasterly winds.
- **Hazards/tips**: Popular beach for day trippers from Gijón.
- **Sleeping**: Playa de España» *p244*.

A popular beach that works through the tides and can produce fast and hollow waves up to 5 ft. Its quality waves and pretty setting means that there is always a crowd here when the waves are on.

13 Playa de Peñarrubia

- **Break type**: Left reef break.
- **Conditions**: Medium to big swells, offshore in south/southeasterly winds.
- **Hazards/tips**: Can be very polluted.
- **Sleeping**: Gijón» *p244*.

16 Playa de Xivares

This rocky left-hander can be a quality break and handles swell up to 6-9 ft. Works best at mid tide. Found between Cabo San Lorenzo and Punta Cervigon.

14 El Mongol

- **Break type**: Point break.
- **Conditions**: Big swells, offshore in southerly/southeasterly winds.
- **Hazards/tips**: Crowds, localism, experienced surfers only.
- **Sleeping**: Gijón» *p244*.

A right-hand point that breaks over rocks. Waves up to 9 ft can be found here. It is a popular spot that produces long, quality waves, found along the Paseo Marítimo. With a name like 'the Mongol', it's obviously a break for experienced surfers only.

15 Playa de San Lorenzo

- **Break type**: Beach break.
- **Conditions**: Medium to big swells, offshore in southeasterly winds.
- **Hazards/tips**: Crowds.
- **Sleeping**: Gijón» *p244*.

Gijón is a big town with a big surfing community so this city beach always attracts surfers into the line-up, and gets busy when good. Works best at low tide to mid tide with lefts and rights breaking along the seafront. Beach disappears at high tide. Parking and showers on seafront.

16 Playa de Xivares

- **Break type**: Beach break.
- **Conditions**: Medium to big swell, offshore in southerly/southwesterly winds.
- **Hazards/tips**: Pollution, smells.
- **Sleeping**: Gijón» *p244*.

A popular, quality beach break that can produce fast and hollow waves at all states of tide. Works best up to 5 ft. It is a pleasant looking beach but is very close to the industrial plants that ring Gijón. Needless to

say the air is pretty foul, and on offshore days the smell of sulphur and other chemicals is overwhelming. A stream runs into the sea here from the direction of the industrial plants. Has cafés and a first-aid point.

17 Playa de Luanco

- **Break type**: Beach break.
- **Conditions**: Big and storm swells, offshore in westerly/southwesterly winds.
- **Hazards/tips**: Very sheltered spot.
- **Sleeping**: Gijón/Luanco» *p244*.

This beach north of Gijón faces northeasterly and so needs a big swell to get going. It also has a huge breakwater that cuts out the swell even more. This means that it is the ideal spot to head for in big westerly or northwesterly storms. A low tide town break, with fast, hollow rides when everywhere else is maxed out. The town beach has seafront parking. Not the prettiest of towns.

18 Verdicio

- **Break type**: Beach breaks with rocks.
- **Conditions**: Medium swells, offshore in a southeasterly wind.
- **Hazards/tips**: Uncrowded spots.
- **Sleeping**: Avilés» *p245*.

Two northwesterly facing beaches, **Playa de Tenrero** and **Playa de Aguilera**, that both work in medium swells and are separated by a rocky finger. The sandbanks can produce some great waves and are worth checking. Usually uncrowded, with parking at the eastern end of the beaches.

19 Playa de Xago

19 Playa de Xago

- **Break type**: Beach break.
- **Conditions**: Small to medium swells, offshore in easterly winds.
- **Hazards/tips**: Busy in summer.
- **Sleeping**: Avilés ▸▸ *p245*.

Due to its exposed location, this beach picks up even the smallest swells. This popular spot is busy in the summer when there is always a good chance of a wave. Although busy, the atmosphere is usually pretty good as it is a real family location with BBQ areas and cafés and bars. It is offshore in any easterly wind. It is also a very popular weekend destination even out of season. The drive into Xago is very unpromising as you pass a big industrial zone but you are soon in a beautiful ecological sanctuary. The beach has many facilities nestled under its eucalyptus trees, such as cafés and a modern wooden shower and toilet block. The eastern end of the beach is overlooked by a beautiful, towering, rust-coloured cliff face and sand dunes act as a buffer between the sea and the forest.

20 Playa el Espartal

- **Break type**: Beach break.
- **Conditions**: Medium swells, offshore in southeasterly winds.
- **Hazards/tips**: Not the cleanest stretch of water, worse after the rains, localism when busy.
- **Sleeping**: Avilés ▸▸ *p245*.

Needs a medium, northwesterly swell but when it's on the quality waves will draw a large local crew. The sandbanks will produce peaks,

24 Playa Los Quebrantos

lefts and rights. Offshore in southeasterly winds, but can take light easterlies and northeasterlies. All tides. This is part of the town beach at Salinas, which is a pretty unremarkable place. This stretch of beach runs from the rivermouth south to Playa de Salinas.

21 Playa de Salinas

- **Break type**: Beach break.
- **Conditions**: Medium swells, offshore in southeasterly winds.
- **Hazards/tips**: Pollution, crowds, localism, urban break.
- **Sleeping**: Avilés ▸▸ *p245*.

Works in the same conditions as Espartal and is as popular and suffers from localism when busy. Not the prettiest location with tower blocks and sea defences overlooking the beach. There is a midi-ramp near the beach.

22 Playas de Santa María del Mar

- **Break type**: Beach break.
- **Conditions**: Medium swells, offshore in southerly winds.
- **Hazards/tips**: Relatively quiet breaks.
- **Sleeping**: Avilés ▸▸ *p245*.

Playa de Santa María del Mar, **Playa Bahinas** and **Playa Munielles** are three beaches heading from east to west, each requiring a bit less swell to get going. Quality sandbanks change with the swells but are pretty consistently good and work through all tides.

23 Playón de Bayas

- **Break type**: Beach break.
- **Conditions**: Small to medium swells, offshore in easterly winds.
- **Hazards/tips**: Long stretch of sand which joins up with Los Quebrantos.
- **Sleeping**: Avilés ▸▸ *p245*.

This beach faces northwesterly and picks up plenty of swell. It works through the tides and has banks that have lefts and rights. Isla de la Diva sits at its eastern end.

24 Playa Los Quebrantos

- **Break type**: Beach break.
- **Conditions**: Medium swells, offshore in south/southeasterly winds.
- **Hazards/tips**: Crowds when good.
- **Sleeping**: Avilés/Cudillero ▸▸ *p245*.

This beach works up to 6 ft when excellent lefts can be had. In smaller swells the usual peaks and beach break fare is on offer. Big breakwater at Ría de Pravia.

25 Playa Aguilar

- **Break type**: Beach break.
- **Conditions**: Medium swells, offshore in southerly/southeasterly winds.
- **Hazards/tips**: Quiet spot, rocky.
- **Sleeping**: Cudillero ▸▸ *p245*.

Two small, sandy bays, separated by rocks that work at all states of tides. This is a quiet, pretty location with peaky waves including lefts and rights breaking in front of a large rock. Worth checking in clean, medium swells. The road to this secluded bay winds down through dense trees with parking and a beachfront café.

26 Playa de Cueva

- **Break type**: Beach break with rivermouth.
- **Conditions**: Small to medium swells, offshore in southeasterly winds.
- **Hazards/tips**: Isolated spot.
- **Sleeping**: Luarca ▸▸ *p245*.

This pebble and sand beach has good lefts at the western end of the beach and rights at the eastern, rivermouth end at low to mid tide. Needs a small to medium northwesterly

25 Playa Aguilar

swell to get going but will work in easterly winds. This is a beautiful, isolated spot overlooked by pastureland and cliffs. Has great potential.

27 Playa de Otur

- 🌀 **Break type**: Beach break.
- 🌊 **Conditions**: Small to medium swells, offshore in southerly winds.
- ❶ **Hazards/tips**: Consistent spot.
- 💤 **Sleeping**: Luarca ›› *p244*.

Take the winding road from Luarca to Playa de Otur off the N-634 to this picturesque bay with a quiet, dark-sand beach. It has shifting banks that work on all tides. Can be excellent when conditions combine. It is sheltered from winds, but best in a southerly. Good lefts at the western end and rights at the eastern end, with many peaks in between. Has parking on the beach and a bar open in the summer.

28 Playa de Barayo

- 🌀 **Break type**: Beach break.
- 🌊 **Conditions**: Medium swells, offshore in southerly winds.
- ❶ **Hazards/tips**: National park, no parking at beach, quiet break.
- 💤 **Sleeping**: Luarca/Navia ›› *p244*.

Barayo is a real gem. The beautiful valley and the beach are in an area of ecological special interest and as such it is not possible to drive down to the break. You can, however, check the waves from the car park, before your 30-minute walk to the beach. This is a great, consistent beach break that works at all states of tides and can produce quality banks, especially at the rivermouth. There are two

car parks, one on the eastern side of the beach and one on the west (access via Vigo). No dogs or camping allowed in the park.

29 Playa de Frejulfe

- 🌀 **Break type**: Beach break.
- 🌊 **Conditions**: Small to medium swells, offshore in southerly/southwesterly winds.
- ❶ **Hazards/tips**: Known as Frexulfe in Asturian, litter-strewn car park on the headland.
- 💤 **Sleeping**: Navia ›› *p245*.

Beach break to the west of Puerto Vega with some excellent sandbanks producing fast barrelling. Doesn't get too crowded. Works on all tides except for high. Has a small stream at the eastern end where there are some wedgy rights. A finger of reef towards the western end allows sand to build up, producing some nice high tide waves.

30 Navia

- 🌀 **Break type**: Beach breaks
- 🌊 **Conditions**: All swells, offshore in southerly winds.
- ❶ **Hazards/tips**: Navia can be checked from the headland, then take the small road round to Moro.
- 💤 **Sleeping**: Navia ›› *p245*.

Playa del Moro is a low tide rocky break that produces hollow rights in most swells. Works up to 9 ft. Moro picks up more swell than Navia to the east. Playa de Navia is a good quality rivermouth beach break with lefts and rights that is best at low tide. Navia is more sheltered. The water can be polluted.

31 Playa de Tapia

- 🌀 **Break type**: Beach and reef.
- 🌊 **Conditions**: Medium to big swells, offshore in southeasterly winds.
- ❶ **Hazards/tips**: Crowds.
- 💤 **Sleeping**: Tapia de Casariego ›› *p245*.

Tapia is a sheltered rivermouth break with a peak in the middle of the beach. Best at low tide. There is also a left-hand reef that can hold waves up to 8 ft. A big local surfing population ensure that it's always crowded. This is a contest venue with good facilities and car parking overlooking the break. Tapia has a large and committed surfing population.

32 Playa de Peñarronda

- 🌀 **Break type**: Beach break.
- 🌊 **Conditions**: Medium swells, offshore in southerly winds.
- ❶ **Hazards/tips**: Picks up more swell than Tapia, but is more exposed.
- 💤 **Sleeping**: Tapia de Casariego ›› *p245*.

This is a big bay with an island at the western end. Good waves can be had in southwesterly winds at all tides but high and it doesn't get too crowded. Rights and lefts break up to about 5 ft. Also worth checking is **Puente de Los Santos** in a big northwesterly swell. Low tide rights can be found in southerly or southwesterly winds.

27 Playa de Otur

26 Playa de Cueva ›› *p241*

28 Playa de Barayo

31 Playa de Tapia

Listings

Andrín

The first port of call along Asturias's 145 km of coastline is Andrín. Accessed from N-634 it has a good off-season free-camp potential. Mid Jun through mid Sep try **Camping Río Purón** to the east of the beach which also has cabin accommodation, T985 41 71 99.

Llanes

Continuing along the N-634 Llanes is the first main town you hit. This pretty working fishing harbour has a walled medieval centre interspersed with cafés and shops and housing the tourist office as well as the 15th-century Basílica de Santa María.

✪ Flat spells

Golf To the east between Cue and Andrín lies the 18-hole **La Cuesta Golf Club**, T985 417 084, www.golflacuesta.com.

⬤ Sleeping

D-E **La Guia**, on Plaza Parres Sobrino is a pensión in an ideal, central location and open year round, T985 402 577.
E **Puerto de Llanes**, on the harbour front, above the local *sidrería* which is heaving in the evening and worth dropping into, T985 400 883.
Camping There are plenty of places to camp in and around the town. **Las Bárcenas**, Jun-Sep, offers cabins, T985 402 887. **Entreplayas**, between Llanes's 2 beaches, Christmas to 30 Sep, T985 400 888. Just east on the AS-263, **El Brao**, Jun-30 Sep, is based in Portilla, T985 400 014. Heading west towards Poo, **Las Conchas** with cabins is open year round, T985 402 290. Heading further west to Celorio, **Camping María Elena**, Christmas to 30 Sep, T985 400 028. Taking the LLN-11 from Celorio to Barro are year round **Playa de Troenzo**, T985 401 672, and **Sorraos**, Apr-30 Sep plus Christmas week, T985 401 161.

⬤ Eating

For breakfasts, coffee or snacks, head to **Café Xana** on the harbourfront. **Sidrería Alloru** on

Gutiérrez de la Gandara is a popular place to head for a snack or a serious meal and is heaving at the weekends. A popular local spot is **Casa**, on Manuel Cue, just off the harbour, offering a good *menú de la noche* for about €12 including wine.

Ribadesella

Ribadesella is divided by the Río Sella which not only gives the town its name but also attracts hordes of canoe fans from across the globe. The first Sat in Aug is given over to the Canoe Festival or International Descent of the River Sella. Eat, drink and sleep in the old part of Ribadesella and get a good fish supper on the harbour front.

✪ Flat spells

Caves Loved by canoeists and anthropologists alike, Ribadesella is also famed for its Jurrassic remnants and prehistoric art hidden in the **Tito Bustillo** caves. The caves are open Apr-Sep except Mon and Tue. Entry costs about €2 and is limited to 375 visitors per day. **Golf** Heading west to Berbes on the N-632, get 9 holes in at **La Rasa de Berbes Golf Club**, T985 857 881.

Los Picos de Europa The Picos de Europa (the peaks of Europe) consist of 3 main limestone massifs, shaped and eroded over 300 million years by glaciation. The peaks cover 64,660 ha, 3 provinces – Cantabria, Asturias and León – are barely 20 km from the sea in parts and are a walker's/caver's/potholer's/nature lover's paradise. Head south on the N-634 to **Cangas de Onís**, the Asturian base of the national park's visitor centre, which is open year round, T985 848 614.

⬤ Sleeping

Camping There are a couple of camping options on the west side of the river, in Sebreno. **Ribadesella**, Jul-30 Sep plus Christmas week, offers cabins, T985 858 293, www.camping-ribadesella.com. **Los Sauces**, between San Pedro and the beach, 15 Jun-30 Sep, offers cabins, T985 861 312.

DEMI TAYLOR

Navia bird

West along the N-632 **Playa de Vega**, Jul-15 Sep, T985 860 406.

Rodiles

Signed from the A-8 motorway and the N-632 coast road, Rodiles sits nestled among eucalyptus trees on the east bank of the tidal Ría de Villaviciosa. With great peak-season facilities – toilets, showers, plenty of parking, cafés and bars, including **El Carabu** – Playa de Rodiles is a popular summer destination. Inland, the biggest town is Villaviciosa, an important cider producer. It offers all facilities including banks, larger food stores and a Wed morning market plus limited cheaper accommodation.

⊛ Flat spells
Golf 9 holes, a driving range and a putting green can be found at the **Villaviciosa Golf Club** just off the N-634, T985 358 289.

⊜ Sleeping
Camping/apartments As it is a nature reserve, free-camping along the tree-lined beach is officially prohibited but there are plenty of official camping options. **La Ensenada** is just back from the beach and open year round, T985 890 157. **Fin de Siglo**, T985 876 535, is larger and has cabins but is only open 15 Jun-15 Sep. **Nery** is much smaller, open Jun-30 Sep, on the road out to Selorio, T985 996 115. **La Casona del Terienzu**, 2 km from the beach, opposite bar/restaurant Casa Covian, offers apartments for up to 5 people from €84–105, www.casonadelterienzu.com.
Villaviciosa F-G Pensión Sol, on Sol, T 985 891 130, and **F-G Pensión El Charcon**, on Piedrafita, T985 974 950. Good food and cider can be had around the town hall.

⊕ Directory
Internet: €3 will buy you an hour's internet access at **Hotel la Ría** on Marques de Villaviciosa. **Rodi Ride Surf Boards** shape and fix boards on the Rodiles-Villaviciosa road, T985 890 986. **Tourist information**: summer only on Parque Vallina.

Playa de España

Heading west along the AS-256, turn towards Marines along the VV-2 or VV-3 for camping **Playa España**, Mar-30 Sep, T985 894 273.

Gijón

This is the largest town within Asturias and has a friendly rivalry with the official capital, Oviedo. Gijón is relaxed and stylish and has enough beautiful people clogging up the sand in the summer to give it a feel of Biarritz.

⊛ Flat spells
Golf There are a couple of golf clubs here including the 18-hole **La Lloreda Municipal Golf Course** on the N-632 between Gijón and Villaviciosa, T985 333 191, www.golfallloreda.com. South of Gijón the 18-hole **Real Club de Golf Castiello** in Castiello de Bernueces comes complete with a driving range and putting green, T985 366 313, www.castiello.com.
Side trip to Pajares Under 2 hrs from the coast, you can hit the snow. From Oviedo head south along the A-66 then the N-630 to Pajares to the **Estación Invernal y de Montaña Valgrande-Pajares** for a spot of snowboarding. T985 957 095/123.

⊜ Sleeping
In terms of cheap places to stay, head for Gijón's old town between the port and the west end of the beach. San Bernando has a few places to stay including **E-G González**, T985 355 863.
Camping Camping Gijón on the Punta del Cervignon to the east of Playa de San Lorenzo is open Jun-30 Sep with good access to both San Lorenzo and Peñarrubia, T985 365 755. Heading out of Gijón on the N-632, **Camping Deva-Gijón** is smaller and open year round, offering cabins, T985 133 848, www.campingdeva.com.

⊘ Eating/drinking
The old town is the place to head for good food, drink and ambience. **La Turuta** on Av María out on the headland has a fantastically relaxed ambience while the Plaza Mayor offers a wide selection of alternatives.

⊙ Shopping
Servicing a thriving surf community, there are plenty of shops to pick up essentials in Gijón, including **Secret Spot Surf Shop** on Juan Carlos heading west out of town. **Surfactivity** is handily placed slap bang in the middle of San Lorenzo on Juan Alonso with **New Tablas** right on the seafront along Paseo del Muro de San Lorenzo.

⊕ Directory
Internet: Ciber del Muelle on the harbour, reasonable hourly rate. **Post office**: a couple, one near the Plaza de Toro on Av de Castilla, the other nearer the centre on Fernández Vallín. **Tourist information**: head to the port for year-round information on the whole region.

Luanco

⊜ Sleeping
Heading north along the AS-239 towards Cabo Peñas, Luanco is not the prettiest town but there are a couple of **campsites**. Just south in Antromero is **El Penoso**, Jun-15 Sep, T985 880 164. To the north, at Playa de Bañugues, is **El Molino**, May-30 Sep and Christmas week, also offers cabins, T985 880 785.

Spain Asturias Listings Rodiles to Luanco

Airports → Madrid T913-936000; Bilbao T944-869661; Málaga T952-048804. **Buses and coaches** → Eurolines, T020-7730 8235, www.gobycoach.com. **Car hire** → Avis, T0870-6060100; Hertz, T08708-448844; National, www.nationalcar.com. **Ferries** → Brittany Ferries, T08705-360360; P&O, T0870-242 4999, www.poportsmouth.com. **Rail links** → RENFE, www.renfe.es. **Petrol prices** → €0.80-95/litre.

Avilés

If you miss the turning for Avilés, don't worry, you'll see the 'eternal flame' burning and the smoke rising from the factories. Behind its ugly veneer is a beautiful, historic centre, home to one of the best carnivals in northern Spain. With high pollution levels, this might not be enough to tempt surfers into its fold or its water although there are plenty or surf shops as a substitute including **Deportes Valentín** and **Vertical Surf Shop** on Av Los Telares. Across the river to the east, the industrial zone gives way to a sanctuary at Playa Xago with a large eucalyptus-shaded car park, facilities block and busy beach bar **Mari Mar**. Heading out of Avilés to Salinas on the busy N-632 you can pick up all your basics at the **Lidl** and **Día** supermarkets.

🛌 Sleeping

Camping West of Avilés there are a couple of campsites open year round – **Las Lunas** in Naveces, T985 519 771, and the larger **Las Gaviotas** in Santa María del Mar, T985 519 491.

Cudillero

This pretty cobblestoned village 20 km west from Avilés hangs above its fishing port, where freshly caught skate are stretched out to dry as *curadillo*. Although small, Cudillero has banks and food stores and the Fri market is a great place to pick up fresh produce.

🛌 Sleeping

Accommodation is fairly pricey here, one of the cheapest year-round options is **Casa Miguel** to the west at Concha de Artedo, T985 596 350.
Camping Just to the east in El Pito there are a couple of campsites. **L'Amuravela** is open year round and offers cabins, T985 590 995. **Cudillero**, on the road from El Pito to Playa de Aguilar, cabins, Jun-15 Sep as well as Christmas week, T985 590 663.

To the west **Yolimar** is just inland at Artedo, Jan-30 Sep, T985 590 472. **Los Pradones** is just back from Playa de Artedo, cabins, 15 Jun-15 Sep, T985 591 108.

🍴 Eating

You can pick up breakfast from **Bar Julio** on the main plaza and in the evening **Sidrería El Patrón** goes off. For good food with ambience, head to the harbour – **Bar Julio** does a roaring trade.

Luarca

Head west along the N-632 to the pretty town of Luarca which winds out along the Río Negro. With an important fishing past and present the focal point of the town is the harbour, lined with cafés, bars and the fish market.

🛌 Sleeping

E Moderna, on Crucero, is one of the cheapest *pensiones*, T985 640 057.
Camping There are a couple of good campsites near the town including the excellent year-round **Playa de Tauran** to the west in San Martín which also has cabins, T985 641 272, www.campingtauran .com. **Los Cantiles** on the N-634 in Luarca is also open year round, T985 640 938, www.conectia.es/cantiles. West along the N-634, camping **Playa de Otur** in the village of Otur is open 20 Mar-15 Sep, T985 640 117, www.inicia.es/de/cotur.

Navia

Navia combines a large commercial port with a pretty old town. Winding inland along the river is a series of historic hill forts some of which are more than 2,000 years old. Navia itself is not particularly beautiful but as a town can be a good place to stock up, especially at the **Consum** supermarket where a lunch menu will set you back about €6. To the east in Puerto de Vega is the summer campsite **El Ancla**, 25 Jun-10 Sep, T985 648 205.

Tapia de Casariego

Tapia is a place that attracts travelling surfers who have seen the contest photos in the European surf mags, and rightly so as it is a relaxed town with several good beaches. As a result it has a decent surf scene – with shops **Uluru** and **Picante Surf** – and plenty of locals to fill the waves. As with most places, eat, drink and be merry around the harbour.

🛌 Sleeping

D Puente de los Santos, on the main road, is the cheapest hotel with rooms as little as **G** out of season, T985 628 155.
Camping/apartments Camp at **Playa de Tapia**, Jun-15 Sep, T985 472 721, or try the year-round apartments **Casa Germana** on the main road Av Primo de Rivera. The apartments are for up to 4 people, €53–90, T985 628 181, www.casagermana.com. To the west, **Playa Peñarronda** is a campsite in the vicinity of the beach with the same name, Apr-Sep, cabins an option, T985 623 022. Inland towards Barres is **La Viña**, a campsite which is open year round offering cabins, T985 623 280.

Off the beaten track . . .

DEMI TAYLOR

Galicia

Surfing Galicia

Galicia quite simply delivers. "The unique geography of the this coast and its situation with respect to the powerful Atlantic storms singles Galicia out as a land with one of the greatest wave potentials in Europe and a place in which virgin waves still exist," explains Fernando Muñoz of Spanish surf magazine, *Surfer Rule*. It has an undulating coastline full of rivermouths, bays, inlets and headlands. It has lush green forest and spectacular points that seem more like northern California than northern Spain, and many of these excellent breaks have small dedicated crews that are friendly to respectful travelling surfers.

Looking at Galicia it is obvious that this is a land dominated by the elements. Houses in many coastal villages have stones strategically placed on their roofs to prevent tiles being blown away in winter gales. Exposed to the full force of the ocean, and accompanying weather fronts that sweep in from the Atlantic, coastal communities have for generations harvested the rich pickings from the sea. Today major ports like A Coruña and Vigo supply Europe with high quality sea produce, which can be sampled in the local bars and restaurants. A Coruña is a lovely city to visit with some great bars, a relaxed atmosphere and a large surfing community.

Galicia has a Celtic heritage that extends beyond the huge annual rainfall to a history that even includes bagpipe music.

Galicia board guide

Short board
Shaper: Peter Daniels for Pukas

➤➤ 5´11" x 18" x 2⅛" for Eneko Acero.
➤➤ Ideal for Doniños and beach breaks.
➤➤ Squash tail, low entry, low box rails and single concave for tight surfing in the pocket and boosting airs.
➤➤ Version for a 75 kg surfer, normal level 6'2" x 18⅜" x 2¼".
➤➤ Version for big guys: 6'7" x 19" x 2⁷⁄₁₆".

Gun
Shaper: Rawson for Pukas

➤➤ Designed at Pipeline on the north shore, but great for hollow wave breaks around the world like Tahiti, Indonesia and places in Spain like "La Machacona".
➤➤ Features a slight double concave bottom along with my hollow wave rocker and fin positioning.
➤➤ Aritz rides a 7' 0" board very similar to this design.

ⓘ Boards by **Pukas**
Factory: Olatu, Oyarzun, Euskadi, Spain
T00 34 (0)943-493255, www.pukasurf.com

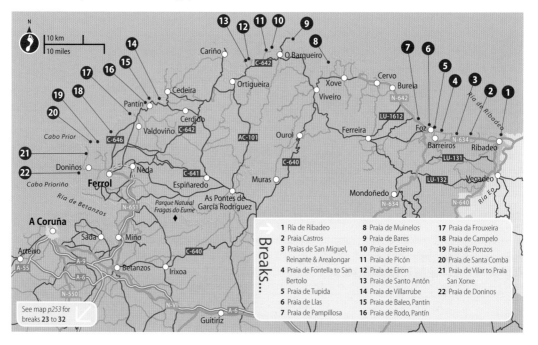

Breaks...

1 Ría de Ribadeo	8 Praia de Muinelos	17 Praia da Frouxeira
2 Praia Castros	9 Praia de Bares	18 Praia de Campelo
3 Praias de San Miguel, Reinante & Arealongar	10 Praia de Esteiro	19 Praia de Ponzos
	11 Praia de Picón	20 Praia de Santa Comba
4 Praia de Fontella to San Bertolo	12 Praia de Eiron	21 Praia de Vilar to Praia San Xorxe
	13 Praia de Santo Antón	
5 Praia de Tupida	14 Praia de Villarrube	22 Praia de Doninos
6 Praia de Llas	15 Praia de Baleo, Pantín	
7 Praia de Pampillosa	16 Praia de Rodo, Pantín	

See map p253 for breaks 23 to 32

Coastline

Northern Galicia between Ortigueira and Viveiro is a lush green landscape of eucalyptus trees and sheltered coves, a real gem. The coastline from Cedeira to Ferrol, however, has more of a Celtic feel to it. The countryside is more open with smallholdings and large beaches. The geography of the open west coast with its fjord-like inlets means it has massive surf potential, one that few travelling surfers venture far enough west to sample.

Localism

Few breaks in Galicia suffer the population pressures that have led to localism at other breaks in Europe. Many surfers are friendly and will be inquisitive towards travelling surfers, especially out of season. There are a couple of spots where a few locals have developed a reputation for localism. Pantín and Doniños are known among Spanish surfers as a place where pressures in the water can lead to drop-ins and other acts of localism. One Galician surfer from a nearby break said, "It can be bad at Pantín sometimes, but if it continues, when those surfers try to come and surf our breaks, we will not let them."

In Galicia, the arrival of every new swell opens up new surfing possibilities as wind and waves combine to provide endless variety. It is a place that still leaves room for discovery.

Willy Uribe, top Spanish photojournalist.

Top local surfers Luis Rodríguez, Gony Zubizarreta, Milo Castelo, Jaji Iglesias, Victor **Iván Pombo** and **Pipo Domínguez.**

Getting around

There really is only one way to explore Galicia and that is by road. Luckily the roads are very good with an expanding motorway system and a good network of minor roads hugging the coastline.

DEMI TAYLOR

10 Praia de Esteiro – empty perfection ▸▸ *p249*

Breaks

1 Ría de Ribadeo

- **Break type**: Rivermouth.
- **Conditions**: Big swell, offshore in southerly/southwesterly winds.
- **Hazards/tips**: Urban break, water quality varies.
- **Sleeping**: Ribadeo ▸▸ *p255*.

This rivermouth break needs a big northwesterly swell to get going. The sandbanks form at the rivermouth where left-handers break at low tide. There is some protection in westerly winds. Parking by the break in this pretty unremarkable town.

2 Praia Castros

- **Break type**: Beach break.
- **Conditions**: Small to medium swells, southerly/southwesterly winds.
- **Hazards/tips**: Gets busy in the summer.
- **Sleeping**: Ribadeo to Foz ▸▸ *p255*.

Castros is the first in a series of beaches along this stretch, following the coast road. It is a small, cliff-lined cove with a sandy beach that throws up some nice peaks. There are a few scattered rocks. Park overlooking the break.

3 Praias de San Miguel, Reinante and Arealongar

- **Break type**: Beach break.
- **Conditions**: Small to medium swells, offshore in south/southwesterly winds.
- **Hazards/tips**: Busy in summer.
- **Sleeping**: Ribadeo to Foz ▸▸ *p255*.

The Estrada da Costa is a well signposted road that hugs the shore and links a series of pretty beach breaks separated by rocky headlands. These sandy bays work best on low to mid tide, but there are waves at high. There are scattered rocks on some of the beaches and parking overlooking each break. Some have showers. Praia Reinante even has a brothel next to the campsite – don't mistake it for a 'club' in the traditional sense of the word.

4 Praia de Fontella to San Bertolo

- **Break type**: Beach breaks.
- **Conditions**: Medium swells, offshore in south/southwesterly winds.
- **Hazards/tips**: Massively popular in the summer.
- **Sleeping**: Ribadeo to Foz ▸▸ *p255*.

Galicia

Air ——— Sea ———

°F Averages   °C

90			30
70			20
50			10
30			0

J F M A M J J A S O N D

| 4/3 Boots | 3/2 | Shortie | 3/2 |

DEMI TAYLOR

3 Praia Reinante

Continuing west on the Estrada da Costa is another series of fine, white sand beach breaks. Again, they work best on low to mid but some still work at high tide, whereas others disappear. The beaches at the eastern end of this stretch pick up most swell. There are campsites, cafés and car parks galore.

5 Praia de Tupida

- **Break type**: Beach break and rivermouth.
- **Conditions**: Big swell, offshore in southwesterly/southerly winds.
- **Hazards/tips**: Parking on the seafront, rips when big.
- **Sleeping**: Foz ⟩⟩ *p255*.

Follow signs for the Moby Dick restaurant. On the eastern side of the *ría* looking over at Foz is this sandy beach with peaks and a rivermouth bank with lefts.

6 Praia de Llas

- **Break type**: Beach break.
- **Conditions**: Medium swells, offshore in southwesterly winds.
- **Hazards/tips**: Crowds.
- **Sleeping**: Foz ⟩⟩ *p255*.

On the west side of Foz is this large, white sandy beach with a few rocks. The beach works on all tides but high and can produce some nice rights. Beachfront has undergone extensive renovation with new toilets and walkways. There is parking overlooking the beach. Foz has an active surfing community and this is a popular break.

7 Praia de Pampillosa

- **Break type**: Beach break with rivermouth.
- **Conditions**: Medium to big swells, offshore in southerly/southwesterly winds.
- **Hazards/tips**: Break visible from the N-642.
- **Sleeping**: Foz ⟩⟩ *p255*.

Pampillosa is a long beach with a rivermouth

at the western end and a pretty, scrub-backed stretch of sand with peaks at all tides. This is a quality break where reeling lefts can be found in big swells.

8 Praia de Muinelos

- **Break type**: Beach break.
- **Conditions**: Small to medium swells, offshore in a southeasterly/easterly wind.
- **Hazards/tips**: Beautiful location, faces west, picks up plenty of swell.
- **Sleeping**: Viveiro ⟩⟩ *p255*

Low tide sees high quality lefts breaking along a sandy beach with some rocks. **Praia de Esteiro**, the next beach, is also worth checking and works in similar conditions. These are the first breaks in Galicia that face west and are both set in fantastic locations, evergreen forest, parking and beautiful clear water.

9 Praia de Bares

- **Break type**: Beach break.
- **Conditions**: Huge swells, offshore in a westerly/northwesterly wind.
- **Hazards/tips**: Beautiful location, stunning scenery, parking at the beach.
- **Sleeping**: Viveiro ⟩⟩ *p255*.

Easterly facing beach break with a small harbour at its northern end. This is a good place to head for if Galicia is being pounded by one of its huge westerly storms. This beach disappears at high and works best from low to mid on a rising tide.

10 Praia de Esteiro

- **Break type**: Beach break.
- **Conditions**: Medium swells, offshore in easterly winds.
- **Hazards/tips**: Quiet spot.
- **Sleeping**: Viveiro ⟩⟩ *p255*.

This bay is hemmed in by cliffs at each side and backed by dunes producing a quiet and beautiful beach with an excellent peak. Short rights and long lefts peel here at low tide. Great location with parking on the beach. Not to be confused with the other Praia de Esteiro, north of Xove.

5 Praia de Tupida

9 Praia de Bares

2 Praia Castros

10 Praia de Esteiro

Spain Galicia Breaks Praia de Tupida to Praia de Esteiro

11 Praia de Picón

- **Break type**: Beach break.
- **Conditions**: Small to medium swells, offshore in south/southeasterly winds.
- **Hazards/tips**: Rocks, quiet beach.
- **Sleeping**: Viveiro/Cedeira ›› p255.

Turn left in the tiny village of Picón to the cliff top where access can be gained down to this beach break. This is a rocky beach with peaks that work on all tides. When the swell gets over 5 ft it tends to close out. There are scattered rocks of various sizes. Parking is on the clifftop.

Picón telephone exchange

15 Praia de Baleo, Pantín

12 Praia de Eiron

- **Break type**: Beach break.
- **Conditions**: Small to medium swells, offshore in southerly/southeasterly winds.
- **Hazards/tips**: Rocks.
- **Sleeping**: Viveiro/Cedeira ›› p255.

Rocky beach which works on low tide. Lefts peel off a rocky outcrop and rights break on the beach. Part of the same bay as Santo Antón, but needs more swell as it is more sheltered. Has showers and a toilet.

13 Praia de Santo Antón

- **Break type**: Beach break,
- **Conditions**: Small to medium swells, offshore in south/southeasterly winds,
- **Hazards/tips**: Less rocky than Eiron,
- **Sleeping**: Viveiro/Cedeira ›› p255

Sheltered from winds except northwesterly. Works on all tides. Town break with parking and toilets at the western end of the bay.

11 Praia de Picón

14 Praia de Villarrube

14 Praia de Villarrube

- **Break type**: Beach break.
- **Conditions**: Big and huge swells, offshore in a south/southwesterly wind.
- **Hazards/tips**: Can be checked from the C-646 to Pantín. Spectacular location.
- **Sleeping**: Cedeira ›› p256.

This is a beautiful sandy beach at the mouth of the estuary south of Cedeira. It needs a big northwesterly swell to get into the Ría de Cedeira, but when it does, long peeling rights reel off the northern end of the beach. The surrounding eucalyptus-covered hills offer good protection from the wind. Works best at low tide. There is also a left at the southern end of the beach.

15 Praia de Baleo, Pantín

- **Break type**: Beach break.
- **Conditions**: Small to medium swells, offshore in southeasterly winds.
- **Hazards/tips**: Rips, localism, crowds.
- **Sleeping**: Cedeira ›› p256.

Pantín is the most famous surf destination in Galicia. Baleo is a popular, medium sized sandy bay that can produce excellent rights and lefts. It works on all tides and in all westerly and northwesterly swells up to 6 ft. It picks up more swell than Rodo but is less crowded. A big peak can break in the middle of the bay with long lefts and rights. In bigger swells there are rips at the north and south of the bay. Parking overlooking the bay with picnic area.

12 Praia de Eiron

16 Praia de Rodo, Pantín

- **Break type**: Beach break.
- **Conditions**: Small to medium swells, offshore in an easterly/southeasterly wind.
- **Hazards/tips**: Localism, crowds.
- **Sleeping**: Cedeira » *p256*.

The WQS event traditionally held here has made Pantín Galicia's best known break. Rodo is more popular than Baleo, but is also a larger bay. There are peaks along the bay that can get crowded during the summer and at weekends. Works on all tides. Depending on who you talk to, Pantín is either a localized spot, or a break with a few grumpy guys who try to intimidate non-locals. The consensus seems to be that if you are chilled and don't go in big groups, you will be OK.

17 Praia da Frouxeira

- **Break type**: Beach break.
- **Conditions**: All swells, offshore in southerly winds.
- **Hazards/tips**: Whole beach can be checked from C-646.
- **Sleeping**: Cedeira » *p256*

This massive, dune-backed beach just south of Pantín, stretches out for 3 km to the west and can have quality peaks all the way along. At the eastern end is a rivermouth that opens into a lagoon. This is a quality beach that picks up loads of swell and has some excellent banks with fast lefts and rights. At the town end of the shore a right breaks towards the rocky island in big swells. This end is usually the busiest, but off season the rest of the beach can be very quiet. This bay works on all tides and all swells. Massive potential.

19 Praia de Ponzos

18 Praia de Campelo

- **Break type**: Beach break.
- **Conditions**: All swells, offshore in south/southeasterly winds.
- **Hazards/tips**: Rips when big.
- **Sleeping**: Cedeira/Ferrol » *p256*.

An excellent beach break that picks up heaps of swell and has some sick banks waiting to produce long, hollow rights and lefts. Rights reel off the eastern end of the beach and lefts further down to the western end. A quality set-up. The cliff-lined beach virtually disappears at high tide but it continues to break in big swells. Works best at low to mid tide. Car park overlooks bay. Access is off the C-646 down a small signposted road.

19 Praia de Ponzos

- **Break type**: Beach break.
- **Conditions**: Small to medium swells, offshore in a southerly wind.
- **Hazards/tips**: A beautiful, quiet location.
- **Sleeping**: Cedeira/Ferrol » *p256*.

17 Praia da Frouxeira

21 Praia de Vilar to San Xorxe » *p252*

Big, sandy bay with dunes and rocky headland at the south. Picks up lots of swell and works on all tides. Peaks break all along the bay and there is a low tide left that breaks off the headland at the south. Parking by the beach at the south end.

20 Praia de Santa Comba

- **Break type**: Beach break.
- **Conditions**: Medium to big swells, offshore in southerly winds.
- **Hazards/tips**: Very quiet out of season.
- **Sleeping**: Cedeira/Ferrol » *p256*.

Another beautiful, dune-backed bay

18 Praia de Campelo

19 Praia de Ponzos

20 Praia de Santa Comba

separated from Ponzos by a rocky headland. This long, sandy bay works on all tides, but is not as good at high. It is more sheltered from swell than Ponzos and has a rocky finger towards the southern end. There is parking at the northern end overlooking the bay with a right-hander in front of the car park. Excellent potential in a stunning location.

21 Praia de Vilar to San Xorxe

- **Break type**: Beach breaks.
- **Conditions**: All swells, works in easterly/southeasterly/southerly winds.
- **Hazards/tips**: A big bay with big potential.
- **Sleeping**: Cedeira/Ferrol ›› p256.

A series of small coves leading to the massive beach at San Xorxe. **Vilar** faces west and picks up the least amount of swell. Moving south,

Fragata and Esmelle are the next two coves which pick up more swell and have rocky fingers separating them. All work best on low tide with lefts and rights breaking off the rocks. Xorxe is a long, crescent-shaped sandy beach that picks up a lot of swell despite being in the shadow of Cabo Prior. It works on all tides and the shape of the beach gives it loads of potential in different swell and wind directions. The car park overlooks this dune-backed beach.

22 Praia de Doniños

- **Break type**: Beach break.
- **Conditions**: All swells, offshore in east and southeasterly winds.
- **Hazards/tips**: Rips, crowds, localism.
- **Sleeping**: Ferrol ›› p256.

This beach is very popular with surfers from the Ferrol area and gets crowded in the

summer and at weekends. It's a 2-km long beach with excellent peaks that picks up lots of swell. It works on all tides. High quality beach break with some of the region's best waves. Beach has bars, cafés, parking and a bus link to Ferrol, which means this spot is always busy. Has a reputation as a localized spot and beware of rips. Worth checking off-season.

23 Praia de Sabón

- **Break type**: Beach break.
- **Conditions**: Small to medium swells, offshore in south/southeasterly wind.
- **Hazards/tips**: A busy break that can be packed on small summer days.
- **Sleeping**: A Coruña ›› p256.

This beach is just south of the city of A Coruña and picks up any swell going, making it a popular summer spot. Works on all tides.

16 Praia de Rodo, Pantín ›› p251

24 Praia de Baldaio/Razo

- ◔ **Break type**: Beach break.
- ◔ **Conditions**: Small to medium swells, offshore in a southerly/southwesterly wind.
- ◔ **Hazards/tips**: A great stretch of coastline to explore.
- ◔ **Sleeping**: Malpica » p257.

A huge stretch of beaches with fantastic dunes, great banks and beautiful scenery. Picks up loads of swell. Can have excellent rights and lefts in even the smallest swells.

25 Praia de Malpica and Canido

- ◔ **Break type**: Beach break.
- ◔ **Conditions**: Medium swells, offshore in south/southwesterly swells
- ◔ **Hazards/tips**: Parking by the beach.
- ◔ **Sleeping**: Malpica » p257.

A busy summer beach that is quiet out of season. Works on medium, northwesterly swells. A great stretch of beach that joins up with Canido. Access via the AC-414.

26 Praia de Nemiña

- ◔ **Break type**: Beach break.
- ◔ **Conditions**: Medium to big swells, offshore in an easterly wind.
- ◔ **Hazards/tips**: Consistent, quiet, rips when big.
- ◔ **Sleeping**: Muxía » p257.

A beautiful stretch of dune-backed beach that picks up plenty of swell and reaches down to the Ría de Lires. Along the beach are numerous peaks that break on excellent banks, while the rivermouth can have a classic left at low to mid tide. A great, consistent spot that is usually pretty uncrowded.

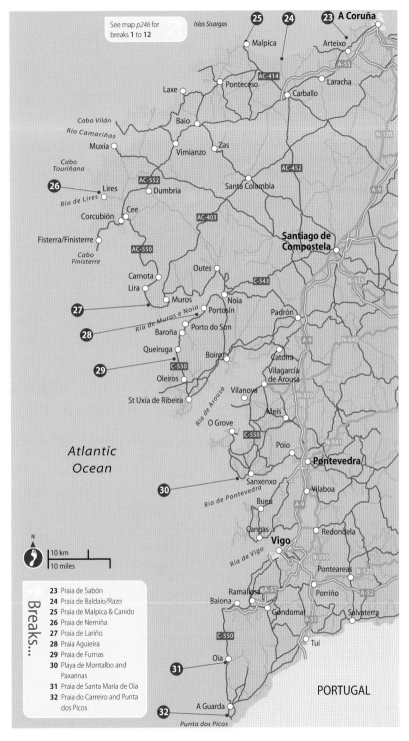

Breaks...

23 Praia de Sabón
24 Praia de Baldaio/Razo
25 Praia de Malpica & Canido
26 Praia de Nemiña
27 Praia de Lariño
28 Praia Aguieira
29 Praia de Furnas
30 Playa de Montalbo and Paxarinas
31 Praia de Santa María de Oia
32 Praia do Carreiro and Punta dos Picos

DEMI TAYLOR

27 Praia de Lariño

- **Break type**: Beach break.
- **Conditions**: Medium to big swells, offshore in a northeasterly.
- **Hazards/tips**: Visible from the main coast road, quiet spot.
- **Sleeping**: Muros » *p257*.

West-facing stretch of beach just off the C-550 that is usually very quiet. Set in beautiful countryside. Needs a swell from the west or south or a big swell from the northwest. From here north there are many spots worth checking just off the C-550. Try **Suresco, Lira, Xaxebe** and **Carnota**.

22 Praia de Doniños » *p252*

26 Praia de Nemiña » *p253*

30 Praia de Montalbo

28 Praia Aguieira

- **Break type**: Beach break.
- **Conditions**: Huge swells, offshore in southerly winds.
- **Hazards/tips**: It's only worth checking here in the biggest of swells.
- **Sleeping**: Porto do Son » *p257*.

Heading south from Noia you will find the beautiful Praia Aguieira. Set in pine forest, this excellent dune-backed beach has quality waves that come to life when the big swells roll in. Awesome location.

29 Praia de Furnas

- **Break type**: Beach break.
- **Conditions**: All swells, offshore in south/southeasterly/easterly winds.
- **Hazards/tips**: Stunning, unmarked stretch of coastline, crystal-clear water.
- **Sleeping**: Porto do Son » *p257*.

Furnas picks up loads of swell and is one of many high quality breaks on this stretch of coastline. Works best at low tide. When it's on it has fast, hollow rides on a beautiful, uncrowded beach. Other breaks worth checking include **Baroña** and **Queiruga** to the north and **Portinos**, **Ladeira** and **Ferreiras** to the south.

30 Praia de Montalbo and Paxarinas

- **Break type**: Beach break.
- **Conditions**: Medium to big swells, offshore in east/northeasterly winds.
- **Hazards/tips**: Crowds, rips when big.
- **Sleeping**: Sanxenxo » *p257*.

Close to the town of Sanxenxo sit the beaches of Montalbo (Montalvo) and Paxarinas. **Paxarinas** has an excellent, hollow left-hander that gets going in big swells and draws surfers from across the region. **Punta Montalbo** is a rocky point that throws up a hollow right-hander at low to mid tide. The beach is also home to some excellent waves.

This is a spot that can get very busy. There is parking at the beach, signposted from the main road.

31 Praia de Santa María de Oia

- **Break type**: Reef.
- **Conditions**: All swells, offshore in south/southeasterly winds.
- **Hazards/tips**: Rocky reef, powerful waves.
- **Sleeping**: A Guarda » *p257*.

This is a stunning stretch of coastline with a rich maritime history, where beautiful bays are separated by rocky points. The beach break at Oia has a reef that works in northwesterly swells producing beautiful, crystal-clear lefts up to 9 ft. The wave is tackled by a small but committed local crew.

32 Praia do Carreiro and Punta dos Picos

- **Break type**: Beach and point break.
- **Conditions**: All swells, offshore in easterly winds.
- **Hazards/tips**: These are the last breaks in Spain before crossing into Portugal.
- **Sleeping**: A Guarda » *p257*.

The beach at Praia do Carreiro is always worth checking for quality waves, as is Punta dos Picos. This works in a northeasterly wind and, in big swells, can have some excellent walling rights. Head south from A Guarda and follow signs.

Birds on the beach

Listings

Eating on the hoof

Ribadeo

Crossing over the Ría Eo into Galicia on the N-634, the first place you hit is Ribadeo which has a regional **tourist office** in the centre on Praza de Espana, www.turgalicia.es.

🛏 Sleeping

In peak season, accommodation can be fairly pricey.
E-G **El Pinar**, on Villaframil, one of the cheapest pensions, T982 131 157.
Camping Ribadeo, summer campsite to the west of the town, Jun-Sep, T982 131 167, also offers cabins.

Ribadeo to Foz

The Ribadeo to Foz stretch is packed with trucks hurtling towards A Coruña. With signs off the N-634 to the beaches placed fairly late, you'll need to keep your wits about you and hit the Estrada de Costa (coast road) as soon as possible.

🛏 Sleeping

East of Foz, camping **Nosa Casa Reinante**, on Playa Reinante, is open year round and has the option of cabins, T982 134 005. Heading towards Foz, campsite **A Gaivota**, 15 Jun-20 Sep, is between Playa de Barreiros and the N-634. It has full facilities as well as cabins, T982 124 451. The large year-round campsite **Benquerencia**, between Benquerencia and Barreiros, is the largest site in the area, T982 124 450. In terms of alternative accommodation, Praia de Fontela on the Estrada de Costa offers **Bar/Hostal Luzan**, which is pretty basic but well-placed.

Foz

This is a fairly unremarkable fishing town with a large port servicing a cluster of good seafood cafés and restaurants. It also has a couple of surf shops and campsites.

✺ Flat spells

Side trip to Lugo An hour south from the coast, the Roman town of Lugo still retains its walled centre – erected in the 3rd century AD – as well as the remains of Roman baths. Grab a bite to eat on the Rua Nova which stretches down towards the cathedral.

🛏 Sleeping

There is not a wide choice of cheap accommodation here.
D **Hotel Leyton**, on the main Av Generalisimo, is a good bet. It looks like a knocking shop from the outside, is pricey in the peak period but drops to E off season, T982 140 800.
Camping Rapadoira-Llas, just back from Praia Llas, is the smaller of the 2 campsites, 24 Jun-1 Sep, T982 140 713. To the west, **San Rafael**, by Praia de Peizas, May-15 Sep, T982 132 218.

🍴 Eating

Asador on the N-634 before Foz is a popular and reasonable place to grab half a chicken and chips. Heading out of town on the N-642, the large **Consum** supermarket is a good place to stock up on essentials or grab a coffee and a cheap snack.

Viveiro

The drive from Xove to Viveiro is an aromatic experience – the road is thickly lined with eucalyptus trees which freely release their heady scent. Viveiro, a busy working port, rests at the neck of the river and nestles in a lush green valley.

✺ Flat spells

To rid yourself of surfer's ear, head for the old town and visit the replica Lourdes grotto. Locals leave offerings in return for good health. **Go-karting** At Arifran, just west of Viveiro, signed from the C-642.

🛏 Sleeping

E **As Areas II**, on the west side on Av Santiago, has parking and reasonable off-season rates, T982 50 523.
F **Hotel Vilar**, on Nicholás Montenegro, is one of the cheapest places to stay

off-season, T982 561 331.

Camping Viviero, at Praia de Covas on the west of the town, Jun-Sep, T982 560 004.

🍴 Eating

Eat good cheap fish along the waterfront – check out the **Galicia Café**, on Av García Navia Castrillón and, for basics, stock up at the **Haley Hiper** supermarket on the main road. On the main road by **O Barqueiro**, the clean, friendly café **O'Boliche** does a great *menú del día* for about €6.50.

🛒 Shopping

There are a couple of **surf shops** here including **T. Hachece** opposite the bridge on the east side of town and **Koala** on Av Ferrol.

Cedeira

Bypassing Ortigueira, Cedeira on the C-646 is a good base for exploring Pantín and the surrounding breaks as it has all the basic amenities including banks and supermarkets.

🛏 Sleeping

E **Chelsea** is not the prettiest place, but it is friendly, functional and one of the cheapest places to stay, T981 482 340.

Camping Heading west, campsite **A Lagoa**, just back from Praia Frouxeira, Jun-15 Sep, T981 487 122. Off the C-642, **Valdoviño**, Jun-Sep, has plenty of facilities including cabins, T981 487 076. Further along, **Fontesín** is simpler and cheaper, Jun-Sep, T981 485 028.

🍴 Eating

Pizza Lanus on the riverfront of the old town does a good pizza as well as a selection of pasta and salads. **Café Plaza** on Praza Sagrado is a great place to grab a coffee and a *napolitana* for breakfast. Heading west towards the village of Pantín, café **Casa Ramos** overlooking the WQS

break, Praia Rodo, is an interesting place to get a beer or a coffee and have a game of pool after a surf.

Ferrol

The drive from Cedeira crosses moorland, rugged countryside and bypasses jagged cliffs interspersed with large expanses of beach. Ferrol itself – the birthplace of Fascist dictator, Franco – is home to a large port, but is fairly unremarkable. There is a large surf community and as such has plenty of surf shops.

✴ Flat spells

Head south to the pretty river town **Pontedeume** and explore the **Parque Natural Fragas do Eume**. **Golf**   Get a few rounds in at **Club de Golf Campomar** on Nicaragua, T619 659 832.

🛏 Sleeping

G **Da Madalena**, on Madalena, T981 355 615, open throughout the year and one of the cheapest options around.

Camping   Try **As Cabazas** on the Cobas-Ferrol road, Jun-15 Sep, also has cabins, T981 365 706.

A Coruña

A Coruña is a relaxed, beautiful city surrounded by water, 155 km north of Vigo. A warren of seafood restaurants and *tapas* bars is headed up by a square paying tribute to the city's saviour, María Pita, who stopped the city from being ravaged by the plundering English in the 1500s. To the north, the Torre de Hércules looks out towards Britain and is said to be the oldest working lighthouse in the world, having been erected by the Romans in the 2nd century AD, though most of the structure dates from the 1700s. You can actually climb to the top and look out over the world.

✴ Flat spells

Head to the **Domus** on Santa Teresa for the museum of mankind and catch a movie at the **Imax** cinema, T981 189 840.

Football   Watch former La Lija champions **Deportiva La Coruña** at Estadio de Raizor just back from Praia de Raizor. **Golf**   Get some practice at **Golpe Pitch & Putt** in Carballo to the southwest of A Coruña, T981 739 699, www.carballo.org, or a full round at the **Campo Municipal de Golf Torre de Hércules**, Av da Torre, T981 209 680.

🛏 Sleeping

A couple of cheap options can be found on Praza de Galicia near the church of St Lucía including **F-G Pazo de San Antonio**, T981 122 358, and **F-G Palacio**, T981 122 338. Closer to the action check out Rua Nueva including **E-F Carbonara**, clean and massive, T981 22 52 51. **Camping**   Camp out of town in Arteixo at Valcobo on Lugar de Valcobar, Apr-Sep, T981 601 040.

🍴 Eating/drinking

Sandwiched between R Nueva and Plaza María Pita is the *tapas* zone and the best place to head for ambience. A Coruña is all about the seafood, especially octopus or *pulpo* and C Franja off the square is the place to sample it. If fish doesn't float your boat, head to **El Serrano** on Galera, which, as the name and the ceiling suggests, is a *jamonería* serving a good selection of *tapas* and *raciones*. In the early evening the Plaza is a popular spot to have a beer and watch the world go by.

🛒 Shopping

There are plenty of surf shops here including **Surf & Rock** and **Fresh** on Alfredo Vicente back from Praia de Raizor. One road back, on Fernando Macías, are **Raz Surf Gallery** and **Silver Surf**. There are also several **Nevada** stores dotted around the city including one on the main Juan Florez.

 Airports → Madrid T913-936000; Bilbao T944-869661; Málaga T952-048804. **Buses and coaches** → Eurolines, T020-7730 8235, www.gobycoach.com. **Car hire** → Avis, T0870-6060100; Hertz, T08708-448844; National, www.nationalcar.com. **Ferries** → Brittany Ferries, T08705-360360; P&O, T0870-242 4999, www.poportsmouth.com. **Rail links** → RENFE, www.renfe.es. **Petrol prices** → €0.80-95/litre.

Parking

As with most cities, it's best to dump your car as quickly as possible and use your feet to get around. There are plenty of car parks dotted along the main arteries of the city including underground car parks at Plaza de María Pita and Av de la Marina.

Directory

Internet: access can be found at **Estrella Park** on Estrella. **Post office**: just opposite the tourist centre on Av de la Marina. **Tourist information**: Av de la Marina, www.turismocoruna.com.

Malpica

Malpica is on the Costa da Morte, or 'coast of death', at the end of the AC-414 from Carballo. Offshore, Islas Sisargas is a haven for birds.

Sleeping

F Hostal JB, C Playa, is one of the cheapest hotel options with rooms overlooking the beach, T981 721 906.
Camping Sisargas, large, seasonal campsite open Jun-15 Sep, also offers cabins, T981 721 702.

Muxía

South of the Río Camariñas, Muxía is home to a couple of campsites. **Lago Mar**, between Merexo and Muxía. offers cabins and is open Jun-Sep, T981 750 628. **Playa Barreira** in Lires is reasonable, open year round and has cabins, T981 730 304. For a change of scene, head to the 'end of the world', **Cabo Finisterre**. The peninsula is a dramatic place to walk around and experience the power of the Atlantic.

Muros

Set on the Ría de Muros e Noia, this pretty fishing town can be accessed by either the C-550 or the AC-403 and has plenty of eating and accommodation options.

Sleeping

F-G Hostal Playa Atlantica, on San

Francisco de Louro, offers some of the best room rates, T981 826 451.
Camping San Francisco, by the beach, 20 Jun-20 Sep, T981 826 148. **A Bouga**, on the road down from Finisterre, T981 826 284. **Ancoradoiro**, the smallest of the 3, Jun-Sep, on the road from Corcubión, T981 878 897.

Porto do Son

Heading south on the C-550 this is a pretty place to stay and one of the most lively around the Ría de Muros e Noia.

Sleeping

Accommodation here is not particularly cheap with **D-E Hotel León II**, by Praia Ornanda, one of the most cost effective, T981 766 188.
Camping Camp year round at **Punta Batuda** near Praia de Ornanda-Gaviotas. The large site has great facilities as well as cabins to rent, T981 766 542. The summer site **Cabiero** to the north of the town is smaller, has fewer facilities, but is cheaper, T981 767 355. Heading south towards the Parque Natural Complexo dunar de Corrubedo e Lagoas de Carregal e Vixán there is also camping mid Jun-15 Sep at **Las Dunas**, T981 868 009.

Sanxenxo

Overdeveloped and slightly disappointing, this resort town is a popular spot, indicated by the high number of campsites crammed into such a small area. The waterfront is packed with bars and cafés and there are hundreds of places to stay so shop around for a deal and take your pick.

Flat spells

Hang out in **Pontevedra**, a pretty city, complete with a beautiful 16th-century church, Basílica de Santa María a Maior.
Golf Get a round in at **Golf a Toxa** on Isla da Toxa near O Grove, T986 730 818, www.latojagolf.com.
Sidetrip to Vigo It's all about the fish and as one of the world's largest fishing ports it's no

surprise that you can pick up some good quality, reasonably priced seafood – head for the market on R de Pescadería or check out the cafés nearby. There's also an abundance of surf shops here including **Cuyagua** on Martín Echegaray, **West Peak** on Av Camelias, **Nova Lobas** on Pintor Laxeiro, **Pui Pui** on Progreso and **Surf Spot** on García Lorca.

Sleeping

Camping Highlights include the all-singing, all-dancing **Boavista**. Open Apr-Sep, with cabins, this site is handily placed by Praia Montalvo, T986 720 478. The lower grade **Montalvo Playa**, Jun-Sep, is again near the beach, T986 724 087. Year-round **Monte Cabo** is just north of Portonovo by the Punta Faxilda, T986 744 141. **Airinos do Mar**, between Pontevedra and O Grove, is fairly small, open Jun-Sep, but does have cabins, T986 723 154.

Shopping

Inland at Pontevedra there are several **surf shops** to pick up essentials including **Puerto Escondido** on Salvador Morno, **Mission** on Sagastra. In Poio in the commercial centre is **Sinsemilla**.

A Guarda

Sitting at the bottom of the C-550, this is the last Atlantic town in Spain.

Flat spells

Trek up the **Monte Santa Trega** to the south for great views across the river and out to sea. There are also the remains of a Celtic village.

Sleeping

Camping Camp out year round in **Salcidos** at Santa Tecla which is crammed full of amenities including cabins to rent, T986 613 011. Heading north, Oia also has a couple of campsites: **O Muinoz**, on the C-550, with cabins and more facilities than you can shake a tent pole at, open Christmas to Sep, T986 361 600; and **Pedra Rubia**, just inland at Mougas, Jun-Sep, offering less, which is reflected in the price, T986 361 562.

Andalucía

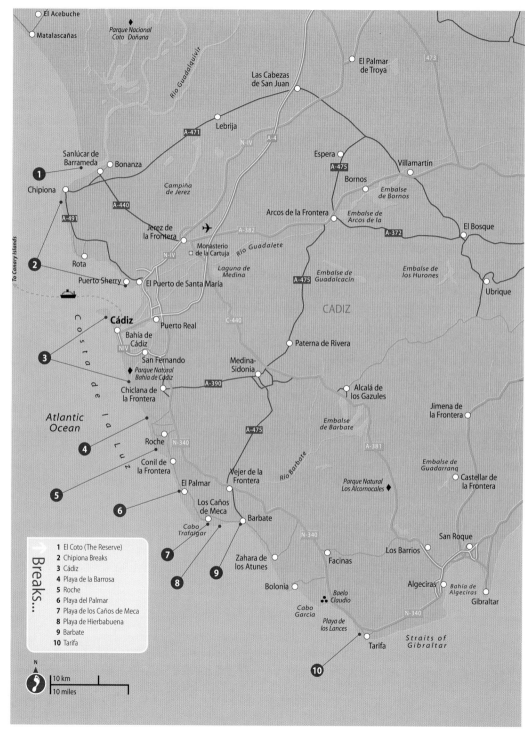

El Acebuche

Matalascañas

Parque Nacional
Coto Doñana

Rio Guadalquivir

Las Cabezas
de San Juan

El Palmar
de Troya

473

A-471

Lebrija

N-IV

A-4

Espera

A-475

Villamartín

Sanlúcar de
Barrameda

Bonanza

Bornos

Embalse
de Bornos

1

Chipiona

Campiña
de Jerez

Arcos de la Frontera

Embalse de
Arcos de la

A-372

El Bosque

A-440

A-491

Jerez de
la Frontera

A-382

Rio Guadalete

2

Rota

N-IV

Monasterio
de la Cartuja

Embalse de
Guadalcacín

A-475

Embalse de
los Hurones

Puerto Sherry

Laguna de
Medina

CADIZ

Ubrique

El Puerto de Santa María

Cádiz

Puerto Real

C-440

Bahía de
Cádiz

N-IV

Paterna de Rivera

3

San Fernando

Medina-
Sidonia

Alcalá de
los Gazules

Jimena de
la Frontera

Parque Natural
Bahía de Cádiz

A-390

Chiclana de
la Frontera

Embalse
de Barbate

A-381

Embalse de
Guadarranq

Costa de la Luz

**Atlantic
Ocean**

A-475

Roche

N-340

Castellar de
la Frontera

4

Conil de
la Frontera

Vejer de la
Frontera

Rio Barbate

Parque Natural
Los Alcornocales

5

El Palmar

6

Los Caños
de Meca

Barbate

San Roque

Cabo
Trafalgar

N-340

Los Barros

Facinas

7

Zahara de
los Atunes

Algeciras

Bahía de
Algeciras

8

Bolonia

Baelo
Claudio

N-340

Gibraltar

9

Cabo
Garcia

Playa de
los Lances

To Canary Islands

10

Tarifa

Straits of
Gibraltar

Breaks...

1 El Coto (The Reserve)
2 Chipiona Breaks
3 Cádiz
4 Playa de la Barrosa
5 Roche
6 Playa del Palmar
7 Playa de los Caños de Meca
8 Playa de Hierbabuena
9 Barbate
10 Tarifa

N

10 km
10 miles

Surfing Andalucía

The southwestern Atlantic coastline of Spain is a completely different experience from the northern provinces. While Green Spain has a Celtic feel and landscape, Andalucía is a province that has been shaped by the north African Moorish culture. The geography is also more African than European. Long dry summers and mild winters lead to a landscape dominated by tinder-dry pines, scrubland and a coastline of long sandy beaches.

This region has had a turbulent past. It was the first to fall to the Moors in AD 711 and the last to be reconquered – Granada was liberated in the late 15th century. Moorish architecture and culture dominate Andalucía with walled cities and palaces set around tiled courtyards with fountains and shady palms. A perfect example is the Alhambra in Granada, one of the region's biggest tourist draws. The nearby Sierra Nevada, with its spectacular mountain ridges, provide some great terrain for snowboarding.

   The western coastline is dominated by the city of Cádiz to the north and the town of Tarifa to the south. Cádiz has an amazing old centre and some excellent city beaches. Locals will tell you that the endless winds make Tarifa the suicide capital of Spain but it has also meant that the picturesque walled town is Europe's windsurfing Mecca. It overlooks the busy shipping lanes of the Straits of Gibraltar and the heights of the north African continent only 14 km through the haze. It has become a traditional overnight stop for those making the trip south to Morocco, and a first glimpse of an exciting new continent.

Coastline

The coastline of Andalucía is a mixture of long, dune-backed, sandy beaches and rocky points. The region around Cádiz is dominated by massive tracts of beach break. This area picks up less swell than the south due to the blocking effect of Cabo San Vincente in Portugal. The rocky points around Cabo de Trafalgar and Cabo Garcia can have some excellent point breaks in good swells and the southern stretch of beach towards Tarifa, although not Europe's most consistent stretch of coastline, can have great waves set against the backdrop of Africa's Northern Rif mountains.

Localism

Many of the breaks are pretty relaxed and there are many uncrowded spots out there to be discovered. Spots in Cádiz and at Roche can get very busy and the coastline has developed a bit of a reputation for car crime. Park with care and don't leave valuables in the car.

Top local surfers Mario Aguilar and Alberto Fernández.

It is a unique location in the surfing world. You can sit in a line-up on one continent and look across a short stretch of water to another – just 14 km separate Europe from Africa.

Peter van Basten, Dutch travelling surfer

Andalucía board guide

Small wave shortboard
Shaper: Rawson for Pukas

» 5'11" x 19¼" x 2⅜" wing swallow.
» Perfect for those small, mushy days that are normally ridden on a longboard or a traditional fish.
» Design works well as a twin fin with back stabiliser, or as a 'quattro' style, using the F.C.S fin system and is now becoming popular on the US East Coast..

Spanish south swells
Shaper: Peter Daniels for Pukas

» 5'10" x 18½" x 2³⁄₁₆" for Iker Fuentes.
» Wider swallow (5½") with less rocker.
» Fuller rails for softer beach breaks and fast, quick turns.
» For long floaters and very stable in 1–2 ft weak waves
» Version for a 75 kg surfer, normal level 6'0" x 19" x 2⅜'.
» Version for big guys: 6'4" x 20" x 2⅝".
» A 'must' for any serious surfer.

ⓘ Boards by **Pukas**
Factory: Olatu, Oyarzun, Euskadi, Spain
T00 34 (0)943-493255, www.pukasurf.com

Getting around

The city beaches in Cádiz are accessible on foot, but if you really want to get out and explore the region you will need wheels. The N-340 south runs parallel to the coast with smaller roads accessing the beaches. Some spots are accessed via rough pistes.

Breaks

Andalucía

Air ——— Sea ———

°F Averages °C

90 — 30

70 — 20

50 — 10

30 — 0

J F M A M J J A S O N D

3/2   3/2   Shortie   3/2

1 El Coto (The Reserve)

- **Break type**: Rocky right-hand break.
- **Conditions**: All swells, offshore in northeasterly winds.
- **Hazards/tips**: Busy wave in national park.
- **Sleeping**: Chipiona ›› p262.

This mid to high tide wave needs a westerly or southwesterly swell but produces walling right-handers. The wave breaks at the northern mouth of the Río Guadalquivir on the edge of the Parque Nacional Coto Doñana. This is a quality wave that can get busy but is pretty chilled.

2 Chipiona Breaks

- **Break type**: Beach breaks.
- **Conditions**: All swells, offshore in northeast/easterly winds.
- **Hazards/tips**: Quality breaks south of Chipiona.
- **Sleeping**: Chipiona ›› p262.

Playa de Regla is a white-sand urban beach best at mid to high tide. On the same stretch of beach to the south is **Playa de Tres Piedras (Three Stones)**, a beach break with some rocks, backed by sand dunes. It has lefts and rights and is best at mid to high tide. Both need winds from the northeast or east and southwesterly or westerly swells. To the south again breaks a quality right-hander, **Cien Metros (One Hundred Metres)**. It is a fast and powerful wave that breaks between mid and high tide. **Playa de la Ballena** is a mid to high tide break. These beaches are

2 Chipiona Breaks

found north of Cádiz on a long stretch of coast between Chipiona and Rota.

3 Cádiz

- **Break type**: Beach breaks.
- **Conditions**: All swells, offshore in easterly winds.
- **Hazards/tips**: This huge stretch of beaches becomes less busy as you head south.
- **Sleeping**: Cádiz/El Puerto de Santa María ›› p262.

Cádiz sits on the northern end of a peninsula, which provides a huge expanse of sandy beaches that stretch south all the way to the river at Sancti Petri. The town beach, **La Playita**, has two boulder groynes along which the sand builds up. It works best at low to mid tide. **Las Caracolos** stretches to the south of the city and works best on a mid to high tide. At the end of Playa de la Victoria is **La Cabañita**, a hollow, right-hand high tide wave. **Torregorda** and **Campo Soto** are both picturesque dune-backed beaches with golden sand.

3 Cádiz

6 Playa del Palmar

4 Playa de la Barrosa

- **Break type**: Beach break.
- **Conditions**: All swells, offshore in northeasterly winds.
- **Hazards/tips**: Picks up less swell.
- **Sleeping**: Chiclana de la Frontera ›› p263.

A continuation of the sandy beaches heading south, La Barrosa has peaks that work best at low to mid tide. This is a quiet spot that needs a bigger swell to get going.

5 Roche

- **Break type**: Beach break.
- **Conditions**: All swells, offshore in easterly winds.
- **Hazards/tips**: Crowds, localism when busy.
- **Sleeping**: Conil de la Frontera ›› p263.

Roche is a popular beach break that is one of the region's most consistent waves. It has powerful, high quality lefts and rights that are best from low to mid tide. Take the turning off the N-340 for Roche.

6 Playa del Palmar

- **Break type**: Beach break.
- **Conditions**: All swells, offshore in northeasterly/easterly winds.
- **Hazards/tips**: Gets busy at peak times.
- **Sleeping**: Conil de la Frontier ›› p263.

Palmar is a popular spot that can produce high quality lefts and rights, with powerful and hollow waves breaking consistently on the sandbanks. Works on all tides with a high tide shore break, but is best from low to mid tide.

7 Playa de los Caños de Meca

- **Break type**: Reef break.
- **Conditions**: All swells, offshore in a north/northeasterly wind.
- **Hazards/tips**: Gets busy when it's working.
- **Sleeping**: Barbate ›› p263.

This is a long, sandy beach but the break is a flat slab reef that works best from low to mid tides. It is a left that can be fast and have tube sections.

8 Playa de Hierbabuena

- **Break type**: Right-hand point.
- **Conditions**: Big swell, offshore in northerly/northeasterly winds.
- **Hazards/tips**: Crowds, car crime.
- **Sleeping**: Barbate ›› p263.

This point is hidden away among scrub and pine trees west of Barbate. It is a rocky break that can produce excellent long right-hand walls on all tides, but needs a good swell to get going. Breaks up to 6 ft. At the end of a long sandy track – you'll need to go by foot unless you have a 4WD. This area has a reputation for car crime. Don't leave any valuables in sight.

9 Barbate

- **Break type**: Rivermouth.
- **Conditions**: Medium to big swells, offshore in northeasterly winds.
- **Hazards/tips**: Busy break, may have localism when crowded.
- **Sleeping**: Barbate ›› p263.

Left-hand walls peel along the sandbank at the mouth of the river here. Barbate is one of the region's most famous breaks and many travelling surfers visit here, drawn by photos of this mini Mundaka-like set-up. The wave works through the tides.

10 Tarifa

- **Break type**: Beach break.
- **Conditions**: All swells, offshore in northeasterly/easterly winds.
- **Hazards/tips**: Windy, packed with windsurfers, can be damp in winter.
- **Sleeping**: Tarifa ›› p263.

From Tarifa north is a huge stretch of sandy beach with the occasional rocky points. This coastline is peppered with campsites and draws windsurfers from all over the world. However there can be waves when the wind drops and the swell picks up. At the northern end of the beach is a right-hand point accessed in front of the Jardín de Las Dunas campsite. This stretch is offshore in a light northeasterly wind. Great views across to Morocco and if you feel the need to learn to kitesurf, this is the ideal place.

DEMI TAYLOR

10 Tarifa: where the wind blows

Spain Andalucía Breaks Playa de la Barrosa to Tarifa

DEMI TAYLOR

Andalucía secret spot

Listings

Chipiona

Heading south from Sevilla on the A4/E5 toll road, the A-471 will bring you onto the Costa de la Luz or 'coast of light'. Less built-up than the high-rise Costa del Sol to the east, Andalucía's west coast is an easy stopping point before heading south to Morocco. Chipiona, south of the Río Guadalquivir, is the first coastal port of call and with four long white sandy beaches is a popular summer resort.

🏄 Flat spells
Beach racing   Nearby town Sanlúcar de Barrameda is home to some intense beach horse racing in August – hit the tourist office on Calzada del Ejército for more info.
Drinking   While in Sanlúcar de Barrameda, enjoy a glass of *manzanilla* sherry which has helped make a name for the place.
Nature reserve   Across the Río Guadalquivir in the Huelva region lies the **Parque Nacional Coto Doñana**, the largest nature reserve in Spain. Home to flamingos, birds of prey and lynx among others, the best way to see (a bit of) the park is by boat tour from the Bajo de Guía quay in Sanlúcar de Barrameda. Tickets for the 4-hr tour are about €14 and need to be pre-booked on T956 363 813, or at the park exhibition centre on the Bajo de Guía.

🛏 Sleeping
The large **Camping El Pinar de Chipiona** is open year round on the road south to Rota, T956 372 321

El Puerto de Santa María

Given its close vicinity to Cádiz, this pretty town is a popular spot with urban holidaymakers and weekenders. It's also a popular spot for anyone interested in sampling the local **sherry** – drunk very cold and very dry – in one of the many bodegas that line the river and road into town.

🏄 Flat spells
Golf   Get 9 holes in at **Vista Hermosa Golf**

nestled in the Bahía Cádiz, T956 541 968.
Sidetrip to Jerez   Jerez is all about horses and sherry – in almost equal quantities. The **Horse Fair** in May is a grand affair and sees horses put through a series of events and shows. More laid-back entertainment can be found at one of the many **bodegas** in the birthplace of sherry where a tour and generous product sampling can set you back about €6. One of the best known is **Pedro Domecq**, T956 357 016, www.domecq.es. Head to the tourist office on Larga, the main road, for help organizing a tour.

🛏 Sleeping
Camping Las Dunas, on the Paseo Marítimo La Puntilla, is fairly large, just back from the beach and open year round, T956 872 210.

🍴 Eating
Around the harbour are plenty of good places to grab a fish supper, try the relaxed **Romerijo** on the Ribera del Marisco.

🛍 Shopping
On the main road into the town check out the retail park which houses a **Decathlon** sports store – worth checking out if you want just about anything for any sporting activity. They also do a cheap range of own-brand wetsuits, boots and gloves as well as a few boards. Surf/skate store **Kalima** on Av del Descubrimiento can sort out your basic needs.

Cádiz

Set out at the end of a long peninsula, Cádiz is an important port town and, having been settled by the Phoenicians in 1100 BC, is also one of the oldest towns in Spain. Head to the Plaza de San Juan just back from the port, where the streets are a warren of watering holes and beds for the night.

🛏 Sleeping
F **Pensión Las Cuatro Naciones** on Plocia, T956 259 061, is one of the best sleeping options where rooms range from about €17.
Camping   El Pinar is the nearest campsite,

11 km away in Puerto Real on the N-IV from Madrid, T956 830 897.

🍴 Eating
Look out for *freidurías* – fried fish shops where you can eat in or, better still, take your meal away with you wrapped in a paper cone.

🛍 Shopping
Sitting at the top of a long stretch of breaks, Cádiz is home to a healthy surf community and has plenty of **surf shops** including **Arrecife**, heading south out of the city on Av Fernández, **Cádiz Surf Shop** on Villa de Paradas, **Hot Water** along the waterfront on Paseo Marítimo and **Tavarua** on Tolosa la Tour.

🔵 Directory
Post office : Plaza de Topete. **Tourist information**: on Ramón de Carranza, just off the plaza San Juan de Dois, www.andalucia.org and www.andalucia.com.

Chiclana de la Frontera
🛏 Sleeping
Heading south on the N-340 from Cádiz to Tarifa, there is **Camping La Barrosa** on the road from Barrosa, open May-Sep, bungalows to rent, T956 494 605.

Conil de la Frontera
This whitewashed fishing village, where the beach flows from the town front, has a laid-back attitude and is fast becoming a favourite with holidaying locals. As such there are plenty of reasonable places to eat, drink and be merry along the beachfront. There are also a couple of internet posts.

🛏 Sleeping
Camping Plenty of campsites here including year-round **Cala del Aceite** with cabins, T956 440 972, www.caladelaceite.com. **La Rosaleda**, on road to Pradillo, open year round, T956 443 327, as is **Roche**, on Pago del

Zorro with cabins, T956 442 216, www.campingroche.com. **El Faro**, on Puerto Pesquero near the beachfront, 1 Jun-30 Sep, T956 232 090, www.campingelfaro.com. **Los Eucaliptos**, on El Padrilo, Apr-Sep, has cabins, T956 441 272. Off season, the police seem to tolerate responsible free-camping near the beach but move vans on in the run up to the summer. **Camping El Palmar**, better placed on the coast off the Conil-Caños de Meca road at Playa El Palmar, 1 Jun -15 Sep, T956 232 161.

🍴 Eating
Keep a look out for *chiringuitos* dotted all along the seafront – fairly seasonal beach bars along the coast where you can pick up a cheap and tasty lunchtime or evening snack of fried fish. There is also a good supermarket, as well as local fish and vegetable markets..

Barbate
On the run down to Tarifa, Barbate is a popular spot to stop and as well as campsites has a couple of surf shops including **Coco's** on Av del Generalísimo.

🛏 Sleeping
Camping Faro de Trafalgar, on the Vejer-Caños de Meca route, Apr-15 Sep, T956 437 017. Just down the road is **Caños de Meca**, with cabins, Apr-5 Oct, T956 437 120. **Camaleón**, in Caños de Meca, 1 Apr-30 Sep, T956 437 154. **Bahía de la Plata**, south at the fishing village of Zahara de los Atunes, open year round, T956 439 040, www.campingbahiadelaplata.com.

Tarifa
Separated from Africa by a 14-km stretch of water, the Moors' influence on this old walled town is obvious. The constant hammering of the levante winds from the east and the poniente winds from the west has brought Tarifa international acclaim within the world of windsurfing. Spring sees the Playa los Lances overrun with some of the world's best windsurfers for the **Redbull**

Skyride, which includes a race across the Straits of Gibraltar. Tarifa's a great place to stop off if you want to try kitesurfing or stock up on surf essentials before heading off to Morocco.

☀ Flat spells
Sidetrip to Morocco If you're not heading south for the winter, take a day trip to Morocco or overnight there. You can book a return to Tanger for about €40 from any one of the kiosks along the main road or at the harbour front. Ask at the tourist office for more information.
Skiing Head east and hit the slopes on the Sierra Nevadas where night skiing is on offer, www.sierranevadaski.com.

🛏 Sleeping
Camping The N-340 into Tarifa is littered with year-round campsites on both sides of the road but as a popular windsurfing destination seems pricey.
Jardín de las Dunas is just off the main road at Playa de Valdevaqueros, near a popular free-camping site, T956 689 101, www.campingjdunas.com.
Paloma has cabins, T956 684 203, www.campingpaloma.com.
Río Jara, T956 680 570, on N-340, is just down the road from Tarifa, T956 684 778, www.camping-tarifa.com.
Torre de la Peña I has cabins, T956 684 903, www.campingtp.com.
Torre de la Peña II, popular with windsurfers, runs onto the beachfront, T956 684 174.

🔵 Shopping
Plenty of windsurf/surf shops, including a **Quiksilver Boardrider** and **Rick Shapes**, **Art of Surfing, Xtrem**, **Surf Division** and **Fly Cat** on Batalla del Saludo.

🔵 Directory
Internet: Check the charts online at **Bar El Trato** on Sancho El Bravo and post your last cards from Europe at the **post office** on Coronel Moscardo. The **tourist office** is on Paseo de la Alameda.

Canary Islands

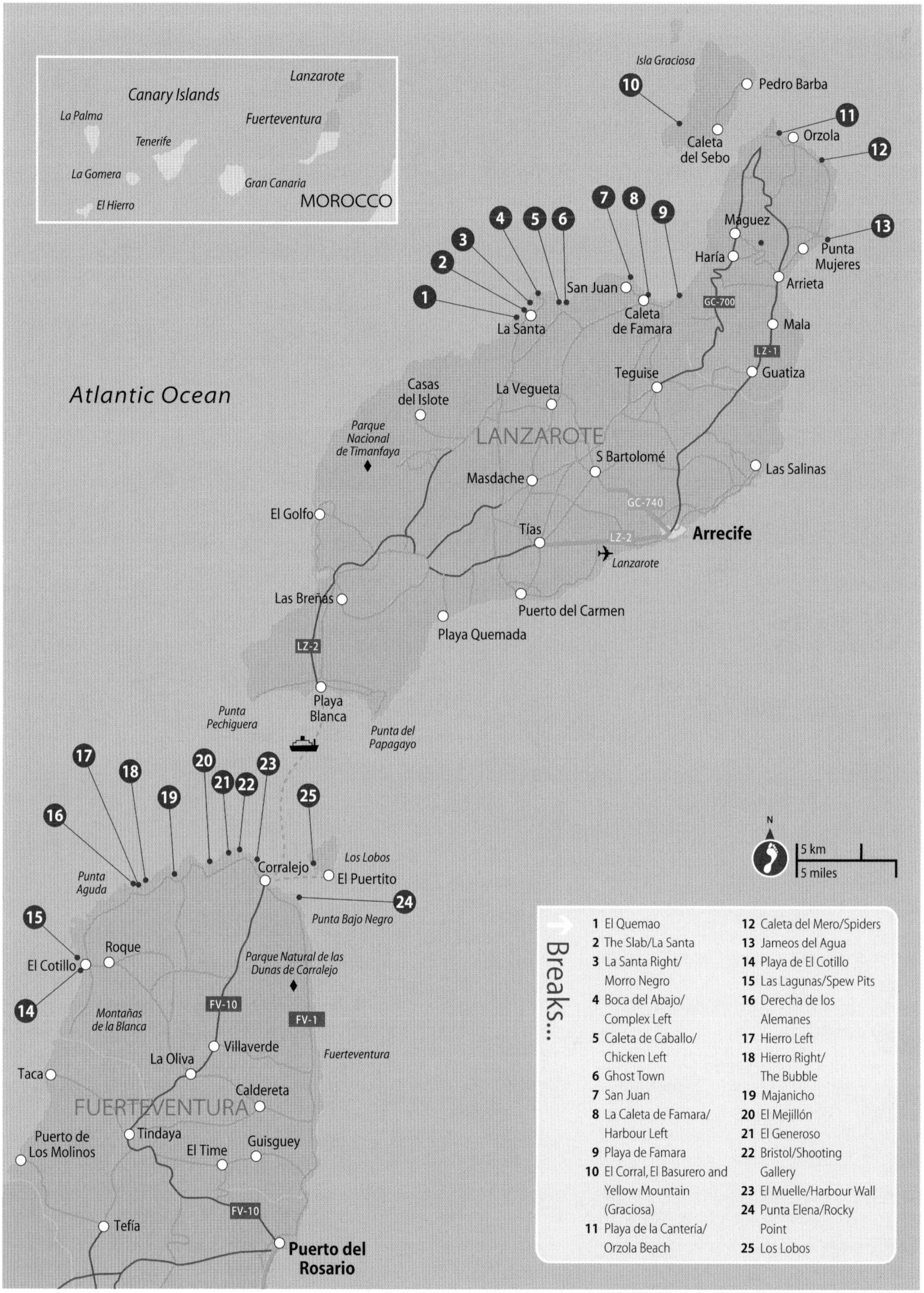

Canary Islands

La Palma
Tenerife
La Gomera
El Hierro
Gran Canaria
Lanzarote
Fuerteventura

MOROCCO

Atlantic Ocean

LANZAROTE

Isla Graciosa
Pedro Barba
10
11
Orzola
12
Caleta del Sebo
Máguez
7 **8** **9**
13
Haría
Punta Mujeres
Arrieta
4 **5** **6**
3
2
San Juan
Mala
1
Caleta de Famara
La Santa
GC-700
Guatiza
LZ-1
Casas del Islote
La Vegueta
Teguise
Las Salinas
Parque Nacional de Timanfaya
Masdache
S Bartolomé
El Golfo
GC-740
Tías
LZ-2
Arrecife
Lanzarote
Las Breñas
Puerto del Carmen
Playa Quemada
LZ-2
Punta Pechiguera
Playa Blanca
Punta del Papagayo

17
18
20 **23**
19
21 **22**
16
25
Los Lobos
Corralejo
El Puertito
Punta Bajo Negro
24
Punta Aguda
15
Roque
Parque Natural de las Dunas de Corralejo
El Cotillo
14
Montañas de la Blanca
FV-10
FV-1
Villaverde
Taca
La Oliva
Fuerteventura
FUERTEVENTURA
Caldereta
Puerto de Los Molinos
Tindaya
Guisguey
El Time
FV-10
Tefía
Puerto del Rosario

N
5 km
5 miles

Breaks…

1 El Quemao	12 Caleta del Mero/Spiders
2 The Slab/La Santa	13 Jameos del Agua
3 La Santa Right/ Morro Negro	14 Playa de El Cotillo
4 Boca del Abajo/ Complex Left	15 Las Lagunas/Spew Pits
5 Caleta de Caballo/ Chicken Left	16 Derecha de los Alemanes
6 Ghost Town	17 Hierro Left
7 San Juan	18 Hierro Right/ The Bubble
8 La Caleta de Famara/ Harbour Left	19 Majanicho
9 Playa de Famara	20 El Mejillón
10 El Corral, El Basurero and Yellow Mountain (Graciosa)	21 El Generoso
11 Playa de la Cantería/ Orzola Beach	22 Bristol/Shooting Gallery
	23 El Muelle/Harbour Wall
	24 Punta Elena/Rocky Point
	25 Los Lobos

Surfing the Canary Islands

"To explore the full surfing potential of the Canary Islands would take several lifetimes. There are many world-class waves concentrated on the the north shores of Fuerteventura and Lanzarote. But to really experience the Canaries, the travelling surfer must push out and explore. There are still many unsurfed breaks out there to discover. Geographically the Canary Islands are part of Africa, but politically and sociologically they are European. This archipelago of Spanish sovereignty lost its African roots many years ago. The islands' original inhabitants disappeared under the pressure of European conquerors many centuries ago and with them went their culture, way of life and language." Willy Uribe, surf photographer

The Canary Islands are the European tropics. It is a land of hot summers and mild winters popular with young holidaymakers and an ideal location for retirement. For surfers, it is a land of great possibilities. They are known as the 'Lucky Islands' for their excellent climate and year-round sun, but for the wave rider they offer more than sun loungers and jacuzzis. Volcanic reefs and points are designed perfectly to produce fast, hollow and shallow waves that are definitely not for the faint-hearted. To take on the jagged reefs, you must have the heart of a toreador and the hide of a bull.

An important aspect of surfing in the Canary Islands is the 'localismo' that has taken hold at some of the waves. "Localism is present at many waves all over this planet, but luckily not all," says Willy. "The *surfista* visitor should used their common sense and also their imagination. There are uncrowded waves out there for those who are prepared to look, and with a bit of time management it is even possible to ride the most famous breaks when the numbers of local *surferos* are low."

Visiting surfers tend to head straight for the north coast of Lanzarote or to the south coast of Tenerife, where the waves are already busy. Bear in mind that there are many other surfing possibilities on the islands. Central and southern coasts of Fuerteventura, the north coast of Tenerife, the greater Chinijo archipelago and other islands that are not quite so famous. As Willy Uribe explains, "It is important to leave the main highways and to explore. To look for and to lose the time looking for... and to be surrounded by silence, the intense vision of the sea or the blazes of colour that the sun reveals in volcanic earth. This is all a part of the Canaries surfing experience."

Coastline

The Canary Islands are a group of volcanic islands sitting 100 km off the African coast. They are the tips of volcanoes, some of which are still active, protruding above the Atlantic waves. Fuerteventura is the closest to Africa and sand from the Sahara has built up on the eastern

I think my favourite place is the Canary Islands. It has really good waves and an excellent climate – the water is warm the whole year round. Tenerife has some great waves but Lanzarote is better. The localism is really bad there but it's only really at the main spots like La Santa. There are so many waves – if you go around the island with the same swell and same conditions you can go to other breaks and be alone.

Eneko Acero, top Basque surfer and ex European Champion

Canary Islands board guide

Semi-gun
Shaper: Peter Daniels for Pukas

» 6'3" x 18" x 2⅛" round pin for Aritz Aranburu.
» Smooth rocker and narrower tail to get into wave early and pigdogging barrels.
» Perfect for when the points fire or when the hollow reefs get over 6 ft.
» Version for a 75 kg surfer, normal level: 6'6" x 18" x 2⁵⁄₁₆".
» Big guys: 7'2" x 19" x 2".

Hi performance shortboard
Shaper: Peter Daniels for Pukas

» 6'0" x18" x 2⅛" for Hodei Collazo.
» High bumpwing squash for fast turning, curvy bottom for looseness, boosting big airs and pulling into barrels.
» No rail catching, no problemas.
» S-concaves.
» Great all round performer for when the surf is at a ripable size.
» Version for a 75 kg surfer, normal level: 6'3" x 18⅜" x 2⁵⁄₁₆".
» Big guys: 6'8" x 19" x 2".

 Boards by **Pukas**
Factory: Olatu, Oyarzun, Euskadi, Spain
T 00 34 (0)943-493255, www.pukasurf.com

seaboard to provide idyllic tourist beaches. The lava rock reefs that fringe the island make for excellent surfing but are definitely not for beginners. Lanzarote is the least mountainous of the islands and, as such, doesn't catch as much rainfall as the others and is therefore less green. It has 300 volcanoes and the northeast corner of the island is home to some comparatively fresh, savagely jagged lava reefs. The north shore is often compared to Hawaii as swells hit the islands with full force, unhindered by a continental shelf to slow them down. Again, not a place for beginners.

Localism

Unfortunately, when discussing surfing in the Canaries the subject of localism always comes up. There have been some very unsavoury incidents over the years and everyone knows someone with a story to tell. The locals maintain that if you surf respectfully, you will have no problems. Avoiding certain breaks at peak times will minimize the risks and many surfers who visit report no problems. On Lanzarote, the locals now only allow certain visitors to surf the two main breaks at La Santa. "If you respect, you won´t have problem with locals, but don´t try to surf in La Santa left or El Quemao if you don't wanna have problems," says José Gonzáles, editor of *Radical Surf* magazine based in the Canaries.

An influx of non-local surfers is frustrating, but it is not a problem unique to the Canaries. It is frustrating for locals who work long hours, wait for the good swells to kick in and then find the breaks crowded with tourists. However, this situation occurs at breaks all over the world every day. Many of the surfers who go to the Canaries on holiday have the same problem at their home breaks without resorting to violence. This is why the rules and etiquette of surfing evolved. If a visiting surfer comes to a break, surfs respectfully, doesn't drop in or take more than their share of the waves, there should be no problems. It is therefore disturbing when respectful surfers, in small groups, are verbally and physically attacked with no provocation. It is also disturbing when surf spots become no-go zones for non-locals. After all, what is the difference between El Quemao and breaks like Bundoran, Coxos, Porthleven or Graviere?

Top local surfers Jonathan González and Adelina Taylor have both made big impressions on the international stage. According to José González, editor of *Surf Radical*, other top riders include **Lenny Perdomo, Franito** and **José María Cabrera** on Lanzarote and **José Casillas** (Pecas), **David Hernández** and **Sonnia** on Fuerte.

Getting around

To get to the breaks on Lanzarote and Fuerte you will definitely need a hire car, preferably a 4WD if you intend surfing the more out of the way spots. The main roads are pretty good, but the dirt tracks, including Fuerteventura's infamous North Track, can be very poor. Make sure you fill up with gas and take all the provisions you need for a full day on the road.

THE GILL

25 A local going loco at Los Lobos ▸▸ *p272*

Breaks

Lanzarote

1 El Quemao

- **Break type**: Left-hand reef.
- **Conditions**: Big westerly swells, offshore in southeasterly winds.
- **Hazards/tips**: Crowds, localism, heavy wave, shallow, experts only.
- **Sleeping**: La Santa » p273.

Considered to be the Pipeline of the Canaries, this is the wave that showcased the surf in Lanzarote to a worldwide audience. Comes to life in big swells, with westerly swells being from the optimum direction. Heavy, hollow fast lefts reel along the sharp, unforgiving reef, but there are also occasional very fast, very hollow rights. This is also one of the most localized waves in Europe and there have been violent incidents here. The waves break out in front of the village of La Santa with the harbour providing a good vantage point.

2 The Slab/La Santa

- **Break type**: A-frame reef.
- **Conditions**: All swells, offshore in easterly winds.
- **Hazards/tips**: Heavy, shallow, powerful, heavy localism.
- **Sleeping**: La Santa » p273.

Visible from the road, this is a heavy, thick A-frame offering serious barrels. Definitely a wave for experienced surfers. Not surfable at

> ❝❞
>
> **Lanzarote has a volcanic heart, which means the island is alive. If you bother to look past the reputation you will find something very special.**
>
> *George Sohl, surf photographer*

low tide but good from mid to high. If you choose to surf here, best to ride here alone as it is considered by the area's surfers to be a 'locals only' wave, probably the most localized on the island. Best to park away from the break as cars have been vandalized.

3 La Santa Right/Morro Negro

- **Break type**: Right-hand reef point.
- **Conditions**: All swells, offshore in southeasterly winds.
- **Hazards/tips**: Heavy wave when big, tricky entry.
- **Sleeping**: La Santa » p273.

This is an excellent, long right-hand point/reef that works through all tides and is offshore in southeasterly winds. More of a long, walling wave than a hollow one, but in bigger swells it can really fire with the three sections joining up to form one huge wave.

THE GILL

1 El Quemao

THE GILL

7 San Juan

One of the island's best known waves. Jump off the rocks to get into the line-up or take the safer option of the long paddle round. Not as localized as El Quemao so surf with respect and you should have no problems. A serious wave in big swells – surfers have drowned here in the past.

4 Boca del Abajo/Complex Left

- **Break type**: Left-hand reef.
- **Conditions**: All swells, offshore in southerly winds.
- **Hazards/tips**: Heavy wave.
- **Sleeping**: La Santa » *p273*.

Found on La Isleta by La Santa's sports complex, this is another awesome, high quality left reef that breaks into a sheltered bay. It can hold a big swell, when it becomes a huge barrelling impression of Padang Padang in. Used to be pretty quiet but is now more localized and busy. Pictures of Tom Curren charging here were seen in surf mags worldwide.

5 Caleta de Caballo/ Chicken Left

- **Break type**: Reef break.
- **Conditions**: Medium swells, offshore in southwesterly swells.
- **Hazards/tips**: Crowds, sharp reef.
- **Sleeping**: La Santa/Famara » *p273*.

This is a pleasant spot close to La Santa that breaks left and right, nestled in the western end of the bay. The left point breaks over a rocky reef and works up to 6 ft. It does get crowded, especially at peak times, as it is a less intense, less 'performance' wave. The right can be fast and hollow. Likes north swells.

6 Ghost Town

- **Break type**: Right reef.
- **Conditions**: Medium to big swells, offshore in southerly winds.
- **Hazards/tips**: Heavy reef.
- **Sleeping**: La Santa/Famara » *p273*.

On its day, this reef does a thundering imitation of Backdoor or Off The Wall. Can break between 4-10 ft over a rocky reef. Again, it can get pretty crowded when working.

7 San Juan

- **Break type**: Left reef.
- **Conditions**: All swells, offshore in southerly winds.
- **Hazards/tips**: Shallow, heavy, crowded.
- **Sleeping**: La Santa/Famara » *p273*.

This is a quality left reef with long, hollow waves breaking over a huge slab reef that is urchin encrusted. Consequently this makes this wave one for the experts only. The inside section gets shallower as the tide drops, going dry at low, but the outside is still surfable. Not a good place to get caught inside in a decent sized swell. This can be a localized break and has parking in front. The venue of the La Santa Sport 4 star WQS surf contest.

THE GILL

8 La Caleta de Famara/Harbour Left

8 La Caleta de Famara/ Harbour Left

- **Break type**: Left-hand point reef.
- **Conditions**: Big westerly swells, offshore in southerly winds.
- **Hazards/tips**: Crowds when good.
- **Sleeping**: La Caleta de Famara ›› *p273*.

Harbour Left doesn't break that often but when it does it reels off long, good quality lefts. Works best in a big westerly swell where it wraps along the reef and is best surfed at high tide. As the tide drops, areas of the wave section and dry out. A crowded wave when it's good.

9 Playa de Famara

- **Break type**: Beach break.
- **Conditions**: All swells, offshore in southerly/southeasterly winds.
- **Hazards/tips**: Safe at southern end.
- **Sleeping**: La Caleta de Famara ›› *p273*.

The south end of the beach is a safe area of crystal-clear waves popular with the island's surf schools. Works on all tides. Further north the beach picks up much more swell and can have good peaks. Probably the only place you are guaranteed to have no localism issues.

10 El Corral, El Basurero and Yellow Mountain (Graciosa)

- **Break type**: Lefts and rights.
- **Conditions**: All swells, offshore in southerly winds.
- **Hazards/tips**: Localism.
- **Sleeping**: Isla Graciosa ›› *p274*.

Once a deserted idyll, this island off the northwest coast of Lanzarote is home to some excellent surf and has great potential. The main breaks – **El Corral**, a long perfect left, **El Basurero**, a thumping right-hander, and **Yellow Mountain**, with its pipe-like barrels – are now popular spots. Localism can be a problem here.

11 Playa de la Cantería/ Orzola Beach

- **Break type**: Beach break.
- **Conditions**: Medium swells, offshore in southwesterly winds.
- **Hazards/tips**: Quiet beach.
- **Sleeping**: La Caleta de Famara ›› *p274*.

A beautiful beach in a stunning location that has some great waves from mid to high tide. There are lefts at the western end, rights at the eastern end, and peaks in the middle section of the beach, all of which are usually pretty quiet.

12 Caleta del Mero/Spiders

- **Break type**: A-frame reef.
- **Conditions**: Big swell, offshore in westerly/southwesterly winds.
- **Hazards/tips**: Sharp reef, tricky entry/exit.
- **Sleeping**: Puerto del Carmen ›› *p274*.

This is an A-frame peak breaking over a

9 Playa de Famara

12 Caleta del Mero/Spiders

13 Jameos del Agua ›› *p270*

jagged lava reef. There is a sucky take-off into grinding lefts and fast hollow right. Works best at mid tide. The rock in this area is very sharp fingers of lava (like a spider's legs), which is hard to walk on and makes entry and exit a bit tricky.

13 Jameos del Agua

- 🌀 **Break type**: Reef break.
- 🌊 **Conditions**: Big swells, offshore in westerly/southwesterly winds.
- ❶ **Hazards/tips**: Rocky reef with urchins.
- 🛏 **Sleeping**: Puerto del Carmen ▸▸ p274.

In the heart of the Malpaís de la Corona – literally 'bad lands' – the waves here break over urchin-infested fingers of solidified lava. There is a big outside left that picks up loads of north swell, an inside left point that works at mid to high tide, and a short, fast right. Crowded at times.

Fuerteventura

14 Playa de El Cotillo

- 🌀 **Break type**: Beach break.
- 🌊 **Conditions**: All swells, offshore in easterly winds.
- ❶ **Hazards/tips**: Heavy waves when big, crowds.
- 🛏 **Sleeping**: El Cotillo ▸▸ p274.

Excellent waves can break on this sandy beach to the south of the village of Cotillo on the western shore of the island. Waves here are pretty powerful and pretty hollow as they come out of deep water, producing some long barrels. Picks up plenty of swell and can still work in a northeasterly wind that blows out the north shore. As with many spots, can get crowded.

15 Las Lagunas/Spew Pits

- 🌀 **Break type**: Shallow lava reef with left or rights.
- 🌊 **Conditions**: All swells, offshore in easterly wind.
- ❶ **Hazards/tips**: Very shallow reef, advanced surfers only, crowds.
- 🛏 **Sleeping**: El Cotillo ▸▸ p274.

This is a sucking, dredging hollow barrel with a difficult take-off and very unforgiving reef. As if that wasn't enough, it can also get very crowded with local surfers and bodyboarders. It does, however, produce some sick waves with hollow lefts or rights on offer, depending on the swell direction. Look for the break just north of Cotillo.

16 Derecha de los Alemanes

- 🌀 **Break type**: Right-hand reef.
- 🌊 **Conditions**: All swells, offshore in south/southwesterly winds.
- ❶ **Hazards/tips**: Crowds, sharp reef, localism.
- 🛏 **Sleeping**: El Cotillo/Corralejo ▸▸ p274.

A hollow right wave breaking over a lava reef. It picks up plenty of swell and works through the tides. Follow the track along the north shore past the Bubble. As this spot takes longer to reach and is further out of the way, it is usually less crowded than other breaks. Gets its name from the fact that it is popular with German surf camps.

THE GILL

14 Playa de El Cotillo

ALEX WILLIAMS

15 Las Lagunas/Spew Pits

17 Hierro Left

- ◉ **Break type**: Left-hand reef.
- ◎ **Conditions**: Small to medium swells, offshore in southerly winds.
- ❶ **Hazards/tips**: Crowds.
- ◉ **Sleeping**: Corralejo » *p274*.

Sometimes just known as Hierro, this spot is a walling left-hander that works well in small and medium swells. A fun wave that's not as intense as many on the north shore, so can get crowded. Along with los Alemanes, Hierro is a gentle introduction to the reefs of the Canaries.

18 Hierro Right/The Bubble

- ◉ **Break type**: Reef break with rights and lefts.
- ◎ **Conditions**: All swells, offshore in southerly winds.
- ❶ **Hazards/tips**: Crowds, sharp reef, board breaker.
- ◉ **Sleeping**: El Cotillo/Corralejo » *p274*.

The Bubble is one of the best known waves on the island, attracting many visiting surfers and locals. At its best, this wave is a picture-perfect A-frame with a fast hollow right and less intense left. Waves come out of deep water and hit the reef with a lot of power. The small take-off zone doesn't help the crowding problems, which are worse at mid to high tide – the safest time to surf as there is more water covering the reef. Follow the road west from Majanicho.

ALEX WILLIAMS

The Bubble is one of the best known waves on the island, attracting many visiting surfers and locals

THE GILL

Spain Canary Islands Breaks Hierro

17 Hierro Left

18 Hierro Right/The Bubble

19 Majanicho

- **Break type**: Reef breaks
- **Conditions**: All swells, offshore in southerly winds
- **Hazards/tips**: Sharp reef, crowds
- **Sleeping**: Corralejo ›› *p274*.

The little fishing village of Majanicho lies at the end of the pitted North Track. Head out of town on the eastern side and you'll find this

THE GILL

25 Los Lobos

THE GILL

24 Punta Elena/Rocky Point

long, right-hand reef. Produces nice walling waves at high and gets hollower and less forgiving as the tide drops. There is also a big outside left reef point.

20 El Mejillón

- **Break type**: Reefs with lefts and rights.
- **Conditions**: Medium to big swells, offshore in southerly winds.
- **Hazards/tips**: Heavy hold-downs.
- **Sleeping**: Corralejo ›› *p274*.

Shifty lefts and rights that really come alive when bigger swells kick in. Not for the inexperienced as the hold-downs can be long, the waves heavy and there's a lot of water moving around. Picks up a lot of swell.

21 El Generoso

- **Break type**: Left reef.
- **Conditions**: All swells, offshore in southerly winds.
- **Hazards/tips**: Rocky.
- **Sleeping**: Corralejo ›› *p274*.

A great, long, walling left that really comes alive when the swells hit. There is also a short right off the peak at high tide, heading towards the rocks. A less intense wave with a less intense vibe.

22 Bristol/Shooting Gallery

- **Break type**: Left reef.
- **Conditions**: All swells, offshore in southwesterly winds.
- **Hazards/tips**: Crowds.
- **Sleeping**: Corralejo ›› *p274*.

A long, left-hand reef break that really attracts the crowds when it's on. At low it is intense with barrel sections, at high it is more forgiving with long walls. Popular with local surfers.

23 El Muelle/Harbour Wall

- **Break type**: Left reef.
- **Conditions**: All swells, offshore in southwesterly winds.
- **Hazards/tips**: Crowds.
- **Sleeping**: Corralejo ›› *p274*.

This fast, hollow, shallow left-hander breaks by the harbour wall in Corralejo and due to its easy access is always very popular. It will break in a huge range of swells, up to 10 ft. Hollower at low, more walling at high, there will always be a crowd here.

24 Punta Elena/Rocky Point

- **Break type**: Reef with lefts and rights.
- **Conditions**: Medium to big swells, offshore in south/southwesterly winds.
- **Hazards/tips**: Crowds.
- **Sleeping**: Corralejo ›› *p274*.

This spot has fast and hollow rights that tend always to draw a crowd. Gets crowded when big swells hit the north shore as it needs a decent swell to get going. Head southwest from Corralejo to Punta Elena.

25 Los Lobos

- **Break type**: Right point.
- **Conditions**: All swells, offshore in southeasterly winds.
- **Hazards/tips**: Breaks on offshore island.
- **Sleeping**: Los Lobos ›› *p275*.

Awesome, long, right-hand point break that can produce waves up to 300-m long in ideal conditions. Northerly or northwesterly swells peel down the western side of this offshore island, producing walling waves with hollow sections. In big swells the waves become much more powerful and hollow. Access to the island is via a ferry from Corralejo which leaves daily at 1000 to make the 2-km crossing and returns at 1600.

Lanzarote

Named after the Genoese sailor Lancelotto Malocello who landed here in the 1300s, Lanzarote is the most easterly of the main islands and, despite its arid landscape, is home to a UNESCO biosphere reserve, see page 205.

✪ Flat spells

Casino Flashing lights, gaming machines, coinage – it's all here at **Casino de Lanzarote**, on Puerto del Carmen's Av de las Playas.

Cesar Manrique This artist has taken some of the island's most awesome, natural phenomena and 'enhanced' them, reflecting 'man's harmonious actions on nature'. They are pricey but worth exploring, including **Jameos del Agua**, T928-848020, a gallery of caves shaped by lava tubes more than 3,000 years ago, and the nearby **Cueva de los Verdes**, T928-848484, a lava tunnel complex now also used as a concert venue.

Offering great views over to Isla Graciosa the **Mirador del Río**, perched on a cliff edge is definitely worth experiencing.

Fishing There are plenty of deep sea fishing charters on the island including **Ana Segundo**, based in Puerto del Carmen on C Teide, T928-513736.

Go-karting Head to **Gran Karting Club Lanzarote**, just to the west of the airport, T619-759946, where you can hit 80 kph.

THE GILL

2 La Santa, Lanzarote ▶ p267

Golf Get a round in at the 18-hole **Golf Costa Teguise**, T928-590512, www.lanzarote-golf.com.

Horse riding **Lanzarote a Caballo**, on the Arrecife-Yaiza road, T928-830314, www.alturin.com, offer treks from €25 and, bizarrely, paintballing.

Montañas del Fuego Visit the island's volcanic heart in the centre of the 50 sq km lava-encrusted Parque Nacional Timanfaya.

Yoga If you need to unwind, try one of the **Yoga Lanzarote** classes held in Costa Teguise and Playa Blanca from €10 a session, T928-843360.

La Santa

La Santa, on the north shore, is a small village with 2 surf shops on the high street, **Sefon Surf Shop** and **Sense Surf Shop**. Sefon offers hardware and clothing, ding repair and has a shaper in house. Grab a bite to eat at **Riminis Italian Restaurant**, on the main street, offering reasonably priced pizzas and pasta.

Caleta de Famara

Famara is a small fishing village flanked by a cliff of the same name and a 3-km stretch of beach.

🛏 Sleeping

E **Playa Famara Bungalows**, T928-591617, are a groovy looking selection of 1970s style bungalows ranging in price and size for 2-6 people.

F **Famara Surf Shop**, info@famarasurf.com, can organize basic but clean accommodation for up to 3 people within walking distance of the nearby breaks.

🍴 Eating/drinking

Casa García Restaurant, close to the beach opposite Famara Surf Shop, is a relaxed spot offering tapas and Spanish/Italian food.

Restaurant Casa Ramón, is a more formal and expensive option a few doors down on Av El Marinero but it does have excellent seafood.

Shopping

There are a couple of surf shops here. **Famara Surf Shop**, on the main Av El Marinero, is a small and friendly shop selling clothing and hardware as well as dealing with board rental. **Lennys** stock all the usual kit and offer **internet** access.

Isla Graciosa

Separated from Lanzarote by the straits of El Río, Graciosa is a quiet island with limited facilities. The **Lineas Marítimas Romero** ferry runs a service 3 times a day between Orzola, on the northern coast of Lanzarote, to Caleta del Sebo – the focus of island life. It takes about 20 mins and costs about €12, T928-842070.

Sleeping

There are a couple of *pensiones* in Caleta de Sebo including F **Pensión Girasol**, T928-842101, right on the seafront. **Camping El Salao**, T928-842000, is pretty basic.

Puerto del Carmen

About 30 mins' drive from the north shore breaks, this is the main tourist development on the island, with wall-to-wall cooked English breakfasts, so it has the most to offer in terms of nightlife and tourist accommodation.

Sleeping

Most of the accommodation in town is monopolized by the tour operators. D **Pensión Magec**, C Hierro, T928-513874, is clean and comfortable.

Eating/drinking

The bars really get going around 2300. Check out Av de las Playas for most of the bars, clubs and the casino. **Hawaii Bar** is on the main road at the north end of town. It plays funky tunes, has friendly staff and DJs at the weekend. **San Miguel Bar** is situated in the old town and is a smart bar serving food with good music and a big screen to boot.

Directory

Bike hire: Renner Bikes in Centro Comercial Marítimo. **Internet**: get on line at **Cyber Jable** on C Bernegal. **Post office**: C Guardilama. **Surf shops**: El Niño and **Blue Planet** on the main drag. **Tourist information**: Av de las Playas.

Fuerteventura

Fuerteventura, named after the 'fuerte' (strong) 'viento' (wind), certainly lives up to its name, especially in the summer months when the island becomes overrun by windsurfers. The beaches of this arid island are littered with circular stone shelters, which offer some protection from the relentless onslaught.

Flat spells

Biking The barren landscape makes this ideal terrain for a bit of off-roading. Get some pedal power at **Vulcano Bikes** on C Acorazado España in Corralejo.
Diving There are a couple of dive centres dotted along the island including **Dive Centre Corralejo**, on C Nuestra Señora del Pino, T928-535906. **Golf** Get a round in at the **Fuerteventura GC** at Caleta de Fuste, just south of the airport, T928-163461.
Lucha Canaria Catch men in leotards wrestling 'Canaries style' in one of the *Terreros* (wrestling rings) across the island. Check out www.federationluchacanaria.com for listings or call Terrero de Lucha in Puerto del Rosario, T928-851104.
Mirador Morro Velasco Just off the FV30, this vantage point serves up weird and wonderful views across this lunar landscape.

El Cotillo

This sleepy little village on the northwest coast is home to the **Onit Surf Shop** on C 3 Abril 1979. As well as offering all the usual surf shop facilities, they hire bikes, run a book swap, have clothes washing facilities as well as internet access for around

€0.10/min. There are a couple of sleeping options here including the chilled out E **La Gaviota**, T928-538567.

Corralejo

Corralejo was a small fishing village but is now a resort town full of bars, facilities and Brits abroad. South of the town the sand dunes of the protected Parque Natural de las Dunas stretch out like a mini Sahara towards Puerto del Rosario.

Sleeping

If you're not on a package holiday it can be hard trying to find affordable accommodation in the town. D-E **Hotel Corralejo**, on the seafront at C la Marina, with beach views, T928-535246. D-E **Hostal Manhattan**, on C Gravina. E-F **Hostal Sol Y Mar**, just behind C Milagrosa, is the cheapest place to stay on the island and has room for boards as well as a communal kitchen and lounge. Popular with kiteborders. *Radical Surf* magazine, T928-535877, reservas@radicalsurfmag.com, have a couple of basic apartments to let. **Apartamento Guarda Mar** sleeps up to 4 (1 room) while **Apartments San Rafael** can squeeze in up to 6 bodies.

Eating/drinking

The main Av General Franco is littered with large pubs, bars, clubs and eateries including **Festers**, where you can get your dose of sports and footy on the big screens, **Corky's Surf Bar**, which screens surf flicks, and reasonably priced grill house **Parilla Poco Loco**. Just off the main drag on C Iglesia. **Blue Rock** has live bands playing regularly.

Shopping

Los Corales supermarket on C General Franco has all the basics. **Surf shop**s are pretty thick on the ground on Av General Franco with **No Work Team International**, **Deportes Chacón**, **Matador**, **Kalvan**, **Sixties Surf Shop** and **Local Wave**. There are also **Home Grown**, on R Jose Segura Torres and **Puro Nectar**, on R Juan de Tustria.

Directory
Banks/ATMs: C General Franco. **Internet**: get on line at the **Orange Projekt** on C General Franco. **Pharmacy**: on the main C General Franco and Primero de Mayo. **Post office**: C Lepanto. **Tourist information**: Plaza Grande de Corralejo.

Los Lobos

This tiny island, which takes about 2½ hrs to walk around, lies in the El Río Strait between Lanzarote and Fuerteventura and is named after the seals that used to frequent these shores. A couple of daily ferry services run to the island from Corralejo port including the glass-bottomed **El Majorero** (around €10 return). There are few facilities on the island but there is a good *chiringuito* serving reasonably priced fresh fish. If you want to camp, you'll need to get a permit from the Oficina del Medio Ambiente in Puerto del Rosario (see below).

Puerto del Rosario

Sleeping
Close to the airport, this port town is the island's capital. There's not a lot going for it but it does have a couple of affordable sleeping options close to the waterfront, handy if you've just flown in and haven't booked ahead, including **E Hostal Tamasite**, on C Leon y Castillo, T928-850280.

Eating
You could grab a pizza at the nearby **Pizzeria El Patio**.

Directory
Airport: C B Matorral, T928-860600. **Pharmacy**: Primero de Mayo. **Police**: C Herbania. **Post office**: Primero de Mayo. **Tourist information**: Av de la Constitución.

Peniche warm-up session
▶▶ *p298*

DEMI TAYLOR

Portugal

Atlantic Ocean

p286

MINHO

Viana do Castelo

Braga

Guimaraes

TRAS OS MONTES

Bragança

Póvoa de Varzim

Porto

DOURO

Villa Real

p287

BEIRA LITORAL

BEIRA ALTA

Aveiro

Viseu

Guarda

p287

Figueira da Foz

Coimbra

Covilhã

★1

Leiria

BEIRA BAIXA

Nazaré

Batalha

Fátima

Castelo Branco

p296

Peniche

★2

ESTREMADURA

RIBATEJO

★3

Ericeira

★4

Portalegra

p307

Estoril

Lisbon

★5

Elvas

SPAIN

Setúbal

Évora

ALENTEJO

Sines

Beja

p316

Lagos

Portimáo

ALGARVE

Sagres

Faro

Golfo de Cádiz

N

30 km
30 miles

Motorway
A Rd
B Rd
Minor Rd
✈ Main Airports
⛴ Main Ferry Routes

Star breaks...

★1 **Supertubos** Heavy, fast, heavy, hollow and heavy. In a big swell it does as good an impression of Pipeline as you'll see in Europe, but don't think the sand bottom is any less painful than a reef ➤➤ *p299.*

★2 **Coxos** Awesome and heavy wave with long barrels and equally long hold-downs. This right-hand reef break sees waves come out of deep water onto a shallow point ➤➤ *p301.*

★3 **Ribeira d'Ilhas** Very popular beach/point set-up that can have long, walling right-handers and an easy paddle out. Venue for world tour event ➤➤ *p302.*

★4 **Pedra Branca** Sitting near the heart of Ericeira, this is a goofy footer's dream. Hollow and shallow, a true barrel fest ➤➤ *p303.*

★5 **Carcavelos** Supertubos look-a-like at the heart of the Lisbon surfing scene ➤➤ *p311.*

Portugal is a classic late developer. Travelling through vibrant, modern Portugal today, it is hard to believe that until the mid-1970s the country was stagnating under a military dictatorship. Until the revolution of 25 April 1974, Peniche – now famous the world over for its barrelling beach break – was better known for its political prison, a walled fortress with a bird's-eye view of Supertubos. Lisbon is today a city of culture, from the traditional fado of Bairro Alto to hip young designers. Away from the capital, Central Portugal can be a harsh environment, arid and hot, with landscapes dominated by rusty earth and brown-green leaves. It is on the coastal fringes that the country really comes to life with a riot of spring flowers, bustling coastal communities in whitewashed villages and golden, sandy beaches fringed by crystal-blue waters.

In surfing terms, Portugal has caught up with her European cousins at lightning speed. Now she has a surf community as committed as any, and waves of world renown. Guys like Ruben Gonzales, Miguel Fortes and Tiago Pires charging waves like Supertubos, Coxos and Carcavelos feature in magazines across the continent. But the best thing about Portuguese surf culture is that local surfers will still take travellers at face value. While you probably won't be welcomed with open arms, if you are friendly and respectful you will find that Portuguese surfers are among the most hospitable and stoked in the whole of Europe.

Best time to visit: **West coast** - autumn. Great waves and warm weather. **Algarve** - autumn/winter. Constant swell and constant sunshine.

Portugal Rating

Surf
★★★★

Cost of living
★★

Nightlife
★★★

Accommodation
★★

Places to visit
★★★

Essentials

Position

The westernmost country in continental Europe, Portugal is bound by the Atlantic ocean on the south and west coast and shares borders with Spain on its northern and eastern flanks.

Language

Portuguese is the language of the country and although about half the population have a working knowledge of English (films are often shown in English with Portuguese subtitles) efforts to speak the local language are greatly appreciated. Spoken by about 190 million people worldwide, Portuguese is also useful for trips to Brazil, Angola and Mozambique among others.

Crime/safety

As with many urban areas in Europe, pickpockets and petty criminals are the main problems in Portugal's city centres. It pays to be careful and to avoid gangs of kids in Porto and Lisbon after hours, especially around the Bairro Alto and Alfama districts. If you do have any problems head for the **Policia de Seguranca Publica** (PSP) in the cities, clad in smart blue uniforms, or the **Guarda Nacional Republicana** (GNR) in smaller towns. Generally their English is limited/not forthcoming and they demand respect. While possession of small amounts of drugs for personal use has been decriminalized, do not light up in public areas unless you want to spend your holiday money on a hefty fine.

Health

EU residents need a stamped E-111 from their home country to certify that they are entitled to free (or reduced cost) healthcare. Chemists or *farmacias* can advise on minor matters and sell many prescription drugs, including antibiotics, over the counter. Large towns will have at least one pharmacy open 24 hours.

Opening hours

As with Spain, lunch is king, reflected in the opening hours which are generally 0900-1300 and 1500-1900 Monday to Friday, shutting up shop for the weekend at 1300 Saturday. Banks follow their own schedule opening 0830-1500 Monday-Friday. If it's flat on a Monday it could be dull as most museums and monuments will be closed.

Sleeping

Portugal has a good range of accommodation – *o alojamento* – to suit any budget and operates on similar principles to neighbouring Spain. *Pousadas* are high-end, government-run establishments, usually a former castle or palace and not really suited to most surfers' needs or budgets, www.pousadas.pt. Still at the premium end of the scale,

5 best trips

① **Lisbon** Grab a ride on a tram from the docks and take in the view from the top of an Elevador ▸▸ *p314*.

② **Sintra** Crazy, chocolate-box town – like a Moorish theme park designed by Michael Jackson ▸▸ *p313*.

③ **Estoril** Take in the Portuguese Grand Prix at the world-famous circuit ▸▸ *p314*.

④ **Obidos** Picturesque, walled, hill-top village just half an hour from Peniche ▸▸ *p305*.

⑤ **Lagos** Great food, great bars, great weather and great atmosphere ▸▸ *p327*.

Elevador in Lisbon

hotels – graded 1-4 stars – can break the bank in the height of the summer but are worth checking out off season when rates can drop considerably. The most popular choices are the *pensão* or *residencial* which offers affordable **B&B** style accommodation randomly graded 1-3 stars. You'll usually be shown the most expensive room first – normally with an en suite bathroom – but cheaper options may be available with just a sink in the room or a shared bathroom down the hall. Slightly cheaper are *hospedarias* (boarding houses) or *quartos/dormidas*, a room in a private house, usually advertised in the window. There are a limited number of *pousadas de juventude* (**youth hostels**) dotted around Portugal, for which you need a Hostelling International (HI) card. There tends to be a curfew, and when compared with the cost of a double in a *pensão* they are not usually the cheapest choice. There are plenty of cheap *parque de campismo* (**campsites**) across Portugal. Although some do close off season, you can usually find a municipal or state-run site open year round – these are always a cheap option. Responsible **free-camping** away from tourist spots (and 1 km away from official campsites) is legal except in the Algarve where it has been banned.

Eating and drinking

If coffee and a roll is your idea of a great breakfast then you'll be in heaven in Portugal. If you're after more of a sugar rush, head to a *pastelaria* (cake shop) for a *pasteis de nata* or a custard tart. Lunch – massive portions, high on carbs and protein, low on vegetables – is usually taken between 1230 and 1500, with the *pratos do dia* (dish of

Fact file

→ **Currency** Euro (€)
Capital city Lisbon
Time zone GMT
Length of coastline 830km
Religion Roman catholic
Emergency numbers
  Police 115/112
Electricity 220v continental
  dual pin

the day) usually the cheapest option around €5. Snack bars have a selection of *pratos combinados* – filling and basic 'with chips' dishes. Dinner is an earlier affair than in Spain with restaurants serving between 1900 and 2200. If you are going to eat out then opt for the **fish**, which will usually be excellent and fantastic value – Portugal is a nation of fishermen. *Sardinhas assadas* (grilled sardines) is one of the most popular and cost-effective dishes. The **meat** can be more of a lottery with some dishes such as *papas de sarrabulho* (a bizarre blood and bread combo) not being the type of meal you want to order accidentally. *Churrasqueira/churrascaria* (grill houses) are the showcase and most towns have them. Post surf, order half or quarter of a *frango assado* (roast chicken) served with rice and/or chips with a beer or a coke for about €4 and you won't be disappointed.

Where drinking is concerned, there are two main brands of beer, Superbock and Sagres, which are cheap and strong. In terms of wine, you can't leave Portugal without trying the **port** – a fortified wine hailing from the Douro valley, which lies inland from the city of Porto, giving the drink its name. But if you want to put hairs on your chest, ask for a glass of the local *aguardente* or firewater!

Festivals/events

Portugal has its fair share of *festas*, *feiras* and *romarios* – festivals, fairs and religious events – throughout the year. And, as well as the usual public holidays, Portugal also celebrates its freedom with Liberty Day on 25 April – the anniversary of the 1974 people's revolution against the dictator Salazar – and Independence Day on 1 December, relating to the restored independence from Spain in 1640.

Getting there

Air Portugal has three main airports – Porto to the north, Faro on the south coast and centrally based Lisbon. There are no direct flights from Australia, New Zealand or west coast America so journeys will need to be broken via another European destination, with the UK offering some of the cheapest options into Faro. **Ryanair**, www.ryanair.com, run weekend flights between Dublin and Faro. From France, **Air Portugal (TAP)** and **Air France** run daily flights between Paris and Lisbon or Porto and from Spain, **Portugalia**, www.pga.pt, **Spanair**, www.spanair.com, **TAP**, www.tap-airportugal.com, and **Lufthansa**, www.lufthansa.com, operate services between Madrid and Lisbon.
From UK: most of the budget airlines offer daily scheduled flights to Faro, making this the cheapest and easiest route into the country, especially if you can avoid peak summer, Easter and Christmas periods. Look at **easyJet**, www.easyjet.com, **Fly Be**, www.flybe.com,

Top tips

◉ I would advise visiting surfers to rent a car and to start from Peniche/Baleal and drive until Sagres, passing through Ericeira, Praia Grande, Guincho, Carcavelos and Arrifana. Portugal is a special place to surf because of the good waves we have and because it's a small country, it's easy and fast to go from one spot to another. Also the landscapes are pretty good and we have really good food and wines. *Rodrigo Bravo Pimento, Billabong Portugal*

◉ Go explore. Avoid the better known places or at least don't limit yourself to those. There are lots of other breaks to be surfed, if you have the time to look for them. *João da Câmara Valente, Editor Surf Portugal magazine*

◉ Enjoy it as much as possible because travelling and surfing is the best thing you can do. Travel as much as possible. You meet all kinds of people and it makes you appreciate home more. You see all kinds of things - good things, bad things, sometimes the best aspects, sometimes the worst, but it makes you realize where you are in the world and where you come from. *Tiago Pires, Portuguese pro surfer*

◉ As a traveller, the same as anywhere else on this planet, be pleasant and fair with others and 99% of the time you will enjoy and be enjoyed by others. Portuguese people in general are warm folks. The invasion of foreign surfers has taken its toll a bit on certain locations so there is a bit of bitterness these days. Do not travel in mobs and don't hog waves even if you are a better surfer. Keep an eye on your gear and your vehicle. *Nick Urrichio, Semente Surfboards*

and **Monarch**, www.flymonarch.com, who offer returns to Faro for £40-140, depending on availability and timing – and budget airlines do charge board carriage. **British Airways**, www.ba.com, and **TAP** are also worth looking at for direct flights to Lisbon and Porto.

Road There are plenty of routes leading from Spain into Portugal depending on how far along the coast you get. From Galicia, crossing near Valenca do Minho, the A3/E1 will lead you to Porto on toll roads. Alternatively, avoiding tolls, take the coastal N13 leading to the IC1 and Porto.

Train Train travel can be a fairly pricey way to get to Portugal (£225-300 for a London-Lisbon return taking around 24 hours on a clear run). The easiest route, using Paris as your main connection, is to take the **TGV Atlantique** to Irun/Hendaye, then catch the **SudExpress** to Lisbon or Porto.

Red tape Portugal is a Schengen state (see European Red Tape).

Getting around

Driving (right-hand side) A full driving licence or International Driving Permit is required plus adequate insurance and ownership papers. Thanks to generous EU funding, Portugal's road network is rapidly improving and expanding. There are, however, still plenty of dirt tracks to explore along the coast as well as substantial stretches of road on popular, main routes that are potholed and in serious need of maintenance and modernization. One of the worst is the notorious **coastal 'N' route** from the northern border of the Algarve to Sines. A more serious issue than the roads themselves is the drivers on them – Portugal has the highest rate of road accidents in Europe, which is no surprise when you've experienced overtaking à la Portuguese. If there's a blind bend in the road or you're on the crest of a hill, you can guarantee someone will want to pass you. If you're in a slow moving vehicle like a van, pull over towards the edge of the road and let them pass. Always give way to the right.

Motorway (*auto estrada*): running north to south, the A3/E1 covers almost the entire length of Portugal from the Spanish border near Valenca do Minho towards the Algarve, with offshoots running east towards the main border with Spain. The toll roads, or *portagem*, prefixed with an A, are fast and well built, but the €3-9 charges soon add up. **Speed limit 120 kph.**

Estrada Nacional: **N** or **EN** roads are improving but can often be slow, clogged with vehicles avoiding tolls and in need of resurfacing. **Speed limit 90 kph/50 kph urban areas.** Due to the high accident rate, speed limits are vigorously enforced and fines are readily doled out.

Other roads: quality varies wildly between dirt *piste* and very good – take your chances. **Speed limit 90 kph/50 kph urban areas.**

Car hire There are plenty of car rental companies operating here including all the big multinationals such as **Hertz**, www.hertz.com, and **Europcar**, www.europcar.com, who have offices in all the main towns and airports. Rental starts at about €400 for two weeks but usually you do need to be over 25. Hire cars are especially attractive propositions to thieves so be extra vigilant and try to remove obvious signs, stickers and logos.

Public transport

The public transport system in Portugal is fairly efficient, especially in the southern half of the country. The state-run **railway** Caminhos de Ferro Portugueses (CP) is the cheapest, if not always the quickest, option for long distance travel and will usually try to accommodate your board, www.cp.pt. Lisbon is serviced by the handy **metro**, www.metrolisboa.pt, from 0600-0100 daily. The **bus** services are fairly consistent, largely managed by **Rede Expressos**, www.rede-expressos.pt, and fairly affordable – about €15 from Lisbon to Porto or Faro. Board carriage however may be difficult, so if you do have to go public, try to stick to trains.

Key phrases

Key words/phrases

Yes	sim
No	não
Please	se faz favor/por favor
Thank you	obrigado/a
Sorry	desculpe
Hello	olá
Goodbye	adeus
Good	bom
Bad	mau
I don't understand	não percebo
I'd like…	queria…
Do you have…	tem…
How much is it?	quanta custa?
Where is…	onde é?
Mens	Homens
Ladies	Senhoras
Left	esquerda
Right	direita
Straight on	sempre en frente
Night	noite
Room	quarto
Pitch	lote
Shower	ducha
Toilet	lavabos/casa de banho
The bill	a conta
White coffee	café com leite
Beer	cerveja
Red wine	vinho tinto
White wine	vinho branco
Mineral water	agua mineral
(still/sparkling)	(sem/com gás)
Orange Juice	sumo de laranja
Sandwich	sandes
Ham	fiambre/presunto
Cheese	queijo
Toasted cheese/ham	tosta mista
Help!	socorro!
Beach	praia
Point	punta
River	rio
Wind	vento
Wave	onda
Board	prancha
Wax	cera
Tide	maré
High	alto
Low	baixo
Mid	meio
North	norte
South	sul
East	leste
West	oeste

Numbers

0	zero
1	um/uma
2	dois/duas
3	três
4	quatro
5	cinco
6	seis
7	sete
8	oito
9	nove
10	dez
11	onze
12	doze
13	treze
14	catorze
15	quinze
16	dezasseis
17	dezassete
18	dezoito
19	dezanove
20	vint
21	vint e um
22	vint e dois
30	trinta
40	quarenta
50	cinquenta
60	sessenta
70	setenta
80	oitenta
90	noventa
100	cem
200	duzentos
1000	mil

Days of the week

Monday	segunda-feira
Tuesday	terça-feira
Wednesday	quarta-feira
Thursday	quinta-feira
Friday	sexta-feira'
Saturday	sábado
Sunday	domingo

Surfing Portugal

"Surfing in Portugal is unique in its geographical set-up. If we look at the distance between, let's say, Carcavelos and Peniche with Ericeira in the middle, we are talking about 100 km. Depending on swell size and wind conditions you can pretty much find a place to surf on any wind direction and most swell directions without having to do a major drive. The coastline is beautiful and there are also a lot of mellow beaches from north to south." Nick Urrichio, Semente Surfboards

Portugal has always been one of the world's great seafaring nations and the coastal communities that fringe the rich waters of the Atlantic have an enduring and timeless bond with the ocean. Although the coastline has some of the best surfing geography in Europe, it took a little while for surfing to become firmly established in Portugal, with small communities springing up around Carcavelos, Peniche and Ericeira in the 1970s. Following a huge surge of interest in the 1990s, brands like Semente and Polen are now known worldwide and surfers like Tiago Pires are pushing hard for a place on the WCT. Today, Portugal is one of Europe's most popular surf destinations. Its combination of amazing reefs, consistent swells, unique culture and great climate has proved to be an irresistible draw to surfers from around the globe.

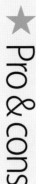

Pro & cons

Pros …
- ✔ Massive variety of breaks on offer in every region.
- ✔ Excellent quality reef breaks.
- ✔ Main breaks very busy but still plenty of scope to explore quiet spots.
- ✔ Warm, sunny winter climate and mild water temperatures.
- ✔ Good surf close to thriving Lisbon.
- ✔ Great climate.
- ✔ Fantastic food.
- ✔ Good nightlife in the cities.

… and cons
- ✘ Some localism around certain areas.
- ✘ Pollution in urban areas.
- ✘ Main breaks can be very busy.
- ✘ Getting more expensive as a destination.

Climate
Warm summer days with cool glassy waves, that is the classic Portuguese scenario. Typically Portugal has a dry sunny climate, but ocean currents conspire to keep the ocean temperatures at a refreshing level year round.

Best seasons to go
During the **summer** months Portugal is a wonderful place to be, with

THE GILL

Sunset at Cova Vapor on the Costa da Caparica ▶▶ *p312*

warm sun, cool seas and occasional swells coming from Atlantic low pressure systems pushing northwesterly swells onto the more exposed breaks. Beaches around Peniche, Guincho and Costa da Caparica are bustling with both holidaymakers and surfers alike and the heaving cafés and bars of Cascais and Ericeira are lively into the early hours of the morning.

Autumn is the best time to head for Portugal. The days are long, the temperatures are more than comfortable, and powerful swells regularly peel along the world-class reefs and beaches that abound along the huge coastline. It is during this season that streams of vans and campers descend upon the car parks and campsites of the central coastline from all across northern Europe and Spain. Line-ups become a collage of nationalities and locals seek out those secret breaks to escape the crowds.

In the north, late **winter** and **spring** brings chilly winds and rain as far south as Lisbon. This is a good time to check out the Estoril coast when the big swells wrap into the Lisbon coastline and the urban breaks like Carcavelos come alive. During these chilly months, a 4/3 wetsuit is essential to keep out the cold and a warm *café com leite* or white coffee is always welcome after a classic session. However, heading south, the Algarve is the sunniest corner of Europe and hence one of the continent's most popular holiday destinations. The fact that it still picks up loads of swell makes the southwest corner of Portugal an ideal winter escape.

Boards
Portugal has a wide variety of breaks so flexibiltiy is the name of the game. A staple would be a beach break board that works in everything from knee high to overhead. A back-up would be a semi-gun pin tail for when the points or hollow beaches fire.

Good charts for surf
Portuguese surfers scan the charts for two scenarios. In line with the rest of Europe, low pressures tracking across the north Atlantic will push swell south and onto the breaks and beaches with a northwesterly or westerly aspect. Many Portuguese breaks will also pick up southwesterly swells coming from low pressures out in the Atlantic to the south, especially those breaks along the southwest coastline and along the Algarve.

Geography and the breaks
The key word when it comes to the Portuguese coastline is variety. Although the north has some excellent beaches, the coastline south of Figuiera da Foz is an amazing patchwork of rocky reefs, interspersed with long sandy bays, cliffs, points and rivermouths. As João da Câmara Valente, Editor of *Surf Portugal* magazine, explains: "The uniqueness of surfing in Portugal is directly related to its geography. Although it is a somewhat small coast, it displays an enormous variety of breaks within very short areas. Point breaks, reef breaks, beach breaks, rivermouths, whatever – Portugal has it all. Sometimes I think

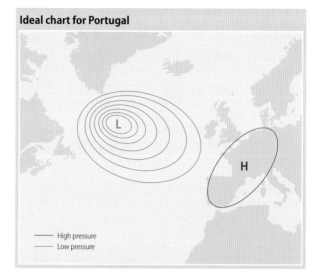

Ideal chart for Portugal

High pressure
Low pressure

DEMI TAYLOR

Windmills are a good way of gauging the weather

to myself how lucky we are that the whole Portuguese coast is not made of just an enormous beach break monotony. Also, for its

5 underground classics

1 **Canal das Barcas** Right-hand, rocky, point break next to a big offshore rock. Produces long, walling waves in good swells ▸▸ *p319*.

2 **Carrapateira** Excellent lefts peel in front of the headland, with powerful, hollow rights across the channel. Usually uncrowded - why? ▸▸ *p322*.

3 **Santa Cruz** Quality beach break hidden between Ericeira and Peniche ▸▸ *p300*.

4 **Buarcos** Big, right-hander at Figueira da Foz where rides of up to 200 m are possible. Catch it before the rest of the surfing world does ▸▸ *p292*.

5 **Cabedelo do Douro** Sleeping beauty found in the mouth of the River Douro. Needs flooding to build up the bank, then a big swell to fire. But when it does it can be a reverse Mundaka ▸▸ *p290*.

Buarcos ▸▸ *p292*

. . . one to remember

number of surfers, it's amazing how many spots remain uncrowded – once one decides to step away from the 'sheep-factor'. Surfing in the south can also be an inspiring experience for its wildness, being the most preserved stretch of coast in Europe."

Surfing and environment

Portugal has some of Europe's most wonderful and pristine coastal regions. Areas of the southwest and the Algarve explode with spring flowers and the crystal-clear waters are alive with dolphins and myriad seabirds. However, around major urban areas the picture is not quite so healthy. As with many spots in Europe, urban beaches can be badly polluted, and the ones around Porto and Lisbon are especially bad. Lisbon is a capital city and has all the usual pollution issues that other major urban areas face. Many local surfers strongly advise against surfing the city beaches in Porto, which can be grim in the extreme.

Localism and surf communities

Portugal is widely considered to have one of the friendliest surfing communities in Europe and is one of the rare places where surfers and bodyboarders happily coexist. While travelling surfers may not exactly be welcomed like a long lost brother, if you are respectful and friendly, local surfers have a tendency to respond in kind. "Break the locals' ice with a smile and a little talk," recommends João. "Even if they don't react immediately, they eventually will and you should be in for some great new friends and, who knows, easy access to some secluded spots." Remember that surfers have been coming to Portugal since the 1970s. Locals have been dropped in on and visiting vans have left litter and waste. It is understandable that you may have to prove you are here to share waves and not take waves. Sagres is one place in Portugal that has earned a reputation for random acts of localism and even violence. However, this has not put off visiting surfers. It may even have had the reverse effect in that many travellers now tend to go there in groups, while Sagres locals are facing hostility when they venture onto other breaks. Random localism and heavy handedness has never solved overcrowding issues.

Surf directory

Surf Portugal, founded in 1987, is one of the most established surf magazines in Europe.

Portugal: a brief surf history

1950s ➔ Portuguese surfers Pedro Lima and Antonio Jonet begin surfing in Costa de Caparica while to the north of the Rio Tejo, Paulo Inocentes begins surfing Carcavelos. **1976** ➔ US based *Surfer Magazine* runs images of awesome waves in Portugal bringing the surf potential of the country to the attention of the world stage. **1977** ➔ Portugal hosts its first international surfing contest in the waves of Peniche. **1979** ➔ Nick Urrichio and Antonio Perira Caldas create Portugal's first surfboards under the 'Lipsticks' label in Costa de Caparica. **1980** ➔ Aleeda in Costa de Caparica becomes Portugal's first surf shop. 1982 - Nick Urrichio and Miguel Katzenstein set up Semente Surfboards who today sponsor, among others, Tiago Pires. **1987** ➔ *Surf Portugal* magazine is established, reflecting the national growth of the sport. **1988** ➔ The Costa brothers and Fernando Horta set up Polen Surfboards who today sponsor, among others, top surfer Justin Mujica. **1994** ➔ The Surf Experience sets up camp in the Algarve. **1996** ➔ Portugal hosts and wins the Junior European Championships. **1997** ➔ Following on from the previous year's success, Portugal wins the Senior European Championships. **Today** ➔ Portugal has a thriving surf industry and a massive surf scene spanning the country. Tiago Pires is one of Europe's top three surfers. Following his impressive second placing in the 2000 Rip Curl Sunset Pro, Tiago has become a respected surfer world wide with a truly international reputation.

Northwest Portugal

Surfing northwest Portugal

The northwest coast of Portugal is a huge expanse of open coastline with amazing surf potential. While the focus of the surfing world has centred further to the south, local surfers have carried on enjoying the consistent swells and high quality waves of this region. Only Figueira da Foz, with its big right-hand point and world tour surfing event, has been in the limelight in this area.

Porto is the country's second city with a population of over 250,000 and a strong surfing community. The 'Port' in Portugal comes from this hardworking, northern city but this industrial workhorse also has a more attractive side. The historical district Ribeira, in the town centre, has been designated a World Heritage site. While the urban breaks are polluted – some of the most polluted in Europe and often closed by the government – they are still popular with the hardcore surfers and the rivermouth wakes periodically to produce a wave of mythical status and legendary quality.

Northwest Portugal board guide

Beach break board
Shaper: Nick Urrichio, Semente Surfboards

» 6'3" x 18⅞" x 2⅜"
» Choice of Semente team rider José Gregorio (Portuguese national Champion 2004) for day-to-day surfing.
» Bump wing squash tail full concave bottom and stand up loose rails through back.
» Rocker is very low in this board with nice release through the tail for vertical attacks.

Fish board
Shaper: Nick Urrichio, Semente Surfboards

» Helping to make the most of any small wave situation.
» Semente's 'big boy' (again José Gregorio) model is 6'0"x19½"x2½" swallow tail.
» Rolled vee up front with soft 50/50 rails, running into concave mid to double barrel concave between fins to a slight vee on release on tail.
» Rocker is very flat for speed and volume distributed for major paddling and wave catching ease.
» Rails are blocky with a hard bottom edge through the back to keep it loose.
» Smaller surfer's version: 5'10"x 18¾"x2¼".
» 'The wave magnet' has become a must for soul surfers and pros travelling through Europe in the summer months.

ⓘ Boards by **Semente Surfboards**
Factory: Rabo da Raposa, Ribamar, Ericeira, Portugal
T00 351 (0)261-863 552 www.semente.pt or contact semente@ip.pt

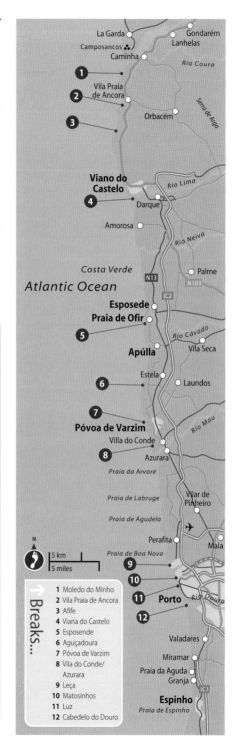

Breaks...

1 Moledo do Minho
2 Vila Praia de Ancora
3 Afife
4 Viana do Castelo
5 Esposende
6 Aguçadoura
7 Póvoa de Varzim
8 Vila do Conde/ Azurara
9 Leça
10 Matosinhos
11 Luz
12 Cabedelo do Douro

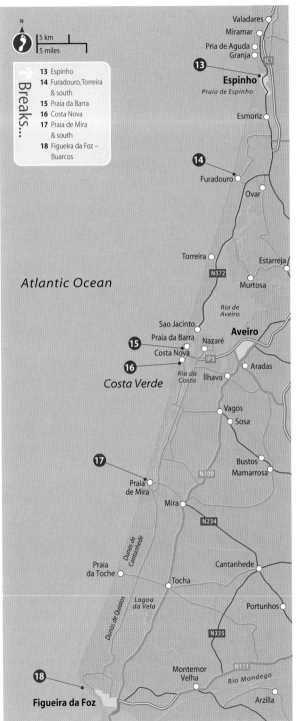

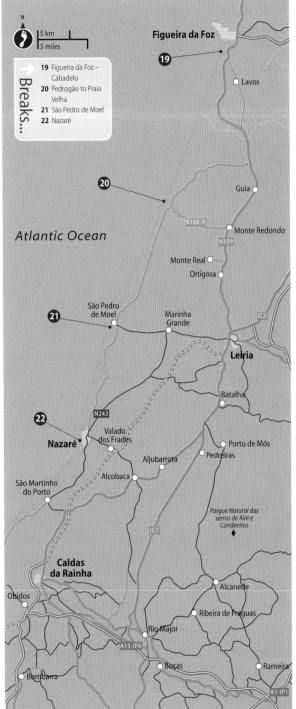

Portugal Northwest Surfing

Left map (images 1):

N
5 km
5 miles

Breaks...

13 Espinho
14 Furadouro, Torreira & south
15 Praia da Barra
16 Costa Nova
17 Praia de Mira & south
18 Figueira da Foz – Buarcos

Valadares
Miramar
Pria de Aguda
Granja
IC1

13 Espinho
Praia de Espinho

Esmoriz

14 Furadouro
Ovar

Atlantic Ocean

Torreira
N372
Estarreja
Murtosa

Ria de Aveiro

Sao Jacinto
Praia da Barra **15**
Nazaré
Aveiro
Costa Nova
IP5
16
Ria da Costa
Ílhavo
Aradas

Costa Verde

Vagos
Sosa

17
Bustos
Mamarrosa
N109
Praia de Mira
Mira
N234

Praia da Toche
Tocha
Cantanhede
Dunas de Cantanhede
Portunhos
Lagoa da Vela
Dunas de Quiaios
N335

18
Montemor Velha
N111
Rio Mondego
Arzilla

Figueira da Foz

Right map (images 2):

N
5 km
5 miles

Breaks...

19 Figueira da Foz – Cabadelo
20 Pedrogão to Praia Velha
21 São Pedro de Moel
22 Nazaré

Figueira da Foz
19

Lavos

20
Guia

Atlantic Ocean

N109-9
Monte Redondo
N109

Monte Real
Ortigosa

São Pedro de Moel
21
Marinha Grande
IC2

Leiria

Batalha

22
N242
Nazaré
Valado dos Frades
Porto de Mós
Aljubarrota
Pedreiras
Alcobaca

São Martinho do Porto

Parque Natural das serras de Aire e Candeeiros

IC2

Caldas da Rainha

Alcanede
Obidos
Ribeira de Fraguas

Rio Major
A15-IP6

Bombarra
Bocas
Rameira
A1-IP1

Coastline

The area to the north of Porto has been christened the **Costa Verde**, due to the green landscape. The coastal area is one long strip of beach, much backed by sand dunes. Areas of the dunes are cultivated and fertilized with seaweed to produce excellent crops. There are occasional rivermouths and resort villages, but many beaches are virtually empty outside the holiday month of August. **Porto** is an industrial city and the water around the rivermouth and urban beaches is very polluted. Heading south the sandy beaches continue on what is known as the **Costa de Prata**, the silver coast, until **Figueira da Foz**. These unspoilt stretches of beach break are again backed by dunes and pines, with spots like **Costa Nova** perfect for those wanting to escape the crowds.

Localism

While endless miles of this stretch of coastline are very quiet, the only real crowds will probably be centred around the breaks near Porto. Here there have been problems with car crime in the past, so make sure no valuables are left in the car or on show in the van.

Top local surfers   The northwest, with its combination of long, open beaches and competitive urban breaks, has a number of top surfers. **João Guedes** is an all-round competitive surfer, up-and-coming talent, **Abílio Pinto**, is a solid big rider, while **Nuno Figueiredo 'Strutura'** is the local tube master.

Getting around

From the northern border with Spain, the A3-E1 toll road runs south and inland to Porto, where the A1-E80 takes over – a good way to cover a large distance in little time. There are plenty of other more scenic routes, including the N13 hugging the coastline from the border south to Porto.

To live in the northern coast of Portugal feels like a privilege to me because we have waves every day of the year. Even in the smallest swell, we can get a knee-high beach break. The thing I like the most here is that if the break is crowded and you search just a little further you can surf alone with your friends. But the crowds here are no problem. Everyone is gentle if respected. Here in the north of Portugal you can see smiles on the faces of everyone in the water, at the beach and in the day to day life in the city.

Francisco Garcia, local surfer

DEMI TAYLOR

5 Esposende

Breaks

1 Moledo do Minho

◉ **Break type**: Beach break.
🌊 **Conditions**: All swells, offshore in easterly winds.
❶ **Hazards/tips**: Rips near the river.
🛏 **Sleeping**: Vila Praia de Ancora ▸▸ *p293*.

A fairly consistent, busy beach that gets crowded in the summer. Shifting sandbars work through the tides with left-handers to the south. There is reputed to be a wave in the rivermouth though it is very inconsistent.

2 Vila Praia de Ancora

◉ **Break type**: Beach break.
🌊 **Conditions**: Small to medium swells, offshore in easterly winds.
❶ **Hazards/tips**: Consistent beach suitable for all surfers.
🛏 **Sleeping**: Vila Praia de Ancora ▸▸ *p293*.

A short trip south on the N13 brings you to Ancora. This is a long, consistent beach break that breaks through the tides.

3 Afife

◉ **Break type**: Beach break.
🌊 **Conditions**: All swells, offshore in easterly winds.
❶ **Hazards/tips**: Easily blown out.
🛏 **Sleeping**: Vila Praia de Ancora/Viana do Castelo ▸▸ *p293*.

This beach break is the place to come when there is a small swell. **Praia do Bico** has a

good local reputation for always having a wave and also producing high quality, hollow waves. In easterly winds and clean swells, the beach will turn on and can hold a big swell. Susceptible to the wind.

4 Viana do Castelo

◉ **Break type**: Beach break.
🌊 **Conditions**: All swells, offshore in easterly winds.
❶ **Hazards/tips**: Nice town with excellent waves.
🛏 **Sleeping**: Viana do Castelo ▸▸ *p293*.

Rivermouth divides beach breaks that can both hold quality waves. The beach to the south, **Cabadelo**, has a breakwater that can produce quality rights in big northwesterly swells. The beach stretches south and can be worth exploring for good peaks. Works on all states of tide.

5 Esposende

◉ **Break type**: Beach breaks.
🌊 **Conditions**: All swells, offshore in south/easterly winds.
❶ **Hazards/tips**: Quiet beaches with good banks. Usually uncrowded.
🛏 **Sleeping**: Esposende ▸▸ *p293*.

If the swell is small and the wind southerly, this is the place to check. To the south of Esposende stretch miles of quiet beaches, broken by rock breakwaters. Check **Praia de Ofir** where the sandbanks can be very good with both lefts and rights on offer.

6 Aguçadoura

◉ **Break type**: Beach break.
🌊 **Conditions**: All swells, offshore in easterly winds.
❶ **Hazards/tips**: Quiet beaches with good banks.
🛏 **Sleeping**: Póvoa de Varzim ▸▸ *p294*.

Take the turning off the N13 and a coastal road opens up a whole stretch of excellent

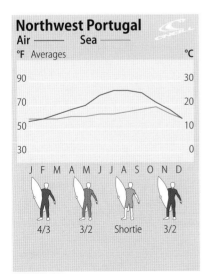

Northwest Portugal

Air —— Sea ——
°F Averages °C

90			30
70			20
50			10
30			0

J F M A M J J A S O N D

4/3 — 3/2 — Shortie — 3/2

DEMI TAYLOR

6 Aguçadoura

quality beach-break waves. Works through the tides and usually uncrowded.

7 Póvoa de Varzim

🌀 **Break type**: Left reef and beach.
🌊 **Conditions**: Medium swells, offshore in easterly winds.
❶ **Hazards/tips**: Crowded, rocky.
🛏 **Sleeping**: Póvoa de Varzim/Vila do Conde ▸▸ *p294*.

A left-hander breaks off the rock in the middle of the beach but needs a decent size swell to get going. Has a small take-off zone and can get crowded easily. Popular with bodyboarders. A short wave that works best on a mid to high tide, but rocky and not a classic. Watch out for rocks. There are other waves worth checking on the beach.

8 Vila do Conde /Azurara

🌀 **Break type**: Beach break.
🌊 **Conditions**: Medium swells, offshore in easterly/northerly winds.
❶ **Hazards/tips**: Rocks and rips.
🛏 **Sleeping**: Vila do Conde ▸▸ *p294*.

Praia Azul at Vila do Conde is a west-facing beach break that produces excellent lefts and rights on all tides. Shouldn't get too crowded but is popular with bodyboarders. **Azurara**, just to the south, is the place to head for if the

wind is coming from the north as there are excellent banks with some nice right-handers.

9 Leça

🌀 **Break type**: Beach break.
🌊 **Conditions**: Medium swells, offshore in easterly winds.
❶ **Hazards/tips**: Dangerously polluted.
🛏 **Sleeping**: Porto ▸▸ *p294*.

An urban beach located near the harbour, Leça is a polluted and crowded wave. Very poor water quality

10 Matosinhos

🌀 **Break type**: Beach break.
🌊 **Conditions**: Medium swells, offshore in north/northeasterly winds.
❶ **Hazards/tips**: Urban waves with poor water quality.
🛏 **Sleeping**: Porto ▸▸ *p294*.

When the swell is over 6 ft, Matosinhos Bay is the place where the local surfers head. As local Francisco Garcia at attitude-surf.com says: "Here you can choose the size of waves you want to ride since the waves are bigger as you walk south on the beach. On the north side of the beach there is a right point break, in the centre of the beach there is a right and left beach break, and at the southern end

where the waves are biggest, you can surf a right beach break and left point."

11 Luz

🌀 **Break type**: Right point.
🌊 **Conditions**: Big swells, offshore in easterly winds.
❶ **Hazards/tips**: Pollution.
🛏 **Sleeping**: Porto ▸▸ *p294*.

In downtown Porto, this high tide, right-hand, urban point break can handle big swells. As with other breaks in this area, the poor water quality is a massive drawback – often outweighing the quality of the wave.

12 Cabedelo do Douro

🌀 **Break type**: Rivermouth.
🌊 **Conditions**: Medium to big swells, offshore in easterly winds.
❶ **Hazards/tips**: Rips and pollution, experts only.
🛏 **Sleeping**: Porto ▸▸ *p294*.

A sandbar at the mouth of the Douro can produce epic, barreling right-handers peeling away from the rivermouth with shorter lefts. The water is coffee brown in colour and polluted. The wave only comes to life when conditions conspire every couple of years, but when it does it is one of the country's best. It needs heavy rains followed by a big swell but when it does it will give northern Spain's Mundaka a run for its money.

13 Espinho

🌀 **Break type**: Beach break and jetty.
🌊 **Conditions**: Medium to big swells, offshore in easterly winds.
❶ **Hazards/tips**: Localism and car crime can be a problem.
🛏 **Sleeping**: Espinho ▸▸ *p294*.

An average beach break that works on all tides but is easily blown out. A right-hander breaks off the southern jetty which is reputed to hold big swells. If you get it early on a mid

DEMI TAYLOR

8 Vila do Conde / Azurara

or low tide it can be a good wave. Easterly winds are offshore and the jetty offers a little protection from the northwesterlies. The crew here are quite tight but there aren't real localism problems. Not an affluent area so keep valuables hidden.

14 Furadouro, Torreira and south

- ◑ **Break type**: Beach break and jetties.
- ☁ **Conditions**: Small to medium swells, offshore in easterly winds.
- ❶ **Hazards/tips**: Water quality is poor.
- ⬭ **Sleeping**: Furadouro ▸▸ *p295*.

"Maceda next to Furadouro always, and I mean always, has a wave waiting for you," says Francisco Garcia. The other breaks are average beaches broken occasionally with jetties and sand-covered rocky breaks. Good waves may be found alongside the jetties but the area easily maxes out and is affected by wind.

15 Praia da Barra

- ◑ **Break type**: Sand bars.
- ☁ **Conditions**: All swells, offshore in easterly winds.
- ❶ **Hazards/tips**: Start of a huge stretch of beach.
- ⬭ **Sleeping**: São Jacinto/Costa Nova ▸▸ *p295*.

Banks form near the breakwater, which provides some shelter from the northwesterly swells that this region hoovers up. High tide can close out but mid to low can see good quality waves.

16 Costa Nova

- ◑ **Break type**: Beach break and jetties.
- ☁ **Conditions**: Small swells, offshore in easterly winds.
- ❶ **Hazards/tips**: Rips when bigger.
- ⬭ **Sleeping**: Costa Nova ▸▸ *p295*.

The longshore drift on this coastline is kept in check by a series of jetties that allow sandbanks to build up on either side. These banks change according to swell direction but can produce some excellent waves. Better in smaller swells and susceptible to winds from directions other than the east. A nice resort that is fairly uncrowded during the week but can get busy at weekends and during the summer. The open beaches are more prone to rips.

DEMI TAYLOR

> There are probably only a couple of breaks from this whole region that surfers from outside Portugal will have heard of, spots like Figueira da Foz and Espinho. But there is a big surf community up there with plenty of breaks to choose from. It's just that travellers are focusing more and more on the south of the country. Not that the local surfers from the northwest are complaining.

Ian Coutanche, surf traveller
Channel Islands

Praia de Mira and south

- **Break type**: Beach break and jetties.
- **Conditions**: Small swells, offshore in easterly winds.
- **Hazards/tips**: Rips in bigger swells.
- **Sleeping**: Costa Nova/Figueira da Foz ▶ *p295*.

The breaks at Praia de Mira are again a series of jetties, which break better off high tide. To the south is an open expanse of beach fronted by sand dunes. It is an exposed

16 Costa Nova ▶ *p291*

stretch best in small summer swells with either no wind or light easterly winds.

18 Figueira da Foz – Buarcos

- **Break type**: Right-hand, sand-covered rocky point break.
- **Conditions**: Medium to big swells, offshore in easterly/southeasterly winds.
- **Hazards/tips**: Rips when big.
- **Sleeping**: Figueira da Foz ▶ *p295*.

Buarcos is a long, sand-covered rocky point that can produce excellent, long walls on medium to large swells. Works on mid to low tides when rides of 100-200 m may be possible. When large swells wrap round the headland the peeling rights can be an impressive sight. Rips can push down the headland making a long paddle just that bit harder. May be crowded in the summer, but not too bad out of season. However, with an expanding surf population, this will probably change.

19 Figueira da Foz – Cabadelo

- **Break type**: Breakwater with sandbanks.
- **Conditions**: Medium swells, offshore in easterly winds.
- **Hazards/tips**: Crowds and pollution.
- **Sleeping**: Figueira da Foz ▶ *p295*.

A huge breakwater runs out to sea at the southern mouth of the Rio Mondego. It provides shelter from big northerly swells and northerly winds, allowing some quality sandbars to be deposited in its shadow. Can produce some excellent waves and is a very popular spot, home to both regular surfing competitions and a thriving local surf scene. Works on all

22 Nazaré

states of tide, but due to its proximity to the rivermouth water quality can be poor.

20 Pedrogão to Praia Velha

- **Break type**: Beach breaks with some jetties.
- **Conditions**: Small swells, offshore in light easterly winds.
- **Hazards/tips**: Rips on the open beaches can be a problem.
- **Sleeping**: Figueira da Foz ▶ *p295*

A long stretch of beach, occasionally broken by jetties. The area picks up loads of swell but, like the beaches to the north, it is easily maxed or blown out. Works best off high tide in small swells and an easterly or no wind. Sandbars can be found around jetties and spread along the open sandy beaches.

21 São Pedro de Moel

- **Break type**: Beach breaks.
- **Conditions**: Small to medium swells, offshore in easterly winds.
- **Hazards/tips**: Rips in bigger swells.
- **Sleeping**: Figueira da Foz ▶ *p295*

Rocky outcrops help hold sandbanks and produce pretty consistent waves on the town beaches. A good place to check in small to medium swells. Best in easterly winds and works at all states of tide.

22 Nazaré

- **Break type**: Beach breaks.
- **Conditions**: All swells, offshore in easterly winds.
- **Hazards/tips**: Bad rips when big, powerful waves.
- **Sleeping**: Figueira da Foz ▶ *p295*

An underwater trench channels swell into this region north of the town, producing big and powerful beach-break waves. However, in big swells there is a lot of water moving around on the beaches and bad rips. The town beaches are a more sheltered option.

Listings

Vila Praia de Ancora

Sitting on the N13, at the very northern tip of the Costa Verde, this pleasant resort town has a not so pleasant past. Legend has it that King Ramiro II had his unfaithful wife drowned here with an anchor tied around her neck for good measure. Anchor beach is overlooked by 2 ruined forts and is popular with Portuguese holidaymakers in the summer, but quiet out of season.

Sleeping
The **tourist information** office is on Largo da Estação and will provide a list of rooms available.
D-E Albergaria Quim Barreiros, Av Dr Ramos Pereira, T258-959100, is a reasonably priced place to stay with sea view and a good location.
Camping Vans tend to congregate and free-camp by the Fortim de Cão but there is also the official **Parque de Campismo do Paço**, T258-912697, open Apr-Oct.

Viana do Castelo

Overlooked by the basilica atop the Monte de Santa Luzia, this popular town at the mouth of the Rio Lima makes a good base. It has plenty of accommodation and is still lively out of season with plenty of bars and restaurants in which to while away autumn evenings after a day of classic surf.

Sleeping
E-D Residencial Jardim, Largo 5 de Outubro, T258-828915 , is close to the river with clean, en suite rooms.
E-D Residencial Magalhães, R Manuel Espregueira, T258-823293, is good value and centrally located.
F Residencial Dolce Vita, T258-824860, has a great location opposite the tourist information.
F Pensão Guerreiro, R Grande, T258-822099, is another good cheap option with clean and good size rooms and café attached.
Camping Orbitur Viana do Castelo, on the Cabedelo side of the river, T258-322167, also offers cabins, has a good location on the beach, and is near the ferry across to the town.

Eating/drinking
Dolce Vita, R do Poço, is a good value restaurant with a selection of basic and filling pasta and pizzas. The café at **Pensão Guerreiro** serves seafood and regional specialities involving goat. For coffee and pastries try **Pastelaria Brasileira** on R Sacadura Cabral and for a late night check out the nightclub **Viana Sol**, on R dos Manjovos, or **Foz Café** on the beach at Cabedelo.

Shopping
For supplies head to the daily **market** on R Martim Velho. There are a couple of surf shops here including **Omni Surf Shop**, R do Poço, with surf gear and mountain bike hire. Also check out **Viana Locals Surf Shop** in Complexo Turistico Minho Hotel, **Scandal Surf** on R Santo Antonio and **Stress Off** on Av Combatentes G. Guerra.

Directory
Banks: with ATMs on the Praça da República. **Post office**: opposite the train station on Av dos Combatentes da Grande Guerra, has **internet** access. **Tourist information**: R Hospital Velho, T258-822620.

Esposende

Heading south on the coastal N13, this relaxed resort sitting at the mouth of the Rio Cávado has plenty to offer. The dune-backed beaches are a couple of km away stretching to the north, with the beautiful white sands of Praia Ofir stretching out from the Pin forests to the south.

Sleeping
F Residencencial Acrópole, close to the tourist office on Praça Dom Sebastião, T253-961238. Just south of the river is the year-round **Campismo Fão**, T253-981777.

Póvoa de Varzim

Close to Porto, this resort is modern and bustling – even off season – with the beachfront a popular area with Porto surfers. It is much more built-up than resorts further north so has plenty of accommodation.

✿ Flat spells
Gambling Put on your sharp threads and place a bet at the **Casino da Póvoa** on Av da Braga and catch some cabaret. **Golf** Get a round in at **Estela**, T052-601814 – head north along the N13 and take the turning to Rio Alto.

● Sleeping
Cheap rooms can easily be found along the main road, R Paulo Barreto, including F **Hospedaria Jantarada**, T252-622789, clean with a handy restaurant below. Otherwise check out the **turismo** on Praça Marquês de Pombal which has a comprehensive list of rooms available. **Rio Alto Orbitur Campismo**, T252-615699, is just up the coast towards Estela.

○ Shopping
To the north at A-Ver-o-Mar is a handy surf shop, **Backwash**, on R Jose Moreira.

Vila do Conde

Close to Porto, this bustling, popular fishing town has managed to maintain its historic, seafaring heart and is a more relaxed stopover than nearby Póvoa de Varzim.

● Sleeping
F **Pensão Princesa do Ave**, R Dr António José Sousa Pereira, T252-642065, good value. F **Le Villageois**, T252-631119, has a couple of rooms above an excellent restaurant serving seafood.
Camping There are a couple of year-round campsites to the south of the town.
Campismo Ârvore, near Praia Arvore on R Cabreiro, T252-633225. Further south still and slightly cheaper is **Campismo Vila Cha**, R do Sol, T229-283163.

❀ Festivals
The first weekend in Jun and last weekend in Jul sees the streets cordoned off and the roads taken over for the annual motor racing festival.

Porto

Portugal's second largest city, Porto, lies at the heart of the Douro region and sprawls across the bank of the Douro River, towards its sister town Vila Nova da Gaia. Porto is an industrial, hardworking place – it gave the county its name, to the world it brought port, and it hasn't stopped grafting since. Although the Ribeira district, complete with cobbled streets, has been presented with a world heritage title from UNESCO, the city itself is not the most glamorous of destinations and you do need to watch your pockets.

✿ Flat spells
Cinema Catch a movie at **Cinema Batalha** on Praca da Batalaha. **Golf** Get 9 holes in at the beachside **Miramar** golf course, just south of Porto on Av Sacadura Cabral, T227-622067.
Port You can't leave here before you've done the tour, drunk the stuff and got the T-shirt. Head over the river to Vila Nova da Gaia and try **Caves Ramos Pinto** on Av Ramos Pinto, T223-707000, or British producers **Taylor's**, R do Choupelo, T223-70867, for a cellar tour and tasting.

● Sleeping
There is plenty of accommodation in the city, some of which at the cheapest end can be fairly grotty so ask to see the room before you agree to staying.
E **Pensão Astorio**, R Arnaldo Gama, T222-008175, near the old town walls, offer a friendly stay.
E **Pensão Porto Rico**, on the main R do Almada, T223-394 690, have extremely good room rates for up to 4 people.
E-F **Pensão Duas Nações**, Praça Guilherme Fernandes, T222-081616, centrally based near the north bus station, is clean, modern and offers internet access.

✪ Eating/drinking
In a city this size there is something for everyone. For cheap chicken 'n' chips or other grilled delights, check out **Pedro dos Frango** on Bonjardim, just up from the tourist office near Praça Dom João. At the other end of the scale on Cais do Riberira, **Taverna dos Bebos** – literally tavern of the drunks – dates from the 19th century and serves up generous portions of traditional fare and fish suppers, some of which can be pricey. Way out east on R Bonfim is a vegetarian's delight, **Suribachi**, dishing up cheap, macrobiotic fare.

○ Shopping
For provisions, there's a **Pingo** supermarket on Pasos Manuel or head to **Mercado Bolhao**, the daily market, for fresh goods. There are several **surf shops** in the area. To the north, check out **Surf Local Surf Shop**, Av Dr Fernando Aroso, in Leça or the **Waimea Surf Shop**, R 1 Dezembro, at Matosinhos. South, in Vila Nova de Gaia, head for **Malibu Surf Shop**, on R Padua Correia.

● Directory
Banks: plenty on the central Av dos Aliados. **Post office**: Av dos Aliados. **Tourist information**: there are a couple of helpful offices, the main one on R Clube Fenianos, another in the Ribeira district on R Infante D. Henrique, www. portoturismo.pt.

Espinho

On paper, Espinho has little going for it. It's a pretty rundown, 1970s-style resort that has become a suburb of Porto. The roads are arranged in a grid system and numbered – not named. The water is polluted and these harsh conditions have bred tough surfers, especially the breakwater right-hander. Although the area can have an intimidating feel, local surfer Francisco Garcia says, "It can be very crowded, it's true, but there is no localism. Here in the north we don't have any localism. When I go to Espinho I leave my board on the top of my car and go eat far from the car, where I can't see my board. I've never had a problem. What more can I say about it being safe to stay here?"

☸ Flat spells

Golf If you're feeling flush, head south out of town on the N109 and get a round in at **Oporto GC**, T027-342008 , one of the oldest courses in the country.

⊖ Sleeping

The reasonably priced F **Hotel Mar Azul**, T227-340824, is on the romantically named Av 8.

○ Shopping/directory

Espinho has one of the largest **markets** in the region which takes place on a Mon on Rua 24, 23 and 22. There are a couple of surf shops here, **Omni Surf Shop**, Centro Commercial California, and **Invert Surf Shop**, Rue 32, by the municipal swimming pool. The **tourist information office** is on Rua 6.

Furadouro

Heading 5 km west from the pretty market town of Ovar lies Praia de Furadouro, home to the beachside **Campismo Furadouro**,T256-596010, a shady spot nestled among the pine trees. In Ovar itself is the **Animal Surf Shop** on R Gonçalo Velho stocking boards, essentials and clothing.

São Jacinto

Heading south on the coastal N327, the port town of São Jacinto is backed by a bird reserve. Camp at the **Orbitur** site, T324-331 220, open 15 Jan-15 Nov, which also has cabins to rent.

São Jacinto/Costa Nova

Just to the south of Aveiro on the coast, Costa Nova is a small and pretty resort that is busy during the weekends with day trippers from the city. With a huge beach stretching from Praia da Barra to the north all the way down to Figueira da Foz, Costa Nova makes a good base for a couple of nights. There is a large and well equipped **Campismo Costa Nova**, T234-369822, which is open year round and a surf shop in town, **Loja da Tribo do Sol**.

Figueira da Foz

Sitting at the mouth of the Rio Mondego, this lively fishing port is a popular Portuguese resort and regular staging ground for national, European and WQS events.

☸ Flat spells

Beach football If you're here in the summer, you may catch the world beach football championships (or if not just recreate your own). **Casino** Put on a shirt and some shoes and head for the slot machines at the **Casino da Figueira** on R Bernado Lopes, also home to a cinema.

⊖ Sleeping

There are plenty of rooms available in private houses if you are willing to hunt around. There is also a good selection of accommodation around R Bernado Lopes including C-D **Pensão Central**, T233-422308, with large rooms. Alternatively try the more basic. E **Pensão Bela Figueira**, R Miguel Bombarda, T233-422728, with good beach access.

Camping There are several good campsites in the area including the inland **Camping Municipal**,T233-402810, and **Foz do Mondego**, set across the river near Praia Cabedelo, T233-402740, open 15 Jan-15 Nov. Further south at Gala is the year-round **Orbitur** site which also offers good rates on cabins off season, T233-431492. Heading north to Praia de Quiaisos is another cheap, year-round **Campismo**.

☻ Eating/drinking

If you feel a long way from home and are in need of a curry, head to the reasonably priced **Pensão Bela Figueira**. To sample the delights of the sea venture out to the fantastic **Dory Negro** at Largo Caras Diretas in Buarcos.

⊙ Shopping/directory

Ze Surf Shop, Centro Comercial Atlantico. **Banks**: a couple overlooking the river on Av Foz do Mondego. **Post office**: the most convenient is on R Miguel Bombarda, running parallel to the beach. **Tourist information**: Av 25 de Abril just back from the seafront.

Airports → Porto, T229-432400; Lisbon, T218-413500; **Faro**, T289-800800. **Buses and coaches** → Rede Expressos, T707-223344, www.rede-expressos.pt; Algarve Eva, T289-800800, www.eva-bus.com; **Car hire** → Auto Jardim, T800 200613, www.auto-jardim.com; **Rail** → Caminhos de Ferro Portugueses, T808-208208, www.cp.pt. **Petrol prices** → €0.90/litre unleaded.

Peniche & Ericeira

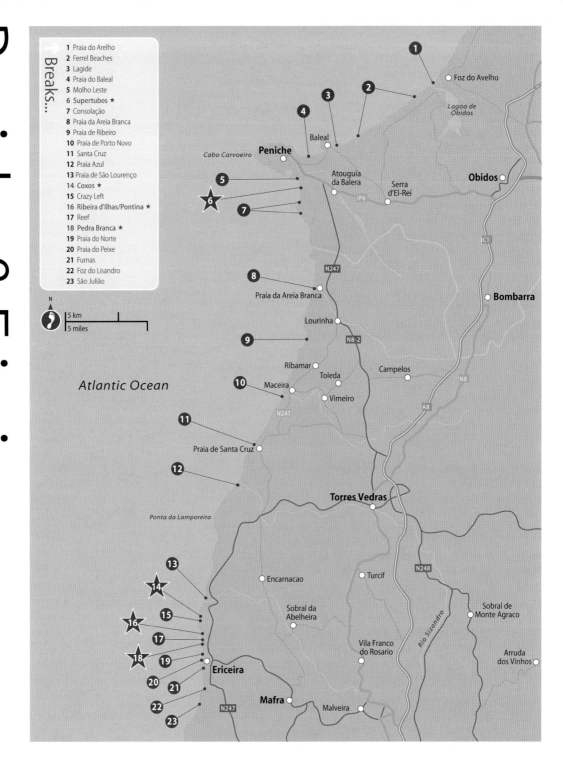

Breaks...

1 Praia do Arelho
2 Ferrel Beaches
3 Lagide
4 Praia do Baleal
5 Molho Leste
6 Supertubos ★
7 Consolação
8 Praia da Areia Branca
9 Praia de Ribeiro
10 Praia de Porto Novo
11 Santa Cruz
12 Praia Azul
13 Praia de São Lourenço
14 Coxos ★
15 Crazy Left
16 Ribeira d'Ilhas/Pontina ★
17 Reef
18 Pedra Branca ★
19 Praia do Norte
20 Praia do Peixe
21 Furnas
22 Foz do Lisandro
23 São Julião

N

5 km
5 miles

Foz do Avelho

Lagoa de Óbidos

Baleal

Cabo Carvoeiro   **Peniche**

Atouguia da Balera

Serra d'El-Rei

Obidos

IP6

IC1

N247

Bombarra

Praia da Areia Branca

Lourinha

N8-2

Ribamar

Toleda

Campelos

N8

Maceira

Vimeiro

A8

Atlantic Ocean

N247

Praia de Santa Cruz

Ponta da Lamporeira

Torres Vedras

N248

Encarnacao

Turcif

Sobral da Abelheira

Sobral de Monte Agraco

Vila Franco do Rosario

Rio Sizandro

Arruda dos Vinhos

Ericeira

Mafra

Malveira

N247

Surfing Peniche & Ericeira

Putting Peniche and Ericeira in the same section is purely for geographical convenience. For, although each is undoubtedly a world-class surfing destination, it is for very different reasons. Ericeira is a thinking surfer's destination – whitewashed fishing cottages and cobbled streets, fine reefs where subtle changes in swell direction have to be taken into account, but still with the punch to humble even the world's best wave riders. Peniche on the other hand is a grey working town, raw and unrefined – fish-processing factories unapologetically fill the skyline, their odour drifting across the brutally powerful beach break at Supertubos. Yet sitting in the line-up at Lagide, a subtle and almost refined reef break just to the east, the view as the sun goes down reveals Peniche, with its formidable city walls, in stunningly beautiful profile.

Both areas have been at the centre of Portuguese surfing since the earliest days. Today they are home to large populations of committed surfers who charge the world-class waves on their own doorsteps, waves which now draw legions of travelling surfers and the attention of the world's surfing media. Every year, both Peniche and Ericeira host legs of the world surfing tour. Local surfers have also made the step up to international level, led by Tiago Pires from Ericeira.

Coastline
Peniche is one of the country's most flexible surf locations. The town is built on a rocky island on the end of a sand peninsula and at the western end of a huge crescent-shaped bay. The idea was to make it an impregnable fortress town, but the geography conspired to produce some great beach breaks. At the eastern end of the bay sits the village of Baleal, also on a peninsula. This geographical set-up means that there are beaches facing almost every direction. The result is a very consistent area of high quality waves.

Ericeira is very different. The jagged coastline faces due west and is made up of a series of high quality reefs with occasional sandy beaches. It lacks the flexibility of its neighbour to the north, but the sheer class of the waves on offer here more than compensates. The flat, jagged rock reefs are unforgiving and many have a carpet of urchins thrown in for good measure. Between these two surfing hot spots are plenty of beaches offering high quality waves but without the crowds.

Localism
Although the line-ups at Coxos and Supertubos are super competitive and the standard of surfing is high, travelling surfers who follow the rules and surf respectfully will have no problems. As Nick Uricchio from Semente says, "As a traveller, the same as anywhere else on this planet, be pleasant and fair with others and 99% of the time you will

enjoy and be enjoyed by others. Portuguese people in general are warm folks. The invasion of foreign surfers has taken its toll a bit on certain locations, so there is a bit of bitterness these days. Do not travel in mobs and don't hog waves even if you are a better surfer." Nick also advises visitors to make sure they don't leave valuables on display in their vans or cars. "Keep an eye on your gear and your vehicle."

Top local surfers Tiago Pires is the biggest name to come out of this region and indeed this continent. His success on the WQS circuit and his performances at events like the Rip Curl Pro at Sunset Beach have established him as one of the world's best. Other well known surfers include Miguel Fortes, João Pedro and José Gregorio.

Getting around
The N247 allows access to the breaks around Ericeira and then heads north past the Semente factory and nearby Coxos. Follow the coast road north (or the faster main road that runs inland) and soon the bustling fishing port of Peniche comes into view. Access to the breaks around Peniche is straightforward, with the local council even providing convenient signposts to Supertubos from the main road.

Peniche & Ericeira board guide

Tiago Pires model
Shaper: Nick Urrichio, Semente Surfboards

» Tiago Pires model 6'6" x 18" x 2⅛" pin tail, smooth unexaggerated rocker.

» A good travelling board for the better side of surfing Portugal, in other words 'thick filthy barrels', with fast, vertical take-offs, i.e. Coxos, Supertubos etc.

» Planeshape with nice draw through the tail for serious carving, slight vee on nose entrance to concave bottom with a slight flat spot on tail release. Fixed fins for power.

» We breed a lot of these animals for the home boys that like to spend serious time in the shade of Coxos barrels.

Beach break board
Shaper: Nick Urrichio, Semente Surfboards

» 6'3" x 18⅞" x 2⅜".

» For José Gregorio for everyday surfing.

» Bump wing, squash tail, full concave bottom and stand up loose rails through back.

» The rocker is very low in this board with nice release through the tail for vertical attacks.

» José is a big lad - for a smaller, lighter surfer run this around 6'1" x 18" x 2⅛".

 Boards by **Semente Surfboards**
Factory: Rabo da Raposa, Ribamar, Ericeira, Portugal
T00 351 (0)261-863 552 www.semente.pt
or contact semente@ip.pt

Breaks

I remember going to
Peniche in the seventies and
surfing Supertubos, before
it was even called
Supertubos. We camped
near Mohlo Leste and just
surfed these epic waves all
summer. It's one of my
favourite places.

Phil Jarratt, former Tracks editor

Peniche & Ericeira

Air ——— Sea ———

°F Averages °C

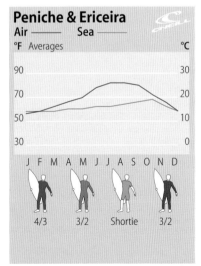

4/3   3/2   Shortie   3/2

Peniche

1 Praia do Arelho

- **Break type**: Beach break.
- **Conditions**: Small to medium swells, offshore in easterly winds.
- **Hazards/tips**: Quiet spot with good waves.
- **Sleeping**: Baleal/Peniche ›› *p304*.

Good spot next to Lagoa de Obidos to check as it is very consistent and usually pretty uncrowded. Can have excellent and powerful beach break waves.

2 Ferrel

2 Ferrel Beaches

- **Break type**: Beach breaks.
- **Conditions**: Small to medium swells, offshore in southeasterly winds.
- **Hazards/tips**: Tricky access, localized spots.
- **Sleeping**: Baleal/Peniche ›› *p304*.

This is a long stretch of beach breaks with some excellent quality waves. Turn left at the 58 surf shop and follow the *piste* roads. Left turns lead down to a series of beaches popular with local surfers. Pick up a lot of swell. You may see some locals-only graffiti – at **Oesuer** a sign proclaims 'Native Locals Only'. **Praia da Almagreira** has nice, sucky, sandbars. Park above the breaks. Show respect to locals, don't turn up in large groups. Access may get tricky after heavy rains.

3 Lagide

- **Break type**: Left-hand reef break.
- **Conditions**: Small to medium swells, offshore in southeasterly winds.
- **Hazards/tips**: Urchin-infested reef.
- **Sleeping**: Baleal/Peniche ›› *p304*.

Lagide is a very popular, good quality left-hand reef that can produce long walling waves that break in front of the car park at Baleal. This is a very nice, easy to surf wave with a tiny take-off point – hence it can be a bit of a mess on the peak with surfers taking off on the wrong side of the peak and lots of drop-ins. There's an easy rip out to the peak just to the west of the break.

3 Lagide

On the other side of the channel the beach can have some great little waves in small to medium swells but it easily closes out when the swell picks up.

4 Praia do Baleal

- ◉ **Break type**: Beach break.
- ◉ **Conditions**: All swells, offshore in winds from the west/south/east.
- ◉ **Hazards/tips**: Rips when big.
- ◉ **Sleeping**: Baleal/Peniche » p304.

A fantastically flexible, crescent-shaped bay that picks up loads of swell. Parts of the bay will be offshore in winds from the west through to the east. A fast, hollow right breaks near Baleal. Further round a nice left works in all swells and the rest of the bay consists of many banks that work through all tides.

5 Molho Leste

- ◉ **Break type**: Beach break.
- ◉ **Conditions**: Small to medium swells, offshore in easterly winds.
- ◉ **Hazards/tips**: Small take-off point, localized spot.
- ◉ **Sleeping**: Baleal/Peniche » p304.

A right-hand sandbar at the mouth of the stream alongside the harbour wall south of Peniche. This can be a great wave in smaller swells but tends to close out in bigger swells. There is a large local crew here who have the tiny take-off zone wired and always seem to be in the best place for the best set waves, so it can be frustrating trying to snag a few waves.

4 Praia do Baleal

6 Supertubos

- ◉ **Break type**: Sandbar with lefts and rights.
- ◉ **Conditions**: All swells.
- ◉ **Size**: 2-10 ft.
- ◉ **Length**: Up to 50 m.
- ◉ **Swell**: Southwesterly to northwesterly.
- ◉ **Wind**: Easterly.
- ◉ **Tide**: All tides, but better around mid tide.
- ◉ **Bottom**: Very shallow sandbar.
- ◉ **Entry/exit**: Off the beach.
- ◉ **Hazards/tips**: Very shallow, very hollow and powerful, board breaking, crowds.
- ◉ **Sleeping**: Baleal/Peniche » p304.

Supertubos is now firmly on the world surfing map, it is even signposted from the road into town. Follow the track down to the sand and look south to see the crowds on the beach and in the water. Currents on this stretch of beach conspire to keep this incredible sandbar replenished and waiting for the next swell to unload on it. Depending on the swell direction it can be a right, a perfect peak or a left, but whenever it's on, it is fast, hollow and shallow. The locals seem to have an uncanny ability to pick off the gaping barrels from between the exploding close-outs. This is really a wave for experienced surfers and broken boards are not uncommon.

When 'Supers' is breaking at 3-4 ft it will be very busy, but the crowds thin out as the swell picks up. At 10 ft it really is a sight to behold, with cavernous stand-up barrels doing a great impression of Pipeline. In ideal conditions there can be a fast hollow right firing to the south of the peak with a left breaking the other way towards a channel. To the north of the channel another hollow right can break, but the rest of this long stretch of beach can be surprisingly free of good quality waves.

Recently a new harbour excavation led to thousands of tons of sand being deposited on the beach here but it doesn't appear to have affected the quality of the waves too much.

ⓘ **If you like** Supertubos, try Carcavelos in Portugal (see page 311) and La Gravière (see page 180) and Les Cavaliers (see page 189), both in France.

7 Consolação

- ◉ **Break type**: Left- and right-hand point breaks.
- ◉ **Conditions**: Medium to big swells, offshore in easterly winds.
- ◉ **Hazards/tips**: Rocky breaks with urchins.
- ◉ **Sleeping**: Baleal/Peniche » p304.

Consolação is a peninsula with a left point down the north side and a right on the southern side. The left can be a quality wave with long, peeling walls that work at all states of tide. It is usually uncrowded and has easy access. The right point breaks in big swells and although the set-up looks promising, the

Peniche Prison

6 Supertubos inside

6 Supertubos

waves look better than they actually are. There is a big drop on take-off after which the wave flattens out and it can be hard work making it through to the inside.

To the south of Consolação is another right-hand point that comes alive in the biggest swells. Access is tricky and the point breaks over rocks. For experienced surfers only.

8 Praia da Areia Branca

- **Break type**: Beach break.
- **Conditions**: Small to medium swells, offshore in easterly winds.
- **Hazards/tips**: Quiet beach with rips in big swells
- **Sleeping**: Praia de Areia Branca ›› p305.

Follow the N247 south to this excellent and underrated beach break. It is a great place to escape the crowds of Peniche and usually has some decent banks (near the rivermouth). Check the whole beach from the cliff top.

9 Praia de Ribeiro

- **Break type**: Beach break.
- **Conditions**: Small to medium swells, offshore in easterly winds.
- **Hazards/tips**: Sheltered beach with few surfers.
- **Sleeping**: Praia de Areia Branca/Santa Cruz ›› p305.

A sheltered sandy beach with a peak in the middle that has lefts and rights. Doesn't break at high tide.

10 Praia de Porto Novo

- **Break type**: Beach breaks and rivermouth.
- **Conditions**: Small to medium swells, offshore in easterly winds.
- **Hazards/tips**: Take a packed lunch and water!
- **Sleeping**: Praia de Areia Branca/Santa Cruz ›› p305.

Porto Novo has a rivermouth break at the northern end and a massive stretch of beach heading south, which has various peaks working at different states of tide. A great place to get away from the crowds and explore.

11 Santa Cruz

- **Break type**: Beach break.
- **Conditions**: Small to medium swells, offshore in easterly winds.
- **Hazards/tips**: Heavy waves, rips.
- **Sleeping**: Santa Cruz ›› p305.

A place with such a surf-related name should be home to quality waves, and this town certainly doesn't disappoint. The beaches to the north of the town are home to some powerful, high quality breaks. There are a series of sandbanks and sand-covered reefs. There is even the sand-covered shipwreck of a boat that sank just after the Second World War and produces an excellent sandbank. Sitting between two surf Meccas, Santa Cruz has managed to avoid attention and is a great place to escape the crowds.

12 Praia Azul

- **Break type**: Beach break.
- **Conditions**: Small to medium swells, offshore in easterly winds.
- **Hazards/tips**: Heavy when big, rocks.
- **Sleeping**: Santa Cruz ›› p305.

One of the most consistent breaks in the area and can have some excellent peaks. Always worth checking in small, clean swells. There is also a reef at the north end of the bay.

7 Consolação ›› p299

8 Praia da Areia Branca

11 Santa Cruz

In Portugal they have so many good waves, it's like a paradise. That's one of the reasons Tiago Pires is so consistent. I surfed with him five years ago and he was good then, but now – he is like a knock-out punch!

Patrick Bevan, French pro surfer

Ericeira

13 Praia de São Lourenço

🌀 **Break type**: Sand-covered reef.
🌊 **Conditions**: Medium to big swells, offshore in easterly winds.
❶ **Hazards/tips**: Big-wave spot, rocks, rips.
💤 **Sleeping**: Ericeira ▸▸ *p305*.

This is a big right-hand reef break that only gets going when big swells kick in. It has heavy, walling waves that peel through to the beach but the peak can shift around a lot and getting caught inside is not a pleasant experience. Doesn't usually get that crowded. For experienced surfers only.

DEMI TAYLOR

14 Coxos

14 Coxos

🌀 **Break type**: Right-hand reef.
🌊 **Conditions**: Medium to big swells.
◐ **Size**: 3-12 ft.
🔄 **Length**: 50-100 m plus.
🐚 **Swell**: Northwesterly to southwesterly.
🌀 **Wind**: Easterly/southeasterly.
💨 **Tide**: Low to mid tide.
☯ **Bottom**: Sharp rock reef.
Ⓦ **Entry/exit**: Off the point (with good timing) or from the inside.
❶ **Hazards/tips**: Heavy waves, sharp rocks, rips, crowds.
💤 **Sleeping**: Ericeira ▸▸ *p305*.

Coxos ranks as one of Europe's very best waves. Swell lunges out of deep water and jacks up onto a ledge where it unloads a powerful, hollow right-hand barrel that reels along a slanting reef into the bay. Depending on the swell direction it can be either a long, walling wave or a fast, heavy, hollow wave with barrel sections. "My favourite break in Europe has to be Coxos," says local pro surfer and WQS star Tiago Pires. "Coxos every time. Eight to ten feet on a southwest swell – perfect!" It wasn't by chance that the Semente factory set up shop just a two-minute hop from this break.

Like any class wave, Coxos has a tight crew of excellent surfers who will be on it every time it fires. There isn't any localism towards travelling surfers who are respectful in the water but in smaller swells the line-up can get crowded and the atmosphere can become a bit strained. In bigger swells it's worth watching the wave and assessing

Hendy and Uricchio on Coxos

"I was on a photo shoot with *Carve* magazine," says top UK surfer James Hendy. "The surf was pretty big but with good lulls. I waited for a gap in the sets and jumped off the point into the line-up. From nowhere a set reared up in front of me and started sucking all the water out from under me. I just managed to scramble under it, otherwise I would have been smashed against the rocks. I took the whole set on the head before finally being washed along the point and paddling into the line-up. One of the local guys smiled and said, 'Good practice for the session.' It just shows you that the swell comes out of deep water and sets can just suddenly appear."

14 Coxos

DEMI TAYLOR

Nick Uricchio, founder of Semente Surfboards, recalls many classic sessions at his local break, Coxos. "There have been too many classic sessions in all these years to pinpoint any one in particular. I do remember one dead flat, windless, beautiful day that my partner [Miguel Katzenstein] and I drove down to Coxos with our boards and a huge amount of 'faith'. There were a bunch of travelling surfers and some locals just hanging out there. We both just had this major feeling that the surf was going to happen, so we put our wetties on and paddled out – to the awe of all watchers or maybe to their jeers. We got about 30 m out when a little half-metre set rolled through. After a little lull, another arrived. Then it was just non-stop. The swell just kept growing every time a set came in. We could not stop laughing as we watched people scrambling for their gear. It was a clean 6 ft by the time we bailed. A once in a lifetime experience!"

honestly whether you'd be out of your depth in the line-up. Many surfers have stories of how they underestimated the power and size of the waves here. Travelling NZ surfer Mike Brown had heard of Coxos and paddled out for a few waves. "It was completely different experience than what I expected. It's a heavy wave, shallow reef – getting in again was pretty scary."

ⓘ *If you like* Coxos, *try* Porthleven *in England (see page 88) and* Crab Island *in Ireland (see page 130).*

15 Crazy Left

- **Break type**: Reef break.
- **Conditions**: Medium swells, offshore in easterly winds.
- **Hazards/tips**: Shallow, heavy, rocky.
- **Sleeping**: Ericeira ▸▸ *p305*.

Rarely surfed left-hand reef found in the same bay as Coxos. It is fast, shallow and hollow and needs a swell from a southerly direction to work. Best left to the experts. It's not called Crazy for nothing.

16 Ribeira d'Ilhas/Pontina

- **Break type**: Sand-covered reef.
- **Conditions**: All swells, offshore in easterly winds.
- **Length**: Up to 200 m.
- **Swell**: Westerly/northwesterly.
- **Wind**: Easterly.
- **Tide**: All.
- **Bottom**: Sand covered reef.
- **Entry/exit**: Off the left-hand side of beach – use rip.
- **Hazards/tips**: Crowds.
- **Sleeping**: Ericeira ▸▸ *p305*.

When looked at from the cliff-top lay-by, this bay has an uncanny resemblance to Bells Beach. Pontina is the right-hand, sand-covered reef to the north of the bay with the main break, Ribeira, peeling south from the middle of the bay. Pontina works best in medium swells, being accessed at low tide by foot along the reef, or by paddling north from the bay. Ribeira is a long, walling, semi-point break right-hander that starts working at 3 ft and can hold swells up to 10 ft comfortably. In the right swells, rides of 200 m are possible and the flexibility of the spot, the ease of access and the fact that it is a very easy wave to surf makes it the region's most popular surf spot. It works through all tides, but is better near low, and there is a nice rip to the south of the wave allowing an easier paddle out. In the late summer the crowds can be heavy. It is also popular with longboarders and hosts a WQS contest. There is parking by the beach as well as good seasonal café.

17 Reef

- **Break type**: Right-hand reef.
- **Conditions**: Small to medium swells, offshore in easterly winds.
- **Hazards/tips**: Shallow reef with urchins.
- **Sleeping**: Ericeira ▸▸ *p305*.

Just to the south of Ribeira, this shallow right-hand reef sees waves coming out of deep water and peeling along a sharp, rock ledge producing hollow waves that finally empty onto virtually dry land. Popular with bodyboarders and experienced surfers only. Access via the same road as Pedra Branca.

14 Coxos Inside ▸▸ *p301*

14 Coxos Outside ▸▸ *p301*

16 Pontina

18 Pedra Branca

- ◉ **Break type**: Left reef.
- ◎ **Conditions**: Small to medium swells, offshore in easterly winds.
- ◉ **Length**: 75 m.
- ◉ **Swell**: Westerly/northwesterly.
- ◉ **Wind**: Easterly.
- ◉ **Tide**: Mid/high.
- ◎ **Bottom**: Rock reef.
- ◉ **Entry/exit**: Paddle off the rocks.
- ◉ **Hazards/tips**: Very crowded, shallow, urchins.
- ◉ **Sleeping**: Ericeira ⟫ *p305*.

An excellent, left-hand reef break, where the swell comes out of deep water onto a shallow ledge producing hollow, fast waves. It can hold a swell up to 8 ft plus but gets shallow at low tide, especially in smaller swells. It has a jacking take-off followed by a long barrel section. Definitely for advanced surfers when it's on. In the summer it can be a pleasant, playful, walling wave; when the autumn swells kick in, it is transformed into a world-class performer. Exposed to winds. Take the short dirt *piste* road opposite the campsite down to the headland. Popular with bodyboarders.

19 Praia do Norte

- ◉ **Break type**: Beach break.
- ◎ **Conditions**: All swells, offshore in easterly winds.
- ◉ **Hazards/tips**: Popular wave, easy access from village.
- ◉ **Sleeping**: Ericeira ⟫ *p305*.

Praia do Norte has a long right-hander that peels in front of the car park on the northern edge of the village. This can be a good quality, walling wave and is one of the area's most consistent spots. Best from quarter to high tide. To the north is a short, hollow left that's worth checking at mid tide. Not considered one of the area's prestige waves and as such can often be overlooked.

20 Praia do Peixe

- ◉ **Break type**: Beach break.
- ◎ **Conditions**: Massive swells, offshore in easterly winds.
- ◉ **Hazards/tips**: Crowds.
- ◉ **Sleeping**: Ericeira ⟫ *p305*.

This break only works in the biggest swells when the rest of the coast is closing out. There is a left peeling actually inside the harbour, but the water quality isn't great and there is bound to be a crowd.

The winter of 2001-02 was the best winter I've ever managed in my life. There was three months of off-shores and the waves didn't drop the 4 ft range! I had some days where I would surf perfect 6-8 ft Coxos in the morning low tide, surf Pedra Branca in the midday high tide and then have another perfect low tide evening surf at Coxos – that would make me touch heaven at night, I couldn't stop laughing!

Tiago Pires

18 Pedra Branca

19 Praia do Norte

Portugal Peniche & Ericeira Breaks Pedra Branca to Praia do Peixe

21 Furnas

- ◉ **Break type**: Beach break.
- ◉ **Conditions**: Big swells, offshore in easterly winds.
- ❶ **Hazards/tips**: Check in big swells.
- ◉ **Sleeping**: Ericeira ▸▸ *p305*.

A right-hand wave breaking off the breakwater and assorted beach-break waves to the south of Ericiera. Can be the only place working in big northwesterly swells, but not a high quality spot.

22 Foz do Lisandro

- ◉ **Break type**: Beach break.
- ◉ **Conditions**: Small to medium swells, offshore in easterly winds.
- ❶ **Hazards/tips**: Fickle rivermouth.
- ◉ **Sleeping**: Ericeira ▸▸ *p305*.

Just south of Ericeira, this rivermouth is worth checking because when it's working it is a high quality beach without the crowds found to the north. Best from low up to three-quarter tide.

23 São Julião

- ◉ **Break type**: Beach break.
- ◉ **Conditions**: Small swells, offshore in easterly winds.
- ❶ **Hazards/tips**: Very consistent spot.
- ◉ **Sleeping**: Ericeira ▸▸ *p305*.

This is a very consistent spot that works through the tides. A good place to check in smaller conditions as it hoovers up the swell, but doesn't handle bigger swells. Can be excellent when the banks are right with hollow lefts and rights on offer.

Listings

DEMI TAYLOR

Baleal

Sitting just to the east of Peniche, this small village has spilled off the island peninsula it occupies onto the mainland. It makes a good base for a surf trip to Peniche. Popular with day trippers and surfers, the car park overlooking Lagide is a busy focal point during the day and noisy free-camping area at night.

◉ Sleeping

Baleal Surf Camp, T969-050546, on the mainland near the car park, offers accommodation. **Campismo Baleal**, T262-769467, is on the coastal road and nearby is the D-E **Hospedaria Baleal a Vista**, T262-769467. There are a few rooms available, the best being in the old village, over the causeway. Try C-D **Pequena Baleia**, T262-769370, or C **Casa das Marés**, 3 separate establishments in a large white building overlooking the sea, T262-769371/769200.

❷ Eating/drinking

Danau Bar is a popular if unspectacular bar that has live music and good views of the surf at sunset. There are also a couple of restaurants close to the causeway.

◯ Shopping

58 Surf Shop sits just inland on the main road east.

Peniche

Peniche is one of the centres of the Portuguese surf scene, but lacks a touristy feel, despite its excellent beaches. Once an island, it became a pretty, fortified fishing town that has since been spoilt by fish factories and building developments. Sometimes the aroma of putrifying fish can hang over parts of the town like a bad fart. Despite its faded beauty, it has a definite charm and a proud working-class feel to it. The main road into town now crosses a peninsula of sand that helps to make it such an excellent surfing destination. There are signs to the most famous breaks in the area.

☺ Flat spells

Cinema Small cinema on R Dr João de Matos Bilhau showing the latest films, usually in English.

Fortaleza If you want to know more about the history of the country check out the 16th-century fortress, converted into a notorious political prison by General Salazar and in use until 1974.

Obidos Don't miss this walled hilltop village, so pretty it was once given as a wedding present. It used to overlook the sea before the bay silted up and is now 20 mins inland. **Skating** A concrete skate park with mini-ramp, rails, banks and funbox sits under the city walls on Av 25 de Abril.

☺ Sleeping

There are plenty of budget sleeping options in town.

D-E Katekero, Av do Mar, T262-787107, has good, clean rooms and is in a great location for restaurants, with parking available at the marina or just over the bridge. In the same area are **D Residencial Maciel**, R José Estevão, T262-784685, and **E Residencial Rima Vier**, R Castilho, T262-789459, which has good value double rooms.

Camping Parque Municipal de Campismo, T262-789529, is a decent and very cheap campsite on the EN114. Open year round, it has free hot showers and is a popular option with surfers in vans as it is only 2 mins from Supertubos. **Camping Peniche Praia**, T262-783460, on the far side of town, not as convenient for the surf.

☺ Eating/drinking

There are some great seafood restaurants on R do Mar including **Restaurante Populaire**. Check out the fish kebab or pick any fresh fish or seafood and watch it cooked in the open kitchen. Any of the numerous fish restaurants on this road are pretty good, but if seafood isn't your thing there's a fairly good **Italian** restaurant on the roundabout at L do Muncipal. The best place for a post-surf binge is **Inter Churrasco**, Av 25 de Abril, near the skate park, eat in or take out excellent grilled chicken or ribs, cooked over

charcoal, with chips, rice and Coca Cola (from a glass bottle) – all for €4.

☺ Shopping

Rip Curl Surf Shop, on R Alexandre Herculano just up from the *turismo*, has hardware and clothing including a great backroom with new/old stock. **Safari Surf Shop** is a few doors down on the same side of the road. There is a large open-air **market** on the last Thu of each month near Fortaleza. The **Intermarche** on EN114 has all the essentials including a little café.

☺ Directory

Banks: with ATMs just off the square near the *turismo*. **Hospital**: R General Humerto Delgado. **Internet**: internet café on R António Cervantes. **Tourist information**: open year round on R Alexandre Herculano.

Praia da Areia Branca

A good size beach sits in front of this modern village, which is an amazing cocktail of architectural styles and very quiet out of season. There are a number of rooms available; an **E Hostel**, T261-422127, near the beach, and a good campsite, **Campismo Municipal da Praia da Areia Branca**, T261-412199, near the beachfront at the bottom end of town.

Santa Cruz

Heading south on the coastal N247, the town of Santa Cruz is set atop cliffs overlooking a fine stretch of beaches.

Although very popular with Portuguese holidaymakers in the summer, it is very quiet out of season when cheap rooms can be found by asking in the local bars. The campsite, **Campismo Praia de Santa Cruz**, T261-930150, on the edge of town, is busy in the summer and quiet off-peak. It's well shaded, full of caravans, but fairly expensive. R José Pedro Lopez is home to a bank, mini-mercado and a number of cafés. **SPO Surfboards**, based near Santa Cruz, T261-937160, www.sposurf.com, are a co-operative of European based shapers who sponsor David Luis and João Antunes.

Ericeira

Since the 1980s, Ericeira has become the epicentre of Portuguese surfing. This picturesque, whitewashed fishing village has expanded to become a popular holiday town, with new developments and holiday apartments set back from the old centre.

☺ Flat spells

To be honest, there is little to do in Ericeira on flat days except sit in the square and drink coffee. There is a **cinema** on the main square. Films are usually in original English but check when you buy tickets.

☺ Sleeping

D-E Hospedaria Vinnu's, on R Prudencio Franco da Trindade, north of the central square, T261-863830, has pleasant, clean rooms available above a bar in a good central location. On the same road try **D-E Hospedaria Casa do Sol**, T261-864400,

Walls of Peniche

Ericeira chapel

good rooms at the top end of the road, near the bus stop from Lisbon.

D-E Hospedaria Bernado, T261-862378, is close to the square and has nice, clean rooms and friendly owner.

D-E Hospedaria Gomes, just south of the *turismo* on R Mendes Leal, T261-863619, is a slightly faded but still attractive residence. The tourist office will also supply a comprehensive list of **apartamentos**.

Camping Parque Municipal de Campismo de Mil Regos, T261-862513, is a large, popular and cheap campsite at the northern edge of town on the N247 coast road. Out of season it is probably just inhabited by surfers but it remains full of empty caravans and feels a bit cramped. It's only a short walk across the road to the breaks around Pedra Branca.

⑦ Eating/drinking

Seafood in Ericeira is excellent and there are many fish restaurants, though these are generally more expensive than in Peniche due to the number of Lisboêtas who come into town for the weekend. Any restaurant busy with locals is a sound bet. **Mar a Vista** on Largo das Ribas has good fish, particularly its grilled sardines or monkfish. Sitting outside **Patios dos Marialvas**, next to the tourist information office, you can enjoy shellfish while watching everyone file into the square for the evening. **Restaurante Chines Guang Yuan** is a surprisingly good Chinese restaurant near the shopping centre on the N247. There is the obligatory **Casa dos Frangos**, on R de Santo Antonio, doing takeaway gilled chicken and chips.

During the week there are some great cafés and bars to sit outside on the main square. At the weekends, **Bar Big Waves** on Praça dos Navigantes is popular while **Disco-Bar Uriço** heaves with local and visiting surfers as well as young people visiting for the weekend.

◯ Shopping

Ericeira Surf Shop, on R Prudencio Franco da Trindade, has a wide selection of hardware and clothing. **Semente Surfboards** can be found on the N247 at Ribamar, about 2 km north of Ericeira. They are the country's top board manufacturer and can also do board repairs. There's a **supermarket** and **24-hr shop** on the N247 towards the northern edge of town.

⑥ Directory

Banks and ATMs: on the main square. **Police**: R de Outubro. **Post office**: R Prudencio Franco da Trindade. **Taxis**: available from the main square back to the campsite. **Tourist information**: large, modern and very helpful office on the main square, P da Republica, open year round.

Ericeira fishing harbour

Ericeira school colours

Airports → Porto, T229-432400; Lisbon, T218-413500; **Faro**, T289-800800. **Buses and coaches** → Rede Expressos, T707-223344, www.rede-expressos.pt; Algarve Eva, T289-800800, www.eva-bus.com; **Car hire** → Auto Jardim, T800 200613, www.auto-jardim.com; **Rail** → Caminhos de Ferro Portugueses, T808-208208, www.cp.pt. **Petrol prices** → €0.90/litre unleaded.

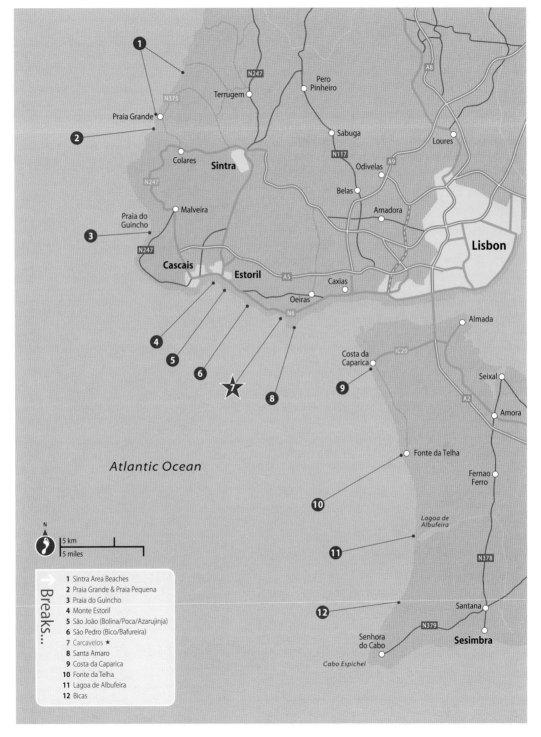

Lisbon

1 Sintra Area Beaches
2 Terrugem
Pero Pinheiro
Praia Grande
Sabuga
Loures
Colares
Sintra
N117
Odivelas
Belas
Amadora
Praia do Guincho
Malveira
Lisbon
Cascais
Estoril
A5
Caxias
Oeiras
N6
Almada
Costa da Caparica
Seixal
A2
Amora
Atlantic Ocean
Fonte da Telha
Fernao Ferro
Lagoa de Albufeira
N378
N379
Santana
Bicas
Senhora do Cabo
Sesimbra
Cabo Espichel

N

5 km
5 miles

Breaks...

1 Sintra Area Beaches
2 Praia Grande & Praia Pequena
3 Praia do Guincho
4 Monte Estoril
5 São João (Bolina/Poca/Azarujinja)
6 São Pedro (Bico/Bafureira)
7 Carcavelos ★
8 Santa Amaro
9 Costa da Caparica
10 Fonte da Telha
11 Lagoa de Albufeira
12 Bicas

O'NEILL

Surfing Lisbon

Lisbon is a city of many faces and a mass of contradictions. Chic, plain, bustling, sprawling, grubby, dour, ornate, poor and wealthy all at once. Climb the hill from the dockside and a wealth of esplanades and cobbled back streets offer an endless opportunity to explore, each criss-crossed by the rickety trams that climb to the very top of the city. The mixture of new and old is a result of the earthquake and tidal wave that destroyed the city in 1755. But the waves of immigration from Portugal's colonies help to make this a culturally rich and diverse city.

The N6 doggedly hugs the seafront as it heads over 30 km due west from the bustling heart of the Lisbon docks through the trendy suburbs of Cascais. Along the way it passes through the heartland of Lisbon's surfing communities from the urban sprawl of the suburbs to Oeiras, Carcavelos and Estoril. Once past the Ponta da Laje, the water quality starts to improve and the breaks become a lot more consistent. Carcavelos quickly became one of the country's best known breaks with photos of the classic barrels drawing surfers to explore this coastline.

The combination of the 1990s surf boom, a massive urban population sitting on the doorstep and easy access meant that these breaks were soon thronging with surfers, especially bodyboarders. Today the waves are rarely uncrowded, but for those who like to combine their surf trips with a bit of lively entertainment, Lisbon can offer a heady cocktail of excellent surf and excellent nightlife.

As João da Câmara Valente, Editor of *Surf Portugal* explains "Lisbon is basically the same as any other city break in the world, but it is the only European capital that sits right on the shore. It means lots of crowds at the main spots and considerable pollution levels (in both the air and sea). On the positive side, Lisbon is probably the place that best illustrates the variety of breaks Portugal's coast has to offer. To the south, we have the jetty breaks and beachbreaks of Caparica and also the Tagus rivermouth break. To the north, besides the awesome beach break of Carcavelos, there are lots of reef and point breaks around the Linha do Estoril coast. Both coasts welcome a huge variety of wind conditions. Besides that, it is just a 45-minute drive to Ericeira and one hour to Peniche."

Coastline

Lisbon sits in an amazing natural harbour in the Rio Tejo, protected from even the fiercest Atlantic storms. The region's surf spots are congregated around two areas. The first stretches from Ponta de Laje to Cascais and is made up of a series of sandy beaches, piers or rocky points fronting a long stretch of urban coastline. There is easy access to the beaches via the main stations on the Linha de Cascais or along the busy N6. This area needs big northwesterly or any southwesterly swell to get going, with winds from a northerly direction. The second area runs north from the large, exposed beach at Guincho, a popular windsurf Mecca in the summer, through to the Sintra beaches at Praia Grande. These

beaches are home to powerful waves and strong rips, as the full power of the Atlantic unloads on them. Between these two huge beaches sits the Cabo da Roca, the most westerly point in Europe.

Localism

Some breaks in the Lisbon area, especially around Carcavelos and Estoril, are very busy and very crowded. There are regular drop-ins and collisions are common. On busy days it's worth watching for a while to assess whether you want to enter the fray. A short walk down the coast can often yield a much less crowded option.

Top local surfers The highly competitive and high quality breaks of the Lisbon area has bred some of the country's best surfers including Ruben Gonzales, Justin Mujica and João Macedo.

Getting around

The A5 is a quick and easy way to get out of Lisbon to the west coast. This modern motorway is a reasonably charged toll road that runs nearly all the way to the coast near Guincho. The N6 is a busy main road that follows the coast out to Cascais and allows access to the urban breaks as do the cheap and regular trains on the Linha de Cascais.

"Carcavelos, my home break, is one of the most consistent spots in Portugal and ties together the coast of the north and the south. In the winter, with its powerful and hollow peaks stretching right along the beach, it is as good as any beach break in the world."

Justin Mujica, Portuguese pro surfer

Portugal Lisbon Surfing

Lisbon board guide

Beach break board
Shaper: Nick Urrichio, Semente Surfboards

▸▸ 6' 3" x 18⅞" x 2⅜"
▸▸ Choice of Semente team rider José Gregorio for day-to-day surfing.
▸▸ Bump wing, squash tail, full concave bottom and stand up loose rails through back.
▸▸ The rocker is very low in this board with nice release through the tail for vertical attacks.
▸▸ José is a big lad - for a smaller, lighter surfer run this around 6'1" x 18" x 2⅛".
▸▸ A beach break board for the good and bad days and the slop that sometimes prevails on the dream surf trip gone sour!

Tiago Pires model
Shaper: Nick Urrichio, Semente Surfboards

▸▸ A good travelling board for the better side of surfing Portugal, in other words 'thick filthy barrels', with fast, vertical take-offs, eg Carcavelos.
▸▸ Depending on your size and weight, a board from 6'5" to 6'8".
▸▸ Tiago Pires model 6'6" x 18" x 2⅛" pin tail, smooth unexaggerated rocker.
▸▸ Plane shape with nice draw through the tail for serious carving, slight vee on nose entrance to concave bottom with a slight flat spot on tail release. Fixed fins for power.
▸▸ We breed a lot of these animals for Tiago Pires and the home boys that like to spend serious time in the shade of barrels.

 Boards by **Semente Surfboards**
Factory: Rabo da Raposa, Ribamar, Ericeira, Portugal
T00 351 (0)261-863 552 www.semente.pt or contact semente@ip.pt

Breaks

Check out the bizarre fantasy city of Sintra, sit in the cafés on the seafront at Cascais, eat great seafood, ride the trams, listen to fado in the back-street clubs of Lisbon and surf the many urban breaks. Lisbon will keep you entertained whether there's surf or not.

Nat and Steve, travelling surfers

1 Sintra Area Beaches

- ◐ **Break type**: Beaches and reefs.
- ◑ **Conditions**: Small to medium swells, offshore in easterly winds.
- ❶ **Hazards/tips**: Rocks, rips and access can be a problem on some of these beaches.
- ◐ **Sleeping**: Praia Grande ▸▸ *p313*.

Stretching south from Ericeira are a series of beaches, coves, rivermouths and reefs. They are offshore in easterlies and work at various tides. Explore **Magoito, São Julião, Adraga** and **Praia das Maças**. You will find many of them work better at low and are usually uncrowded. Most don't handle big swells and prefer small, clean surf.

2 Praia Grande/Praia Pequena

- ◐ **Break type**: Beach breaks.
- ◑ **Conditions**: All swells, offshore in easterly winds.
- ❶ **Hazards/tips**: Crowds, powerful board-breaking waves.
- ◐ **Sleeping**: Praia Grande ▸▸ *p313*.

As the name suggests, **Praia Grande** is a large, sandy beach and has some great banks at low tide that can produce fast, hollow waves. Popular beach with surfers and bodyboarders. Can have a heavy shore break. The beach picks up lots of swell making it the preferred destination for the area's surfers. **Praia Pequena** is a smaller bay at the north end of the beach. Again the sandbanks here work through the tides, but a right-hander breaks off the northern point at low tide. This can be a quality wave so is worth checking in a decent swell. Park on top of the cliff. Very busy in the summer, both in and out of the water, so be careful where you park as it is easy to get blocked in.

3 Praia do Guincho

- ◐ **Break type**: Beach break.
- ◑ **Conditions**: All swells, offshore in easterly winds.
- ❶ **Hazards/tips**: Exposed beach, powerful waves, dangerous rips.
- ◐ **Sleeping**: Guincho/Cascais ▸▸ *p313*.

This large, exposed beach break picks up loads of swell and the waves can really pack a punch. It works through the tidal range with low often being better. Guincho is famed for its strong rips and swimmers do drown here every year – take care. Not recommended for beginners. In the summer it's common for roaring winds to scour the beach in the afternoons so it's worth getting in early for the morning glass. This makes it a windsurfer's Mecca. At the southern end of the beach is **Little Guincho**, a smaller bay that can also have good banks.

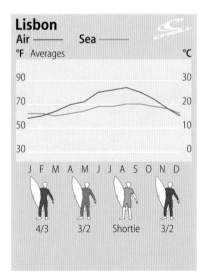

Lisbon

Air —— Sea ——

°F Averages   °C

90			30
70			20
50			10
30			0

J F M A M J J A S O N D

| 4/3 | 3/2 | Shortie | 3/2 |

DEMI TAYLOR

3 Praia do Guincho

Lisbon

4 Monte Estoril

- **Break type**: Right, sandy-bottomed reef peeling along jetty.
- **Conditions**: Medium swells, offshore in northerly winds.
- **Hazards/tips**: Rocks at low tide.
- **Sleeping**: Cascais/Estoril/Lisbon ⟩⟩ *p313*.

Walking east from Cascais you will come to a jetty, which occasionally has rights breaking off the far side. Access is from the end of the concrete pier but watch out for rocks as the tide drops. Water quality is poor as there is a sewage pipe in front of the break.

5 São João (Bolina/Poca/Azarujinja)

- **Break type**: Sandy reefs.
- **Conditions**: Medium to big swells, offshore in northerly winds.
- **Hazards/tips**: Urchins, crowds, pollution.
- **Sleeping**: Cascais/Estoril/Lisbon ⟩⟩ *p313*.

The breaks at São João need a decent size swell and northerly winds to work although the water quality of each of these breaks is dubious. **Bolina** is the first spot in São João, a shallow, hollow wave over a rocky/sandy reef. It's a crowded spot, popular with bodyboarders, that is best at mid tide. **Poca** is the next break, a good left and fast right with a steep take-off. Very popular spot so respect the locals. Rocky reef that works through the tides but better at mid. Restaurant and bar on the beach. Just a short walk to the east, **Azarujinja** is a powerful right and left that breaks over a sand-covered reef. It's a quality wave that breaks best at mid to low and is therefore very busy and can suffer from localism.

6 São Pedro (Bico/Bafureira)

- **Break type**: Both right-hand sandy reefs.
- **Conditions**: Medium to big swells, offshore in northerly winds.
- **Hazards/tips**: Crowded and poor water quality.
- **Sleeping**: Cascais/Estoril/Lisbon ⟩⟩ *p313*.

Bico is a fat right-hander that produces fun waves but closes out easily. It gets very crowded even though the waves lack power and the water quality is fairly bad. Next to Bico, **Bafureira** is the less crowded right-hander, with shorter but better waves – probably an all-round better bet.

7 Carcavelos

- **Break type**: Hollow left.
- **Conditions**: Medium to big.
- **Size**: 3-10 ft.
- **Length**: 50 m plus.
- **Swell**: Southwesterly or northwesterly.
- **Wind**: Northeasterly.
- **Tide**: All tides.
- **Bottom**: Sandbank.
- **Entry/exit**: Off the beach.
- **Hazards/tips**: Powerful, crowded, polluted.
- **Sleeping**: Cascais/Estoril/Lisbon ⟩⟩ *p313*.

Carcavelos is a long, sandy beach on the edge of Lisbon, with a fort at the eastern end where the most localized break, the **Zone**, sits. Known mainly as a left, waves breaking on this sandbar can be high quality, very hollow and very crowded. Carcavelos was one of the first waves in Portugal to reach the attention of the world and now attracts surfers and bodyboarders from all over the capital. Not really a summertime wave, but comes to life during the autumn and winter when it can be quite consistent. You have to be on it at first light to beat the locals. In big swells the wave can be a board breaker so obviously a wave for experienced surfers only. The sandbars shift around and swell

THE GILL

6 São Pedro (Bico/Bafureira)

THE GILL

7 Carcavelos

Surfers' tales

The taxi hit the motorway and the driver hammered the accelerator. I was just about to say "Slow down" when there was a bang from the roof and we turned round to see our boards bouncing down the fast lane of the motorway. The decrepid roof rack had died, scattering our precious boards, which were now acting as speed bumps for a succession of BMWs and Range Rovers. So far on this trip we'd had to deal with the horrors of public transport, flashers and either no surf or huge gales. Then, when the surf finally did get cranking, one of our party was dragged out to sea in a horrendous rip and had to be rescued. After risking life and limb to retrieve our battered, broken boards we arrived at Lisbon airport to be greeted by the departures screen flashing "All flights cancelled". A great end to a great surf trip – penniless, in the middle of a massive airport strike.

Damian Tate, *Freeride* magazine

direction can also affect the types of waves formed. When the banks are properly aligned the beach produces long, hollow powerful lefts and sometimes rights.

Nearby **Parede** is a high quality right-hand point break that comes to life in huge swells. Raved about when conditions combine to produce classic conditions here.

This stretch of coastline used to be home to the elite of Lisbon until a boom in development in the 1980s saw the area expand rapidly. The extra sewage waste from the new housing was simply dumped in the sea. The area has suffered from pollution issues ever since, but now local surfers are speaking out. As João Valente points out: "In the winter it can be very bad, especially with a southern swell. Sometimes you can see the waves are brown – polluted with sewage."

ⓘ *If you like* Carcavelos *try* **Supertubos** *in Portugal (see page 299),* **Hossegor** *in France (see page 178) and low tide* **Croyde** *in England (see page 75).*

8 Santa Amaro

- ◐ **Break type**: Right-hand point.
- ◑ **Conditions**: Big swells, offshore in northerly winds.
- ❶ **Hazards/tips**: Very heavy, polluted, debris, localism.
- ◉ **Sleeping**: Cascais/Estoril/Lisbon ▸▸ *p313*.

Works only on the biggest swells producing hollow, powerful waves for experienced surfers only. Works best at mid to high tides, when long, punchy rights are ridden by Lisbon's best surfers. When it's on, everywhere else will be maxed out. Has a heavy reputation as one of the best waves in Lisbon. Rideable in 10-ft plus range. The bottom here is rocky with metal debris. The water is very polluted and the wave is the realm of the area's most experienced surfers.

Costa da Caparica

9 Costa da Caparica

- ◐ **Break type**: Beach break.
- ◑ **Conditions**: All swells, offshore in easterly winds.
- ❶ **Hazards/tips**: Crowds and pollution at the northern end.
- ◉ **Sleeping**: Costa da Caparica ▸▸ *p315*.

Crossing the bridge allows access to a huge stretch of open sand, a very popular destination for Lisbon's surf community with miles of endless beach breaks. This northern end of the bay has groynes to trap the sand and produce reliable sandbars. Each section may have a regular crew of bodyboarders or surfers, but the further south you go, the more the crowds thin out and the water quality improves. Easterly winds are offshore and the beach picks up southerly, westerly or large northerly swells. Works through all states of tide.

Five minutes from Caparica is **Cova do Vapor**, a left that breaks along a rocky groyne. It's the best wave in the area, producing fast and hollow lefts at low tide. Dominated by a large pack of bodyboarders, it gets very crowded and non-locals may find they get dropped in on. The beach is suitable for surfers of all abilities. Some of the groynes (**Vapor**) for experts only.

7 Carcavelos ▸▸ *p311*

9 Guts at Costa da Caparica

10 Fonte da Telha

- **Break type**: Beach break.
- **Conditions**: Small to medium swells, offshore in easterly winds.
- **Hazards/tips**: Shifting peaks.
- **Sleeping**: Costa da Caparica ▸▸ *p315*.

Driving south about 10 km you come to Fonte da Tehla. Towards the middle of the bay the peaks tend to shift around more without the groynes. Still crowded but less polluted. Low tide tends to be a better option but some high tide peaks do form. A much better bet in smaller swells but can work in medium and bigger swells as well. Much less crowded than the Costa Estoril.

11 Lagoa de Albufeira

- **Break type**: Beach break.
- **Conditions**: Small to medium swells, offshore in easterly winds.
- **Hazards/tips**: Rips in big swells.
- **Sleeping**: Costa da Caparica ▸▸ *p315*.

Hollow, fast waves near the mouth of the lagoon. Works on all tides but can get busy at the weekend or in the summer. In the winter it is usually quiet. Produces nice rights when the lagoon opens into the sea and fickle sandbars when the lagoon mouth is closed.

12 Bicas

- **Break type**: Left reef break.
- **Conditions**: Big swells, offshore in easterly winds.
- **Hazards/tips**: Watch out for rocks.
- **Sleeping**: Costa da Caparica ▸▸ *p315*.

Rocky left reef that works best on low to mid tide. Bicas can handle a big northwest and westerly swell, needing 3-5 ft waves to really get going. Only breaks a few times a year but can produce high quality waves. The nearby beach has waves with a left and hollow right.

3 Praia do Guincho ▸▸ *p310*

Praia Grande

Sitting on the edge of the N247 this resort is packed in the summer and quiet out of season.

Flat spells

Sintra With it's crazy Moorish architecture and only 20 mins inland, Sintra makes a good day out if the surf is flat.

Sleeping

Rooms are available in the village but try first **C-D Maria Pereira**, 19 Av Maestro Frederico de Freitas, T21-290 319. The rooms are great and there are also apartments available.
Camping Praia Grande Campismo, on the EN135 Sintra–Praia das Maças road, T21-929 058, is a good size campsite open year round.

Guincho

This windswept beach is busy in the summer.

Sleeping

Except for the expensive L **Fortaleza do Guincho**, T21-487 0431, accommodation near the beach is limited. Better options are in nearby Cascais.
Camping Just behind the beach and set in tree-topped dunes, **Orbitur Campismo Guincho**, T21-487 0450, is a large site with some shady pitches and good facilities including cabins to rent. A good option if you want a cheap place near Lisbon. Has bus access to the train station in Cascais, for regular 30-min train service to Lisbon.

Cascais

Cascais has traditionally been an upmarket suburb of Lisbon due to its excellent transport links to the centre, great bars, restaurants and beachfront culture. It makes a great base for a surf trip to the Lisbon area with good links to beaches on the Estoril and west coasts.

DEMI TAYLOR

✿ Flat spells

Bike rides Rent a bike from **Aerial** on Cascais Marina. **Cinema** Catch a film at Cascais Shopping's multiplex where most of the films are in English. **Golf** Quinta da Marinha, T21-486 9881, is an excellent par 71, 18-hole course just off the N247 road out of Cascais towards Guincho. **Horse riding** Centro Hipico, Quinta da Marinha, T21-486 9433. **Lisbon** Explore Lisbon which is only 30 mins away by train, €3 return. **Motor racing** Check at the *turismo* to see what's on at Estoril.

⬤ Sleeping

There are plenty of expensive options in Cascais as it attracts the posh set, but there are good value options around if you explore.
F Residencial Avenida, R da Palmeira, T21-486 4417, is probably the best value and has some good double rooms in a central location. Nearer the beaches in the older part of town is **D-E Residence Parsi**, R Afonso Sanchez, T21-484 5744. A good but noisy location. Also try **E-F Adega do Goncalves**, T21-483 1519, north on the same road above a restaurant of the same name.

DEMI TAYLOR

Praying for a good wave . . .

❼ Eating/drinking

Grilled fish, especially sardines, *sardinhas assado*, is a local speciality. Check out **Esplanada Santa Marta** for their grilled fish served on a terrace overlooking the tiny beach of the same name. **Jardim dos Frangos**, Av Com. da Grande Guerra, is the obligatory grilled chicken establishment, a popular spot with tables outside. **Dom Monolo's**, Av Marginal, offer a good value menu with grilled fish and meat. Recommended are the catch of the day and the grilled chicken all served with chips and salad. More expensive but recommended is the seafood restaurant **Beira Mar** on R das Flores.

⬤ Shopping

The old **fish market** is definitely worth checking out as is Wed's weekly market on R do Mercado. The out of town mall, **Cascais Shopping**, has 2 **surf shops**, restaurants, fast food eateries as well as a multi-screen cinema showing films in original English version. **Aerial Wind and Surf**, Marina de Cascais, rent out boards and wetsuits.

⬤ Transport

There are regular **trains** into central Lisbon with stops at all the best breaks along the Costa Estoril. The train station is on the EN6/Av Marginal.

❶ Directory

Tourist information: R Visconde da Luz.

Estoril

Estoril has traditionally been a haunt of Europe's rich and famous. With its villas, Ferraris and beaches, it is not the cheapest place to be based.

✿ Flat spells

Casino If it's flat, hit the casino, Europe's biggest, but you'll need to dress smart – it's the kind of place you expect to see James Bond playing blackjack.
Golf The *turismo* can give you the run down on the many local golfing possibilities and arrange golf passes.

⬤ Sleeping

Probably the best place to stay is the reasonably priced and very pleasant **C-D Pensão Residencial Smart** on R Jose Viana, T21-468 2164.

⬤ Shopping

Aerial Wind and Surf, Av Egas Moniz, sells boards, wetsuits etc. The area is also home to **Atlantico Surfboards**, T21-460 0975, www.atlanticsurf.com, a respected company that has shaped for some of Europe's top riders.

❶ Directory

Tourist information: opposite the train station, can find accommodation.

Lisbon

Lisbon is a bustling city best seen on foot. A good idea if you are in a van is to leave it in Cascais and get the cheap and regular metro train into the centre. The station (Cais do Sodré) is near the river and just a short walk east to Baixa. This is the heart of the city and is dissected by the pedestrianized R Augusta, which runs from the river up to Rossio near the main railway station. Walking through the archway on Praça do Comércio, you enter the bustling city centre where shady characters appear and offer counterfeit watches before melting away. There are cafés and restaurants along the length of what is the heart of the rebuilt city. There are some good cheap accommodation options in this area and it makes a great base from which to push out and explore.

⬤ Sleeping

D New Aljubarrota, R da Assunção, T21-346 0112, is well located just off R Augusta, has a selection of great rooms with or without showers, and does triples as well. Breakfast included.
D Residencial Duas Nações, T21-347 0206, has a great location in the pedestrianized area close to R Augusta.
E Pensão Norte, R dos Douradores, T21-887

8941, has a wide selection of rooms with either a shower or bath and is close to Rossio.
E **Pensão Prata**, close to Praça Comércio on R de Prata, T21-346 8908, a good budget option.

⊘ Eating/drinking
Rei do Frangos on Trav De Santo Antão really is king of the chickens. If it's vegetarian food you're after, check out **Refeições Naturais e Vegetarianos**, R dos Correios, a good value self-service eatery in Baixo. Sit outside and drink in the atmosphere over lunch at **Académica** on Largo do Carmo in Bairro Alto. Enjoy a coffee and pastry for breakfast or a lunch of grilled sardines. **Suica** on Rossio is another popular café serving excellent pastries.

Lisbon has an amazing assortment of bars and clubs and with new ones opening practically every week, there's something for everyone. There are Jazz clubs, Fado bars and even a new club part-owned by John Malkovich. It's best to get out and explore.

⊘ Directory
Internet: Espaço Agora, on the seafront at Av Brasilia (opposite the train station), is late opening and reasonably priced.
Medical facilities: Hospital Britanico, R Saraiva de Carvalho, has English-speaking doctors or ask at the *turismo* for one.
Police: 24-hr tourist police in the Foz Cultura at Praça dos Restauradores. **Post office**: Praça do Comércio, with internet access. **Tourist information**: Praça do Comércio – pick up a copy of *Follow Me Lisboa*, a free guide to what's happening.

Costa da Caparica

Cross the Ponte 25 de Abril and come face to face with Jesus – well, a 28-m high statue of him (think Rio de Janeiro). Costa da Caparica itself is a huge beach backed by numerous campsites. In the summer and at weekends the northern end of the stretch is packed with holidaymakers, *Lisboetas* and surfers. The further south you head the more the crowds thin out.

❄ Flat spells
Golf Get a round in at the 18-hole **Aroeira GC** in Fonte da Telha, just to the south on the N377, T21-297 1314. **Jesus** If you've got a head for heights, hand over your €2 to climb up inside him to take in the views.

⊜ Sleeping
Camping Orbitur Costa da Caparica Campisimo, T21-290 3894, is well located just outside the town, open year round with the option of cabins to rent. Just south at Fonte da Telha is camping **Costa Nova**, T21-290 3021, open Jan-Nov. Other campsites worth checking include **Campismo da Praia da Saude**, by the beach of the same name, T21-290 2272, open year round, and **Campismo Un Lagara o Sol**, T21-290 1592, open mid Jan-mid Dec.

◐ Shopping
Several **shapers** are in this area. In São João try **Polen Surfboards**, R Infante D. Henriques, T21-291 4083, established in 1988, who shape for some of Portugal's most exciting riders including Justin Mujica and Ruben Gonzales. Also in São João are **Fusion Surfboards**, T966 329255, and **Lufi Surfboards** T21-290 0402, www.lufisurfboards.com, on R João Inacio de Alfama.

⊘ Directory
Tourist information: Av da Republica.

DEMI TAYLOR

One of Lisbon's emblematic trams

Airports → Porto, T229-432400; Lisbon, T218-413500; **Faro**, T289-800800. **Buses and coaches** → Rede Expressos, T707-223344, www.rede-expressos.pt; Algarve Eva, T289-800800, www.eva-bus.com; **Car hire** → Auto Jardim, T800 200613, www.auto-jardim.com; **Rail** → Caminhos de Ferro Portugueses, T808-208208, www.cp.pt. **Petrol prices** → €0.90/litre unleaded.

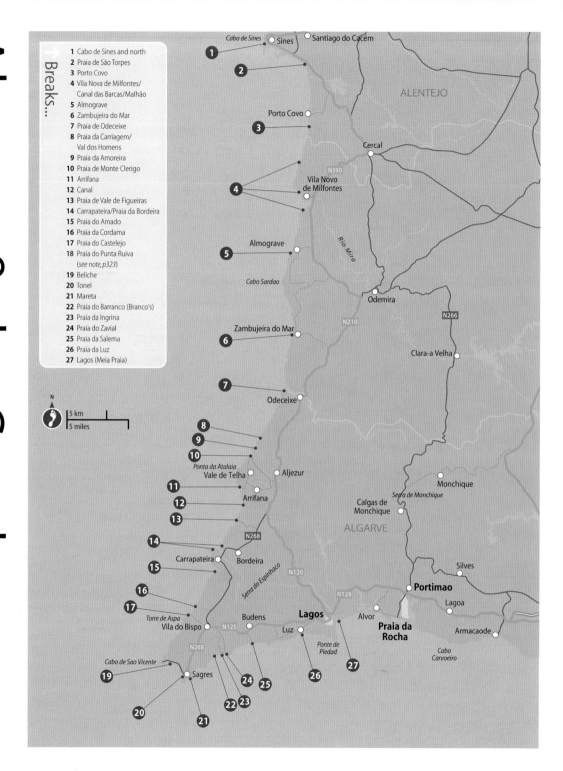

Breaks...

1 Cabo de Sines and north
2 Praia de São Torpes
3 Porto Covo
4 Vila Nova de Milfontes/
   Canal das Barcas/Malhão
5 Almograve
6 Zambujeira do Mar
7 Praia de Odeceixe
8 Praia da Carriagem/
   Val dos Homens
9 Praia da Amoreira
10 Praia de Monte Clerigo
11 Arrifana
12 Canal
13 Praia de Vale de Figueiras
14 Carrapateira/Praia da Bordeira
15 Praia do Amado
16 Praia da Cordama
17 Praia do Castelejo
18 Praia do Punta Ruiva
   (see note, p323)
19 Beliche
20 Tonel
21 Mareta
22 Praia do Barranco (Branco's)
23 Praia da Ingrina
24 Praia do Zavial
25 Praia da Salema
26 Praia da Luz
27 Lagos (Meia Praia)

5 km
5 miles

Cabo de Sines
Sines
Santiago do Cacém
ALENTEJO
Porto Covo
Cercal
N390
Vila Novo de Milfontes
Rio Mira
Almograve
Cabo Sardao
Odemira
N266
N210
Zambujeira do Mar
Clara-a-Velha
Odeceixe
Ponta da Atalaia
Vale de Telha
Aljezur
Monchique
Serra de Monchique
Arrifana
Calgas de Monchique
ALGARVE
N268
Carrapateira
Bordeira
Serra do Espinhaco
N120
Silves
N128
Portimao
Lagoa
Torre de Aspa
Budens
Lagos
Alvor
Armacaode
Vila do Bispo
N125
Luz
Praia da Rocha
Cabo Carvoeiro
N268
Ponte de Piedad
Cabo de Sao Vicente
Sagres

Surfing Algarve & the South

When you think of Europe's top surfing destinations, the Algarve isn't the first place that springs to people's minds. Holiday brochures are full of images of crystal-clear waters and tranquil bays with grey-haired couples strolling hand in hand along the golden sand. When travelling surfers first explored Portugal, it wasn't the southwest that they immediately headed for. However, the region couldn't remain a secret for long and now it is home to a hardcore and very dedicated surfing population, one of the country's most controversial breaks and a number of surf camps.

Cast aside thoughts of concrete resorts and cafés serving up greasy breakfasts. The western Algarve is a vast region of pristine coastlines, whitewashed villages and rough tracks winding down to quiet bays. A good sturdy vehicle or 4WD is a definite advantage here and helps to open up the massive potential this coastline has to offer. The southwest of Portugal is one of the most unspoilt coastlines in Europe and it is still possible to find empty bays overlooked by a patchwork of flower-filled, pristine pastureland.

The amazing thing about southwest Portugal is that the western coastline picks up so much swell that the south coast can sometimes be the only place to surf. Not that the western coastline is without its big-wave spots. "I think my most memorable experience in Portugal was a session in the late 1980s with two close friends at a big-wave spot called Montanhas (Mountains), on the southwest coast," explains *Surf Portugal* Editor João da Câmara Valente. "For two days we surfed 2-3 ft waves in the first week of October wearing trunks, due to an uncharacteristic warm current passing through the coast. On the third day, however, the swell jumped almost instantaneously to a solid 12 ft. A friend of mine suggested we should check this fabled outside reef he had surfed on his own. When we arrived, we saw in the distance these giant, perfect glassy 12-15 ft peaks breaking on the outside of a bay that was itself lining up a perfect 8-10 ft right point break on its inside. It was an amazing view. We surfed for three hours, trying to figure out a line-up, dodging sets and eating a lot of shit (the biggest board we had was my 6'6"). I remember that on our way back to shore, we surfed a few rights on the point break and they felt so easy and mellow in comparison. I have never seen 'Mountains' break so perfectly again."

Coastline

The western coastline from the industrial port of Sines down to Arrifana is a mixture of rocky coastline interspersed with small bays and attractive beaches. The potential of this area is incredible, with secret points and heavy beach breaks that have somehow never

The Algarve has two coastlines and is in the top three swell-receiving areas in the world. In the winter it is also the warmest place to be in Europe and it is relatively cheap. What more do you want?

Toby Millage, the Surf Experience

Algarve & the South board guide

Fish board
Shaper: Nick Urrichio, Semente Surfboards

- If you are going to spend a lot of time on southern shores, or for the micro-mush days that exist in any part of the world, a fish board will help you make the most of the situation.
- Semente's 'big boy' (again José Gregorio) model is 6'0" x 19 ½" x 2½" swallow tail.
- Rolled vee up front with soft 50/50 rails, running into concave mid to double barrel concave between fins to a slight vee on release on tail.
- Rocker is very flat for speed and volume distributed for major paddling and wave catching ease.
- Rails are blocky with a hard bottom edge through the back to keep it loose.
- 'The wave magnet' has become a must for soul surfers and pros travelling through all of Europe in the summer months.

Beach break board
Shaper: Nick Urricho, Semente Surfboards

- 6'3" x 18⅞" x 2⅜".
- Choice of Semente team rider José Gregorio for day-to-day surfing.
- Bump wing, squash tail, full concave bottom and stand up loose rails through back.
- The rocker is very low in this board with nice release through the tail for vertical attacks.
- Jose is a big lad - for a smaller, lighter surfer run this around 6'1" x 18" x 2⅛".
- Beat those summertime blues!

 Boards by **Semente Surfboards**
Factory: Rabo da Raposa, Ribamar, Ericeira, Portugal
T00 351 (0)261-863 552 www.semente.pt or contact semente@ip.pt

made it onto the surfing map. From Arrifana south to Torre de Aspa, two huge expanses of sandy beach are exposed to the full onslaught of the Atlantic Ocean. These are some of the most powerful breaks in Europe and only worth checking in small to medium swells.

Sagres, on the southwest toe of Portugal, has an amazing seafaring history and is home to a sometimes overly protective surf community. The breaks here are sandy bays nestled below sheltering cliffs, watched over by an impressive fortress.

The south coast between Ponta de Sagres and Lagos is, again, an impressive series of beaches and points, some in front of picturesque villages, many hidden away down dirt tracks. The water is warm, clean and crystal clear and the sun seems to shine every day. Sitting in the line-up here, you can see why more and more people are attracted here in search of winter paradise.

Localism

Incredibly for an area with so much surf potential, and one that receives so much swell, the area around Sagres has had real localism issues. There are very few places in Europe where there have been incidences of violent localism but this is one of those areas. Members of the local surf community have threatened and intimidated and, on a couple of occasions, assaulted surfers from outside the area.

However, many people report no problems in or out of the water. The trouble is probably confined to a small number of highly strung locals with vested interests in protecting their patch. The karmic wheel does like balance and one local surfer explained that on a trip to Lisbon some of the worst offenders found themselves meeting a reception committee made up of Lisbon surfers they had previously threatened. When it comes to Sagres, the message seems to be, if you go and surf respectfully, you should have no problems.

Top local surfers The Algarve and southwest Portugal has produced some very good surfers such as **João Mealha** and **Nuno Fontaínhas**. **Marlon Lipke,** who grew up surfing on the Algarve, is now one of Europe's top young competitive riders.

Getting around

The N125 is a modern highway that runs just inland from Lagos to Vila de Bispo and allows quick access to the south coast. The N268 heads north to Arrifana and is a good quality road, but it is worth topping up with petrol as there are no filling stations on this section of the west coast until you get to Aljezur. Some of the breaks are hard to access with rough *pistes*, potholes and muddy slopes to negotiate. Signs to beaches are routinely removed.

Lagos town walls ▸▸ *p327*

Breaks

Algarve & the South

Air ——— Sea ———

°F Averages   °C

90 ————————————————————————— 30

70 ————————————————————————— 20

50 ————————————————————————— 10

30 ————————————————————————— 0

J F M A M J J A S O N D

3/2   3/2   Shortie   Shortie

1 Cabo de Sines and north

- **Break type**: Beach breaks.
- **Conditions**: All swells, offshore in light easterly winds.
- **Hazards/tips**: Access to sections of the beach can be difficult.
- **Sleeping**: Porto Covo ▸▸ p325.

Sines was once a pretty port town that is now dominated by surrounding petrochemical plants and a large harbour complex. Cabo de Sines is a very smelly rock point with spectacular waves crashing on the rocks. North of this point starts a huge crescent-shaped beach that runs north all the way to the Peninsula de Troia, just south of Setubal. The further north you travel, the more Cabo Espichel cuts out the swell. The beaches here are virtually unsurfed and fully exposed to wind and swell. At high tide the waves tend to turn into shore dump. This stretch of coastline is one of Europe's last real unexplored areas.

2 Praia de São Torpes

- **Break type**: Beach break.
- **Conditions**: Medium to big swells, offshore in easterly/northeasterly winds.
- **Hazards/tips**: Pollution.
- **Sleeping**: Porto Covo ▸▸ p325.

To the south of Sines stretches a long sandy beach that picks up more swell as you head further south. This area is offshore in northeasterly winds and offers some protection from big northwesterly swells. A

4 Canal das Barcas

good spot to check are the jetties in front of the power plant on the N120 just south of Sines. Sand builds up next to the jetties producing some quality waves. The piers are usually uncrowded, as are the beaches nearby. The water quality here can be poor due to the huge petrochemical plants in Sines.

3 Porto Covo

- **Break type**: Beach breaks and reefs.
- **Conditions**: Medium swells, offshore in easterly winds.
- **Hazards/tips**: Rocky reef.
- **Sleeping**: Porto Covo ▸▸ p325.

This is a very pretty fishing settlement that has metamorphosed into a holiday village of white painted cottages and small cafés. Around the village are numerous coves and reefs, some of which may only come to life a couple of times a year. The most famous break in Porto Covo is a sheltered mid tide reef break with rights and lefts, found in the shadow of Ilha Do Pessegueiro (Peach Tree Island). This peak needs a decent swell to break and is offshore in easterly winds. There are also peaks to be found on the beaches to the north and south of this spot. Time spent exploring could be rewarding. A quiet spot with campsites and free-camping possibilities. Busy with tourists in the summer but quiet off season.

4 Vila Nova de Milfontes/Canal das Barcas/Malhão

- **Break type**: Rivermouth, beach and point break.
- **Conditions**: All swells, offshore in easterly winds.
- **Hazards/tips**: Excellent potential.
- **Sleeping**: Vila Nova de Milfontes ▸▸ p325.

South of the Rio Mira is a beach break accessible via the road to Furnas, which leads to parking in the dunes. There are peaks around the beachfront café. The rivermouth has a left, which is of variable quality depending on the swell and tidal flow. There

DEMI TAYLOR

are also a couple of further breaks in front of the town north of the river. They can all be checked from the seafront at the rivermouth.

Leave the town via the small coastal road and follow the signs north for the harbour and you come to **Canal das Barcas**. This is a right-hand rocky point break that can have excellent, long waves. These peel in front of a huge rock and when a big, clean swell combines with easterly winds, it will fire. This is one of the area's quality waves so respect is needed in the line-up. **Praia do Malhão** is a long, popular beach that works at all tides and picks up a lot of swell. Follow the *piste* off the main road north of the town.

Vila Nova is a great town with cinema, surf shop and great cafés and bars. Vans can be seen free-camping in the dunes south of the river. This area doesn't get a huge amount of travelling surfers so be friendly to the surfers and they will be friendly in return.

5 Almograve

- ◉ **Break type**: Rocky beach break.
- ◉ **Conditions**: Small to medium swells, offshore in easterly winds.
- ◉ **Hazards/tips**: Fickle and rocky bay but usually very quiet.
- ◉ **Sleeping**: Vila Nova de Milfontes/Zambujeira do Mar ›› *p325*.

This rocky beach break has a number of peaks worth checking in different swells and tides. There can be a left to the south near the Restaurant de Pescador and a rocky right towards the middle of the bay. It's worth checking the point to the north.

6 Zambujeira do Mar

- ◉ **Break type**: Beach break.
- ◉ **Conditions**: Small to medium swells, offshore in an easterly wind.
- ◉ **Hazards/tips**: Campsite in village.
- ◉ **Sleeping**: Zambujeira do Mar ›› *p326*.

This beach is the last break in the Alentejo region before crossing into the Algarve. It's a protected beach within rocky outcrops. A left breaks off the cliff to the south and can produce some quality waves and there can also be a peak in the middle of the bay depending on the sandbar. Headlands provide some protection from winds from the north or south. The village is not unattractive and has all the usual amenities. Some vans free-camp on the cliff-top car park south of the beach. There are beaches north and south worth checking.

Algarve

7 Praia de Odeceixe

- ◉ **Break type**: Rivermouth beach break.
- ◉ **Conditions**: Small to medium swells, offshore in easterly winds.
- ◉ **Hazards/tips**: Fickle break, rips in bigger swells.
- ◉ **Sleeping**: Odeceixe ›› *p326*.

Turn off the N120 onto the new road to Praia de Odeceixe and park up overlooking the break in the village. The beach here is sheltered by cliffs at the northern end and

offshore in an easterly wind. Peaks work best at low tide on the push and tend to shift about almost daily. This pretty beach is usually uncrowded making it a nice spot to escape the crowds both in and out of the water. The beach can also be accessed by taking the first left right before the bridge on the N120.

8 Praia da Carriagem/ Val dos Homens

- ◉ **Break type**: Beach breaks.
- ◉ **Conditions**: Small to medium swells, offshore in easterly winds.
- ◉ **Hazards/tips**: Long drive on rough *piste*.
- ◉ **Sleeping**: Aljezur ›› *p326*.

Turn off the N120 at Rogil and follow the *piste* down to these two breaks. **Carriagem** is a beach break worth checking. It works on all tides but is exposed to the wind. **Val dos Homens** is a rocky beach with a scar where the waves break. Park at the top of the cliff. Susceptible to winds unless from the east.

9 Praia da Amoreira

- ◉ **Break type**: Rivermouth beach break.
- ◉ **Conditions**: Small to medium swells, offshore in easterly winds.
- ◉ **Hazards/tips**: Safe beach for learners on small days. Vans sometimes free-camp in car park.
- ◉ **Sleeping**: Aljezur ›› *p326*.

Amoreira is a beach break with a left-hand sandbar at the mouth of the river under the

8 Praia da Carriagem

9 Praia da Amoreira

10 Praia de Monte Clerigo

headland and a reef in the middle of the bay. The left can work in big, clean swells peeling for up to 100 m. On clean, small days any number of peaks can pop up in the bay. The waves can be empty when big but popular with local surfers when small.

10 Praia de Monte Clerigo

◉ **Break type**: Beach with sandbanks and reefs.
◉ **Conditions**: Small to medium swells, offshore in easterly winds.
◉ **Hazards/tips**: Quiet break. Rips in large swells.
◉ **Sleeping**: Aljezur/Arrifana ›› *p326*.

Take the right turn at the top of the hill coming up from Aljezur to Arrifana and follow the road to the small village of Monte Clerigo. It has cafés and a beautiful, quiet beach. There is an assortment of waves here from reefs to sandbars, so on a clean swell with light easterlies you could be spoilt for

choice. At the south end of the beach at low tide is a reef with lefts and rights. On the beach are a number of banks, good from low up to high, and at the north end of the beach breaks another right. This beach is exposed and strong winds can be a problem.

11 Arrifana

◉ **Break type**: Beach-break peak and right point.
◉ **Conditions**: Medium to big swells, offshore in easterly winds.
◉ **Hazards/tips**: Rocks on the point. On the peak, problems are from other surfers.
◉ **Sleeping**: Arrifana ›› *p326*.

Probably the best known spot in southwest Portugal, this is the area's most versatile and consistent wave. In an area that gets so much swell, it is one of the few places that is sheltered in big swells. It is also sheltered from northerly winds and therefore usually crowded. The undemanding beach break

attracts surfers of all abilities and the peak can often see local and travelling surfers hassling over waves. Works at all states of tide. The point is a large right that breaks over rocks and boulders in massive swells. Doesn't start working until the waves are over 6 ft on the point. One huge rock sits right in the line of the wave, so the bigger the swell, the more chance of making it around the rock. A wave for experienced surfers only.

12 Canal

◉ **Break type**: Beach with right point.
◉ **Conditions**: Small to medium swells, offshore in easterly winds.
◉ **Hazards/tips**: Rips when big.
◉ **Sleeping**: Arrifana ›› *p326*.

Sheltered under the cliffs to the south of Arrifana, Canal can be home to some quality waves. The right works in medium, clean northwesterly swells. The beach runs all the way to Vale de Figueiras to the south.

10 Praia de Monte Clerigo

11 Arrifana

13 Praia de Vale de Figueiras

- **Break type**: Beach break and sand-covered reef.
- **Conditions**: Small to medium swells, offshore in easterly winds.
- **Hazards/tips**: Rips when big. Isolated so never surf alone.
- **Sleeping**: Arrifana » *p326*.

Take the turning off the N268 for Monte Novo and follow the long, rough *piste*. Can be a mission to find but the tricky access does keep crowds down to virtually zero. Can have quality lefts and rights at low tide. This spot gives access to a huge expanse of beach where you can walk and find a peak. Works best on a small to medium swell. Waves break over sand or sand-covered reef and are offshore in easterly winds.

14 Carrapateira/Praia da Bordeira

- **Break type**: Left point and long beach.
- **Conditions**: Small to medium swells, offshore in easterly winds.
- **Hazards/tips**: Powerful waves and strong rips. Not for inexperienced surfers.
- **Sleeping**: Carrapateira » *p326*.

At the south end of the beach is a car park that overlooks a left point. The wave peels in front of a cliff towards the rivermouth and is best from low on the push. It can produce some excellent, long rides in small to large swells. Heading north from the headland is a long sandy beach that is usually virtually empty. At the rivermouth, a hollow right breaks, producing excellent board-breaking waves in clean swells. Looking north there are sandbanks producing excellent waves along the length of the beach in light, easterly, offshore winds and clean, northwesterly swells. The beach is, however, exposed and susceptible to strong winds. Overall one of the region's top spots. There are rips near the river and rocks on the point.

15 Praia do Amado

- **Break type**: Long beach break.
- **Conditions**: Small to medium swells, offshore in easterly winds.
- **Hazards/tips**: Crowds.
- **Sleeping**: Carrapateira » *p326*.

Very popular beach just to the south of the village of Carrapateira. Amado is home to a surf school and café and in the summer is packed with surfers of all nationalities, particularly Spanish surfers during their holidays and on long weekends (convoys of five or six cars are not uncommon). The wave quality here varies a lot with shifting sandbars. Picks up less swell than Carrapateira to the north, and the sandbars are usually not as good. Works best on small swells. Peaks near car park get very busy. Overly popular for its wave quality. Also a popular free-camping area with motorhomes and vans.

14 Praia da Bordeira

12 Canal » *p321*

15 Praia do Amado

15 Praia do Amado

16 Praia da Cordama

- ⦿ **Break type**: Beach break.
- ⦿ **Conditions**: Small to medium swells, offshore in easterly winds.
- ⦿ **Hazards/tips**: Rips when big, rocks.
- ⦿ **Sleeping**: Carrapateira/Sagres ⤞ *p326*.

A series of empty beaches lead south to Cordama. All good at low tide with some working through until high, depending on local sandbars and rocks. Most work well in small to medium, clean swells and are offshore in easterly winds. Various points and reefs can be found if you have the time to check out the *piste* roads north. Some of the beaches are quite isolated so never surf alone. Can have rips when big and isolated rocks.

17 Praia do Castelejo

- ⦿ **Break type**: Left-hand, sand-covered rocky point.
- ⦿ **Conditions**: Small to medium swells, offshore in easterly winds.
- ⦿ **Hazards/tips**: Cliff top between here and Cordama gives views of the whole coastline.
- ⦿ **Sleeping**: Carrapateira/Sagres ⤞ *p326*.

This west-facing bay is home to a long, shallow, rocky left point break at the south of the bay. Can be classic in small to medium clean swells. Towards the northern end, a right-hand sandbar can produce good waves.

18 Praia do Punta Ruiva

- ⦿ **Break type**: Right-hand point break.
- ⦿ **Conditions**: All swells, offshore in southerly winds.
- ⦿ **Hazards/tips**: Hidden down miles of rutted *piste*.
- ⦿ **Sleeping**: Carrapateira/Sagres ⤞ *p326*.

An exposed point break that picks up loads of swell but is susceptible to wind. Signs are switched round so it can be a mission to find. Respect the locals if you do. It is not marked on our map.

19 Beliche

- ⦿ **Break type**: Beach-break peak.
- ⦿ **Conditions**: Medium and big swells, offshore in northeasterly winds.
- ⦿ **Hazards/tips**: Crowds and localism.
- ⦿ **Sleeping**: Sagres ⤞ *p326*.

Small, sandy cove that picks up less swell than Tonel. The peak here can be very good, producing hollow waves, but consequently gets very crowded depending on the time of day (lunch and evenings). Faces south so is offshore in northerly winds. Beach can disappear at high tide.

20 Tonel

- ⦿ **Break type**: Beach break.
- ⦿ **Conditions**: Medium swells, offshore in easterly winds.
- ⦿ **Hazards/tips**: Localism and crowds.
- ⦿ **Sleeping**: Sagres ⤞ *p326*.

A west-facing beach overlooked by an imposing fortress, this cliff-lined cove is home to some excellent surf. There are many

sandbars at low tide but fewer at high as most of the beach disappears. Northwesterly swells will be smaller here than on the west coast. It can get very busy and there are lots of local bodyboarders with attitude. There is even a local bodyboarding school. Peaks nearest the parking are always the busiest so check out the far end if you want some waves to yourself.

21 Mareta

- ⦿ **Break type**: Beach break.
- ⦿ **Conditions**: Medium to big swells, offshore in northwesterly winds.
- ⦿ **Hazards/tips**: Localism.
- ⦿ **Sleeping**: Sagres ⤞ *p326*.

Mareta is a cresent-shaped beach south of Sagres that faces southeast. It has peaks along its length which break in medium southwesterly or big northwesterly swells. It's a very popular break as it works during northwesterly winds which blow out the west coast. Has a reputation for localism, not just to foreign surfers but to travelling Portuguese as well. As a result some

16 Praia da Cordama

17 Praia do Castelejo

19 Beliche

20 Tonel

x

travelling surfers avoid the area, but if you keep your eyes open and are respectful you should be OK. Cafés on the beachfront and cliff top overlook the breaks with parking and showers beachside.

22 Praia do Barranco (Branco's)

- **Break type**: Right-hander in pebble bay.
- **Conditions**: Medium swells, offshore in northerly winds.
- **Hazards/tips**: Access along a rutted track, can be a problem in wet weather.
- **Sleeping**: Sagres/Luz/Lagos ›› p326.

Popular mid to high tide beach. Can get crowded as people will head here when the west coast is big or when a good southwesterly swell is running. Popular as a free-camping area as it is a trek to get too.

23 Praia da Ingrina

- **Break type**: Left reef.
- **Conditions**: Bigger swells, offshore in northerly winds.
- **Hazards/tips**: For experienced surfers only. Bar overlooks break.
- **Sleeping**: Sagres/Luz/Lagos ›› p326.

Wave breaks in front of a large rock and into a small cove. Popular with boogers in small swells, as they can take off on the backwash off the rock. Better for surfers when a bit bigger and clean.

24 Praia do Zavial

- **Break type**: Right point and beach.
- **Conditions**: Medium swells, offshore in northerly winds.
- **Hazards/tips**: Popular beach which gets crowded.
- **Sleeping**: Sagres/Luz/Lagos ›› p326.

Sandy cove at low tide with right point at the west, which can produce some quality waves at mid tide. Waves peel from headland towards beach along this sand-covered reef. Peaks in the bay tend to close out in bigger swells. The best spot on the south coast when west coast gets too big. Café overlooks beach with parking. Walk out onto the rocks to check the point, which is obscured from the car park.

25 Praia da Salema

- **Break type**: Beach break.
- **Conditions**: Big swells, offshore in northwesterly winds.
- **Hazards/tips**: Car park on seafront in village.
- **Sleeping**: Luz/Lagos ›› p327.

Small village with sheltered beach. Peaks on seafront can be good depending on banks. Picks up less swell than Zavial.

26 Praia da Luz

- **Break type**: Left point, beach and right point.
- **Conditions**: Big swells, offshore in northerly winds.
- **Hazards/tips**: Rocky point best left to experienced surfers.
- **Sleeping**: Luz/Lagos ›› p326.

Luz is a holiday village just outside Lagos off the N125. The beach break can have nice peaks helped by a small rivermouth. The sloping right reef on the western edge and long, rocky left point on the eastern end both work in big, clean, southwesterly swells.

27 Lagos (Meia Praia)

- **Break type**: Long, sandy beach break.
- **Conditions**: Big swells, offshore in northerly/northwesterly winds.
- **Hazards/tips**: Fairly safe beach for beginners.
- **Sleeping**: Lagos ›› p326.

This big beach works well in big northerly or southwesterly swells. At the Lagos end sandbars can be found near the harbour/rivermouth where the sea wall can provide protection. Further along, the horseshoe-shaped beach picks up more swell. Better on a low tide. Beach is packed with tourists in summer, but off season it's quiet and free-camping is possible in the car park behind the beach. A good place to check if big northerlies are battering the west coast.

DEMI TAYLOR
22 Gemma Pasierb at Branco's

DEMI TAYLOR
22 Praia do Barranco (Branco's)

DEMI TAYLOR
25 Praia da Salema

Listings

Mullens restaurant in Lagos ▸▸ *p327*

Sines

Part of the Alentejo region, Sines is a once pretty town now blighted by petrochemical plants and refineries. The town centre is still attractive and overlooked by an impressive castle, but unless you fancy a day trip on a flat day, it is probably best bypassed.

Porto Covo

Sitting on the coast to the south of Sines, this pretty whitewashed fishing village makes a great base for a surf trip. Although it is becoming a tourist resort with modern housing and developments springing up on the edge of the village, it has retained most of its charm and has plenty of accommodation.

✪ Flat spells

Santiago do Cacém Head north to Sines and inland along the IP8 to this town complete with the Roman ruins of Mirobriga (€2, closed Mon) and a Moorish castle with good views along the coast.
Evora One of the country's most impressive and picturesque towns, though getting there is a serious inland trek.

⬤ Sleeping

C-E Porto Covo Hotel Apartamento, R Vitalina da Silva, T269-959140, www.hotelportocovo.com, year-round apartments and rooms with very reasonable off-season rates. Slightly more upmarket than the basic
E-F Pensão Boa Esperança, R Conde Bandeira, T269-905109.
If you are in a group, check out
F Apartment Rosa, R de Farmacia, T269-905125, for a cheap option or on R Vasco da Gamma try apartments **Abelha**, T269-905108, or **Capitao**, T269-905179.
Camping Camping Porto Covo, T269-95136, is open year round and has cabins for rent. **Ilha do Pessegueiro Camping**, T269-95178, open year round, overlooks the island south of Porto Covo and also has cabins.

❼ Eating/drinking

La Bella Vita Pizzeria, R Vasco da Gama, offers good evening meals while **O Balneario** at Baia dos Pescadores is a *casa de frango* (offering good value grilled chicken with chips or rice) that also serves pizzas against the backdrop of the fishing port. **Restaurant O Rosas**, R Vasco da Gama, is a very popular seafood eatery with good fish dishes. **O Marques** is a popular café on the main square which does good coffees and pastries – a nice spot for breakfast.

❶ Directory

Tourist information: on Praça Mercado Municipal (the main square) with the library, www.costa-azul.rts.pt, also has **internet** access. There are also a couple of **ATMs** (Multibancos) in the village as well several mini-mercados to stock up on provisions.

Vila Nova de Milfontes

The N390 heads towards the coast where it hits the Rio Mira at this popular coastal town. Sitting on the north bank of the estuary, Vila Nova makes a good base with excellent waves close to the town and plenty of accommodation and facilities to hand. The resort is popular with Portuguese holidaymakers but is off the travelling surfer's European trail and out of season manages to keep the feeling of a normal, pleasant working town.

⬤ Sleeping

E-F Pensão do Cais, R do Cais, T283-996268, is busy in the summer so book ahead. It's cheaper off season with good, clean rooms and is one of the best options in town.
E Casa Dos Arcos, also on R do Cais up from the Jardin do Cais, T283-996264, offers B&B with pleasant rooms but is slightly more expensive.
For an apartment try **Duna Parque**, on R Eira da Pedra, T283-996451, which has modern, well-equipped, if somewhat pricey rooms that sleep 4.
Camping Parques de Milfontes,

T283-996104, is the larger of the 2 campsites with excellent facilities, electric hook-ups etc., while nearby **Campiferias**, T283-996409, is smaller but similarly priced. Vans also free-camp off season south of the river, near the seafront, and are serviced by a mobile shop/van that can supply most basic requirements, from water to tinned foods and fruit.

Eating/drinking
A Choupana on Av Marginal is a popular eatery specializing in good value, local seafood. For a post-surf binge of grilled chicken and chips try **Churrasqueira A Telha** on R da Pinhal. **Miramar** is a café-restaurant near the castle that does good coffees and snacks. **O Pescador** on Largo da Praça is a very good seafood restaurant popular with locals – a bit pricey, but worth it, especially for the seafood stew.

Bars & clubs
The town has plenty of nightlife with the weekends really coming to life. **Café Azul**, on Rossio, plays good music, is popular with local surfers and stays open until the early hours, as does the busy **Pacifica Bar** on R Dr Barbosa. If you fancy somewhere a bit more chilled, check out **Café Turco** on R Dom João II which has good live music and a relaxed atmosphere.

Directory
Banks/Post office: on R Custodio Bras Pachego. **Tourist information**: the *turismo* is on R Antonio Mantas.

Zambujeira do Mar

Heading south on the main road, take the turning to this coastal resort that sits on cliffs overlooking a sheltered cove. While busy in the summer, the town – which has supermarkets, public toilets and a bank with ATM – can be extremely quiet off season. Campsite **Parque de Campismo da Zambujeira** on the edge of town is open Apr-Nov, T283-961172.

Odeceixe

Crossing the River Seixe, the N120 leaves Alentejo behind and enters the Algarve at this popular summer holiday retreat. The village, a couple of km inland, has shops, a bank with ATM and a post office. For a cheap place to stay try F **Residêncio do Parque** on R da Estrada Nacional, T282-947117.
Satellite village **Praia de Odeceixe** sits at the mouth of the river. It has a couple of cafés, including **Dorita**, with views over the beach. There are also showers, toilets and changing areas for surfers on the cliff top.

Aljezur

This village is a regional centre and sits on the busy N120 where the road squeezes over the small, shady bridge across the River Cerca. The picturesque older parts of Aljezur are set back up the hill leading to the Moorish castle. There is a great daily indoor market by the river that sells local produce and fresh seafood.

Sleeping
The *turismo* provides a list of available rooms – there are always plenty of places to stay at very reasonable rates.
E-F **Hospedaria S. Sebastião**, on the busy main road, T933-264943, has decent rooms and is conveniently placed.
Camping Parque de Campismo do Serrao, north of Aljezur off the N120, T282-98612, is very quiet off season with pitches in among the rows of eucalyptus trees. It also has apartments available.

Eating/drinking
Restaurante Ruth, on R 25 de Abril near the bridge, does good seafood. **Primavera**, just to the south on the main road, does excellent *frango* (grilled chicken). For coffee check out the neighbouring **Pastelaria Mioto** café which has a terrace.

Shopping/directory
There are 2 petrol stations and a couple of

multibancos on the main road through town. The *turismo* is just off on the main road near the market. **Adrenalina Surf Shop**, on the main road, stocks boards, wetsuits and clothing.

Arrifana

This is a small cliff-top village of whitewashed cottages and holiday homes, some hugging the cobbled road that winds down to the beach. There are cafés and some villas for rent, but little else. The beach is very popular and if it's working will be crowded. **Café de Praia** has the ultimate position at the bottom of the hill overlooking the sea. It's a great place to grab a post-surf beer and snack – the savoury pancakes are recommended. **Café Restaurant Fortaleza** serves fresh seafood overlooking the sea and has apartments for rent. The **Brisamar Café** at the top of the cliff may also have rooms available. **Camping Vale da Telha** on the road from Arrifana to Monte Clerigo is a bit run down and grotty.

Carrapateira

Just inland on the N120, this is a great place to be based for access to the main beaches, the surprisingly quiet Bordeira and the surprisingly busy Amado.
E-F **Pensão das Dunas** on R da Padaria, T282-973118, has a number of rooms available but if you ask around in the cafés there are sure to be rooms available in the village. For a post-surf eat, **Restaurant do Cabrita**, on the road to Bordeira, does good seafood and grilled chicken. On the beach at Bordeira, **O Sitio do Rio** restaurant has a wide menu including vegetarian options. There is also the **Carrapateira Surf Shop** in the village.

Sagres

This settlement on the southwest tip of Portugal dates back to pre-Roman times and was used as a base by Prince Henry the Navigator, who built the Fortaleza on the headland. This fortress was sacked by Sir Francis Drake in 1587 and was subsequently damaged in the earthquake of 1755, which destroyed much of the town. Sagres isn't the prettiest of towns and doesn't have an amazing amount to offer.

🛏 Sleeping
A-E Hotel Baleeira, overlooking the beach at Baleeira, T282-624212, has cheap rooms off season but is expensive in the summer. Also try **E Pensão Sagres**, R do Beco da Olaria, T282-624536, or **E Pensão Navegante II**, T282-624 442.
Villa Martinhal is a lovely self-catering villa overlooking the beach and sleeps 8. T+0044 (0)20-8673 1027.
Camping There is a good campsite north of the town, **Parque de Campismo Sagres**, T282-624371. There are a couple of areas where vans free-camp including the car park for Fortaleza. When free-camping it's always safer to camp where all the other vans are, and make sure you don't leave any mess behind.

🍴 Eating/drinking
Casa de Pasto A Grelha, on R Comandante Matoso, does the obligatory grilled chicken and chips – essential after a hard day's surfing. **Bossa Nova**, on R da Mareta, offers good pizzas and pasta and even has a vegetarian option. **Nortada** on Martinhal beach has a flexible menu serving seafood through to steaks and pizzas. There isn't a huge range of bars in Sagres but two worth checking out are the **Last Chance Saloon** and **Polvo Dreams**.

🛍 Shopping/directory
Planet Surf Shop, on the main route N268 into town, offers hardware and clothing. **Banks**: with ATMs on R Comandante Matoso. **Post office**: R Comandante Matoso. **Tourist information**: *turismo* on R Comandante Matoso. There is also a privately run **Turinfo** on Praça da Republica offering a room booking service as well as bike hire, internet access and boat trips.

Luz

This is purely a resort town in the typical western Algarve style of whitewashed apartments and plenty of cafés and bars.

🛏 Sleeping
Off season there are plenty of apartments and rooms to let as well as a couple of campsites to choose from. If you need a room or apartment ask around in the pubs.
Camping Coming into town, **Camping Valverde**, T282-789213, is a large, shady site run by Orbitur but it's about 1.5 km from the beach. They also have cabins for rent.
Camping de Espiche, on the main N125, T282-789265, is a large site with some shaded pitches and a great second-hand shop if you need to stock up on books. You may find vans free-camping near the seafront west of Luz.

🍴 Eating/drinking
The **Bull**, just off the main square, does steak and kidney pie, steaks and home made puddings and has Sky sports and a balcony.

Lagos

When looking at a map of the Algarve, the ancient town of Lagos doesn't appear to be the ideal base for a surf trip, but this place has everything. Picturesque cobbled back streets, lively bars and clubs, cheap accommodation and easy access to the west and south coast breaks. Lagos was founded around its natural harbour and has been both a Phoenician and Moorish trading post. Today it is a popular tourist destination, busy in the summer and comfortably lively off season.

🛏 Sleeping
Surf camp The Surf Experience, T282-761943, surfexperience@hotmail.com, is a central Lagos based surf camp with over 10 years' experience. They offer transfers, accommodation and 4WD transport to the best surf locations. They can also point out the best bars and restaurants.
B-D Pensão Lagos-Mar, R Dr Faria e Silva, T282-763523, en suite, TV, some have balconies.
E-F Pensão Caravela, R 25 de Abril, T282-763361, good basic accommodation at reasonable prices.
Camping Limited options. **Parque de Campismo da Trindade**, T282-763893, is a shabby, walled, shaded site on the western side of town by the Sagres road, next to the football stadium. In the winter there is usually a corral of vans free-camping in the car park behind Meia Praia, but the police do come and move them on occasionally.

🍴 Eating/drinking
Fools and Horses, just north of the square, do great evening meals and Sunday roast. **Mullen's**, on R Cândido dos Reis near the cinema, is a very popular restaurant with good reason – it has an excellent menu with fish and meat dishes and converts into a great drinking hole when the eating is over.

🎵 Bars & clubs
As with every major city in the world, there is an Irish pub, the **Irish Rover**, which also has internet access. Toby Millage can be found DJing occasionally at **Eddies Bar** on R 25 de Abril – but as he says, "Lagos is full of great bars. Just head out and explore."

🛍 Shopping/directory
Blue Ocean Diving and Kayak Centre, T282-782718. **Banks**: with ATMs on Praça Gil Eanes. **Bike trips**: available through Eddies Bar. **Internet**: access available at Gélibar on R Lançerote de Freitas as well as the Irish Rover. **Post office**: on Praça Gil Eanes. **Tourist information**: centrally located on Largo Marques de Pombal.

Morocco

Laurent Miramon at Sidi Bouzid
↠ *p350*

THIERRY ORGANOFF

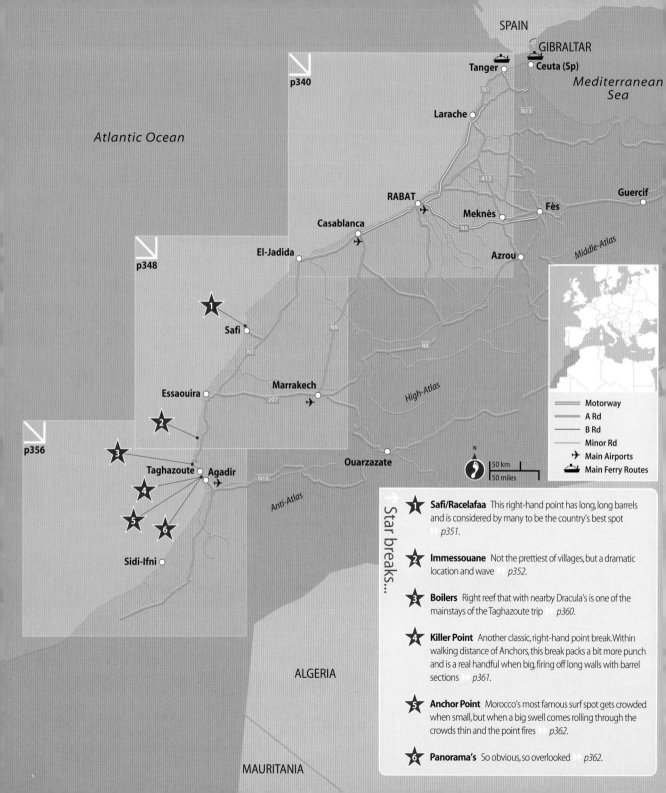

SPAIN

GIBRALTAR

Tanger · Ceuta (Sp)

Mediterranean Sea

Larache

N1

N13

Atlantic Ocean

p340

RABAT

Casablanca

Meknès · Fès

Guercif

413

Azrou

Middle-Atlas

N6

El-Jadida

p348

★1

Safi

N9

N1

N8

Essaouira

Marrakech

High-Atlas

207

★2

p356

★3

Taghazoute · Agadir

Ouarzazate

N

50 km
50 miles

★4

N10

Anti-Atlas

★5

★6

Motorway
A Rd
B Rd
Minor Rd
✈ Main Airports
⛴ Main Ferry Routes

Sidi-Ifni

Star breaks...

★1 **Safi/Racelafaa** This right-hand point has long, long barrels and is considered by many to be the country's best spot ▶ *p351*.

★2 **Immessouane** Not the prettiest of villages, but a dramatic location and wave ▶ *p352*.

★3 **Boilers** Right reef that with nearby Dracula's is one of the mainstays of the Taghazoute trip ▶ *p360*.

★4 **Killer Point** Another classic, right-hand point break. Within walking distance of Anchors, this break packs a bit more punch and is a real handful when big, firing off long walls with barrel sections ▶ *p361*.

★5 **Anchor Point** Morocco's most famous surf spot gets crowded when small, but when a big swell comes rolling through the crowds thin and the point fires ▶ *p362*.

★6 **Panorama's** So obvious, so overlooked ▶ *p362*.

ALGERIA

MAURITANIA

Emerald green waves peeling along burnt-red rocky points overlooked by twisted and gnarled Aragon trees. Although technically part of another continent, Morocco has been part of the European surfers' beat since the 1970s, when its classic, warm winter breaks first came to the world's attention. Since then it has become one of surfing's ultimate winter destinations. The line-ups around Safi and Taghazoute are now a vibrant mix of all Europe's languages and dialects, with many faces returning year after year for the excellent waves and Berber hospitality.

The geography of the Moroccan coastline conspires to make it the land of the right-hand point break. Endless, walling right-handers can fire for weeks on end under the onslaught of a constant stream of swells down from the north Atlantic. In the winter peak season the café terraces of Taghazoute become a melting pot of cultures sipping mint tea after an early morning session or morning call to prayer. The standard of living is cheap by European standards, yet browse the souks and you will find fruit and vegetables better than any back home.

The Moroccans have taken a while to make it into the line-ups but things are changing. Abdel El Harim ranks as one of the best surfers on the European tour and many local surfers now ride to a high standard. The Royal Moroccan Surfing Federation is actively engaged in competitive surfing at home and abroad, but the pace of life remains relaxed here and the spirit of 'In shallah' highly infectious.

Best time to visit: Winter - busiest around Christmas, but by mid January great weather, plenty of swell and cheaper flights.

Introduction

Morocco

Morocco Rating

Surf
★★★★

Cost of living
★

Nightlife
★

Accommodation
★★

Places to visit
★★★

Essentials

Position

Physically, Morocco occupies the northwestern edge of Africa while spiritually it forms the westernmost pillar of Islam. Separated from Europe by just 14 km of water it is bordered by the Mediterranean to the north, the Atlantic to the west and the less hospitable Algeria and Mauritania to the east and south.

Language

Arabic is the official language of Morocco, with French, as taught in the schools, the language of business. In cities, towns and tourist zones, French is generally spoken and understood. In the mountains, Amazizh is spoken and the Berber languages are also an influence. Spanish is understood in the north.

Currency

Dirham (dh), divided into 100 centimes. There are 1, 5 and 10dh coins and 10, 20, 50, 100 and 200dh notes – study them hard as it is easy to mistake a 20dh note for a 100dh note. A dirham is split into 5, 10, 20 and 50 centime coins. It's pretty hard to get hold of currency before you enter Morocco and you're not allowed to take it out of the country again but you can change Euros on the ferry or hit a hole in the wall (*guichet automatiques*) once in Morocco. There are plenty of ATMs in the cities and main towns and this is probably the easiest way to get hold of cash in Morocco. €1 will get you about 10dh.

Crime/safety

Violent crime isn't a serious problem in the majority of Morocco but you do need to be aware in major towns and cities like Tanger, Rabat, Agadir and Casablanca especially around cash machines. The main issues usually involve pickpockets (buses, busy areas), con artists and seemingly helpful 'guides'. May 2003 saw Casablanca targeted by extremist suicide bombers killing more than 40 people – a reality of the world today. While authorities have not advised against travel to Morocco, it pays to travel respectfully, keep an eye on the media and avoid being in and around political demonstrations and rallies.

If you are travelling in a van, break-ins are a frequent occurrence and carried out with an artful dodger style opportunism. While the majority are not violent, do not assume that because you're asleep in your van, it will put off potential break-ins – thieves have become very adept at removing seals from windows and creeping in. Don't leave your money/camera/stereo out on display – it can be a tempting invitation.

For women travelling alone in Morocco, or even separated from friends by a few feet, you can quickly attract a lot of attention – Moroccan women are rarely seen out alone and the majority of Moroccan women in nightclubs are pay to play. Dress modestly (topless is not an option here) and be firm but fair.

5 best trips

1. **Marrakech** Weird and wonderful walled city and tourist Mecca with impressive mountain backdrop ▸▸ *p355*.
2. **Paradise Valley** Great day out from Agadir on a flat day ▸▸ *p366*.
3. **Essaouira** Beautiful walled médina with a real colonial feel. Nearby Diabat, the town Jimi Hendrix tried to buy, is worth missing though ▸▸ *p354*.
4. **Atlas Mountains** Stunning scenery and good snowboarding ▸▸ *p355*.
5. **The Desert South** Southeastern Morocco has incredible, 'Lawrence of Arabia' Saharan sand dunes ▸▸ *p369*.

Got any slippers?

Health

Before entering Morocco, make sure your jabs are up to date – recommended are Polio, Tetanus, Typhoid and Hepatitis A/B. If you're driving in from Europe, pick up some antibiotics or similar from the pharmacist as a fallback.

The general standard of health care is not as high or widely available as in Europe. If you take regular medication, take enough with you to see you through your trip. Pharmacists do not generally have top-notch training but if you know what you need they should be able to sell it to you. If not, the majority will be able to give you the contact details for a good *médecin généraliste* (GP). Most major cities have access to private healthcare in the form of SOS Médicins.

Water needs to be boiled/sterilized before use, whether you're going to drink it or just clean your teeth with it. The best bet though is to buy bottled water – about 5dh per litre.

The most common complaint in Morocco is food poisoning/diarrhoea caused by bad food hygiene or surfing in sewage-contaminated water (common around urban breaks). Rehydration and rest is the key but generally if it goes on for more than three days or if you're passing blood, go see a doctor.

Opening hours

Here everyone stops for lunch. Monday to Friday, banks and post offices are generally open 0830-1130 and 1430-1700; shops 0900-1200 and 1500-1900. Saturdays are generally half days. During Ramadan working hours are shortened and many restaurants close during the day.

Factfile

Currency Dirham (dh)
Capital city Rabat
Time zone GMT
Length of coastline 3,230km
Religion Islamic
Emergency numbers
  Police 19
  International Operator 12
Electricity 240v French style dual pin

Sleeping

Levels and prices of accommodation vary wildly, from exclusive villas in the Palmeraie district of Marrakech frequented by the likes of David Bowie to basic scrubland free-camping areas watched over by local guardians. In between, there are plenty of low cost apartments and **hotels** that can easily be sourced through word of mouth for as little as 100dh a night. The standards vary from 'room with a view' to 'prisoner cell block H', so check it out before you agree to anything. There are plenty of official **campsites** along the Moroccan coastline – popular with foreign tourists during the winter and locals throughout the summer months. Generally, the standards are basic – hole in the ground toilets, limited shower facilities (if any). and are comparatively pricey. They are, however, watched over by the site's guardian, offering a degree of security.

Eating and drinking

A hangover from the days of French rule, breakfast is usually a simple affair of baguette/bread and jam or even croissants if you're lucky. Bigger towns boast patisseries while smaller villages have spawned entrepreneurial kids who do a mean trade in doughnuts. Moroccan cooking is all about spices and for the most part lunch is a bigger affair than dinner. A popular staple of cafés are *kebabs* or *kefta* (non-specific meat on sticks) usually served with *couscous* or chips. Another cheap and popular choice (especially during Ramadan) is the *harira* soup, which can take pretty much any form but usually contains lentils, veg and meat bits. For a more substantial meal at lunch or dinner opt for a *tagine*. This Moroccan style casserole is cooked in a conical clay pot over embers for a couple of hours (although they do make stainless steel versions to sit on the top of hobs). Usually chicken, meat (non-specific) or fish cooked with vegetables and spices, tagines are traditionally prepared by the men. They are eaten using fingers of the right hand only (the left has other less palatable uses), shared straight from the pot with hunks of bread. In a café, a tagine for two shouldn't set you back more than about 40-50dh. If you're self-catering you can buy a tagine set for about 15-20dh in most markets. The climate ensures that the fruit and vegetables you eat are both tasty and cheap. Red meat is more of a rarity and, with limited refrigeration and hygiene standards, is best avoided.

Tea is the lifeblood of Morocco and is drunk all day long. Made with a palm full of green tea, a fist full of mint and enough sugar to make your teeth dissolve – it is poured from a height and enjoys the local name 'Berber whisky'. Although an Islamic state, *alcohol* is not actually banned and is available from supermarkets such as *Marjane*, as well as in top-end hotels, tourist bars and a select few discreet off-licences. Morocco produces local lagers like Flag and Castel, as well as wines – usually a bit rough and ready and pricey (better to stick to the beer).

Festivals/events

Religious festivals are scheduled around a lunar calendar – shorter than the solar year – and events can move by a few weeks each year. The month of **Ramadan** is the biggest and sees Muslims fasting during daylight hours (this also includes abstaining from things like smoking). Cafés close, the roads become even more dangerous, but by night the cities come alive.

Getting there

Air There are plenty of airlines flying into Morocco's main airports, the most useful for surfing being **Casablanca** and **Agadir** with full bureau de change and transport services. The national airline **Royal Air Maroc**, www.royalairmaroc.com, has good European cover as well as offering flights between New York and Casablanca – a 6½ hour journey. Other major airlines servicing Morocco include **Air France**,

THE GILL

Spice up your trip

www.airfrance.com, who offer good deals between Casablanca and Paris, **British Airways**, www.british-airways.com, **KLM**, www.klm.com, and **Lufthansa**, www.lufthansa.com.

From UK: flights between London and Casablanca take about 3 hours and about 3½ hours to Agadir. Prices can vary wildly between about £150-350 depending on when you go so shop around. A cheaper option might be to look at charter flights or package holidays to Agadir with accommodation thrown in.

Sea Making the intercontinental journey from Europe to Morocco means negotiating the busy Straits of Gibraltar. As a foot passenger you have a wide selection of embarkation options including hydrofoils from Tarifa and Gibraltar, but as a driver there are really only two choices: Algeciras to Tanger or Algeciras to Ceuta, www.transmediterranea.es. (**Sea France** offers a route from Sete in France to Tanger but on a crossing lasting nearly 40 hours with a price tag to match you're better off driving south to Spain.)

Algeciras to Tanger is the busier of the two crossings, takes twice as long as the Ceuta route and is more expensive. If you're still tempted, prices for a car and two people start at around €150 for a return and go up to about €315 for two plus a large camper van. Foot passengers can travel for about €25. The crossing takes 2-3 hours and there are up to 10 crossings a day. Tickets can be bought in the UK from **Southern Ferries**, T020-7491 4968, or in Algeciras up to the day of travel from one of the various kiosks in the city or ferry terminal. An open return costs the same as two singles.

Ferry departures are usually late so take this into account when planning your onward journey. The ships are basic with cafés and lounge areas. You will be given a disembarkation form to fill in and you must also have your passport stamped by the police official onboard. The official is available for only a short part of the journey ensuring everyone gets a chance to queue together in the lounge area. This queuing practice will come in handy for disembarkation and customs. The onboard bureau de change will open 'sometime' during the journey – details are vague so be prepared to loiter.

Disembarkation and Moroccan customs is an experience. Allow 60-90 minutes to get yourself and your vehicle through the unique system of 'official' paperwork and a queue of people expecting a tip for their services (see Red tape, below and page 10). In the ferry terminal is a bureau de change with a bank outside if you missed the service on the ferry.

Algeciras to Ceuta seems to be the most popular crossing with seasoned surf travellers. The 90-minute crossing to the Spanish enclave of Ceuta is a bit cheaper than the Tanger run with up to nine services a day. There are no customs to go through on disembarkation as you're still officially in Spain, but you will have to fill in the same paperwork when you reach the inland border (see Red tape). You'll also have to wait until the border to change your Euros into dirham.

Red tape A valid passport is required but citizens of the UK, USA, Canada, Australia, New Zealand and most EU countries don't need a

Top tips

- The water in Morocco is colder than you think. We were cold in shorties; you really need a 3/2 or a 4/3. *Gabe Davies, ex British Champion*

- Avoid surfing spots that are out of your ability range, as it seems many people do drown there. It's dangerous for everyone. *Toby, the Surf Experience*

- Bring reef boots, sun cream, toilet roll, Imodium, basic first aid kit and cool water wax - not warm water. A few words of French can be a great help and always drink bottled water. As surf shops are not overly stocked bring spare leashes, fins, but repairs are cheap and of good quality. Also any gifts for the local kids can go a long way such as stickers, T-shirt etc. *Chris and Den, Moroccan Surf Adventures*

- Buy a tagine as soon as you get here - they cost about £2. Get spices, fresh veg and some chicken or fish and you'll eat really well. *Paddy Butler, travelling surfer*

- Micky's Burger in Agadir is the best burger place you'll ever go to. They make the burger from fresh meat, cook it in front of you, use fresh organic buns, they chip the potatoes and fry them as you watch - it's awesome. Just what you want after a day's surfing. *Paul McCarthy, Irish surfer and Morocco regular*

visa. At the border you need to hand in a green entry form with your details and destination. Passports are also checked and stamped. You can enter Morocco for up to three months after which you must either leave and re-enter, or apply for an extension at the Immigration or Bureau des Etrangers department in larger towns. **NB** Check you have been allocated your full three-month stay when your passport is stamped.

If you are driving, you need to fill in a D16 form for the temporary importation of your vehicle – valid for a maximum of six months per year. You'll also need to present your ownership documents and a green card showing valid insurance cover for Morocco. If your insurance doesn't stretch that far, you can always get cover at the port or border crossing. The registration number and details of the vehicle will be logged in the owner's passport and checked when you leave the country to ensure the vehicle has not been sold without the full taxes being paid. **NB** Make sure the correct registration number has been recorded to ensure a hassle-free return.

Up to a couple of years ago, items of value had to be declared at the border and checked on departure. Surfers had to declare surfboards, meaning any broken boards had to be brought home so they could be checked out again by customs – again designed to prevent the sales of expensive items without the payment of taxes. This seems to have stopped so you can now leave your old boards for aspiring local grommets.

Getting around

Driving (right-hand side) You need a full licence plus liability insurance which is checked at the border. The quality of roads varies from a high quality toll *autopista* to thousands of kilometres of *pistes* or unsurfaced tracks – useful for exploring more out of the way breaks, just watch the ground clearance of your vehicle. Morocco is not the safest place to drive in, with ten times as many fatal accidents as France. Driving at night should be avoided at all costs as there can be various hidden obstacles lurking around the next bend – people in *djellabas*, animals, carts, boulders, trucks etc.

Motorway (*autopista*): stretches along the west coast from north of Larache south to Casablanca. The motorway is shared by cars, the odd cart, and truck drivers with suicidal tendencies and regularly crossed by families of kamikaze pedestrians. In a country of resourcefulness the central reservation isn't wasted either – animals are grazed and mint is grown and harvested. **Speed limit 120 kph.**

Other roads: P roads are major trunk roads of a fair standard, generally single track, and can take you direct to Agadir from Casablanca. **S** (secondary) roads of varying quality hug the coast south from Casablanca to Essaouira. **Speed limit 100 kph/40 kph urban areas.** Speed limits are enforced and tourists can be hit with hefty on-the-spot penalties.

Parking In towns a guardian, looking like a bus conductor, will watch your vehicle for you day and night in lieu of metered parking – 5-10dh should cover it.

Car hire This is not a problem here although it is pretty pricey. About £200-300 for two weeks will hire a standard issue white Fiat Uno, although a bit of haggling might get the price down. The big companies like **Hertz**, www.hertz.com, and **Europcar**, www.europcar.com, operate in Morocco, with smaller ones more open to negotiation.

Public transport

Morocco has a good rail network run by **ONCF**, www.oncf.org.ma (poor website), but only runs as far south as Marrakech. A journey from Casablanca to Marrakech takes about 3½ hours and costs around 90dh. From Marrakech, a bus network – **Supratours** or **CTM** – links you to most major destinations. Luggage (i.e. your board) will generally be stowed on the roof or in a luggage locker –at their discretion – so travel off peak and remember to tip the baggage man to avoid breakages. Taking the local bus is like taking your life in your hands but can be a cheap way to hit the town to pick up supplies – Taghazoute to Agadir sets you back 3-4dh and is an adrenaline rush the whole way. **Petits taxis** (little painted hatchbacks) are metered, licensed to carry three passengers and can get you around town. Colour coded by town they are orange in Agadir, red in Casablanca and beige in Marrakech. **Grands taxis** (old Merc saloons) are long distance vehicles, licensed to carry six cramped passengers at a reasonable price, that travel between set destinations – agree the price and pick them up from the taxi ranks in town.

Key phrases

Key words/phrases

Yes	wakha
No	la
Please	min fadhlek
Thank you	shukran
Hello	salamalaykoom
Goodbye	bisslema
Good	mezyan
Bad	khaib
I don't understand	mafhemtsh
I'd like…	bghit
Do you have…	wash 'andkom…
How much is it?	bshhal
Where is…	fayn kayin…
Left	liser
Right	limen
Straight on	sir nishan
Night	lil
Room	el-beet
Campsite	lmukheyyem
Shower	duzh
Toilet	bit lma
The bill	fatura
White coffee	kahwa bil-halib
Beer	bira
Red wine	hmer shrab
White wine	byed shrab
Mineral water	lma ma'dini

Numbers

0 sifr
1 wahed
2 zou or tnine
3 tlata
4 arba
5 khamsa
6 setta
7 saba
8 tmaniya
9 ts'oud
10 ashra
11 hedash
12 t'nash
13 t'latash
14 rb'atash
15 kh'msatash
16 settash
17 sb'atash
18 t'mentash
19 ts'atash
20 'ashrine
21 wahed ou 'ashrine
22 tnine ou 'ashrine
30 tlatine
40 'arba'ine
50 khamsine
60 sittine
70 temenine
80 temenine
90 t'issine
100 miya
200 miyatayn
1000 alf

Tea	atei
Juice	'aseir
Sandwich	kaskrut
Egg	bída
Cheese	frumazh
Help!	teqni
Beach	laplazh
River	wad
Wind	rih
Wave	muzha
High	'ali
Low	habt
North	shamal
South	zhanub
East	sherq
West	gherb

Days of the week

Monday	nhar el itnayn
Tuesday	nhar ettlata
Wednesday	nhar el arba
Thursday	nhar el khemis
Friday	nhar el jema'
Saturday	nhar essebt
Sunday	nhar el had

Arabic is the official language of Morocco but nearly all Moroccans with a secondary education have enough French to communicate with. For key French words and phrases ▸▸ *p153*

key French words and phrases ▸▸ p153

Morocco Essentials

Surfing Morocco

"In 1976 I went to Taghazoute with Chops (Lascelles) and we had six weeks when the surf never dropped below eight feet," says Mike McNeill, who had just left Lightning Bolt Surfboards on the North Shore. *"There were six to eight of us surfing. It was one of the best surfing experiences I'd ever had – and I'd come from Hawaii."*

As Europe's small surfing community grew in size, so they pushed out and began exploring further afield. Inevitably the trail led to the sunshine and relaxed atmosphere of Morocco. Slowly but surely, van loads of Aussie and French surfers pushed south from the northern beaches to the points of Taghazoute and the word was out. Since the 1970s, Morocco has drawn surfers from all over the world to its famous right-hand point breaks and laid-back culture. Morocco was the soul surfers' nirvana. Cheap living, cheap drugs and friendly people – it was no accident that the hippy trail led here. In the 1969 movie *Evolution*, Nat Young and Wayne Lynch brought a glimpse of what Morocco had to offer and surfers wanted to see more. Morocco has now become the culmination of every travelling Aussie surfer's 'year in Europe' and the ideal winter break for those wanting to escape northern Europe's darker months.

Pros & cons

Pros …

- ✓ Long and rugged coastline that picks up loads of swell from Atlantic low pressures.
- ✓ Seemingly endless surfing possibilities with classic right-hand points as good as any in the world.
- ✓ Rugged and deserted surf spots.
- ✓ Warm, sunny winter climate and mild water temperatures.
- ✓ Relaxed pace of life.
- ✓ Cheap cost of living.

… and cons

- ✗ Key breaks get busy during winter holidays.
- ✗ Food hygiene can be poor at some restaurants.
- ✗ Some breaks polluted by industrial and sewage waste.

However, while Morocco has recently made leaps forward in terms of education and healthcare, it is still a developing country. The roads are genuinely dangerous and the police can be loathe to get involved with petty crime such as burglary or car break-ins. They may, however, be keen to enforce the anti-drugs laws. Although the hash is high quality and low cost, it is illegal and rarely tolerated – bear this in mind.

Russell Winter at the Source ▸▸ *p361*

Climate

Morocco is a land of contradictions – towards the desert south, hot days convert into cold nights; dry riverbeds can be brought back to life during flash floods, and just as quickly disappear; and regions that are geographically close can experience massive seasonal differences. While the tourist haven of Marrakech can top 40°C, the snow-topped High Atlas mountains that overlook it boast a number of good ski resorts with boarding possibilities. While the northern plains are lush and green in their mild winter months, the south of the country opens into the spectacular harsh surroundings of the Sahara Desert.

For the surfer, the coastal regions are less extreme and benefit from an almost endless supply of sun, with the huge mass of the North Atlantic acting as a heat sink, helping to keep temperatures extremely comfortable. Agadir has become a popular winter destination for holidaying Europeans because of the warm winter days and cool evening temperatures.

Best seasons to go

The peak seasons to hit Morocco are autumn and winter. In **summer**, temperatures are high, the Atlantic swells are inconsistent and the wind can be tortuous, but as **autumn** arrives the hot nights start to cool and the waves begin to filter through. Morocco's fabled points around Safi, Immessouane and Agadir really come to life during this period, the swells seem to be never ending and the sun seems to shine every day. Long, clean walls reel with glassy waves anywhere between 3 ft and 10 ft. Numbers in the line-up around popular destinations like Taghazoute reach bursting point during the two weeks over **Christmas and New Year**. As northern Europe freezes, January and February sees Morocco enjoying warm days and the peak of the swell season. However as March starts to melt into April, the winds kick in and the surf quality decreases, heralding the departure of the few remaining campers.

Board

A good two-board selection for Morocco would have a thruster and a pintail as the mainstays. A good, rounded squash tail or swallow tailed thruster, about 18½" wide, will give plenty of range. For the big days, or for when the points fire, a good semi-gun will definitely be a help, something between a 6'4" to 7'0" pin tail. For board advice check out the Gulfstream website at www.gulfstreamsurfboards.co.uk.

Good charts for surf

During the winter season Morocco picks up heaps of swell. It has a vast, open coastline that faces northwest, so every low pressure that tracks across the north Atlantic pushes swell towards it. A big low sitting in the middle of the Atlantic should bring even the more sheltered points to life. Morocco is far enough south that even a low tracking across into the Bay of Biscay will still produce clean, lined-up swell when it hits the north African coastline.

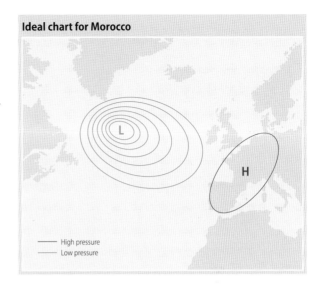

Ideal chart for Morocco

— High pressure
— Low pressure

Geography and the breaks

In general, northern Morocco is a series of beach breaks interspersed with a few rocky points and reefs. From Tangier down to Bouznika, huge stretches of sand see few surfers until the urban breaks of Mohammedia appear. Here the points and reefs are popular with local bodyboarders and surfers with only the occasional traveller stopping for a few waves. Casablanca is a huge urban sprawl with polluted breaks but once past the shanty towns and crazy driving, the countryside opens up again and the undulating rocky coastline offers incredible opportunities. Many unknown spots break between the points at El Jadida, Safi and Immessouane.

From Immessouane the landscape changes. The rugged coastline here is home to the thorny Argan trees, whose nuts are harvested to produce a versatile, but expensive cooking oil. Goats climb into the Argan trees to eat the nuts which are actually harvested from their droppings – a flavour, some say, that stays with the oil. It is among the

DEMI TAYLOR

Surf juice

Morocco Surfing

5 underground classics

① **Tifnite** Half an hour south of Agadir and a whole world away. This sleepy village overlooks some epics waves. Picks up loads of swell and is usually empty ⇥ *p365*.

② **Desert Point** Secret, right-hand point that reels off leg-numbing walls ⇥ 366.

③ **Cap Sim** Right-hand point near Essaouira ⇥ 352.

④ **Royal Groynes** Semi-secret spot with sandbars forming fast, hollow, barreling waves ⇥ 365.

⑤ **Panorama's** So obvious, but so underestimated. ⇥ *p362*.

DEMI TAYLOR

Tifnite

Argan trees that Morocco's most famous waves break, at spots like Anchor Point and Killers.

Below Agadir the desert south beckons. From here beaches expand, temperatures rise and the numbers of surfers drops off to virtually zero. Pistes lead to dried-up rivermouths while long expanses of beach breaks, some backed by cliffs, are only broken by the occasional points and reefs.

Surfing and environment

Morocco is a developing country and as such lacks a lot of the infrastructure many take for granted. Water purification and sewage treatment are basic at best. Tap water is not safe to drink – bottled water is not seen as a luxury but a necessity. Homes in Taghazoute have water delivered in tankers from a well in neighbouring Banana Village. In dry seasons the water becomes more concentrated with contaminants, so even boiling the water before drinking may not be a good idea.

In a lot of areas sewage is discharged straight into the sea, so urban breaks can be badly polluted. Many large villages and towns have outfalls near the line-ups and are best avoided, especially after heavy rains, while waves further away from urban centres are usually as clean as you'll find anywhere. However make sure you are up to date on your jabs before you leave home.

Localism and surf communities

Moroccans are generally very friendly and hospitable, but also fairly determined, and this extends into the line-up. It would be unusual to experience localism here from local surfers, unless it is at one of the very busy urban breaks near Casablanca or Safi. In fact you are more likely to be dropped in on by a travelling surfer, some of whom take on the role of 'honorary local' after a few weeks of free-camping.

Over the past five years, surfing around Taghazoute has undergone a massive explosion. While line-ups on the whole are relatively aggro free, some surfers who are used to more competitive line-ups are beginning to cause tensions among both the locals and other visitors. For Morocco to remain a mellow winter escape it is important to take on board a relaxed and respectful attitude in and out of the water. Otherwise, like Ireland, it may be that a once-mellow country adopts the ways of the more aggressive visitors.

Surf directory

Morocco has yet to develop a surf industry infrastructure of magazines, shapers and surf brands. It does have a number of surf shops and board repair businesses as well as many regional surf clubs. As the president of the Royal Moroccan Surfing Federation, Hicham El Ouarga, sums up: "We do not have any shapers yet, but I am sure that this will happen with time." There are surf shops springing up and even **Quiksilver Boardriders** and **Rip Curl** stores in Casablanca.

Morocco: a brief surf history

1950s ➔ US soldiers based in Kénitra begin to explore the surf potential of Morocco. **1969** ➔ Paul Witzig's seminal film *Evolution* presents Morocco as a place of untapped surf potential and sees the country firmly placed on the surf explorers' itinerary. **1988** ➔ National surf contests are held in Rabat, Mohammedia and Casablanca. **1990** ➔ Association Marocaine de Surf established. **1991** ➔ Cap Surf Morocco is founded and Morocco participates in EPSA contest. **1991** ➔ The first Moroccan surf camp, Surfland, opens in Oualidia. **1997** ➔ Agadir surf club is founded. **2004** ➔ World Masters Championships to be held at Safi.

Surfers' tales

Killer Point ▶ p361

Killer whales, Killer roads and Killer waves

"I looked up and the fin was easily a metre high. It sank underwater about ten feet away from me and then surfaced again. My next conscious thought was, I'm on the rocks and I'm still paddling." Former Lightning Bolt glasser Mike McNeill on surfing with the killer whales off Ankor Point, 1976.

Mike Brown, a 27-year-old Kiwi surfer, had been in Morocco a week when he saw a busy bus get washed away and two people drown in a flash flood. A couple of weeks later he was sitting around a campfire looking over at Killer Point. Little did he know that later that evening it would be living up to its name. "We were chatting around a fire when one of the guys jumped up and shouted 'Look!'" The road from Taghazoute winds past Anchors and over the cliffs that look down on Killer Point. "We turned to see a huge truck mid air. It missed a bend in the road, severed a telegraph pole like a match and disappeared into a ravine. We looked at each other – I don't think we quite believed what we'd just seen – and ran up to the point where the truck left the road. It was lying at the bottom of a chasm." One person had been thrown clear of the wreckage. About twenty feet away sat the massive diesel engine. It had been ripped clean out of the truck. "If we hadn't have gone, I don't think anyone would have – a bus went by and didn't even stop. One of the guys was still in the truck and looked in a really bad way." The group did the best they could to tend to the two injured men while someone went to get the police from town. They spent twenty minutes in the police station until they managed to convince them to come out to the crash. "The passenger survived his injuries but the driver was not so lucky. I thought, I've only been in this country a couple of weeks and I've already seen three people die! It made me realize that we hadn't just crossed into a different country, we were in a whole different culture."

"I was down in Morocco, one year, staying in Taghazoute," remembers top UK surfer, James Hendy. "I got up early one morning and there was a massive pack at Killers sitting way out back with eight foot waves coming through. It was inconsistent but I had a brand new 7'2" from Australia – it was my pride and joy and I hadn't had a chance to ride it so I paddled out. It's a major paddle out there when it's big. I had a couple of quick waves – really nice, long walls, really fast, clean – and I just got a little bit cocky. A few surfers were sitting deeper than the pack, and decided I'd paddle deeper with the other guys and get into a late one.

"A set appeared and I paddled into the first wave and took off. Suddenly the whole section just shut down. I got to the bottom, realized I wasn't going to make it, jumped off my board, and as I was bailing, the eight foot wave unloaded behind me and just snapped my leash. I came to the surface and knew there were probably six waves in the set and I was miles out. When it's big at Killers it breaks 350-400 yards out in front of the cliffs. But as I looked around, all I could think about was where's my 7'2" – I was so far out it could just disappear anywhere. I turned to see this next wave pitching right in front of me and it landed virtually on my head, opened my wetsuit all down my back, and filled my suit with water. It ballooned my legs, and the water's quite cold in Morocco, and I'm under the water like balloon man. I came up just in time for the next wave and proceeded to get another four waves on my head.

"When I finally came up again I was really cold and tired, but the set had passed. I was still 300 yards out, and couldn't see my board anywhere and rather than thinking about survival, I decided I had to try and find it. I swam to the cliffs and scrambled up the base in my bare feet. The waves were surging up the rock face and pushed me up the cliff. I grabbed hold of the cliff face with my hands and feet, like a cat, and the water dropped away, sucking out about ten or twelve feet and leaving me clinging to the rocks. Then the next wave came in, hit me, launched me over this outcrop about ten feet and dragged me down the other side. I was frantic, still thinking, Where's my 7'2"? My feet were lacerated, my hands were lacerated and I sat on the rocks bleeding, thinking this is stupid, I'm going to kill myself. I jumped off, made the long swim back to the beach and hobbled the mile and a half back to Taghazoute. Later I went back up to Killers, still gutted, and met a Kiwi surfer who'd just unwedged my board from the back of a cave. It just had a bit of damage to the nose and tail, so I was really lucky – all round."

Surfing Northern Morocco

Tanger is a crazy, hectic, wild, frantic, frenzied, exciting, chaotic, confusing and frenetic introduction to Morocco. So much condensed energy is waiting to greet the traveller, hot off the ferry with a pocket full of freshly changed dirham, that the onslaught of sales pitches hits before vehicles have even cleared customs.

After two hours in the queue, filling in forms and dealing with the bewildering array of 'officials', it is great to finally get on the road and out of town. Before you know it the crazy world of Morocco's principle port has been left behind and the northern coastline beckons. On the roadside, camels nonchalantly wander by. This is truly the gateway to Africa.

Camel crossing

DEMI TAYLOR

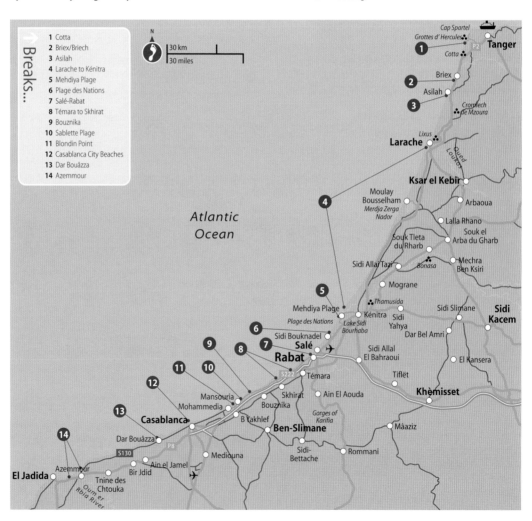

Breaks...

1 Cotta
2 Briex/Briech
3 Asilah
4 Larache to Kénitra
5 Mehdiya Plage
6 Plage des Nations
7 Salé-Rabat
8 Témara to Skhirat
9 Bouznika
10 Sablette Plage
11 Blondin Point
12 Casablanca City Beaches
13 Dar Bouàzza
14 Azemmour

30 km
30 miles

Atlantic Ocean

The travelling surfer often bypasses the open, sandy coastline between Cap Spartel and Kenitra, but these beaches, rivermouths and occasional points are a great place to explore. The people are friendly and in the winter months the land can be surprisingly lush and green following the rains. These empty breaks are a complete antithesis to the chaos of the major cities. The traffic around Casablanca has to be seen to be believed - cars exit the motorway where there are no junctions while people and animals wander the central reservation.

The breaks around the edges of Rabat and Casablanca are popular destinations for holidaying Moroccans and can be very busy at weekends. This also means that there are plenty of campsites and cheap hotels. Many beaches near Casablanca have vibrant surfing communities, especially around Mohammedia and Bouznika. One drawback to urban breaks is that there can be pollution from sewage and industrial plants, however local surfers are usually very friendly and it always helps to carry a few extra blocks of wax.

Coastline

The northern coastline in Morocco is considered to have beaches among the most beautiful in the country. This endless stretch of beach breaks is broken by the occasional rivermouth and reef just waiting to be surfed. The far north picks up less swell than the region near Casablanca, where reefs and points are more common and the number of surfers increases dramatically. Unfortunately the water quality can be poor.

Localism

More and more local surfers are taking to the water every year and certain breaks are already crowded, but in general the atmosphere is pretty good, especially if you go with a relaxed and friendly attitude. Bouznika, Sablette and Dar Bouâzza can get very busy at weekends but, although there may be the odd drop in, there is not the level of localism found in certain regions in Europe.

Top local surfers French WQS surfer **Micky Picon** was born in Casablanca and learned to surf at the city's breaks. Eighteen year old **Abdel El Harim** from Rabat was the 2002 Moroccan Champion, finished 15th on the 2003 EPSA Tour and is aiming for a slot on the WQS. Local hotshots **Sahoui Abderahmane, Redouane Taieb** and **Khilaji Mohammed** have all surfed for the Moroccan team.

Getting around

An excellent toll motorway runs from Asilah south to Casablanca. It has regular service stations, which can be a good place for vans to overnight on the journey down. Driving in central Casablanca is best avoided. Hire cars are available at Casablanca airport for those flying in, but it is always advisable to book in advance. Compared to the general prices of things in Morocco, fuel prices are relatively expensive - on a par with those in Europe. Watch out for things in the road - people,

Morocco is only a short plane ride away from Europe, but it's a whole world away in terms of culture, climate and surf. It's not just a surf trip, it's a whole experience.

Russell Winter, former WCT professional surfer

Northern Morocco board guide

Fish
Shaper: Jools at Gulf Stream Surfboards

»» 6'0" x 19½" x 2⅜"
»» A fast, loose board perfect for when the waves are small on the northwest beach breaks..
»» It can turn an average or onshore day into an epic one.
»» Ideal for small days at Bouznika and Blondin points or beach breaks like Sablette or Plage des Nations.

Shortboard
Shaper: Jools at Gulf Stream Surfboards

»» 6'2" x 18¼" x 2¼"
»» One of our most popular shortboard templates.
»» Ridden by a lot of our team riders.
»» Perfect for punchy beach breaks and small to medium points.
»» A 'must' for any serious surfer.

 Boards by **Gulf Stream Surfboards**
Factory/shop: 12 South Street, Woolacombe, Devon, UK
T00 44 (0)1271-870831 www.gulfstreamboards.co.uk

donkeys, rocks and dogs. Getting around by bus and train is really best left to those unaccompanied by a surfboard. In this region access to breaks is usually via piste roads leading off the coast road. It's sometimes worth exploring tracks used by fishermen that allow coastal access to some of the more out of the way spots.

Breaks

1 Cotta

- ◉ **Break type**: Beach break.
- ◉ **Conditions**: Small to medium swells, offshore in easterly winds.
- ❶ **Hazards/tips**: Rips when big, major sand excavation from beach.
- ◉ **Sleeping**: Tanger ⇒ *p344*.

Long stretch of sandy beach that works on all tides. Picks up northwesterly swells and has some nice peaks. Usually no other surfers here. Take the turning off the P2 south of Tanger and follow the road to the coast. Brings you out south of Grottes d'Hercules (which has a campsite).

2 Briex/Briech

- ◉ **Break type**: Beach break.
- ◉ **Conditions**: Small to medium swells, offshore in easterly winds.
- ❶ **Hazards/tips**: Rips when big.
- ◉ **Sleeping**: Asilah ⇒ *p345*.

A good beach break north of Asilah that is visible from the road. Works on all tides and is usually uncrowded.

3 Asilah

- ◉ **Break type**: Beach breaks.
- ◉ **Conditions**: Easterly winds are offshore.
- ❶ **Hazards/tips**: Access difficult to breaks to the south of the town.
- ◉ **Sleeping**: Asilah ⇒ *p345*.

Again works on all tides. The picturesque tourist destination of Asilah has a 45-km stretch of deserted beach breaks to the north, with easy access from the P2.

4 Larache to Kénitra

- ◉ **Break type**: Beach, rivermouths and reefs.
- ◉ **Conditions**: All swells and easterly winds.
- ❶ **Hazards/tips**: Access via pistes to breaks.
- ◉ **Sleeping**: Larache/Moulay Bousselham/Kénitra ⇒ *p345*.

A long stretch of coastline with a wide variety of breaks to explore. There can be a good right-hand wave inside the rivermouth at Larache. A great place to explore but bring a good map and a sturdy car. Worth checking rivermouth at Moulay Bousselham.

Northern Morocco

Air —— Sea ——

°F Averages °C

J F M A M J J A S O N D

4/3   3/2   Shortie   3/2

1 Cotta

3 Asilah

4 Larache South

7 Salé-Rabat

5 Mehdiya Plage

- **Break type**: Right-hand sandbank by jetty.
- **Conditions**: Jetty needs a big swell. Offshore in an easterly/southeasterly wind.
- **Hazards/tips**: Access via S212 about 10 km from Kénitra.
- **Sleeping**: Kénitra ▸ *p345*.

American servicemen surfed here first in the 1950s. Long rock jetty can have excellent hollow waves breaking through all tides. Beach can also be worth a look. Not many local surfers but a popular holiday beach in the summer. Great place to check on the way south.

6 Plage des Nations

- **Break type**: Beach break.
- **Conditions**: Offshore in southeasterly wind.
- **Hazards/tips**: Busy tourist beach in summer.
- **Sleeping**: Kénitra/Salé-Rabat ▸ *p345*.

This is a popular beach which has good quality waves that works on all tides. Turn off the P2 to Sidi Bouknadel halfway between Kénitra and Rabat.

7 Salé-Rabat

- **Break type**: Beach breaks.
- **Conditions**: Medium to big swells. Offshore in easterly/southeasterly winds.
- **Hazards/tips**: Busy city breaks with poor water quality, especially after rains.
- **Sleeping**: Salé-Rabat ▸ *p346*.

There are a series of rocky groynes with waves peeling off them and beach breaks in between. Can produce fast and hollow rides on all tides. There are surf clubs based in both Rabat and Salé. These are popular urban breaks with a large population of surfers and bodyboarders. The water quality here can be not very good.

8 Témara to Skhirat

- **Break type**: Beach break and left off jetty.
- **Conditions**: Southeasterly winds are offshore.
- **Hazards/tips**: Access to this stretch off the motorway or the S222 south of Rabat.
- **Sleeping**: Témara ▸ *p346*.

A stretch of beach break with banks that work through the tides. Skhirat has a jetty with a long left that is best at low to mid tide.

9 Bouznika

- **Break type**: Right-hand point break.
- **Conditions**: Medium to big swells. Offshore in easterly winds.
- **Hazards/tips**: Water quality not great, can get crowded, urchins.
- **Sleeping**: Mohammedia ▸ *p346*.

Popular and well known, low to mid tide flat rock point that attracts local surfers and bodyboarders. Access is from the beach or off the point. Motorway exit signposted Bouznika.

10 Sablette Plage

- **Break type**: Beach break.
- **Conditions**: Small to big swells. Offshore in southeasterly wind.
- **Hazards/tips**: Very busy break with a large local crew.
- **Sleeping**: Mohammedia ▸ *p346*.

This is a popular beach north of

Mohammedia that works on all tides. Strong surfing tradition here – top French WQS surfer Micky Picon was born in Casablanca and learned to surf here. "Sablette Bay is suitable for beginners and good surfers," says Amine Afal of Mohammedia surf association FAST. "Both left- and right-hand waves can be hollow, but the current is sometimes strong. Moreover, the waves change dramatically from low to high tide."

11 Blondin Point

- **Break type**: Right point break.
- **Conditions**: Offshore in southerly/southeasterly wind.
- **Hazards/tips**: Mohammedia has a large petroleum refinery, so the water quality is not good.
- **Sleeping**: Mohammedia ▸ *p346*.

Popular right-hand point that works on all tides. The beaches here and at Sablette are popular weekend and holiday destinations, so can get very busy. There are lots of campsites around Mansouria.

12 Casablanca City Beaches

- **Break type**: Series of beach breaks.
- **Conditions**: Offshore in southerly winds.
- **Hazards/tips**: Rips when big, pollution and crowds.
- **Sleeping**: Casablanca ▸ *p347*.

The beaches are studded with rock jetties that can create decent sandbars working

DEMI TAYLOR

13 Dar Bouâzza ▸ *p344*

through the tides. The city beaches are very competitive and quickly become crowded with bodyboarders. Casablanca is Morocco's surf capital, home to the Cap Surf Association, with no shortage of surf shops.

13 Dar Bouâzza

- ◉ **Break type**: Left point break
- ◉ **Conditions**: Offshore in southerly winds.
- ❶ **Hazards/tips**: Gets crowded, especially at weekends.
- ▭ **Sleeping**: Casablanca ›› p347.

Long lefts peel in clean swells, best at low tide. One of the area's best known waves but watch out for sharp reef and urchins. Another spot worth checking is Jack's. Carry on along the S130 south until you hit **Jack's Beach**, a good beach break that hosts the occasional surf competition.

14 Azemmour

- ◉ **Break type**: Beach break.
- ◉ **Conditions**: Offshore in southeasterly winds.
- ❶ **Hazards/tips**: Rips when big.
- ▭ **Sleeping**: Azemmour ›› p347.

Haouzia beach stretches south with the mouth of the Oum er Rbia River to the north. Works on all tides. About 1 km from Azemmour, follow the coast road or face a half hour walk from the town.

Listings

Tanger

The gateway to Morocco, Tanger is a wild entrance to Morocco and has always attracted hedonists, hippies and artists among them Marlene Dietrich, Oscar Wilde, Ian Fleming, Cecil Beaton, Matisse, Jack Kerouac, Tennessee Williams and Yves St Laurent. As a busy intercontinental port servicing a steady stream of native tourists and day trippers it's also home to a high concentration of hasslers and hustlers both at the port and in the city itself. If the hassle doesn't put you off, there are plenty of places to soak up the atmosphere. Head up the main road – Av Mohammed V/Blvd Pasteur – and on up the R de la Liberté north towards the Grand Socco and on to the médina or city centre and fortified kasbah.

✺ Flat spell

Caves West of Tanger on the S701, **Grottes d'Hercules** was once a party venue for the rich, famous and decadent and is now known for its inverted Africa-shaped portal through which you can look out over the sea. A nominal charge will get you entry to the caves – sunset is the showcase. **Golf** Get a round in at **Tangier Royal Golf Club**, T039-944484.

▭ Sleeping

G The **youth hostel** on R Antaki off Pl des Nations is clean, easy and about 40dh a

Moroccan spring time

night, so make sure you book in advance,T039-946127. There are plenty of cheap but very basic pensions on **R de la Plage** running up towards the Grand Socco. G **Murinia**, south of the port on R Magellan, T039-933537, is next door to **Tanger Inn**, made famous by Kerouac. **Camping Achakar**, 12 km west towards Cap Spartel, T039-333840. Pricey, and the toilet block is basic, but handy for exploring the northern beaches. Be aware that the sand from this northwest strip is regularly excavated by building contractors.

🍴 Eating/drinking
Africa on R de la Plage is a reasonable and fairly reliable place to grab a simple taste of Morocco. If you're still hungry, head to one of the many cafés on Blvd Pasteur. Grab a coffee and watch the world go by at these former artists' haunts: **Café de France** on Pl de France, **Café Central** in the Petit Socco, or **Detroit Café** at the north of the médina on R Sultan.

🛍 Shopping
North Shore Surf Shop on R Kacem Guenoun has all the basics. The **fruit stalls** lining R de la Plage are a good place to pick up fresh provisions for the trip south, while the **Marjane** on the P2 south to Larache is a European style supermarket.

ⓘ Directory
Banks: Av Mohammed V/Blvd Pasteur – the BMCE has a good bureau de change. **Car hire**: Av Mohammed V/Pasteur are home to the biggies. **Internet**: Cybercafé Momnet on Moulay Abdallah and Cybercafé Adam off Blvd Pasteur. **Police**: T19. **Post office**: Av Mohammed V. **Tourist office**: Blvd Pasteur, 0800-1400, Mon-Sat.

Asilah

South on the P2 this pretty fishing port was a former Portuguese outpost. The ramparts surrounding the town were built by the Portuguese in the 15th century and their influence can still be seen in the town's white and blue houses, reminiscent of

Portugal's coastal town Ericeira. Once popular with pirates, the town is now popular with wealthy Moroccans who flock to Asilah every August for the **International Festival of Asilah**. The Thursday souk is good for provisions.

🛏 Sleeping
G **Marhaba**, close to the médina on R Zelaka, has bright, basic rooms. **Camping** There are plenty of options heading into town from Briex – **Camping International** and **Camping Atlas** are closest to the beach and have fair but limited facilities.

Larache

Having been occupied by the Spanish and part of their protectorate, Larache still has a certain Spanish influence, most notably in the cooking. This port town is popular with families returning from Europe in the summer but quiet in the winter. From here the autoroute continues south to Casablanca – about 100dh in tolls in a van.

🏄 Flat spells
Head 5 km northeast to **Ancient Lixus**, a site of Roman ruins and legendary Garden of Hesperides where Hercules is said to have killed a local dragon and picked golden apples.

🛏 Sleeping
G **Hotel Cervantes**, near Pl de Libération, is fair, T039-910874. G **Pension Atlas**, in the médina, T039-912014. Crossing the Loukos estuary to the north, the beach road yields a **camping** area.

🍴 Eating
Hit the port to eat delicious, fresh grilled sardines or try one of the cheap Spanish-style cafés near the médina.

ⓘ Directory
Bank and **tourist office** on the main Av Mohammed V.

Moulay Bousselham

This low-key summer beach resort is 85 km south of Larache on the autoroute. To the south, the lagoon Merdja Zerga (blue lagoon) stretches over 30 km and is an important place for wintering birds. A main street running to the beach and lake divides the town and is filled with grill cafés.

🛏 Sleeping
Camping Moulay Bousselham is summer opening only, basic and a real mozzie haven. A better (and free) bet is a motorway stopover – try the coastal stretch to the south.

🍴 Eating/drinking
Eat at one of the little restaurants such as **L'Ocean** for fresh fish snacks and grab a drink at the lagoon-edged **Hotel le Lagon**.

Kénitra

About an hour and a half south of Larache, Kénitra has its roots in the military and was an important post initially for the French. In the 1940s the Americans set up a naval base (and sparked an interest in surfing). It remained for more than 30 years but now the Moroccans have it back – the city and the surfing. A sucker for consistency, the city centres around 2 roads, Mohammed V and Hassan II, for eating, sleeping, shopping and being.

🛏 Sleeping
G **Hotel de France** on Mohammed V, worth a try. Post your letters just up the road and

DEMI TAYLOR

What's in a name?

get your cash out on the corner of Mohammed V and Hassan II.

South of the Oued Sebou, **Mehdiya Plage**, about 11 km from Kénitra, has the summer opening **Camping Medhia** and is backed by Lake Sidi Bourhaba – a winter home to hundreds of ducks. Further south along the P2, the **Plage des Nations** and **Sidi Bouknadel** are accessed via a 2-km surfaced track.

Salé-Rabat

Twin towns separated by the Oued Bou Regreg, Rabat is the hardworking political capital to Salé's old walled city. Both though are fairly conservative and favour early nights. Rabat's main road, Av Mohammed V, packed with big stores runs north from the new town, past the train station and impressive 18th-century As-Sunna Mosque to the walls of the médina.

☼ Flat spells
Cinema Catch the latest Bollywood sensation at one of the cinemas on Av Mohammed V. **Culture** Rabat has some beautiful sights including the Kasbah des Oudaias set in the walls of the médina on the banks of the river – great views down the coast. **Golf** Get a round in at one of the largest courses in Morocco, the upmarket **Royal Golf Dar Es Salam**, 12 km out of town, about 500dh, T037-755864. **Salé** Take a boat across the river and explore the médina (petits taxis can't transport you between the towns).

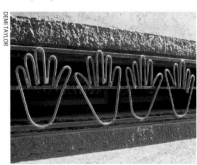
DEMI TAYLOR
Hand of Fátima

☻ Sleeping
Sleeping is centred around Av and Blvd Mohammed V while the médina has plenty of cheap but dodgy options.
G **Hotel Dorhmi**, one of the best affordable choices and close to good eating options, is just inside the médina off Mohamed V, T037-723898.
G The **youth hostel** just inside the southwest corner of the médina is very basic but offers B&B from about 40dh IYAH members, T037-725769.

☻ Eating
Mohammed V has more pâtisseries and crémeries offering juices and sandwiches than you can possibly sample. For good old home-cooked pizza or pasta, head to **La Mamma** just off Av Mohammed V. If you'd rather sample home-cooked, traditional Moroccan fare, try **Restaurant El Bahia** in the médina wall – set lunches are tasty, filling and good value.

☻ Shopping
Carpets Get haggling on R des Consuls in the médina on a Thu morning. Hit the **Marjane** supermarket on the airport road between the 2 towns – there is even a **Pizza Hut** there and for fresh fruit and veggies you can't beat the Sun souk at Rabat médina.

☻ Directory
Banks: Mohammed V has a steady supply of cashpoints. **Chemists**: 24-hr chemist on rotations. **Internet**: Cyberplanet, Av d'Alger next to the tourist info, has a reasonable connection and is not too pricey. **Post office**: Mohammed V. **Tourist information**: Av d'Alger near Pl de Golan.

Temara

South along the S222 or take the No 17 bus from Hassan II in Rabat, this is a popular weekend beach stop with Rabat residents. There are several campsites here including **Camping de Temara**, **Camping La Palmeraie** 100 m from the beach T037-749251, **Camping Gambusias** and –

south at Ech-Chiahna, near the mouth of the Oued Yquem – **Camping Rose-Marie**. Head south to Skhirat for the souk on Sun.

Mohammedia

Just incase the former king didn't have enough roads named after him, they turned this town into a namesake as well. After Skhirat, the coastal road to Mohammedia is less developed with simple sandy tracks running down to Bouznika and Dahomey Plages. Mohammedia however is not so simple. Port Blondin at the mouth of the Oued Nefifikh marks the start of the 3-km stretch of Mohammedia sands. Although a popular and pretty summer retreat from Casablanca, a thriving petrochemical industry and oil refinery shadows the town.

☼ Flat spells
Casablanca is just a short hop by train, bus or grand taxi if you fancy a day in the city. **Golf** Get 18 holes in at the **Royal Mohammedia Golf Course**, about 250dh for a round, T022-322052

☻ Sleeping
Camping Camping International Loran is 100 m from the beach, T022-322957. In the summer, villages of tents spring up along the length of the beach. North at Mansouria are **Camping Oubaha** and **Camping Mimosa** who also have chalets. If you ask nicely, they may even let you grab a hot chalet shower when they're quiet. And they are dead quiet during the wintere months.

☻ Eating
In Mohammedia get a brochette at one of the pavement cafés at the entrance to the kasbah – try **Tiznit** or **Tarfaya**. For a coffee and a snack try **Le Dome** café by the station. "The best bar is the pizzeria **Santa Monica** which is both a bar and a restaurant and where some of the local surfers relax," recommends Amine Afal of the Mohammedia-based FAST surf association.

Directory

Banks: get your cash on R Rachidi. **Post office**: Av Mohammed Zerktouni. **Tourist information**: R Al Jahid.

Casablanca

Casablanca – the 'white house' – grew from a trading port into a sprawling, hustling, traffic-filled, cosmopolitan metropolis. South of the port, the walled médina stretches out towards the main square, Pl Mohammed V, from which the rest of the city seems to radiate. To the west, the showpiece Hassan II Mosque stands watching over the Atlantic. Continuing west along the seafront Blvd Corniche you hit Plage Ain Diab and the significant nightlife district. Surrounding the city the *bidonvilles* or shanty towns spread out, and mark a stark contrast, while above the city, pollution hangs like a fog.

Flat spells

Football Catch a match between rival city teams **Raja Club Athletic**, T022-259954, and **Wydad Athletic Club**, www.wydad.com. **Golf/horse racing** Travel 10 mins south along the S130 to the suburb of Anfa and the **Anfa-Casablanca Racecourse** with races on Sun. Sharing the course is **Royal Golf d'Anfa**, 9 holes, T023-365355.

Sleeping

Head to R Allal Ben Abdallah behind the médina and just off Pl Mohammed V and try: G **Hotel Touring**, T022-310216, G **Bon Reve**, T022-311439 or G **Negociants**

– basic but fair rooms and well placed for cheap eating options.
G The **youth hostel** on the eastern edge of the médina is a fair bet, clean and does beds from 45dh a night.
Camping Not a practical option in the city. **Camping International**, T022-330060, is about 15 km south of the city, 100 m from beach, and popular in the summer.
Camping Deserte des Plages is just before Dar Bouzza while **Camping Tamaris** is further along the 1122 at Hajra Khala, handy for Jack's Beach.

Eating

Café Anwal on Allal Ben Abdallah does a good traditional set menu while **Snack Amine** on R Chaouia is the place for fried fish. If you feel the need for **McDonald's** golden arches take a stroll on the corniche above Ain Diab beach. For coffee or ice cream try **Oliveri** on Hassan II.

Shopping

Check out the covered market on Av Mohammed V for fresh provisions or head to the Twin Centre for the **Marjane** hypermarket where you can also pick up booze. There are plenty of **surf shops** in the city including a **Quiksilver** and a **Rip Curl** store as well as the **Malibu** surf shop on R el Fourat, **Balibongo** on Daoud Dahiri, **Pipeline** on Blvd Rahal el Meskini and **Moby Dick** on R de l'Atlas Maarif.

Transport

The major International Airport Mohammed V is to the south of the city at Nouasseur.

The train journey to Casa-Port station in the centre of the city takes about 40 mins and costs about 20dh. A *grand taxi* in the evening after the trains stop running should cost about 300dh.

Directory

Banks: there are plenty dotted around including Av Mohammed V. **Chemist**: 24-hour chemist on Mohammed V. **Internet**: several choices on Allal Ben Abdallah. **Post office**: Av Mohammed V. **Tourist information**: Av Mohammed V.

Azemmour

Heading south on the coastal S130 the white médina of Azemmour sits on the banks of the river Oum er Rbia. The main road Mohammed V runs up to the central Pl de Souk and the médina. The ramparts surrounding the médina offer great views north up the coast to Casablanca while to the south the popular, long sandy beach is about half an hour's walk through eucalyptus trees.

Sleeping

There are a couple of hotels here:
G **Hotel de la Poste**, as the name suggests, is by the post office, and G **Hotel Victoire**, by the mosque, both just off Mohammed V.

Eating

There are a couple of good cafés by Pl de Souk including **El Manzah**.

 Airports → Tangier, T039-393720; Casablanca, T022-539040; Agadir, T048-839112; Marrakech, T044-447865. www.onda.org.ma. **Buses and coaches** → CTM, T022-458881, www.ctm.co.ma. **Car hire** → Avis, T0870-6060100; Europcar, T0970-6075000. **Ferries** → Southern Ferries, T0044 (0)20-7491 4968; Transmediterranea, T039-931142, www.transmediterranea.es. **Rail links** → ONCF, www.oncf.org.ma. **Petrol prices** → 10dh/litre.

Surfing Central Morocco

At El Jadida the S121 begins its long, winding journey south to Essaouira. This stretch of road follows a coastline that for decades has been relatively unknown to all but a few hardy travellers and dedicated locals who have consistently kept quiet about the potential of this area. However, with world-class waves it is only a matter of time before word gets out. Despite the best attempts of some locals, Safi has exploded into the surf magazines world wide, and a major surf contest is scheduled to take place there at the end of 2004.

"We stayed at Oualidia and it's about an hour to the wave at Safi," says Gabe Davies. "There are a few beaches along the way but nothing that special. However, the wave at Safi is something else. I surfed with Tom Carroll and Spencer Hargreaves and it was eight to ten feet for a week. Tom compared it to Burleigh, but way longer and more barrelly."

Top French surfer Didier Piter's favourite spot in Morocco is Safi. "This wave is a train to heaven, peeling perfectly for 300 metres." Local camp owner Laurent Miramon warns however that the wave is best left to advanced surfers. "The wave is a real world-class break and when it's solid, it's seriously difficult. It's hard to make the wave from the start. The first 200 metres are really very intense, and the surfer must be under the lip if not deep in the barrel – that's why just a few riders can do it. I can tell you I have twice ended up

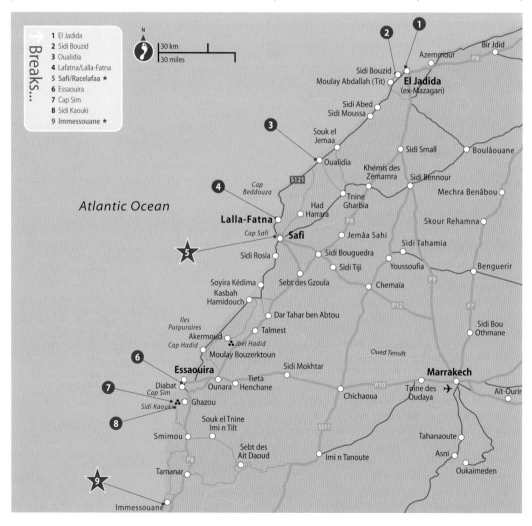

Breaks...

1 El Jadida
2 Sidi Bouzid
3 Oualidia
4 Lafatna/Lalla-Fatna
5 Safi/Racelafaa ★
6 Essaouira
7 Cap Sim
8 Sidi Kaouki
9 Immessouane ★

head first on the rocks (last one was this winter, and I'm lucky to be alive!)."

South of Safi, the picturesque town of Essaouira, with its walled medina and bustling port, is a wonderful place to experience the atmosphere and culture that attracted so many of the worlds great writers and artists over the years. Orson Welles filmed here, Jimi Hendrix chilled here and now a new generation can be found enjoying the freshly caught seafood in the wonderful harbourside restaurants. The *alizée* winds make this one of the windsurfing world's most popular destinations, but during the winter the area boasts some fantastic surf spots.

For those who like their surf straight up, with no mixer, Immessouane is the place. This tiny, functional, if a little unattractive, village is home to a quiet campsite and three quality, uncrowded waves. Whether it will remain this way is in some doubt as a proposed new Japanese development threatens a huge expansion of the village and dredging of the harbour. This could destroy two of the waves that make Immessouane such a surfing gem.

Coastline

The Central Moroccan coastline south of El Jadida is composed of long stretches of exposed beaches broken by rocky outcrops and cliffs. The beaches are powerful and usually facing northwest so they pick up plenty of swell, but the quality of the banks is very variable. The waves between Cap Beddouza and Safi are more sheltered and require bigger swells to work. From here the northwest facing rocky coastline heads southwest again and is home to a mixture of surf spots broken by occasional points. From Essaouira the coastline turns and heads south into a region where many unridden, quality waves break along rocky points. Here access to the coastline becomes difficult and a good map and local knowledge become invaluable. Local surfers may offer advice and tips to respectful travellers.

Localism

Safi is home to one of the most localised spots in the country. The right hand point has been somewhat controversial over the years and now attracts a crowd whenever it breaks. Be patient and there should be plenty of waves to go around. Bear in mind that there have been some nasty scenes here. As you head south to spots like Immessouane the line-up couldn't be more different. Obviously it only takes a couple of hassling surfers to turn up to ruin any session, but in general this section of Morocco is pretty chilled.

Top local surfers Karim Laaleg is a 23 year-old surfer sponsored by Quiksilver. Karim 'Ghier' Chaibat is an excellent rider who moved to the USA, but comes back to the region whenever he can. "He's a Moroccan legend and example for up and coming surfers," says Laurent Miramon.

Getting around

Access to the breaks in central Morocco is pretty straightforward. The

There are fewer quality breaks in Safi compared to Taghazoute, it's less consistent, and mainly beach breaks. However, the point at Safi wipes the floor with Anchor Point. There are barrels from 300 to 500 metres. Like a reverse Mundaka.

Gabe Davies, travelling pro surfer

Central Morocco board guide

Gun
Shaper: Jools at Gulf Stream Surfboards

» 7'2" x 18¾" x 2½".
» When heading for Safi you need a serious board for serious waves.
» This is for when things get serious during those big winter swells.
» Modelled on team rider Sam Lamiroy's Sunset gun for Hawaii.

Shortboard
Shaper: Jools at Gulf Stream Surfboards

» 6'6" x 18½" x 2¼".
» A good all rounder that can be ridden in a wide range of conditions.
» Has a bit of length for when the good points like Sidi Bouzid and Immessouane are working.
» Flexible enough for the beaches.
» Ideal for the surfer travelling light.

(i) Boards by **Gulf Stream Surfboards**
Factory/shop: 12 South Street, Woolacombe, Devon, UK
T00 44 (0)1271-870831 www.gulfstreamboards.co.uk

coastal roads are of good quality and allow easy access to many spots. However there are breaks where access is limited to hiking. Make sure you leave your vehicle in a safe place or with a guardian. Don't leave any valuables visible.

Breaks

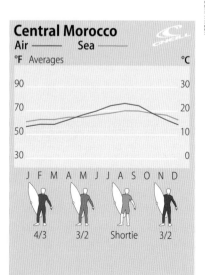

1 El Jadida

- **Break type**: Beach break.
- **Conditions**: Medium swells, offshore in southerly winds.
- **Hazards/tips**: El Jadida can suffer from pollution from the nearby port.
- **Sleeping**: El Jadida ▸▸ *p353*.

Northeast-facing beach with decent waves and a right that breaks off a sandbar alongside the jetty. Popular in the summer with Moroccan families.

2 Sidi Bouzid

- **Break type**: Point and beach.
- **Conditions**: Medium swells, offshore in southeasterly winds.
- **Hazards/tips**: The resort has limited sewage facilities so the water can be heavily polluted with household waste.
- **Sleeping**: El Jadida ▸▸ *p353*.

Well known, good quality right-point break that works in northwesterly swells. It breaks over a sand-covered rock reef. The beach has peaks and is popular with local bodyboarders at high tide. Developed seafront, popular with holidaying Moroccans in the summer.

3 Oualidia

- **Break type**: Beach break.
- **Conditions**: Small to big swells, offshore in southeasterly winds.
- **Hazards/tips**: Location of Surfland surf camp.
- **Sleeping**: Oualidia ▸▸ *p353*.

Exposed stretch of beaches with powerful waves working on all tides. Beaches front a very sheltered lagoon that has reform waves suitable for beginners in a big swell. Beautiful location with dolphins and flamingos.

4 Lafatna/Lalla-Fatna

- **Break type**: Beach break.
- **Conditions**: Big swells, easterly winds.
- **Hazards/tips**: Rips and rocks.
- **Sleeping**: Safi ▸▸ *p353*.

South from Cap Beddouza, the rocky headland protects a series of cliff-backed sandy coves. Lalla-Fatna is a 2-km descent from the S121 coast road. Westerly facing beach that needs a big swell to work as it is sheltered by the headland. Produces mainly right-hand sandbanks. If camping on the beach, be aware of tidal range.

Central Morocco

Air ——— Sea ———

°F Averages °C

90	30
70	20
50	10
30	0

J F M A M J J A S O N D

4/3 · 3/2 · Shortie · 3/2

DEMI TAYLOR

The entrance to the harbour at Essaouira ▸▸ *p354*

Tales round the campfire

"So there I was, stark naked, towelling myself down, and I turned round to see this chap making off with my mini-Malibu board."

It's amazing the people you find yourself camping next to. Ken was an ex-pat, retired, long grey hair in a pony tail, battered old Land Rover, voice booming like Brian Blessed. He was telling us about an incident that had happened to him a couple of weeks before.

"He was trying to get it into his car so I grabbed my revolver from the Land Rover and shouted at him to stop. He just ignored me so I loosed off a couple of rounds into his car. The old Northern Ireland training kicks in you know. Well he shot off at top speed – but left my board behind.

"A few days later I reported that I had discharged a firearm and I asked the policeman what would have happened if I had actually shot the bugger. He explained that this would not have been good. I asked him what would have happened had I used my crossbow instead. He said this would have been OK. They would have assumed that the thief had a knife, and using a crossbow would not have been seen as escalating the confrontation."

All we could think was 'You have a crossbow *and* a revolver?'

"Anyway, I have a pot of coffee on, care to join me?"

Well we weren't about to say no to a guy with a mobile arsenal in his vehicle.

"Milk? Sugar? You know, when you've seen a man blown apart before your eyes . . . it changes you."

We decided there and then that we would be moving on at first light.

Chris Nelson and Demi Taylor

5 Safi/Racelafaa

- **Break type**: Right point break.
- **Conditions**: Big to huge swells.
- **Size**: 4-12 ft.
- **Length**: 300-600 m.
- **Swell**: Northwesterly.
- **Wind**: Offshore in northeasterly/easterly winds.
- **Tide**: Low to mid.
- **Bottom**: Sand and rock point.
- **Entry/exit**: Good timing off the rocks.
- **Hazards/tips**: Access, rocks, localism, heavy wave, advanced surfers only.
- **Sleeping**: Safi »» *p353*.

Low to mid tide, right-hand reef that produces long, long, hollow barrels that reel along the point in big swells. Head north out of Safi on the S121 and you come to what is considered by many to be the best spot in the country. Although an inconsistent wave that only breaks in the biggest swells, when it does fire, "It wipes the floor with Anchor Point," says top pro Gabe Davies.

For decades the waves at Safi avoided the media spotlight and travelling surfers bypassed this gem, heading straight to Taghazoute. However, over the past few years the wave has featured in all the major European surf mags and word has spread of the sheer quality of the waves here. Unlike many Moroccan points that offer long, walling rights, Safi produces big, hollow barrels. It is for this reason that many of Europe's top pros have been drawn here and it has been pencilled in as the site for the Quiksilver World Masters.

For many reasons, this is a wave for advanced surfers only. It has had some localism issues over the years, which at times have been quite extreme. Travelling surfers have been threatened in the past, but things seem to be less extreme lately. "When I surfed there the locals were pretty heavy, you had to be respectful and choose your waves so that you didn't get dropped in on, but the waves were like a mix between Kirra and J Bay," says top French rider Didier Piter.

The point only starts to work when the swell hits 10 ft at Oualidia. The waves are fast and hollow, and a huge swell can see 12 ft waves barrelling for 300-500 m. Tom Carroll described the wave as being "like Burleigh only longer and more hollow", and Gabe Davies compared it to "a reverse Mundaka".

If you like Safi, try Killer Point in Morocco (see page 361) or La Santa Right in Lanzarote (see page 267).

THIERRY ORGANOFF

This wave is a train to heaven, peeling perfectly for 300 metres.

5 Safi/Racelafaa

6 Essaouira

- **Break type**: Beach break
- **Conditions**: Medium to big swells, offshore in easterly winds.
- **Hazards/tips**: Surfboards (Bics) available for hire on northern end the beach.
- **Sleeping**: Essaouira ›› p354.

Long, crescent-shaped beach that works on all tides. An offshore island cuts out swell. The southern end towards Diabat picks up the most swell and has the best banks. This is a famous windsurfing spot so don't expect too many glassy days. Best in the winter when there is less wind. There is a local crew of surfers worth talking to about other spots around the town.

The road to Rabat

7 Cap Sim

- **Break type**: Right-hand point.
- **Conditions**: Medium to big swell, offshore in easterly/southeasterly winds.
- **Hazards/tips**: Access is difficult. Store valuables somewhere safe.
- **Sleeping**: Sidi Kaouki ›› p354.

Cap Sim needs a decent sized swell to get going but produces long, walling rights over a sand-covered rock bottom. Works on all tides but best on low. Access is from the road to Sidi Kaouki. Turn right onto the *piste* road towards the point, then the final part is on foot. Quality waves. Be friendly to the locals and you will be received well.

8 Sidi Kaouki

- **Break type**: Beach break.
- **Conditions**: All swells, offshore in easterly winds.
- **Hazards/tips**: Exposed, few facilities.
- **Sleeping**: Sidi Kaouki ›› p354.

This long beach, which works on all tides, can produce some good banks but is exposed to the wind. Can have excellent waves with rights at the northern end and peaks along the length. Parking, with a guardian, at the northern end of the beach. Check the wind direction before making the long drive from Essaouira. Keep an eye on your belongings.

9 Immessouane

- **Break type**: Right-hand point breaks.
- **Conditions**: Medium to big swells.
- **Size**: 3-10 ft.
- **Length**: 50-300 m plus.
- **Swell**: Northwesterly.
- **Wind**: Southeasterly/easterly.
- **Tide**: All tides.
- **Bottom**: Sand/reef.
- **Entry/exit**: Off the rocks/from the harbour.
- **Hazards/tips**: Rarely crowded.
- **Sleeping**: Immessouane ›› p355.

A series of good quality waves that work on different swells and tides. The first point is in front of the campsite and produces some nice right-hand walls through the tides. Offshore in an easterly wind. Access off the rocks near the campsite.

The second wave is a heavy, barrelling right that peels in front of the harbour wall. The take-off is steep and fires through to the harbour mouth where it peters out. Winds from the east or southeast are offshore and it works in big swells at mid to high tide. For experienced surfers only. Harbour wall wave one of the heaviest in this region.

Inside the bay is the most popular and longest right-hander. It starts to break at the southern end of the harbour and peels through to the beach at low tide. Suitable for all surfers, this is an excellent, long walling wave breaking over sand and rocks. This wave is sheltered from northerly and northeasterly winds by cliffs and is also the most sheltered from swell.

(i) *If you like* Immessouane, *try* Inch Reef *in Ireland (see page 141) or* The Gare *in England (see page 66).*

9 Immessouane

6 Essaouira

Listings

9 Immessouane

El Jadida

This busy port town is still protected by the ramparts of the Portuguese médina built in the 1500s. It is also a popular summer spot with holidaying Moroccans who set up makeshift tent villages along the beaches surrounding the Sidi Ouafi lighthouse. The bus station sits to the south of the town and the No 2 can take you south a couple of km to Sidi-Bouzid Plage. Further south – about 15 km – lies the port Jorf Lasfar and a phosphate processing plant, which means the water in this region can be less than clean.

✪ Flat spells
Golf Get 18 holes in at the **Royal Golf Club** (cheaper during the week) just north of El Jadida, T023-352251.

🛏 Sleeping
There are a couple of cheap options here: G **Hotel de Maghreb**, just off Pl Mohammed V, G **Hotel Suisse**, on the main R Zerktouni, which has rooms with showers. **Camping Camping International**, T023-342755, on the road into town not far from the beach, also has option of cabins.

🍴 Eating
For cheap eats head to Pl El Hansali, just up from Mohammed V. You could try **La Broche** or **Chahrazade** for simple Moroccan and fish dishes.

🍶 Directory
Banks: there are plenty here including several around Pl Mohammed V. **Post office**: Pl Mohammed V. **Souk**: head to the lighthouse on a Wed to stock up on provisions. **Tourist information**: just off Pl Mohammed V on Av Rafi.

Oualidia

Travelling south, the coastal S121 passes a series of quiet beaches and rocky outcrops, backed by dunes. Around Sidi Moussa, the scenery encompasses saltpans and hot houses nurturing tomatoes. To the south, Souk el Jemaa is named after its Friday market. The quiet town of Oualidia hugs the edges of a tidal lagoon, which fills through two gaps in the spit of land separating it from the ocean. Beyond this stretches miles of empty beach. Famous for its oysters and flanked by a 17th-century kasbah, built by Saltan El Oualid, Oualidia is also slowly becoming an upmarket holiday resort – hence accommodation may seem pricey.

🛏 Sleeping
Camping Surfland, T+212 6114 6461, surfland@iam.net.ma. The tented surf camp run by Laurent Miramon, offers first-hand knowledge of the area and tuition, as well as half board. As Laurent explains, "Surf conditions in Safi–Oualidia are sensitive to tides, wind, and sandbar position so local knowledge is important. There are different classes of waves for all levels with the advantage of the lagoon of Oualidia. When it's too powerful or too big, beginners and kids can find good conditions at Oualidia." In the summer, **Camping International de Oualidia** offers fair facilities just back from the lagoon.
Other alternatives include:
F **Hotel Restaurant l'Initial**, T044-366246.

🍴 Eating
Grab some pasta at **Hotel Restaurant l'Initial** or for good cheap eats head to **Thalassa** for their set menu. If you want to pick up a few basic supplies check out the Sat market.

Safi

Winding along the road south, the sea and hidden stretches of deserted beach are intermittently hidden by sand dunes. Cap Beddouza offers a lighthouse, views along the coast, a pricey auberge as well as a protective rocky headland, sheltering small sandy coves southwards to Cap Safi. Safi itself is a fairly industrialized, unattractive working port town dealing with fertilizer factories and sardine-canning plants so surrounding coast is fairly polluted. Fort Dar el Bahar offers good views along the coast to Essaouira while the seafront médina is the place to pick up pottery. Outside of the médina, life centres around two main squares – Pl de l'Independence near the seafront crammed with shops, cafés and banks and the more sensible Pl Mohammed V, inland and south of the médina with the post office and tourist office leading off it.

Sleeping

The cheapest places to sleep are squeezed between the médina and the seafront. **F Hotel de Paris**, T044-462149, one of the best with big clean double rooms. The campsite a couple of kms north at Sidi Bouzid has good facilities.

Eating

Café M'Zoughan, on Pl de l'Independence, is a good pâtisserie and a nice place to get breakfast while **Café El Bahia** is the place to grab a snack and watch the world go by.

Essaouira

Travelling via the coastal road or the faster P8 from Safi, Essaouira makes a great stopover for atmosphere alone. And, known as Africa's windy city, if you're into windsurfing then this place is surely heaven. (The wind is known locally as the *alizée*).

The white walled médina, entered by 5 main gates, is all about ambience and has been a bohemian lure since Jimi Hendrix stayed here in the 1960s. Next to the médina the busy fishing port is also a rehabilitation zone for boats whose wooden hulls are ripped apart and rebuilt. From the kasbah a wide beach – a popular spot for a game of football – follows the main road south towards Cap Sim. Offshore the Îles Purpuraires, named for their ancient production of purple dye, are home to a colony of falcons.

Flat spells

Diabat At the south end of Essaouira's beach sits the village of Diabat, overlooking a castle ruin sinking slowly into the sands. The ruin was the inspiration for Hendrix's 'Castles in the Sand' and this village was the one he tried to buy before being deported for drugs offences. The village is fairly uninspiring but the castle is worth a look.

Sleeping

Essaouira is becoming popular again with the young, free and monied so accommodation is generally geared to the higher end. There are however a couple of good options that won't break the bank. **F-G Chez Brahim**, on R Mourabatine at the southern end of the médina by Bab Marrakech entrance, T044-472599. Double rooms surround a courtyard and there's a board room for storing equipment. **G Hotel Smara**, inside the ramparts on R Skala, has clean double rooms and a roof terrace – as with all rooms see it before you agree to it. **Camping** Camping d'Essaouira, southbound on the road out of town, about 2 km from the médina. A small, walled site with good showers and toilets (even if it does feel a bit like a prison complex) and a good place to stop overnight. Alternatively, you can overnight in the carpark near the harbourfront, watched over by guardians for about 10dh.

Eating/drinking

Unquestionably the best place to eat here is at one of the fish grills set up between the port and the médina. Sitting at a communal table at midday or early evening, eat fresh fish off the boats from about 20dh and watch the world fly by. On Moulay Hassan head to **Restaurant Essalam** for a cheap 3-course set menu of *harira*, couscous and fruit. **Pizzeria L'As Dos** off Av l'Istiqlal can fulfil your pizza needs cheaply. **Chez Ben**

Mustapha on the main square is a great place to get a *nes-nes* or white coffee and soak up some jazz.

Festivals

In June Essaouira is taken over by the **Gnaoua music festival**, a traditional form of music – but you'll probably be relieved of a few dirham by a troupe doing the rounds of the main squares throughout the year.

Shopping

There are a couple of **windsurfing shops** here including **L'Ocean Vagabond** on the seafront and **Palais d'Ocean**, where you may be able to pick up basic surf equipment and hire bikes. For fresh fruit and provisions head to the market in the médina on R M Zerktouni near entrance Bab Doukkala. Essaouira is famous for its gnarled and knotted **thuya wood** creations (everything from lighters to backgammon sets to full-blown dining suites) so it's a great place to pick up a few souvenirs – about 30dh will get you a wooden box, 5dh a basic lighter holder.

Directory

Banks: Pl Moulay Hassan. **Pharmacies**: a few on the main drag through the médina, Av l'Istiqual. **Post office**: Av Lalla Aicha parallel to Mohammed V. **Tourist information**: Av du Caire.

Sidi Kaouki

Sidi Kaouki is a one-horse town 15 km south of Essaouria with camels for hire. Other than that, it has a guardian for parking, a teleboutique, the surf-inspired café **Point Break**, a tat shop and a *marabout* said to cure female infertility. **F Residence Le Kaouki**, T044-783206, is near the beach and is popular with German windsurfers. All this may change though as Sidi Kaouki is earmarked for development.

Airports → Tangier, T039-393720; Casablanca, T022-539040; Agadir, T048-839112; Marrakech, T044-447865. www.onda.org.ma. **Buses and coaches** → CTM, T022-458881, www.ctm.co.ma. **Car hire** → Avis, T0870-6060100; Europcar, T0970-6075000. **Ferries** → Southern Ferries, T0044 (0)20-7491 4968; Transmediterranea, T039-931142, www.transmediterranea.es. **Rail links** → ONCF, www.oncf.org.ma. **Petrol prices** → 10dh/litre.

Marrakech

The city of the south, with its wild médina, has always had a hypnotic draw. Everyone from leaders – Churchill and Roosevelt – to creatives – The Stones, Blur, YSL, even Alfred Hitchcock – have been intoxicated by Marrakech and for many it is their first introduction to Morocco.

The skyscape is dominated by the High Atlas mountains while the spiritual and physical heart of Marrakech is the Jemaâ el Fna or 'assembly of the dead' – 'La Place'. Previously the site of public executions the market square is an almost filmic experience filled with weird and wonderful smells, sights, sounds and tastes. Grill cafés rub shoulders with snake charmers and watersellers. 'Dentists' with molars piled high on rugs by their feet compete with storytellers, fire breathers and the Gnaoua musicians. With all these distractions you need to watch your wallet (although security has much improved in recent years). Watching over the square is the 12th-century Koutoubia minaret which, legend has it, bled its spirit into the city, giving it its colour. To the north of the square are a series of souks for every occasion. Although they are oppressive, with 'guides' trying to offer tours or traders trying to sell their wares, take a deep breath as they are definitely worth a look. Surrounding the city, the ramparts stretch for 16 km defending Marrakech from the encroaching desert.

✿ Flat spells

Give yourself at least a day to soak up the atmosphere of the city and explore the souks before heading off to the coast. **Golf** The 3 courses should leave you satiated: **Royal Golf Club**, 5 km south on the road to Ouarzazate T044-4404705; **Palmeraie**, on the road to Tizi-n-Tichka, T044-4301010; and the **Almekis**, closest to the city on Blvd Mohamed Zerktouni, T044-404414. **Snowboarding** Head to the High Atlas resort of **Oukaimeden**, a 2-hr drive south of Marrakech on the S513, to enjoy a Nov-Mar powder session.

⊙ Sleeping

There are good cheap places to find around the pedestrianized R Bab Agnaou just off the Jemaâ el Fna but places do get packed out so try to book in advance.
G La Gazelle, R Beni Marinine – parallel to Bab Agnaou, T044-441112, is clean.
G Afriqua, off Bab Agnaou, T044-442403, is a cheaper choice with a roof terrace.
East off the square are a couple of good, similarly priced choices: **G Mimosa**, R des Banques, T044-426385, and **G Mounir**, R el Kennaria, T044-444356.

⊘ Eating

For atmosphere, the only place to eat is at one of the open-air grills on the Jemaâ el Fna. The standards are pretty safe but if you're worried choose something cooked to order. Former *Tracks* editor, Phil Jarratt, recommends: "**Stylo** in the souk. It's not too expensive and is an amazing experience. **Café Argana** on the square – you can't miss it – has great views especially at sunset and reasonable snacks. Just off Mohammed V, **L'Escale** does a great chicken 'n' chips – you can even get a beer here!"

⊙ Shopping

Marjane Hypermarket, just north on the P7 Casablanca road, has everything you need or try the **Gueliz** food market off Mohammed V for fresh fruits and veg.

⊖ Transport

Marrakech-Menara **airport** is just 5 km

southwest of the city and has the usual facilities such as car hire and bureau de change. It's about a 50dh cab ride away from the médina. The **train station** is on the edge of Guéliz, the new town – west of the médina. A *petit taxi* into the médina should cost about 10dh. Next door the **bus station** can offer long-distance solutions south to Agadir.

❶ Directory

Banks: in Guéliz there are plenty around the main Av Mohammed V while in the heart of the médina you can find them just off the main square. **Pharmacy**: Pharmacie Centrale, 120 Av Mohammed V in the new town ; all-night pharmacy, **Dépôt de Nuit**, open next to the Police on Jemaâ el Fna. **Internet**: Cyber Behja on R Bani Marine can connect you for about 15dh/hr. **Post office**: on Jemaâ el Fna as well as the main one in Guéliz on Pl du 16 Novembre. **Tourist information**: on Av Mohammed V.

Immessouane

Another sleepy one-horse town, but this one is due for a makeover by a Japanese fishing company that will threaten this spot's quality waves. Other than fishing, the village has a small café and an exposed and dusty **campsite** with basic facilities on the headland and the G **Auberge Kahina**, T048-826032. If you are coming to stay, come prepared!

Mohammedia pit stop

Heading home on the P8

Surfing Taghazoute & the South

When surfers' minds conjure up images of Morocco, there is one place that they see in wide-screen Technicolor – the fabled points of Taghazoute. It was these breaks that first brought the *Freeride* generation here in the 1970s and, over thirty years on, is still the country's surfing Mecca. The constant influx of western surfers has had a profound effect upon this small village. Possessing a flair for capitalism that would bring a rush of pride to the hardest Thatcherite heart, the locals now service the booming surf culture throughout the winter season with cafés, restaurants and

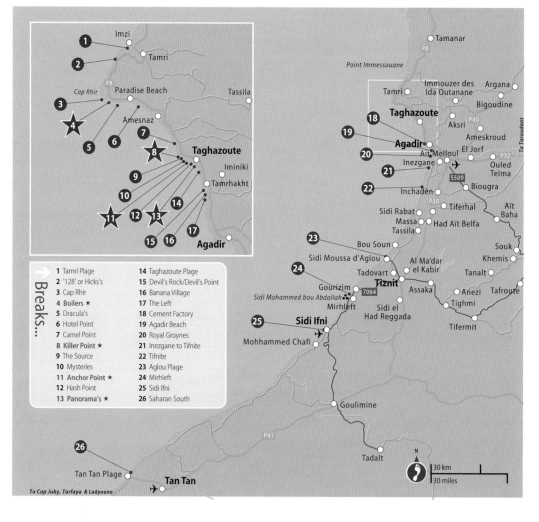

→ Breaks...

1 Tamri Plage	14 Taghazoute Plage
2 '128' or Hicks's	15 Devil's Rock/Devil's Point
3 Cap Rhir	16 Banana Village
4 Boilers ★	17 The Left
5 Dracula's	18 Cement Factory
6 Hotel Point	19 Agadir Beach
7 Camel Point	20 Royal Groynes
8 Killer Point ★	21 Inezgane to Tifnite
9 The Source	22 Tifnite
10 Mysteries	23 Aglou Plage
11 Anchor Point ★	24 Mirhleft
12 Hash Point	25 Sidi Ifni
13 Panorama's ★	26 Saharan South

B&Bs, and even surf shops have sprung up along the high street. Taghazoute has even changed colour from a patchwork of white and blue, to a uniform terracotta. The sheer number of apartments available for rent has financed the migration into the surrounding hills and the spread of utilities, like electricity, to the neighbouring villages. There is always talk of big projects coming to the village. Hotels, Club Med, huge swathes of beachfront, high-rise complexes – so far these have not materialized, but the locals believe such 'progress' is inevitable.

The many reefs and points around the region make this a true surfers' paradise – an often-used cliché applicable to few places on earth. Anchor Point and Killer Point are headline acts that draw surfers of all nationalities. Paddle out into the line-up and you'll hear French, Arabic, German, Portuguese and Spanish voices as well as English spoken with Australian, American or Irish accents. The region around Taghazoute is as wave rich and diverse as the line-ups. Breaks at Mysteries, Boilers, Panorama's, Devil's Rock and Killers can be truly awesome and the seemingly endless sunny days and the clear, green water only serve to increase the allure. Add to this the mix of local culture and it is no surprise to see the same faces appearing in cafés of Taghazoute year after year, drawn by the classic surf, the perfect climate, cheap living and the welcoming people.

The major resort of Agadir, just to the south of Taghazoute, is the first port of call for many surfers arriving in the country. Some merely glance at it from the window of the hire car as they hightail it to one of the villages to the north that will be home for their Moroccan adventure. Agadir can hardly be called picturesque – with its McDonald's and nightclubs, it is hardly typical of a major Islamic city – but it still has a lot to offer the traveller. This winter resort town is the gateway to the vast south of the country. From here on, the coastline opens up with unlimited surfing potential, and the number of surfers, even at well known breaks like Tifnite, drops off to virtually none. If you want to lose the crowds and have a real surf adventure, just follow the road south but make sure you're well stocked up on water and supplies – the desert can be unforgiving.

Coastline

The geography of this coastline produces a closely packed series of rocky points and reefs to the north, with incredible stretches of sandy beach opening up to the south of Agadir. The breaks north of Cap Rhir consist of a series of reefs and a beach that receive the full force of wind and swell. However, once round the point, the cape aligns itself into a series of points, each with slightly different characteristics. The sand builds up on the rocks and gives rise to breaks that can vary greatly year to year, or even within the same swell season. A point that failed to break one year, may fire the next.

Agadir shelters in the lee of Cap Rhir which means the huge, crescent-shaped sandy bay is an ideal tourist beach for those who descend upon the town looking for some winter sun. Heading south,

The more you see of Morocco, the more you realize that Taghazoute is unique. The hippies have been coming here since the sixties and the surfers since the mid seventies. Money has come into the village. They've had access to western culture, language ... one local dude even became a frisbee champion.

Hugo Martin, travelling surfer

Taghazoute & the South board guide

Fun board
Shaper: Jools at Gulf Stream Surfboards

▸▸ 7'0" x 20¼" x 2⅞"
▸▸ The name say it all - fun.
▸▸ Beat the hungry pack at Christmas.
▸▸ Perfect in a wide range of conditions, from smaller days at the beaches to overhead days at the points.
▸▸ A wider nose template`and added volume throughout makes this board perfect for the larger surfer or novices looking to improve.

Semi-gun
Shaper: Jools at Gulf Stream Surfboards

▸▸ 6'8" x 18¾" x 2⅜"
▸▸ A great mid-range semi-gun for when points such as Killers and Anchors are going off.
▸▸ Perfect for deep barrels, fast walls and control at high speed.

 Boards by **Gulf Stream Surfboards**
Factory/shop: 12 South Street, Woolacombe, Devon, UK
T00 44 (0)1271-870831 www.gulfstreamboards.co.uk

the coastline merges into a series of beaches, rivermouths and points that pick up masses of swell. The point at Tifnite can be double overhead when Anchor Point is 3 ft. Sidi Ifni is a town that some intrepid surfers head for, with its relaxed line-up and excellent surf potential. But from here on, the only limit is time and road access. With a 4WD and a full tank of petrol, a whole world of possibilities open up.

Localism

Breaks like Anchor Point, Killers and Mysteries can get extremely crowded, especially over the Christmas and New Year break. Weekends also see numbers increase as Moroccan surfers arrive from nearby cities. But you are more likely to experience drop-ins from tourists. "There are two sorts of travelling surfer that increases the tension in the line-up," says Irish surfer Paul McCarthy. "Those who feel that, having spent a few weeks here, it makes them local and those who have the 'I'm only here for a week so must get as many waves as possible' attitude. Neither outlook wins friends." Luckily, problems are rare here and despite the crowds it is still generally a very relaxed line-up. To the south of Agadir, the only thing to worry about is making sure you have enough sun cream on.

Top local surfers According to Laurent Miramon, 10-year-old **Ramzi Boukhiam** from Agadir is a future champion. "I've seen thousands of kids over the 14 years I've coached, but this one is a monument of style, motivation and vibes. He's lucky to live in Agadir, with very cool parents, so he can surf three or four days a week minimum." **Aurelie Magnen** is one of Morocco's hottest female surfers and a former Moroccan surfing champion. She is a member of both the Agadir and Hossegor surf clubs, where she is now spending more of her time.

Getting around

Taghazoute is one of the few places in Morocco where you can happily exist without a car, if you don't mind being limited to the breaks around the village. Anchors, Killers and Mysteries are all within walking distance. However they can be crowded and a car allows the surfer to fully appreciate the breaks around the area. The roads around Taghazoute are generally very good and the P8 allows access to all the breaks. Those without a car can take one of the regular buses from the village square to either Aourir to the south or to Boilers and Tamri Plage to the north. Tickets are cheap and the buses run every 30 minutes. For a trip into Agadir you may want to experience a *grand taxi* ride. These blue and white Mercedes saloons are scarier than any Disney theme ride.

The only beach accessible on foot in Agadir is the flat city beach. Once out of town, a solid car or 4WD is needed for some of the *piste* roads and tracks that lead to the breaks. Tifnite is serviced by a modern, tarmac road, which finishes at the southern end of the bay. The only way to the point is by 4WD over the sand dunes, or by foot. Vehicles are not allowed to park at the Royal Groynes due to its proximity to the palace. A surf check means a long walk, but this does help keep the crowds down.

THE GILL

Banno at Boilers ▶▶ *p360*

Breaks

1 Tamri Plage

- **Break type**: Beach break, left and right sandbanks and dried rivermouth.
- **Conditions**: Small swell, offshore in easterly winds.
- **Hazards/tips**: Crowded when working.
- **Sleeping**: Taghazoute ⇢ *p366*.

Tamri Plage can be disappointing. It looks like it should be home to some quality waves, but often it flatters to deceive. Works on all tides but better nearer low tide, easily maxes out in bigger swells. Waves begin to break out from the rocks to the south of the beach as the tide drops and there may also be a right-hander in front of the rivermouth.

Park in the lay-by on top of the cliffs at the southern end of the beach, just off the main road, but be prepared to be hassled by local kids for dihram. Tamri picks up more swell than any break in this area so if everywhere else is flat, others will be there too. Weekends can be a zoo but weekdays should be OK. Best peaks usually form in front of the cliffs.

1 Tamri Plage

2 '128' or Hicks's

- **Break type**: Short, right-hand reef break.
- **Conditions**: Small, clean swells, no wind or light easterly winds.
- **Hazards/tips**: Rocky reef, shallow, urchins and difficult access.
- **Sleeping**: Taghazoute ⇢ *p366*.

Low tide reef that easily maxes out and is easily blown out. Access by jumping off the rocks; come in over the shelf just to the south of the break. Always wear boots as the reef and shelf are both urchin infested. The expression "Three's a crowd" was invented for this break. If people are already in, try somewhere else. When heading north from Taghazoute, turn left at the 'Essaouira 128 km' sign. Park on the cliff top and you should see a right-hand reef breaking at low tide.

3 Cap Rhir

- **Break type**: Large, right-hand point break.
- **Conditions**: Medium and big swells, offshore in southeasterly and easterly winds.
- **Hazards/tips**: Big powerful waves, tricky access, rocks.
- **Sleeping**: Taghazoute ⇢ *p366*.

Tides depend on swell size. Cap Rhir has long, right, point break waves that are not for the faint-hearted and are rarely surfed. It's a good place to escape the crowds and produces some epic waves in big swells. Access is best by 4WD or sturdy hire car. Explore north from Boilers or south from the lighthouse. Sharp, urchin-infested reef – access to the break is tricky, as is entry and exit from the water.

2 '128' or Hicks's

3 Cap Rhir

Taghazoute & the South

Air —— Sea ——

°F Averages   °C

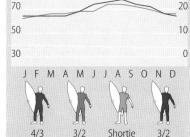

90			30
70			20
50			10
30			0

J F M A M J J A S O N D

4/3   3/2   Shortie   3/2

Morocco Taghazoute & the South Breaks Tamri Plage to Cap Rhir

4 Boilers

- **Break type**: Quality right-hand reef break.
- **Conditions**: Medium swells, offshore in easterly wind.
- **Size**: 3-8 ft.
- **Length**: 50-100 m plus
- **Swell**: Northerly/northwesterly/westerly.
- **Wind**: Easterly.
- **Tide**: All tides.
- **Bottom**: Rocky reef.
- **Entry/exit**: Paddle out between huge rock and boiler, in over rocks.
- **Hazards/tips**: Sharp reef, urchins, difficult exit in big swells, crowds.
- **Sleeping**: Taghazoute ▸ p366.

Boilers is clearly visible from the coast road. Named after the huge ship's boiler that sits next to the peak, this spot is a great indicator reef. If Boilers is maxed out, head for Taghazoute; if too small, head for Tamri. This right-hander can be classic on its day. If the wind is calm and a 6-ft swell is running, it can reel off perfect wave after perfect wave. Works at all tides but better nearer low. If the swell picks up the wave can section and exiting the water can be a problem. Boilers can also be very crowded during peak periods and weekends.

Boots are essential here as access in and out is over the rocks. Paddle out between the boiler and the large rock during a lull in the sets – good timing is needed in a big swell.

Boilers can have a weather system all of its own so is always worth a check. Due to the effect of the surrounding hills it can be onshore everywhere else and offshore here. It can also be calm one minute and howling offshore the next.

(i) *If you like Boilers, try Punta dos Picos in Spain (see page 254) or Easkey Right in Ireland (see page 128).*

5 Dracula's

- **Break type**: Fickle, right-hand reef break.
- **Conditions**: Medium swell, offshore in east/northeasterly wind.
- **Hazards/tips**: Tricky access, shallow with urchins, experienced surfers only.
- **Sleeping**: Taghazoute ▸ p366.

Working on all tides, Dracula's is a right point just south of Boilers and can be a good bet if Boilers is big and crowded. Has become more popular as Boilers gets busier. Access is tricky here but the waves are suckier and have a bit more punch. Park just south of the break in the small fishermen's car park.

6 Hotel Point

- **Break type**: Right-hand point.
- **Conditions**: Big swell, easterly or northeasterly winds.
- **Hazards/tips**: Rips when big, sheltered from winds, rocks.
- **Sleeping**: Taghazoute ▸ p366.

Hotel Point is a mid to low tide, right point located where the road bends out along the point towards Boilers. It needs a big swell to break, but it can be calm and glassy even on the windiest of days due to the sheltering hills. Breaks in front of the small village.

On a big swell, long barrels are there for the taking but beware of rips. It is rarely surfed as it works when many other points are firing.

4 Canno at Boilers

6 Hotel Point

4 Boilers

THE GILL

THE GILL

DEMI TAYLOR

7 Camel Point

- 🌐 **Break type**: Right-hand point break.
- ☁ **Conditions**: Small to medium swells, offshore in easterly winds.
- ❗ **Hazards/tips**: Suitable for all surfers.
- 💤 **Sleeping**: Taghazoute ▸ *p366*.

Camel Point is at the north end of the first beach north of Killers. This right-hand point works well on a low to mid tide in small to medium swells. The take-off point is out level with the end of the headland and can be ridden through to the beach on good days. Not a world-class wave, but a great place to leave the crowds behind. Good spot for intermediate surfers as it has a sand bottom and easy access from the beach.

8 Killer Point

- 🌐 **Break type**: Right-hand point break.
- ☁ **Conditions**: All size swells.
- ⊕ **Size**: 2-10 ft.
- ⊕ **Length**: 50-300 m.
- 🌀 **Swell**: Northerly/northwesterly/westerly.
- 🌀 **Wind**: Easterly.
- 〰 **Tide**: All tides.
- ⚒ **Bottom**: Sand-covered reef.
- ⊛ **Entry/exit**: Paddle off the beach at the Source not from the cliffs.
- ❗ **Hazards/tips**: Crowds, rips when big, heavy wave.
- 💤 **Sleeping**: Taghazoute ▸ *p366*.

Like many of the area's waves, Killers is a sand-covered reef. Quality of the waves varies from year to year, but can resemble a picture book version of everything a right point should be. It works on all tides but is better at

low. On small days, Killers has a short right just around the headland that hoovers up swell but on a medium to large swell, Killer Point really comes to life. A steep take-off and fast bowl section leads onto endless walls all the way through to the inside. It's a long paddle off the beach and surfers taking on Killers at 8-ft plus may find a strong rip pushing down towards Mysteries.. This is a wave for competent and advanced surfers only. Legend has it that Killer Point is named after the killer whales that are occasionally seen here (see Surfer Tale on page 339).

ⓘ **If you like** *Killer Point*, try *Safi* in *Morocco* (see page 351) or *Roca Puta* in *Euskadi* (see page 213).

9 The Source

- 🌐 **Break type**: Peak.
- ☁ **Conditions**: Small to medium swells, offshore in easterly/northeasterly winds.
- ❗ **Hazards/tips**: Crowded, suitable for all surfers.
- 💤 **Sleeping**: Taghazoute ▸ *p366*.

I thought 'I've only been in this country a couple of weeks and I've already seen three people die!' It made me realize that we hadn't just crossed into a different country, we were in a whole different culture.

Kiwi surfer Mike Brown

This sand-covered reef works in small to medium swells at low to mid tides and gets its name from the natural spring that emerges on the shore nearby. Breaking both left and right, the Source can be one of the few places where goofy footers may pick up a few front-side waves. A fun wave that tends to get crowded as it's in front of the Mysteries free-camping area.

7 Camel Point

Secret spot

Fishing boats in Taghazoute harbour

7 Camel Point

9 The Source

10 Mysteries

- 🌀 **Break type**: Right-hand, sand-covered reef.
- ☁ **Conditions**: All swells, offshore in east/northeasterly winds.
- ❗ **Hazards/tips**: Crowded, inconsistent.
- 🛏 **Sleeping**: Taghazoute ▸ *p366*.

Mysteries can be classic in the years when the sand has built up in the right way. Best surfed with water on the reef, so from mid to high tide. A staple diet of the Mystery free-campers and, as such, gets crowded. The small take-off zone doesn't help.

11 Anchor Point

- 🌀 **Break type**: Classic right hand point break.
- ☁ **Conditions**: Medium to big swells, offshore in east/northeasterly winds.
- ⊕ **Size**: 2-12 ft.
- ⬌ **Length**: 50-200 m.
- ⤳ **Swell**: Northerly/northwesterly/westerly.
- ➰ **Wind**: Easterly/northeasterly.
- 〰 **Tide**: Low to three-quarter tide.
- ⬤ **Bottom**: Sand-covered reef.
- ⊗ **Entry/exit**: Jump off the big rock near the end of the point.
- ❗ **Hazards/tips**: Crowds, rips when big, access and exit.
- 🛏 **Sleeping**: Taghazoute ▸ *p366*.

Anchor Point (Anchors/Ankas) is one of the few waves of world-class potential in the area. This long, rocky point stretches from the edge of Taghazoute out to the old Anchor factory, which gives the wave its name.

Property disputes have left this building derelict on what must be one of the country's hottest pieces of real estate. Anchors works best from low to three-quarter tide and picks up less swell than the other waves in the Taghazoute area. It doesn't really get going until it's over 4 ft, and if it's small it will be packed. The bigger it gets, the more the crowds will thin out. Anchor Point at 6 ft plus is great, at 8-10 ft even better. Wait for a lull and jump off the rock at the end of the point and make for the line-up. Waves start breaking way out beyond the point and can fire through to Hash Point in the village. Don't expect many barrels as this wave is all about big walls. To exit the water in a big swell, aim for the small beach near Taghazoute.

ⓘ *If you like Anchor Point, try Doolin Point in Ireland (see page 131) or Skaill Bay in Orkney (see page 50).*

12 Hash Point

- 🌀 **Break type**: Right-hand point break.
- ☁ **Conditions**: Medium swells, easterly winds.
- ❗ **Hazards/tips**: Pollution from village, but an easy-going atmosphere.
- 🛏 **Sleeping**: Taghazoute ▸ *p366*.

Hash Point is in Taghazoute village in front of a picturesque beach where the local fishermen keep their multicoloured boats. A wave of variable quality, depending on the sand and swell direction. Usually uncrowded and can be a great place for an evening session for those staying in the village. On good years it may even join up with Panorama's.

13 Panorama's

- 🌀 **Break type**: Right-hand point break.
- ☁ **Conditions**: Medium to large swell.
- ⊕ **Size**: 3-8 ft.
- ⬌ **Length**: 50-150 m.
- ⤳ **Swell**: Northwesterly to westerly.
- ➰ **Wind**: Northeasterly.
- 〰 **Tide**: Low to mid.
- ⬤ **Bottom**: Sand-covered rock point.
- ⊗ **Entry/exit**: Paddle off beach or jump off rocks in front of apartments.
- ❗ **Hazards/tips**: Not usually crowded, rips pushing south when big.
- 🛏 **Sleeping**: Taghazoute ▸ *p366*.

When the groundswell finally hits Taghazoute, an exodus of surfers can be seen walking north out of the village along the short stretch of road to Anchor Point. Many have come to the region for this one wave alone. Yet at the southern tip of the village sits a more low-key challenge that is faster and hollower and – though far less glamorous – can deliver some of the most exciting waves in the area.

Panorama's is named after the Panorama Café that overlooks this right-hand point break – or used to overlook, as it no longer enjoys the view it once did. A new apartment block has somehow managed to squeeze in between the café and the water's edge, obscuring the view from this once idyllic watering hole.

Currents and swell conspire to deposit sand around the point where the rocky headland meets the long, flat beach. This stretch of sand is popular with holidaymakers and has a seemingly endless soccer game in progress. If Anchor Point is firing, Panorama's should be too. This low tide break can resemble an Indonesian reef as barrel after barrel spins off the point, but at size it is not for the faint-hearted. A rip pushes away from the take-off point by the apartments and a difficult, steep take-off leads into a fast, driving section. Blow the take-off on a big day and you'll have a nightmare paddle all the way round again from the inside. Make the drop, pull in and you'll be rewarded with a barrel to rival any in the region.

11 Chris Mason at Anchor Point

11 Anchor Point

Morocco Taghazoute & the South Breaks Mysteries to Panorama's

THE GILL

McCarthy on Panorama's

Irish surfer Paul McCarthy has been coming to Taghazoute for many years and believes Panorama's is the most underestimated wave in the area. "I think that so much attention is focused on Killers and Anchors that spots like this are forgotten, but for me, some of the best waves I've seen in this country have been peeling around Panorama's point."

But Paul has a word of warning. "As with many waves in this area, Panorama's relies on the sand building up in the right way. If the currents or storms displace the sand it may section or close out."

However, the gods of surfing believe in balance and the beauty of this area is that if one break is underperforming, another will be all-time.

The region around Taghazoute is as wave rich and diverse as the line-ups.

16 Russ at Banana Village ▶▶ *p364*

If you like Panorama's, try Devil's Rock in Morocco (see page below) or Lafitenia in France (see page 193).

13 Panorama's

14 Taghazoute Plage

- **Break type**: Beach break.
- **Conditions**: Small to medium swells, offshore in east/southeasterly.
- **Hazards/tips**: Poor water quality.
- **Sleeping**: Taghazoute ▶▶ *p366*.

Taghazoute Plage is found at the north end of a long stretch of beach that finishes at Devil's Rock. Can have some nice peaks in small swells at low tide but tends to close out when the swell picks up. Water quality here may be affected by the run-off from the campsite toilets and from the free-campers further along the beach, but having said that there is probably less pollution than comes from Taghazoute itself. Banks can be found in front of the cafés and the campsite.

15 Devil's Rock/Devil's Point

- **Break type**: Right-hand point break.
- **Conditions**: All swells, offshore in easterly winds.
- **Hazards/tips**: Crowds, outer section shallow reef.
- **Sleeping**: Taghazoute ▶▶ *p366*.

Devil's Rock is a very underrated wave that works in all conditions from small to large swells. It breaks along a headland and is clearly visible from the marketplace at Aourir.

15 Devil's Rock

15 Devil's Rock

Morocco Taghazoute & the South Breaks Taghazoute Plage to Devil's Rock

The point has two sections that join up to produce one long wave in the right conditions. The outside section has a steep take-off and barrels along the reef until it hits the corner of the headland, where it mellows into a long wall that peels through to the beach. The point breaks on all states of tide, but the outside section is at its most hollow at low tide. The headland provides a great vantage point to view the action and access to the water is down a cliff track. It can get pretty crowded on the inside section when other spots aren't working or at weekends. Popular with surfers of all abilities as the mellower inside section can be easily accessed from the beach.

16 Banana Village

- ◉ **Break type**: Long left and short right, sand-covered reef.
- ◉ **Conditions**: Small to medium swells, offshore in an easterly/northeasterly wind.
- ◉ **Hazards/tips**: Can get crowded.
- ◉ **Sleeping**: Taghazoute ⇢ p366.

Banana Village is a reef that has a good left and short right. Works well in small and medium swells providing a change of scenery from the right points. Banana Village gets its name from the market town of Aourir, which has banana stalls lining the main road through it. The reef can be checked from the main coast road south towards Agadir. Parking is possible right in front of the break, accessed through the market/car park at the roundabout.

17 The Left

- ◉ **Break type**: Left-hand, sand-covered reef.
- ◉ **Conditions**: Small to medium swells, offshore in easterly winds.
- ◉ **Hazards/tips**: Avoid Wednesday – Souk day!
- ◉ **Sleeping**: Taghazoute ⇢ p366.

The Left can be found just to the south of Banana Village and is a short, powerful barrel. It is a popular wave with local bodyboarding grommets and is one of the true barreling left-handers on this stretch of coastline. Wednesday afternoons are packed as the kids from the local school have surfing as part of their school sports.

Agadir to the Saharan South

18 Cement Factory

- ◉ **Break type**: Right-hand point break.
- ◉ **Conditions**: Medium to big swells, offshore in easterly winds.
- ◉ **Hazards/tips**: Pollution and access.
- ◉ **Sleeping**: Agadir ⇢ p368.

On the way into Agadir from the north, the coast road passes an industrial area with a cement factory overlooking a Camping Gaz works. Beyond the shanty town sits a bay fringed by shipwrecks with a harbour wall at the southern end and an excellent right point at the northern end. This sand-covered rock point fires in big swells and some say it is the best wave on this whole stretch of coastline. It can throw up endless J-Bay like barrels and reeling walls. Works in all tides and is offshore in southerly through to easterly winds. Due to the bay's position in a run-down part of town and its proximity to these industrial plants, this wave is rarely surfed. However, those who have surfed it big are full of praise. "I surfed it once at ten foot and it made Anchor Point look ordinary," says Irish surfer Paul McCarthy.

DEMI TAYLOR

Taghazoute seafront

DEMI TAYLOR

16 Banana Village

19 Agadir Beach

- ◉ **Break type**: Beach break.
- ◈ **Conditions**: Big swell, northeasterly winds are offshore.
- ❶ **Hazards/tips**: Pretty poor, flat beach.
- ▣ **Sleeping**: Agadir ➤ p368.

This sheltered, crescent-shaped flat beach should not really be on your agenda. It is usually either flat or closing out. You may see local grommets out.

20 Royal Groynes

- ◉ **Break type**: Beach break with groynes.
- ◈ **Conditions**: Small to medium swells, offshore in easterly winds.
- ❶ **Hazards/tips**: Access by car depends on whether the King is in residence.
- ▣ **Sleeping**: Agadir ➤ p368.

Heading south out of town, with a little bit of exploring you will find the Royal Groynes, a semi-secret spot consisting of a series of waves that break on the sandbars that form around the huge stone breakwaters. Works through the tides and picks up plenty of swell. The first wave is a right-hander that peels off the most southerly groyne and can produce excellent hollow waves. The other side of the breakwater sees a fast, barrelling left and across the channel peels another barrelling right. This break picks up more swell than the breaks around Taghazoute.

21 Inezgane to Tifnite

- ◉ **Break type**: Beach breaks.
- ◈ **Conditions**: Small to medium swells, offshore in easterly/southeasterly winds.
- ❶ **Hazards/tips**: Isolated spots, don't surf alone.
- ▣ **Sleeping**: Agadir ➤ p368.

A stretch of exposed beaches that work on all tides and pick up heaps of swell. This is a huge stretch of beach break that is very rarely surfed. Access is via rough *piste* roads off the main P30 south from Agadir.

22 Tifnite

- ◉ **Break type**: Right point and reef.
- ◈ **Conditions**: Small to big swells, offshore in easterly/southeasterly winds.
- ❶ **Hazards/tips**: Isolated waves that can be powerful.
- ▣ **Sleeping**: Agadir ➤ p368.

The long, right-hand point wraps into the bay and picks up loads of swell, working in easterly and southeasterly winds. The point can see long walls breaking over 10 ft, with the take-off point moving outside the bay. Just north of the bay sits **Outsides**, a fast, hollow, right-hand break that holds swell up to 8 ft. There is also a left in front of the army post at the southern end of the bay. Outsides consists of a couple of reefs that pick up a huge amount of swell. The main break is a right but there is also a left and a peak. These waves work from 3-12 ft with easy access from the north side of the village. On big days, watch out for 'outside' sets sneaking through. This spot is very rarely surfed and just checking the spot usually attracts a few villagers keen to pass the time of day.

To get there, head south on the P30 and turn right at Inchadèn. Tifnite is like stepping back in time. The small village sits on a headland at the northern end of a crescent-shaped bay with no road access. Either park at the army post and walk, or four wheel it along the beach or over the dunes. Access is off the point or from the bay. Although the wave is well known, it is still rarely surfed due to the one hour drive down from Taghazoute, making it a great place to escape the crowds.

23 Aglou Plage

- ◉ **Break type**: Beach break with rivermouth.
- ◈ **Conditions**: Small to medium swells, offshore in southeasterly winds.
- ❶ **Hazards/tips**: Very quiet break.
- ▣ **Sleeping**: Tiznit ➤ p369.

Aglou is definitely worth checking on the trip south. It works through all tides and the rivermouth can have some excellent waves depending on the banks. Access from Tiznit on the 7062.

24 Mirhleft

- ◉ **Break type**: Beach break.
- ◈ **Conditions**: Small to medium swells, offshore in southeasterly winds.
- ❶ **Hazards/tips**: Picks up heaps of swell, very quiet spot.
- ▣ **Sleeping**: Tiznit/Sidi Ifni ➤ p369.

Heading south on the coast road to Sidi Ifni uncovers plenty of surfing potential. Breaks

20 Royal Groynes

22 Saharan south

22 Tifnite

like Mirleft pick up loads of swell and, depending on the banks, can produce excellent, hollow waves. Not a place to go alone. The south is best tackled with more than one vehicle in case of problems.

25 Sidi Ifni

- **Break type**: Beach and reef breaks.
- **Conditions**: Small to medium swells, offshore in southeasterly winds.
- **Hazards/tips**: Pollution, access, isolation.
- **Sleeping**: Sidi Ifni ▸ *p369*.

This collection of breaks around the southern town Sidi Ifni are predominantly offshore in southeasterly winds but gets mixed reviews from many who go there. Some surfers like the laid-back attitude and relaxed line-ups here. "North of Sidi Ifni, look out for the white vans," says Hugo Young. "There's a spot that's like Apostles in Oz. Lovely location and quiet." Others see it as overrated and there are problems with sewage pollution. "We spent a week down there," says Mike Brown from NZ. "After three or four days all the surfers got sick. There's also not many places to surf. We had a perfect 4-ft swell running but we checked all over and access can be a real problem." A good place to escape the crowds but can be a harsh environment to surf on your own.

26 Saharan South

- **Break type**: All types.
- **Conditions**: All swells, offshore in southeasterly or southerly winds.
- **Hazards/tips**: Isolation, go with other surfers for safety.
- **Sleeping**: South of Sidi Ifni: ▸ *p369*.

As a veteran of many 4WD southern Saharan trips, Gabriel, a German surfer, gives this advice: "It is possible to do it in a van but you should go with at least one other vehicle. Go with plenty of water, food and spare fuel. There will be no other surfers down there and the potential is amazing. However, access can be a problem in certain areas as parts of the coast are cliff lined."

Listings

The souk at Taghazoute

Taghazoute

Travelling along the P8, Taghazoute lies about 150 km south of Essaouira and 15 km north of Agadir (see below). Hippies and surfers have been heading to this unremarkable looking village since the 1970s, creating a unique micro-community where men in *djellabas* share a table with boardshorted surfers. This relaxed tourist trade sets it apart from the more frantic and hedonistic Agadir, just a bus ride away. It is a fully contained community complete with cafés, general stores, a mosque, surf repair shops, even an internet café, all centred around the main drag bisecting the village. (In fact the only thing lacking is an ATM.) Most of the houses in town have electricity and running water and there is an increasing trend for the town's locals to move back up into the hills and rent out their homes to visiting tourists and surfers.

Flat spells

Agadir Take a trip into the big bad 'sin city' (see below). **Barber** Get a cut-throat shave and a haircut at the barber in Taghazoute just off the main square – about 15dh for a shave, 25dh for a haircut. **Golf** Get 9 holes in at **Royal Club de Golf** near Inezgane, T048-241278. **Paradise Valley** Head into the hills on the road between Aourir and Tamrhakht to **Imouzzer des Ida Outanane** and the seasonal waterfalls that can be tempted into life in the winter after rains.

Sleeping

There are good apartments in Taghazoute overlooking the sea for around 1200-1800dh a week for 2 (higher prices during Christmas week when demand is greater). There are also cheap rooms in private houses – check how secure your room will be. Don't worry if you are stuck for somewhere to stay. As Chris and Den from **Moroccan Surf Adventures** explain, "Newcomers to the village will soon have plenty of offers of accommodation from the local agents all vying for your business."

DEMI TAYLOR

G Hotel Atlantique, 'upmarket' and clean, can supply you with breakfast.

G Residence l'Auberge Abdoullah, T062-418452, overlooks Hash Point and is a popular and cheap B&B experience at about 60dh a night.

Surf camps Many surf camps have sprung up in and around Taghazoute. The Portugal-based, Brit-run **Surf Experience**, www.surf-experience.com, and UK-based **Moroccan Surf Adventures**, www.morocsurf.com, offer a good quality service with airport transfers, transport to the breaks and half board in Taghazoute and Tamrhakht respectively. **Dynamic Loisirs** in Tamrhakht, T048-314655, is a popular camp with French surfers. Watch out for less experienced camps trying to cash in on the Moroccan experience. One surf camp was offering blow-up air mattresses on the floor, no transport and poor food – all for a couple of hundred quid! Make sure you know exactly what you are getting before you book.

Camping Mysteries, about 2 km north of town, is still a popular free-camping spot, despite the fact that break-ins are an almost nightly occurrence. If you do get broken into here, the police will not be particularly interested, as in their eyes you have deliberately put yourself at risk. Mysteries is, however, serviced by entrepreneurs – you can get your daily bread delivered straight to your (van) door. Mohammed V on his motorbike carries just about everything you need, from chocolate bars to processed cheese, or any other requests you may have made. It may sound idyllic but there is

growing resentment among locals who see comparatively rich westerners abusing the local environment by defecating in the bushes, emptying their chemical toilets into the sea, leaving rubbish and used toilet paper scattered around and not even contributing to the local economy in return. It is amazing to see this level of environmental disregard from a group of people usually associated with championing environmental awareness.

Camping Taghazoute, south of the village, overlooks Taghazoute Plage. "It's a big, dusty bowl with sparse cover, the toilets aren't great, the site is full of Germans, but it is pretty safe," explains travelling UK surfer Paddy Butler. Although you have to pay (about 15dh a night) you do have access to water brought in every couple of days from Aourir, basic toilets as well as protection against break-ins. You also get the daily rounds from locals touting everything from carpets and rugs to fruit, fish and jewellery. Servicing the site are beachfront cafés, where you can get a beer and a plate of fried calamari for a few dirham, as well as a couple of general stores stocking all basic essentials. To the south is another unofficial, post-apocalyptic free-camping site where motorhomes jostle for space near the 'guardian' whom they pay for protection from 'Berber bandits'. Break-ins happen here regularly and there are no facilities.

❶ Eating/drinking
There are plenty of cheap cafés and restaurants in the village, though with variable hygiene standards eating out can

be a bit of a wheel of fortune. As Toby from the Surf Experience sums up, "Eating out can be pretty dodgy – there's **Café Florida** on the main road where the majority of people seem to get sick, eventually, plus a whole bunch of other small ones at your own risk. But **Panorama's** on the seafront, overlooking the point, has in my eyes the best dish in town, Calamare Tagine." For the less adventurous, **Panorama's** also has a 'with chips' range of snacks. "For those who like a drink with their meal, **Restaurant Sables d'Or** on the road between the village and the campsite is good with superb views over Panorama's as the sun sets," recommend Chris and Den of Moroccan Surf Adventures.

❍ Shopping
The **Ankor Surf Shop**, opposite Café Florida on the main road, is basic (everything is second-hand) and a bit pricey but has wax, boards, leashes and boardies as well as basic camping equipment. The **board repair shops** that spring up each season are normally pretty reasonable – about 500dh will fix a clean break. The **main square** in town has a good range of basic food stores (for tinned food, bread, processed cheese, tea, mint, water etc.) as well as an ice-cream shop and a tobacconist. The **fish market** on the square is just a couple of tables but has some great bargains that vary daily depending on the catch – 2 tuna steaks or a big bag of prawns will set you back about 15dh. Get there by midday and remember to smell it for freshness. The **chicken** shop just off the square will kill and pluck a

DEMI TAYLOR

Flying goats

DEMI TAYLOR

General stores

DEMI TAYLOR

Camping de Taghazoute

chicken for you while you wait for about 30dh – guaranteed fresh meat if you can handle the 'still warm' feeling.

Head a couple of kilometres south to **Aourir** (also known as Banana Village) on a Wed for the **seafront souk** where you can pick up fresh fruit, veg and spices as well as a tagine and other essentials.

⊖ Transport
Bus: the No 14 bus runs north to Tamri every half hour from outside the mosque. Buses next to the main square run south to Agadir for about 3.20dh. **Petrol**: Afriqua in Aourir. **Van repairs**: if you're in a van that needs some TLC, get it done here at one of the mechanics on the road south to Tamrhakht – welding, roof racks, resprays and repairs are extremely cheap.

❶ Directory
Chemist: well stocked chemist with all the basic essentials at the south end of the village just off the main road. **Internet**: on the main road, connection isn't fast but it's always full. **Police**: just off the main square.

Agadir

Agadir is the royal choice. The King of Morocco, Mohammed VI, has his summer palace to the south of the town, while the Saudi royal family favours northern Agadir – so much so that they had the road rebuilt, connecting their palace to the town, thereby creating a decent stretch on the P8 between Taghazoute and Agadir. A massive earthquake in the 1960s destroyed the town and some 15,000 of the population. In the rebuild the entire town shifted south and, with a 9-km beach out front, was constructed with tourism in mind. With its coastal climate and relaxed drinking laws, it is a hotspot for visiting Europeans and Arabs alike and with casinos, nightlife and attached sex industry is considered the 'sin city' of the Muslim world.

✱ Flat spells
Cinema If you want some good, cheap entertainment, try heading to the cinema where you can catch some great Bollywood classics for about 8dh. **Golf** There are 3 courses in Agadir: the 9-hole **Royal Club de Golf**, about 12 km outside Agadir, T048-241278; the snootier **Golf les Dunes**, on the road to Inezgane, T048-834690, with 3 9-hole courses; or the newly opened **Golf du Soleil**, chemin Oued Souss, T048-843005. **Hammam** Chris and Den of Moroccan Surf Adventures recommend a "hammam with a mud scrub and a massage" at the Millennium Hotel on the south side of Agadir by Baie des Palmiers which is reasonably priced for non-residents.

⊜ Sleeping
Package deals to Agadir usually come with a fair standard of room and can be the cheapest option for a 2-week stay. Given the option, though, this is not the best place to base yourself for a surf trip – Taghazoute offers more 'surf friendly' accommodation. However, if you want a room for the night there are plenty of choices, including **F-G Hotel El Bahia**, R El Mahdi Bin Toummert, T048-822724, and the cheaper **G Hotel Amenou**, R Ya qub al Mansour, T048-823026.

Camping **Camping Caravaning International d'Agadir** on north end of Av Mohammed V is not a bad bet for a night. It's got good facilities, great showers, is near the town but is a bit pricey and cramped.

❷ Eating/drinking
Head to the port at the north end of town for the **fish restaurants**. Menus are based on the day's catch and the restaurants, set up back to back on long plastic covered trestle tables, compete for business. Open midday to early evening, the food is good and cheap. **Mickey Burger**, Hassan II, is the best burger and chips in town and possibly the world. They mince the meat for each burger only after you place your order and the potatoes are freshly chipped and fried. The daddy of burgers comes complete with a slice of melted cheese and a fried egg on top – spice it up with piripiri and wash it down with an ice cold, neon Fanta. **Pâtisserie Tafarnout**, Hassan II, is the

DEMI TAYLOR

10 Free-camping at Mysteries ▸▸ *p362*

showcase place for a morning pain au chocolate and milky coffee; check out all the pastries on offer inside. **Restaurant Mille et Une Nuits** (1001 nights), R 29 de Fevrier, is a good place to head for affordable but authentic Moroccan fare including tagines and couscous. There is even a McDonald's on Mohammed V, while Chris and Den recommend the **Taco Loco** just off Blvd 20 Aout for Mexican food and live music.

Bars & clubs

In terms of nightlife, there are discos usually at the big hotels but make sure that the person you're chatting up isn't 'pay to play'! Clubs include **Le Central** and **Foukets** on Av 20 Août. No town is complete without the mandatory 'Irish Bar'. This and other drinking holes can be found nearby.

Shopping

Uniprix supermarket on Hassan II is a good place to stock up on food and alcohol. The other alternative is the **Marjane** heading south out of town on the Mohammed V towards the airport. This French style supermarket is stocked full of home comforts and alcohol. There's also a big garage there where you can stock up on wash water. Agadir's **souk** on the southern edge of town is open every day and plays towards the tourist. This walled, covered market is half fruit and veg and half tat, among which there are few bargins to be had. **Marine and Sport** on the seafront has a few surfing basics.

Transport

Air: Agadir Airport, about 30 km southeast of Agadir on the road to Taroudant, is a popular entry point for many visiting surfers given its proximity to Taghazoute (about a 50-min drive). The airport has basic essentials – bureau de change, ATM and car rental etc. A *grand taxi* to Agadir should cost about 170dh – a bit more at night. It's licensed to take up to 6 people and won't leave until it's full or until you agree to pay for the empty spaces. Some will accommodate boards – for a fee – but remember to take board straps. **Bus/taxi**: to most Moroccan destinations from Pl Salam. To get to **Taghazoute**, jump on bus 12 or 14 (about 3.50dh). **Car hire**: about 6 hire companies, mainly on Mohammed V and Hassan II, get ready to haggle. **Train station**: R des Orangers.

Directory

Ambulance: T15. **Chemist**: 24-hr pharmacy next to the post office on Prince Moulay Abdallah. **Fire**: T150. **Newspapers**: corner Av Mohammed V and Av Prince Sidi Mohammed for day-old European and international newspapers. **Police**: R 18 Novembre, T190. **Post office**: corner Av Prince Moulay Abdallah and Av Prince Sidi Mohammed. **Tourist information**: Office du Tourisme, Pl Prince Heritier Sidi Mohammed, T048-822894. Syndicat d'Initiative, Av Mohammed V, T048-840307.

Tiznit

Heading south from Agadir the P30 runs inland to Tiznit, a market town known for its silver jewellery – check out the open air souk on a Thu or Fri just south of the walled médina. To the west of the médina, Pl de Mechouar is the focal point with banks, a post office and a tourist information office as well as cafés.

Sleeping

G **Hotel des Tourists** is probably the best bet out of a few cheap options.

There is also a **campsite** just south of the médina which is basic but fine. Aglou Plage is about 15 km northwest of the town with cheap accommodation available at the **Motel d'Aglou**.

Sidi Ifni

Travelling west from Tiznit towards the sea, the 7064 runs south along the coast from Gourizim to Sidi Ifni passing Mirleft – once the border between the Spanish enclave of Sidi Ifni and Morocco. Sidi Ifni itself was Spanish controlled until 1969 and is now a quiet, crumbling port town. The Sun souk, on the corner of Mohammed V and Hassan II, is worth checking out for provisions.

Sleeping

F **Hotel Suerta Loca**, just off Plaza de la Marina, T048-875350, which also does good food, or the cheaper G **Hotel Ifni** on Mohammed V next to the bank. There is a basic **campsite** just south of the town as well as plenty of cheap places to stay.

South of Sidi Ifni

South of Sidi Ifni, heading towards Plage Blanche the coast road turns to rough *piste* which is fairly inaccessible without a 4WD. Heading south along the main P41, the next major town you hit after Sidi Ifni is Tan Tan which used to be the southernmost town in Morocco before the Sahara to the south was reclaimed. It is pretty uninspiring but has banks, food stores, accommodation and cafés as well as an airport to the west. Continuing west along the sand-blown P41, Tarfaya at Cap Juby is backed by the Sahara and has only basic facilities including a few stores, basic cafés and very basic accommodation.

Directory

Footprint
6 Riverside Court,
Bath, BA2 3DZ England
☎(01225) 469141
www.footprintbooks.com

Footprint are the publishers of this guide.
For more titles, the occasional special offer
and plenty more, go to the website …
Footprint are making waves...

Wales

Odd - Surfboards (Freelap)
Unit 9, South Cornelly Industrial Estate
Bridgend, Porthcawl, Wales
☎(01656) 744691
Email: alby@tinyworld.co.uk
www.oddsurfboards.co.uk (under
construction)

Specialises in customised surf boards of
any length for both professionals and
amateurs.

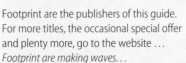

1 Beach Terrace,
Anglesey, LL64 5QD
☎(01407) 810899
Email: Bucky@funsport.fsnet.co.uk
www.funsport.fsnet.co.uk

Funsport shop has been around for about 20 years
and sells a comprehensive range of windsurfing,
kitesurfing and surfing products. When it is windy
the beach is busy with windsurfers and kitesurfers
from all over the country. When the swell hits there
are a number of sweet spots for all surfing abilities.

Langland Cove Guest House
4 Rotherslade Road, Langland
Swansea, SA3 4QN, Wales
☎(01792) 366003
gill@eurotelemail.net

We run an up market 5 bedroom (non-smoking)
B&B, with two rooms that sleep 3 sharing. Next
door is a self catering cottage sleeping up to 4.
Situated a minutes walk down the hill from the
multiple surf-breaks of Langland Bay. Best time to
come for surf is Autumn, Winter and Spring. With
25 years of experience in this area I could send
you to the best spots in the region on any given
day. Party animals need not apply.

Scotland

clan

0141-339 6523

www.clanskates.co.uk
45 Hyndland St, Partick, Glasgow, G11 5QF
Glasgow's most premier surf, skate and snow shop. 16 years old and still going strong. Hire, sales and repair. B.S.A certified surf school.

Ireland

Lahinch Surf Shop
Old Promenade, Lahinch, Co. Clare, Eire
☎ 00 353 65708 1543 Fax 00 353 65708 1684
Surf report on 00 353 (0)818 365 180
Email: bear@iol.ie www.lahinchsurfshop.com

Lahinch Surf Shop was the first surf shop to open in Ireland. It is also closer to the surf than any surf shop anywhere according to visitors who have been in surf shops all over the world. At times it is too close as the storm waves try to come in the door. We are open all year round.

Portugal

The Surf Experience
Rua dos Ferrieros
No 21, 8600 Lagos
Algarve
Portugal

☎ 00351 282761943
Fax: 00351 282761943
Email: enquire@surf-experience.com
www.surf-experience.com

Morocco

Moroccan Surf Adventures
Tamaraght, Agadir, Morocco
UK: ☎ (01323) 469439 (all year)
Morocco: ☎ 00212 48315163 (Oct-April)
Email: info@morocsurf.com
Website: www.morocsurf.com

Hassle free surf trips in the perfect winter location. Our camp is situated near numerous world class point, reef and beach breaks. Run by two well-travelled and experienced surfers who appreciate the requirements of a great, hassle-free surf trip.

Bold italic entries denote breaks. Countries are indicated in brackets: **GB** = Britain; **Can** = Canary Islands ; **Fr** = France; **Ire** = Ireland; **Mor** = Morocco; **Port** = Portugal and **Sp** = Spain.

Index

Footprint credits

Text editors: Tim Jollands and Alan Murphy
Map editor: Robert Lunn
Picture editor and layouts: Patrick Dawson

Publisher: Patrick Dawson
Editorial: Alan Murphy, Sophie Blacksell,
Claire Boobbyer, Felicity Laughton, Laura Dixon, Davina Rungasamy
Cartography: Sarah Sorensen, Robert Lunn,
Claire Benison, Kevin Feeney, Sean Feeney
Design: Mytton Williams
Advertising: Debbie Wylde
Finance and administration:
Sharon Hughes, Elizabeth Taylor

Photography credits

Front cover: Willy Uribe
Back cover and flap: Demi Taylor
Inside images: Alex Williams, Chris Gregory, Estpix, Paul Gill (The Gill), George Sohl, Jakue Andikoetxa, Stuart Norton, Scott Wicking, Thierry Organoff and Willy Uribe. Our thanks also go to O'Neills who provided the images of Sam Lamiroy on page 15 and Justin Mujica on page 308.

Print

Manufactured in Italy by Printer Trento
Pulp from sustainable forests

Ordnance Survey® This product includes mapping data licensed from Ordnance Survey® with the permission of the Controller of Her Majesty's Stationery Office © Crown Copyright. All rights reserved. Licence number 100027877.

The weather charts have been prepared based on information supplied by the Met Office © Crown Copyright. The publishers acknowledge with thanks the help given by the Met Office.

Footprint feedback

We try as hard as we can to make each Footprint guide as up to date as possible but, of course, things always change. If you want to let us know about your experiences – good, bad or ugly – then don't delay, go to www.footprintbooks.com and send in your comments.

Publishing information

Footprint Surfing Europe
1st edition
© Footprint Handbooks Ltd
August 2004

ISBN 1 904777 07 4
CIP DATA: A catalogue record for this book is available from the British Library

® Footprint Handbooks and the Footprint mark are a registered trademark of Footprint Handbooks Ltd

Published by Footprint

6 Riverside Court
Lower Bristol Road
Bath BA2 3DZ, UK
T +44 (0)1225 469141
F +44 (0)1225 469461
discover@footprintbooks.com
www.footprintbooks.com

Distributed in the USA by

Publishers Group West

The colour maps are not intended to have any political significance.

Every effort has been made to ensure that the facts in this guidebook are accurate. However, travellers should still obtain advice from consulates, airlines etc about travel and visa requirements before travelling. The authors and publishers cannot accept responsibility for any loss, injury or inconvenience however caused.

Complete title listing

Footprint publishes travel guides to over **150** destinations worldwide. Each guide is packed with practical, concise and colourful information for everybody from first-time travellers to travel aficionados.

The list is growing fast and current titles are noted below.

Available from all good bookshops and online at **www.footprintbooks.com**
(P) denotes pocket guide.

Latin America & Caribbean

Argentina
Barbados (P)
Bolivia
Brazil
Caribbean Islands
Central America & Mexico
Chile
Colombia
Costa Rica
Cuba
Cusco & the Inca Trail
Dominican Republic
Ecuador & Galápagos
Guatemala
Havana (P)
Mexico
Nicaragua
Peru
Rio de Janeiro
South American Handbook
Venezuela

North America

New York (P)
Vancouver (P)

Western Canada

Africa

Cape Town (P)
East Africa
Libya
Marrakech & the High Atlas
Marrakech (P)
Morocco
Namibia
South Africa
Tunisia
Uganda

Middle East

Egypt
Israel
Jordan
Syria & Lebanon

Australasia

Australia
East Coast Australia
New Zealand
Sydney (P)
West Coast Australia

Asia

Bali
Bangkok & the Beaches
Cambodia
Goa
Hong Kong (P)
India
Indian Himalaya
Indonesia
Laos
Malaysia
Nepal
Northern Pakistan
Pakistan
Rajasthan & Gujarat
Singapore
South India
Sri Lanka
Sumatra
Thailand
Tibet
Vietnam

Europe

Andalucía
Barcelona

Put Steven Spielberg, Charles Darwin and Claude Monet in a room with six bottles of vodka and a party pack of recreational drugs and combined, they could not come close to the concept of New Zealand…
Footprint New Zealand

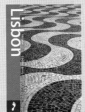

Welcome to Footprint

For **81 years**, Footprint have been leading and innovating at the forefront of travel guides.
The South American Handbook, Footprint's flagship title, has been published annually
for 81 years and is the longest running travel guide in the English language.

Footprint has **unrivalled** experience within the travel market and an uncompromising
reputation for providing reliable and relevant information to inspire, inform and entertain.

With over **100 titles** throughout the world from the super-chic style capitals of Paris,
New York and London through to exotic countries from Argentina to Venezuela, Footprint
guides are available worldwide.

Footprint enjoys ongoing **critical acclaim** in the national and specialist press as well as from
hardened travellers and has won several awards.

Surfing Europe is the first of many in our new lifestyle series.

---

66 99

Seriously well researched, the best of the lot.
The Observer

*Great travelling companions, constantly
entertaining and they know what they're
talking about.*
Michael Palin

The best of the best.
Le Monde, Paris

**The 81st Edition
South American
Handbook 2005**

Footprint
South American
Handbook 2005

"Sets the pace for
the rest to follow."
Michael Palin